ECONOMY AND SOCIETY
IN PREHISTORIC EUROPE

ECONOMY AND SOCIETY IN PREHISTORIC EUROPE

Changing Perspectives

Andrew Sherratt

PRINCETON UNIVERSITY PRESS
PRINCETON, NEW JERSEY

For my teacher

DAVID L. CLARKE
1937–1976

Hinc lucem

Published in the United States of America
by Princeton University Press,
41 William Street, Princeton, New Jersey 08540
In the United Kingdom,
published by Edinburgh University Press,
22 George Square, Edinburgh

This book has been composed in Sabon
by Nene Phototypesetters

Library of Congress Cataloging-in-Publication Data
Sherratt, Andrew.
    Economy and society in prehistoric Europe : changing perspectives /
    Andrew Sherratt.
        p.   cm.
    Includes bibliographical references and index.
    ISBN 0–691–01697–6 (alk. paper)
    1. Prehistoric peoples—Europe.   2. Economics. Prehistoric—
Europe.   3. Prehistoric antiquities—Europe.   4. Europe—
Antiquities.   I. Title.
GN803.S5   1997
936—dc21   97–8494

Princeton University Press books are printed on
acid-free paper and meet the guidelines for
permanence and durability of the Committee
on Production Guidelines for Book Longevity
of the Council on Library Resources

Printed and bound in Great Britain

1   3   5   7   9   10   8   6   4   2

CONTENTS

Preface   vii

Acknowledgements   xi

Introduction   Changing Perspectives on European Prehistory   1

SECTION I   CYCLES OF INTERPRETATION   35

1   V. Gordon Childe: Archaeology and Intellectual History (1989)   38

SECTION II   ECOLOGICAL IMPERATIVES?   67

2   Socio-economic and Demographic Models for
Later Prehistoric Europe (1972)   70

3   Water, Soil and Seasonality in Early Cereal Cultivation (1980)   85

4   Resources, Technology and Trade: An Essay on
Early European Metallurgy (1976)   102

5   Social Evolution: Europe in the Later Neolithic and
Copper Ages (1984)   134

SECTION III   DISCOVERING THE SECONDARY PRODUCTS COMPLEX   155

6   Plough and Pastoralism: Aspects of the Secondary
Products Revolution (1981)   158

7   The Secondary Exploitation of Animals in the Old World
(1983, revised)   199

8   Wool, Wheels and Ploughmarks: Local Developments or
Outside Introductions in Neolithic Europe? (1987)   229

9   Two New Finds of Wooden Wheels from Later Neolithic
and Early Bronze Age Europe (1986)   242

SECTION IV   PATTERNS ON THE GROUND   249

10   Mobile Resources: Settlement and Exchange in Early
Agricultural Europe (1982)   252

11 The Development of Neolithic and Copper Age Settlement
    in the Great Hungarian Plain   270
    I: The Regional Setting (1983)   270
    II: Site Survey and Settlement Dynamics (1984)   293

12 Neolithic Exchange Systems in Central Europe,
    6000–3500 BC (1987)   320

13 The Genesis of Megaliths: Monumentality, Ethnicity and
    Social Complexity in Neolithic North-West Europe (1990)   333

14 Instruments of Conversion? The Role of Megaliths in the
    Mesolithic–Neolithic Transition in North-West Europe (1995)   354

SECTION V   INVISIBLE FLOWS: LANGUAGES,
             CULTURE AND DRUGS   373

15 Cups that Cheered: The Introduction of Alcohol to
    Prehistoric Europe (1987)   376

16 Sacred and Profane Substances: The Ritual Use of Narcotics
    in Later Neolithic Europe (1991)   403

17 Metal Vessels in Bronze Age Europe and the Context of
    Vulchetrun (with T. Taylor, 1989)   431

18 Troy, Maikop, Altyn Depe: Early Bronze Age Urbanism and
    its Periphery (1991)   457

19 The Archaeology of Indo-European: An Alternative View
    (with E. S. Sherratt, 1988)   471

SECTION VI   A CONVERSATION WITH CHILDE   487

20 Gordon Childe: Right or Wrong? (1995)   490

        Bibliography   506
          Index   552

PREFACE

*'Meine Absicht ist nicht, zu beweisen, daß ich bisher recht gehabt habe,
sondern: herauszufinden, ob.'*

Bertolt Brecht, *Leben des Galilei*

This book consists of papers written, roughly one a year, over the first two decades of my academic life. They are largely concerned with the great changes which affected the cultures of the western Old World in the fourth millennium BC: a time which saw the appearance of the first civilisations in the Near East, and a fundamental transformation of life in prehistoric Europe. They range, however, rather widely, exploring the history of archaeology and the origins of farming, prehistoric uses of narcotics or the spread of Indo-European languages, as well as early trading systems and the changing uses of domestic animals. Disparate though these aspects may appear to be, they are all interlinked in sometimes surprising ways; and that is the justification for publishing them together.

Although part of my argument is that these pieces have stood the test of time, they are nevertheless easily attributable to their respective dates of composition, or at least to a sequence of phases within the recent development of prehistoric archaeology in the English-speaking world. This in itself provides an interesting exercise for the typologist and intellectual historian. But there is a deeper and more fundamental interest which I hope that this historical sequence of essays will demonstrate. The volume carries the subtitle *Changing Perspectives* because, in those decades since I first went into print, archaeological interpretations have changed very considerably. Topics which were once at the centre of debate have been displaced by others; explanations which once seemed convincing have been abandoned or revised. Only in part is this due to the growth of knowledge by new observations; rather it is due to changes in the way that these observations are approached – in archaeology as in the humanities and social sciences in general, and indeed in society at large. Such shifts are summed up in the polemical labels adopted by the schools of thought which claim responsibility – 'processualist' or 'post-processualist' – and in the changing proportions of certain key words in the texts of their publications. (The main title that I have chosen, *Economy and Society*, is itself deliberately emblematic of the period in which these papers were composed.) Broadly, this shift has been manifested in a move from economic calculations about how the bulk of the population acquired their food, to a more nuanced concern with how individuals manipulate their positions and symbolise their thoughts.

One effect of this fashionable shift in interests is that whole areas of knowledge can fall into relative neglect in the general archaeological community, and become confined to specialists. There is thus a danger that topics such as the beginnings of farming or its later developments will become ghettoised among archaeo-osteologists and palaeobotanists. This would be a disaster: for while reconstructions of prehistoric activities must rest on specialist techniques and knowledge, in the end the processes involved can only be understood by combining all of the insights available to the prehistorian. We should never abandon the interpretation of the economy to economists, or 'economic' prehistory to biologists. This principle works both ways: archaeologists interested in symbolism can only grasp the potential meanings of prehistoric phenomena by understanding their material effects. To succeed in his or her trade, the prehistorian must always be a generalist. That is perhaps the most important message of the book.

There is, then, a particular advantage to looking backwards at changing interpretations of important episodes in prehistory: for shifting perspectives can reveal the three-dimensional structure behind the cardboard-cutout caricatures which deceive the eyes of a single generation. Looking back on my interpretations of the fourth millennium, for instance, it is perhaps only now – fifteen years after publication of 'Plough and Pastoralism' (Chapter 6) – that I can claim to understand it in a three-dimensional way. That is why the essays on megaliths and narcotics are as fundamental to this volume as those on farming and settlement-history; and why increasing age (as well as its penalties) really does bring its advantages. Paradoxically, an approach via culture and value makes the idea of a secondary products complex *more* viable and useful as a concept than one based simply on calculations of energetics and economic efficiency. On the other hand, a purely 'cognitive' approach can only confess defeat in the face of larger questions about the reasons for farming and urbanisation. The way forward lies in combining the different insights of successive generations in the most sophisticated way possible.

It is in the belief that archaeology makes it feasible to write a coherent history of prehistoric times that these essays have been compiled. Nevertheless, it is perhaps too soon to write a seamless narrative as if all archaeologists were agreed on the conclusions presented. I have sometimes been horrified in the past to see the secondary products revolution treated as a tangible fact rather than as a mental construct, or to see myself quoted as (or criticised for not being) an authority on soils or sheep. I am neither of these things, only an intelligent generalist. These accounts are rhetorical and dialectical, in that they are intended to change a prevailing set of assumptions and to challenge an accepted picture, and my tone throughout is one of advocacy. That is why I have tried to maximise their usefulness to students by preserving their fidelity to the time and objective of their composition, while at the same time pointing out new facts, revised interpretations, and the interconnections between papers. I have therefore left the texts themselves largely unaltered, save for editing out overlaps and digressions, and removing ambiguities or inaccuracies in wording; and I have indicated new material by the use of square brackets. Introductions – to the volume as a whole, to its constituent sections, and to individual papers – express my current views and how these papers relate to them.

This series of contributions covers what have been exciting times in archaeology: from 1960s optimism to 1990s uncertainty as the turn of the millennium approaches. It seemed right, therefore, both to begin and end with Gordon Childe and his position in the streams of archaeological thought. One of the better by-products of uncertainty is a search for intellectual roots, and an attempt to situate archaeology within the other dialogues that have accompanied and made possible its growth. Childe saw the landscape of European prehistory all the more clearly because it was not then covered with the forests of information which now sometimes obscure the view; and the clarity of his vision often compensates for a lack of facts. The first chapter is a study of his role in the history of archaeology, the last one an attempt to relate these papers to his own conception of the prehistory of Europe and the Near East. Between these two polar points, I have grouped the essays roughly by chronology and theme, moving from the ecological emphasis of a processualist outlook, through the analysis of patterns in space, to a more recent set of topics concerned with consumption and larger patterns of emulation and interaction.

What is common to these papers is an attempt to go beyond the archaeological evidence. To deal only with what survives is to espouse a naive positivism; but to leave the evidence in favour of pure imagination is to go into free fall. The alternative to both is to develop a sensitivity to time and an awareness of anachronism, and to realise how different things were at successive stages in the past. It was this attitude which fuelled my interest in how different early farming systems were from those when secondary products had become important; and it is this awareness which must inform any attempt to reconstruct the less tangible aspects of human culture and society. This outlook, above all, I owe to my teacher David Clarke at Cambridge, to whose memory these essays are offered.

While the factual basis of these arguments grows increasingly robust as observations accumulate, the interpretation is always open to new insights from unexpected quarters. These papers are therefore presented in the spirit of Bertolt Brecht's Galileo quoted above: my intention is not to prove that I have been right up to now, but to find out whether I have been. Or not.

Witney, Oxfordshire, 1996

ACKNOWLEDGEMENTS

A book such as this one has accumulated many debts over the years. It was on the shelves of my father's study that I first discovered Gordon Childe's *What Happened in History* and Herbert Spencer's *First Principles*; and I am sorry that he did not live to see this fruition. Professor Sir Grahame Clark, whose generosity made it possible for me to study pollen analysis with J. Troels-Smith in Copenhagen before taking up a history scholarship at Peterhouse, has also passed on; while David Clarke, who taught me so much there, died twenty years ago. *Requiescant.* Among those who were acknowledged for their stimulus and help in writing the original papers, I note certain recurrent names: Betchen Barber, Richard Bradley, Cyprian Broodbank, David Clarke, Joost Crouwel, Robin Dennell, György Goldman, Fred Hamond, Ian Hodder, John Howell, Nándor Kalicz, Kristian Kristiansen, Jim Lewthwaite, Mary Littauer, Roger Moorey, Joan Oates, Sebastian Payne, Stuart Piggott, Colin Renfrew, Neil Roberts, Mike Rowlands, Steve and Sue Shennan, Sue Sherratt, Nick Starling, Tim Taylor, István Torma, Michael Vickers and Norm Yoffee. To all these (and many others), thanks – but no responsibility for my errors and opinions.

I am especially pleased to include here two pieces of work done in collaboration, one with my wife Susan Sherratt and another with Timothy Taylor. I must make special mention of Colin Renfrew for his unflagging liveliness in making European prehistory exciting and interesting, and for his personal interest in my sometimes wayward interpretations. When I contemplate how consistently I have controverted his views (while sympathising with his intentions) in the papers that follow, I realise what an exceptional debt I owe – and how much I learned at the 'University of Sitagroi'. I have been especially fortunate, too, in the head of my Department in the Ashmolean: Roger Moorey is a scholar whose knowledge I could not hope to equal, but from whom I have received constant and unstinted help.

The papers collected here were published for the first time in the volumes listed below.
1 'V. Gordon Childe: Archaeology and Intellectual History', *Past and Present* 125 (1989), 151–85.
2 'Socio-economic and Demographic Models for Later Prehistoric

Europe', from D. L. Clarke (ed.) *Models in Archaeology* (London: Methuen, 1972), pp. 477–542.

3 'Water, Soil and Seasonality in Early Cereal Cultivation', *World Archaeology* 11 (3) (1980), 313–30.

4 'Resources, Technology and Trade: An Essay on Early European Metallurgy', from I. Longworth, G. Sieveking and K. Wilson (eds) *Problems in Social and Economic Archaeology* (London: Duckworth, 1976), pp. 557–81.

5 'Social Evolution: Europe in the Later Neolithic and Copper Ages', from J. Bintliff (ed.) *European Social Evolution* (Bradford University, 1984), pp. 123–34.

6 'Plough and Pastoralism: Aspects of the Secondary Products Revolution', from N. Hammond, I. Hodder and G. Isaac (eds) *Pattern of the Past: Studies in Honour of David Clarke* (Cambridge: Cambridge University Press, 1981), pp. 261–305.

7 'The Secondary Exploitation of Animals in the Old World', *World Archaeology* 15 (1) (1983), 90–104.

8 'Wool, Wheels and Ploughmarks: Local Developments or Outside Introductions in Neolithic Europe?', *Bulletin of the London University Institute of Archaeology* 23 (1987), 1–15.

9 'Two New Finds of Wooden Wheels from Later Neolithic and Early Bronze Age Europe', *Oxford Journal of Archaeology* 5 (1986), 243–8.

10 'Mobile Resources: Settlement and Exchange in Early Agricultural Europe', from A. C. Renfrew and S. J. Shennan (eds) *Ranking, Resource and Exchange* (Cambridge: Cambridge University Press, 1982), pp. 13–26.

11 'The Development of Neolithic and Copper Age Settlement in the Great Hungarian Plain (Part I: The Regional Setting; Part II: Site Survey and Settlement Dynamics)', *Oxford Journal of Archaeology* 1(3) (1983), 287–316; 2(1) (1984), 13–41.

12 'Neolithic Exchange Systems in Central Europe, 6000–3500 BC', from G. Sieveking and M. Newcomer (eds) *The Human Uses of Flint and Chert* (Cambridge: Cambridge University Press, 1987), pp. 193–204.

13 'The Genesis of Megaliths: Monumentality, Ethnicity and Social Complexity in Neolithic North-West Europe', *World Archaeology* 22 (2) (1990), 147–67.

14 'Instruments of Conversion: The Role of Megaliths in the Mesolithic–Neolithic Transition in North-West Europe', *Oxford Journal of Archaeology* 14(3) (1995), 245–60.

15 'Cups that Cheered: The Introduction of Alcohol to Prehistoric Europe', from W. Waldren and R. Kennard (eds) *Bell Beakers of the Western Mediterranean: The Oxford International Conference 1986* (BAR Int. Ser. 331, 1987), pp. 81–106.

16 'Sacred and Profane Substances: The Ritual Use of Narcotics in Later

Neolithic Europe', from P. Garwood, D. Jennings, R. Skeates and J. Toms (eds) *Sacred and Profane: Proceedings of a Conference on Archaeology, Ritual and Religion*, Oxford University Committee for Archaeology Monographs 32 (1991), 50–64.

17 'Metal Vessels in Bronze Age Europe and the Context of Vulchetrun', with T. Taylor, from J. Best and N. de Vries (eds) *Thracians and Mycenaeans* (Leiden: Brill, 1989), pp. 106–34.

18 'Troy, Maikop, Altyn Depe: Early Bronze Age Urbanism and its Periphery' (written 1991), to appear (in Russian) in V. M. Masson (ed.) *Majkopskaya Kultura-fenomen Drevnej Istorii Kavkaza i Vostochnoj Evropy* (St Petersburg).

19 'The Archaeology of Indo-European: An Alternative View', with E. S. Sherratt, in *Antiquity* 62 (no. 236) (1988), 584–95.

20 'Gordon Childe: Right or Wrong?' (written 1995), to appear (in Polish) in Jacek Lech (ed.) Conference volume on Gordon Childe, Warsaw; English version also in *Archaeologia Polona* (1997).

Changing Perspectives
on European Prehistory

During the fourth millennium BC, the western Old World underwent a series of changes which were in many ways comparable in magnitude to the beginning of farming there some five millennia previously,[1] and were in large part a consequence of it. In a roundabout way, this book is about how those changes are best described. To understand what difference they made, it is essential to define what went before and to characterise the nature of the earliest forms of farming. To describe how and where the differences became evident, it is necessary to look for the often indirect traces of innovation and to track the patterns of their spread. Over and above these tasks, however, is the need to come to terms with what kind of changes we are talking about. Were they primarily economic advances, either forced on a growing population by sheer necessity, or alternatively constituting a breakthrough in production which allowed population to expand? Or were they essentially changes within society itself: either in social relationships, or in the way in which the world was perceived, which then came to have material effects? Were they, on the other hand, primarily concerned with material possessions – in effect, a consumer revolution in which people discovered a need for things they had never before experienced? All of these descriptions have some appeal, and yet fall short of a full characterisation – in part because they are presented as exclusive alternatives, either/or. They relate to habits of thought developed in the unusual circumstances of the western world after the Industrial Revolution, when these aspects of life have assumed a certain autonomy – a division which is a positive hindrance

---

This opening essay reviews how the themes treated in the following chapters have been conceptualised by archaeologists, and offers a viewpoint which reconciles economic and symbolic interpretations. It offers an assessment of the role of the Near East, and an outline of the structure of European prehistory from 7000–2000 BC.

in understanding an earlier world. This introduction is an attempt to bring them back together again.

FROM SUBSISTENCE TO SYMBOLS: FALSE DICHOTOMIES

That these interpretations present themselves as such stark alternatives, with party labels attached (economic, processualist, diffusionist, autonomist, cognitive, etc.), is itself an interesting phenomenon of intellectual history which it is worth stopping for a moment to ponder. Each generation considers that its predecessor made fundamental interpretative errors, which can now be expunged. In part this is simply the dynamics of factionalism and the challenge for power; but it is made easier by the fact that the real world changes and time moves on – the questions of the new generation are unlike those of their predecessors because their world is not the same. When gender roles are being renegotiated, it is not surprising that interest focuses on what they have been like in the past, for instance, to a far greater degree than when they are stable and apparently self-evident. At certain times – usually periods of prosperity – great abstract schemes seem a natural way of summarising knowledge; at others, when the world seems to be coming apart, such schemes seem an artificial imposition. Thus one generation emphasises abstract principles, the next one the reality of material conditions. In this way the circumstances of the present time give rise to the prevalent metaphors for the past.[2]

Such principles can be seen at work in the period over which the essays in this volume have been composed.[3] The movements which had their origins in the 1960s (various forms of New Archaeology) represented a kind of abstract sociological system-building with natural science as its model and endogenous change as its mechanism. Explanations favoured demographic pressure and environmental carrying capacity, within a metaphor of diversification and integration. The papers in Section II, and to some extent in Section III, show the influence of this background. This is not necessarily a bad way of accumulating observations about important aspects of life in the past, but it does not lead to the most sophisticated explanations. It verges on Panglossianism ('everything works for the best, in this best of all possible worlds'), and it encourages a certain naivete of interpretation, for instance the belief that prehistoric cemeteries provide a direct reflection of living social structures. After the 1970s Oil Crisis, we were much more ready to believe that elites could be exploitative as well as benevolent, and indeed that culture itself could lie – in the sense that cemeteries and grave-goods, as much as wall-paintings and praise-songs, are attempts at self-definition and contain an important element of negotiation and propaganda. The movements which broke surface during the 1980s were explicitly concerned with individualism, expression, symbolic structures and contextual relativism with a concern for historical specificity. The

2

papers of Section V show a much greater awareness of this dimension. But while its best exponent has retained the ability to write on a broad canvas and engage large themes (Hodder 1990), some of his students and imitators have espoused a more nihilist outlook and explicitly condemn such wider vision, in favour of a personal engagement with particularities and the spirit of place.

Although some accounts of recent interpretative changes in archaeology by 'post-processual' archaeologists tend to cast them, quite against the letter of their own relativistic pronouncements, as straightforward, uni-linear advances in understanding, I am myself more struck by the extent to which they replay a classic cycle in intellectual history (see Chapters 1 and 20). Its paradigm is the Enlightenment/Romantic succession, but this *Auseinandersetzung* has been regularly repeated and has manifested itself for instance as the swing from Positivism to Nationalism at the end of the nineteenth century, and only most recently as the move from Modernism to Postmodernism in our own times. Figure 0.1 presents the succession of intellectual movements in modern European history as a dialectic between these two polar models of intellectual activity, related to the social and economic circumstances of the societies which gave birth to them (see Chapter 1). Each of these cycles shows the oscillation between system-building and deconstruction, between attempts to create general models and the desire to create interpretative metaphors. That this cycle is so con-tinuously repeated suggests to me that both approaches have elements which are useful and necessary, and that each acts to correct the excesses of the other. Together, they convey an essential truth: history must be under-stood both from the outside and from the inside, as a set of constrained possibilities and as a sequence of meaningful actions. We should beware, then, of simply following interpretative 'fashion' (or rather the dictates of the *Zeitgeist*) in choosing either a purely demographic or alternatively a symbolic explanation – the Neolithic as a response to population pressure or as a drama of culturing the wild; for the prominence given to these features is no more than a reflection of cyclical changes of interest within our own society. Rather, we should address posterity by trying to integrate the benefits of approaches which up to now (for the purposes of rhetoric or academic politics) have largely put themselves forward as being mutually exclusive. Genuine progress can come from their integration – not in a soggy compromise,[4] but in a critical combination of their respective merits.

We are thus faced with a confrontation between generalisation and particularism, models and metaphors, *grand récit* and *petites histoires*. Do we simply shift our attention from the large phenomena such as the origins of agriculture or urbanism which dominated the '60s agenda, to the meaning of particular pieces of rock art in Arizona or Scandinavia; or do we attempt to rethink the nature of these larger processes using the insights

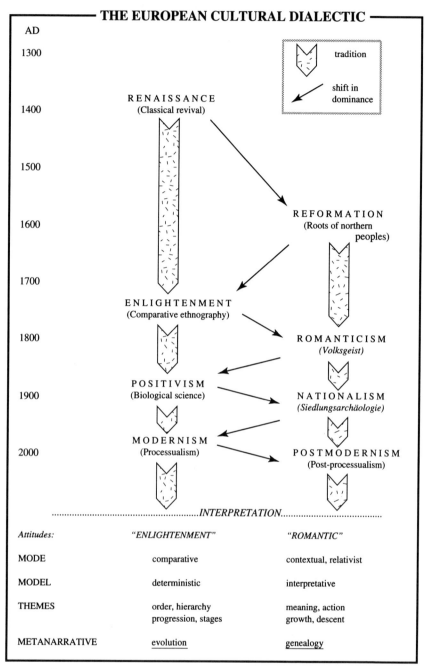

THE EUROPEAN CULTURAL DIALECTIC

AD

1300

tradition

shift in
dominance

RENAISSANCE
(Classical revival)

1400

1500

1600

REFORMATION
(Roots of northern
peoples)

1700

ENLIGHTENMENT
(Comparative ethnography)

1800

ROMANTICISM
(Volksgeist)

POSITIVISM
(Biological science)

1900

NATIONALISM
(Siedlungsarchäologie)

MODERNISM
(Processualism)

2000

POSTMODERNISM
(Post-processualism)

....*INTERPRETATION*...

Attitudes:	"ENLIGHTENMENT"	"ROMANTIC"
MODE	comparative	contextual, relativist
MODEL	deterministic	interpretative
THEMES	order, hierarchy progression, stages	meaning, action growth, descent
METANARRATIVE	evolution	genealogy

0.1 *Intellectual currents in modern European history as an alternation of attitudes and intellectual traditions. The 'modernist' or Enlightenment stance is character- istic of established and economically dominant regions, the 'postmodernist' or Romantic one more typical of less self-assured (rising or declining) cultures on their margins. The former emphasises equilibrium, the latter, disruption of established patterns.*

which we have gained in contemplating the smaller ones? It seems to me that the latter presents the greater and more worthwhile challenge.

How might we proceed? A useful beginning would be to examine some of the categories within which we work and to remove the artificial contrasts which have been built into them. Our entire vocabulary is suspect. The common word 'settlement', for instance, contains an implied contrast with a time of ceaseless wandering – literally how prehistory was conceived in the nineteenth century. Perhaps 'habitation', therefore, would be a better word. Our opposition of 'settlement-site' and 'cemetery' is also an ethnocentric one, for the construction of symbolic spatial order and the elaboration of structures sheltering either the living population or the remains of the dead are particular conjunctions and not universal regularities (see Chapter 14). The terminology collapses as soon as we press it. The common usage of 'trade' and 'exchange', where the former is taken to imply a profit motive and the latter a socially embedded network of gifts, can easily lead to a prehistory in which there are no gainers from material transactions. The conceptions which are embodied in these choices of words impoverish past worlds by constructing them in antithesis to the present. By far the most culpable term in our vocabulary, however, is the word 'subsistence'.

It was economic anthropologists who drew a distinction between *market* economies and *subsistence* economies. The former were linked to international patterns of trade; the latter were supposed, by contrast, to have no external links and no production beyond that required for survival.[5] Clearly, this picture is a caricature, based largely on heavily-taxed peasantries in third-world countries which are themselves the victims of global capitalism. It was in any case an artificial division between activities that were already intertwined, trying artificially to reconstruct the 'primitive condition'; but the label has stuck. 'Subsistence' farming, by definition, seems to be concerned only with scratching a living, and any changes it might undergo should thus be concerned only with improving the provision of staples. This assumption simplifies energetic calculations, since it deals only with a few crops and principally those which provide the calories; but it is a fundamentally misleading conception of human behaviour to accept even for the present day, and still less to project backwards across the millennia. Populations *exist*; most *persist*; only a few (mostly as a result of international exploitation) merely *subsist*: the word should be banned from the archaeological vocabulary. It creates a fundamentally misleading dichotomy between the activities of getting food and exchanging items between productive units – 'subsistence' *versus* 'trade' – and in so doing has driven a wedge between two fundamental and closely related aspects of human activity. The concept of consumption is so important because it remakes the link, and emphasises the importance of the rarer items, for which people negotiate, in creating what is actually consumed (Goodman, Lovejoy and Sherratt 1995).[6] What this reformulation does is to remove the barrier between the processualist, calorie-based models of optimised mass behaviour, and the individualist, meaning-sensitive contextual analyses of motivation and value, which have been artificially held apart by our very terminology.

This realisation fundamentally transforms the nature of the inquiry, for it becomes clear that it is no longer possible to parcel up the questions into a set of conventional categories. The problem of 'escaping the Malthusian trap'[7] raised (though not in those words) in Chapter 2 is an artificial one, if population levels are not autonomously generated but rise in relation to economic activity, and food is found by intensifying production in response to this stimulus. The core of the question is thus concerned with consumption and its motivation as much as production and its constraints. It is thus misleading to conceptualise any human situation simply in terms of the relationship between population and food resources, without adding a middle term for those non-staple items which people desire, and for which they often compete: organic items such as spices or drugs, or inorganic materials used for ornaments. Nor can clothing and shelter be considered neutral 'necessities', for they likewise have an expressive dimension which goes far beyond protection from the elements: hence the long-term elasticity in demand for them, over and above the effects of demographic growth. Even what are now staple crops were once rare and desirable items to be acquired by trade (see Chapter 10). Curt Runnels and Tjeerd van Andel (1988) have come nearest to this viewpoint in their discussion of 'Trade and the origins of agriculture', when they assert: 'In a sense we are saying that "cash crop" farming was a phenomenon as old as, and perhaps older than, subsistence farming' (1988, 97). In effect, *all* crops are potentially 'cash crops', even in a cashless economy; the beginning of the Neolithic was the original Consumer Revolution, and the secondary products revolution (Chapter 6) was its second round.

A SECONDARY PRODUCTS SCENARIO[8]

With these considerations in mind, it is perhaps appropriate here to sketch how I currently envisage the phenomena discussed in the following chapters. Since these chapters themselves describe the nature of the evidence, the account given here will be an exercise in pattern-recognition as well as evaluation.[9]

My description of the nature of early farming from 9000–7000 BC (PPN A and B) in Chapter 3 seems to me still to be broadly correct: though my narrative accounts of how it came about (Sherratt 1980b; 1996a) now appear deficient in discussing only calories and population pressure rather than trade (for instance in obsidian and cowries) and the possibly antecedent traffic in plants yielding fibre, oil, sugars or natural drugs – but that is another issue. Pulses may have preceded cereals as domesticates, and sickles may have been used to harvest cereals because the stems were used for basketry – of a type known from PPN B Nahal Hemar, along with evidence of linen (Kislev and Bar-Yosef 1988). As Runnels and van Andel point out (and as Barbara Bender had earlier implied), cereal grains themselves would have been 'luxury' items of trade, quite differently perceived from the staple commodity they were to become. The 'dispersal' of cultivated forms would have been, like that of the domestic cattle discussed in Chapter 10, a social process of economic transaction and negotiation, and not just a passive 'spread'. Cultivation seems to have started in the southern Levant, and may even have begun specifically in the uniquely propitious conditions at Jericho. For these two thousand years, during which (in somewhat more humid conditions than today) village-based cultivation spread over an area from southern Anatolia to western Iran, sites remained scattered and restricted to locations with the narrow set of conditions suitable for simple cereal-growing. Hunting sites, marked by kite-shaped stone-built traps, proliferated in adjacent desert regions. Domestic animals, principally ovicaprids, were slowly integrated into the farming system from PPN B onwards, but still showed little evidence of selective breeding (and they only appeared in the desert area after 5000 BC, in the Chalcolithic, when more specialised breeds may have been available). This early farming must still be reckoned as having been of a most primitive kind; and in the Levant it seems to have ended in a phase of crisis or catastrophe which was not due to climatic change but which may reflect over-exploitation of this narrow range of habitats.

The seventh and early sixth millennia were a phase of rapid adjustment which saw the expansion of farming villages into the Balkans and as far as Baluchistan, and the appearance of complex, pottery-using sites like Çatalhöyük in central Anatolia or the onager-hunting site of Umm Dabaghiyah in Assyria. The full integration of domestic animals into the farming economy now took place, including larger species such as cattle; and free-threshing wheat was now becoming available in addition to the more primitive varieties of cereals. In the later part of the seventh millennium there was a remarkable proliferation of sites within the Fertile Crescent – on the Assyrian steppes and the alluvial fans spreading from the Zagros foothills – belonging to the painted pottery complex of Hassuna-Samarra-Halaf. Free-threshing wheats of *durum* type now became dominant in the Near East.[10] Farming settlement of the Mesopotamian floodplain was also well advanced, though massive alluviation has obscured the picture. Excavations at the Samarran site of Choga Mami near Mandali in eastern Iraq revealed irrigation canals to spread water across the fan. Since the more northerly sites are rain-fed and not suitable for simple irrigation, the implication is that they were supported by some comparable technique; and use of the plough is a plausible inference for this specific arc of northern Mesopotamia. As well as still plentiful quantities of obsidian, small copper objects circulated well beyond their source areas.

In the later sixth and fifth millennia, as European farming spread across

10 000 BC cal.	FERTILE CRESCENT
	(Younger Dryas)
9 000	*(Holocene)*
	EARLY CULTIVATION OF PRIMITIVE CEREALS...
8 000	...AND FIRST INTEGRATION OF DOMESTIC ANIMALS
7 000	*- CRISIS TRANSITION -*
	SPATIAL EXPANSION & SPREAD OF INNOVATIONS (cattle & free-threshing wheat) ○
6 000	DEVELOPMENT OF PLOUGH CULTIVATION AND IRRIGATION (first farmers in the delta plain) ○
5 000	DIVERSIFICATION OF PRODUCTS: (tree crops and secondary live animal products) ○
4 000	DENSE NETWORK OF EXCHANGES OF NEW PRODUCTS AROUND FERTILE CRESCENT ○ RIVERINE BYPASS TRADE (centrality of plain/delta) ○
3 000	GENESIS OF CENTRE/ PERIPHERY INTERACTION (colonies) ○ RIVAL SECONDARY STATES AND MILITARISATION ○
2 000	FIRST EMPIRES

0.2 *The emergence of secondary farming: innovations in plant and animal husbandry, 9000–2000 BC: (a) chronological chart; (b) map sequence. The first three maps indicate the growing diversity of crops around the Fertile Crescent in the periods leading to the emergence of urbanism in Mesopotamia; the last, contemporary with the spread of city-centred trading networks, shows the domestication of new animals for transport (see Chapter 7).*

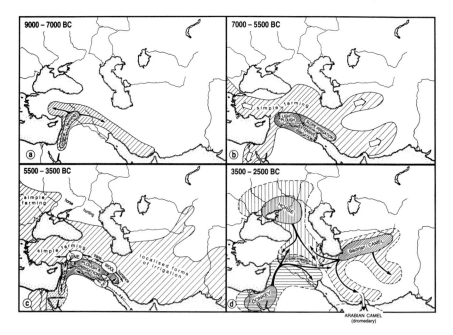

the loess-lands and consolidated its position there, the expansion of cereal cultivation around the inner rim of the Fertile Crescent made possible a process of diversification and interaction which by 4000 BC had given rise to major innovations. Arguments set out in subsequent chapters point to a series of areas, arranged apparently around the edge of the zone where advances in cereal cultivation had occurred (Figure 0.2), in which new plant and animal products, often capable of being stored or processed, were pioneered. Several of these were new tree-crops, propagated vegetatively to fix desirable strains: olive, fig and almond in the Levant; vine and pomegranate in the Upper Euphrates and Tigris catchments in south-east Anatolia; perhaps dates in the extensive natural palm-groves at the head of the Persian Gulf (dates were found in Ubaid levels at Eridu). One, in particular, was an animal product: wool-bearing sheep seem to have had their origin in western Iran, perhaps in Kermanshah where the upland valleys are most conveniently linked to the Mesopotamian plain. Such articulation is likely to have been a critical stimulus to specialisation – not at the level of bulk transport, but at the level of exchanging innovations that were valuable because of their very novelty, and because they contributed to a wider range of consumable products. It is the variety, not the bulk, that explains the interest. These innovations were thus propagated around the network, so that at Nahal Mishmar in Israel there is evidence for olives, dates and wool by 4000 BC. It is not accidental that these finds occurred in association with a hoard of spectacularly innovative metal objects (arsenical copper, cast by the lost-wax process), for the circulation of metals would have provided economic liquidity to such a series of exchanges. With the incentive to keep greater quantities of livestock, milk and its products apparently became more important, and could also provide special products, storable and to some degree negotiable as trade items with neighbouring groups (cf. Lees and Bates 1974; Bates and Lees 1977; for the growing literature on ancient cheese, see Nissen et al. 1990; Stol 1993; Teuber 1995; Englund 1995). Even cereals were discovered to have a new potential, and for similar reasons. Two new micro-domesticates, *Lactobacillus* and *Saccharomyces*, made possible on the one hand the production of yoghurt and cheese (the latter requiring salt as a preservative), and on the other hand the making of beer and leavened bread (see Chapter 15). It seems likely that yeasts from the fruit crops were important in the latter instance (Figure 0.3); and the drinking of beer is first evidenced on a sealing from Tepe Gawra, c.4000 BC. All this contributed to the diversification of desire. The increasing networking of these areas into a regional interaction sphere is indicated by the spread of the pottery complex termed Ubaid, from southern Mesopotamia around the Fertile Crescent and in local versions into Iran; and the willingness to travel is summarised in a clay model of a boat with a mast-socket from a grave at Eridu (then on the coast), implying use of the sail also by 4000 BC. Ubaid pottery made its appearance at several points

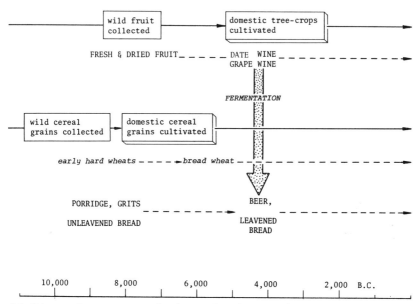

0.3 Dietary changes as a result of secondary farming: the interaction between cereals and tree-crops (Sherratt 1985, unpublished).

along the Gulf coast down to Qatar and Oman, indicating a sphere of maritime interaction as well as the extensive overland contacts.

The potential for a fundamental transformation in the way of life of the populations of greater Mesopotamia is thus evident; and the major shift came about in the fourth millennium – during the period in which, in Europe, farming first spread into the North European Plain. Two related processes were principally responsible. One is what Tom Beale (1973) has neatly termed the 'bypass phenomenon' – the concentration of multilateral contacts into a few principal channels – best exemplified in the increasingly axial role of the great rivers themselves, especially the Euphrates, which drew a chord across the arc of the Fertile Crescent, effectively linking the sub-tropical Gulf with the Mediterranean hilly flanks. This focusing of traffic made possible, and was itself promoted by, a second phenomenon which I have called (1995, 17–20) the principle of intervening opportunity: in an otherwise rather unattractive region (the lower Mesopotamian plain) the opportunity arose to concentrate on added-value production, princi- pally in the form of textiles, supporting its labour-force by an expansion of irrigated farming. This created an increasing contrast (as Childe had per- ceived)[11] between a manufacturing core area and a raw-material supplying hinterland, altering the economic and political character of the interaction. Within the core, it produced a technological explosion as a whole range of new manufacturing processes were explored, from the mass-production of wheelmade pottery to more elite products such as wheeled vehicles or granulated goldwork. These, in turn, required increasing quantities of raw materials from the (mostly highland) periphery, which could only be acquired by the active setting up of colonial stations to alter local tastes and mobilise supplies. This was what happened in the Uruk period, which saw the emergence of true cities, writing systems and the formal characteristics of civilisation (Algaze 1993; Frangipane et al. 1993). The scale of this expansion, which drew in valuable materials like lapis lazuli from as far afield as eastern Afghanistan, began to involve two new alluvial agrarian cores which rapidly developed into independent centres of activity with their own immediate peripheries: Egypt and the Indus valley. In the dry spaces which separated these three nuclear areas, two new forms of overland animal transport came into use – the donkey and the camel – which spread rapidly around different parts of the urbanising area to complement the riverine routes and their boats, which, at least in certain directions, made use of the sail (see Figure 0.2). Where this network of routes met the sea, in the (then unalluviated) bay of the lower Orontes in the Amuq, a cradle of maritime activity was created in the Mediterranean.[12] The scale of this expansion had repercussions on all the surrounding areas (see Chapter 18), and in my view gave the stimulus to horse-domestication on the Pontic steppes;[13] and it was at this time that the features of secondary farming appeared more generally in the western Old World. It is this fusion and explosion of the constituent elements of this complex which give it its revolutionary nature.

Such, in brief, is the story of the emergence of secondary farming, secondary products and secondary consumption patterns. It was summarised in a diagram that I prepared in 1984, and reproduce again here as Figure 0.4. This emphasises the structure, which I had always envisaged, of a multilinear emergence of secondary features in different parts of the Near East, and their integration and further spread in package form – just like the original spread of primary farming. (Chapter 20 considers whether this was 'revolutionary', and what kind of revolution it was.) All of the crucial developments before 4000 BC (with the possible exception of horse domestication) seem to have taken place within the theatre of greater Mesopotamia: the Tigris/Euphrates catchment and its hilly flanks (including the Levant); though their appearance beyond this focal area seems to have taken place very rapidly after 3500. In my view of things, that looks like a nuclear/ margin process: that is to say, it seems that these features did not develop indigenously in areas like temperate Europe (though given time they might have done), but in fact appeared as a result of external intervention. It is to this more controversial aspect that I now turn.

HOW MUCH CENTRICITY?

One of the issues which seems to fire up European prehistorians more than any other is the question of autonomy. It relates to a long debate within

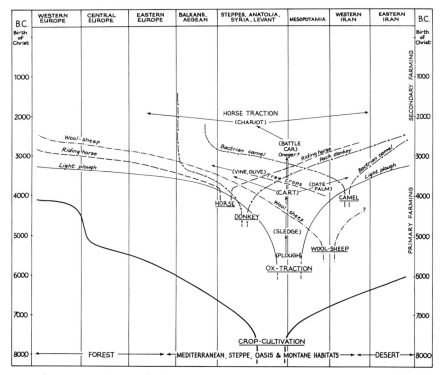

0.4 The origins and spread of secondary farming: note the multiple origins, integration, and explosive spread (from Sherratt 1987b, corrected).

European prehistoriography (and the split between 'classics' and oriental studies: see Chapter 1 and Bernal 1987) between indigenists and diffusionists. Despite the fact that 'Europe' appeared as an ideological entity only with the spread of Christianity, and has only the faintest geographical justification as a physical unit, a set of myths going back to the Trojan War (reinforced both by the Persian invasion of Greece and the Turkish takeover of Byzantium) have set along the Sea of Marmara an imaginary line which marks the division of Europe from Asia. It has thus sometimes (e.g. Reinach 1893) seemed to be a matter of honour, emotion and continental pride whether any population movement or cultural influence has crossed the Aegean or not.[14] The issue is still one of contemporary interest because the ecological orientation of New Archaeology took it as axiomatic (see Chapter 2) that local conditions were crucial to explaining change, and that diffusionism had too easily invoked typological similarities to tell a tale of missionaries and colonists in deep prehistory. This seems to me to be largely true; but it does not preclude the possibility that processes outside the region may have played a crucial role in determining the nature of local opportunities. I have argued elsewhere (1995b) that the belief in autonomism is closely associated with a form of evolutionism involving a stadial model of change, and I have suggested instead that important innovations more usually start at particular, unusual points on the Earth's surface where rare sets of conditions coincide, and spread outwards from there. It seems inherently probable that the unusual conditions of the Fertile Crescent have consistently given rise to innovations in a way that the more uniform landscapes of forested Europe have not (Sherratt 1996a; in press b). This is the picture that I would wish to suggest for the features of secondary farming described in the previous section. The proposal can only be evaluated by considering the alternatives.

It leads at once to questions of methodology. All of the features of secondary farming which spread to Europe, although important as innovations, are inherently quite hard to demonstrate.[15] Evidence for milking is probably so ambiguous that until extensive biochemical analysis of food-residues trapped within pottery fabrics has been undertaken on a large scale (and it will revolutionise archaeology in the early twenty-first century), it is practically impossible to tell; and so far only plant-lipids have been detected on the ceramic sieves sometimes interpreted as milk-strainers (Rottländer 1995). The arguments are set out in Chapter 7, but it seems likely that milking only took place on a large scale when animals were kept in large numbers, and often for other reasons. Wool is rather more tangible in the archaeological record, though its remains are rare. A spread to Europe during the third millennium is accepted by experts (Ryder 1983; Barber 1991), though its abundance at that time is harder to gauge. Domesticated horses seem to have spread at about the same time, and new studies of faunal assemblages by various methods are introducing greater precision. Chapter 7 again summarises this. The features that we can most easily identify seem to have been essentially third- or late fourth-millennium introductions. Whilst milking is a practice that might be taken up anywhere that domestic cattle and ovicaprids were kept, both riding and wool production depended, to the contrary, on the introduction of a new species and a new subspecies respectively, and are therefore inevitably exotic. The crucial test for indigenism is the plough.[16]

Evidence for use of the plough is in fact surprisingly common (Thrane 1989; Tegtmeier 1993). More than a hundred third- and second-millennium round-barrows with plough-marks are known in Denmark alone, along with similar evidence from twelve Middle Neolithic passage graves from the second half of the fourth millennium, and ten attributed to EN C[17] or Fuchsberg from the middle of the fourth millennium. There are none under earlier long-mounds, though these are admittedly rarer. This excellent sequence seems to suggest a rather precise date, of the order of 3500 BC, which fits well with the half-dozen pieces of iconic evidence for animal traction from Hungary and Poland, which date to 3500–3000 BC (Boleráz and Classical Baden). Indeed, the very interest in representing them could be seen as symptomatic of their novelty and social importance (cf. Hodder 1988).

Why, then, the reluctance to recognise this horizon (e.g. Midgley 1992, 388–90), shortly before the appearance of wool and horses? To some extent it reflects an ignorance on the part of European prehistorians of any wider setting for their studies. One constantly quoted reason, however, is the single mid-fifth-millennium radiocarbon date[18] from an ambiguous ('complex') stratigraphic context for the possible furrows under a Wiórek long mound at Sarnowo in central Poland. The fragility of this straw obstacle suggests that the real reason is a prior expectation that the plough *should* be older,[19] because indigenous; and it is this expectation which underlies Chapman's belief that it appeared in the Balkans in the early fifth millennium. His principal reason for seeking it at this date is the widespread horizon of settlement-pattern change associated with the beginning of Vinča-Pločnik and the Tisza culture, which is discussed in Chapter 11 and interpreted there as a culmination of earlier trends towards settlement nucleation, and the northwards extension of tell-building. It is not the most marked change in settlement patterns, however, better candidates for which would be the local mid-fifth-millennium shift to a 'Copper Age' dispersed pattern of small settlements and large cemeteries, or on a much more radical scale the fundamental shift of the mid-fourth millennium, which affected both local and regional patterns. It was, in fact, the scale of this latter phenomenon which first attracted my attention (Sherratt 1976).[20]

Yet even if a fifth-millennium date were to be demonstrated for Balkan ploughing, it could still be seen as the extension of an innovation originally made in the heartland of western Old World agriculture, extending to Europe at a time of inter-regional linkup (northern Ubaid) in greater Meso-potamia, and perhaps accompanied to the Balkans by the first use of copper and a fashion for dark-faced pottery that is perhaps symptomatic of some other new material technology. This alternative seems to me to be less appealing, however, because the plough does not seem universal at that time in the Near East. (Tom Levy has denied its existence in the Chalcolithic of the southern Levant, for instance, making it improbable in Egypt; the most radical changes in Anatolian settlement patterns are also later: Figure 2.3.) The most probable scenario on an inter-regional scale would still be the massive extension of contact-radius which took place during the fourth millennium, when many other innovations reached Europe. Metallurgy, for instance, having developed in south-east Europe along entirely indigenous lines in terms of the technique and design of its products, was transformed by the arrival of Near Eastern innovations like the the two-piece mould (Chernykh 1992). These seem to me to be strong reasons for accepting the empirical indications offered by Danish ploughmarks.

The choice of an interpretative framework nevertheless seems in the end to depend as much on quasi-metaphysical assumptions about the nature of change (stadial *versus* spatially punctuated) as it does upon empirical evidence; those who believe that the plough came into existence whenever it was made necessary by the pressure of population (following the model elaborated by Boserup in 1965) will not be impressed by the apparent coincidence of the first ploughmarks with the arrival of new elements of material culture from Anatolia, and they would in any case deny the element of diffusion even were it possible to demonstrate a perfect pattern of concentric extension, by postulating a common demographic threshold which required intensified production. What might decide the issue, however, is a shift of perception: if these various features which I have grouped as parts of a secondary products revolution are seen, not as features of more efficient farming practice adopted under pressure, but much more as expressions of a demand for new consumables and new elements of what was primarily elite display.

CONSUMING SYMBOLS AND SUSTAINING HABITS

My outburst against 'subsistence' in an earlier section now becomes central to the argument. The concept of populations 'on the breadline' is one which relates to social systems involving large-scale exploitation – relatively massive transfers of resources from one part of the population to another, whether it is within a class relationship or one of regional dependency. Whilst famine and disease were ever-present dangers (at least at certain times), it may be doubted whether this constant penury was the permanent condition of humankind before the rise of urbanism and the state. Without elaborating a myth of primordial sufficiency, it may nevertheless be asserted that life has only rarely been so dire as actually to compel the adoption of new ways of life; more usually they have been initially chosen because they presented opportunities in which certain people saw an advantage, and only later were they taken over (perhaps under pressure) by whole populations who thus become locked in to such practices.[21] These advantages have been both bodily, in terms of taste and nutrition, and social, in terms of what Wolfgang Schivelbusch has called 'performance in the process of enjoyment': in a word, they were concerned with consumption – whether in the literal sense of consuming food or in the derived sense of consuming automobiles and ox-carts.

One of the apparent associations in the European evidence is the contemporaneity of the first evidence for ploughs and that for wheeled vehicles. Whilst both employ yoked oxen and require an appropriate herd-structure to supply them, these two machines do not necessarily have any further association, unless they were in some sense perceived as being closely related. It is unlikely that such expensive items as carts and waggons were initially simply pieces of everyday farming equipment (even if they eventually became so), and the association of wheeled vehicles with elite burials indicates that they were seen as prestige equipment (Piggott 1992), either belonging to individuals or in outer Europe perhaps under communal ownership (as certain contrasts between Baden and the megalith-builders would hint: Chapter 16). What, then, of ploughs: prestige ploughing? Ostentatious cultivation? The concept does not seem to me to be inherently absurd in the context of the Baden culture, any more than the idea of their ritual significance in northern Europe. Even in Mesopotamia, the plough was recognised as a minority instrument, confined to those prosperous enough to afford it – as discussed in the Sumerian literary text called 'The disputation between the plough and the hoe'.[22] In northern Europe, it so happens that there has been a continuing discussion (Pätzold 1960; Randsborg and Nybo 1986; Rowley-Conwy 1987; Rausing 1988; Kristiansen 1989) of 'ritual' ploughing as part of Neolithic and Bronze Age funerary ceremonies, on the assumption that this was the opposite of some 'secular' usage. Could it be that these were in fact one and the same? Whilst neither 'ritual' nor 'prestige' fully convey the nature of what is involved, neither does the simple instrumentalist[23] conception of the plough as the solution to a technical problem of preparing the soil. That is not to deny that it had practical usefulness, which probably became increasingly apparent as it was employed more widely; but initially it was particularly powerful because of its combination of mental and material qualities. It was no doubt the focus of social and religious practices connected with fertility (since the simile of the ard-share as penis is unlikely to have been lost on Neolithic minds), and its adoption was as much a conceptual and performative change as the adoption of the cart with which it was apparently associated. One corollary of this is that the invention of wheeled vehicles, with their universal appeal to the human (male?) psyche, was a significant factor in the spread of the plough to Europe.

This immediately begins to make much better sense of the pattern of evidence. As Chapter 6 indicates, the scatter of early (late fourth millennium) indications of paired draught in Europe largely falls along the axis which was to become the first trans-continental route of contacts at the beginning of the Reinecke Bronze Age (late third/early second millennium: Sherratt 1993, fig. 6). Not merely do the figurines and paired-cattle burials mark out the route, but certain items like the Oldenburg vases and the Bytyń ox-figures imply long-distance contacts, the latter apparently as far back as Anatolia (Chapter 7). Even the Bronze Age pattern of fortified sites on important passes through the mountain chain (Sherratt 1993, fig. 7) is prefigured in the existence of impressive sites like Hlinsko on the upper Morava with its elaborate defences and evidence for textile production. Moreover, the Baden paired-cattle burials are particularly associated (Chapters 8 and 15) with drinking-sets, which specifically resemble metal vessels (Chapter 17) that were manufactured in Anatolia but not in the Balkans; and the most explicit cart-models are in fact cups. The common characteristic of these elements is their restriction to privileged social groups. There could hardly be clearer indications of the fact that paired draught was associated with new, exotic consumption-habits, and that these spread among what must have been a relative minority of literally well-connected people (Figure 0.5).

The reason for the explosive dispersal of such features at the time of the Uruk colonies thus becomes clearer: while the direct search for raw materials to supply growing lowland cities was directed to the immediate mountain periphery, it was part of the strategy of acquiring them to impress the 'natives' with large temples like those on Jebel Aruda, and with new practices, consumption habits and consumer needs: wheeled vehicles, alcoholic drinks, textiles, metalwork. The dynamic of core and periphery depended on the export of added value and the stimulation of new needs. The features of secondary farming and the manufacturing technologies of the new urban communities came together to transform the material environment of the areas around the Fertile Crescent. This new material culture, however, had its own dynamic; and it spread in a material trans-formation of life in a zone beyond this periphery – what I have called, following Jane Schneider, the *margin* – including much of temperate Europe. What is impressive, and must surely have been preceded by even earlier networks of contact which we can only dimly discern, is the speed and directionality with which innovations spread across Anatolia and up into central Europe. In south-east Europe within the Carpathian arc – the area of the Balkan-Carpathian Copper Age – there was an instant transformation of culture and settlement-pattern: the Baden-Cernavoda-Ezero complex, the beginning of the Bronze Age in Balkan (but not Carpathian) terminology.[24] Despite the continuing rapidity of their spread to the north as far as Denmark, these features did not cause such a discontinuity in the megalith-building cultures of the North European Plain and western Europe.[25] Instead, the existing pattern was elaborated, before being decisively altered with the spread of the Corded Ware culture some 500 years later (see below, and Chapter 16).

All of the introduced novelties are likely to have been relative luxuries, restricted to elite groups in society: woollen clothes, the consumption of alcoholic drinks, the use of traction- or riding-animals.[26] In south-east Europe all these features may have been more or less coincident, along with some tree-crops in the Mediterranean parts and perhaps the donkey too; the horse was slightly later. (Tree crops remained confined to the Mediterranean, and their subsequent westward spread was closely con-nected to the extension of trade, social complexity and the mobilisation of capital; the plough and cart, however, had spread to northern Italy by 3000, as shown by statue-menhirs from the Adige region.) Beyond the Carpathians the appearance of these elements was less closely synchronous, with the plough appearing before the others, in the middle of TRB. As noted above, there is disagreement amongst faunal experts as to when milking began, and when it became widespread. In northern Europe most of the other features appeared with Corded Ware, and further west with Bell-Beakers; though

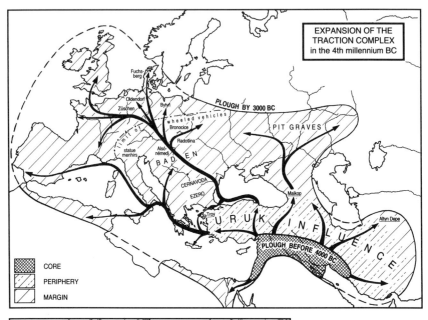

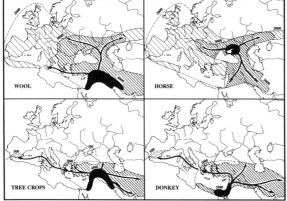

0.5 The spread of secondary farming in Europe: above, re-constructed routes for the spread of the traction complex (plough and wheeled vehicles; cf. Fig. 6.7) in the fourth millennium BC; below, estimated dispersal-patterns for other secondary live products, 4000–500 BC.

wool in particular seems to have remained a relative rarity for a long time in the far west. Wheeled vehicles seem also to have lagged behind the plough in spreading to north-west Europe. The notion of a European 'horizon' therefore applies particularly to the plough, which was accompanied in the Carpathian Basin and the Balkans by a major change in settlement patterns. A shift of comparable magnitude only occurred half a millennium later in northern Europe, and up to a millennium later on the Atlantic coastlands to the west. These major social and economic shifts in each area, successively from 'inner' to 'outer' Europe, each marked the inception of a pattern of settlement and burial type that was to characterise their development for much of the Bronze Age, down to around 1300 BC.

The sharpness of this threshold serves to point up particularly clearly the 'otherness' of what had gone before – a continent whose culture was much closer in many respects to those which Europeans would encounter in the New World in the sixteenth century AD, in its manual cultivation systems, its lack of riding and draught-animals, and less tangibly in a smoking of narcotic substances rather than a widespread use of alcohol, and religious beliefs which might broadly be described as shamanism. If I am correct in my model, these changes were not simply the result of inherent trends in earlier prehistoric European practices, but came about because of a specific historical conjunction. It is not satisfactory, therefore, simply to tell a tale of local developments: change, when it came, was a surprise and could not have been predicted from antecedent local conditions.

THE PATTERNING OF EUROPE

As a final element in this introduction, to provide a framework within which to insert the various studies which follow, a brief sketch of 'what happened in Europe' is perhaps of use. Chronology is of the essence, for the world moves on and each period is different from its predecessor; but spatial contrasts, especially in the Neolithic and Copper Age, were striking, too, and it is important to establish the spatio-temporal limits of a generalisation (Figure 0.6).

Farming first spread to Europe in its phase of diversification and elaboration in the seventh millennium BC, which saw the effective integration of livestock (and the continuing domestication of cattle in several different areas) but preceded the development of ploughing and irrigation which subsequently took place in greater Mesopotamia. The first European farming was still, therefore, a relatively simple form of cultivation, best described as horticulture, and spreading in a series of rapid leaps because of the limited spatial extent of land to which it could be successfully applied: the restricted areas of high surface- or ground-water within a Mediterranean environment.[27] Neil Roberts (1991) has seen the somewhat different settings of Çatalhöyük and Hacılar – respectively on an alluvial fan and beside a seasonally enlarged lake – as a microcosm of the larger contrast between the Near East,[28] where the use of river-waters was to be extended by irrigation, and south-east Europe, where a series of Balkan lake-basins offered stepping-stones to central Europe. In this latter zone, probably in the Carpathian Basin,[29] a new pattern of rain-fed horticulture, appropriate to temperate Europe, had emerged by the middle of the sixth millennium, at about the same time as some Near Eastern farmers were also turning to rain-fed cultivation, but probably using the plough. Europe thus conserved and propagated older forms of hand-cultivation, pioneered in the formative phases of farming; which is why the introduction of more advanced methods was to come as such a radical change in the mid-fourth millennium.

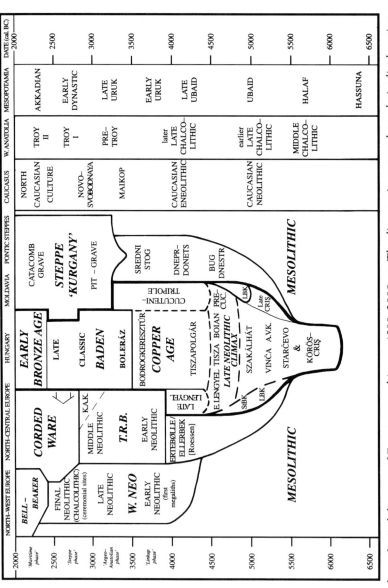

0.6 A chronological diagram of European prehistory, 6500–2000 BC. The diagram is arranged as a latitudinal section across the centre of the continent, to show the symmetry between developments on the eastern and western sides, following the introduction of farming. The thicker line encloses 'intrusive' cultures; the widening spread indicates successive incorporation and cultural transformation of indigenous populations. Influences from the Near East and from the steppe region interrupt the course of these local developments.

(LBK = Linienbandkeramik   A.V.K. = Alföldi Vonaldíszes Kerámia

STBK = Stichbandkeramik   K.A.K. = Kugelamphorenkultur)

In a recent article (1995), van Andel and Runnels have summarised the model expounded in the early chapters here, and fitted calibrated radio-carbon dates to a pattern of spread through southern Anatolia by 7500 BC and across the Aegean by 7000 BC. Equally importantly, they report the results of geomorphological investigations in Thessaly (see also van Andel et al. 1994), which confirm the suggestions put forward in Chapters 2 and 3 concerning the nature of floodplain farming;[30] some tells had actually been situated on actively aggrading floodplains. The same is true of central Anatolian sites like Çatalhöyük and its contemporary neighbour Can Hasan III (Roberts 1991). This pattern of association with very specific environ-mental niches suggests relatively low (though locally concentrated) popu-lation densities, and makes plausible a dispersal model in which small-scale population movements played a critical part. This is certain in the cases of Cyprus and Crete, and very likely true of Thessaly. On the mainland, these populations were inserted into finite spaces within already occupied lands, but in parts which were often of secondary interest to hunters (some, indeed, probably so disease-ridden that only the greater fecundity of farming popu-lations allowed their colonisation: see Chapter 2). Recent research has begun to reveal traces of such Mesolithic populations in certain parts both of Hungary and Thessaly. On the other hand, it is likely that in optimal areas indigenous populations achieved some density, especially on the coasts; and it should be remembered that the Black Sea was only fully united with the Mediterranean after 5500 BC, when waters flowed across the spillway of the Bosphorus to drown extensive coastlands which are now under 200m of water. Here, surely, was the focus of a Mesolithic population which is at the moment evident as much by its negative effects as by its demonstrable artefactual presence (much of which is presumably now underwater): the way in which Neolithic penetration – just as in the Baltic region – conspicuously avoids the Black Sea coasts of Anatolia, Bulgaria and Romania, where Neolithic cultures are later and which even in the fifth and fourth millennia retained a distinctive character, partly due to their own independent network of external maritime contacts.

A whole spectrum of relationships with such indigenous Mesolithic groups may therefore be expected. Small numbers of hunters, on lands where farming had a decisive advantage, may have been immediately absorbed into farming populations; others, in more remote locations, no doubt continued as a small and relatively isolated minority. Between these two extremes, various patterns of symbiosis with farming groups are likely, and some selective adoption of their innovations. This can be most clearly seen, on a larger 'external' scale, with the 'Sub-Neolithic' groups of the Pontic steppes like the Dnepr-Donets culture (whose heartland was pre-sumably in the now drowned northern Black Sea coastlands); and their 'internal' equivalents are exemplified in settlements like Lepenski Vir, con-temporary with the first farmers but in locations where they had the advantage, and from which they could transact with farming groups to some extent on equal terms. As farming populations increased, however, the balance of this relationship began to alter and such groups were increasingly absorbed – retaining, however, a certain regional distinctiveness, like Hamangia and subsequently Varna in coastal Bulgaria, with its own ostentatious burial habits even when using similar items of material culture to those of its inland Chalcolithic contemporaries (Price 1993). Some contribution of older traditions (e.g. in the making of organic containers) may be evident in the changing decorative syntax of painted pottery; but the dominant process was nevertheless one of accommodation to the introduced pattern. Habitation-monuments (tells), with their more formal patterns of existence such as the use of chairs and tables and elaborate painted pottery, tended to spread even to those areas whose initial Neolithic had been marked by a strong continuity with indigenous lifeways, like Körös/Criş.

Farming thus spread by a balance between these two processes of insertion and adoption; and the preponderance of one or other of them affected the regional character of the cultures that were created. Both were social processes, one based on internal reproduction and the other on external recruitment. Broadly speaking, insertion dominated along the axis from Anatolia through the Balkans to the loess-lands of central Europe; elsewhere, adoption by existing populations played a larger part. This was the dominant mode in the Mediterranean, where many caves occupied both in Mesolithic and early Neolithic (Cardial) times testify to such continuity. It was also the pattern in the outer arc of Europe, along the Atlantic coast-lands, the Baltic and the lakes and rivers of eastern Europe. Western and northern Europe were distinctive, however, in that the spread of farming to the dense indigenous populations which had grown up there by the fifth and fourth millennia BC continued to propagate the *structure* of farming communities as it had spread across the central European axis of the loess-lands: that is, a pattern centred on permanent artificial points inscribed in the landscape. Instead of 'habitation monuments' of timber longhouse villages, the structure was continued by the building of megalithic funerary monuments (see Chapters 13 and 14). It may be that 'farming', too – in the sense of cereal cultivation and domestic livestock keeping – also became somewhat ritualised and token, with much food still coming from the wild; only later (perhaps with the arrival of the plough) did cereals and livestock become the staple: the Mesolithic communities of outer Europe were initially re-structured, rather than being immediately transformed economically. The distribution of megaliths picks out those areas of western and northern Europe where indigenous populations were densest, and made their greatest demographic and cultural contribution to the emerging pattern; and they were mirrored, in the east, by the Sub-Neolithic groups on the Pontic steppes who developed in a quite opposite direction – not by espousing a sedentary monumentality but by embracing increased mobility – through hunting, and ultimately domestication, of the horse.

This balance between the two processes was important in creating the character of different regions of Europe, and their receptiveness to new influences from outside these regions. Within the Carpathian Basin and in south-east Europe where a single cultural pattern predominated, the tell cultures reached their climax in the early fifth millennium, and the south-east European Copper Age developed after 4500 BC. It was in this region that renewed contacts with the expanding Near Eastern world system had such instantaneous and many-sided effects a millennium later, around 3500 BC. Beyond this region, however, the pattern was much more complicated by relationships with the often numerous Mesolithic populations, and the possibility of forming 'alternative' networks amongst 'outsiders'. This rather dialectical pattern of cultural change continued to characterise this area until the Bronze Age.[31] The initial spread of farmers across the loess-lands had been in many respects a pioneer extension of a Balkan (and ultimately Near Eastern) pattern, accommodated to the rather different conditions of central Europe but still based on a highly selective use of a rather similar set of landscapes (Figure 0.7a), and avoiding areas of dense Mesolithic occupation. It was initially reinforced after 4500 by the spread of elements from further south, most conspicuously in the form of small quantities of copper; these impulses spread north-westwards, in the footsteps of the *Bandkeramik* pioneers, and also by demographic expansion on a new axis north-westwards from the Carpathians along the forest-steppe margin towards Kiev, in the form of Cucuteni-Tripole groups. Both movements intruded increasingly on to territories where Mesolithic groups lived in larger numbers; but the reactions were very different. Around the western and northern margins of the loess-covered plains – from the Paris Basin to Poland – loess-land farmers increasingly merged with their neighbours and embraced a much greater diversity of food-getting practices, though unified socially through the common symbolism of funerary monuments which seems to have been an essential element of this process of cultural fusion. The thin strip of loess-covered territory ceased to be the lifeline to cultural innovation, and it now became more integrated with surrounding areas (where former Mesolithic populations were in the majority) as new cultural blocs formed on the basis of this neolithicisation of outer Europe (Figure 0.7b). In Moldavia and the Ukraine, however, no such accommodation could be observed: indeed, quite the reverse, as increasingly nucleated and defended Cucuteni-Tripole settlements protected a provincial version of Balkan culture from Sub-Neolithic (becoming Sub-Copper Age) steppe neighbours such as Sredni Stog and its contemporaries.

In the early centuries of the fourth millennium, closely connected with the first spread of farming to Scandinavia, a chain of connections developed from the Balkans through the Carpathian Basin to Denmark. It is evident in a continuum of Balkan and Carpathian cultures with connections reaching up into Poland, and characteristically including sets of drinking-vessels (Chapter 15).[32] It is possible that this series of links began in Late Chalcolithic northern Anatolia, connecting with these others through the Cernavoda I culture in the lower Danube. These links mark the first emergence of an axis which was to become a dominant feature of European development down until the mid-second millennium: a chain of connections along which news of the traction complex seems to have travelled. This latter event, in the middle of the fourth millennium, can thus be seen as the impact of a specific style of elite culture (metal vessels, wheeled vehicles) on a pre-existing set of relationships and already-spreading practices. Its directionality (along a line from Turkey to Denmark) is shown by the way in which the Tripole block in the Ukraine did not participate in these developments, and after 3500 BC remained for a whole phase (CII) isolated between Baden and Pit-Graves, gradually splitting into local groups and losing the coherence of its already old-fashioned painted pottery style.[33]

The reception of new elements was very different north of the Carpathians from that south-east of them, where a relatively homogeneous set of cultures underwent a rather uniform set of changes. In the North European Plain, even a novelty as radical as the plough was absorbed (and its usage no doubt transformed) within a pre-existing pattern – either that of TRB villages within the loess-lands, or megalith-centred communities beyond. True, the monuments became more elaborate (like Nordic passage-graves); but the really radical change in culture, behaviour and settlement-patterns was deferred for another half-millennium (Chapter 16). It seems likely that already initiated processes of change were still continuing: enclaves of Mesolithic hunting populations were still being absorbed, and beyond the margins of farming cultures a further belt of Sub-Neolithic groups was also being generated. As well as regional differences in culture, therefore, some diversity in lifestyles between partly symbiotic groups was probably coming into existence, as a complex pattern of often inter-digitating cultural distributions between TRB and new groupings would suggest. In the centuries following 3500 BC, a broad band of related communities developed across much of the North European Plain, from Hamburg to Kiev, called after its distinctive liquid-container, the globular amphora. The territory of the Cucuteni-Tripole culture was now divided between the Globular Amphora culture and the Pit-Grave culture (created on the steppes from Sub-Neolithic groups by the transmission of Near Eastern innovations via the Caucasus), bringing the two into direct contact; and the eastern, mobile, steppe model played an important part in transforming certain groups within the North European Plain into the new pattern of dispersed, tumulus-building Corded Ware cultures, with their characteristic single-graves containing drinking-cups and battle axes. After the predominantly north/south pattern of contacts in the fourth millennium,

24

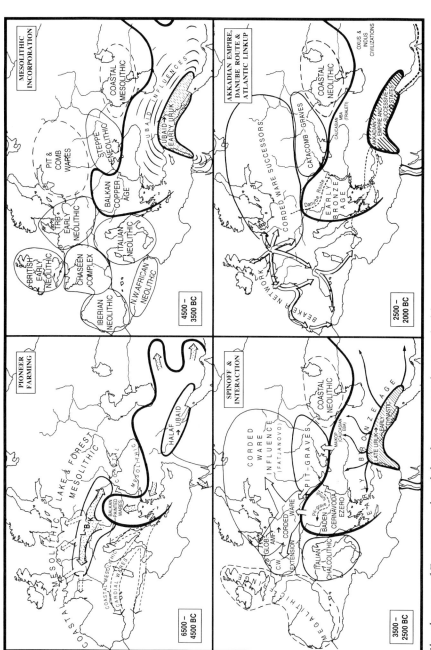

0.7 Sketch-maps of European cultural development: (a) the spread of farming, 6500–4500; (b) the formation of new cultures by interaction with indigenous populations, 4500–3500; (c) spinoff effects from Near Eastern urbanisation and interactions with steppe groups, 3500–2500; (d) the spread of these innovations in the west, as south-east and central Europe became indirectly linked to maritime networks centred on the Akkadian Empire, 2500–2000 (cf. Fig. 18.1).

therefore, the third millennium was characterised by a broadly east/west pattern of interaction, in which the new pattern extended both westwards into Germany, eastern France and Switzerland, and also eastwards towards Moscow (Figure 0.7c). In many respects the spread of Bell-Beakers in the far west can be seen as an extension of this process, carrying a new pattern of mobility into the heartlands of megalithism, and setting up its own network of riverine links within the Continent (Figure 0.7d). Even as this was happening, however, further impulses along the north/south axis via the Danube, starting from an Anatolian town now established on the threshold of Europe, at Troy (Chapter 18), began to introduce fresh novelties and to initiate the changes which central European archaeologists recognise as the beginning of the Bronze Age.

Although my account of fourth-millennium cultural changes emphasises the importance of new long-distance contacts, it is very far from 'diffusionism', in the sense in which the term has fallen into disrepute through its neglect of local conditions and contexts. Even the spread of farming into Europe, undoubtedly a process which began in the Near East, can only be understood by reference to the different reactions of the indigenous populations. So, equally, with later contact-episodes, contact and context must be evaluated together: it takes two to tango. Many changes came about as consequences of the spread of farming itself – the demand for raw materials like stone, and especially axes for forest-clearance, the growing formality of the domestic setting, with tables and flat surfaces – while even the propensity to experiment with metallurgy was inherent in the pyrotechnology of potting and the interest in brightly-coloured stones (Sherratt 1994b). The Copper Age pattern, therefore, with its network of elite exchanges for particularly desirable materials, seems to have been essentially independent of any further input from outside. (The counterpoint between 'successional' and 'contact-induced' changes is explored in Chapter 5.) Indeed, what is remarkable is the relative independence between phenomena like the use of the plough, and the sort of individualising, copper-using, prestige-goods society which tempts us to call it Chalcolithic – whether fifth-millennium like Tiszapolgár or third-millennium like Bell-Beaker. Plotted on a chronological chart, the two horizons cut across one another: one steeply sloping, one relatively flat (Figure 0.8). The south-east European Copper Age is metallurgy without the plough, the Danish Middle Neolithic is the plough without metallurgy; Baden and Corded Ware have both, and witnessed the more profound transformation: it was the combination of a source of capital and a medium of exchange which gave these cultures their potential for growth, and allowed their cultural patterns to spread so widely. By the early second millennium, many of the regional contrasts which are so characteristic a feature of the fourth and third millennia had become much less evident. The diverse origins both of the populations and cultural elements which came together in Europe had been submerged in what

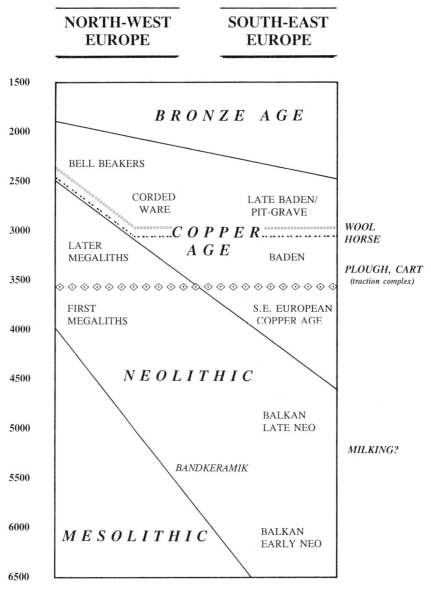

NORTH-WEST EUROPE

SOUTH-EAST EUROPE

0.8 A chronological diagram of European prehistory, 6500–1500 BC, aligned along the main axis of contact with the Near East, showing the postulated dates of introduction of selected features of secondary farming. The rapid introduction of innovations in the fourth millennium cuts across the slower pattern of social and cultural developments.

was now a common inheritance: a pattern of mixed farming and herding over a variety of landscapes, whose elites espoused similar objectives and used what was to a remarkable extent a common language of material culture. Seen from this perspective, the fourth millennium was the climax of regional diversity, resulting both from internal processes and new external contacts.

THE EMERGENCE OF 'MODERN' EUROPE

What sort of story, therefore, emerges from this discussion and the pages that follow? It is one which requires a broad spatial setting, for only within such a large framework does the local detail make sense. But the local detail cannot just be read off from the abstract generalisations: it is what constitutes the larger processes and determines their outcome. The story is 'evolutionary' not in the Spencerian sense of evolutionist gradualism with predictable stages of progress, but in the Darwinian sense of constrained genealogical paths with often unpredictable conjunctures and unexpected outcomes – which nevertheless, with the benefits of hindsight, show some regularities both of form and of direction. It is necessary to stress that the regularities are retrospective: they are not principles which are manifested in development, like a constant search to maximise energy, or population, or whatever; nor, therefore, can they be used to explain it. Rather, they are the structured outcomes of choices made from recognisably human motives. The structure is created, in a particular environment, by the potential of what has been invented, as it is realised in a set of emergent properties which were not necessarily apparent at the beginning of the process. It is important not to over-rationalise the past: the philosophy of history as a chapter of interesting accidents is more convincing than one which sees it as planned progress.

Important, also, to recognise how different it all was: in L. P. Hartley's famous phrase, the past is a foreign country, and things are done differently there. At the beginning of the Holocene, no-one had ever farmed before. Everything had to be worked out from scratch, and at first things changed only slowly. To give two small, but symptomatic examples: until quite recently, cows would only let down their milk in the presence of a calf; and horses, as herd animals, needed to stay in a group. Hence, perhaps, the famous transitional sequence, recorded on Assyrian reliefs, from paired horses as draught animals for chariots, through paired animals for riding (both being controlled, as in a chariot, by a groom, whilst the warrior looses his bow), and finally to our 'logical' expectation of single animals controlled by single riders (Littauer and Crouwel 1979, 136). Whether this slow development depended on equine psychology or simply on the way in which concept and practice were limited by previous experience, change was not simple. To go from A to C requires an intervening B, which is often an unstable, transitional phase that is probably an 'extinct practice' which is nowhere represented in the contemporary spectrum of human behaviours. This was certainly true of the earliest farming, with its incongruous combination of cereal-cultivation and gazelle-hunting. Ethnography, which necessarily describes situations that are themselves the outcome of long developmental sequences, is often not a good guide to the deep past. The mobility of many recent hunting groups, for instance, relates to their relatively recent occupation of marginal habitats, and in some cases actually depends on techniques acquired from farming or pastoral groups. Animal-based societies, whether hunters or pastoralists, have probably become more mobile during the Holocene; intensive collectors, in the same way as agriculturalists, have probably become more sedentary. The only universally valid generalisation is probably that global diversity has tended to increase – until the sixteenth century AD, when that trend began to be catastrophically reversed.

When, therefore, did Europe acquire the distinctive character that it was later to impose on much of the rest of the world? Surely the answer must be: in the fourth millennium BC, as part of the general transformation of the western Old World. Much of the cultural distinctiveness of this area can be summed up in two words: animals, and alcohol. Animals first: one of the most telling illustrations in Fernand Braudel's *Civilisation and Capitalism* is a graph (taken from Pierre Chaunu) of the populations of Indians, cattle, goats and sheep in Mexico after 1500. While the indigenous human population fell, in a steep, hollow curve following the Spanish conquest, the numbers of introduced ungulates climbed in a classic logistic growth pattern. As they said in England in the fourteenth century, 'sheep do eat up men'. Europeans used their domestic livestock to create 'Neo-Europes' in the lands they conquered overseas – usually at the expense of the natives (Crosby 1986). These large numbers of domestic animals relative to human populations are an Old World characteristic, and typical especially of the western rather than the eastern part, since in east Asia there is a sharp division between the agrarian Chinese, with few animals (mainly pigs and water-buffalo, and otherwise beans for protein), and their specialised pastoralist neighbours on the steppes. The western Old World has a more intimate mixture of arable and pastoral, either as symbiotic (often ethnically distinct) groups in the Near East, or as mixed farming (sometimes with transhumance) in temperate Europe. These large numbers of animals make sense in the system because of the variety of products they yield, both food and non-food. Animal labour replaced human labour, with the added advantage of the labourers being edible.[34] Domestic livestock extended the power of the family and lineage, almost like fictitious kin, and simultaneously provided capital capable of generating growth. As Peter Bogucki has pointed out in a thoughtful article (1993), these properties became increasingly evident in European societies after the fourth millennium. The growing numbers of animals, as well as people, are fundamental to understanding the social changes of later European prehistory (cf. Halstead 1995).

Finally, alcohol: arguably the most fundamental constituent of western civilisation, inebriating drink is at the core of its culture (see Chapter 15; also Goodman, Lovejoy and Sheratt 1995). Wine is the life-blood of the Mediterranean, and its proscription by a conquering Islam is eloquent testimony to its deep symbolic significance, both secular and religious. What makes the civilisations of the New World seem so alien, despite their outward similarity in possessing criteria such as cities, monumental architecture, writing etc., is the nature of their religion, which resembles a scaled-up version of the shamanism of native American tribal society. One aspect of this is the consumption of psychotropic substances and a consequent ecstatic emphasis. Such practices have some echoes in Old World civilisations, but they are memories of a world long passed. It was alcohol, that is both drug and food, which domesticated the ecstatic experience and converted it from private trance to public conviviality. Archaeology shows that the uses of traction animals and the conspicuous consumption of liquid refreshment were essentially co-eval. Alcohol and animal traction, drinking and driving – associated then and forever after[35] – were the most powerful of the cultural attractions which impinged on Europe in the mid-fourth millennium BC; and the images of the Alsónémedi graves and the Szigetszentmárton waggon-cup, which recur throughout the papers which follow, are symptomatic of a Europe which, though still prehistoric, is increasingly recognisable to its present-day inhabitants.

NOTES

1. Extension of a calibrated radiocarbon timescale to the beginning of the Holocene and tentatively beyond it (the former on the basis of the European pine sequence and the latter from marine carbonates) has given a new realism to estimates of time in this period (Stuiver and Reimer 1993). Since the offset between 'raw' and calibrated radiocarbon estimates is of the order of a millennium in the earlier Holocene, and even more at its onset, currently acceptable dates may differ substantially from some earlier published estimates.
2. This is well illustrated in the search for 'rank' and 'hierarchy' in the archaeological record; presumably there will soon be a discovery that prehistory was full of flexible, task-oriented workteams. *Plus ça change, plus c'est la même chose!*
3. I have explored these ideas more fully in Sherratt 1990b and 1992b, and in a recent David Clarke Memorial Lecture – Sherratt 1995b – and will do no more than sketch them here.
4. One example of which is, I fear, Braudel's stratified degrees of determinacy, from long-term geological processes to political events: this is too simple. It is paralleled by some recent American pronouncements.
5. '*Subsistence farming*: farming which directly supports the farmer's household without producing a significant surplus for trade' (Shorter OED).
6. The current emphasis on consumption is, of course, a child of its time and reflects the contemporary economics of the supermarket and hypermarket; just as the emphasis on production in a previous generation reflected the relative deprivation of the Great Depression and post-war rationing. Clearly, both parts of the cycle need to be considered in a balanced account.
7. I.e. how to prevent population growth from eating up increased productivity: but what is productivity for if not to be eaten up? The real question is: who eats it?

8. In Greenfield's (1988, 573) concise definition: 'Secondary products are products for which animals may be utilised repeatedly over the course of their lifetimes. In contrast, animals used for primary products (meat, bone and hide) must be slaughtered, yielding the product only once.' In saying that animals before the secondary products revolution were used 'primarily for meat', I naturally do not exclude other uses of the carcase (as at least one over-literal reader has assumed) nor even *ad hoc* uses such as carrying or dragging loads; the contrast I am drawing is with maintaining an appropriate population structure for milking, wool-bearing, draught, etc.

9. I hope that this formulation will make explicit features of my model which were perhaps not sufficiently emphasised in Chapter 6, and gave rise to the following comment from L. K. Horwitz and E. Tchernov (1989, 283): 'In two highly stimulating articles, Sherratt (1981; 1983) has proposed that in the fourth millennium BC, the Old World underwent what he terms a "secondary products revolution". This revolution marks the intro-duction of a wide range of activities and uses to which animals had not been put before then such as ploughing, riding and the exploitation of their secondary products such as milk and wool. However, Sherratt's hypothesis has met with some criticism ... The innovations noted by Sherratt do not in fact occur within a circumscribed time period, but rather cover a long span of time and as such do not qualify to be called a revolution but rather a long-term trend or process. Sherratt has combined his data without reference to the historical context of many of these features, i.e. the rise of urban societies.' In fact, Sherratt (1983) – the article reprinted here as Chapter 7 – does just that.

10. Though hulled tetraploid forms – heavy, hard and probably spring-grown – were to continue in Europe and were only slowly displaced by the arrival of bread-wheat (a free-threshing hexaploid) from further east. This process was only completed in western Europe in the first millennium BC.

11. 'In fact not only the products of urban industry, but the new economy that produced them, spread and was bound to spread. To persuade their possessors to exchange the needed raw materials for manufactures, they must be induced not only to demand the latter, but also to adjust their economy to absorb them' (1942, 124).

12. It was probably from here that 'foreign ships' with sails reached Egypt, to be recorded in Protodynastic art. During the third millennium the capacity of maritime shipping increased, and the carriage of larger quantities of goods by sea reduced the importance of some of the early long-distance land-trails; these topological changes caused shifts of urban activity both in the Levant and Iran. The Gulf saw a great density of traffic during the later third millennium. The emergence of secondary states around these networks altered the social and political nature of contacts, in which chains of independent political units passed goods between them. Maritime activity in the Mediterranean expanded greatly in the second millennium, when the sail came into use on the east/west route along south Anatolia, between the Aegean and the Levant.

13. Domestic horses only spread into Europe and the Near East in the third millennium, but until recently were considered to have been domesticated just before 4000 BC on the Pontic Steppes. The evidence is, however, contentious, and is discussed in Chapter 7. Whilst a late fifth- early-fourth-millennium date would make horses perhaps the only case of secondary (non-nuclear) domestication in the Old World that did not form an intimate part of this wider interactive network around the Fertile Crescent, this is not *ipso facto* impossible. On the other hand (as I come to believe), we have perhaps been over-hasty in inferring the domestic status of horses in the Sredni Stog culture, when in fact the domestication process really took place in the following (Pit-Grave) period, when Near Eastern input is evident from the use of wheeled vehicles. See Chapter 7 for details.

14. I have recently been taken to task for supposedly using the occasion of a review of Ian Hodder's *Domestication of Europe* to support neo-diffusionist views! This anxiety about the cultural integrity of Mother Europe can only find its explanation in the concepts expounded by Mary Douglas in *Purity and Danger*; it has little to do with the adjudi-cation of evidence. In any case, the landscapes of Turkey seem to me to have rather more in common with Balkan Europe than Mesopotamia, and there is a strong case for

considering the Taurus as the south-east border of a common entity (e.g. of the area using the vertical, as opposed to the horizontal, loom) in Neolithic times. The burst of new information coming from Turkey is helping to break down the insulating ignorance which separates European from Near Eastern prehistorians.

15. In an exemplary attempt, Margaret Glass (1991) has systematically examined faunal assemblages in central Europe from 5500–2500 BC in an attempt to define patterns of animal exploitation. Her painstaking work is vitiated by a number of factors: (1) by taking a large number of sometimes mediocre assemblages rather than a few good ones; (2) by making a bipolar contrast between 'early' and 'late' – the latter defined as 4000–2000 and thus cutting across the crucial transition; and (3) by analysing diversity as a factor of time rather than location. As a literature-based study of faunal remains, without reference to other classes of evidence and within an evolutionary metaphysic, it nevertheless demonstrates important temporal contrasts. Haskell Greenfield's study (1986; 1988, with CA comments) of Balkan assemblages is more focused and better articulated with culture-historical considerations, though its samples are small and rather uncertain. Its conclusion that there was a relatively sudden shift in exploitation patterns in the later fourth millennium is welcome, though not conclusive, support for the models proposed here. Kenneth Russell's splendid compendium of information (1988) has the merits and disadvantages of cultural materialism: a welcome search for modern comparative data, but a rather deterministic use of them. It does not bear directly on present questions. In a pioneering paper, Smith and Horwitz (1984) attempted to demonstrate milking from changes in bone structure due to calcium mobilisation; this technique awaits systematic application and evaluation. Finally, Chang and Koster (1986) have reviewed 'pastoralism' from the point of view of ethnographers of modern transhumant minorities in the Mediterranean. Their lightning tour of the subject contains useful references, but few insights for prehistorians.

16. Unless explicitly indicated otherwise, I speak of the light plough (technically an *ard*), rather than the heavy plough which was invented in temperate Europe in the early Middle Ages.

17. This term has now disappeared in the typological reform of the Danish Neolithic, being subsumed into EN II, but seems to be largely contemporary with Fuchsberg in areas adjacent to it. Fuchsberg has southern connections, reaching down the spine of Jutland into central Germany, and the pattern of early plough-marks (Thrane 1989, fig. 4) supports a picture of an initial Fuchsberg introduction in east Jutland, spreading to the Islands in MNIb, along with the construction of Passage Graves. Whittle's assertion (1985, 210) that 'the earliest ploughmarks under barrows in Denmark are now dated to ENC, and so substantially before 2700 bc [i.e. 3500 BC]' is thus misleading, since they are at most only a century sooner. The pattern actually fits together very well.

18. GrN–5035, 5570 ± 60 bp (Bakker, Vogel and Wiślański 1969), calibrating to 4530–4340 BC. The mound itself (like the other example overlying plough-marks, Łupawa 15) is from the TRB Wiórek phase, comparable to Salzmünde and Fuchsberg, and dating to c.3600–3300 BC. Jankowska and Wiślański (1991, 64) see this clearly: 'Eine deutliche Veränderung in der Wirtschaftsweise der Trichterbecherkultur wird erst in deren letzten Abschnitten erkennbar.'

19. Midgley suggests (1992, 390) the mid-fifth millennium BC, when Lengyel elements indicate contacts with Hungary, though there is no evidence for the plough there either, at this date.

20. As argued below, introduction of the plough may not in fact coincide immediately with a radical change in settlement-pattern, though it stores up the potential for a large-scale change in the future.

21. Such an assertion is not to deny the obvious fact that, for instance, farming can support greater numbers of people than hunting; it is simply to dissociate its ultimate effects from the reason for adopting it in the first place. The two aspects should not be conflated. Farming, for instance, may well have begun at Jericho because of its crucial position on routes of contact and exchange ('trade'); this localised, humanly created demographic

pressure could long have preceded the regional pressures caused by climatic change, which may well have been the reason for the *general* adoption of farming.

22. The god Enlil defends the superiority of the hoe, which is equally effective, does not break so easily, is more easily repaired and can be used throughout the year – and by all people, not just the wealthy with their draught animals. See Potts (1994, 164) and further references therein. Even with the plough, however, secondary hoeing was apparently necessary in European cultivation systems, since Val Camonica rock-engravings of plough scenes show the plough-team followed by 2–5 people with hoes.

23. That is why it is misleading rhetoric to claim, for instance, that the domestication of the horse had 'an effect comparable in scope to that of the introduction of the steam loco- motive or the private automobile' (Anthony and Brown 1991, 22); all these inventions ultimately (and especially in conjunction, and in an appropriate socio-economic context) had a revolutionary effect on human cultures, but these were usually emergent properties, not an instant effect following their initial introduction, which was often their adoption by a minority. Equally, however, it is important not to fall into the trap of assuming that 'prestige' equals 'useless for practical purposes': in most societies, prestige accrues to effective performance.

24. It is a constant pitfall of European prehistory that terms are used in different ways even for the same material on different sides of a national frontier. Mediterranean usage begins the Bronze Age (well before tin-bronze!) in the mid-fourth millennium; central Europe starts the Bronze Age (following Paul Reinecke) in the mid-third millennium. *Caveat lector.*

25. One of the mistakes of my original attempt (Chapter 6) was to look for a major horizon of change in settlement patterns comparable in magnitude to that in the Carpathian Basin at the onset of Baden. I therefore saw the beginning of TRB as in some way related to use of the plough (e.g. Figure 6.18). This can now be seen as part of a quite different process, the fusion of loess-land Neolithic and indigenous populations in the North European Plain (see Chapter 13). The first use of the plough after 3500 was associated with relatively little change in settlement patterns; only after 3000 did a truly radical change occur.

26. Neither 'luxury' nor 'elite' are quite the right terms, but there is nothing equally comprehensive but more precise for such minority use.

27. Many of these micro-environments had become available at the beginning of the Holo- cene, because of increased runoff and the creation of fine alluvium on fans, or the regular seasonal rise and fall of lakes. It was this, rather than a straightforward fall in the levels of lakes (which had come into being largely as a result of low evaporation rates in the Pleistocene), which provided soils suitable for farming. These changes merely created the possibility of farming; they allowed, but did not determine, its adoption.

28. Because of its intimate association with seasonally abundant streamflows, the earliest farming probably involved some minimal forms of water-control, and was itself a kind of proto-irrigation. Formal types of channel-irrigation, however, emerged in Iraq and Iran, and also in the Levant, but not apparently to any great extent in Turkey. In this respect, Turkey resembles Europe rather than her eastern neighbours. Nevertheless the contrast between west- and east-central Anatolia noted by Roberts in the Neolithic also extended to differing livestock emphases: sheep/goat around Lake Beyşehir (as in Balkan Europe), cattle in the Konya plain.

29. The Körös/Criş culture looks like the last attempt to apply a Mediterranean pattern at its northern limits, supplementing unreliable cereal yields with a variety of collected wild foods; the *Bandkeramik* culture, on the other hand, looks like the rapid expansion of a group which has just worked out a new pattern, suitable for central Europe. It was still, however, very closely related to the river network and to fine-grained, fertile soils.

30. 'Our observations on early floodplain farming were predicted long ago by Sherratt (1980) ... His view was rejected by Barker (1985) based on a geomorphic study by Bintliff (1976) which, however, rested on a model of Holocene alluviation that has since proved unworkable' (van Andel et al. 1994, 140). 'Sherratt ... had realised much earlier (1972; 1980) that Neolithic farmers might have chosen floodplain soils for the water they

stored after the floods of spring. He was ignored because of a pervasive belief that the traditional farming methods of Greece and the southeastern Balkans illustrate prehistoric agricultural practice' (van Andel and Runnels 1995, 483). Commentators working in the Higgsian tradition had failed to realise the extent to which geomorphological change had fundamentally altered the Neolithic landscape (cf. Sherratt 1987f).

31. E.g. TRB / Globular Amphorae / Corded Ware / Bell Beaker: each seems to have been conceived in part in explicit reaction to its predecessor and neighbours, and distribution patterns often show considerable overlap, even at the same period.

32. Ian Hodder (1990, 93, commenting on my diagram reproduced here as Figure 15.6) interprets the proliferation of small, individual serving-vessels as the result of an endogenous long-term trend. This is not necessarily in conflict with the idea of a specific external model: the same developmental potential underlay farming societies in both areas, which broadly developed from small, scattered, intensive forms of cultivation to large and extensive ones, with similar social consequences. What I am suggesting, however, is that older-established areas got there first and provided a pattern for the others.

33. The Usatovo group, around Odessa on the Black Sea coast, did however have direct maritime links to north-west Anatolia and the north Aegean, as shown by its arsenical, riveted daggers.

34. Slavery only took root in areas where insufficient bovids were available, or for intricate tasks (like cotton picking) which required skill as well as power.

35. Down to the present day when, needless to say, the combination is a lethal one.

Section I

CYCLES OF
INTERPRETATION

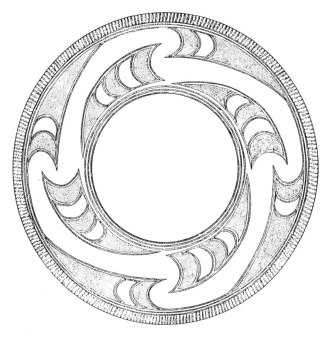

Ornament on the interior of a graphite-painted bowl from Devetaki Cave,
Bulgaria, c.4000 BC (after Mikov and Džambazov).

A preliminary conception, indefinite but comprehensive, is needful as
an introduction to a definite conception. A complex idea is not
communicable directly, by giving one after another of its component
parts their finished forms; since if no outline pre-exists in the mind of
the recipient, they will not be rightly combined.

HERBERT SPENCER (1862)

The study of prehistory requires an approach which owes something to 'history' and something to 'evolution', but in fact must go beyond both. Unmodified, either one of these ways of conceptualising the past is inadequate when faced with the archaeological record. Study of the European Iron Age, for instance, can be simply a hunt for the material correlates of the tribes described by Caesar; projected back into the Bronze Age and the Neolithic (or even the Palaeolithic!), this attitude gives rise to an absurd pseudo-history in which typological tribes are invested with ethnicity and become the equivalents of European nations in old-fashioned nationalistic history textbooks. This approach, while dying, is still not yet dead. On the other hand, however, the evolutionary attitude is equally inadequate, and can be positively harmful. It is easy to treat Palaeolithic populations as automata, predictably responding to climatic change; but the same approach can also be applied in later periods, leading to ecologically reductionist accounts of the beginnings of farming or urban life.

While both approaches co-exist and have long intellectual ancestries, there is a tendency for prehistory to be colonised either from one side or from the other, from the humanities or the sciences, so that at any particular period there is clearly a dominant outlook. Such episodes are not arbitrary, for they correspond to the needs of their time – either to find some underlying progressive regularity to human history as a whole, or else to trace the specific genealogies and experiences of particular groups. Such cycles can be traced in many disciplines: even in biology, for instance, from the abstract 'transformationism' of Erasmus Darwin in 1791, through the genealogical specificity of his grandson Charles Darwin's concept of natural selection in 1859, back again to the abstract, high-Victorian orthogeneticism of Herbert Spencer's version of evolution in 1862. Darwin's vision was in fact a Romantic deconstruction of Enlightenment progressivism, that was in turn lost in Spencer's liberal optimism. These movements thus mirror other aspects of cultural and intellectual history, and the social and economic circumstances behind them; and this insight has a contemporary relevance, in that the interpretative shift which archaeology – in parallel with many other subjects – has recently experienced, from the comparative and deterministic approach of New Archaeology to the cultural particularism of the post-processualists, has many of the characteristic features of the Romantic revolt.

Both approaches have their corresponding advantages and disadvantages, and the success of prehistoric archaeology as a sphere of human knowledge can be gauged by the extent to which it has succeeded in integrating these two enterprises. The prize to be gained from uniting them is nothing less than a comprehensive vision of the whole panorama of nature and culture, and the place of human society within the natural world. This may seem a distant prospect, but there is no doubt that an understanding of prehistory is absolutely central to its achievement. That is why the writings of V. Gordon Childe can be seen to play a crucial part in the intellectual history of the twentieth century. Childe was effectively the first prehistorian simultaneously to see early history in evolutionary perspective and pre-history in historical perspective. Although his works are mainly narrative or methodological rather than theoretical, his constant rewriting of west Eurasian prehistory and early history both defined a field of research and successively tested a whole range of ideas – genealogical, diffusionist and evolutionary – which had been applied to it. Moreover, in developing his own extension of Marxism, he created a model whose coherence could pro-vide a paradigm for the elaboration of many different kinds of explanation. This gift to his chosen subject was perhaps more appreciated by his successors than by his archaeological contemporaries, among whom there were few thinkers of comparable calibre; but it was a precious inheritance to the generations which followed.

1

V. Gordon Childe: Archaeology and Intellectual History

(1989)

If archaeology is the study of the past through its material remains, prehistory is one of its most important branches. Yet prehistory is a very young subject, its very name being little more than a century old (Chippindale 1988). In the story of its development, Gordon Childe occupies a very special place, not only as the most distinguished European prehistorian of the twentieth century, but also as one of the first to combine a professional mastery of the subject with a wider vision of its significance.[1]

Of course there were others before him who studied prehistoric archaeology, under whatever name; but by and large they were concerned with a single period or area – usually that in which they were engaged on excavation. Perhaps because he was not primarily a fieldworker, Gordon Childe had no such encumbrance. As a result of his appointment to a chair at Edinburgh in 1927, he was able to range widely over the prehistory of an area from Scotland to northern India, from the Stone Age to the end of Antiquity. Almost single-handedly he moulded a series of site reports and regional studies into a comprehensive view of the pre- and proto-history of Europe and the Near East. But he did more than merely bring together disparate branches of the same subject, divided by different origins and institutional commitments. In writing a comprehensive prehistory of Europe, he had to choose an appropriate narrative model for the kinds of conclusions which could be distilled from raw archaeological observations.

Gordon Childe was one of the founding members of the board of the historical journal Past and Present, *and this paper arose from a Past and Present Open Lecture delivered at the Institute of Archaeology, London, in November 1987, thirty years after his death. I tried to convey not only the broad intellectual currents which were expressed in his work, but also the sense of idealism and commitment expressed to me by his former colleagues and pupils: Sinclair Hood, Stuart Piggott, Peter Gathercole, Humphrey Case, Cecilia Western, Rachel Maxwell-Hyslop and the late Lady Mallowan.*

For archaeology in Childe's hands was more than just 'piecing together the past' (to use the title of one of his own books [1956] about the craft side of his subject): it was a means of finding answers to some of the great questions about the early history of human societies, which had been central to the European intellectual tradition long before there was any conception of prehistoric archaeology at all. Childe's contribution was to set a growing body of factual material in the context of long-standing debates on matters such as evolutionary models of social development, the relationship between Europe and the Orient, and the significance of technological change, which had been conducted (from the Enlightenment onwards, but pre-eminently by Marx) largely in isolation from firm archaeological knowledge. By placing his work in this larger setting, it may be possible to see why – despite the transformation in prehistoric studies which has taken place since he wrote – he occupies such a crucial position in the history of the subject.

Childe's output, by any standard, was massive. He wrote some twenty substantial books, many of them successively rewritten and updated, and some translated into a dozen languages; and a rapid count of his published articles comes to something around 240: a daunting total.[2] In his writings, he had two audiences in mind: a technical, archaeological one (not only in this country, but also more widely in Europe), and a more popular but educated audience reached by people like Julian Huxley, J. D. Bernal, J. B. S. Haldane, Lancelot Hogben and Hyman Levy through the medium of publishing houses such as the Cobbett Press, the Watts Thinker's Library or Pelican Books. This serious and perhaps rather self-consciously intellectual forum (in which Childe, as a Marxist, found sympathetic company) was viewed with a certain amount of suspicion by many of his archaeological colleagues, but it must be seen as an enterprise in its own right, and not just an exercise in popularisation – of the kind which, with coffee-table books and television, has now grown to industrial proportions. It was an attempt to engage in reasoned debate with a wider world of scholarship than was immediately available in his own subject. As Jaquetta Hawkes put it in 1963, 'Professor Gordon Childe has long been the sole prehistorian with both the ability and the will to draw his subject from its rustic and academic backwaters and make it contribute to the main streams of thought'.[3] In combining these roles he became the natural choice of editors needing a comprehensible account of prehistoric developments in volumes such as the *Cambridge Economic History*, *The European Inheritance*, or the (Oxford) *History of Technology* (Childe 1952; 1954a; 1954b). Through works such as these, his name became widely known beyond his own subject, and still today he is one of the archaeologists most frequently cited in the early chapters of general historical summaries.

In tracing the progress of his thought, it is important to follow it on both levels. Although in terms of his archaeology there is a certain sameness about his output over his last thirty years of work, and Professor Grahame

Clark has gone so far as to say that 'He had achieved what he was going to achieve [in the discipline of prehistoric archaeology] essentially by 1930' (Clark 1976, 4), it is in his more general writings that one can see the way in which he wrestled with the wider significance of his subject. While his professional interests remained circumscribed by the problems in European and Near Eastern archaeology which he set out to tackle in his B.Litt. days, it was in his exploration of new ways of thinking about prehistoric social changes that the larger story lies.

Yet despite the fact that many current schools of archaeology still hail him as a founding father, much of his writing about prehistory has been completely superseded. The progress of archaeological discovery since his death has been remarkably rapid. New information has accumulated at an ever-increasing rate, and with the help of new methods many of his fundamental ideas have been put to the test. The results have not been kind to his theories. It would not be unfair to say that many of his principal conclusions about the European Neolithic and Bronze Ages have been shown to be largely incorrect. One by one, his major postulates about prehistoric European societies have been knocked over. After a generation, not much of his detailed explanatory edifice is left. What remains, however, is his commitment to archaeology as a social science (Childe 1947): if not exactly in the way which he envisaged (for the social sciences have themselves moved a long way from the works in which he found inspiration), at least in a way far removed from the antiquarian condition of archaeology as he found it. It is because his enterprise has been continued that we can now, with hindsight, more clearly discern both the failures and inconsistencies in his position and the positive elements of his achievement.

CHILDE'S CAREER: ARCHAEOLOGY AND POLITICS

It is unnecessary to do more than briefly rehearse the facts of Childe's life, since they have been admirably set out in Sally Green's biography (1981). He was born in 1892 in New South Wales, and had a somewhat oppressive upbringing as the son of the Anglican rector of a parish in north Sydney, a man of High Church sympathies who had emigrated to Australia in 1878. This gave Gordon Childe both an interest in books and an entrenched dislike of established religion which was later to colour his views both of Near Eastern civilisation and the megalith builders of Neolithic Europe. His growing interest in radical politics was thus something that he nurtured in private. He was rather shy, conscious both of his unprepossessing appearance[4] and somewhat indistinct speech, and his academic achievements helped to compensate for a certain social awkwardness. His rebellious attitudes were expressed in a rather idiosyncratic style of dress, a studied shabbiness or – as recorded in later photographs – incongruous combinations of broad-brimmed hat, waistcoat and shorts. At the University of

Sydney Childe excelled both in Greek and philosophy, and was awarded a graduate scholarship in classics tenable at Oxford.

He arrived in 1914, at the age of 22, in a University increasingly emptied by the War, and perhaps manifesting many features of the world which he so much disliked. Yet academically, he had come home. He began work for the diploma in Classical Archaeology, taught by Professor Percy Gardner and J. D. Beazley, famous for his painstaking studies of Greek vases; but much of the excitement in the study of Greek archaeology was coming from the emerging story of the prehistoric Aegean, and specifically from the presence of two scholars of notable vision and archaeological achievement: Professor J. L. (later Sir John) Myres and Sir Arthur Evans, Extraordinary Professor of Prehistoric Archaeology and formerly Keeper of the Ashmolean. Evans' excavations at Knossos had won him world fame; but he was equally notable for the breadth of his knowledge of the surrounding areas – the prehistoric Balkans (where he had travelled widely as correspondent of the *Manchester Guardian*) and the contemporary civilisations of the east Mediterranean.[5] His friend Myres, who was Wykeham Professor of Ancient History from 1910 to 1939, was no less polymathic. Trained in both classics and geology, he had organised the archaeological collections in Cyprus and excavated in Greece before taking up academic posts in Britain. Of his influence on Childe I shall have more to say later on; in fact for much of the War he was on special operations in the east Mediterranean, collecting intelligence and directing Greek irregulars in cattle raids on the Turkish coast, for he combined his scholarship with an intimate knowledge of the realities of life in the Aegean (Myres 1980).

Childe at first took part in military exercises, but already in 1915 he made known his anti-war views and in 1916 moved out of his college, Queen's, to share lodgings with Rajani Palme Dutt, a founding member of the British Communist Party. Childe was an active member of the University Socialist Society and supported the No-Conscription Fellowship, as well as other radical causes. Nevertheless he continued to work hard at his academic studies, and transferred from the Diploma to do a B.Litt. under Myres on 'The influence of the Indo-Europeans in Prehistoric Greece'. Its combination of archaeological evidence with a wider perspective from comparative philology is characteristic of his early work. At the same time he took the examinations for Greats, and was awarded a First. With these achievements he returned to Australia in 1917.

He spent four years there; first, in attempting to find an academic post, which was blocked because of his political views, and then actively engaged in politics as private secretary to the newly elected Labour Premier of New South Wales. Then, in 1921, he was sent to London as Research and Publicity Officer to liaise with European labour movements and prepare press releases; but within two weeks of landing the Labour government had fallen. Childe, seen as a political appointee, was dismissed. He remained in

London, searching for a job in either the political or the academic world. Indeed, he pursued the two activities in tandem, writing *How Labour Governs* (1923), translating archaeological works in French, Italian and Russian, and visiting continental museums. In 1925, through Myres' good offices, he was appointed Librarian to the Royal Anthropological Institute and published his first book, *The Dawn of European Civilisation* (1925), soon to be followed by studies of *The Aryans* (1926) and *The Danube in Prehistory* (1929). It was largely on the strength of *The Dawn* (as it was inevitably known) that Childe was appointed, now thirty-five, to a newly created chair at Edinburgh, and given the security to pursue his research. The chair had been established by a bequest from Lord Abercromby, and it might have been designed for him in its stipulation of a knowledge of European languages and a grasp of European prehistory as a whole. Childe spent nearly two decades in Edinburgh, in a job whose teaching responsibilities were not onerous and where he could largely devote himself to research. He took the opportunity to travel more widely, including visits to the Near East, North America and the Soviet Union, and he continued to write with the same industry as before. He revised *The Dawn*, wrote a companion volume on the Near East (1928, revised 1934), summarised the Bronze Age (1930), explored Scottish prehistory (1931; 1935), and wrote his two masterpieces of popular scholarship, *Man Makes Himself* (1936) and *What Happened in History* (1942). Increasingly his thoughts were directed towards the growth of fascism and the approach of war; *What Happened in History* was a direct response to the conflict, which cut him off from continental contacts and led him to reflect on the vicissitudes of civilisation.

The end of the War coincided with an opportunity to move back to London (where in any case he had spent as much time as possible during the years in Edinburgh). Mortimer Wheeler had since 1927 been trying to set up an Institute of Archaeology as part of the University of London, and it finally took shape a decade later in the august setting of St John's Lodge in Regent's Park (Evans 1987). With Wheeler as its part-time director, it accumulated an impressive range of expertise – albeit on a rather shoestring basis – which successively embraced the fields not only of British, Near Eastern and environmental archaeology, but also the technical disciplines of conservation and photography necessary for a fully professional approach. When Wheeler was appointed Director General of Archaeology in India, the committee charged with finding a successor unanimously put forward Childe's name, and he became the first full-time Director of the Institute in 1946.

It was a happy move. At the Institute there was a full archaeological team and an enthusiastic group of students, in contrast to his lonely archaeological presence in Edinburgh. London also gave more immediate access to a wider network of stimulating friends and the intellectual life of the capital. In his inaugural lecture, 'Archaeology as a Social Science', he stressed the general significance of archaeology to wider concerns. In this period he discovered a common enterprise with other Marxist scholars and was involved in the founding of *Past and Present* (Hill, Hilton and Hobsbawm 1983), and wrote his contributions to general histories of economy and technology (1952; 1954a; 1954b). He wrote accounts of archaeological methodology (1956), and explored ideas of social evolution (1951). His interest in the history of science led him to write a general book on epistemology, *Society and Knowledge* (1956), and he continued to revise his classic, *The Dawn* (1957). These various threads he drew together in his last synthesis, *The Prehistory of European Society*, published in 1958, the year after his death (Piggott 1958).

He was not, perhaps, a natural administrator – an activity which more resembled his style of driving than his skill at writing prehistory.[6] His driving, indeed, was as legendary and as idiosyncratic as his taste in clothes. Edward Pyddocke recounts an incident when Childe, giving him a lift, stopped at a set of traffic lights. After several cycles of red and green he gently intimated that it was perhaps time to move off. 'Oh, sorry – I thought you were driving' was Childe's reply. When the lease on the Institute's premises in St John's Lodge ran out and the move to construct the present building in Gordon Square was contemplated, it was clear that the Institute was entering a new phase, and perhaps needed more practical steersmanship. With characteristic generosity, Childe agreed to give up his post a year before his official retirement, in order to allow his successor to manage the move.

After a climactic year in which he received a Festschrift[7] and the Gold Medal of the Society of Antiquaries, he donated much of his library to the Institute and sold off the rest, and moved to the Athenaeum to contemplate retirement. He visited several of his ex-students abroad, and planned a visit to Australia. Leaving the Institute was the end of a lifetime's work; and as Professor John Evans, its present director, has recently written, 'with his post he gave up, quite literally, his reason for living' (1987, 19). There was also a sense of personal loneliness: in the words of Peter Gathercole, 'he remained to the end quite unreconciled to his bachelorhood' (1982, 198). When he left for Sydney, thirty years after taking up his chair in Edinburgh, it was with a sense of finality; as we now know, he had made a conscious decision to end his life.

Nevertheless, he was not idle. He completed his last book on the voyage, and a recension of it for *Past and Present* (1958c; 1957a). He lectured, and visited old friends in Australia; received an honorary degree and broadcast on Australian Radio. Yet he did not like much of what he saw, and wrote scathingly of Australian society in letters home. He also composed three documents: an autobiographical note, later published under the title 'Retrospect' (1958a); another, giving his view of the main tasks confronting archaeology in Britain, which was given the title 'Valediction' (1958b) –

parallel, as we now know, to a letter which he had written to Soviet archaeologists (mainly about methodology) before his departure from England,
and which caused an embarrassed silence among its recipients (Klejn 1994).
Finally, there was a personal letter to his successor accompanied by a
memoir to be read in ten years' time (later published by Glyn Daniel in an
Antiquity editorial: Childe 1980). In it, he set out his personal attitude to
life in general, and his own in particular. 'Now I have seen the Australian
Spring; I have smelt the boronia, watched snakes and lizards, listened to the
"locusts". There is nothing more I want to do here ... Life ends best when
one is happy and strong'. That life ended in the Blue Mountains, near to his
childhood home.

Childe was unusual in combining an interest, and even starting careers in,
politics and prehistory. Both were expressions of his interest in human
affairs. His approach to the prehistory and early history of Europe was thus
more than an antiquarian curiosity. Although it is a commonplace to assert
that, coming from the antipodes, he saw European prehistory as an outsider
(not unlike the metaphorical observer from Mars), quite the reverse is true.
As the product of a colonial culture – an Anglican rectory and a department
of classics – he was, like many others, in search of his European roots. In a
famous sentence in the preface to the first (1925) edition of his otherwise
highly technical work on *The Dawn of European Civilisation* he defined its
theme as 'the foundation of European civilisation as a peculiar and individual manifestation of the human spirit'. It is a theme, conceptualised with
increasing sophistication, that runs throughout his work. As Michael
Rowlands has made clear in a brilliant essay (1984), it was an attempt to
push back into prehistory the familiar story of 'The Rise of the West' – a
story which goes back to the beginning of European historiography and
continues to occupy historians as diverse as W. H. McNeil, Hugh Trevor-
Roper, and J. M. Roberts. Childe's answers began with the intellectual
assumptions of the Romantic movement, the Aryans and Indo-Germanic
philology, and ended with the answers of the Enlightenment – Oriental
despotism and the progress of science. To translate these ideas into archaeology, with a raw material of broken potsherds and partial house-plans, was
an act of outstanding imagination – the wonder is not that it was done well,
but that it was done at all.

Structuring the past: ancestry and evolution

While histories of archaeology conventionally describe, in classic Whig
fashion, a series of discoveries that lead up to the present sum of knowledge,
a more sophisticated view must attempt to describe the forces which create
and structure knowledge of the past. It is thus necessary to put Childe's
attempt into a longer perspective, and to situate it within a broader
intellectual context.

The growth of a consciousness of the past is one of the features of European development since the end of the Middle Ages, and is intimately connected with three important processes: global expansion, industrialisation, and the creation of ethnically coherent nation states. Each of these has given rise to questions of identity – national, social and cultural – on several different levels. Such identity can be defined in relation to immediate predecessors or neighbours (the French, the Celts, the Germans, the Slavs); in relation to other civilisations (the Classical world, Egypt, Islam, the East in general); or in relation to more distant societies, the 'other cultures' of ethnology and anthropology. These successive encounters and their perception in terms of identity or otherness by dominant groups within western societies (including their use as metaphors for other social conflicts) were instrumental in forming the academic categories within which we still organise our knowledge, as Hugh MacDougall (1982), Martin Bernal (1987) and Edward Said (1978) have recently pointed out in relation respectively to English history, classical studies and orientalism (cf. Thapar 1975). While world encounters have been important in raising general questions such as the definition of 'civilisation', territorial disputes within Europe have focused more immediate attention on ethnic origins and nationality.

The importance of such questions of identity for models of the past lies in their implications for development through time. Such relationships can be visualised in various ways, all of which require some concept of time depth. They may be conceived in terms of common ancestry, expressed as a family tree: identity is here seen in terms of the genealogies of peoples.[8] A different (though sometimes complementary) image is that of superimposed layers, in which a superior or inferior position may take on a moral aspect, with higher groups more worthy of respect than lower ones. These metaphors have not been confined to human identities. Overseas expansion brought about an encounter not just with other societies but with other species as well: the global variety of the animal and plant kingdoms whose systematic classification prompted the questions of relationship and ancestry that were answered by Darwin, and that had their physical exemplification in fossils from different layers of rock. Each of these sets of ideas has interacted with, and provided models for, the others – not always with happy results, as when the confusion of biological and cultural taxonomies produced intellectual racism, and the idea of social stratification gave human inequality an apparently geological permanence.

In translating patterns of contemporary variety into reconstructed relationships in time, however, social theorists were handicapped more severely than biologists. For when evolutionary biologists came to look for exemplification of their theories, they could appeal to the fossil record, long studied in its own right by antiquarians, and increasingly systematised by geologists. Social theorists had access to no such well-ordered body of observations about the remote past. While Biblical narrative and ancient history provided some information about earlier civilisations, it contained only mythological references to events such as the origins of farming or the beginnings of urban life. Social theorists could thus only speculate on these matters; and, as a result, speculative prehistory long preceded the actual evidence of prehistoric archaeology.

Study of the past: Science or Romance?

These multiple questions of relationship did not, of course, all present themselves simultaneously; local problems alternated with a growing scale of external encounters. A consequence is that at some periods attention has been focused on European national problems, as in the early nineteenth century or the early twentieth century; at others, it has been directed outwards to a wider range of overseas questions, as in the mid-eighteenth century or the later nineteenth century. Reflecting these attitudes, writers about the past have alternated between two approaches: a retrospective approach to questions of cultural identity, working backwards to solve problems of immediate ancestry (Who were the Celts? Who were the Greeks?); and a more abstract approach, arguing forwards from first principles to formulate more global questions ('In the infancy of society ...'). Each has produced its own kind of history and archaeology. The first group is characterised by a Romantic attachment to place and often by a direct (and often nationalistic) involvement with the areas of their concern; while the second group is more typified by 'scientific' attitudes and positivist assumptions. Neither side, needless to say, has had a monopoly of truth, and both embody often hidden political assumptions. One emphasises cultural specificity and tradition, the other is more willing to prise its specimens loose from their context for comparative study. Individual disciplines may swing between these attitudes, and the current state of any subject (as with archaeology today) is the result of a continuing dialectic between alternative approaches.

What this means is that, in tracing intellectual history, the threads often seem to skip a generation. There is a nationalist thread, from Luther through Herder to Kossinna and early Childe, interwoven with a rationalist thread, from Montesquieu through Morgan and Marx to later Childe. The following excursion attempts briefly to disentangle them.

From fictitious genealogy to philosophical prehistory

In the Middle Ages, questions of national relationship and ancestry were expressed literally in the form of a family tree.[9] These were the pedigrees of rulers, not peoples, for it was they that defined the polities. The genealogies of leading dynasties were traced back to the Romans, and beyond them the Trojans: hence Geoffrey of Monmouth's interest in Brutus, son of Aeneas, who gave Britain its name and its first national mythology. A shift of emphasis towards ethnicity, however (with a particular concern for language), first became evident at the time of the Reformation, which produced some of the themes that would later serve as arguments for more specific kinds of nationalism: religious reformers and German humanists combined to emphasise the importance and antiquity of the Germanic tradition, hoping thereby to emancipate northern Europe from its dependence on Italy and the Mediterranean. They combined Tacitus' idealised view of the ancient Germans (written as propaganda in his own time) with an extrapolation of Biblical narrative.[10] Luther himself traced the origin of the Germans to Ashkenaz, great-grandson of Noah; Abraham Ortelius held the Teutonic tongue to be the true language of Adam. It is no accident that philology was later to strike such strong roots in German soil.

Biblical narrative and accounts by ancient authors long remained the basis of conceptions of life in earlier times.[11] Speculation about a more remote past, and a more systematic attempt to define the character of early civilisations, came to prominence in the Enlightenment, when European cultures became more aware both of their oriental neighbours and of the inhabitants of their overseas possessions.[12] External observations were again linked to internal concerns, in terms of the idea of progress and the notion of civilisation, defined as the increase of knowledge and the advance of social conditions and morals. This involved investigation of problems such as the origins of language, the early condition of humanity, and the development of laws. In elaborating a universal history, Enlightenment writers sought to bring together both the newly known primitive world and the older civilisations of the Mediterranean and the Orient in the light of their own political agenda. This had important consequences for the way in which the role of ancient cultures came to be viewed.

One aspect of this is the beginnings of the idealisation of Greece. As Michael Vickers has recently pointed out (1985/6), the values of the *ancien régime* were closely bound up with the idea of imperial Rome. As a counterpoint to this, revolutionary interest began to appeal to the republican and democratic ideals of classical Greece. Winckelmann's aesthetic studies gave a new status to Greek art, appropriate to the idealisation of its politics. This libertarian view of the Greeks articulated with another characteristic attitude of the time: the theme of the Orient as other. While this conception had its origins with the Greeks themselves in their confrontation with Persia (and accounts for the longevity of the theme of the Trojan War), it was given contemporary relevance in eighteenth-century Europe by its congruence with the situation of the western powers and the Ottoman Empire, giving new meaning to the old opposition of Europe and Asia, the West and the East, Christianity and Islam, liberty and despotism, industry and stagnation. For behind the egalitarian rhetoric and the universalist interests of the Enlightenment was a firm conception of the superiority of European culture. Seeking a rational explanation of these differences, Montesquieu (*L'esprit des lois*, 1748) found it in climate and geography – the beginning of a long tradition of environmental determinism (Shklar 1987). He pointed particularly to the role of the state in organising irrigation works in Oriental societies, and its consequences in terms of slavery, state ownership of land and despotic rulership. This he contrasted with the relative liberty of Europe, whether under republican or monarchical government. This line of thought has its heirs in Marx's Asiatic mode of production and Wittfogel's Oriental Despotism (1957), both of which have coloured interpretations of early Near Eastern societies down to the present time.

Equally significant as an intellectual framework pre-dating the recovery of direct evidence by archaeology was the emergence of ideas of successive types of society derived from the comparison of contemporary primitive peoples. This was particularly a feature of the Scottish Enlightenment, and is well exemplified in Adam Smith's [1776] categorisations of 'hunters, the lowest and rudest state of society, such as we find it among the native tribes of North America', 'shepherds, a more advanced state of society' and 'a yet more advanced state of society … husbandmen who have little foreign commerce' (1893, 541); and in Thomas Pownall's more picturesque description (1773, 241) of the succession of the 'Woodland-Men' and the 'Land-Workers' who 'as at this day, eat out the thinly scattered race of Wood-Men'. Here, in embryo, is the outline of an evolutionary view of stages of social and economic progress, from savagery to civilisation, through despotism to liberty, that will become important in the scientific social and economic writers of the nineteenth century, including Marx.

Romanticism and the search for roots

What separated Marx from the Enlightenment, and interrupted the continuity of a comparative and relatively deterministic approach, was Romantic nationalism. Here the ethnic concerns raised at the time of the Reformation were again to the fore, this time in the context of empire and of the consolidation of nation states from a polyethnic basis. These interests, combined with other features of the Romantic Movement (such as the reaction from industrialisation and an interest in rural landscapes) brought about the genesis of a systematic study of prehistory. For although Enlightenment speculations about the primitive condition of man seem to cry out for archaeological exemplification, there was, in fact, no systematic archaeology to put to them. It was the Romantic concern with origins, especially local origins and national roots, which led to a methodology capable of investigating prehistoric times, and which was in turn to contribute to the rise of a new science of prehistory in the succeeding phase of later nineteenth-century positivism.

Intellectually, the new attitude can first be discerned in the writings of Johann Gottfried Herder (Berlin 1976, 165ff). Although closely linked to earlier, Enlightenment interests, he had a new conception of the relationship between peoples and places. Human nature is not uniform. It manifests differences of race and national character. Particular peoples have an inherent genius or spirit which derives in part from the land they inhabit, but is not simply determined by it – it is an immutable essence that they carry with them. It is no coincidence that these views were developed in Germany, with its crisis of identity in relation to France and its own disunity, and with an older tradition of ethnocentric concern. Now, in a wider world, this was to be generalised into *Rassenkunde*, the investigation of the varieties of the human species: their physical types, their manners and their customs – the old unity of anthropology.

This gave a new meaning to the metaphor of the family tree. As Martin Bernal has written, 'Trees ... provide the ideal Romantic image. They are rooted in their own soils, and nourished by their particular climates; at the same time they are alive and grow. They progress and never turn back' (1987, 205). The classic application of the tree model is Indo-European philology, part of the Romantic concern with language. The relationship between Sanskrit and the European languages had been explicitly recognised by Sir William Jones in 1786, and interest in it was fuelled both by European nationalism and a growing involvement with India. This discovery was seized with enthusiasm in Germany, where much of the detailed comparative work was done; and *indogermanisch* was used more or less synonymously with Indo-European. The superiority of Indo-European as a vehicle for thought became increasingly explicit in German writings, as a natural extension of the idea of the distinctiveness of cultures and their different roles in world history. Although anti-Semitism was not yet explicit, the two branches of Old World culture – the Indo-European and the Semitic – were often consciously counterposed.

As well as these philological concerns, there were also opportunities for the development of practical archaeology. For Britain and France, the seaborne struggle for the east Mediterranean territories of the decaying Ottoman Empire brought a closer acquaintance with the lands of ancient civilisation, and the beginnings of systematic investigation of their antiquities (Silberman 1982). Napoleon's invasion of Egypt was a comprehensive exercise in cultural and political imperialism, and the plans, drawings and crates of antiquities which he sent back marked a new phase in Egyptology. British intervention in Palestine initiated a similar practical interest in Biblical archaeology, and led to successive waves of military, missionary and academic activity. The strategic importance of Naples to naval activity in the east Mediterranean also gave an opportunity for archaeological work: the British envoy Sir William Hamilton dug at Pompeii and collected 'Etruscan' (actually Greek) vases. Like the Rosetta stone and the Elgin marbles, these ended up in the growing collections of the British Museum.

These strands of political involvement and academic interest coincided in Greece. English Philhellenism fitted well with the Romantic aesthetic and its taste for the cultures and scenery of remote, mountainous and exotic places, and paralleled the enthusiasm for Celtic culture in Scotland and Wales.[13] Libertarian identification with the Greek people brought Romantic involvement in Greece to a new pitch with the outbreak of the War of Independence in 1821, and the commitment of Shelley and Byron. German scholarship canonised a scarcely less Romantic view of ancient Greece, institutionalised in the German university system by Humboldt's reforms which gave *Altertumswissenschaft* a cardinal role in education and the formation of a new ruling class. This new, professional German classical scholarship, building on the tradition of Indo-Germanic philology, began to stress the northern roots of Greek culture, as transmitted by the northern Dorians or their mythical precursors, the Minyans.[14]

Similar ethnic concerns also played a major part in promoting antiquarian and archaeological inquiry within mainland Europe, both as part of the consolidation of empire (the French enthusiasm for the Celts as an indigenous civilisation distinct both from the Germans and the classical world) and as a focus for the aspiration of national minorities in Austria and Prussia.[15] Here the lack of coincidence between national and ethnic or linguistic boundaries began to create increasing tensions, and the post-Napoleonic map of Europe took little account of nationality. Substantial minorities such as the Czechs and Magyars aspired to some degree of autonomy within polyethnic empires: the middle classes were vocal in their protests against alien rule, and in their claims to use their own languages. Germans and Poles, on the other hand, aspired to unification. Both of these factors led to an interest in national origins and national culture, and produced a burst of enthusiasm for Europe's pagan past.

Prehistory was thus explored in the spirit of Goethe's exhortation to 'nurture love for our common fatherland and for the memory of our great forebears'. The French sought out their *monuments celtiques*, the Germans and the Slavs sought a more direct continuity between the historical nations and their prehistoric predecessors with the help of new philological tools, in order to support territorial claims. Each side also exploited classical authors such as Tacitus to the full, and the Czechs supplemented them with forged Old Slavonic epics. Both produced images of an ideal society and its folk heroes, which owe a great deal to the contemporary theatre. One example in a more permanent medium is the gigantic statue of 'Hermann the Liberator' (Arminius the Cheruscan) near to where this Germanic chieftain had defeated three Roman legions in the Teutoburger Wald (Figure 1.1).

These nationalistic motivations were accompanied by a more generalised Romantic concern with the strange and picturesque. There was a great interest in graves, pagan shrines and idols, and sacrificial stones, in much the same spirit as the growing fascination with Gothic architecture and medievalism. Moreover, the soil of Europe was being turned over as never before by quarrying, building and agricultural operations, so that finds of

1.1 The gigantic statue of 'Hermann the Liberator' (Arminius the Cheruscan) in the Teutoburger Wald, designed 1838–46 and completed in 1875 (photo: Heinrich Härke). There is a copy in New Ulm, Minnesota.

archaeological material were increasingly common. Collectors accumulated quantities of prehistoric stone and bronze artefacts, local societies for the study of antiquities were founded, as well as regional and national museums. The sheer quantity of new material made possible a more systematic classification and study, including the recognition of different periods of prehistory. It is significant, however, that it was in Denmark, unaffected by competing nationalisms and with a long pagan period lacking literary sources before the Middle Ages, that these methods were taken furthest. The result was a recognition of three successive 'Ages' in European prehistory, of Stone, Bronze and Iron, used in organising the newly founded National Museum in Copenhagen. This 'Three Age' system was nevertheless met by hostility from German (especially Prussian) archaeologists; and its acceptance outside Scandinavia had to await a less nationally committed prehistory.

Positivist science and 'national science'

Prehistory (though not yet given that name) was thus an offspring of the Romantic movement; but it was a conceptually unsophisticated kind of prehistory, which has left its legacy in popular concepts of the Ancient Britons, or Asterix and Obelix. What was to transform it, or at least to give it a slightly schizophrenic existence (which it still has), was the growth of later nineteenth-century science, particularly biology, and the attitudes of positivism. In reaction to nationalistic and historical models, archaeology found a place among the natural sciences under the rubric of anthropology, and with an ahistorical, comparative emphasis. The science of prehistory (*préhistoire*, *Vorgeschichte*) was counterposed to humane, nationalistic history. Often this was associated with the rise of new institutions or departments – in Oxford, for instance, the Ashmolean was joined by the Pitt Rivers Museum. Prehistoric archaeology formed part of a growing scientific endeavour, based in laboratories and closely associated both with physical anthropology and geology. This reflected both the growing success of science and industry at home, and the changing nature of the colonial encounter, as it moved from adventurism to systematic exploitation. Comparative studies of the native peoples of the colonies began to flesh out some of the generalisations of the Enlightenment: recent hunting and simple farming peoples became evidence for successive transformations of human economy and society.

Of particular importance to these new ideas was the recognition of the high antiquity of the human species and the definition of an early phase of the Stone Age, the Palaeolithic. This extended the prehistoric timescale, and gave scientific status to prehistory by bringing it into relationship with geology and evolutionary biology: recognition of the Ice Age replaced the Flood as a suitably dramatic backdrop of environmental change, and skeletal remains previously dismissed as pathological were recognised as the bones of 'fossil man'. Study of the Palaeolithic was centred in France, whose river gravels and limestone caves provided abundant evidence for a vast period before the lake-villages and megaliths of the later Stone Age, the Neolithic.

Perhaps because of the image provided by geological stratigraphy and the patterns of palaeontology, the idea of successive strata or steps – *Stufentheorie* – became a common motif in both the natural and social sciences, usually allied to the idea of progressive change: from hunting to farming, from household economy to national economy, from magic and religion to science, *Gemeinschaft* to *Gesellschaft*, status to contract, mechanical to organic solidarity. The Three Age system received widespread acceptance because of its congruence with these ideas; yet these schemes were elaborated largely without reference to archaeology, by comparing ethnographic observations and treating 'primitive' societies (*Naturvölker*) as representatives of earlier stages of human progress. In Berlin, Eduard Hahn investigated the contribution of domestic animals to human economies and speculated on the origins of agriculture and the plough (1896); from New York, Lewis Henry Morgan synthesised the variety of human family systems into a series of stages that correlated with advances in material culture – the bow and arrow, pottery, farming, metalworking – and marked the progress from savagery to barbarism and civilisation (1877).

Marx himself, in creating a materialist science of society, was not much concerned about the earlier periods of prehistory; and for the historical periods he drew on earlier conceptions in defining a series of material productive forces and their property relations: 'In broad outline, the Asiatic, ancient, feudal and modern bourgeois modes of production may be designated as progressive epochs of the socio-economic order'.[16] He was, however, interested in Morgan's ideas, and made extensive notes on *Ancient Society*, which after his death were elaborated by Engels in *The Origin of the Family, Private Property and the State*[17] as a materialistic (and largely technologically determined) conception of history. So strong was the idea of progressive evolutionary stages that Darwin's model of descent with modification, which was essentially a tree model, was often accommodated in popular perception to Herbert Spencer's view of evolution as a progression from simple to complex (applied not only to sociology but to sciences as diverse as cosmology and psychology). These assumptions underlay not only the classic works of late nineteenth-century anthropology and prehistory,[18] but also Darwin's own treatment of human evolution in *The Descent of Man*. Nevertheless, the idea of phylogeny did find reflection in anthropology, in Taylor's 'lines of culture' and Pitt Rivers' studies of the ancestry of tools. It was more directly applied in physical anthropology, where a new science of skull-measuring came into being to define the pedigrees of races, with a pseudo-geological classification of 'higher' and 'lower' – which in less scrupulously scientific hands might be translated into 'dear' races and 'cheap' races. In this way biological ideas of human phylogeny reinforced the continuing Romantic belief in a congruence between language, culture and race. The comparative philologist Max Müller, lecturing on 'the science of language', reconstructed an Aryan culture that lay behind the Greek, Roman and Teutonic achievements, allowing historians like E. A. Freeman to trace English liberties to a common root with those of the Greeks themselves (MacDougall 1982, 120; Burrow 1981, 174, 191). And Heinrich Schliemann, Homer in hand, carried the heroic age of Greece (at least to his own satisfaction) back into the Bronze Age.

From 1890 onwards, such nationalistic trends again took over from the wider concerns of comparative anthropology. The term *Vorgeschichte*, indicative of an ahistoric, disinterested, geological approach, began to be replaced by *Urgeschichte*, stressing again the continuities with modern nations. Archaeological images, like those of *nos ancêtres les Gaulois*, became part of the 'mass production of traditions', often by the state itself (Hobsbawm 1983).[19] German imperialism, increasingly conscious of its late arrival in the colonial enterprise and lacking a history of national unity, placed great stress on patriotism and early Germanic history. Relations between the Germanic tribes and the Romans on the imperial frontier were investigated by a *Limeskommission*, and celebrated in the new *Römisch-Germanisches Zentralmuseum* at Mainz. The Slav peoples of the Austro-Hungarian empire also looked to their roots, to define their identities in opposition both to Germans and Magyars. In direct reflection of current territorial questions, much energy was expended on defining the supposed boundary in prehistoric times between the Germans and the Slavs, a critical role being played by the Lausitz culture – a Late Bronze Age group occupying the area between the middle Elbe and the Vistula. The general interests of the German Anthropological Society were overtaken by those of the new German Society for Prehistory, whose aims were exemplified by its founder Gustav Kossinna in his definition of prehistory as '*eine hervorragende nationale Wissenschaft*' (1912).[20]

These trends were paralleled in other areas of German scholarship. There was a tendency for the homeland of the first Indo-Europeans (*Urindogermanen*) to be shifted from central Asia or the Caucasus, where the Romantics and positivists had looked for it, to Germany itself where it could be sought among the various Neolithic groups now recognised on the basis of their pottery. In somewhat similar fashion, the classicist Julius Beloch stressed the indigenous, European nature of Greek culture and its background, independent of the Semitic east Mediterranean; and such academic suspicion of the Semitic contribution to European culture was fuelled by populist anti-Semitism following the mass immigration of east European Jews. Nor were these attitudes confined to Germany. In a widely read article in *L'Anthropologie* for 1893, Salomon Reinach – himself an assimilated Parisian Jew – condemned both the theory of an eastern origin of the Aryans, and the idea of Semitic influence, as two aspects of what he called *le mirage oriental*. He asserted the independence of European civilisation, 'a revindication of the rights of Europe against the claims of Asia' (Reinach 1893).

European archaeology at the beginning of the twentieth century

While there were many common currents affecting the different branches of European archaeology, therefore, there was no consensus on the interpretation, or even the basic structure, of European prehistory. Moreover, differences of interpretation corresponded to a significant extent with national (though not always nationalistic) attitudes. It may be useful here to summarise this intellectual geography.

In France, with its wealth of Palaeolithic material (including the spectacular cave-paintings), prehistory continued its alliance with geology and evolutionary anthropology, and its *loi du progrès de l'humanité*. Reinach's attitudes reflect a more general tendency to see important developments as autochthonous, and prehistoric archaeology as the record of indigenous evolution and achievement. French thought was long to be dominated by Gabriel de Mortillet's conception of prehistory as a geological sequence, with its succession of *âges*, *périodes* and *époques* named after European type-sites – a practice which still to some extent survives in Palaeolithic studies. Its more general application was ensured by the *loi du développement similaire*, which predicted that other areas would essentially conform to the French sequence. Some movement of peoples was allowed, on the analogy of palaeontological migrations, to account for sudden irruptions: the Romans, Celts, or – in the Bronze Age – the supposed ancestors of the gypsies.

Germanic scholarship, however, occupied the heartland of continental Europe, where migrations were of the essence. Kossinna's own training was in philology, and he translated its methodology into prehistory. His retrospective method, which he termed *die siedlungsarchäologische Methode* (i.e. reconstructing the process of occupying a landscape by a particular people), was based on the definition of distinctive sets of artefacts representing particular ethnic groups whose roots could be traced back into the past. Archaeological assemblages could be used to define cultures, which represented peoples. His journal *Mannus* published excellent local studies in the new, detailed manner; technically, much of the new work was of a very high order, yet its generalisations inevitably involved successive waves of Germanic expansion from northern Europe. These attitudes were also manifested even by a moderate German prehistorian, the outstanding figure of Carl Schuchhardt, who was an old enemy of Kossinna.[21] From his position in the Berlin museum, in charge both of Schliemann's Aegean collection and German prehistoric antiquities, he was able to survey the whole of Europe and wrote a magisterial survey, *Alteuropa*.[22] Yet its whole structure was a description of '*die Indogermanisierung unseres Erdteils*', the Indo-Europeanisation of our continent. The ancient Mediterranean was *vorindogermanisch*, and dominated by the Iberians, originally from Africa. Farming came about indigenously among the late Palaeolithic population of Thuringia – there was no consideration of its exotic economic basis (of the kind which Eduard Hahn, for instance, had done so much to illuminate) – and spread south. The west European megaliths were the forerunners of Mycenaean tholos tombs. Troy was an outpost of Europe, its Nordic origins clearly indicated in its architecture, the Homeric *megaron* with its predecessors in Bronze Age Brandenburg.

In contrast to this continental hegemony, archaeologists in Britain and Scandinavia maintained a different emphasis: the former reflecting a map of Europe seen from the sea, the latter eager to articulate an alternative to German nationalism. Both saw much more direct (and often maritime) links to the Orient, especially via the Atlantic route and the Mediterranean. Differing both from French evolutionism and German migrationism, they espoused diffusionism.[23] Danish archaeologists had maintained a critical view of nationalistic archaeology in Germany (despite their central position in the postulated Nordic *Urheimat*), preferring instead to refine the divisions of the Three Age system. But this was never seen as a purely indigenous, evolutionary succession: they looked elsewhere for the origins of these innovations, especially to the ancient Mediterranean civilisations and Bronze Age Greece. Rather than trace migrations of peoples, they looked instead to the peaceful medium of trade as a mechanism by which to outflank the militaristic models dominating central Europe. Instead of dealing with whole cultures, they emphasised the stylistic development of individual artefacts – the typological method – which could be traced across a network of inter-regional contacts (and incidentally thus provide much-needed chronological anchorage points in historically dated sequences). These developments are associated particularly with the Swede, Oscar Montelius (1899; 1903; 1910).

In Britain, where there was a less intimate knowledge of Continental archaeology[24] and more concern with the Mediterranean, these ideas were received sympathetically. The idea of maritime contacts was especially appealing,[25] and Arthur Evans agreed with Montelius' idea of an east Mediterranean origin for the megaliths in the Neolithic period. It is significant that his own work in Crete (and that of Myres in Cyprus and Woolley in the Turkish Hatay) were conceived as building up links along the sea routes from the Near East. As with German nationalism, however, this view could be taken to extremes: the lunatic wing of British archaeology was represented by Grafton Elliot Smith and the Egyptocentric hyper-diffusionists. They believed that the Egyptians (who were essentially Asiatic rather than African) had carried civilisation all over the world, an 'exotic leaven' which was responsible for all cultural change. European megaliths, with their Atlantic distribution, were no more than reflections of the tombs and obelisks of the Ancient Egyptians. Elliot Smith's disciple W. J. Perry was to take this doctrine further, seeing Egyptians as setting out in boats to prosyletise a heliocentric religion. Nonsense? Yet it was reissued under the early imprint of Pelican Books, and was eagerly consumed by a British public in the fading years of overseas colonialism (Perry 1937).

This, then, is the somewhat schizophrenic intellectual environment within which Gordon Childe undertook his early studies of prehistory.

There were many conflicting attitudes, some deeply rooted in earlier modes of thought, and many bodies of knowledge which had never been considered in relation to each other. Above all, there was a growing archaeological record which could be interpreted in very different ways in relation to radically different ideologies.

CHILDE'S SYNTHESES OF PREHISTORY

Childe's achievement was twofold: he brought order to a multitude of local sequences of prehistoric cultures and integrated them into an overall picture; and he explored some general principles of building social and economic models to explain these patterns. Because he never quite overcame the intellectual preconceptions of his background and training, he did not fully achieve the satisfactory synthesis he was seeking; but he nevertheless gave European prehistory a coherence that made systematic progress possible.

His first achievement was based on an unrivalled knowledge of the material evidence, the result of tireless visits to museums all over Europe: *The Danube* alone records research visits to some sixty institutions. By constructing local sequences of cultures and then tying them together over longer distances using typological cross-datings, pivoting on relatively well investigated areas such as Moravia and Bohemia, he was able to build up a framework in a transect across Europe. This integrated account bridged the dichotomies between northern Europe and the Aegean, and between British and Continental scholarship. Without nationalistic preconceptions, he made use of German methods and observations (notably the equation of an archaeological culture with a prehistoric people), taking the best of Kossinna and Schuchhardt without their excesses. In this way he was able to define a succession of periods, and map contemporaneous developments within them. This produced a standard framework, free so far as possible from outside assumptions. The result was complex but objective, comprehensive and explicit; and it provided a means of defining patterns of cultural change (Childe 1925; 1929). Having done this for Europe, he applied a similar methodology to the Near East, using his synoptic viewpoint to integrate observations made by the more diverse and specialised disciplines of Assyriology and Egyptology and write a general account of their prehistory and early history (1928; 1934). This was his technical contribution.

In carrying out this reformation, he did not radically question the assumptions of contemporary prehistoriography: his emphasis in successive books down to 1930 shifted gradually from migration to diffusion, but he invoked conventional archaeological explanations. In looking at the early Near East, however, with its richer pictorial record, he became more aware of technology and its social context, and saw how a Marxist approach to prehistory might be applied. His later work was an elaboration of these themes, in terms both of history and social evolution, through which he attempted to see the significance of his reconstruction of European pre-history. While the answers which he gave were unsatisfactory, partly because of a flaw in his chronology and partly because he did not entirely emancipate himself from earlier ways of thought, he showed how general models could be used to illuminate the detail of prehistoric change.

The early synthesis: culture history

Childe's early approach owed much to J. L. Myres, whose scholarship preserved a Victorian breadth, but also a commitment to philology as the key to history.[26] His interest in ethnology (like his enthusiasm for Herodotus) was based on a belief in the unity of language, culture and race, balanced by a sensitivity to geography. His general writings (e.g. 1911; 1935a; 1935b) were characterised by a reliance on the categories of physical anthropology (Mediterranean, Alpine and Nordic 'races'), and a more fundamental polarity between Indo-European and oriental cultures. The arrival of Indo-European peoples – 'the coming of the North' – was the decisive turning-point in European history, creating the condition for the new civilisations of Persia, Greece and Rome, 'Eastern and Western in name, but held and directed on both sides by long-lost brothers and true kinsmen'. The Indo-Europeans had organisation and rationality, the Orientals had an aptitude for trade but a tendency to religious obscurantism and political tyranny.[27] The Mycenaeans – to Myres totally 'un-Hellenic' (1911, 165)[28] – were part of the earlier, oriental and Mediterranean, story.

Childe's early work shows a tension between his fascination for the Indo-European problem and his ambivalence towards it as an explanation of historical differences. His work at Oxford was directly concerned with the question of the Indo-Europeanising of Greece; he went more deeply into the German and east European archaeological literature than Myres, and favoured (correctly, as the decipherment of Linear B was to demonstrate) a pre-Mycenaean date (Childe 1915; 1916).[29] In writing *The Dawn* for the 'History of Civilisation' series, however, he carried this detailed evaluation of continental scholarship much further but managed to set on one side any talk of Indo-Europeans.[30] Instead, he was more concerned to strike a balance between Orientalists (who ignored prehistoric Europe) and Occidentalists (who downplayed any oriental contribution). Some oriental intrusions, like that of the megalith-builders, he saw as too oriental to survive on western soil; but some immigrants from south Russia, whom he in fact believed to be Indo-European, had brought Mesopotamian metallurgy and new dynamism. The West had thus received inspiration from the East, but not by slavish imitation; they adapted it into a new and original whole, represented by the Bronze Age cultures of the Aegean, the Danube valley, and northern Europe – in whose energy, independence and inventiveness he recognised qualities distinctively European.

But he had not completely exorcised the Indo-European *Volksgeist*. In another volume in the 'History of Civilisation' series, entitled *The Aryans*, he released his pent-up speculation about a problem which continued to fascinate him to the end of his life. While he summarised opposing views with admirable detachment, he showed the extent to which it still influenced his thought; for in the epilogue he eulogised Greek and Persian achievements, and spoke of the Indo-Europeans' possession of 'a more excellent language, and the mentality which it generated'. Appearing in the year after the publication of Hitler's *Mein Kampf*, it was an embarrassment that propelled him to find a materialist model more suited to his Marxism and to seek in the social context of technology the answer to European uniqueness.[31]

The later synthesis: revolutions and their beneficiaries

The book that best represents the originality of Childe's contribution in this phase is *Man Makes Himself*, the fruit of his researches on the Near East. Written during the depressed years of the '30s, it was also an assertion of a deeper trend, underlying the surface events and partisan interpretations of history, which might properly be labelled progress. Over the long term, the increase in human numbers and in their independence from environmental controls is some measure of man's evolutionary success; and just as the Industrial Revolution marked a crucial turning point, so prehistory too was punctuated by periods of sharply accelerated growth. Childe thus visualised the transitions from hunting to farming, and from farming to urban life, as two comparable 'revolutions', which he termed the Neolithic and Urban Revolutions – separating savagery from barbarism, and barbarism from civilisation. In this way he returned to nineteenth-century and Enlightenment ideas: but with the addition for the first time of archaeological evidence for these events.

He was therefore able to describe the early movements of pottery-bearing populations as part of the spread of farming from the Near East (where plants and animals were first domesticated), and the colonisation of Europe by agriculturalists. Farming made possible the first village communities, and the development of crafts such as potting, carpentry and weaving. These societies were relatively egalitarian, with no evidence for chieftainship. But the Near East continued to produce innovations: the plough, the cart and the sailing boat, as well as the cultivation of tree crops. The concentration of fertile land in alluvial basins and oases limited its supply, but made it amenable to improvement by irrigation. Economies became more specialised and reliant on exchange and trade; the settlements larger and more permanent, containing craft workers such as metalsmiths and defended by walls. A new level of social differentiation was now achieved, with rulers, priests and craftsmen supported by the surplus from peasant farming; the power of the temple and the state was expressed in monumental architecture, the complexity of their transactions recorded for the first time in writing. Together, these led to a revolution in human knowledge and the exploration of practical mathematics.

This picture is very broadly correct, and acceptable today as a description of the beginning of urban life. But to take it further, he developed a more specific hypothesis about the role of metallurgy. Despite his use of the term 'revolution', it is clear that he did not see it in Marxian terms, as the resolution of a contradiction: it is a consensualist model in which all parties initially benefited – although unequally – from the change. He thought the concentration of the agrarian surplus was a necessary precondition for the genesis of a metallurgical industry. The contradiction arose later, as a consequence of the relegation of the practical craftsmen to a lower class, divorced from the theoretical expertise of the literary class which was devoted largely to religion: science was thus fettered by subservience to superstition. The result was stagnation and arrested growth; instead of technical progress, a succession of unstable empires competed for control of finite resources, their methods of internal control becoming increasingly totalitarian.[32]

His growing fascination with technology had in the meantime been reflected in study of the developmental sequences of European Bronze Age tools and the diffusion of new techniques (1930). Here he saw a more dynamic picture, the result of free craftsmen able to innovate and experiment. This gave him the clue to how the model might be extended to European prehistory, a theme that he worked out in increasing detail down to his last book, *The Prehistory of European Society*. The Urban Revolution had created the concentration of capital necessary for the formation of a bronze industry; but, once created, its techniques and knowledge could be passed on. Because metallurgical knowledge was diffused from the orient, European metalsmiths did not pay the price of subjection. Knowledge of metalworking techniques was spread by oriental colonists and Mycenaean prospectors; and metalsmiths – because no single community could concentrate the surplus to support them permanently – wandered freely, like the metics of ancient Athens. The hoards of bronzes from prehistoric Europe were their stock in trade, hidden in times of danger. The stimulus to trade given by the need to acquire copper and tin was responsible for the opening up of Europe, and the growth of an unfettered, proto-capitalist economy. Archaeological ages were technological stages; but within those stages the same technology could produce despotism or liberty depending on specific historical conjunctures. Europe benefited from the mistakes of the Orient; and its liberties were founded on the freedom of its craftsmen. That 'peculiar manifestation of the human spirit' had a technological base.

Childe's work: an assessment

Childe's knowledge of his material was immense, and his vision of its importance went far beyond that of his contemporaries. His pages sparkle with erudition and insight. Yet his answer to the problem which he set himself was already old-fashioned. He had come to a subject whose definition was only half a century old, and whose basic information was still accumulating, and gave it a maturity of expression which allowed it to be taken seriously by its sister sciences; but his interpretations were still fixed in the context of the nineteenth-century debates in which the subject had its origins.

One handicap in getting the story right was the lack of an independent European chronology. We now know, thanks to radiocarbon dating, that European Neolithic and Bronze Age cultures were much older – both absolutely, and in relation to the Near East – than Childe thought them. In this sense, Europe's peculiar character was no more than a consequence of his dating: there was no 'slavish dependence' because the originals did not then exist. Thus megaliths long preceded the pyramids, and European bronze industries were already flourishing by Mycenaean times. But it is significant that Childe consciously chose his chronology: in a presidential address to the Anthropology Section of the British Association for the Advancement of Science in 1938 (Childe 1938) he actually set out two schemes, one of which strikingly resembles the present picture and anticipated by three decades the results of radiocarbon; but he rejected it on the grounds that European cultures were always retarded in relation to Near Eastern ones, using detailed and often dubious typological synchronisms. Thus his chronology was already implicit in his choice of model.

Another conceptual block, closely related to this, was the anachronism of many of his models. His idea of the penetration of Europe by oriental colonies has considerable validity as a description of the activities of the Phoenicians in the west Mediterranean in the first millennium BC; but this was quite different from the relationship of the second-millennium Mycenaeans with their European hinterland. To project this picture back to the world of the megalith builders was simply to continue a habit of thought well established in the seventeenth century. Similarly the truly nomadic Scythians were very different from the early inhabitants of the steppe lands, while the metics of ancient Athens were no analogy for the craftsmen of the Bronze Age. These ideas were projected back into very different societies, for which there are no historical analogies, and for which better parallels might be found in other parts of the world; but Childe was inhibited from using ethnographic models by his Eurocentric preoccupation. To him, the Maori or the Melanesians were not like the prehistoric Europeans, because they had no role in the creation of European civilisation. Nor were the Incas and the Aztecs, or even the Chinese, to be spoken of in the same breath. Childe's archaeology, like his upbringing and education, were firmly Eurocentric. The prophet that played him false (in Grahame Clark's phrase)[33] was not Marx but Herder.

Moreover, what he took from Marx was specifically his most typically nineteenth-century aspect, the preoccupation with technology. Marx appealed to him because his own views represented a similar translation of Hegelian dialectic into industrial materialism, a vision of the relationship between East and West expressed in the language of tools and economies. To this Childe added his own anti-clericalism and a rather naive rationalism. He was still fighting nineteenth-century battles, as is clear from his forays into epistemology (Childe 1950):[34] true knowledge is useful in changing the world and therefore survives when error (magic and religion) is burnt out. This stark dichotomy between the usefulness of technology and the encumbrance of religion gives his otherwise sophisticated and well-informed descriptions a painful simplicity: it was not so much technological determinism, but a techno-centricity which caused him to over-emphasise its importance in the societies he studied. It was as if the mystique which formerly attached to the Indo-Europeans had been transferred to metalworking.

As his ideas became more abstract, so his archaeology became more mechanical, failing to do justice to the detail of the archaeological record. The conclusion of his final summary, *The Prehistory of European Society*, was allegory rather than explanation, as he perhaps realised. At the end of his life, he had taken the wrong track too many times to go back. Having surveyed his subject, both its raw material and the ideas which motivated it, he could not go beyond his nineteenth-century inheritance. 'Now I confess that my whole account may prove to be erroneous; my formulae may be inadequate; my chronological framework – and without such one cannot speak of conjunctures – is frankly shaky'. His final disillusionment was intellectual as well as personal.

Archaeology since Childe

Childe died just as the post-war boom began to bring both a rapid growth of archaeological work and the routine application of scientific methods of analysis. New university departments brought an industrial increase in scale to teaching and research, and now his ideas were tested in the field and the laboratory. While everyone was now discussing models of the past, Childe's explanations – the first explicit ones – were easy to criticise. Radiocarbon dating seemed to confirm Europe's cultural autonomy in prehistoric times, as Colin Renfrew hammered home in successive papers (1967; 1968; 1969), and it did not take long for Childe's shaky chronological and intellectual framework to be overturned. In a period of scientific enthusiasm, Childe's humanistic concerns were pushed into the background. A new professionalism made Childe's efforts look amateur. Archaeology as anthropology dealt ruthlessly with his caricature of savage society – the very name consigned it to a different age. Large-scale interdisciplinary work opened up ecological perspectives and revealed sites in their landscapes, filling in a whole dimension of prehistoric life missing from Childe's picture.

This phase of positivist enthusiasm culminated in the New Archaeology, which – while respecting Childe's pioneering attempts to make sociological sense of prehistory – was in many respects an inversion of his ideas. Vague influences from far-off regions seemed less compelling reasons for prehistoric developments than very tangible local processes of population growth and environmental change, summarised in often deterministic models derived from comparative ethnography. The new prehistory, too, celebrated the independence and native inventiveness of Europe: but megaliths and Mycenae alike owed little to the Orient, and the answers lay in endogenous processes of social change.[35]

Inevitably, perhaps, in the perspective of intellectual history, such views have also come to be seen as typical of their time. Recent years have brought about a rediscovery of some of Childe's insights, in respect both of the interpretation of archaeological material, and the wider setting of European prehistory. As enthusiasm for the deterministic models of ecology and systems theory has waned, interest has shifted back to the artefacts themselves, and how culture works. Childe's approach has been seen as foreshadowing a current concern with culture as a socially constructed reality, and the historically specific conditions of its creation (e.g. papers in Hodder 1982). More practically, Childe's grasp of the meaning of archaeological material has been appreciated again: for instance, his discussion of the relation between ostentatious burial practices and political instability (e.g. 1944, 85–7) has been recognised as more fruitful than pseudo-scientific attempts to 'measure' social differentiation from the evidence of burials as if this were a simple reflection of living societies. Such insights have also been applied beyond the field of prehistory, and his observations on the reconstruction of vanished classes of material from their imitations in other media have found some sympathetic echoes even in classical archaeology.

So also with Childe's fundamental concern: the relationship between prehistoric Europe and the Near East. Now purged of the erroneous distractions resulting from a false chronology and anachronistic conceptions, the core of his reconstruction again demands attention. European culture cumulatively absorbed and reinterpreted many features whose origins lay in the Near East, from agriculture to Christianity. A particular complex of features, including the plough, wheeled vehicles, horses, woollen textiles and alcoholic drinks, as well as some of the metallurgical features Childe identified, arrived in Europe shortly after the Urban Revolution and arguably as a consequence of it. This continuing transformation of European culture, together with early commercial contacts by sea with the east Mediterranean, created the conditions in which the societies of historical Europe emerged. To understand this process, with a wealth of new information from a further generation of fieldwork, is a major task for prehistoric archaeology; and it is one that demands a vision as broad as Childe's own.

Childe thus stands halfway between the heroic age of later nineteenth-century prehistory and the anonymous professionalism of the present-day discipline. He combined the breadth of vision characteristic of a formative period of European thought with the grasp of detail required to found a systematic study of prehistoric times. His sense of the importance of the past, derived as much from awareness of an older European scholarship as from the narrower concerns of archaeology, created a subject which still bears his imprint. The writing of prehistory is still a dialogue with the ghost of Childe.

NOTES

1. On Childe's life see Green (1981); for a careful evaluation of the development of Childe's thought and the influences on it, Trigger (1980); a useful survey of his views, McNairn (1980); also Piggott (1958a); for a sympathetic evaluation of his later thought, Gathercole (1971); for a contrary view, Clark (1976).
2. For a list of Childe's publications, see Green (1981, 176–90).
3. Quoted on the cover of the Fontana paperback edition of *Social Evolution* (London, 1963). The book was first published by Watts in 1951.
4. Attributed by Max Mallowan (1977, 235) to a childhood illness. Nevertheless, 'This impractical man, an innocent abroad, clumsy with his hands and an indifferent digger, through his imaginative mental powers shed lustre on any activity in which he was engaged' (ibid., 234).
5. Childe's only fellow student on the Diploma course was Joan Evans, Arthur Evans' younger half-sister, whose *Time and Chance* (1943) gives a history of the Evans family, including an account of her half-brother's archaeological career and that of their father, the eminent prehistoric archaeologist Sir John Evans. She recorded her personal impressions in her autobiography *Prelude and Fugue* (1954), including a poem which she wrote at the time, beginning, 'The science of prehistory's a mysterious kind of game, In which the winner's privilege is to invent a name ...' – a reference to the practice of naming prehistoric groups after eponymous sites.
6. Wheeler spoke of his 'astonishing incapacity' in administrative matters (Hawkes 1982, 321).
7. Volume 21 of the *Proceedings of the Prehistoric Society* (1955).
8. Or, in more abstract form, through the idea of inheritance: for instance the Medieval scheme of the Four Empires, resurrected in Hegel; or the many metaphors of cultural succession: see Wolf (1982, 5).
9. For this section see especially MacDougall (1982).
10. The megalithic tombs of northern Europe (the first prehistoric monuments to invite attention) were traditionally attributed to giants, after the description of the world before the Flood in Genesis VI: 'There were giants in the earth in those days'. This explanation was illustrated by J. Picardt in a description of Drenthe in his *Korte beschryvinge van eenige vergetene en verborgene antiquiteten* ... (Amsterdam, 1660).
11. In maritime western Europe, the Phoenicians were for long to play a role in historical imagination, because of their skills in seafaring; the idea of their trading for Cornish tin appeared already in the sixteenth century, and recurs constantly thereafter (Daniel 1962, 13). This diffusionist paradigm thus grew up in parallel with the Germanic migrationist one.
12. This process had begun much earlier in Renaissance Italy, where early ethnographic observations had recalled Lucretius' description of a mythical Stone Age in *De Rerum Natura*, V, 1282, and even led to the recognition of stray finds of Neolithic axes as ancient artefacts. These speculations were known to French Jesuits in the seventeenth and early eighteenth centuries: see Clarke (1968, 4–7) following Cheynier (1936, 8–10). This was the germ of the evolutionist paradigm.

13. See for instance Trevor-Roper (1983). Comparisons were explicitly made between the 'folk' poetry of Homer and that of the bogus Gaelic bard, Ossian.

14. Notably in the work of Karl Ottfried Müller. The term 'Minyan' was applied by Schliemann to a type of Middle Bronze Age pottery, on which Childe was to publish his first article.

15. For the development of prehistoric archaeology in central Europe, see Sklenář (1983), with special reference to its social and political context; also Kühn (1976); Jażdżewski (1984, Ch. 2).

16. Preface to *Contribution to a Critique of the Political Economy* (1859). This formulation was essentially a continuation of Hegel's idea of world progress. Marx was equivocal about whether the Asiatic mode of production constituted a necessary step in the emergence of the others, reflecting a more general European ambivalence towards the orient.

17. Engels, *Der Ursprung der Familie, des Privateigentums und des Staates, im Anschluss an Lewis H. Morgans Forschungen* (Zürich, 1884).

18. For instance Taylor (1865), Lubbock (1870) and Pitt-Rivers (Myres 1906); these assumptions were perhaps a necessary precondition for developmental discussion of social change, in opposition both to 'degenerationist' views (advanced, for instance, by Archbishop Whately) and the cyclical view inherent in Lyell's uniformitarianism. See in general Burrow (1966) and Ingold (1986).

19. Note that *Gauloises* cigarettes still carry the image of a Late Bronze Age helmet – with added wings.

20. Kossinna was of Lithuanian extraction, born in Tilsit 'am Rande des Deutschtums, dort wo das Deutschtum im Kampfe gegen andere Kräfte lag' (Kühn 1976, 338): a syndrome neatly characterised by T. S. Eliot in *The Waste Land* in a snatch of Bavarian coffee-conversation – *stamm' aus Litauen, echt deutsch*. For a survey of Kossinna's career, and a systematic comparison with Childe, see Veit (1984).

21. Derided for his background in classical archaeology by Kossinna, who found his attitude to German prehistory 'pathological' (Kühn 1976, 339).

22. C. Schuchhardt (1919, with successive editions to 1944). The emphasis on ethnicity only became dominant in the 1935 edition, however, and was perhaps a concession to the climate of the time rather than a personal view.

23. There was a parallel use of this term in ethnology, associated principally with the Catholic, anti-evolutionist *Kulturkreislehre* of Koppers and Schmidt in Vienna, but it made little contribution to mainstream prehistory. Its existence was one reason why Gordon Childe emphasised the concept of progress in the 1930s.

24. This is to put it mildly: in fact there was profound ignorance and provincialism.

25. The Phoenicians had long played a role in English visions of the past, where Romanticism had not bred xenophobia but even encouraged the image of exotic traders bartering for Cornish tin; and by the nineteenth century (in contrast to French attitudes) the Phoenicians were seen as models of maritime enterprise. The relative neglect of their archaeology until recently in Britain relates to the growing exclusiveness of classics from the 1930s onwards.

26. He was instrumental in the formation of a School of Geography at Oxford, and active in attempts to introduce the teaching of anthropology. It is characteristic that when his contributions to the first edition of the *Cambridge Ancient History* (1923) came to be revised fifty years later, it required six specialists to cover the ground.

27. Hence the curious (but still powerful) image of classical Greece as unconcerned with trade and immune to luxury, in which the irrational has to be explained as an anomaly.

28. Presumably because of the 'un-Hellenic' ostentation of the Shaft Graves, with their golden finery. It was only in 1953 that the Mycenaean (Linear B) script was recognised as an early form of Greek. To those who saw Mycenaean Greece as an extension, via Crete, of the Orient, no wonder this discovery was to prove hard to swallow.

29. Childe seems to have convinced Myres that Middle Bronze Age ('Minyan') Greece was at least Indo-European (Myres 1935b, 213).

30. It is instructive to compare Myres' comprehensive, but relatively superficial, account of European prehistory in his *Cambridge Ancient History* chapter (1923) with Childe's detailed cultural sequences in *The Dawn* (1925); but for all that, Myres' higher dates (reflecting his geological knowledge) have proved nearer the truth.

31. In a lecture written in 1933, he defended the practical importance of prehistory precisely because it is 'just the objective and critical study of precisely those data on which the political theories of Houston Chamberlain and Adolf Hitler purport to be built'. The reaction to Nazism effectively ended general acceptance of the equation of race and culture. It is noteworthy that while 'national character' was a common subject for books in the 1920s – for example Ernest Barker, *National Character and the Factors in its Formation* (1927) – by the 1940s it was more common to find titles such as Hamilton Fyfe, *The Illusion of National Character* (1940). The Nazi abuse of prehistory strengthened Childe's belief in an eastern homeland for the Indo-Europeans, and may have contributed to his distrust of high chronologies for prehistoric Europe, which were advocated by German nationalist prehistorians.

32. The analogy with the events then taking place in Nazi Germany was made explicit in his description of the 'oriental centralisation' of the later Roman Empire (Childe 1942, 286).

33. 'Intellectually ... Marxism exerted a seriously inhibiting effect', 'at the end of his life he realised that his prophet had played him false' (Clark 1976, 3).

34. This was the Frazer Lecture for 1949 to the Royal Anthropological Institute: it is perhaps significant that Sir James Frazer, too, was influenced in his unfavourable view of religion by his clerical parentage.

35. This description applies to British and American writing on prehistory; in Germany the rejection of Kossinna and a suspicion of general theory in the post-war period led in effect to a revival of Montelius, and German prehistorians have only slowly accepted the validity of radiocarbon dating.

Section II

ECOLOGICAL
IMPERATIVES?

*Scene from an Egyptian ceremonial macehead of 'King Scorpion', c.3200 BC,
showing the king performing a ritual connected with irrigation
(Ashmolean Museum).*

Horticulture preceded field culture, as the garden (*hortus*)
came before the field (*ager*).

LEWIS HENRY MORGAN (1877)

It is hard, now, for subsequent generations to capture the sense of excitement and optimism in archaeology (especially in Cambridge), and indeed in life itself, which characterised the later 1960s and first few years of the 1970s, before the Oil Crisis gave the first intimation that a newer and post-modern world was arriving. We had New Archaeology; but so did everyone else – New Geography, New History, New Demography, even New Math[ematic]s. It was a mini-Enlightenment, when the books that one wanted to be seen with had titles like Thomas Kuhn's *The Structure of Scientific Revolutions* or Alfred Sauvy's *Théorie générale de la population*, or Lévi-Strauss' *Elementary Structures of Kinship*. Historians had been first off the mark in France, where Braudel's revival of the *Annales* school had pointed to the structures and conjunctures below the surface of mere events; though such history was not much read at that stage – even by historians, but especially not by archaeologists, whose paradigmatic pattern was sought in the life sciences (who had just cracked the genetic code) and the earth sciences (who were just discovering plate tectonics). The Cavendish Laboratory and the Sidgewick Museum neatly bracketed the Department of Archaeology in Downing Street; Peter Haggett and Richard Chorley took coffee just round the corner, opposite Emmanuel College, reinventing geography; Peter Laslett and Tony Wrigley were revolutionising historical demography; David Clarke wrote *Analytical Archaeology*, and a string of key papers and edited books (Clarke 1968; 1979). Ecology and systems theory provided a common language for these common enterprises.

With the benefit of hindsight, the hard sciences were hard and stayed so, while the soft sciences remained soft or got softer. DNA and plate tectonics permanently revolutionised our way of looking at the world; the social sciences swung in the opposite direction and spent the next twenty years condemning the follies of functionalism, evolutionism and systems thinking. The search for deterministic models of human behaviour was replaced by voluntaristic models of human agency, the search for ecological advantage by the search for meaning. Yet it would be wrong to decry the achievements of archaeology in this period. It filled in huge areas of ignorance in our cognisance of ancient times, of how people spent their lives; it invented methodologies which have remained fundamental to all reconstructions of the past; it created links between different branches of archaeology, and between archaeology and neighbouring disciplines; and above all it asked: why are you doing this, and what are you trying to prove? When, eventually, archaeology rediscovered history, it was not the *histoire historisante* of leaders and battles (still all too dominant in schools), but the transformed, ecologically and socially conscious history of *les Annales* (Sherratt 1992). We can recover what was lost, but not lose what was gained.

The principal areas of advance were in the twin areas of investigation which (especially in American parlance) came to be labelled 'subsistence and settlement' and 'trade and exchange'. The former was essentially the discovery for the first time of how people gained a living from the landscape (by analysing their animal-bone and seed residues), and how they distributed themselves over that landscape (by searching more systematically for their traces than archaeologists ever had before). The latter was the detection of imported items (by new forms of petrological and metallurgical examination), and the reconstruction of their circulation patterns, especially by noting associations with particular classes of burial – sorted by age and sex. Each of these operations involved certain naive assumptions (not least that these were separate and unrelated spheres of existence, questioned in Chapter 10 below), which have increasingly been made explicit and actively controlled; but it is arguable that more sophisticated and worldly-wise archaeologists would simply not have made the effort in the first place.

The much more three-dimensional picture of prehistoric Europe produced by this burst of new observations made many of Childe's characterisations seem more like caricatures, and allowed a new range of interpretations to be explored, which, with a rather more sophisticated view of the social, are essential components of a balanced view.

2

Socio-economic and Demographic Models for Later Prehistoric Europe

(1972)

Until recently there was at least a measure of general agreement among European prehistorians on the aims of archaeology and the appropriate framework for its interpretation. The most explicit statements of these aims and methods are to be found in the writings of V. G. Childe, in his series of syntheses of European prehistory from 1925 onwards, and in various later works devoted specifically to methodology (Childe 1925; 1956). Childe's approach was based on three related concepts: the 'stages of culture' classification of Morgan and Engels, the key role of technology in relation to these, and a model of technological change which assumed that innovation was a characteristic of specific types of society. From this point of view, the progress of European societies depended on their proximity to Near Eastern civilisation through the mediation of the 'secondary civilisations' of the Mediterranean, themselves only made possible by the 'Urban Revolution' in the Orient. Thus the whole process depended ultimately on one or two unique events – the achievement of a regular surplus by irrigation agriculture in the alluvial valleys of the Nile and the Tigris–Euphrates.

Both the theoretical basis of this, and the usefulness of these ideas in interpreting the evidence now available, have been questioned. In particular, on the theoretical side, it has become clear that more consideration must be given to factors which in the archaeological record are less obvious than technological change. The use of economic concepts such as 'surplus' cannot

This was written while I was a graduate student at Peterhouse with David Clarke, for his book Models in Archaeology. *It was a heady time, when someone in their mid-twenties was invited to contribute in this way to a major publication. I had just returned from excavating in Turkey, at Can Hasan with David French and Sebastian Payne, and was sharing a house with Robin Dennell. The extracts reproduced here have been chosen to convey the excitement of exploring a whole range of neighbouring disciplines for their relevance to archaeology, and the delight at finding principles and processes of human ecology.*

be separated from demographic questions, such as why this was not ab-sorbed by population increase, or whether the productivity of Meso-potamian agriculture really was inherently greater than contemporary European systems. The role of technology must be assessed in the light of its relation to specific agricultural and economic systems, as it is only in re-lation to these that the significance of particular innovations can be judged.

RESOURCES AND POTENTIAL FOR GROWTH

Economic expansion, far from being a characteristic of all societies, is a rather exceptional occurrence. Small-scale economies appear to be charac-terised both by low levels of labour input and low population densities, even though human populations possess the ability to make use of a great range of food resources. The small fraction of these exploited at any one time makes the use of calculations based on 'carrying capacity' a dangerous pro-cedure. The only alternative is a detailed reconstruction of prehistoric economies based upon evidence of food remains, technology and site locations.

One of the most important factors to be taken into account is the fluctuation in the abundance of available resources. Not merely must population levels be adjusted to the season of greatest scarcity in the year, but the economic strategy must minimise the effects of differences in yield from year to year. The effects of such fluctuations, however, can be cushioned by reliance on a combination of resources which assures the highest return under the most adverse conditions. This is particularly important in determining the balance between animal and plant foods, and accounts for the heavy emphasis on pastoralism in arid regions (Deschler 1965). Although animal resources are less productive than plant ones, being one step higher in the food chain, they possess the advantage of mobility, so that scattered flushes of vegetation in areas of variable rainfall, which are too erratic to be predicted and thus used for cereal growing, can be used to support moving herds. Even where the rainfall is more regular, but the area is still subject to droughts, the use of plant foods such as cereals still needs to be supplemented by a strong pastoral component, in case of crop failure. The types of social organisation typical of such economies embody further security precautions, based on the circulation of animals on loan.

In less marginal areas, however, such considerations are not so important in determining economic strategies and population levels. In particular, there seem to be a number of stable patterns of small-scale exploitation. The lack of complex techniques for storage, for instance, or for intensive forms of cropping, places limits on the development of increasingly productive ways of utilising many types of resources. Although shellfish may be con-veniently gathered from beds exposed intertidally or in shallow water, any more intensive method would involve a 'leap' in technological capacity, including for instance the construction of large-scale dams, cages, etc. Similarly, the most productive method of exploiting an ungulate population is by a ranching technique, in which large numbers of animals are raised to a uniform age at which the gain in meat weight begins to be offset by the continuing cost of providing grazing or fodder. In small-scale exploitation, however, this is impossible: what is required is a regular supply of daily food, which is best supplied by live animal products (blood, milk, etc.) if this is possible, or by occasional culling.

While an increase in yield is therefore possible, it is unlikely to be attempted by most groups practising small-scale economies. Only where there is a set of relatively simple transition possibilities, based upon a series of small modifications to an existing system, are changes likely to occur. Given the tendency of societies to 'fight to stay the same' (Schon 1971, 32), by resisting innovations that would cause large-scale restructuring of established patterns, such possibilities are limited in occurrence, and are conceivable (a) only with resources with a high potential for expansion (elasticity), and (b) with resource systems including complementary resources which allow the problems created by the development of one element in the resource system to be overcome by the provision of – for example – a secure if low-yielding supply of food in case of the failure of the main element.

One of the most striking contrasts in patterns of growth is that between cereal-based economies, and those based on animal resources such as ungulates or shellfish. The root of the contrast lies in the relative elasticity of the resources. With an ungulate population, cropping above a certain percentage of the population will impair the ability of the herd to reproduce itself. The size of the total population can only be raised by drastic changes in the structure of the ecosystem. With cereals, on the other hand, by relatively small changes in the structure of the ecosystem – shifting plants with an annual habit into niches occupied by plants more successful in competition – the yield of useful products can be greatly increased. Moreover, there is a more or less direct relationship between labour input and return: clearance and sowing of small additional areas produces an immediate effect in terms of increased output. Similarly, even relatively minor advances in technology may have the effect of greatly increasing yield, both by allowing more efficient cultivation methods and by making possible the use of hitherto unused types of land.

The significance of the Neolithic Revolution lies in the almost continuous growth possible in cereal-based economies, and the increasing degree of interference with the ecosystem that it entails. The domestication of animals such as sheep provided a resource compatible with a sedentary pattern of exploitation in a system in which settlements needed to be located for access to cereal-growing soils, and provided not only additional protein but also security in case of crop failure. Patterns of animal exploitation were thus adjusted to complement an increased reliance on plant food. Despite the difficulties involved in actually identifying 'domesticated' animals (Higgs and Jarman 1969), the need for greater control over movement, breeding, etc., in this situation is clear, and the distinction between agricultural and 'hunter-gatherer' economies remains valid.

Patterns of growth in agricultural economies are thus closely related to the amounts and distributions of fertile land, which affect both the capacity for further expansion and the kinds of more intensive exploitation that can be developed. In areas of heavy leaching such as the tropics, the potential for growth with a pre-industrial technology is much smaller than in temperate areas, even though in almost every zone there are alluvial soils whose concentration of minerals and water retentive capacity makes them first-class agricultural land. The capacity for further expansion thus depends ultimately on the availability of 'middle range' soils which allow expansion to continue when the first-class ones are filled to capacity. A second factor is present in some areas where a diversity of different zones adjoin (or are connected by easy transport links) and the integration of zones of specialised production is possible through reciprocal redistribution and exchange networks.

The phrase 'the colonisation of Europe' has often been used by historians (e.g. Koebner 1966) to describe the extension of settlement in the Middle Ages into hitherto uncultivated areas. Yet this marginal infilling is but the final phase of a continuous process with its beginning in the Early Neolithic. The demographic crises of the later Middle Ages reflect the increased difficulty with which the extension of the margin of cultivation could be carried out. In many documented instances, population was very close to the ceiling. As Postan and Titow (1959) noted for the estates of the bishopric of Winchester in the thirteenth century, poor harvests were directly reflected in mortality figures. Wrigley (1962) has suggested that the ceiling imposed by competing uses for available land caused a recession until the bottleneck was broken by technical innovation – in this case the development of machines based on coal and iron rather than wood. This was an essential element in a solution involving radical changes in settlement location, land tenure and more intensive systems of agrarian production, complemented by the growth of an imperialist colonial system based on the export of specialist manufactured products and the importation of food and raw materials.

Systems of land use

The economies of prehistoric Europe and the Near East thus belong to a class of economies characterised by the possibility of more or less continuous expansion. It might be expected from this that the economic, social and technological developments that characterise the post-Neolithic sequence could be explained in terms of this process of growth, and that the different patterns that characterise the Near East, the Mediterranean and inland Europe could be related to the geographical background – the distribution of soils, raw materials and transport routes.

An important set of information for the analysis of subsistence agriculture is the labour requirements of the various crops. As there is great variation in these, and as societies are generally unwilling to work harder than is necessary, certain resources possess clear advantages for populations of a given size. Thus it has already been noted that hunter-gatherer groups expend relatively little effort on subsistence in comparison with agriculturalists. The same contrast is true for the various stages of agricultural intensification.

An increase in output can be achieved by two means: either by an increase in the area of land utilised or by intensification – the more productive use of land already cropped. Both require changes in technology and both have implications for social organisation, but intensification makes special demands on labour input. Expansion in a given system proceeds by a balance between the two processes related to the opportunities of an individual environment; but before introducing a spatial element into the model, some characteristics of the intensification process should be noted.

The most thorough discussion of this problem is by Boserup (1965). She points out that with a small population, the most economic agricultural system in terms of labour input is an extensive one, based on swidden (slash-and-burn) cultivation with a simple technology. Intensification is measured by the increased frequency of cropping of a given area, with a consequent shortening of fallow periods. This process has several implications. In the first place little preparation of the soil is necessary for long fallow systems, where cropping is for short periods only and it is not necessary to maintain fertility by manuring during this period, nor even worthwhile clearing tree stumps. In consequence, the use of the plough is unnecessary and the cultivated plot is abandoned when weeds begin to compete seriously with crops or when the nutrients released by burning off the forest are exhausted. For short fallow systems, however, both manuring and ploughing become necessary, as the land is cropped beyond the point at which initial fertility begins to decline, and fallowing is only long enough to allow the growth of grass, presenting problems in tillage. Further intensification, allowing even multi-cropping, depends on the introduction of techniques such as irrigation or terracing involving heavy capital investment.

In an extensive agricultural system, a relatively small labour input is sufficient to produce a good crop. As hoeing and weeding take a large amount of labour time, any increase in these is particularly important in this respect. It is these elements that become increasingly necessary with intensification. In addition, yields are likely to fall somewhat even with manuring. With plough agriculture, considerations of scale are critical – draught animals must be fed and sufficient beasts are required for manuring to make cultivation profitable. In consequence of these, one of the corollaries of intensification is an actual fall in output per man hour. Since labour is in any case low in extensive systems, this is still a possibility, but intensification does imply longer working hours if output is to be increased. Intensification is thus not likely to be undertaken except in a situation where the population cannot be supported by existing systems of cultivation and until other possibilities have been exhausted – or would themselves involve a comparable increase in effort.

Boserup's scheme is artificial to the extent that it neglects local soil variation and presents only an economic analysis of the factors involved in intensification. In the analysis of the agricultural development of a specific area, the range of available land types and their distribution must be an important element. The soils determine the degree to which intensification can proceed with a pre-industrial technology without causing permanent damage. Many tropical soils are easily overcropped, and in consequence the widespread occurrence of extensive systems can be seen in part as due to this. In other areas, however, extensive systems occur on land that would sustain a shorter fallow period: here land is simply abundant in relation to population and there is no need for a system involving higher labour input.

On the basis of African evidence, Allan (1965) has produced a sixfold land classification based on the ratio of crop time to fallow time. Although based on the use of the soils, for the long-settled agricultural areas there is a strong correlation between this and inherent fertility characteristics. An important distinction can be drawn, for example, between *permanent cultivation soils*, and others that require a longer fallow period. The latter range through *semi-permanent cultivation*, *recurrent cultivation*, *shifting cultivation*, and *partial cultivation* to wholly uncultivable soils, requiring progressively longer fallow periods. Although Boserup's model does not admit the existence of ceilings determined by soil type, it is clear that with a pre-industrial technology they must exist. Certainly the more fertile areas could formerly have been cultivated on an extensive system: but as population grew, intensification proceeded only as far as the nature of the soil allowed without artificial fertilisers.

With a small initial population, the richest soils will be settled first, especially permanent cultivation soils if they are available. The growth of population leads to the spread of settlement to poorer and more difficult soils, first on an extensive basis and then on to as intensive a system as the soil will permit. As the good soils are filled up, a choice will open as to whether local intensification or extension of the margin of cultivation is more attractive. This depends on the character and availability of the remaining land – whether it is only slightly less fertile than that already cultivated, or much poorer – and thus on the relative cost-effectiveness of the two possibilities.[1]

The interrelatedness of different aspects of production introduces

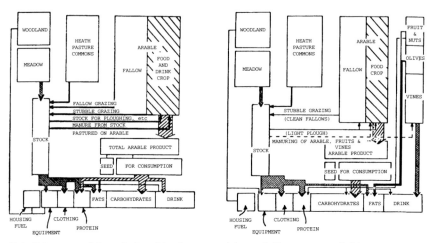

2.1 *Diagram of the relationships between (a) north European and (b) Mediterranean agrarian systems in the medieval period. In the former (here diagrammed as a two-course rotation), arable and pastoral elements are closely interlinked; in the latter they have greater independence (after C. T. Smith).*

constraints on the range of possibilities for expansion. A series of well-documented examples is provided by the farming systems of medieval Europe (see especially Slicher van Bath 1963, 9–18; Smith 1967, 191–256). In an intensive system of north European kind, where manure is utilised and the animals are overwintered largely on special crops and by products of cereal farming (stubble, chaff, etc.), the animal component has to be extended at the same time as the cereal element, and the balance between the two is closely defined. The network of rights over stubble grazing was therefore an important element in assuring maximum utilisation of animal fodder. Figure 2.1a shows the connections between various parts of the system. By contrast, the Mediterranean areas of Europe are characterised by a system where different elements could be developed independently; large areas of upland unsuitable for cereal growing encouraged the use of transhumance, while some lowland areas provided suitable places for fruit growing, often with small-scale irrigation (see Figures 2.1b, 2.2).

For a given set of resources, and techniques for cropping them, there are optimum sizes and locations for settlement units. Regularities in settlement pattern represent the end result of decisions based on the need to minimise unproductive travelling time and the costs of bulk transport; thus locational decisions can be modelled in the same way as decisions on crop strategy. As transport technology, exploitation pattern or social organisation changes, so the factors affecting site location will alter. Stable patterns of locational preference are thus valuable evidence for reconstructing these.

The potential for growth in a particular area and its pattern of development are determined in the first place by the range of soil types and their distribution. For the analysis of specific situations, therefore, a spatial model

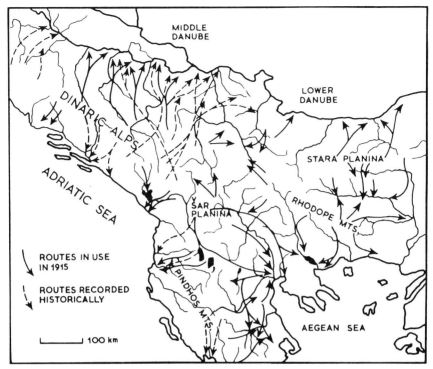

2.2 South-east Europe showing routes used in transhumance in recent times (after Cvijić).

is essential, and data on archaeological site locations offer one of the easiest methods of testing predictions derived from these. Over the last fifty years a great mass of data on archaeological distributions has been collected, some of it of outstanding quality and scholarship. Small-scale distribution maps were not greatly used by Childe, and it is this lack of contact with the pattern of prehistoric settlement 'on the ground', in a regional setting, that is the root of the inadequacy of much of his models today. It is not necessarily possible, however, to compare one kind of distribution map with another, especially when maps of different periods may be constructed in terms of different features – settlement sites, burials, stray finds of various types, etc. What must be compared are the inferred systems of land use deduced from various kinds of map, in conjunction with the analysis of food remains from settlement sites.

THE CHARACTER OF EARLY NEOLITHIC SETTLEMENT

The change to an economy based on planted cereals and pulses and the adjustment of complementary exploitation and settlement patterns, despite the slowness with which the various elements of this strategy were integrated, marks a significant transition to new patterns of demographic and economic growth for which Childe's description of a 'Neolithic Revolution' is not inappropriate. In Europe particularly, the introduction of new plant staples produced a sharply defined economic shift in areas of high agricultural potential, even though this had no immediate effect in areas where the exploitation of animal populations continued to be superior to primitive farming.

The restricted range of environments suitable for early farming systems has not been sufficiently emphasised in discussions of the spread of agriculture, and in particular the significance of soil fertility and moisture content in determining the pattern of occupation. Although the striking correlation between Neolithic settlement and loess soils in central Europe has been the subject of comment since Buttler, this phenomenon of close association with particular soil types is not limited to the Danube region but is a general feature of the initial agricultural colonisation of Europe. A characteristic of early cereal assemblages from Neolithic sites in the Near East is the presence of seeds of *Scirpus*, indicating a very moist immediate environment for cereal cultivation. This evidence is supported by the strong pattern of association between early village sites and permanent cultivation soils near springs, and especially near the backswamps of large lakes or the fringes of old lake basins (cf. Allan 1970). This strongly suggests that an economic yield from cereal cultivation was generally possible only where a sufficient area of such soils was available, and that the recent geological history of the relevant areas should provide significant predictions about the kinds of area where early Neolithic sites are likely to be found.

Central Turkey and the areas of historic Macedonia and Thrace form an ancient crystalline massif against which later sedimentary rocks were intensively folded during the Tertiary mountain building phase, forming chains to the north and south of the original massif. The downfaulted areas of this were for a time occupied by arms of the sea, during which shallow water limestones were deposited in the Tertiary period. The inland basins were then cut off from the sea by further uplifting, and became freshwater lakes – or in some cases saltwater lakes in the case of internal drainage basins, e.g. Tuzgölü in central Anatolia. The levels of these lakes seem to have fluctuated considerably in the course of the Pleistocene, related to changes in temperature and humidity. In general the rise in temperature during interglacial phases would have increased evaporation (Butzer 1970), and a postglacial recession of lake levels has been documented in Anatolia (Cohen and Erol 1969; Cohen 1970) and in the Dead Sea Rift (Vita-Finzi 1969). Similar phenomena are likely to have occurred in the large flat basins of Thessaly and central Bulgaria, and in a multitude of small lakes in the Balkans and Anatolia.

The relationship between the areas of fine alluvium and backswamp soils produced by the Late Glacial recession in lake levels, and the pattern of early

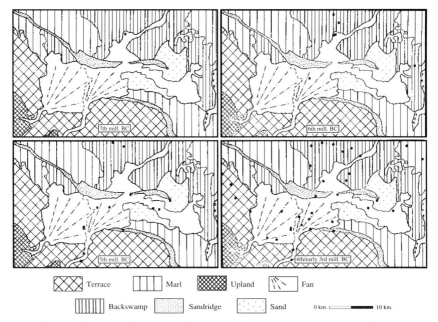

2.3 *The distribution of known prehistoric sites in the Çumra region of south-central Turkey (between Konya and Karaman), after field-survey by Dr D. H. French (1970), with soil boundaries after Driessen and de Meester: (a) seventh millennium* BC; *(b) sixth millennium* BC; *(c) fifth millennium* BC; *(d) fourth millennium* BC *[from Sherratt 1973, with dates corrected].*

settlement, has so far been intensively investigated only in Anatolia (Cohen 1970; French 1970). In the Konya plain, Neolithic settlement seems to be closely associated with backswamp soils, which, unlike the other soil types also associated with the receding lake such as marls, are not subject to strong seasonal desiccation. Although located for access to such backswamp soils, the settlements themselves are typically sited on the edges of alluvial fans which provide raised areas less liable to be flooded. The site of Çatal Hüyük, for example, occupies a highly favourable position on a spur where the fan seems to have broken through a sandspit representing an old shore-line, and the site has ready access to backswamp soils on three sides (Figure 2.3, top left).

One piece of evidence which suggests that such areas were strongly pre-ferred in spite of other disadvantages is the apparent incidence of malaria, for example at Çatal Hüyük and at Nea Nikomedia in a low-lying part of Greek Macedonia. Angel (1968) has suggested that the incidence of porotic hyperostosis in skeletal material from these two sites is associated with a form of anaemia conferring resistance to this disease. Certainly the tectonic basins of Macedonia occupied by the remnants of Pleistocene lakes were until recently highly malarial, as the French and British forces discovered in 1916–18 (see *Naval Intelligence Handbooks: Greece*, vol. I, 272).

Two basic reasons lie behind this pattern of land occupation. First, with low population densities, the model put forward in previous sections suggests that there would be a strong selection for permanent cultivation soils, and that excess population would move to other areas of similarly high-yielding soil before tackling poorer-quality land or changing to a more intensive system of exploitation. Secondly, in dry Mediterranean climates frequent ploughing of land is necessary to prevent run-off and to encourage moisture absorption in order to produce an adequate crop on land where groundwater is not near to the surface (Clark 1952, 100; Stevens 1966, 93). It is most unlikely that the earliest agricultural communities in the Near East and south-east Europe used the plough, in view of Boserup's arguments summarised above. Instead, the initial stage of agricultural development seems to be characterised by a pattern of rapid spread with relatively low population densities, settlement systems being restricted to small areas of land of high agricultural potential, with specialised satellites.

This pattern of settlement has important implications for reconstructions of the types of social regulation and mechanisms for the distribution of goods, as well as being the unstable initial state of a system with great potential for change.

INTERNAL EXPANSION IN ENEOLITHIC AND BRONZE AGE EUROPE

While there was still an adjacent expanding frontier allowing surplus population to emigrate, population levels in a given area would have remained low. In south-east Europe the association of settlement with marshy areas and the consequent prevalence of malaria would in any case have checked growth to some extent. However, over a long time the build-up of population continued, and resulted in changes in economy, settlement pattern and social structure.

Of particular significance is the point at which permanent settlement began to be extended beyond the range of soils typical of the initial settlement of the area. In the Konya plain third-millennium settlements are found for the first time, in any number, on the drier terraces above the plain; doubling the number of sites known from the previous millennium. In the Balkans a shift in the preferred location of settlement occurs, typified by sites on defended promontories on the edge of the basins. In Czechoslovakia, similar hilltop settlements are found extending up the valleys from the fertile Bohemian 'heartland'. In the north European plain, settlement extends onto the sandy heathlands previously avoided.[2] These movements are not closely synchronous even within individual regions, but they represent critical points in a common process at work over the whole area.

The process of agricultural expansion carried with it implications for social organisation. One aspect of this was the competition for colonisable land distributed between the existing centres of population, reflected both in the selection of defensive locations and the development of effective metal weapons as opposed to small copper knives. Another was the occupation of a more diverse range of environments than the initial optimal ones, and the increased necessity for the redistribution of basic products. Even though some of the forested sandy soils taken into cultivation would originally have carried brown earths suitable for cereal cultivation, the agricultural use of these would rapidly encourage podsolisation and reduce their value as arable. In this situation redistributive centres, even if only seasonal markets or fairs under the auspices or protection of a local chief, would take on increasing significance. The role of metal, increasingly a strategic raw material, would in these circumstances have been important in securing low-land cereal products, while the emergence of distributional centres and local chieftains made possible the exchange of specialised materials and objects between centres. In a similar way textiles – evidenced from the increased numbers and size of sheep in the Bronze Age of south-east Europe and from the appearance of loom weights and fittings – would have been an important medium of exchange.

URBANISATION AND ECONOMIC GROWTH

In Neolithic and Bronze Age Europe, the relationship between population and food supply can be expressed schematically as in Figure 2.3a (although the actual course of the curve will of course be far from regular). The cultivated area increases as population grows, and production rises with it. Year-to-year fluctuations produce a temporary surplus in good years: this is the *normal surplus* of subsistence agriculture (Figure 2.3b; cf. Allan 1965). There is little or no large-scale distribution of food over any distance, since all sites are growing similar crops.

By the later fourth millennium, however, certain communities in the Near East had initiated a new pattern of exchanges between regions, notably between the alluvial river-basins and their hinterlands. Such institution-alised exchange introduced a new factor of production for manufacture. A system involving urbanism necessitates the production of a *standard surplus* (Figure 2.4a) by means of additional labour input, in which one region exports specialised manufactured products (often textiles) in return for grain and raw materials. Since the increase in grain production requires considerable additional labour input, it is likely that some element of co-ercion is needed to initiate an exchange system of this kind, even though the system may then be maintained by local elites – the main consumers of luxury products (Figure 2.5). The process of demographic and economic expansion thus has sociological implications which are essential to the general problem of growth, and particularly to the question of regulation of production and exchange. As the maintenance of an agriculturally non-

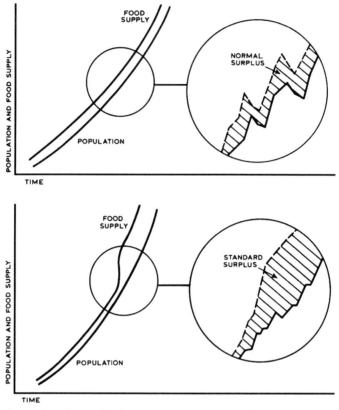

2.4 *Surplus as the relationship between population and food supply: (a) the* normal *surplus – the fluctuating yearly excess over subsistence requirements, and (b) the* standard *surplus, a regularly achieved production for exchange, requiring additional labour input.*

productive class requires more work from those directly involved in agriculture, the development of social stratification can be seen as one of a range of increasingly high-cost solutions to the problem of supporting further growth, and the rarity of such systems in the course of human development is therefore scarcely surprising.

A true urban system, in which the central places are also centres of population and have facilities for continuous storage and manufacturing, is typical of state organisation with bulk interregional exchange. The actual size of such 'cities', however, is a local problem, depending on the concentration of agricultural population. Where only a small agricultural community is resident, these may more aptly be described as palace or ceremonial centres. In Mesopotamia, by contrast, such centres seem often to have been surrounded by a zone empty of villages (Adams 1970), implying that the land was worked by labour from the city, and the difference in size between central and non-central places is largely related to settlement

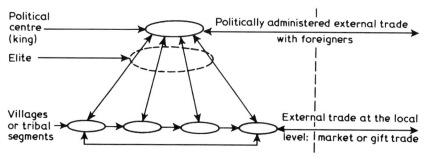

2.5 *Socio-economic transactions in the primitive economy, within a centralised system of political authority (from Dalton 1969).*

nucleation and concentration of population for defence. In other environments, however, this may not be a rational pattern of population distribution. The true 'urban' functions of such sites are represented by the magazines, storage areas, administrative and religious 'core', and specialist manufacturing workshops. (The existence of a network of small 'market towns' is related to the degree to which the villages themselves consume specialist products, and such forms may be typical of a later phase either than fairs or urban centres as defined above.)

With the development of social differentiation and centres of power, new phenomena emerge as it becomes possible for innovations to appeal to sectional interests and emerging elites. Even more striking are the results of changes in the communication infrastructure of societies with a need to find external markets and sources of supply. With the growing disparity between 'advanced' and 'underdeveloped' countries, centre/periphery diffusion systems (Schon 1971, ch. 4) become increasingly common and the scale of their effects becomes increasingly wide. Even so, however, such effects are largely limited to the areas in which they have a direct economic interest, and large areas – even adjacent to the colonising country – may remain relatively uninfluenced if they are outside this sphere of interest. The state seems to be closely related to the degree in which long-distance bulk exchange of products is critical to the functioning of the economy, and typically state organisation begins at nodal points and extends along the routes of trade (cf. Morton-Williams 1969). Historical geographers (e.g. Deutsch 1953; East 1968; Whittlesey 1944) have elaborated models of the genesis of states, which are in fact applicable, with modification, to less centralised systems.[3] State systems exist to cope with large-scale flows of products; thus phenomena of this kind seem to be behind the growth of large oppida in southern Britain in the later pre-Roman Iron Age with the exports recorded by Strabo, a process of local development stimulated by, and progressively amalgamated into, the formal network of an expanding empire. This example illustrates the 'multiplier effect' (Hamilton 1967), by which nodal areas propagate their organisation outwards.

CONCLUSION

The arguments set out in this paper are intended as much to indicate the range of evidence that must be considered in interpreting prehistoric cultural development as to advocate the use of specific models. Without an under-lying framework of assumptions about the role of factors such as population growth, there is no possibility of relating different aspects of prehistoric culture to each other and producing a convincing explanation for the contrasts in development between different areas. Only with this framework in mind can relevant models be selected for specific problems.

NOTES

1. Many of the types of choice made by subsistence farmers in assessing the cost-effectiveness of various types of exploitation are conveniently expressed as programming models (e.g. linear programming, integer programming, etc.). These are techniques for finding the optimum allocation of labour on different resources with different degrees of productivity to give a maximum yield, and they make it possible to work out mathematically a solution found in practice only by trial and error (Joy 1967).
2. Most useful here is Mathiassen's careful study (1948) of the distribution of prehistoric finds in Jutland. The comparison of evidence from different classes of objects and monuments produces an interesting and highly significant pattern related to the three major facies of the Riss and Würm moraine landscape – hill sand, heath sand and clay. At the risk of oversimplification, it is almost possible to see a reflection of Thomsen's 'Three Age System' in the successive occupation phases of these soil types: Neolithic settlement is concentrated largely on the more fertile hill sand; the late Neolithic Corded Ware period sees the occupation of the poorer heath sand areas, and this pattern persists until the occupation of clay areas in Iron Age times.
3. Useful here is the distinction used by human geographers concerned with the genesis of states (e.g. East 1968) between 'core' and 'peripheral' areas.

3

Water, Soil and Seasonality in Early Cereal Cultivation

(1980)

The purpose of this paper is to review current ideas of agricultural development in the sub-tropical and temperate parts of the western Old World and to suggest that the small scale and restricted extent of early cultivation systems gave them a unique character which has not been generally appreciated. Recent studies of prehistoric settlement in the western Old World have shown the basic role of soil moisture in early cultivation, and the association of such sites with riverine and springside locations. The beginning of such a cropping system marked a significant departure from earlier forms of cereal exploitation in the natural habitat zone, and may have involved a difference in growth cycle from that of the wild forms. The kind of cultivation which can be reconstructed as the earliest stage of agriculture is best described as a form of fixed plot horticulture dependent on ground- and surface-water, which differentiated in succeeding millennia into various forms of dry farming and irrigation agriculture. The former path involved the development of cultivation techniques suitable for interfluvial areas, including plough cultivation and swiddening; while the latter involved increasing degrees of water management to enlarge the area suitable for intensive cultivation.

Because the evidence for early cultivation systems is so varied in character

---

The ideas of the previous chapter suggested that early farming, usually thought of as shifting cultivation, had been fundamentally misunderstood. This paper – written by invitation for a World Archaeology *special volume on water management – was an attempt to outline a systematic alternative: that agriculture had begun as a transition from wild cereal populations to floodplain cultivation, and that such horticulture was the primary form of farming. It was actually written after Chapter 6, though published before it – in the same year as the* Cambridge Encyclopedia of Archaeology, *where I used its conclusions in my chapters. It was fuelled by comments from Jim Lewthwaite, Neil Roberts, Joan Oates and David Harris.*

85

and the arguments often speculative, three aspects will be considered separately rather than treated in strict chronological or regional order. After a short discussion of current schemes of agricultural development, the problem is approached first from the settlement evidence, and then from the viewpoint of crop ecology, before discussing the development of methods of water-management. The final section sets these observations in a wider context.

THE CHARACTER OF EARLY CULTIVATION SYSTEMS

Recent discussions of agricultural development, notably those of Boserup (1965), Wolf (1966) and Sanders and Price (1968), have stressed the transition from extensive to intensive forms of land-use. A major theme of this analysis is the move from long-fallow systems, often involving 'slash-and-burn' or swidden farming, to more intensive cultivation with shorter fallows made possible by labour-intensive techniques such as manuring and irrigation. Such transitions have been studied notably in south-east Asia (Geertz 1963) and in tropical Africa (Allan 1965). In applying these ideas to archaeological material, swiddening has usually been seen as the 'primeval' system, and assumed to be typical of the earliest farming groups. This idea has a long history in Europe, where early Neolithic groups have often been assumed to be 'slash-and-burn' cultivators (e.g. Clark 1952, 93). Yet the very fact that swiddening is still widespread in many areas and was only superseded in other areas in historical times should itself argue caution in using this as a model for the systems which were in existence six thousand years before.

A further argument against seeing swidden cultivation as a feature of great antiquity, especially in temperate environments, is its restriction in recent times to the most marginal European habitats, usually under coniferous forest. Its use is known mainly from the Boreal forest areas, for instance in Finland (Sigaut 1975), or else from upland areas of coniferous forest in central Europe such as the Carpathians (Lewicka 1972). In these areas it occurs on soils so marginal that they were not cultivated before the Middle Ages, as can be seen from the distribution of Late-Medieval clearance-names (Smith 1967, 133). It could plausibly be argued, therefore, that far from being a 'primeval' agrarian system, swidden agriculture was a characteristic of the most recent phase of the internal colonisation of Europe, when settlement spread to the least fertile soils which could not withstand any other form of cultivation.

While this phase may be more significant in the tropics, where low-quality soils form a greater proportion of the landscape, the same arguments apply: it is likely that the starting point of the Boserup scheme represents an already developed system of cultivation which is no model for the earliest farming systems.

INFERENCE FROM PREHISTORIC SETTLEMENT PATTERNS

The above arguments receive further support from examination of the archaeological evidence. The most striking feature of early farming settlement is its restricted distribution. By comparison with the proportion of the landscape under cultivation today, only a small fraction was used by early agriculturalists. In the Near East this proportion has grown much larger by the third millennium BC; but in Europe it did not attain anything like its present spread until the first millennium BC or even the Christian era, and the process of infilling continued well into the Middle Ages.

Not only was the distribution of sites in the earlier phases restricted, it was highly selective; and there are consistent patterns of association with certain environments and situations. Alluvial, lake-edge and other locations with high groundwater are characteristic of the Neolithic both in the near East and in southern Europe (Allan 1972; Sherratt 1973).

In the earliest stage of farming villages, many important sites like Jericho and Mureybit fall outside the zone of possible dry-farming altogether. Indeed, when evidence of cereal crops was first found at these sites it was commonly assumed that the grain must have been traded from better-watered hill-country nearby, or else that the climate must have undergone radical alteration. What all such sites possess, however, are abundant supplies of localised surface- or ground-water, such as the seepage area and spring of Ain es Sultan at Jericho or the seasonal wadis and perennially damp Euphrates floodplain at Mureybit. Similar observations apply to the more developed phase represented at Beidha, Tell Abu Hureyra and Bouqras, where local concentrations of surface-water permitted a limited cultivation on suitable fine-grained alluvial soils, especially at wadi-mouths.

The late glacial fall in lake-levels provided suitable terrain on the former lake-margins in many parts of the east Mediterranean. In Anatolia, the earlier Neolithic sites of the Konya Plain, including Çatal Hüyük, cluster in the backswamp region where rivers spread out in the otherwise arid plain; while further west the fluctuating lakes in the upland basins of Pisdia are ringed with sites like Hacılar and Suberde. Early sites in Greece and the Balkans are concentrated in areas of high water-table in the tectonic basins, either by springs at the valley-edge, by stream confluences, or on lower terraces by rivers and seasonally-enlarged lakes. In central Europe, early agricultural settlements occur on levees in the Middle Danube and Tisza floodplains, and by rivers and streams within the loess area. All of these locations give access to hydromorphic soils, and avoid the drier interfluves. Contrary to expectations generated by the model of 'shifting cultivation', such sites are usually long-lived, lasting for hundreds or even thousands of years in some cases. This is as true for *Bandkeramik* sites in north-west and central Europe as it is for the early *tells* of the Near East. Moreover, they often represent surprisingly large communities; sites like Jericho and Çatal

Hüyük are only the most spectacular examples of a general phenomenon. Clusters of agricultural settlement were often widely scattered, but within them population was locally concentrated around critical resources such as fine-grained, well-watered soils.

The implication of all this is that early agriculturalists occupied only a narrow zone of maximum productivity, in an essentially small-scale though locally intensive system of cultivation. In places this was capable of supporting nucleated communities, though in others produced a pattern of hamlets following the exploited zone. This zone of high water-table was of importance not only for cereal-growing but for a variety of resources, including water itself, fish and freshwater mussels, and the range of plant and animal species characteristic of the unusual conditions of the alluvium – in the Near East the game and exploitable perennials of wet conditions, and in Europe the species which could flourish only in the more open conditions where the Atlantic forests were interrupted by wet ground (Clarke 1976). In a sense, therefore, 'Mesolithic' and 'Neolithic' adaptations were parallel rather than successive: the main difference was the possibilities of expansion inherent in systems using cereals (Sherratt 1972, 491).

The characteristics of initial farming systems in Europe are best demonstrated by comparison with the patterns which emerged in succeeding millennia. The results of intensive regional surveys indicate the major changes which took place in the fourth and third millennia BC. A classic study of this kind is the work of Janusz Kruk and his associates in the loess-covered uplands of Little Poland (Kruk 1973). Here the restricted catchments of early Neolithic sites in the river valleys are a clear indication of the focus of interest in this zone, in striking contrast to the pattern which succeeded it in the later fourth and third millennia BC. Kruk notes the restriction of the earliest (early fifth millennium BC) agricultural sites to the lower parts of the valley slopes, immediately overlooking the floodplain – a pattern which continued down to the early fourth millennium, with some expansion to similar positions in small side-valleys. The main change occurred in the fourth millennium with the TRB culture, when there was a shift of activity to the interfluves and sites were located on higher ground above the valleys.

Kruk uses these regularities to reconstruct the economy of the initial settlers (255): 'Because of the limited size of the zone where the activities of the Danubian [fifth millennium BC] people were concentrated, the regular use of burning economy seems virtually impossible. The characteristic concentration of settlements within relatively limited areas also seems to speak against this possibility. Any extensive use of burning as a farming system would involve also the interfluve … However, the higher landscape zone was not systematically exploited by the Danubian people.' Instead, 'it is possible to assume with a fair amount of certainty that amongst the Danubian people the plant cultivation was closely linked with the lowest-lying parts of the ground. Natural conditions of this zone, notably the considerable humidity of soils and their productivity, favoured near larger settlements ... were worked by hand ... Owing to the high and durable edaphic potential of the soils that covered this zone it was possible to use the same portion of land continuously even without fertilizing it.' Such a pattern, with its small amount of forest-clearance and restricted possibilities for grazing, would fit the lack of stone tools suitable for woodcutting and the suggestions of stalled livestock in these early contexts.

There is accumulating evidence (Chapter 6) that the late fourth and early third millennia BC saw the widespread introduction of the plough, and that the extension of cultivation and shift in the focus of settlement to the drier interfluves was associated with plough-cultivation, extensive clearance and increased quantities of livestock. Such observations can be made in most parts of Europe. Their significance for our present purpose, however, is to suggest some important characteristics of the preceding regime. A common feature of early agrarian systems in the western Old World is their spatial restriction and concentration on limited alluvial zones. Soil moisture was evidently a critical feature of their cultivation system, and ground-water as significant as rainfall in the growth of crops. Such environments, while limited in extent, offered unusually high productivity and allowed considerable continuity of cultivation and, in some areas, notable concentrations of population. Such a reconstruction prompts some further speculations about the nature and origins of this type of cultivation.

CEREAL SEASONALITY AND GROWING-CONDITIONS

Wild cereals belong to the group of grasses which have adapted to strong seasonal stress by an annual habit and the development of food-storage in the seed. This allows succeeding generations to 'recolonise' seasonally bare habitats by rapid growth with the onset of rain. Wild wheats and barleys occur as members of open communities, particularly on limestone or basalt slopes and plateaux in the submediterranean park-forest belt. Their mechanism of dispersal is a simple one, in which the spike shatters when the seeds are ripe and they fall to the ground near the parent plant, where the sharp spikelet helps implantation in cracks in the soil. The time of ripening and localised area of dispersal prevent them from taking advantage of otherwise suitable habitats, for instance on seasonally open areas of alluvium. They thus grow mainly on dry hillslopes during the period of winter rainfall and ripen around May, with some variation according to altitude (Zohary 1969).

Under these dry upland conditions, their growing season is spread over nine months. Such a long period is not, however, a physiological necessity: wheat can be grown in only three months (90–100 days) in appropriate conditions, as it was in certain places in antiquity. Such three-month wheat is often called spring wheat, since it grows between March and May.[1] The principal sort of wheat grown in Europe and North America at the present day, however, is winter wheat which is sown in the autumn and harvested in summer. This has a higher and more stable yield than spring wheats (Klages 1949, 345). In most areas of Europe this type of wheat actually requires exposure to cold weather (vernalisation), though this is not so in the Mediterranean. At the present time, spring-sown wheat with a three-month growing season is only grown in any quantity on the northern margin of cultivation where the winter climate is too harsh.

Spring-grown wheat was, however, known in the Ancient World in the Mediterranean. Semple (1932, 382) describes the hard, heavy spring wheats as being typical of limited areas of southern Europe, by comparison with the soft, light grains which were then preferred for food. 'The heavy Boeotian wheat was doubtless spring-sown, as it is today, on the margin of the Lake Copais basin as the winter floodwaters gradually receded and Lake Copais contracted. The rich lacustrine soil and high water-table explained the superior quality of the grain.' The rapid growth of this crop, which did not have to rely on winter rainfall, was possible in the conditions of high ground-water which existed in restricted areas near to bodies of water, especially those subject to marked seasonal changes of volume.

It is tempting to ask whether the system documented for the Copais basin is not a relic of a much more widespread method of cultivation, that was typical of the pre-plough agriculture of southern and eastern Europe and the Near East. Is this not, in fact, the surface groundwater-based cultivation-system inferred from the settlement evidence in the preceding section? Such a form of cultivation would take advantage of the short period of optimum water-availability between winter floods and summer desiccation, allowing the three months' growing in spring which is necessary for a crop. Since less soil preparation is needed with this system than in one using rainwater, and little forest-clearance would be required, this pattern would make sense with low population levels and a simple technology.

This model suggests that the critical innovation in the cultivation of cereals was their transfer from dry environments with a rain-fed, winter, growth pattern to alluvial, lake-edge, riverine or springside locations in which an accelerated (spring) growth cycle was possible. The wild cereals themselves were precluded by their simple dispersal mechanism from colonising such habitats without human aid. The cultivation of crops in damp conditions is indicated by the presence of *Scirpus* seeds in early cereal samples (Flannery 1969, 81), and such deliberate sowing in areas away from their natural habitats was a necessary precondition (along with the use of the sickle for reaping) for the selection of tough-rachis forms, since the naturally-dispersed forms would always predominate in self-seeded populations. The early cultivation of cereals in such habitats was thus a quantum change from other forms of tending and exploitation, in that it operated in effect as a new means of dispersal. It thus opened up a new range of highly productive habitats for the species concerned without involving the massive restructuring of the ecosystem which became necessary in later agriculture; and it involved only a change in the growing-season. A minimum of cultivation, and no clearance of climax forest would have been necessary; and moreover this system had the potential to spread very widely beyond the natural habitat zone of the wild cereals, wherever such alluvial niches were to be found.

The term 'dry-farming', which is often used to describe the phase of cultivation before the development of formal canal-irrigation, is thus misleading: indeed, in the model suggested here, 'dry' (rainfall-dependent) farming was a specialised development parallel to that of irrigation itself. A small-scale horticulture adapted to riverine and lacustrine conditions explains the pattern of early Neolithic distribution in which even restricted areas of fine-grained water-retentive soils were sought for settlement. With initially low population levels, the still relatively sparse settlements could be supported from very limited patches of suitable soil, which could sustain even quite large villages. Such soils tend often to be neglected at the present day because of their small extent, their unsuitability for the cultivation of winter cereals, and their equally important role in providing spring grazing where large numbers of animals are kept and where much of the rest of the landscape is under cultivation.

The technology which such a horticultural system would require is of the simplest. In most cases major forest-clearance would not be needed. The seed would be broadcast, and relatively little weeding would be necessary. Virtually no preparation of the soil would be required, which in many cases would hardly rank even as hoe- or digging-stick cultivation. Where soils are subject to winter flooding and summer desiccation, the deep cracking caused by drying-out would provide natural aeration and make them practically self-cultivating. The labour-costs would thus have been trivial by comparison with later forms of agriculture, especially with the major forest-clearance required by interfluvial expansion in third-millennium Europe which is reflected in the emergence of effective axes and the widespread trade in stone for these tools (Sherratt 1976, 563–7). Such early horticultural systems would always have been spatially restricted, however, with locally high population levels but wide intervening uncultivated areas and with little potential for local growth without radical changes in technique. The main pattern of growth would be first by rapid budding-off and export of population, followed by expansion to smaller and smaller patches of the appropriate high-yielding soils within the occupied area. This is precisely the picture which emerges from studies such as those of Kruk (1973: see also Sherratt 1972, 517, 524).

The rapidity of early agricultural dispersal was not due to shifting cultivation, but to the pattern of restricted (and often linear) habitats suitable for initial farming practices. The spread of cultivation in similar habitats would have allowed a dispersal through a variety of environmental zones with minimal adaptation. It has, for instance, been suggested (Butzer 1972, 580) that the penetration of inland Europe would have involved a major shift from winter-grown crops in the Mediterranean to spring-grown crops in the temperate zone. If both were essentially spring-grown, then no such radical change in the growth period would have been necessary, other than a slight adjustment in the time of sowing.

Developments beyond this initial stage of cultivation involved adaptation to drier habitats which required more soil preparation and the use of fallow-ing or systematic rotation. Such techniques are likely to have emerged in areas where forest-clearance was not necessary. One of the first major steps in this direction was the extensive appearance of sites on the deep brown soils of the moist steppes of northern Assyria in the sixth millennium BC (Oates 1980). Such cultivation would require extensive soil preparation with the hoe, a fallow of one to four years and probably the development of new strains of cereals as cultivation moved out of the zone of abundant ground- and surface-water. Rainfall-dependent growth would have necessi-tated a winter growing season, at least for the wheats, and it is likely that there was a return to the pattern of seasonality characteristic of the wild cereals. Such a move would favour the use of barley, as well as bread-wheat (*Triticum aestivum*) – the 'soft, light grain' which replaced the older and harder forms.

The additional labour required for soil preparation under these circum-stances would have given a powerful incentive to the development of new techniques. As cattle were common domestic animals on these lowland sites, it is possible that the plough came into use in this area by the fifth millen-nium, even though it is only definitely attested from the fourth millennium in southern Mesopotamia (Sherratt 1980). This could be used to pulverise the soil to prevent loss of moisture through capillary action (Clark 1952, 100; Stevens 1966, 93). Only at this stage would the characteristic pattern of 'dry farming' have emerged. While the extension of interfluvial culti-vation in the Mediterranean would have required a winter growing-season, in temperate Europe the higher spring rainfall would have allowed the continuation of a spring-growth pattern (Figure 3.1). The major role played by barley in late Neolithic and Bronze Age agriculture argues in favour of a spring growing-season, as cultivation proliferated on sandy or other light soils which warm up rapidly in spring. The frequency of millet (*Panicum* and *Setaria*) in these contexts in southern Europe (Hartanyi and Novaki 1975) also supports this suggestion. Spring-grown crops would leave a greater area for winter grazing, important in Bronze Age stock economies.

The first definite indication of winter-grown crops in northern Europe is the spread of spelt in the first millennium BC (Applebaum 1954, 104). By this time it is likely that winter varieties of the other wheat species had also

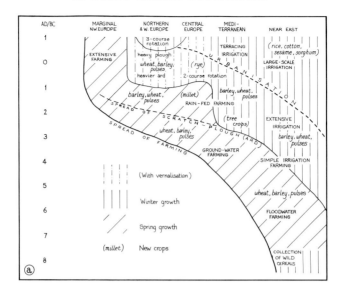

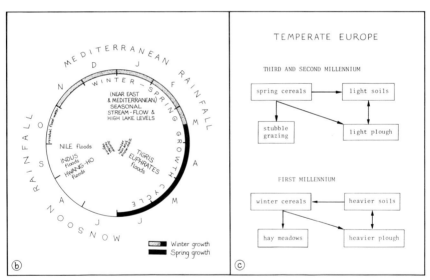

3.1 *The seasonality of cereal-growing: (a) the spread of farming to Europe from the Near East and the postulated shift from spring-grown to winter-grown cereals; (b) growing-periods in relation to rainfall seasonality, and to flood regimes in the major river-valleys; (c) implications of the shift from spring- to winter-grown cereals in temperate Europe: an expansion of livestock-keeping (especially sheep for wool) was a related development [(c) added from Sherratt, 1980, unpublished].*

emerged, involving the evolution of vernalisation mechanisms. This was the point at which the primitive original wheats such as emmer would have been increasingly replaced in Europe by hexaploid species better able to withstand the cold, and barley became relatively less important. Rye also became more common in eastern and central Europe, after a long period of sporadic occurrence as a weed (Jankuhn 1969, 220). Spring-grown crops cultivated with the ard would have survived on the northern margins where the winter was too harsh for the longer growth-cycle. The pressure of grazing caused by winter sowing could have been alleviated by the provision of hay, which would have been increasingly important for the keeping of livestock.

At this point also cultivation began to spread to heavier soils, and more robust and ultimately sod-turning ploughs developed (Figure 3.2). This was important in autumn ploughing, to form clods which would prevent the formation of soil-caps and pans over winter, unlike the spring ploughing where a fine tilth is required. The use of iron for plough-shares also produced a more effective instrument for land-breaking, especially on clays. (Iron shares appeared in the Near East in the early first millennium BC, in central Europe at the end of the first millennium BC, and in northern Europe in the later first millennium AD.) A probable consequence of these changes, and especially (as Susan Limbrey has pointed out) the existence of open ploughed fields at the time of maximum winter rainfall, would have been the massive increase in soil erosion indicated in the extensive accumulation of valley alluvium in temperate Europe. The cropping-system which came into use at this time would be essentially the same as that already in use in the Mediterranean, with a two-course rotation of alternate winter crops and fallow. This persisted until the later first millennium AD, when it was replaced in parts of temperate Europe by the three-course system in which a further field of spring-grown crops – oats (for horses), barley and legumes – was added, which suited the developing needs of animal husbandry (White 1962, 69). The fully-developed pre-industrial agricultural system of northern Europe was by this stage able to sustain comparable population levels to the intensive, though necessarily more restricted, irrigation-based systems of the Near East, and it was associated with the large-scale urbanisation of temperate Europe.

DEVELOPED SURFACE-WATER AGRICULTURE: IRRIGATION

During the time that these developments in rain-fed farming were taking place in Europe, a succession of irrigation-based systems had appeared in various parts of the Near East. It is commonly assumed that irrigation represented a major departure from earlier agricultural systems, involving radical changes in technique. In the perspective adopted here, however, it can be seen as an artificial extension of the conditions which characterised

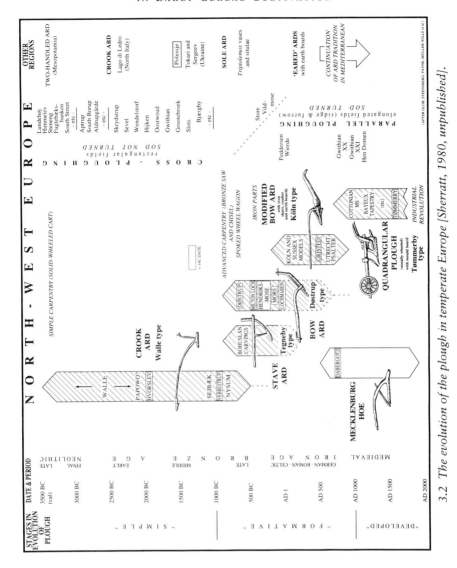

3.2 *The evolution of the plough in temperate Europe [Sherratt, 1980, unpublished].*

the earliest forms of cultivation. A much more continuous pattern of development, by small additional inputs of labour and capital, can thus be postulated (Figure 3.3).

The earliest forms of irrigation are likely to be small-scale water-spreading involving minimum amounts of investment in new facilities. Such are indeed possible in pre-agricultural contexts, as with the Owen's Valley Paiute who divert streams to water patches of self-propagating wild plants (Steward 1929). Similar practices may have been employed from the beginning in locations like that of Jericho. Without modifying the natural drainage by channels, cultivation may also make use of the sheet-flow of

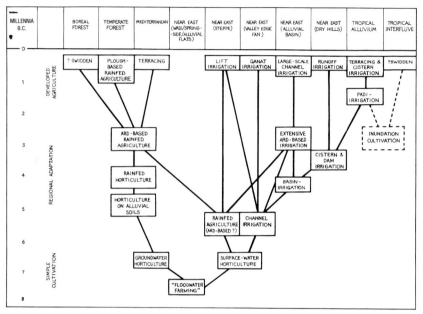

3.3 The differentiation of Old World farming systems: from simple floodwater farming to plough agriculture and irrigation.

floodwaters. This system provided the basis of agriculture among some groups of Pueblo Indians of the south-west of the United States, where the rainfall is too slight to grow crops. As water seasonally overflows from high ground, however, cultivation is possible either at the sides of valleys below escarpments or on alluvial fans at the mouths of gullies (*arroyos*), or else on the valley floor itself where streams overflow their floodplains (Bryan 1929, 445). Such floodwater farming supported communities of the Hopi and neighbouring Indian groups, and was a determining factor in the location of such villages, which might have a population of several hundred. This method of cultivation, however, requires undissected valley-floors and is very vulnerable to gullying in periods of stream-incision (Cooke and Reeves 1976). Vita-Finzi has suggested that suitable conditions for this kind of cultivation obtained in parts of Jordan in the early Holocene during the deposition of the Hasa formation (1969, 32).

The earliest demonstrated examples of channel-irrigation in the Near East are related to the braided streams which flow down alluvial fans on the margins of the semi-arid basins. Cutting transverse trenches to carry the water to a wider area is a simple but effective way of using the gradient to maintain an adequate supply to the fields, either from floodwater or perennial flow. Such a system has been documented at Choga Mami near Mandali in Iraq and dated to the Samarran culture in the sixth millennium BC (Oates and Oates 1976). This form of irrigation is typical of the Early Chalcolithic period in the Near East, when it was also employed on the fringes of the Zagros and of the Kopet Dagh in Turkmenia. In the latter area it sustained the settlements of the Geoksyur culture (Lisitsina 1969). It may also have been used in Anatolia at this time, for instance at sites in comparable positions in the Konya plain (French 1970; Sherratt 1973).

This system is well adapted to the margins of lowland areas fed by streams from nearby better-watered mountains. Similar techniques may have been employed in other areas of low rainfall such as southern Spain by the third millennium BC (Schüle 1967). They are, however, vulnerable to erosion producing channel incision and gully formation. Major extensions of the cultivated area by these methods, moreover, are difficult to obtain and require more complex engineering and higher investment. The system of underground channels or *qanats* in Iran and adjacent areas (e.g. the *falaj* system of Oman) carrying ground-water from valley-edge fans, represents a further attempt to extend these types of water-sources from the first millennium BC onwards (Stronach 1980).

In more marginal environments it was sometimes possible to make use of ephemeral run-off and wadi-flow by the use of dams or small channels. In Baluchistan and southern Arabia, where brief periods of stream-flow result from melting snow in the mountains, the water and fertile suspended silts were trapped by boulder-walls (*gabarbands*) across narrow valleys to allow the growth of a spring wheat-crop (Raikes 1965; Leshnik 1973, 67). A somewhat more sophisticated channel-based system dating to the fifth millennium BC has been found in association with the major Late Chalcolithic settlement at Jawa in the basalt region in the arid zone of Jordan (Roberts 1977). Here, three systems of channels were used to tap the short-lived winter surplus, both by gravity flow from the main wadi and by collecting local runoff, and these were used to supply both fields and cisterns. Comparable systems supported the Bronze Age towns of Palestine, and highly sophisticated methods for utilising runoff were developed in the Levant and western Arabia in the first millennium BC (Evenari et al. 1971).

The greatest opportunities for the extension of cultivation by irrigation, however, lay in riverine environments, especially the major alluvial valleys situated in arid plains but fed by exotic water, like those of the Tigris/Euphrates, Indus and Nile. Despite the environmental similarities of these three basins and the hydraulic civilisations which they produced, however, there are significant differences between them. Most important is the timing of their flood-periods (Figure 3.1). The Indus and Nile both have an essentially autumn inundation, allowing crops to be sown as the waters retreat in time for a winter growing-season, but the Tigris and Euphrates are characterised by inconvenient spring floods.

In the Indus basin, on the south-eastern edge of the distribution of the west Asiatic cereals, crops such as wheat and barley with a winter/spring growth cycle (*rabi* crops) could be grown in the dry winter season only in low-lying areas where they could make use of residual soil moisture from the autumn flood and monsoonal rains (Lambrick 1964, 75). Alluvial silts along the rivers thus provided the basis for Harappan agriculture. Cultivable land could be easily extended by simple methods of inundation irrigation (*sailaba*), especially along inlets and creeks or on the inner sides of river-meanders (Leshnik 1973, 73). 'Thus the whole operation involves an absolute minimum of skill, labour and aid of implements' (Lambrick 1964, 76), and this limited but productive land could support the development of Harappan cities even before the introduction of the complementary summer/autumn (*kharif*) crops such as sorghum.

The Nile, flowing in a more narrowly-defined trench, allowed cultivation of the flood-deposited silts in a series of basins formed by old levees, in which the autumn floods provided natural irrigation for cereals sown as the waters receded by November (Butzer 1976). Simple techniques for retaining the water and increasing the watered area were in use by the third millennium BC, involving the breaching of levees and the canalisation of floodwater by digging overflow channels and constructing dikes. The proto-dynastic 'King Scorpion' macehead shows a ritual scene of this kind (p. 67). More labour-intensive methods of actually raising water from its lower, summer levels began by the mid-second millennium with the use of the *shaduf* (pole and bucket lever), and larger-scale operations were only initiated in the later first millennium BC. In consequence, summer-grown crops were not cultivated before the second or first millennium.

The growth of irrigation systems in the Mesopotamian lowlands has been extensively investigated in recent years (Adams 1974; Gibson 1974; Oates and Oates 1976). The Tigris and Euphrates differ from the Nile and Indus in that their floods, related to snow-melt in the mountains, occur towards the end of the winter growing-season, in April and May. It was thus the perennial flow which was most useful, with floodwater often presenting a problem of dispersal: what started as irrigation had to continue as drainage and crop-protection. Because the rivers deposit large quantities of silt and build up high levees, they actually run above the level of the surrounding plain. It is a relatively simple matter to spread water through breaches in these levees; though this water had then to be dispersed through a system of anastomosing channels. Early settlement 'followed the numerous small, meandering stream distributaries found on any unmodified alluvial plain. Lengthy, branching canal networks are not in evidence, and cultivation seemingly was confined to narrow bands along natural levee backslopes and to favourably situated margins of seasonally filled depressions' (Adams 1974, 2). Mesopotamian irrigation was an extensive system in the sense that it required an alternate fallow to restore the water-table and prevent salination, and that there was more potentially irrigable land than could easily be managed without major investment in flood-control. Indeed, the onset of local salination forced periodic shifts. The fallow and intervening areas allowed a symbiotic pastoralism which was essential to a full exploitation of the region.

These observations apply to lower Mesopotamia – the 'River Plain' of Buringh (1957). The development of irrigation on the Assyrian Steppe was a later feature, because the entrenched character of the rivers necessitated the use of lifting-devices rather than a simple use of gravity-flow. The *shaduf* (used in lower Mesopotamia for watering the levees) was one answer to this problem, and it was in use by the early-second millennium BC (Drower 1954), though only in a limited area adjacent to the major rivers.

In each of these major alluvial basins, the Nile, Indus and Tigris/ Euphrates, there is evidence for the use of the plough (technically the ard or scratch-plough) from an early stage in the development of lowland irrigation: in Mesopotamia at least by the fourth millennium and in the others by the third millennium (Chapter 6). It seems that this instrument was an integral part of these extensive lowland cultivation systems, and perhaps a precondition for their development.

The construction of major artificial watercourses in Mesopotamia dates to the Sassanian period (Adams 1965), when long branching canals argue a significant degree of central control and investment, and are part of the general pattern of intensified inputs of capital and labour and the more elaborate construction typical of all forms of irrigation from the first millennium BC onwards. This was the period in which summer-grown crops such as rice and sesame were introduced from further east. Intensive irrigation led in many areas to substantially higher population densities and an extension of the areas under state control. Many of the features stressed by Wittfogel (1957) as associated with irrigation agriculture may thus be more characteristic of these Iron Age developments than of preceding systems, which were often village-based and local in management.

The growth of irrigation thus followed a natural progression from the earliest surface- and groundwater-based systems through an increasing management of sources of surface-water and its distribution to suitable locations. The earlier forms required only a small input of effort in propitious circumstances, and involved little co-operation beyond individual communities. As with south-east Asian systems, even quite complex arrangements could grow by quite small increments of household investment in each generation (cf. Leach 1959). Small-scale hydroagriculture (in Wittfogel's term) was a widespread though sporadic feature of cultivation in the semi-arid and arid zones from the Mediterranean to central Asia in the third and second millennia BC. Larger-scale projects involving higher investment and wider co-operation were needed to increase the area served by these limited systems, and these did not emerge until the growth of imperial power and investment in rural development by landlords and urban capitalists, especially from the first millennium BC onwards.

Comparison

Starting from similar initial conditions, therefore, cultivation systems in the Near East and Europe became increasingly differentiated as they exploited more fully the particular characteristics of the two regions. In the subtropical zone, where lack of water was the main constraint, large areas of alluvium could be brought into cultivation by irrigation, to support substantial local populations from an early date. In the temperate zone, the most significant agricultural resource was the reservoir of nutrients stored as soil-colloids which could be released by forest-clearance and ploughing. The wide areas of productive forest soils postponed the need for intensive methods of cultivation; though, once introduced, these could support higher overall densities of settlement. In northern Europe the scratch-plough evolved into a heavier and more deeply-penetrating instrument for use on heavy soils whose thick sod required turning to aerate and drain. What had originally developed as a response to the lack of water had become a method of dealing with its over-abundance.

By contrast to the ecosystems of the subtropical and temperate areas, those of the humid tropics are characterised by rapid oxidation and strong leaching: nutrients are stored in standing vegetation rather than in the soil. While significant areas of alluvial and volcanic soils can support permanent cropping, the much greater areas of interfluvial terrain necessitate short periods of cultivation and long fallows. Nutrients can be released from standing vegetation by combustion, used up by crops in a few years, and the plot returned to forest. More permanent cultivation can only be imposed on such soils by large-scale investment of capital and labour. South-east Asian terracing systems with padi-farming are a specialised development of this kind, using flowing water to carry nutrients not available in the soil (Geertz 1963).

The kinds of transition to more intensive systems studied by development economists such as Boserup, therefore, are only partly analogous to the kinds of change inferred in subtropical and temperate regions, and in any case represent a relatively late phase of land-use even in the tropics. Recent research has increasingly emphasised that the earlier stages of tropical cultivation were characterised by systems of fixed-plot horticulture (Harris 1973, 399–402); while ecological arguments and archaeological evidence from several parts of the world have emphasised the importance of low-lying, alluvial areas in early cultivation.

In south-east Asia, rice began as a palustrian species, adapted to semi-aquatic habitats, as did taro. Dry rice, suitable for interfluvial cultivation, was a secondary development. Gorman (1977) has postulated an initial stage of inundation-cultivation in piedmont regions, lasting down to c.2000 BC, followed by an extension of irrigation-systems in the open alluvial plains, with iron and plough-cultivation (using the water-buffalo) spreading in this context in the first millennium BC. Extensive swiddening could be a relatively recent development, as drought-resistant strains of rice allowed a spread to the hills in the first millennium AD.

In Africa, where agriculture developed at a later date than the other areas considered here, the situation is less well understood. Nevertheless, Harlan (1975, 197) has pointed out the importance of fluctuating shallow lakes in the Sahel region of West Africa where many of the indigenous cultigens emerged, which would have been suitable for *décrue* cultivation on moist soil as the floodwaters subsided.

In Mesoamerica (Price 1971) the present importance of swidden contrasts with the types of cultivation inferred for prehistoric and early historic times. Early crops in the dry tropical zone of Mexico were cultivated by floodwater along *barrancas* (wadis). In the Valley of Oaxaca, one of the most intensively-investigated areas, initial cultivation was confined to the alluvial zone with a high water-table, and extended over a limited area by pot-irrigation from wells. In the Late Formative period, settlement spread to the piedmont zone where water from springs could be directed by canals to terraced fields, as in the fossilised system at Hierve el Agua (Kirkby 1973). In the Valley of Mexico, canal irrigation supported the growth of Classic Teotihuacan, while intensive *chinampa* (wet-garden) cultivation sustained Postclassic Tenochtitlan. In the Maya area of the humid tropical lowlands, the supposition that swiddening formed the basis of sites like Tikal has been replaced by a recognition of the importance of shallow lakes (*bajos*) exploited by canals and raised fields as well as a variety of other water-spreading devices (Harris 1978), and the situation is more complex than was previously imagined. In coastal Peru, floodwater farming on the coast was replaced by limited canal-irrigation in inland valleys, and in turn succeeded by larger-scale canal irrigation on the arid coastal plain (Moseley 1974). All these examples show a direct transition from floodwater-cultivation to canal-based systems, with extensive cultivation as a later, marginal development.

Behind the regional variations, therefore, underlying similarities in the development of agricultural systems are becoming evident. They emphasise the importance of an often protracted initial phase of small-scale surface- and groundwater-based horticulture, which ultimately differentiated into hydraulic and rainfed systems of both extensive and intensive kinds.

NOTE

1. The term 'spring wheat' is used in a special sense by plant geneticists, to describe any wheat which lacks a vernalisation requirement, including winter-grown varieties in the Mediterranean and Near East. I am grateful to F. G. H. Lupton of the Plant Breeding Institute, Cambridge, for this and other observations.

4

Resources, Technology and Trade: An Essay on Early European Metallurgy

(1976)

Early European metallurgy has been a topic of debate since the beginning of the study of prehistory. As a fundamental division in the Three-age framework and a crucial contribution to chronology through typological sequences, it was a focus of interest from the mid-nineteenth century onwards. More recently, the application of rapid techniques of micro-analysis has provided a massive body of quantitative data on the composition of early metal objects and new opportunities for interpretation, while the large body of surviving material continues to offer itself as a major source of information – not only about chronology but also about the way of life of Copper and Bronze Age communities.

The abundance of copper and bronze objects from these periods leaves no doubt about their importance in the prehistoric economy, and the reasons for growth in the use of metal are clearly essential in this case to our understanding of economic change in primitive society. The process usually invoked to explain the spread of metallurgy is one of discovery, followed by diffusion of knowledge about the techniques involved, leading to a widespread use of metal because of its superiority for manufacturing tools and weapons. The change in technology would thus have led to a breakdown of economic self-sufficiency, and a consequent reliance on trade as a funda-

---

This chapter was written as a tribute to J. G. D. Clark, Disney Professor of Archaeology at Cambridge and subsequently Master of Peterhouse. (Sir Grahame died in 1995.) It contrasts the metallurgy of the Early Bronze Age with that of the preceding Copper Age, and suggests that the latter differed in no fundamental way from the sophisticated uses and trade in stone achieved in the Neolithic. Grahame Clark had himself illuminated the European stone axe trade by comparison with Australian ethnography, and this paper followed Colin Renfrew's example in applying the anthropological economics of M. D. Sahlins to early metalworking. (See also Chapter 12 for flint exchange-networks in Neolithic and Copper Age Hungary.) The illustrations are notable as experiments in graphical presentation.

mental mechanism. At the same time, increasing productivity of agriculture would have begun to produce a surplus that served both to finance this increased scale of trading activity and to support the specialists concerned.

In its original conception (Childe 1958), this model sought to connect the appearance of metallurgy in Europe with the activities of prospectors from urban societies (in the Near East) whose concentration of capital had fostered the growth of the industry. More recently the reappraisal of European chronologies has suggested a more active role for south-east Europe, and attention has turned to the background of technological skills in high-temperature firing available to Neolithic bakers and potters (Renfrew 1969). But, whatever the circumstances of discovery, emphasis still rests on metallurgical *knowledge* as the key factor in the explanation with the assumption that, once discovered, metal became common because of its self-evident usefulness or inherent attractiveness. Both in Childe's account of this process (1956, 115–20) and in Renfrew's discussion (1972, 308, 483) of the growth of metallurgy in the Aegean, economic change is seen as the *result* of technological change, both through increased efficiency and through its stimulation of 'new needs'.

It may be doubted, however, whether the advantages conferred by a knowledge of the technical processes of metalworking could by themselves have had such far-reaching effects. Early metal tools were not, in practice, more efficient than stone ones, nor are early metal weapons likely to have been decisive in battle. Are there, then, less obvious reasons why a relatively rare raw material such as copper should have achieved so wide a circulation in the third and second millennia? And was this circulation different, in scale or character, from existing networks distributing materials such as fine stone?

The inevitable bias given by a material subject-matter often leads the archaeologist to a view of prehistory in which technology appears as the main element of progress. On the other hand, Professor Clark (1965) has stressed the need to come to terms with the social role of material objects, and to treat prehistoric societies in a total ecological context. From this standpoint, it may be possible to reach a view of the artefactual evidence that relates it to long-term processes of economic and social change, rather than treating technology as an independent sector producing revolutionary repercussions throughout society.

'STONE AGE ECONOMICS'

A key issue in this discussion is the contrast often drawn between the relative self-sufficiency of Neolithic life and the variety of raw materials required for the more complex technical processes of the Bronze Age. If there is a difference in trading activity between the two periods, however, it cannot be summarised as simply as this. Even in the Neolithic there were inherent limitations on self-sufficiency.

This point soon becomes evident from a consideration of site locations. The distribution of a population dependent on agriculture is determined largely by the soils on which its crops are grown, the most suitable zones for cultivation being naturally those with deep soil and an abundant water-supply. In order to make use of these locations, however, another set of resources is required – hard stone for tools, for example, or supplies of salt to offset dietary deficiency. By and large, such resources occur in different environments, and only a limited number of agricultural settlements have direct access to them. For instance, a distribution such as that of the early Neolithic *Bandkeramik* in central Europe (Clark 1952, fig. 45), with its concentration on open loess-covered plains, implies a constant import of materials from sources peripheral to the main concentration of population.

In any case, there are good reasons why, in small-scale societies, individual settlements and clusters of villages should not be isolated from wider contacts. Single units of settlement are naturally vulnerable to the possibility of local disaster, whether due to poor harvest or disease. A continuous exchange of population from village to village creates a network of relationships that can distribute inequalities in local production and provide a wider pool of assistance. As a background to the distribution of rarer materials, a continuous movement of personnel and subsistence products between villages must be envisaged. It is this network which provides the basic carrier for the kinds of material that survive archaeologically in Neolithic contexts.

An important effect of this is the pattern of 'random walk' followed by individual objects in the course of such exchanges. Although there may be a general direction of drift in one class of material as it moves towards an area of scarcity, there is a large number of jumps between the source and the ultimate area of consumption. This lack of a direct link between producers and consumers at some distance from the source implies a strong spatial limit on effective demand with this kind of system. A distribution channel for a particular material is thus likely to have the following structure:

1. *Source:* not necessarily in an area of agricultural production, though accessible from it. Activities: unearthing of material, preliminary reduction of bulk.
2. *Production zone:* settlements concerned in the active exploitation of the material. Activities: working up into an exchangeable form.
3. *Direct contact zone:* area of settlements linked directly to production zone by face-to-face contact. Effective supply as result of close kinship links.
4. *Indirect supply zone:* area of settlements without direct access to the production zone, receiving supplies through intermediaries.

Anthropologists have stressed the basic contrast between the mechanisms connecting zones (3) and (4) with their supplies. Sahlins (1965) has noted the way in which exchanges with close kinsmen, who may be expected to provide assistance, are less concerned with material equivalence than those that take place across tribal boundaries, where a more direct return is sought. Brookfield and Hart (1971, 315), discussing Melanesian evidence, have drawn the contrast between *transfer*, where goods are easily balanced by services, and *trade*, where goods are rarely exchanged for non-material favours. Rappaport (1968, 106) has suggested that production will be sensitive to demand from within the area of direct contact, but not outside it. In a situation where each village is producing a similar range of subsistence goods, there will be an especially sharp division between those able to supply food and services direct to the producers and those beyond this range. Only in the case of particularly important materials is this friction overcome, by the exchange of high-value objects between certain individuals in different local groups (Sherratt 1972, 506).

This lack of direct articulation between supply and demand must have been a characteristic limitation on Neolithic economies, as Rappaport points out for the primitive farming groups of the New Guinea highlands. The problem is to avoid a situation in which an extensively needed commodity is under-exploited because of the lack of items to exchange for it. In overcoming this, the circulation of non-utilitarian goods plays a vital role in mobilising demand. Items of adornment or display that are exchangeable for essential commodities, and can themselves be accumulated, encourage continuity in the production of basic materials even when local needs are filled. They thus act as a kind of 'fly-wheel' for the whole system.

Not only do items not directly concerned with subsistence activities contribute to the maintenance of the system, but essential commodities, such as fine stone, also have non-material functions. Speaking again of the New Guinea highlands, Strathern notes that 'in their area of production axes circulate as items of exchange value, in ceremonial exchange, death compensation, bride-wealth, payments in the settlement of disputes, and they had a similar role in the Enga area' where they were distributed. While ordinary working axes may be given in these contexts, particularly large and fine specimens are considered appropriate for ceremonial and bride-wealth presentations, and in the case quoted by Chappell (1966, 98) these may be up to five times the size of working axes. (Such an axe 30cm in length would require about three weeks' work in grinding.)

The goods in circulation thus carry important symbolic values in a way that is often explicitly organised. Commodities may be accumulated and exchanged in specified quantities for particular situations such as marriage alliances. Such artefacts are not generally exchangeable, as with a true currency, but act as 'standardised entitlements to a series of social prerogatives' (Douglas 1967, 135).

The wider effects of this social aspect of material goods are twofold. In the first place, the system is continuously generating demand both for the commodities with direct symbolic value and for those exchangeable with them, thus helping to overcome the limitations on supplies of useful materials that arise from the lack of direct articulation between producers and consumers. The use of necessary items, such as axes, in ceremonial contexts also ensures a reservoir of raw material in case of shortage. In the second place, by linking the movement of goods with the distribution of marriage partners, the system contributes to demographic equilibrium by adjusting the spatial distribution of women and goods (Rappaport 1968, 108–9).

This tentative sketch of the working of a simple economic system is a starting point for the analysis of the prehistoric European situation. In opposition to the idea that 'a Stone Age community was, at least potentially, self-sufficing' and that 'the objects of Stone Age trade were always luxuries ... at least things that men could have done without' (Childe 1951, 35), it suggests that continuous circulation was a basic pre-condition of such societies, extending even beyond simple material needs.

To be fully satisfactory, however, something beyond a static model is necessary if it is to cope with the evident changes within the prehistoric economy. In the first place, changes occur as new sources of raw materials are discovered and old ones are exhausted. Such changes are especially likely as the area under exploitation itself expands and peripheral groups come into contact with a wider environment. Secondly, any growth in population will also increase effective demand, making worthwhile intensification in the effort involved in unearthing raw materials and the development of larger-scale operations. Perhaps even more important are changes in the sphere of subsistence economy underlying the patterns of distribution in rarer materials. Once again, ethnography provides a clue to the processes involved.

Coastal Melanesia, in particular, shows a high development of long-distance trading links, some of them of extraordinary complexity. For some of the groups involved, participation in these networks is essential, not only at the level of raw materials but also in terms of basic subsistence products. Hogbin (1951) quotes examples from the Huon Gulf of New Guinea where groups survived only by producing pottery and importing food-stuffs, and Malinowski noted the division, within the Trobriand Islands, between the richer agricultural part and the poorer areas of the interior that manufacture wooden dishes, baskets and pots to exchange with it for food. In these cases, the occupation of such poorer areas is possibly only because of a continuing output of non-subsistence products. One consequence of the extension of settlement to marginal environments is the need for a class of products that stimulate the mobility of subsistence goods. Brookfield and Hart (1971, 320–32), in a stimulating discussion of the problem, interpret the complex cycles of inter-island exchange in Melanesia as part of a 'flywheel' mechanism to keep products on the move and so to articulate several kinds of

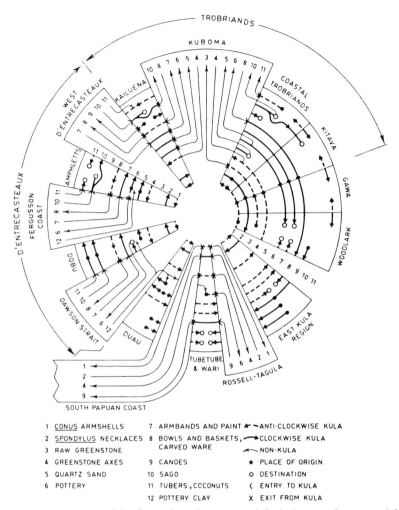

4.1 A reconstruction of the flow of products around the kula *ring: from Brookfield and Hart (1971).*

specialisation within the chain (see Figure 4.1). Such regional differentiation allows areas of lower subsistence potential to survive alongside better-endowed ones. Indeed, the fact that transactions still occur in a series of individual jumps means that opportunities open up for middleman trading, and some areas well connected in the network can survive even without specialist products of their own (e.g. Siassi).

In contrast to the relatively simple situation postulated above for the *Bandkeramik*, with its concentration on a single productive zone and occasional expeditions for raw materials outside this, the colonisation of a wide range of landscapes leads to a situation in which various groups are actively pumping rarer materials and products into the system. The contrast stems, not from a disparity in technology and raw material requirements but from the difference in settlement ecology between the two cases.

One further feature of the Melanesian case may be mentioned – the social mechanisms involved. The actual operation of the trading process is in the hands of individuals: participation in the network depends on the ability to create stocks of trade articles and to manipulate social and ceremonial relationships:

> Leadership and the political structure of groups are not set apart from the sphere of commerce; the rewards of the successful entrepreneur are the highest rewards of power and prestige which the society has to offer; he cannot dominate the political situation without first dominating the market ... This kind of fluidity is not a matter of individuals moving up and down rapidly from one recognized position to another. It is much more an instability in the relationship of actual positions, since each outstanding leader creates his own leadership. (Douglas 1967, 125)

In such systems, which have come to be known as 'big man' systems (Sahlins 1963), richer individuals provide nodes of concentration for circulating goods, without a rigidly hierarchical social structure divided on class lines. The accumulation of subsistence products is a temporary matter, and the climb to prestige is expressed in possession of the items of display, such as valued ornaments, which act as indicators or 'counters' of success. Although the majority of transactions is concerned with subsistence products, the system runs on the movement of symbolic items and these provide a material reading of varying status positions. This situation, one of regional economic differentiation articulated by individuals in small communities, must have been the condition of much of later prehistoric Europe before the emergence of urban centres. How far are such processes reflected in the artefactual record?

THE MOVEMENT OF MATERIALS IN NEOLITHIC EUROPE

The patterns of movement, even in inorganic raw materials, are a field of research hardly yet systematically explored, but some idea of the scale involved can be gained from the major commodities often recognised and from the few areas where detailed studies have been made.

The Neolithic economy required both the cutting and scraping tools for fine work that had been essential to previous hunting economies, and a range of more massive implements for forest clearance and the manufacture of wooden tools. Higher population densities, moreover, demanded a much greater bulk of raw materials. For heavy axes and chisels, either large blocks of flint were necessary or else crystalline massive rocks, mostly of highland occurrence. These included ancient sedimentary rocks such as greywackes; igneous rocks either formed at great depth, such as diorite, or nearer the surface, such as dolerite; and direct volcanic products, such as lavas (e.g. andesite and trachyte); or consolidated fall-out products (tuffs), and meta-morphosed forms of these and other rocks such as amphibolite or schist. The more deeply formed varieties have larger crystals and are hard to flake, while those more rapidly cooled are more likely to approach flint in their flaking properties. Apart from flints and cherts, almost all of the rocks used for heavy tools occur in regions of low agricultural potential, either in ancient massifs or more recently up-thrust blocks.

In different areas, the distribution of agricultural land might be adjacent to such regions or far removed. In the Balkans, with tectonic basins sur-rounded by highland areas, there were many local sources of such rocks in the crystalline massif and volcanic deposits in the Tertiary fold-chains (Sherratt 1972, 518). In addition, siltstones and cherts were used from later sedimentary deposits, while the extensive Cretaceous deposits of north-west Bulgaria provided large quantities of the characteristic brown flint that had been exploited since the Palaeolithic.

The same pattern, on a larger scale, is represented in the Carpathian Basin. Surrounded on all sides by young fold-mountains with local volcanic activity, the basin itself consists of two parts: in the western area of Trans-danubia, flint and chert, along with hard intrusive rocks, occur in the Mesozoic formations of the Bakony mountains; but to the east of the Danube neither these nor massive rocks are locally available, and an area of around 50,000 sq. km provides only river-pebbles. This deficiency is com-pensated for by the richness of the surrounding mountains in raw materials and their direct river links with the Danube Basin. To the north, the volcanic range of the Mátra-Bükk-Zemplén mountains could provide not only trachyte and related rocks for heavier tools but also, in the parts near Tokaj, bombs of obsidian: to the east, Transylvania offered a variety of eruptive rocks within easy access of the plains. Obsidian, as in the Near East, was particularly widely traded.

In the loess plains sought by early agriculturalists further north, inorganic raw materials again came mostly from areas peripheral to the main con-centrations of population. Around the clusters of *Bandkeramik* settlement, sources of hard rocks were plentiful, for instance, in the ancient massif of Bohemia, at various points along the Rhine rift and the Middle Rhine high-lands, and in the central German highlands. There was no useful obsidian in these areas, but cherts from pre-Cretaceous rocks were available, and on the edge of the North European Plain the *Bandkeramik* spread as far as the flint sources in the Low Countries and Little Poland. Local exchange cycles brought these different sources into relationship: for instance, hard volcanic rocks, such as trachyte, tephrite and basalt from the Koblenz region, moved in the reverse direction to the flint of the Belgian Hesbaye; while the occur-rence of import sherds shows how important were the major rivers in articulating such systems (Clark 1952, 251). The recently investigated site

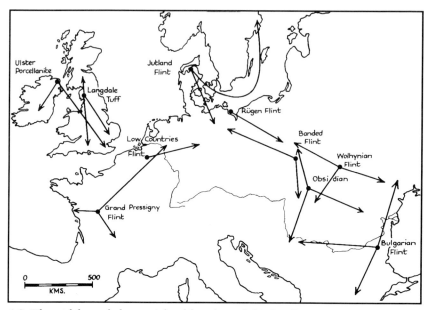

4.2 *The widely-traded materials of fourth- and third-millennium Europe (selection).*

at Müddersheim indicated a supply distance for stone of up to 10km for bulky sandstone objects, 30–40km for basalt, and up to 70km for flint.

As new regions were explored, fresh sources were discovered, and particularly desirable raw materials achieved a circulation over hundreds of kilometres. The results of petrographic studies in the British Isles show how a primary use of local sources was supplemented by the products of distant factories as the network of inter-regional relations grew. Thus, in southwestern Britain, early sites show a dominance of Cornish products, with Welsh and north-west British materials appearing in this area in large numbers in the Middle Neolithic. Less attractive products continued to be worked on a small scale and locally distributed: the Mynydd Rhiw quarry site (Houlder 1961) with an associated flint assemblage implies no more than small-scale seasonal exploitation in times of slack agricultural work, in which the winning of raw materials could be combined with hunting forays. On the other hand, it is clear that more highly organised production was becoming profitable for the commodities widely in demand.

The later-fourth and third millennia in many parts of Europe saw this rationalisation and intensification of production on a large scale (see Figure 4.2). The honey-coloured flint of Bulgaria achieved a wide distribution within the Balkans, up to the north of the Black Sea, and into the southern half of the Carpathian Basin. Obsidian continued to be traded in large quantities, and is found on a very high proportion of the sites of this period, both within the Carpathians and beyond, especially in southern Poland.

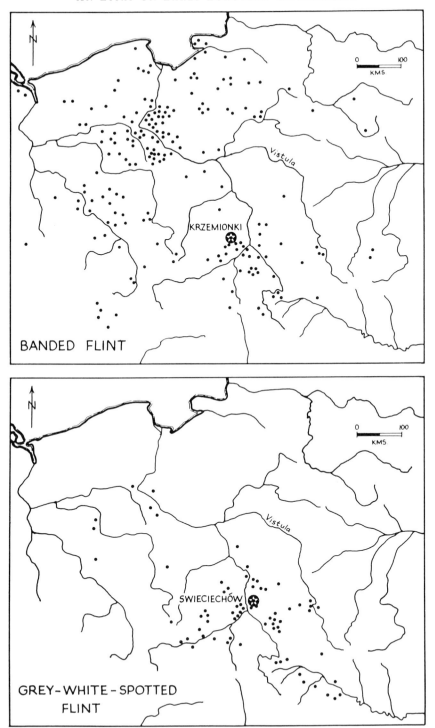

4.3 *The distribution of two kinds of Polish flint; after Sulimirski (1960).*

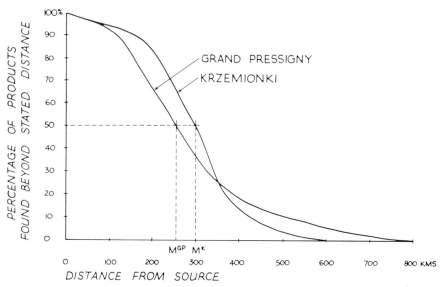

4.4 The distance from source of finds made from two varieties of flint: Krzemionki banded flint and Grand Pressigny honey-coloured flint.

This last area seems to have had – at least in certain phases such as Early Lengyel – a particularly intense exchange with the area of north Hungary and Slovakia just across the mountains, reflecting the complementary character of resources on either side. Going south to balance the obsidian were flint and, probably, salt as well: there are salt-pans from mid-fourth-millennium Lengyel contexts near Krakow in Little Poland (Jodłowski 1971). Supplies of flint became particularly important as settlement increased in the North European Plain from TRB times onwards, for although flint was widely scattered in glacial deposits, it was mostly of poor quality, due to frost cracking. As in north-west Bulgaria, large-scale working and trading took place in response to demand from neighbouring areas lacking, or with inferior, raw materials.

To the west, areas of good flint potential occurred widely in France and the Low Countries within the Cretaceous deposits between the Seine and the Maas; but to the north and east, such sources were more scattered, occurring in north Jutland, Scania, the island of Rügen, south Poland and further east in Wolhynia. Among the south Polish sources, various characteristic types can be distinguished (Sulimirski 1960), mainly from the Upper Vistula region. These include the chocolate-coloured Upper Astartian flint from the Świętokrzyskie (Holy Cross) mountains; Lower Astartian banded flint from Krzemionki, used for axes; greyish, white-speckled Turonian flint from Świeciechów, used for blades; and a banded Jurassic chert from near Krakow. (*Krema*, incidentally, is a common Slav place-name element meaning 'flint'; e.g. Kremikovci, Bulgaria.) Attempts have been made to

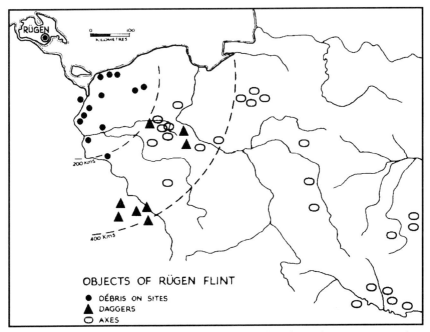

4.5 The differential dispersal of three types of product from the same source: data from Sulimirski (1960) [corrected].

map the distribution of these types of flint from visual identifications. The Świeciechów variety shows a restricted local circulation but the banded Krzemionki variety was exported in bulk, especially to the Middle Vistula/ Notec/Middle Warta area, and examples are known from beyond the Carpathians in Slovakia (see Figure 4.3).

Such distributions can be summarised as curves showing the percentages of objects at given distances from the source (see Figure 4.4). Half of the known finds of Świeciechów flint lie within 100km of the source, while for the banded flint 50 per cent are within 300km, and 75 per cent within 350km. Finds of both types are mainly of third-millennium date, though both start in the later-fourth millennium. Something of the same order of magnitude would hold for the other wide-traded commodities shown in Figure 4.2. An interesting feature of the Rügen flint distribution (see Figure 4.5) is the way different products have a characteristic range of distributions.

Of the western sources, the most easily recognisable and widely-traded variety is the well-known iron-rich flint of Grand Pressigny, used in the later-third millennium for large blades hafted as daggers (see below). This shows a distribution on a similar scale to that of the banded flint, with 50 per cent within 250km and 75 per cent within 350km, despite the fact that stray finds occasionally occur up to 800km away. An analysis of the direction of

113

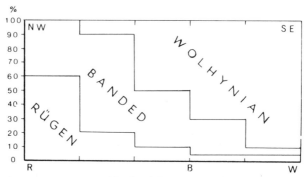

4.6 *Approximate percentages of finds of three types of flint in a* SE–NW *transect across Poland. Each division represents a 100 km² sample cell:* R, B *and* W *mark the positions of the sources. Calculated from maps in Sulimirski (1960).*

movement (Figure 4.7) indicates three major components: up-river, down-river, and across-country north-eastward. The distribution map shows that the down-river component splits at the coast to go either to Brittany or to the Gironde – in neither case more than 200–300km by sea. The largest component is the overland route to centres of population on the Loire and the Seine, and beyond into the Low Countries. Finds become noticeably more scattered on this axis beyond the 350km limit. It is an indication of the special desirability of this material that its main axis of movement should be into areas with local supplies of good flint.

Although there are several sources of bias and inaccuracy in the maps used above, they do give some idea of the scale of later Neolithic trade. While many products were of merely local significance, demand was sufficient to move large volumes of particularly desirable goods over several hundred kilometres. While the banded flint went mainly to a single cultural area, the Grand Pressigny distribution is significantly inter-cultural. Both show the 'pull' of nearby population clusters, but spread beyond these to remoter areas. (Compare, for instance, the banded-flint distribution map with the one of Globular Amphora culture settlements in Wiślański 1970, fig. 56.)

Trading systems on this scale clearly required a considerable quantity of raw material, and a particular expression of the expansion in demand, by the later-fourth millennium and after, is the development of large-scale mining for various materials. Small operations had been undertaken even in Upper Palaeolithic times, as is shown by the two-metre deep pits for colouring material at Lovas in western Hungary. Such workings must have become very common in the Neolithic and, undoubtedly, many more sites remain to be discovered. Typical, for instance, are the two- to three-metre horizontal 'drifts' for jasper in the hard Jura limestone of the Isteiner Klotz, north of Basle (Schmid 1952), the mass of small shafts for limnoquartzite near Miskolc, in north-west Hungary, and the network of three-metre deep

114

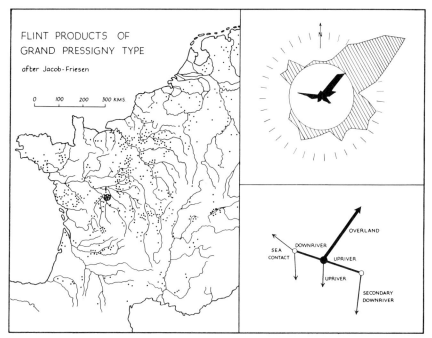

4.7 The distribution of products of Grand Pressigny flint, analysed by direction of movement. The black inner zone of the orientation diagram (top right) includes finds within 200km, the hatched outer zone covers finds beyond this (cf. Figure 4.4).

channels following vertical flint boundaries at Sümeg, in western Hungary (Vértes 1964). All these are probably of third-millennium date, and the last one certainly so. Somewhat larger are the series of shafts for Jurassic chert (radiolarite) at Mauern, near Vienna, some of which reach eight metres in depth and have lateral galleries (Kirnbauer 1958). With the widespread shallow workings alongside, these would have yielded around 1000 tonnes of usable stone, perhaps at the rate of a few tonnes per year. The workings seem to belong to a Lengyel culture local group, and this material was widely used between the Alps and the Danube. That such efforts were not restricted to mining stone is shown by the extensive system of underground galleries at Šuplja Stena, near Belgrade, for the extraction of cinnabarite (red mercuric sulphide), used as a paint. The galleries are definitely dated by finds of Baden pottery to the mid-third millennium, but finds of cinnabarite at the nearby *tell* of Vinča suggest an earlier beginning (Milojčić 1943).

None of these, however, compares with the scale of flint-mining in northern Europe, where shafts were sunk through the relatively soft chalk to up to fifteen metres in depth, with lateral galleries following the horizontal seams. These are found in all the areas where flint could be won direct from the chalk, and range in date from early third-millennium examples, such as the Hov mine in Jutland producing thin-butted axes, to early second-millennium ones like the Aalborg mine 80km away, producing especially daggers and sickles (Becker 1959). Where flint was widely available within a region, activity was not concentrated in one place: where opportunities were rarer, very large operations took place. The extensive use and limited natural occurrence of banded flint is reflected in the scale of mines at Krzemionki Opatowskie, where between 700 and 1000 shafts, some as much as 11m deep, are known in a rather barren area some 10km away from the nearest centres of settlement, where the working-up took place. Such an industrial scale of production (in the Krzemionki case perhaps twice that of Grimes Graves in East Anglia), as much as the wide distribution of the products, indicates the organisation that underlies such a pattern, in which at least groups of villages were gaining special advantages from their nearness to raw materials.

The large volume of material required in northern Europe is partly related to the size of woodworking tools. There is a general decrease in the size of axes further south, where small quadrangular or shoe-last forms were most usually mounted in antler sleeves. In addition, the very large size of some northern examples suggests that the contrast may be exaggerated by non-utilitarian factors. In the New Guinea case mentioned in an earlier section, the ceremonial axes are clearly distinguished by their size, being over 25cm in length as opposed to the working axes, which are generally less than 15cm. Thin-butted axes in Scandinavia and north Germany occasionally occur up to over 40cm in length, weighing around 4kg, clearly in excess of ergonomic requirements. In northern Europe, the large axe had a symbolic role beyond its immediate technical function, and is notable as one of the few representational elements in Megalithic art. Large ceremonial forms, if that is what they are, certainly travelled over long distances; the far-flung Langdale axe from Langwood Fen, in Cambridgeshire, is 28cm long (Fell 1964) and it would be interesting to discover whether the larger forms generally moved further than the smaller 'working' forms. The existence of a complete spectrum from simple working tools to purely symbolic forms is impressively demonstrated by the larger and finer jadeite examples, where use in ceremonial presentations was a sufficiently powerful motive to necessitate the exploitation of a specific raw material – though this explicit differentiation between tool and symbol may be a fairly late feature. The aesthetic qualities of Langdale tuff and banded flint may, in a similar way, have contributed to their major distributions, and the cross-cutting character of the British stone axe distributions (Clark 1965, fig. 1) indicates how one rock was traded against another.

Besides axes that are simply a variation of working forms in a different size or material, other forms appeared in the Late Neolithic that are linked to status through their use as weapons. This is most clearly seen south of the Carpathians, as early as the mid-fourth millennium, where working axes are rather small and axes over 10–15cm in length are almost entirely shaft-hole

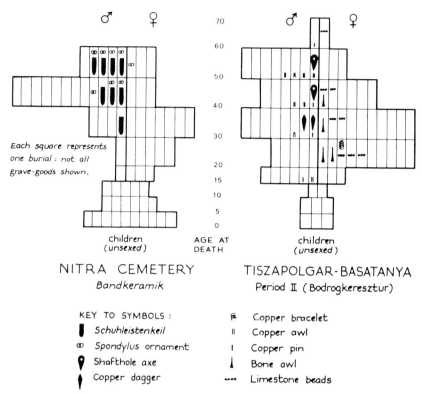

4.8 *The association of grave-goods by age and sex; a comparison of sixth- and later fifth-millennium examples. Data from Pavúk (1972) and Bognár-Kutzián (1963).*

forms and best described as 'battle-axes', since they are clearly intended for fighting or display rather than more mundane tasks. Such stone battle-axes occur in the north from TRB times onwards, becoming increasingly elaborate and distinctive. These axes seem to belong to a stage in the development of a more explicit symbolism of social status, the extension of a phenomenon traceable from the Early Neolithic. The occurrence of various items as common grave-goods allows some observations to be made on this process. An interesting feature of certain classes of artefact is their association with a specific sex and age-range (see Figure 4.8), suggesting that their possession was limited to individuals of a particular status – even if items such as axes could, no doubt, be borrowed by younger men for specific tasks. Such a social dimension of utilitarian objects is well known in anthropological literature, and it is likely that the exchanges that distributed objects such as axes took place only between men of comparable rank.

In the Nitra cemetery example, *Spondylus* ornaments reinforce the pattern of axe distribution: in other contemporary cases further north, however, they occupy a converse position, associated with female and juvenile burials (Pavúk 1972; Kahlke 1954). A particularly elaborate *Bandkeramik* female inhumation grave at Erfurt (*Inventaria Archaeologica* D 85), for example, had eighteen beads and eleven pendants of this shell at the neck, two discs on the breast, and a ring on each upper arm.

Besides the shaft-hole axe, another personal weapon that began to achieve a widespread symbolic significance was the dagger. As early as the fourth millennium in Bodrogkeresztúr contexts (Bognár-Kutzián 1963, 318 'Group 1'), large dagger-blades of up to 18cm in length often accompany male burials. This is another feature that was greatly emphasised in the third millennium of northern Europe. It is significant that one of the most extensively traded materials of the time should be the Grand Pressigny flint, whose characteristic cores were carefully prepared to produce especially long blades, at great cost in flint. Some of the most extensively developed systems of distribution in these stone-using communities were, thus, those connected with status items.

The development of a range of 'socio-technic' items, such as the battle-axe, was a characteristic feature of the artefactual history of the later fourth and third millennia, both north and south of the Carpathians and, as Tabaczynski has said (1972, 59), should be considered 'nicht nur als Ausdruck der Verbreitung neuer Ideen ... sondern auch als eine archaeologischer Hinweis auf die fortschreitende gesellschaftliche Aufgliederung'. The evidence of stonework thus shows a growing scale of trade during the Neolithic, not only in essential products but also in increasing flows of symbolic artefacts. The rise in demand for essentials relates directly to the growth of population, but the indirect results of this are also of importance for the movement of materials in general. From the cultural and environmental uniformity of the earliest Neolithic, expansion and differentiation produced a mosaic of regional groupings and economic zones of great complexity, ranging from farmers on the rich loess-lands or more pastoral groups in sandy areas, to the specialised fishing villages of the Rzucewo culture on the sandspits of the Vistula estuary. The opportunity for fruitful exchange between these groups was thus much greater than in the situation of initial colonisation. The basic exchange channels could usefully carry a much greater volume of subsistence products and, with them, other material items to balance and regulate the flow. The significance of material counters in such situations has been emphasised by Vayda (1966) in discussing the Pomo Indians of central California, where shell beads were exchanged for food between communities concentrating on different staple foods that were in surplus at different seasons. Beads accumulated from a fish surplus, for instance, could be exchanged later with the donor community for inland products, when these in turn were in surplus.

The actual distribution of population on the ground also encouraged and necessitated contact. While Early Neolithic groups in central Europe showed a strong orientation towards the river network and flood-plain edge, the spread of settlement to drier interfluvial regions implied more frequent face-to-face contact between clusters of villages, and a more richly networked overall pattern (Kruk 1973). With more extensive grazing, the maintenance of a wide set of relationships with surrounding communities was not merely possible but essential to a smooth running of the system. Indeed, the widespread distribution of certain ceramic styles, such as the bell-beaker complex, indicates the growing intensity of inter-regional contacts. All these factors promoted an increased turnover in goods, a general quickening in local transactions that increased the power of such networks to carry rarer materials. Such traded items served to emphasise the rank and authority of those who could obtain them.

THE ROLE OF COPPER

To understand the part that copper played in these developments, the distribution and character of its sources must first be appreciated. In the first place, copper ores are – like many of the types of harder stone used for axes – basically of highland occurrence, being 'concentrated in areas of structural complexity and igneous activity' (Park and Macdiarmid 1970). Such deposits are commonly formed by *hydrothermal injection* in periods of tectonic movement, when hot solutions from deep-lying magma chambers penetrate upwards into favourable structural and lithological environments. Many such deposits were formed, for instance, during the Alpine mountain-building phase, and such ores are widespread in the Tertiary fold-chains of southern Europe (Sherratt 1972, 518). Somewhat different ore-complexes, formed at deeper levels, are found in the ancient crystalline massifs such as Bohemia or the Rhodope block: these may also contain copper, often lead, and occasionally tin.

A further factor of importance is the degree to which secondary changes have occurred as a result of weathering. Where an ore vein reaches the surface, a characteristic sequence of 'weathering horizons' develops, as a result of the leaching downwards of impurities. At the top is a zone of pure (*native*) copper, stable because of a thin surface coating of oxide. Below this develop successively zones of oxide and carbonate ores (see Table 4.1 for common minerals) and, below this, a zone of enrichment where impurities accumulate at the water-table. While the higher ore minerals are mostly bright¹y coloured, those of the enrichment zone are characteristically grey and are collectively referred to by the German miners' term of *Fahlerz*. These are sulphide ores, containing also appreciable quantities of arsenic, antimony, often silver and sometimes lead. (Depending on whether arsenic or antimony dominates, these form crystals of the minerals tennantite and tetrahedrite respectively – though owing to chemical replacement within the same crystal structure, tetrahedrite-type crystals may represent either compound: this is important in linking ores with analysed objects.) Finally, below these secondary products, lies the zone of original unaltered sulphide

Ore Type	Chemical Formula	Colour	Approximate Cu Content	Crystalline Schist					Mesozoic							Banat Phase					Neogene											
				Bălan (r. Ciuc)	Băile Borsa (r. Viseu)	Crucea (r. Vatra Dornei)	Lipova (r. Lipova)	Muncelul Mic (r. Ilia)	Gârii Baba (r. Vatra Dornei)	Mina Altin Tepe (r. Istria)	Gemenea (r. Câmpulung)	Căsăreşti (r. Brad)	Mircea Vodă (r. Tulcea)	Pătirs (r. Lipova)	Tulgheş (r. Gheorghieni)	Bâlţa Bihorului (r. Beiuş)	Moldova Moua	Oraviţa Ciclova-Romana	Sasca Montană (r. Oraviţa)	Deogecera (o. Reşiţa)	Ilba (o. Baia Mare)	Cavnic (r. Lapuş)	Baia Sprie (o. Baia Mare)	Deva	Intregalde (r. Alba)	Baia Mare	Stănija (r. Brad)	Hondol (r. Ilia)	Ruda Barzia (r. Brad)	Baia de Arieş (r. Câmpeni)	Bucium (r. Câmpeni)	Băiuţ (r. Lapuş)
Pure Copper																																
Native Copper	Cu	Copper	c. 100%	x						x	x		x		x	x	x	x	x	x	x	x	x				x	x	x		x		x
Copper Oxides																																
Tenorite	Cu O	black	c. 80%	x								x	x			x	x	x	x	x							x						x
Cuprite	Cu₂ O	red	c. 90%	x							x			x		x	x	x	x	x							x	x					
Copper Carbonates																																
Azurite	2Cu CO₃.Cu (OH)₂	blue	c. 55%	x		x	x	x	x	x	x					x	x	x	x	x	x	x	x			x						x	x
Malachite	Cu CO₃.Cu (OH)₂	green	c. 55%	x		x	x	x	x	x	x					x	x	x	x	x	x	x	x			x	x	x		x	x	x	x
Copper Silicate																																
Crysocolla (*Kupferpecherz*)	Cu Si O₃ H₂O	blue	c. 35%							x			x	x		x	x	x	x	x						x				x			
'Fahlerz'																																
Tennantite	Cu₃ As S₃.₄	grey	c. 55%													x	x	x	x	x	x	x	x			x				x			
Tetrahedrite	Cu₃ Sb S₃.₄	grey	c. 55%	x		x		x				x				x	x	x	x	x	x	x	x			x	x	x	x	x	x	x	x
Enargite	Cu₃ As S₄	grey	c. 50%													x			x			x				x							
Bournonite	Pb Cu Sb S₃	grey	c. 15%	x	x						x										x	x	x	x			x	x	x	x	x		
Copper Sulphate																																
Chalcanthite	Cu SO₄ 5H₂O	blue	c. 25%	x			x			x						x	x		x	x				x			x		x	x			
Copper Sulphides																																
Covellina (*Kupferindig*)	Cu S	blue	c. 65%	x	x	x		x		x	x		x	x		x				x		x	x			x				x	x		x
Chalcocite (*Kupferglanz*)	Cu₂ S	grey	c. 50%	x	x	x			x					x			x	x	x	x		x	x	x		x				x	x		x
Bornite (*Buntkupferz*)	Cu Fe S₄	'peacock'	c. 65%	x		x			x					x			x	x	x	x		x		x			x		x		x		x
Chalcopyrite (*Kupferkies*)	Cu Fe S₂	yellow	c. 35%	x	x	x	x	x	x	x	x	x	x	x	x	x	x	x	x	x	x	x	x	x	x	x	x	x	x	x	x	x	x	x
Copper/Arsenic																																
'Whitneyite'	Cu As	reddish-white																											x				
Domeykite	Cu₃ As	grey-white																											x				
Algodonite	Cu₆.₇ As	grey-white																											x				
Pseudomalachite	2Cu As O₄.2Cu (OH)₂	green																x															
Pure Arsenic																																
Native Arsenic	As	white																x				x	x	x			x	x		x	x	x	
Arsenic Oxide																																
Arsenolite	As₂ O₃	grey															x		x														
Arsenic Sulphides																																
Orpiment	As₂ S₃	yellow															x	x		x		x	x	x			x			x			x
Realgar	As₂ S₂	red															x					x	x	x			x			x			x
Arsenopyrite	Fe S As	white					x	x		x			x			x		x	x	x		x	x			x	x – x	x	x	x	x	x
Tin Oxide																																
Cassiterite	Sn O₂	black		x																													

Table 4.1 Selected occurrences of various copper ores in Romania: data from Rădulescu and Dumitrescu (1966). [The age of the metallogenesis will be reflected in lead-isotope values.]

ore, usually chalcopyrite. Secondary sulphides not containing iron may also occur higher up in the series. All sulphide ores require an additional roasting process before smelting, to get rid of the sulphur; and, in addition, the iron-containing pyrite ores present problems with slag. The common secondary ores all have a much higher copper content than the unaltered primary deposits.

The formation of secondary minerals is not inevitable, and ores in different areas show this to varying degrees. In the Alps, for example, unaltered sulphide ores are usual; while in the Carpathians and the Balkans large deposits of secondary minerals were formed, including native copper. Various factors (Pittioni 1957, 8–9) affected this and, in particular, the effects of glaciation in the Alps, in contrast with the more continuous conditions of development further south. As Pittioni (1957, 10) remarks, 'die kulturgeschichtliche Bedeutung dieser lagerstättenkundlich-klimageschichtlichen Feststellungen kann nicht eindringlich genug betont werden'. The most important factor in the early development of copper metallurgy was the availability of a well-developed series of ores from the pure native form, through the easily smelted oxide and carbonate forms, down to enriched and, finally, unaltered sulphides; and, above all, the occurrence of such deposits in locations not too distantly removed from the

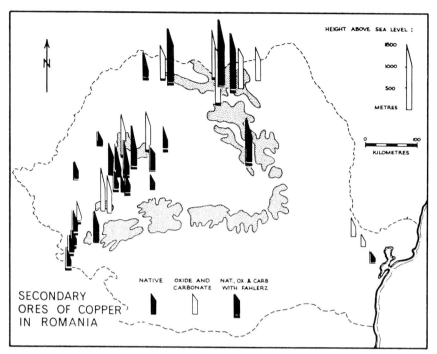

4.9 Relative accessibility of copper ores in Romania as indicated by the heights above sea level of different sources. Data from Rădulescu and Dumitrescu (1966).

early centres of population. In the Balkans and the fringes of the Carpathian Basin especially – as indeed in other centres of early development such as Anatolia and Spain – the exploration of nearby upland regions brought agricultural populations, familiar with the controlled use of heat in firing pottery, into early contact with the brightly-coloured secondary ores of copper.

Some idea of the overall distribution of copper ores within the Carpatho-Balkan and Dinaric chains is given in Figure 4.15. Within this, however, there are important differences in accessibility, and these seem to have been major controlling factors in the development of local metallurgy. An attempt has been made in Figure 4.9 to give a visual impression of the variety within Romania. Two major groupings suggest themselves – a north-east group to the east of Baia Mare, and a south-west group from the Iron Gates to the Munţii Metalici where the densest concentrations occur. The altitudes of these two groups indicate that the latter are much more accessible, and the distribution of copper artefacts (see Figure 4.10) strengthens the impression that these were, in fact, important sources in the fourth and third millennia (see below). The less accessible sources of the north-east group sustained the second florescence of Carpathian copper metallurgy, in the early Bronze Age (Otomani culture).

A similar situation obtained in parts of Bulgaria. Figure 4.11 shows the position of sources exploited in the later fourth millennium (Chernykh

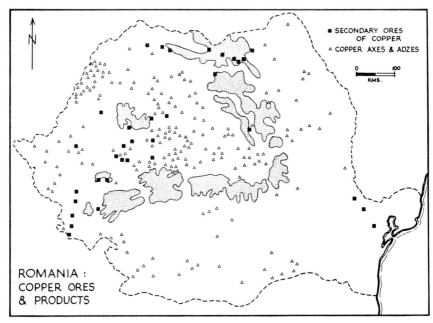

4.10 *The distribution of copper axes of the fifth and fourth millennia in Romania, compared with potential ore-sources. Data from Vulpe (1973), Maczek et al. (1953).*

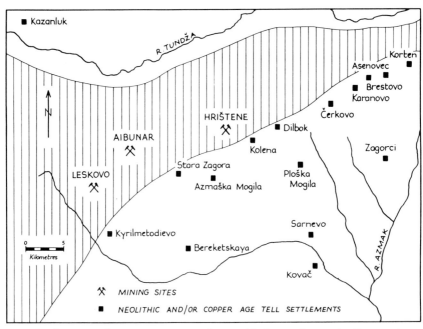

4.11 *Settlement and resources in part of central Bulgaria during the Copper Age: Karanovo and adjacent copper mines in use at the time.*

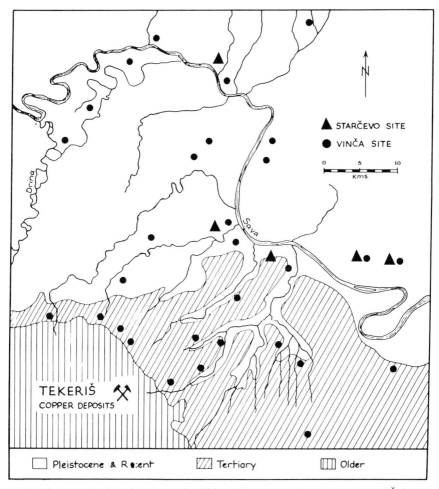

4.12 The spread of settlement in the fifth millennium in the region around Šabac, Serbia. (Sites marked 'Vinča' include also ones with Lengyel affinities.)

1972; also below), in relation to the area of dense prehistoric settlement around Stara Zagora, where a series of important sites, including Azmak and Karanovo, occur along the spring-line at the edge of the basin. In this region, occupied from Early Neolithic times in the later sixth millennium, metal ores as well as hard stone sources occur within 5–10km of long-lived *tell* settlements.

In addition to areas that had this intimate association from such an early date, expansion of settlement brought about similar conditions over a wider area. One example will suffice to illustrate what must have been a widespread process. The Tertiary limestones of Serbia were extensively colonised in the Vinča period (Sherratt 1972, 531). In the area around Šabac shown in Figure 4.12, Starčevo occupation of the sixth millennium concentrates

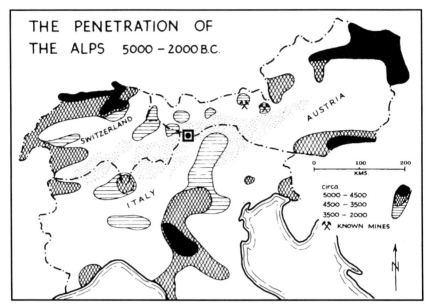

4.13 A schematic attempt to illustrate the extension of upland settlement in the Alps as indicated by archaeological finds; compiled from various sources. [Dates corrected; the location of Copper Age 'Iceman' from the Hauslabjoch has been added as a square symbol.]

along the Sava; but, in the course of the fifth millennium, settlement pushed into the fringes of the uplands. Copper ores are known, not from the limestone area itself, but from the older rocks behind it, for instance at Tekeriš (Maczek et al. 1953). Such deposits would again have been within a 5–10km range from the nearest settlements.

These three situations may be contrasted with the spread of settlement into those regions of the Alps where metal ores occur. In the Mühlbach-Bischofshofen area near Salzburg, for instance, which was the scene of extensive mining and smelting activity in the second millennium, the ores lie between 1000 and 1500 metres above sea level. This is comparable with the group in north-east Romania, and such areas would have seen little human activity before the Bronze Age. Initial Neolithic settlement concentrated on the loess lowlands (see Figure 4.13), spreading in the fourth and early third millennia into the lake districts of the Alpine foreland, and only in the second millennium, with the development of transhumance, were the high pastures systematically used (Pittioni 1973). As the copper deposits in this area were, in any case, mainly sulphide ores requiring a longer roasting process, it is not surprising that Alpine ores did not figure largely in the Copper Age.

In the case of Bulgaria, therefore, with ores that must have been known as curiosities for a millennium before copper-working began, a limiting factor in terms of technology can, indeed, be inferred. The transition from

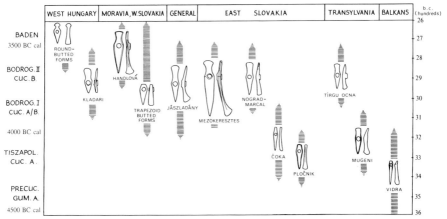

4.14 The succession of Copper Age shafthole-axe types in Balkan-Carpathian Europe, roughly from SE to NW as new sources were opened up (for selected spatial distributions, see following figure); [from Sherratt 1976a].

light-coloured painted pottery fired in an oxidising atmosphere to the dark-coloured reduced wares that became fashionable in south-east Europe and Anatolia in the later fifth millennium probably indicates the critical change involved. The Macedno-Bulgarian region, therefore, where settlement began as early as the sixth millennium in a landscape in which fertile alluvial basins lay scattered among mountains rich in stone and metal, was an area where resources waited for an appropriate technology; but outside this, factors of location and, ultimately, of ore-type were more critical. For resources requiring considerable labour to extract and process them at source, it is unlikely that extensive exploitation could take place within a primitive farming context unless these activities could be integrated within a yearly subsistence cycle. Only where settlement was nearby, or when seasonal movements of stock took men as a matter of routine into the area of occurrence, could such a process begin.

The earliest use of copper is, in fact, very hard to determine, as the kinds of small object made in the experimental stages are rarely found except by careful sieving of excavated deposits. For this reason, the date of the earliest metallurgy is likely, in many areas, to be pushed further back than current evidence allows. In south-east Europe, well-associated finds of beads, probably made from native copper, from the Boian culture cemetery of Cernica (Cantacuzino and Morinz 1963) give a *terminus ante quem* in the earlier fourth millennium, while a find of a copper awl has been claimed in a fifth-millennium Criş context, though this is disputed. The earliest well-dated heavy objects probably made from smelted copper occur early in the second half of the fourth millennium, when the simpler forms of flat and shaft-hole axes make their appearance, along with arm-rings and bracelets.

The typological sequence of copper shaft-hole axes, beginning with simple axe-hammers that were a direct translation of contemporary stone forms, is now well known (Bognár-Kutzián 1963; Schubert 1965 *inter alia*). See Figure 4.14. Some of the earliest associated finds are the three examples from different houses in the early Gumelniţa settlement at Hotnica in Bulgaria, of the so-called Vidra type (Bognár-Kutzián 1972, 144). The Vidra form is typical of the area covered by the Gumelniţa culture in Bulgaria and south Romania. A local form of flat axe has a complementary distribution (see Figure 4.15). Only slightly later are the finds from the Tibava cemetery (Šiška 1964), not far from the copper sources of east Slovakia. Here, from a sample of forty-one excavated graves, come seven examples of the Čoka and Pločnik types (Figure 4.15). Although these forms are known from a wider area at this time, it is significant that they occur in graves only in this immediate region, which would correspond to zone (2) of the distribution model set out earlier. The metalliferous area of eastern Slovakia was, in any case, already an important supply-area for andesite and obsidian (lumps of which occur in contemporary graves at Lučky in this region), and an intermediary in the transmission of brown translucent chert and Wolhynian flint (also in graves, at Tibava: Andel 1961). The copper industry at this stage was thus ancillary to the distribution of a wide range of raw materials, some of which were economically much more important.

With the widespread occurrence of mining for various rocks in mind, it is no surprise that the exploitation of copper should also involve mining activity as early as the fourth millennium. It can plausibly be related to the larger volumes of material required for heavy objects such as axe-hammers, and was probably an essential part of the process of collecting the raw material for smelting, rather than simply hammering small amounts of native copper. As with the stone-quarries, therefore, many more sites must remain to be recognised. The earliest confirmed traces of mining are the six shafts from Rudna Glava near Bor – an important copper-producing area down to the present day – where the Carpathian/Balkan arc swings through north-east Yugoslavia (Jovanović 1971). These shafts are sloping funnels, varying from two metres to half-a-metre in diameter, following the ore veins. One shaft had an access platform partly revetted by a dry-stone wall, and the shafts extend beyond the two to three metres to which they were explored. Fragments of pottery and a 'cult-vessel' (lamp?) datable to the beginning of the Vinča-Pločnik phase of the early or mid-fourth millennium, were found in association with this site (Figure 16.1).

The Bulgarian sites near Stara Zagora, noted above and shown on Figure 4.11, have also yielded traces of mining (Chernykh and Radunčeva 1972). Pottery of Copper Age and Early Bronze Age types has been found in association at the site of Aibunar, though the mine at Hrištene, which has a wide funnel entrance and a shaft nearly 25m in depth, may belong to a later period. Other traces of prehistoric mining activity have been discovered at Špania Dolina, near Banska Bistrica in western Slovakia (Točik and Vladar

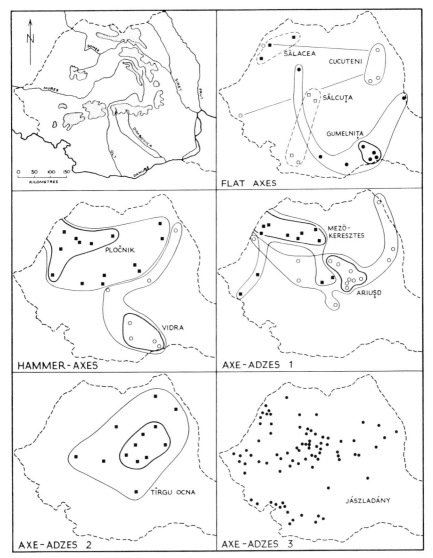

4.15 *The distribution of various types of copper axe in Romania during the fifth and fourth millennia. Heavy lines enclose 50 per cent of the finds of a given type in the country. Data from Vulpe (1973).*

1971), identified by large stone hammers grooved for withy hafts of a kind known elsewhere in Bronze Age contexts. (See map for these sites: Figure 4.16.)

The scale of copper-working and trading grew appreciably, towards the end of the fourth millennium and at the beginning of the third. Typologically, this is indicated by the appearance of larger and more elaborate forms of axe-hammers, usually formed by flattening and fanning out the

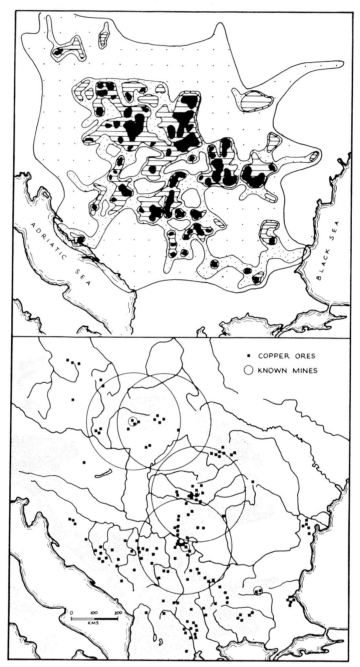

4.16 Above: *clusters of finds of copper axes of the fifth and fourth millennia shown by spatial proximity linkage [joining findspots at successive distance-thresholds – more accurate than a grid isopleth]; dark masses indicate dense clusters. Data from Schubert (1965). Below: the distribution of copper ores (dots) and known prehistoric mines (circles); large circles indicate a 200km radius around the most important sources. Source data from Maczek et al. (1954).*

128

'hammer' end: Figure 4.14. In some cases this method was used to produce an actual working edge, and thus an axe-adze (e.g. Jászladány type); in others, it simply produced a more elaborate terminal (e.g. Mezőkeresztes type). Some examples of the latter – a local development in the upper Tisza area – are up to 32cm in length, indicating the abundance of copper supplies available. These developments took place in the Carpathian Basin rather than in the Balkans, where supplies seem to have been less plentiful and simpler forms continued. The Jászladány type is by far the commonest and most widespread of the stray finds (Figure 4.15), as well as being put into graves in the consuming area (zone 3) in the eastern Carpathian Basin. It was probably produced at a number of centres. Despite the large amounts of metal in circulation, however, there is no reason to believe that the trading mechanisms that distributed them were any more sophisticated than those involved in carrying stone supplies further north. The distribution map (Figure 4.16) for copper axes shows a concentration largely within the Carpathian Basin, and this pattern can be accounted for as the output of a number of sources on its edge whose scale of production was well below that documented for banded flint, for instance. While the use of copper added another new and desirable raw material, it caused no revolution in the sphere of trade.

The development of copper-working in the later fourth and third millennia was the result of the availability of easily-smelted ores in locations already well known. The numerous analyses of hammer-axes, adze-axes and flat copper axes from this period (Patay et al. 1963; Junghans et al. 1968) show a consistent pattern almost without impurities, except for traces of silver. This would be compatible with the use either of native, oxide or carbonate ores, but it is likely that the bulk of copper came from the widely distributed (Table 4.1) ores, malachite and azurite, pieces of which have been found on a number of sites in Yugoslavia (e.g. Fafos: Jovanović 1971). Over a wide area, from Macedonia and Bulgaria in the south to Slovakia in the north, the extensive deposits of ores of this kind allowed a simple metal-lurgy to flourish on an impressive scale. Although smelting was probably confined to areas immediately adjacent to the sources, re-melting probably took place over a wider area, and large objects traded outwards from the sources would, no doubt, at some stage have been broken down, as occasion demanded, into a multitude of smaller forms. No specialised ingots of comparable size are known. The processes involved in the manufacture of finished products are of a simple kind, involving only a one-piece open mould and a good deal of hammering (Coghlan 1961; Charles 1969).

There is some evidence, even from the fourth millennium, of the pro-duction of arsenical alloys. One of the Tibava hammer-axes (SAM No. 3354) contains 1.15 per cent of arsenic, and sporadic values of up to 4 per cent occur in objects from the later Copper Age. Such occurrences in no way imply the kind of regular trade in additives suggested by consistently high tin values in the Bronze Age. As can be seen from Table 4.1, native arsenic and its oxides and sulphides occur commonly in association with the kinds of copper deposit under discussion. Indeed, the green pseudo-malachite mineral with a high arsenic content, similar in appearance to the pure copper carbonate, is occasionally found, and could well have been added quite accidentally. It is also, of course, likely that the effects of adding associated arsenic minerals came to be appreciated and, with the development of closed-mould casting in the later third millennium (see below), the use of this additive became standard practice in south-east Europe (Chernykh 1971) and the Aegean (Charles 1967), where tin supplies were sporadic.

The ores that sustained the output of massive copper axes were naturally limited in extent, and there are indications that by the later third millennium they were in short supply. Copper axes were no longer put in graves, and settlement finds are few. Some continuity was maintained in the north-west part of the basin where axes are found occasionally in Baden contexts in Austria and in Slovakia, and pieces of sheet metal were put in graves. Significantly, one or two pieces from this period are of *Fahlerz*, and while small amounts of purer copper ore remained (probably in relatively inaccessible areas) to be used sporadically for the next half-millennium, its main phase of use was over. The final stages of the third millennium marked a time of scarcity and experiment.

A curious situation then came about: at a time when raw-material supplies in the Carpathian Basin were short, contacts across the Pontic steppes with the Caucasian school of metallurgy (Chernykh 1966) introduced a new range of forms, such as the single-bladed axe (Mozsolics 1967), associated with the technique of closed casting in a two-piece mould. At the same time, local copper-working began over a much wider area of central and north-west Europe. This occurred in areas metallurgically entirely distinct: lacking extensive deposits of purer secondary ores, their industries developed on the basis of a supply of *Fahlerz* copper.

By the beginning of the second millennium, therefore, especially in Bohemia and central Germany but also further west, a second florescence of copper-using was under way. It is this '*Fahlerz* boom' which has marked the Early Bronze Age of central Europe in general, and the Aunjetitz culture in particular, as a phenomenon of special interest to the prehistorian (Childe 1957). Based initially on open-mould casting, this central European school later followed the Carpathian Basin in adopting the two-piece mould, at the same time taking local tin as a standard additive to improve closed castings in the same way that arsenic was adopted in the Balkans.

Spectographic analysis, of little use in identifying specific sources for the purer metals of the Copper Age, has proved of great value in distinguishing several varieties of *Fahlerz* (Otto and Witter 1952; Junghans et al. 1960; 1968). The assemblages of the central European Early Bronze Age are dominated by a limited number of groups, chiefly 'A' or Singen metal and the so-called *Ösenhalsring* metal (Waterbolk and Butler 1965). Neither can be definitely attributed to a specific source: 'A' metal probably covers several sources including, possibly, some in the Harz mountains; but *Ösenhalsring* metal shows a significant geographical patterning. Its concentration on the Upper Danube and in Moravia has been related both to a Slovakian and to an Alpine origin (Neuninger and Pittioni 1963; Bath-Bílková 1973) but, whichever is correct, two features stand out – the large quantities that occur as ingots in hoards, and the contrast between the frequency of these in Moravia and the trickle of this metal that reached the Carpathian Basin. Only appreciably later did a local *Fahlerz* ($F_{A/B}$ or 'Otomani metal') become widespread in the Basin and allow a full expression of the forms that had developed there in the period of intervening scarcity (Schubert and Schubert 1967).

What, then, was the social and historical significance of these changes in the availability of metal, and how do these relate to the questions set out in the opening section? In the first place, the development of a technology of copper-smelting from the purer secondary ores had few wider effects upon contemporary society. It was a local expression of processes widespread in Later Neolithic Europe – the exploration of the landscape, an intensified exploitation of raw materials, and a limited widening of trade networks. It added a new prestige material that was used in much the same way as stone and shell elsewhere. The earliest hammer-axes are a direct translation of the stone forms elsewhere called 'battle-axes', and are clearly the equivalents of these as deposits in graves. It was used for daggers – in phase II of the Tiszapolgár cemetery associated with somewhat younger adult males than the shaft-hole axes (Figure 4.8) – in place of stone blades, and it was used for armbands and beads in place of shell. Its importance was largely symbolic: the medium was the message.

The spread of metal-using further north in the second millennium was equally associated primarily with prestige uses. Again, the axe – in this case, the local flat form rather than a shaft-hole type – and the dagger were among the first applications, along with ornaments and the pins that were at this time becoming fashionable in place of buttons. There are, however, new features that are of significance for the social structure of the Bronze Age proper. The rich grave of Thun-Renzenbühl in Switzerland (Figure 4.17; Strahm 1972) epitomises both old and new features. Axe and dagger retain their symbolic role, reinforced by a headband and belt-terminal which themselves have antecedents in the later Copper Age. Cloak-pins of specific regional types no doubt proclaim local loyalties, but the six neck-rings introduce a new element of special importance. Such neck-rings (*Ösenhalsringe*) were evidently both traded as ingots and worn as ornaments. They occur in hoards of up to 600 (Schubert 1966) and are clearly counters as much as symbols of individual authority. In the Copper Age, groups of more than two or three axes found together are rare, and the 'hoard' of thirteen flat

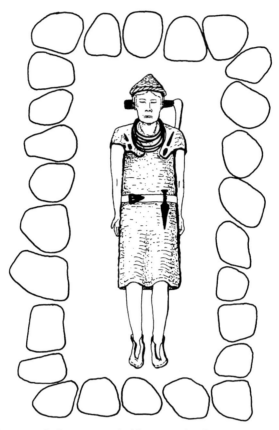

4.17 The rich grave of Thun-Renzenbühl, Switzerland; [reconstructed, initially after Strahm (1972), updated].

axes from the Pločnik settlement is unique. This is consistent with their inferred use as indicators of ascribed status. With the *Ösenhalsringe* we have for the first time an element of accumulation, the achieved position of a 'big man' superadded to other inequalities. Contemporary with the *Ösenhalsringe* are the massive axe-hoards of the Saale region, such as that of Gröbers-Bennewitz, with 300 flanged axes, or the Dieskau II hoard including also daggers and halberds (Brunn 1959). Such collections are typical of the mixture of ingot-counters and display equipment that dominates European Bronze Age hoards down to the occurrence of industrial collections ('smiths' hoards') which mark the system of rapid recycling necessary when bronze was used as a workaday material (Rowlands 1971).

It is unlikely that the goods that survive archaeologically moved in isolation: the greater concentration of metal in the Early Bronze Age, which for the first time saw the extensive import of metal objects to large areas, such as Denmark and north Germany, without local resources, must indicate also a greater mobility in other commodities, probably including subsistence products and textiles. The greater mobility offered by extensive transhumance and seafaring, the widespread use of the horse, all helped to make possible a wider network of exchange and trade. In the Aegean, the sudden flowering of inter-regional contacts in the later third millennium (Renfrew 1967) surely indicates the beginning of the type of complex maritime exchange-cycles so familiar to ethnographers (Figure 4.1).

The division of prehistory into Stone, Bronze and Iron Ages has had a remarkably long life since the scheme was first put forward in 1832. Seen as symptomatic of underlying ecological and social changes, rather than simply as a technological advance, the beginning of the Bronze Age retains its significance as a critical point in European development.

<u>5</u>

Social Evolution: Europe in the Later Neolithic and Copper Ages
(1984)

Although archaeological information about the later Neolithic and Copper Ages[1] has increased enormously since the later part of the last century, its interpretation in social terms has remained at a relatively primitive level. While the need to deal with underlying social processes has been increasingly stressed in recent years, many of the concepts employed have been no more than revivals of nineteenth-century schemes. Technological change and the unilinear development of increasingly hierarchical forms of society still lie at the base of many current interpretations.

One symptom of this is the frequent appearance of the term 'chiefdom', covering a wide range of social forms from the groups encountered by the Romans in the later Iron Age to the Copper Age inhabitants of Bulgaria or the megalith-building Neolithic farmers of western Europe. Looking for 'the indian behind the artefact' (in Robert Braidwood's phrase) has become increasingly difficult when there is nothing to be seen but chiefs.

This uncertainty as to when social ranking actually arose is symptomatic of the problems of describing European prehistory by comparison, say, with that of the Near East. While we have a fairly refined vocabulary for dealing with the various stages in the emergence of complex urban societies, Europe's stubborn failure to organise itself until just before the arrival of the

---

This paper was prepared for a conference on social evolution organised by John Bintliff. It was the first sketch of a pan-European picture, with attention to social process; and it was stimulated especially by the work of Richard Bradley, Ian Hodder, Kristian Kristiansen, Michael Rowlands and Stephen Shennan – an astonishing concentration of talent on a set of related problems. (The article by Mike Rowlands in the same conference volume is now a classic, and has profoundly influenced my own perceptions ever since.) It tried to go beyond the ecological and functionalist views which had dominated my earlier work, and pointed the way to some of the themes which would emerge in the following decade.

Romans leaves us with some 6000 years of social development for which a simple division into 'tribal' or 'chiefly' seems hopelessly inadequate. It is especially primitive by comparison with the sophistication of our typological and chronological analyses, which allow us to divide this same period into nearly twenty major cultural divisions, many themselves subdivided into three or four phases.

The temptation in interpreting the archaeological record of the later Neolithic and Copper Ages is thus to see some sort of cumulative growth of social complexity, with evidence such as monument-building or minority burial reflecting emerging hierarchies. Terms such as 'chiefdom' have become stretched to include earlier and earlier examples of prehistoric societies. The account presented here takes a different point of view: it tries to explore the variety in early agricultural societies in terms of non-hierarchical forms of social organisation. Although social change did not benefit all sections of the population equally, it is misleading to see prehistory simply in terms of the increasing domination of an elite. We need to look more closely at the problems faced by communities in different circumstances and the sorts of power relations that emerged in each case.[2] While such societies may demonstrate a considerable degree of cultural complexity, this does not necessarily take the form of centralisation, ranking and stratification.

STAGES AND ZONES

A problem common to many discussions of 'social evolution' is the use of categories derived from contemporary ethnography and their application to long-term archaeological sequences. From Lewis Henry Morgan (1877) onwards evolutionary writers have put forward schemes defining successive 'stages of culture': savagery-barbarism-civilisation (Clark 1946); band-tribe-chiefdom-state (Service 1962); egalitarian-ranked-state (Fried 1967); and so forth. While differing in detail, they share the same logic: they attempt to convert static snapshots into a dynamic sequence. Such schemes are now increasingly under attack. The band to state sequence – that most used by archaeologists – has now been trenchantly criticised by its own author (Service 1968, 169). Recent bands, he noted, were often the smashed remnants of more complex systems dislocated by western colonial impact. Tribes, in the sense of discrete political units, were often created by interaction with more organised units (Fried 1978); chiefdoms and simple states frequently arose in reaction to slave-raiding and the trading opportunities offered by contact with the west (Stevenson 1968). Even if we do not treat the whole band-tribe-chiefdom-state continuum simply as a reflection of the differential impact of colonial contact, these arguments at least point to differing degrees of social complexity in the ethnographic record as being largely related to positions within the 'macro von Thünen rings' of a recent world system – a geographical zonation as a result of historical interaction around a few major centres.

The difficulty of interpreting archaeological sequences in social terms is thus that of mapping an observed spatial variability onto an inferred chronological sequence of social forms reconstructed from artefactual remains. Not only do the two bodies of evidence – ethnographic and archaeological observations – differ in their raw material, but they also reflect different parts of the process of global development. Many of the 'chiefdoms' of the ethnographic record reflect secondary consequences of the existence of states that cannot be projected back into periods before the emergence of the state. The time has now come to reassert the independent validity of archaeological data, which offer too multivariate a pattern to be constrained within arbitrary partitions of a homogenised universal succession. For this reason the following discussion takes a more inductive view of the archaeological evidence, in searching for internal contrasts before seeking external comparisons in world ethnography.

Many apparently stadial phenomena need to be considered from a spatial point of view, as they result from the rapid imposition of systems developed in nuclear areas on less fast-moving peripheries. For instance, the contrast between 'Mesolithic' and 'Neolithic' ways of life is in fact as much geographical as chronological, as economies based on cereals increasingly intruded into neighbouring areas whose subsistence was based on the increasingly intensive cropping of local resources. In other parts of the world, this process was less abrupt and indigenous sequences were able to develop further before being radically restructured by outside contact. Temperate North America offers a relevant example, where the florescence of monument-building and trading in exotica that characterises phenomena such as Hopewell, for instance, preceded rather than resulted from the spread of cereal cultivation from further south. Indeed, it is now suggested that the apparent 'cultural decline' of the later Woodland period in fact represents a period of increased stability and security in food supplies, with cereal cultivation requiring a less complex and certainly less spectacular socio-cultural system.

There are two points to note here. One is the way in which a 'Mesolithic' system, if preserved from outside interference, may manifest far more complex properties than would be inferred from the truncated sequence of early postglacial Europe. The other is the way in which new subsistence elements that may actually raise population levels and energy flows can at the same time cause a simplification or decentralisation of social structures. It is this kind of variability which characterises semi-isolated regions such as the woodlands of Europe and North America. Structural principles which were rapidly superseded in nuclear areas may have continued to be important in the more drawnout sequences of social change where urbanisation was a relatively late feature. Rather than trying to see in the European prehistoric sequence an increasingly ranked series of societies in which successively more powerful chiefdoms succeeded one another at each opportunity, it may be more profitable to explore alternative descriptions of social organisation.

One of the striking features of the west European archaeological record is the abundant evidence of ritual monuments which are not accompanied by elaborate individual burials or residences. Instead of always looking for hierarchisation, it may become appropriate in such contexts to look for a different principle, that of ritual formalisation as the basis of social order. To equate certain artefacts – monumental tombs, rare or craft-made items (Renfrew 1973) in the later Neolithic of western Europe – with 'chieftainship' may be to miss the essential character of such societies, and to obscure both their essential similarity to earlier Neolithic societies and their contrast with contemporary groups further east.

It is clear that this approach requires European prehistory to be treated as a whole, and that it is necessary to go beyond the artefactual manifestations to postulate underlying similarities in social organisation which may cross-cut conventional divisions. Such social forms may have no direct correspondence to that of any particular group within the ethnographic record; but while this makes the task of such reconstruction more difficult, it also makes the attempt more worthwhile as a contribution to the general study of pre-literate societies.

Evolutionary pathways

The basic regional structure of Neolithic and Copper Age societies was established by the arrival of agricultural groups and their interaction with native communities.[3] Along the main axis of agricultural spread, in the Balkans and the central European loesslands, the dominant process was one of colonisation. By 5000 BC the unity of 'Danubian' cultures across the loess, from western Hungary in the south to the Low Countries and the western Ukraine in the north, was already established. Cultures of the Balkan group with a core area of tell settlements in Bulgaria and southern Jugoslavia extended northwards into Romania and eastern Hungary. In the central and west Mediterranean (Lewthwaite 1982), the successive adoption of sheep and pottery by native littoral groups was increasingly supplemented by cultivation as the complex expanded from its coastal base. The main surviving zone of hunting and collecting groups lay in a broad arc from the British Isles, across Scandinavia and the North European Plain, to the marshes of eastern Europe which drain into the Black Sea. As the Atlantic forests thickened and the climax trees of the mixed oak forest shaded out pioneer species such as hazel, the nuts and game resources of forest areas declined in productivity and concentrated the attention of native groups on coasts, lakes and rivers where fish and molluscs provided a substantial part of the diet.

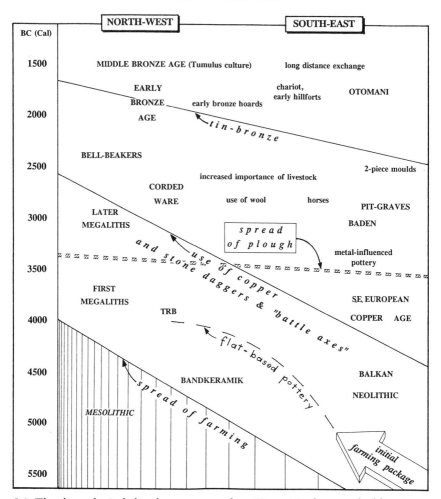

5.1 *The chronological cline between* SE *and* NW *Europe in the spread of farming, metal use and features of the secondary products complex [from Sherratt 1995, fig. 4].*

Two processes, therefore, dominated the development of European societies in the period following this initial establishment of agriculture: one was the differentiation and linkage of the increasingly copper-using groups of south-east and south-central Europe; the other was the expansion of agricultural groups and their interaction with native populations in the outer arc. As a result of these processes, the relative regional homogeneity of the first agricultural communities gave way to a diversity both within and between regions that reached its climax during the fourth millennium BC before giving way to a degree of uniformity within the new corridors of contact which were opened up – the Mediterranean, the North European Plain, the Steppes and the Atlantic Seaboard.

South-east Europe, 5500–4500 BC

The first question, therefore, is the nature of the changes that were taking place in south-east Europe during the fifth millennium BC. This period encompasses the climax of the pattern established in the Balkans during the seventh and sixth millennia, and illustrates a relatively pure 'successional' change in that these societies then underwent an important transformation without interference from adjacent zones. The climax of the tell cultures is represented by a variety of groups whose ceramic distinctiveness is a hall-mark of the period. There is a profusion of substantial settlement sites, rich in the imported materials of everyday life: obsidian, greenstone axes, shell beads. Female figurines, often in elaborate settings of painted clay altars and shrines, are a characteristic feature; though burials (often still in household clusters within settlements rather than in formal cemeteries) are not marked by large accumulations of grave goods. I have tried elsewhere (Chapter 10) to sketch how these systems may have operated. There is no reason to sup-pose that these groups were composed of anything other than autonomous communities and lineages. What is evident is an elaboration of material culture, particularly the decorative elements, at the same time as an increase in regional trade: an intensive production of locally specific pottery types, the production of local specialities like salt and perhaps linen textiles, and a massive transfer of materials like obsidian and flint between adjacent highland and lowland zones. There is also a special emphasis on ritual elements – figurines and house decoration, in south-east Europe, and also some of the first ritual monuments like Kyjovice Těšetice (Moravia), Schalkenburg (central Germany) or Kothingeichendorf (Bavaria) in the related area of the central European loess belt (Höckmann 1972).

These two elements, regional trade and ritual, give a clue to the social mechanisms that organised and linked such communities. The wealth of everyday objects, manufactured to high standards of craftsmanship, repre-sent more than satisfaction of material needs. The flow of such items was clearly vital to social reproduction as much as material survival. This would explain the large quantities of items at the top end of the range of utilitarian goods – well-finished axes, fine pottery, good flint or obsidian tools – that occur in such profusion. Such quantities of valuables were generated by social rather than economic needs (cf. Douglas and Isherwood 1978). Anyone who has a small child is familiar with this principle: every visitor or relative sends another toy digger, fire engine or teddy bear on social occasions, quite beyond the propensity of the child to consume such wealth (he has boxes full upstairs). Similarly with these Neolithic settlements: every site is a bonanza to the archaeologist, who finds great quantities of museum-worthy objects (stored in boxes downstairs) that originally circulated to cement alliances, to purchase wives, or to compensate for offences.

If relations between communities rested on alliances and the flow of material valuables, the proliferation of items with ritual associations suggests that this was important in regulating social life within the community. The common forms of figurines suggest that these ritual codes were widely shared between groups. Indeed, the contrasts between archaeological cultures in this context (e.g. Vinča and Tisza, to take two classic Childean examples), which are evident in their figurine designs and decorative styles but not in their more mundane objects, are likely to reflect not breaks in social interaction (Hodder 1982a) but the limits of particular, consciously held, ideological systems. The general form of these ideologies was probably very similar in the different areas in which they were expressed, since the typical female figurines are all variations on a theme. The basic features of this cult may even be reproduced in very different cultural contexts, though similar social circumstances, in other parts of Europe for which the shadowy presence of a mother goddess has been inferred. We shall return later to the megalithic temples of Malta, but it is perhaps worth noting the association of such Neolithic societies with the worship of female deities or earth spirits. It is this kind of association that lies behind older views – going back to Lewis Henry Morgan and surviving in the canon of Marxist orthodoxy – which describe Neolithic society as 'matriarchal' (e.g. Neustupný and Neustupný 1961). In settlement terms, this phase was characterised by big sites – large communities of several lineage groups with their own burial areas – aggregating for co-operation and defence. In such acephalous groups, intensification of warfare is the other side of the coin from the intensification of trading and ritual activity, and competition between communities for the acquisition of material goods involved both alliance and hostility (Chapter 10).

This, then, is what I mean by ritual formalisation in an east European context. The actual structures that underlay these archaeological manifestations remain to be defined, but we may bear in mind the elaboration of cross-cutting ties – clans and sub-clans, moieties and ceremonial associations – that ethnography suggests may be relevant, and that do not involve hierarchy. Their material evidence, in the form of ceremonial houses, dancing grounds, symbolic oppositions or totemic signs, should not be beyond the perception of archaeology. The hallmark of this type of system – which archaeologically we may term the 'mature' Neolithic, to respect its time-transgressive character and avoid regional terminologies – is the presence of an abundance of material items, mostly of an unspectacular kind, that are imported but not rare, moved by active regional trading networks and circulating as small valuables. Allied to this is the pervasive ritual and symbolic character of material culture in general, which nevertheless lacks the marks of individual rank and achievement.

4500–3500 BC

Some time around the middle of the fifth millennium BC this system was radically changed, marking the beginning of what is locally termed the

'Copper Age' (Chapter 10). The tight regional groupings disappeared; settlements dispersed or became less continuously occupied; burials received greater emphasis (often being easier to find than the settlements); the bulk of regionally traded products was replaced by smaller quantities of exotic items (notably copper and gold); objects symbolising individual status appeared (shafthole axes); the figurines became more schematic and less overtly female; and there are greater contrasts in these new forms of wealth both within regions and in individual cemeteries. The use of ritual within established and long-lived communities was thus replaced by an apparently more fluid system in which more explicit statements about rank were necessary, and a wider range of competition was possible. Even so, there is little indication of hierarchy: the rich burials are the end of a continuum, and occur within the same cemeteries as the others – there was no mobilisation of labour for a Fürstengrab like Helmsdorf or Łęki Małe. Nor are there hoards in the same way as in the Bronze Age.

This pattern continued into the fourth millennium when agricultural settlement was expanding onto the Steppes and the North European Plain. These movements of expansion on the periphery did not take place in isolation: for the increasing scale of inter-regional trade from the Carpathian Basin and the Balkans reached even the outer margins, in Denmark and the Ukraine. These long-distance links were associated with shifts in the centres of prosperity within south-east Europe. Instead of the central agricultural areas, in Thrace or the Körös depression for instance, the areas which rose to prominence were on the edges, at nodal positions between regional systems: in east Slovakia, at Tibava by the critical passes through to the Ukraine (modern frontier crossing-point at Užgorod); on the Black Sea coast at Varna, with its spectacular, gold-filled graves perhaps indicating access to the Anatolian gold; in Kujavia (Brześć Kujawski) on the interface with the North European Plain. Access to metal sources and control of the trade routes was the key to economic and social success, as the rich graves in these areas testify, and the products which crossed regional boundaries included Wolhynian flint in eastern Hungary (Kaczanowska 1980) – especially the long flint dagger blades – and also the first horses (Bökönyi 1978), in return for the Balkan/Carpathian copper objects which appeared at this time as far afield as Ukraine and in Early Neolithic contexts in Denmark.

3500–3000 BC

Although this theme is clearly relevant to the developing picture in northern Europe, we will follow through the sequence in south-east Europe down to the end of the fourth millennium BC; for there follows a classic example of a discontinuity caused by the incorporation of new features from a neighbouring region. That region was the Steppes, where major developments were now occurring. The expansion of population into the dry interfluves altered the economic role of this region in a fundamental way. It now came to act as a bridge between the peripheral Near Eastern cultures of the Caucasus and those of south-east Europe: and many of the features involved in adaptation to the steppe landscape were also relevant to the increasingly open parts of temperate Europe. The early transfer of horses has already been mentioned, though these early specimens – doubtless objects of wonder and curiosity – did not survive as a local breeding stock. Equally important (though contacts with Anatolia may have been equally relevant here) were new breeds of sheep that are evident from the increased size of European stocks at this time (Bökönyi 1974).

In any case, a radical change in the settlement structure of south-east Europe took place at this time, which accelerated the divergence of truly Mediterranean areas (where tree crops now became important) from inland areas. In the Carpathian Basin, the change is manifested in a major shift of population to previously marginal areas both on the edges of the Basin and the surrounding valleys penetrating into the uplands, and on the sandy inter-fluves within it like the area between the Danube and Tisza (Chapter 10). Within the interstices created by this shift, some actual penetration of Steppe tribes seems to have occurred (Ecsedy 1979), for example on the Tisza and lower Danube. As with the Late Woodland phenomenon mentioned above, the effect of a more secure subsistence base was to render some of the spectacular efforts of the previous period largely unnecessary: there is no later-fourth-millennium equivalent to the Varna cemetery, and indeed a relative recession in the copper industry. Social differences were now perhaps evident in more basic ways – between village headmen buried with their draught oxen and their local followers in the Alsónémedi cemetery (Figure 8.1) for instance – than between generally wealthy communities in nodal regions and poorer populations in the hinterlands. Such a foundation had the potential for a taller edifice of social structure, in which hierarchical divisions could cut deeper than ever before – the beginning of the Bronze Age pattern – though it was another millennium before these divisions were to become evident in the rich, fortified centres of Early Bronze Age Hungary, Romania and Slovakia.

Central and northern Europe, 5000–3000 BC
While the south-east had a protracted early agrarian sequence unaffected by neighbouring developments, north-west Europe was from the beginning in contact with a wider network. It was also an area of greater diversity, from the relatively dense coastal native populations to the pioneer farmers of the loess bridgehead. Inevitably, therefore, it did not simply replicate the stages defined for Balkan and Carpathian Europe; though at a deeper level there are some significant resemblances. The sequence on the loess corridor of central Europe has something of a transitional character: it reflected some of the developments of the south-east, but its limited area rather reduced its

importance in the fourth and third millennia when the surrounding regions were opened up. This change in role makes it difficult to treat as an independent entity and it will therefore be considered in conjunction with its northern and western hinterlands. The increasing aggregation of settlement that was characteristic of the early fifth millennium in the Carpathian Basin (Chapter 10) was repeated during the later fifth and early fourth millennia in the central European zone. The clusters of hamlets that were characteristic of the pioneer phase, for example in the Rhineland, were replaced by nucleated, enclosed villages of long-houses. Already, however, small groups were penetrating northwards into the interstices of established Mesolithic groups around the lakes of the North European Plain, and a complex pattern of interaction was beginning.

The origins of the northern Neolithic cultures (TRB) have conventionally been sought either in continuity from local Mesolithic groups or in some fresh wave of agricultural population from further south (e.g. Troels-Smith 1952; *contra*, Becker 1954). The present picture suggests that the new pattern of farming cultures that united both the North European Plain and the northern loesslands, actually originated from interaction on the interface between the two. In some areas, such as Scandinavia, the expansion of farming seems to have followed a relative collapse of local resources (Rowley-Conway 1984); in others, such as Brittany, some kind of fusion seems to have occurred; in the south-east of the British Isles, some colonisation into empty niches seems more likely. Despite these diverse origins, a strongly convergent pattern came about, in which scattered hamlets were focused on small burial-monuments and enclosures that provided continuing points of integration between a diversity of exploited zones. Already, however, there were significant regional exchange systems, which at certain points articulated with long-distance chains reaching back to central and south-east Europe; though these imported objects did not serve to mark an elite in the same way as in Hungary or Bulgaria (Randsborg 1979).

These relatively small-scale systems, limited in territorial extent, were greatly enlarged at the same time as the radical shift which transformed Balkan and Carpathian Copper Age groups. The appearance of plough-marks in northern Europe suggests that these phenomena had a common cause, and that in both areas the use of plough cultivation greatly enlarged the area which could be exploited for agriculture. The effect of this technological innovation, on two contrasting socio-economic systems, was very different: rather than changing the direction of development, as in the south-east, this more extensive form of agriculture actually intensified propensities already present in north-western Europe.

One effect was greatly to extend the area under cultivation, absorbing in the process many of the remnant communities of hunters and fishers. This was accomplished, however, within the existing framework: the megalithic tombs became larger and more elaborate, taking the form of passage-graves rather than simple burial-chambers; the enclosures which seem to represent a level of local integration above that of the monumental tombs reached a peak and then declined; and existing methods of exploiting raw materials either for tools (e.g. flint) or ornaments (e.g. amber) were greatly enlarged. In the loess area this progress was manifested in a shift from the riverine strip to the edge of the interfluvial zone (Kruk 1973; 1980); though since this area lacked the local diversity of the north-western landscape, the foci of this process were nucleated (and now often defended) villages (Bronocice, Dölauer Heide) rather than burial monuments. The common basis of all these societies, however, was an attachment to place and the rituals which were performed there, rather than to individuals of a particular rank.

How were these societies integrated, and in particular how do they compare in this respect with the various stages defined for south-east Europe? My impression is that despite their contemporaneity with the Copper Age and Early Bronze Age groups of that area, they were fundamentally more similar to those of the late Neolithic tell climax, in which ritual (manifested both in the monuments and the artefacts), rather than rank, was the organising principle. As with these earlier 'mature' Neolithic communities, the artefactual repertoire does not distinguish symbols of individual rank, but rather offers a broad range of often finely-made domestic items – such as decorated pottery, stone axes and amber beads – which did not themselves act as sumptuary markers of a particular rank, but served to structure social relations through their use as valuables. Burials were not accompanied by impressive quantities of wealth objects associated with particular individuals, although burial itself was a focus of ritual which involved both monumental construction and the disposal of wealth. The tombs are usually communal, and convey meaning by the arrangement of the bones, rather than by varying quantities of personal grave-goods, which often take the form of offerings at the monument as a whole. Emphasis was on the community rather than the individual, and effort was expended not to commemorate powerful leaders but to enhance corporate prestige and territorial integrity. Moreover, burials in monumental tombs probably represent only a part of the total population; though this in itself does not imply a system of social stratification. The tombs should not be considered as a means of disposing of the dead, but rather of giving significance to selected people whose death was of importance to the groups involved. There was often a considerable interval between death (and exposure of the corpse, which was perhaps the usual means of disposal) and interment in a tomb. The remains selected for such treatment were probably not those of people who occupied a particular rank in their own lifetime, but venerated ancestors who stood in critical genealogical positions in relation to group fissioning.

The main contrast between 'mature Neolithic' groups in south-east and north-west Europe, then, is the elaboration of mortuary ritual which characterises the latter. It can be argued that this is more an expression of local ecology than of fundamental differences in social organisation. Funerary monuments are typical of areas of early agricultural settlement beyond the loess, and are associated with the particular conditions of the North European Plain and the Atlantic coastlands – unlike the defended centres, which also occur on the loess. Monumental tombs are characteristic of areas where settlement was still constrained – note their occurrence in clusters and linear arrangements in relation to river-valleys – but where large aggregated communities were not possible. They represent foci and territorial markers for an expanded (though not dispersed) pattern of settlement, particularly in core areas like the Danish islands where settlement was relatively dense. Other types of non-monumental 'earth-graves' occur in less densely settled zones like western Jutland (Randsborg 1975), where a seasonally mobile way of life may have persisted, that was perhaps also characteristic of the earliest phase of settlement in the core area. The monuments thus mark a phase of saturation and the crystallisation of defined territorial units.

Such monumental tombs served not only to legitimate rights to particular territories, but were also agents of social control within the groups. One striking feature, both of long barrows and 'causewayed' enclosures, is the composite nature of their construction – reflected in discontinuous quarry ditches as well as constructional compartments[4] that seem to relate to corporate work-groups involved in their construction. Rather than simply representing the tombs of different lineages, therefore, the tombs may be the products of cross-cutting local associations which provided a focus of political allegiance. This would be particularly important if surviving Mesolithic groups retained a corporate existence within the agrarian territorial structure, and such monuments would thus be particularly developed in areas where native populations were integrated into Neolithic societies at a local level.

This interpretation of the social basis of the megalith-building groups of north-west Europe does not imply that such groups were essentially egalitarian – in the sense that there was no conflict of interests between different status- and kinship-groups – for it is basic to the idea of such ritual-centred organisations that competition took place between (probably ex-ogamous) local units, and that certain sections of the population (notably senior men) exercise dominance within them. But authority was localised, and there was no hierarchy in the sense of successive tiers of authority: rather, dominant groups promoted a common ideology which supported their own interests within the unit, and left them free to engage in competition for prestige between units. This probably took the form of competitive feasting – 'fighting with wealth' – involving both consumption of subsistence goods and the ritual destruction of material items, e.g. pot-smashing. Differences in wealth between units (whether communities or lineages) are therefore to be expected and are indeed manifested in the different quantities of offerings associated with communal tombs, just as there are notably 'wealthy' settlements among the Neolithic villages of south-east Europe. Such differences in wealth, however, do not add up to a conical pattern of ranking between communities and these must still be considered as largely autonomous.

3000–2500 BC

This parallelism with the 'mature Neolithic' phase of the south-eastern sequence is even more striking in its transition to a pattern which reversed many of these elements – the disappearance of large, central sites and the dispersal of population; the decline in ritual elements and the appearance of status-symbolic artefacts; the development of long-distance trade (especially in metal) rather than in common regional items. These new features characterise the Corded Ware cultures that succeeded the variety of megalith-building groups throughout the North European Plain and initiated the pattern that was to characterise the second millennium BC; and in this sense, it may still be useful to describe the Corded Ware and Beaker periods as 'Copper Age'.

One evident feature of this period was a major phase of internal colonisation penetrating more deeply into the interfluvial areas of the loess and cover sands, and extending agrarian occupation to the outwash sands of the North European Plain. Settlement had a greater fluidity, with less substantial and long-lived sites, and a shorter-term investment in burial monuments: single graves under round barrows[5] rather than long megalithic or earth-built structures. Material culture had a more segmentary character; a consistently replicated series of status-kits comprising a personal drinking vessel and weapon (battle-axe) which accompanied a large number of males to the grave. These symbols became internationalised to a much larger extent, even integrating neighbouring hunting and fishing groups within a single framework of status codes, as in central Scandinavia and the Baltic regions.

This pattern did not emerge in a uniform way over the whole of the North European Plain. It seems to have crystallised earlier in the east, perhaps in central Germany and eastern Poland, and to have spread like a domino effect westwards into the megalithic heartlands, as far as the North Sea. This complex seems to have penetrated within and around the established TRB communities of the Low Countries and Scandinavia, before absorbing them into the new pattern. It opened up a new east–west corridor that articulated at its eastern end with the expanding Steppe groups, transmitting horses and woolly sheep (as well as artefacts such as hammer-headed bone pins) directly across the open landscape of northern Europe, and restructuring the communities of the adjacent loess belt. It did not, however, penetrate westwards as far as the British Isles or large parts of northern France (Seine-Oise-Marne culture), where the earlier pattern of territorially focused communities persisted (Howell 1982).

146

This linkage, from the forest Steppe to the Atlantic sea-board, was a manifestation of the speed of forest clearance on the lighter soils of the North European Plain. The increased size of cultivated area followed a greater development of the pastoral sector of a mixed farming economy based on light plough agriculture, with an emphasis on the male role in warfare and protection of an acquired territory. It produced a similar, segmentary social structure over a large interconnected area, with the ability to penetrate and corrode the more static structures of surrounding groups. In the following centuries, this pattern was to spread, and be further enriched, by contact along the Atlantic coast, the Rhone, and across the western Alps: the Bell Beaker network.

The central and west Mediterranean, 5000–3000 BC

It is now time to consider the third major geographical division, the central and western Mediterranean. During the earlier fourth millennium there was no major opening-up of new areas for settlement as in northern Europe, and a relatively stable pattern of large villages with stone or rock-cut tombs occupied the more fertile zones within it, at a relatively low overall density. Exchange networks carrying material such as obsidian linked islands such as Sardinia with the adjacent mainland, but these had a limited, regional scope. Some signs of the elaboration of territorial foci were in evidence, in the beginning of megalithic construction in Iberia and in the prototypes of the trefoil-shaped temples in Malta.

As in north-west Europe, the mid-fourth millennium saw an increase in the scale of these activities, without a discontinuity of developmental trajectory. Tomb and temple construction became more elaborate, with a concomitant appearance of small cult objects such as female figurines. Craft production developed, with copper axes supplementing stone ones and pottery bearing a profusion of ornamental and symbolic signs including the 'oculus' motif.

These features bear a general resemblance to those of the megalithic cultures of north-west Europe and they probably shared a similar form of social organisation. Increasingly, however, a further process of spatial expansion and inter-regional linkage introduced new elements, both from northern Europe and from the east Mediterranean. This expansion can plausibly be attributed to the use of the light plough, which assisted in the opening-up of the interfluves in the same way as in other areas of Europe at this time, and to specific features of the drier Mediterranean environment: the cultivation of tree crops along with an expansion of sheep rearing, and also fishing. An important outcome was the colonisation of new areas, particularly highlands like the limestone plateaux of Languedoc and islands like Lipari, which acted as nodal points in inter-regional contacts. Fortification was a notable feature of Mediterranean settlement patterns, both at large villages such as Los Millares (Almeria)[6] and smaller fortified enclosures like Zambujal (Portugal) and Lébous (southern France). The new external links promoted the rapid spread of particular features such as bastion fortification which can be traced throughout the length of the Mediterranean. These contacts can also be seen in portable artefacts, like the distribution of Castelluccio bone plaques.

This growing network of regional links within the Mediterranean began to be articulated with the long-distance routes reaching down from northern Europe. The characteristic combination of drinking vessel (sometimes a beaker but often a local form of handled cup) and personal weapons (now a dagger and arrows rather than a battle-axe) began to appear in male graves, though normally these were rock-cut tombs more appropriate to a Mediterranean environment than the earthen barrows of the north. This emphasis on the male warrior began to replace that on the female figure in representations, stelae and rock engraving.[7] The transition was most rapid in Italy and southern France, with their more direct northward connections, but also penetrated to the islands (e.g. Corsica). In Iberia the change was less clear-cut, and was only fully complete in the second millennium with the appearance of the Argaric culture with its male warrior burials. The pattern of settlement in the Mediterranean, however, continued to be based on defended centres now often positioned on spectacular heights.

As with the British Isles in relation to the North European Plain, there were spatial limits to this penetration, and in peripheral areas an older stratum survived and continued to develop along its own lines. In Malta the temples serving a female divinity reached a peak of elaboration in the earlier third millennium, culminating in the massive structures of Tarxien and the nearby Hypogeum. The stability of these temple-centres, of which over a dozen are known, is indicated by their cumulative rebuilding and extension, and this territorial stability must be related to the finite size and relative isolation of the island; these laboratory conditions allowed the undisturbed growth of perhaps the most complex of these ritual-centred organisations.

The British Isles

Britain itself must also be considered as part of the archaic fringe to which continental innovations were introduced at a relatively late stage, and which continued to develop along its existing trajectory to take an older pattern to new heights of elaboration. While large enclosures and other monuments to territorial stability largely disappeared in adjacent areas of the continent during the third millennium BC, many parts of the British Isles saw a renewed phase of monumental construction, either of large passage graves like Maes Howe or Newgrange in northern and western Britain in the later fourth millennium, or of henges like Avebury or Durrington Walls – the latter being significantly close to earlier territorial foci – in the south in the third millennium BC. The scale of such construction, however, was entirely new; and the ritual landscapes of the British chalklands – for instance the triangle of Avebury and its avenues, the 'Sanctuary' and Silbury Hill – represent a concentration of effort unparalleled before. In this case, the relative isolation from the Corded Ware 'domino effect' was reinforced by the local setting of continued territorial expansion, which was internally focused within the chalklands and adjacent gravel terraces, rather than externally directed to the large areas of outwash sands as it was in the North European Plain. This elaboration of ritual and territorial foci seems to have been an alternative to the segmentary organisation reflected in Beaker 'status-kits', which began to be represented in parts of Britain, outside the main henge areas. This 'Beaker' pattern led to the formation of rich individual burials in Wessex itself shortly before 2000 BC, associated with the erection of stone settings in the earlier earth and timber henges, e.g. at Avebury and Stonehenge. The 'Beaker' pottery lost its role as a status item and merged with the rest of the domestic pottery assemblage to form the basis of the Bronze Age wares of the second millennium. These were associated with a major spatial expansion into more marginal areas outside the earlier chalkland foci, in the manner of Corded Ware and Early Bronze Age expansion on the Continent.

This third-millennium phase of ritual monuments represented by henges, like the Maltese temples discussed above, clearly went beyond the simple, relatively autonomous character of earlier ritual-centred forms of social organisation. They may well have been associated with a specialised ritual caste with access to esoteric (e.g. astronomical) knowledge, rather than simply being run by lineage heads or village elders in the way that may be imagined for earlier Neolithic ritual monuments. But although they were able to mobilise impressive quantities of labour, this apparently did not extend to the accumulation of surplus produce or the extensive patronage of manufacturing operations based upon it. These properties, and the 'conical' patterns of ranking that underlay them, only emerged from the more explicitly individualising warrior-centred form of organisation associated with Corded Ware and Beakers.

CONCLUSION: SPACE, TIME AND SOCIAL STRUCTURE

This brief review of the contrasts between successive and contemporary groups in different parts of Europe demonstrates the difficulty of applying any simple scheme of social evolution to this phase of maximum diversification. Nevertheless, some common elements have been identified, as well as trends which were to result in a much greater degree of convergence during the Bronze Age.

A basic theme of discussion has been the contrast between east and west. Many of the most conspicuous artefacts of this phase – the megalithic and earthen monuments of western Europe – have no direct parallels in the east.

Yet the types of society which they represent may, at a deeper level, have a fundamental resemblance to already superseded stages of social development in those parts of Europe which had been settled by agricultural communities at an earlier date (Figure 5.1). The evident contrasts stem from the historical and environmental setting of their respective developments, and the relative isolation of the western periphery which allowed a further elaboration of social forms which in other areas had been rapidly extinguished.

These contrasting trajectories determined the different reactions of the various areas to the major technological and economic innovations of the period, the secondary products complex (Chapter 6). The rapid spread of features like the plough and woolly sheep cross-cut local successions of social development, and they were integrated into local systems in different ways. In the east, they caused something of a recession in the production of spectacular elite items such as the goldwork of Varna; in the west they accelerated and increased the scale of monument construction and territorial demarcation, giving a further twist to the elaboration of ritual integration. In this way the effect of these innovations was to increase regional contrasts, even though in the longer term it was to provide a more uniform basis for convergent development.

Although elites of different kinds were produced by the various processes which have been defined, with a measure of ranking both within and between communities, there are no signs of substantial contrasts between different levels of society that would deserve the term 'stratification'; nor of the cumulative addition of levels of executive authority that could be described as a hierarchy. The basic building block of Neolithic and Copper Age societies was the community or lineage, and the bonds between them were the fragile ones of exogamy and alliance.

Within this framework, however, there was a variety of ways in which social relations might be organised. An important variable was the layout of settlement on the ground. Although Europe went through a protracted process of 'filling up', this did not produce a simple linear increase in population pressure and stress on land: instead, we can observe small cycles of infilling within particular zones, followed by the unlocking of further zones either within or beyond the region. The plough in particular opened up extensive areas for cultivation (incidentally increasing the pastoral component of agricultural economies) which allowed a more rapid process of spatial expansion than was characteristic of the often river-based patterns of initial land-taking. Paradoxically, therefore, analogies with slash-and-burn farmers in the tropics may be more relevant to the later Neolithic than to the early Neolithic, whose constrained commitment to zones of primary productivity is perhaps more analogous to that of the lowland rice farmers.

The implication of these patterns of expansion can be taken further. In an illuminating article on stateless societies in West Africa, Horton (1976) has discussed the circumstances under which lineages and corporations based on principles other than descent become important media of social organisation. He contrasts the conditions of unconstrained expansion, in which dispersed settlement is the norm and spatial and genealogical distance maintain an approximate equivalence, with constrained expansion where 'leap-frogging' and disjunctive migration become necessary. In the former case, segmentary lineages can occur in which a single genealogical scheme can embrace many thousands of people; in the latter, aggregates composed of several lineages are formed, which must be integrated by cross-cutting ties and a genealogical definition of landholding rights is replaced by a territorial one. Co-residence, rather than common descent, becomes the focus of political allegiance.

Such territorially-based societies may be of two kinds: those where the political community coincides with a large, nucleated village, and those where its members are scattered in a number of smaller settlements. In the former case, the role of lineages is subordinated to cross-cutting institutions based on age grades, secret societies, and especially ritual groupings – 'a cluster of adaptations to the problem posed by the presence in the community of strong and rivalrous lineages' (ibid., 96). In the latter, the lineages maintain their importance as social groupings within the territorial unit, whose role in this potentially fissiparous situation is stressed by the cult of an earth spirit that unites the constituent descent groups. In this case, the head of the leading lineage usually acts as cult priest and presides over internal affairs.

Now these distinctions correspond in a rough way to some of the contrasts which have emerged in discussing the societies of later Neolithic and Copper Age Europe. While there are no equivalents here to the pioneer societies of the earlier Neolithic, there are striking resemblances between the institutions that have been inferred for the large Neolithic villages of south-east Europe and the loess area, for instance, and those of stateless groups in West Africa such as the Kalabari. The problems of scattered, but territorially defined, groups like the Lodagaa are paralleled by the megalith-building communities of north-west Europe, and were apparently solved in a similar way, through a focus in territorial ritual.

Can the properties inferred for 'Copper Age' societies (both the fourth-millennium examples from south-east Europe and third-millennium examples from the North European Plain) be related to a pattern of segmentary lineages (Kristiansen 1982)? Settlement was both dispersed and expanding in space, producing the (temporary) conditions under which genealogical reckoning was an effective way of maintaining an expanding series of relationships, and reducing the emphasis on territorial definition. In such a system there is no permanent political community, but rather adventitious combinations for particular threats, drawing on as large a kinship range as necessary. This equivalence of segments and relativity of political grouping – overlapping egocentred units – leads to a predominance of leadership over authority: political position is a matter of external negotiation rather than internal control. In such circumstances, the role of individual lineage heads becomes crucial, both as a widespread status position (marked by an appropriate set of sumptuary artefacts?) and as a potential focus for wider allegiances in a shifting configuration of political structures (with the possibility of achieving individual prominence in the process). In this context, we can understand the emergence both of inter-regional symbols of rank, such as stone or copper battleaxes or decorated drinking vessels. The deposition of these items in graves (as Shennan, 1982, remarks) was important in the process of defining succession to these ranks and their acquired prestige. Moreover, this type of organisation has the property of being able to spread at the expense of surrounding groups – Marshall Sahlins (1961) has called it an 'organisation of predatory expansion'. This seems a particularly appropriate description of the spread of Corded Ware and its impact on the ritually focused megalith-builders.

The main contrast in the European succession is thus between two sorts of societies. The first was characterised by stable flows of regionally-acquired goods, and was organised on an established territorial basis, with public rituals and symbolic analogies based on female images. The societies which superseded them were characterised by a greater emphasis on exotic goods and longer-distance trading contacts often of a less stable and more adventitious kind, in which information-carrying items took precedence over more basic commodities. Their territorial basis was less stable, their ethos was a competitive and self-aggrandising one, with sumptuary codes of artefact use and symbolic analogies based on the image of the warrior male. More generally, we can perhaps discern in these European sequences an underlying shift from societies organised primarily on the basis of community (whether a single settlement or several sites with a common focus) to an increased emphasis on the potential of kinship for forming wider networks of alliance than had hitherto been realised.[8] This is perhaps the clue to the new properties which emerged in Copper Age systems in temperate Europe.

This latter type of social structure provided the basis for Bronze Age development, in which the scale of inter-regional exchange was expanded from a primary concern with symbolic items to include a greater volume of 'consumer durables' like textiles and bronze tools. This involved a greater organisation of local production for inter-regional exchange, with regional specialisation in commodities and manufactured products which were more widely available but still supplied through an elite. With the gradual filling-up of the continent during the second millennium, differential access to productive land became more significant and provided preconditions for the emergence of true stratification. At the same time the expansion of urban trading networks from the east Mediterranean started a process of interaction with indigenous European communities, to produce the core-periphery pattern of the first-millennium Iron Age (Frankenstein and Rowlands 1978).

The societies of later prehistoric Europe thus provide an extended series of examples of the processes operating in the early stages of social differentiation. Such societies are arguably poorly represented both in the ethnographic record, and in the archaeological evidence from nuclear regions where these types of society were rapidly superseded. European Neolithic and Bronze Age archaeology thus represents a prime source for the study of such phenomena. It may be complemented by the study of other areas – for instance Polynesia – whose relative remoteness from expanding core areas of states and empires allowed indigenous sequences to achieve a measure of social complexity. An understanding of social change requires a continuing dialogue between the evidence of ethnography and archaeology. By a better definition of their own material, archaeologists will be in a better position to understand the relevance of other branches of anthropology to it.

NOTES

1. The terminology of period divisions in European prehistory has been elaborated over more than a century and is still inconsistent. 'Neolithic' was first defined as the later part of the Stone Age in opposition to 'Palaeolithic'; the idea of a 'Copper Age' before the beginning of the Bronze Age grew up as a local concept both in Ireland and Hungary in the 1870s. National terminologies have incorporated this usage (often in the form 'Chalcolithic' or 'Eneolithic'), but these usages are often mutually inconsistent and in any case do not precisely conform to the beginning of copper use in any particular area. This article uses calibrated radiocarbon dates to give absolute ages. The terms 'mature Neolithic' and 'Copper Age' are used in a descriptive sense to denote particular types of social systems that are defined in the text. 'Copper Age' thus denotes a system in which copper objects are used in a particular way, rather than a period defined by the first use of metal.
2. Recent social theories (Giddens, A. 1979, *Central Problems in Social Theory*, London, Macmillan; Harré, R. 1979, *Social Being*, Oxford, Blackwell) have attempted to overcome the essentially static nature of conceptions of social structure based on fixed roles and functions, determined by efficient adaptation to external (usually economic) circumstances. Instead they have proposed a more dynamic view in which individuals and groups manipulate their shifting advantages in a continuous process of negotiation (called 'structuration' by Giddens) which itself creates and defines the patterns of social life. While this overcomes some of the problems associated with the endless search for a 'prime mover' of social change, it has yet to be formulated in a way which is relevant to changes on an archaeological ('evolutionary') timescale.
3. For a more systematic general account of European prehistory and that of adjacent areas (with references), see Sherratt (1980).
4. Such compartments are seen both in earthen long barrows, where they are defined by hurdling, and cairns like the Severn-Cotswold barrows, where the mound was constructed of dry-stone cells filled with material from the quarry-ditches, themselves dug in a series of intersecting pits. This suggests an organisation of several co-operating groups, perhaps on the scale postulated by W. Startin (*PPS* 1978, vol. 44, pp. 143–59), for construction of a *Bandkeramik* longhouse. Such a co-operating unit, itself segmentary in character, would represent a political community but not necessarily a co-resident group. This may be the logic behind the settlement clusters definable in Neolithic settlement patterns in several areas.

5. Such tombs still had a 'monumental' aspect in that they were covered with earth mounds, which might form small cemeteries through the accumulation of satellite and secondary burials. A role as territorial markers is evident from their occurrence on interfluves and on sight-lines, but not all such burials were marked by mounds. In some areas where spatial expansion was not occurring, flat graves are found – sometimes in large cemeteries – e.g. Vikletice, Bohemia.

6. The Almerian collective burials in tholoi (nearly ninety at Los Millares) differ from other European megalithic tombs in their direct associations with a large adjacent settlement: in this case the tombs may directly reflect lineages within the community. These appear to be ranked in wealth and this pattern is probably associated with the continuing importance of limited areas of wet bottomlands in this arid environment.

7. This occurs on menhirs in the west Mediterranean, and also on Cycladic figurines.

8. This is not to deny the existence of extensive kinship networks in earlier times, especially among Upper Palaeolithic hunters in open environments; but it suggests that an initial effect of the introduction of agriculture (or other forms of existence involving large, sedentary communities) was to place the emphasis of social organisation foremost on community. This would be the case both in the large settlements of the Neolithic of central and south-east Europe, and in the Neolithic of western Europe where 'big monuments' replaced 'big sites'. The formation of more extensive kinship networks would then represent a shift to forms of social organisation that were less tied to patterns of residence and the existence of large, stable settlements.

DISCOVERING THE SECONDARY PRODUCTS COMPLEX

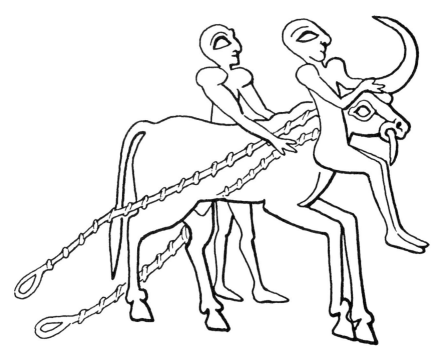

Impression of a cylinder-seal of the Uruk period, c.3500 BC, showing two men harnessing an ox (British Museum: drawing by Ann Searight).

Als man Milch trank, und den Ochsen an den Pflug spannte, waren wesentlich alle Bedingungen für unsere asiatisch-europäische Kultur vorhanden.

(When milk was drunk, and the ox yoked to the plough, all the conditions for our Asiatic-European culture were present.)

EDUARD HAHN (1896)

'Our understanding of Old World animal management after the initial provision of a captive meat supply was put on a new footing by Andrew Sherratt's now classic study of 1981', wrote Stuart Piggott (1992, 13), having earlier (1983, 34) called it 'important and stimulating' but the phenomenon in question 'unhappily named'. Alas, quite true – but deliberately so. I have tendentiously titled this section '*Discovering ...*', but it would be more in tune with contemporary terminology if I had written '*Inventing* the Secondary Products Complex' – or Secondary Products Revolution, as I even more tendentiously termed it at the time. The rhetorical flourish of an admittedly ugly title was a necessary strategy to ensure the visibility of the concept.

That strategy apparently succeeded; for not only is the concept enshrined in the new *Oxford Companion to Archaeology* (with which I have no editorial links), but the term is used in several British universities to structure their teaching of later European prehistory. There is obviously a need to find punctuation points within the long sequence of agrarian communities before the arrival of bronze – a period which has successively increased in length with every advance in absolute dating since the invention (or discovery?) of radiocarbon dating. It clearly, therefore, fulfils a need in current expository schemes: but did it ever really happen?

That depends, of course, on how it is conceived. 'This was a time of considerable intensification of farming production, using a whole range of devices and inventions in agriculture and in animal husbandry. Some of these are well encapsulated in Sherratt's term the "secondary products revolution"', writes Colin Renfrew (1994, 159–60), presenting a minimalist interpretation – for he goes on to qualify his acceptance of the idea: 'but unfortunately his exposition involves the diffusionist assumption that the innovations in question had an eastern origin, a point that has been effectively countered (Chapman 1982; see Bogucki 1988). As noted above, these diffusionist arguments rest as much on faith as on material evidence, and the positive features of his model are just as well described under the rubric of the intensification of farming systems.'

In this minimalist form, it still fulfils one of the intentions which I had in (well, yes, frankly) inventing the concept: to emphasise the *otherness* of early farming. Terms such as 'hunting' or 'farming' carry a heavy baggage of contemporary images and assumptions, which it is anachronistic to retroject deep into the past. On the one hand, it is necessary to choose some term from contemporary language; on the other, any term cannot quite fit earlier circumstances – for instance the combination of cereal cultivation and gazelle-hunting practised by the early inhabitants of Jericho. Bundling together all the features now characteristic of Old World farming – but not present at the beginning, nor represented, for instance, in native North American farming – was a convenient way of summarising the very different character of early Old World cultivation systems. Use of the term 'revolution', however, suggested a stadial, evolutionary model underlying it, which it was not part of my intention to convey; and this would be the core of my disagreement with Colin Renfrew, for I do not believe that these changes could have happened if Europe had remained in complete isolation.

Fundamental to my conception of why the SPR did happen, and why its successive impacts in mid- and late-fourth-millennium BC Europe were so concentrated, was its intimate connection to Gordon Childe's Urban Revolution in Mesopotamia. This, as I suggest in the final chapter in this volume, is the 'revolution' to which its European impact is due – just as the fundamental impact which farming itself had on Europe some three millennia earlier was due to the Neolithic Revolution in the same area. It was the unique characteristics of that intimate intermixture of the desert, the steppe and the sown which made the area between the Mediterranean and the Persian Gulf into such a power-house of innovations (Sherratt 1996).

6

Plough and Pastoralism: Aspects of the Secondary Products Revolution

(1981)

The contrast between the development of agriculture in the Old and New Worlds is an instructive one. In both, the domestication of a cereal crop allowed a massive increase in population, first in village communities and later in towns and cities. The major difference lay in the role of animal domesticates. In the New World there were few counterparts to the range of domesticated animals which were an integral part of Old World systems; in North America only the turkey, and in South America the guinea-pig and the Andean camelids, played a comparable role to the sheep, cattle and equids of Eurasia.

The first implication of this contrast is the primary role in the 'Neolithic Revolution' which was played in both hemispheres by the domestication of plants, and especially cereals. Cultivation alone, without the extensive use of domestic animals, was able to sustain even complex urban societies. But it is not without significance that the next threshold, that of industrial-isation, was attained only in the Old World; for the employment of animal-power as the first stage in the successive harnessing of increasingly powerful sources of energy beyond that of human muscle was only possible where these animals were domestic, not wild. The critical differences between the

David Clarke's death in 1976, at the age of 38, was a devastating blow. Ian Hodder and I discussed compiling a volume of papers. I wanted to write the best paper of which I was capable, and this was it. (Even Glyn Daniel – no admirer of New Archaeology – liked it, as I discovered from an unfinished review tucked inside his copy, sold after his death.) It builds on comments that David made on my Ph.D. thesis, about the fundamental nature of the transition from the Balkan Copper Age to the Early Bronze Age, and continued in the comparative (and interactionist) way which he encouraged. The paper would not have been possible without the pervasive influence of David Clarke. Many of its ideas had their roots in his suggestions and remarks. His enthusiasm and criticism were sadly missed in writing it.

utilisation of animals in the Old and New World lay less in their uses as a source of meat than in their emergent properties when other applications were explored – their 'secondary products'.

The distinguishing feature of agrarian development in the Old World, therefore, is the interaction between plant and animal domesticates. Of major importance in this process is the plough – the first application of animal-power to the mechanisation of agriculture. Closely connected with this is the use of the cart, with its contribution not only to more intensive farming but to the transportation of its products. These two innovations resulted from a new application of domesticated cattle. Comparable advances in transport resulted from the domestication of the equids and their use as draught- and pack-animals. Also, secondary features of domesticated ovicaprids – notably the development of wool in sheep – allowed a new range of uses for these animals in providing fibres suitable for textiles. Finally, the regular milking of domesticated animals provided a variety of storable products and made possible a continuous flow of food without slaughtering the stock.

These features were not part of the original complex of plant and animal domestication in the Old World. Archaeological evidence for this range of secondary uses and products of domesticated animals is naturally very varied and of uneven value. Nevertheless, where these features can be dated, it is apparent that they only appear five millennia or so after the beginnings of agriculture in the Near East, and some three or four millennia after its introduction to Europe. There was thus a long primary phase of agricultural development before the secondary uses of domesticated animals were discovered and applied. Moreover, many of these features appeared within a similar span of time, some four to five thousand years ago. While they are by no means exactly contemporary, their appearance together at approximately the halfway point in the development of agriculture in the Old World, marking the beginnings of a phase of interaction between the plant and animal components and the earliest non-human sources of energy, perhaps deserves some explicit recognition: and it is in this spirit that I venture to burden an already over-taxed archaeological vocabulary with yet another revolution – the Secondary Products Revolution of the Old World.

These secondary products had important applications both in the intensification of agricultural production and in the sphere of transport, trade and personal mobility. The plough increased production and made economic the cultivation of a range of poorer-quality soils; it thus resulted in the colonisation of a wider area than had been possible under previous systems of cultivation. Both the ox-cart and the horse, as well as the pack-donkey, opened up new possibilities for bulk transport and reduced the friction of distance. They made economic a range of locations and settlement types, including systems with cities, which would otherwise have involved huge amounts of effort. The development of textiles made from animal fibres

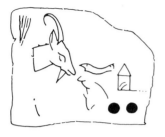 

6.1 *Clay tablets from Uruk with symbols in pictographic script, including the sign for 'cart'. Uruk period, late fourth millennium* BC *(after Falkenstein 1936).*

gave for the first time a commodity which could be produced for exchange in areas where arable production was not the optimal form of land use. The use of milk made much larger herds economical, making use of exhausted and otherwise marginal land and encouraging the development of the pastoral sector with transhumance or even nomadism.

This bundle of innovations produced two types of society and subsistence systems which were unknown in pre-contact aboriginal America: plough-using agriculturalists, and pastoralists. The two were frequently in geographical proximity and interaction and their relations, both of conflict and symbiosis, are a recurring theme in the history of the Old World. Anthropologists have long recognised (and are increasingly emphasising; Goody 1976) the importance of plough agriculture as a predictor of social systems involving new mechanisms of inheritance as a result of the importance which the transmission of land acquires in such economies. Groups with a major pastoral component, too, have characteristic social features, such as strongly patrilineal descent groups, which are unlikely to have been associated with earlier hoe cultivators. The revolution was thus not simply a matter of subsistence and economics: it was a threshold of social development as well.

It would be surprising if so radical a set of changes were without evident traces in the archaeological record. While the secondary utilisation of animals can be shown from representations, or occasionally glimpsed directly where the evidence is favourably preserved, the striking changes in the distribution and character of settlement in Europe in the third millennium BC are eloquent testimony to a major alteration in the condition of life. Coming at a time when settlement in many of the older-settled areas had expanded to its limits, and long-term soil deterioration had begun to set in, these changes define a 'second generation' of agrarian economies in Europe, and the beginnings of a new cycle of expansion in the Bronze Age.

The 'secondary products revolution' thus separates two stages in the development of Old World agriculture: an initial stage of hoe cultivation, whose technology and transportation systems were based upon human muscle-power, and in which animals were kept purely for meat; and a second stage in which both plough agriculture and pastoralism can be recognised, with a technology using animal sources of energy. The former mode of life is now extinct in the temperate and sub-tropical parts of the Old World, though it may have important analogies with agriculture or semi-agriculture as practised in aboriginal temperate North America. The secondary products revolution marked the birth of the kinds of society characteristic of modern Eurasia.

DATING EVIDENCE

The use of animal traction

Although cattle were fully domesticated at least by the sixth millennium BC, they were not systematically used as traction animals until the later fourth millennium, when a specific technology was developed to make use of this. The most important applications were to the plough and the cart. The evidence will be reviewed separately here, but it is clear that the two spread as a closely related complex.

The cart. Earliest unambiguous indications of the use of the cart (Figure 6.1) come from archaic Sumerian pictograms from Uruk in southern Mesopotamia (Falkenstein 1936, signs 742–5). These date to the first half of the fourth millennium BC. From the succeeding Early Dynastic period there is a wealth of evidence from representations and actual cart burials. Clay models of vehicles with two or four solid wheels occur at this time over a wide area including northern Syria, northern Iraq, eastern Turkey, northern Iran and Transcaucasia. Mesopotamian examples are mostly vehicles for use in war, but the ones from further north include 'covered wagon' forms well suited for use in regions at the junction of steppe and forest (Piggott 1968 [and now 1983 for the early history of wheeled vehicles in general]).

Comparable vehicles are known to have been used at least during the third millennium BC on the steppe-lands north of the Caucasus and the Black Sea. Several groups of barrows near Elista on the Kalmuk steppe between the Caucasus and the Volga have produced evidence of carts. The most famous example, Tri Brata, contained both wooden wheels and a model of a two-wheeled cart. A somewhat later example from Kudinov on the lower Don contained a complete four-wheeled wagon. Similar finds occur on the lower Dnepr.

In Eastern Europe the most striking evidence is the handled drinking-cup in the form of a four-wheeled wagon from Budakalász near Budapest in Hungary, now with another example (Figure 6.2a) from Szigetszentmárton (Kalicz 1976). These belong to the Baden culture, as does the cemetery of Alsónémedi with its double bovid burial [cow and calf in Alsónémedi graves 3 and 28, two calves in the comparable grave 3 at Budakalász – presumably

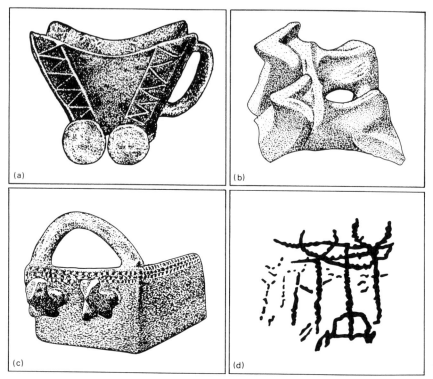

6.2 *Early evidence of ox-traction in Europe: (a) cup in the form of a wagon from a Baden culture grave at Szigetszentmárton, Hungary; (b) handle in the form of two yoked oxen,* TRB *culture Krężnica Jara, Poland; (c) pottery 'cart' with two protomes, Baden culture, Radošina, Slovakia; (d) pecked scene of oxen drawing a cart, from a megalithic cist at Züschen, Germany; after Kalicz (1976), Němejcová-Pavúková (1973) and Uenze (1958).*

to avoid killing valuable draught-oxen] indicative of paired draught (see below Korek, Behrens 1964). [It is notable that there are several pedestalled cups whose bowl is a wheel-less wagon body (Banner 1956, plate 114 nos 1–7); and also that the Budakalász wagon-cup had its own grave (no.177) – a cenotaph without a body.] A somewhat larger vessel in the form of a wagon, without wheels but with two animal (ox?) protomes protruding from the front, comes from Radošina in Slovakia (Figure 6.2c), from an early Baden (Boleráz) context (Němejcová-Pavúková 1973, fig. 3). Radio-carbon dates for this culture indicate a date of 3400–3100 BC. Double ox burials appear at the same time in over a dozen examples in the Globular Amphora culture in Poland and central Germany (and may be present in Middle Neolithic Denmark, though bone is less well preserved). Evidence from representations is also available in the form of a pottery handle show-ing a pair of yoked oxen from Krężnica Jara, Lublin (Figure 6.2b), in the context of the south-east TRB group, datable to the later fourth millennium BC, and also from a stone with a pecked schematic scene (Figure 6.2d) in

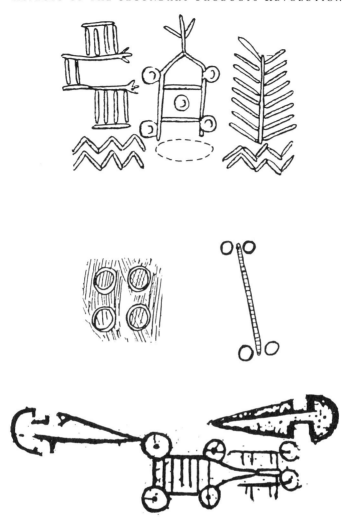

6.3 Above: *representation of a four-wheeled wagon on a* TRB *pot from Bronocice (Phase III, 3500–3100), Little Poland: Milisauskas and Kruk 1982;* middle: *motif in schematic form on contemporary Polish* TRB *pots from Inowrocław-Mątwy and Ostrowiec Świętokrzyski (Midgley 1992, figs 13 and 108);* below: *wagon-representation from below the belt of a statue-menhir from Lagunda, Alto Adige, Italy (other examples have a plough in the same position): [new drawing].*

a Hesse collective-burial cist at Lohne (Züschen) with a similar dating (Uenze 1958). The scene is a vertical view of pairs of oxen yoked to what are probably carts. A similar view of a four-wheeled vehicle has recently been found in a TRB context at Bronocice in south-east Poland (Milisauskas and Kruk 1978: see Figure 6.3).

Finds of actual cart components have been made in Europe only in water-logged contexts. Wheels from the Netherlands and Denmark have been dated by pollen analysis and radiocarbon dating to the third-millennium BC

6.4 *Clay tablets of the fourth millennium* BC *with symbols in pictographic script, including the sign for 'plough': above,* from Uruk, Mesopotamia (Uruk period); *below,* from Susa, Khuzestan (proto-Elamite period). After Falkenstein (1936) and Scheil (1923).

Corded-ware period (van der Waals 1964; Rostholm 1977). Two yokes, one from Switzerland (Vinelz) and one from Lower Saxony (Petersfehn), may also be of third-millennium date (Gandert 1964).

Turning east, there are many examples of models showing solid-wheeled carts from the Harappan culture of the mid-third millennium BC in northeast India. In China, however (as also apparently in Egypt), the wheel only arrived in its spoked form in the second millennium. This spread across central Asia was associated with the use of the horse, and is considered below.

The evidence thus suggests that wheeled vehicles were first produced in the Near East in the fourth millennium BC, and that they rapidly spread from there both to Europe and India during the course of the third millennium, and across the central Asian steppes in the second. The occurrence of

6.5 *Third- and second-millennium ploughs:* left, *impression of a cylinder-seal showing two-handled plough (ard) with sowing-funnel, Akkadian period, late third millennium* BC *(Ashmolean Museum);* right, *sole-ards in Cretan hieroglyphic script, early second millennium (after Evans).*

model wheels in New World contexts, indicating that the principle was known even though wheeled vehicles were not used in transport, shows that the availability of draught animals was the critical factor in this technology.

The plough. Again, earliest indications are in pictograms (Figure 6.4) (Falkenstein 1936, sign 214; Scheil 1923, signs 668–77). The basic model seems to be the same in both cases, with two stilts (handles) and a composite draught-pole. Representations of such ploughs (or, more accurately, ards) are plentiful as ritual scenes on cylinder-seals in the Akkadian period around 2300 BC, both in Mesopotamia and Assyria. These sometimes show a developed form with a sowing funnel (Figure 6.5), a device for sowing in regular lines which was especially useful with irrigation and generally in semi-arid conditions because of the deep implantation of the seed (Christiansen-Weniger 1967).

The plough, also in a two-handled version, is first evidenced in Egypt in the mid-third millennium, in a third-dynasty representation (Hartmann 1923). The construction of the Egyptian plough owed features of design like the rope binding to earlier hoe types.

In contrast to these Near Eastern forms, the earliest European ones are simpler and have only a single handle (Figures 6.6, 6.7). In the Mediterranean region it consisted of a flat sole into which were inserted both the stilt and the draught-pole. Further north, the even simpler design of the crook-shaft was used – a branch with a recurving projection, carved from the trunk itself, into which was set the stilt. As in Egypt, this resembled local hoe types, and was indeed the basic form of hafting in use at the time.

Ploughs of the sole-ard type are demonstrated from Early Bronze Age Cyprus from small terracotta models [e.g. Vounous: Karageorghis 1982, fig. 29], and the signs of the Cretan pictographic and Linear A scripts (Figure 6.5; Evans 1909) make it clear that this design was also in use there in the Bronze Age. It is not known what form was in use in Anatolia, but it was probably also a one-handled type. The crook-ard is known to have been in

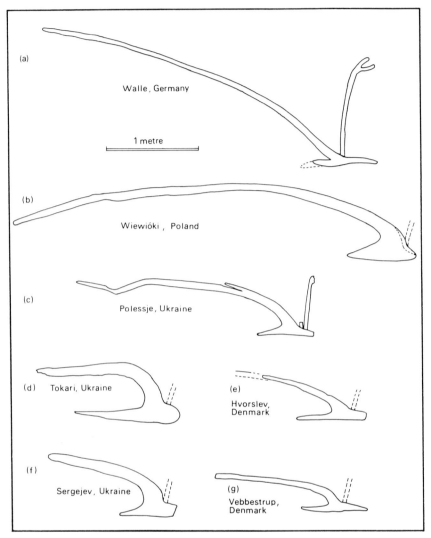

6.6 *Finds of ards of crook-ard type from northern Europe and the Ukraine:*
(a) Walle, Germany; (b) Wiewióki, Poland; (c) Polessje, Ukraine; (d) Tokari,
Ukraine; (e) Hvorslev, Denmark; (f) Sergeiev, Ukraine; (g) Vebbestrup, Denmark.
After Glob (1951) and Šramko (1971).

use in the second millennium north of the Black Sea in the area around Kiev,
as shown by finds from Polessje, Tokari and Sergeiev, the first radiocarbon
dated to the early second millennium BC (Šramko 1971). There is no reason
to suppose that it was not in contemporary use in the better-watered parts
of the true steppes further south.

The use of the plough in the later third millennium in Harappan India has
recently been demonstrated by finds of plough-marks at Kalibangan in the
Punjab (Steensberg 1971). Its arrival in China, however, seems even later

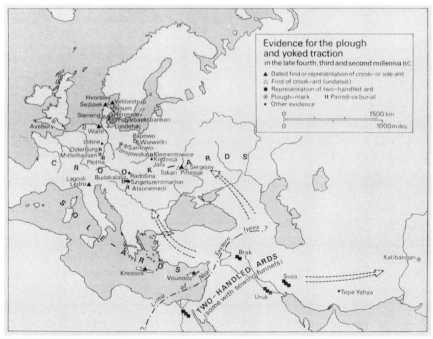

6.7 *Map of plough-marks and of ard finds and representations, showing the division between two-handled Near Eastern forms and European sole- and crook-ards [cf. Fig. 0.5].*

than that of wheeled vehicles, and occurred only in the first millennium BC.

In southern Europe, finds of ploughs and plough-like objects are known from second- and third-millennia circum-Alpine lakeside-village sites such

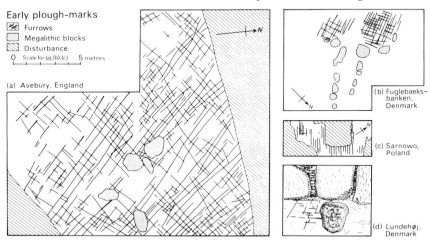

6.8 *Plough-marks preserved under north European long-barrows: (a) Avebury, England; (b) Fuglebaeksbanken, Denmark; (c) Sarnowo, Poland; (d) Lundehøj, Denmark. After Evans (1967), Ebbesen and Brinch-Peterson (1973), Ørsnes (1956) and Dąbrowski (1971).*

Plough-marks	Paired-ox burials	Yoke model	Cart drawing	Cart models	Plough finds	Wheels	Date BC

Plough-marks: South Street (G B), Fuglebaeksbanken (Denmark), Steneng (Denmark), Himmelev (Denmark), Lundehøj (Denmark), Sarnowo (Poland)

Paired-ox burials: Mittelhausen (E Germany), Osterburg (E Germany), Plotha (E Germany), Klementowice (Poland), Pitkutkowo (Poland), Zdrojowka (Poland), Alsonemedi (Hungary), Budakalasz (Hungary)

Yoke model: Krężnica Jara (Poland)

Cart drawing: Lohne (Züschen) (E Germany)

Cart models: Budakalasz (Hungary), Szigetszentmarton (Hungary), Radošina (Czechoslovakia)

Plough finds: Walle (W Germany), Hvorslev (Denmark), Lago de Ledro (Italy), Polessje (U S S R)

Wheels: Nieuw-Dordrecht (Holland), De Eese (Holland), Midlaren (Holland)

Date BC: 45, 44, 43, 42, 41, 40, 39, 38, 37, 36, 35, 34, 33, 32, 31, 30, 29, 28, 27, 26, 25, 24, 23, 22, 21, 20, 19, 18, 17, 16, 15

t.p.q

Legend: ● Direct C14 dates; ⬢ Indirect C14 dates

6.9 *Summary of evidence on the date of early ox-traction in Europe (scale in hundreds of dendro-calibrated C14 years).*

as the Lago di Ledro near Trento and Seeberg-Burgäschisee Süd near Berne. The former yielded a crook-ard, the latter a rather similar 'hand-ard' or *Furchenstock* (Battaglia 1943; Müller-Beck 1965). The most extensive series of early plough finds, however, comes from the North European Plain (Glob 1951). Four crook-ards are known from Jutland, of which two are dated to the second millennium. Another, three metres in length, came from Walle in East Friesland, Germany. Two more examples are known from the bend of the Vistula in Poland.

These finds of actual ploughs do not date the introduction of the implement. It has long been known that traces of criss-cross plough-marks are preserved under third-millennium round-barrows in north-west Europe; but

B.C.	North-central Europe	Carpathian Basin	Western steppes	
4000	Roessen	Tiszapolgár	Tripole BII	
3500	Early TRB	Bodrogkeresztúr	Tripole CI	
3000	Middle Neolithic	Baden	Tripole CII (Usatovo)	⇐ Plough Cart (Milk?)
	Corded-ware/ Beaker	Vučedol	Pit-graves	⇐ Wool Horse Tumuli Alloying
2500	Early Unětice	Nagyrev	Catacomb-graves	
2000	Late Unětice	Otomani	Timber-graves	⇐ Chariot

Table 6.1 The earliest cultural contexts of features of the secondary products complex in Europe.

now six examples preserved under late fourth-millennium long-barrows are known, from Britain to Poland (Figure 6.8). At Sarnowo in Kujavia a trapezoid barrow of the Wiórek phase of TRB overlay parallel plough-furrows. A radiocarbon date for a pit beneath the barrow gave a *terminus post quem* in the fifth millennium BC (Bakker et al. 1969, 7; Wiślański 1970) and a more direct date is suggested from a nearby Wiórek site at Zarębowo dated to 3400 BC (2674 ± 40 b.c.). In Denmark four examples are known, dating to the Middle Neolithic, around 3400–3200 BC. They are Lundehøj on Møn (MN II–IV: Ørsnes 1956), Fuglebaeksbanken on Stevns in west Zealand (MN Ib: Ebbesen and Petersen 1973), Himmelev 53 in central Zealand (MN Ib) and Steneng in south Jutland (Skaarup 1975, note 239). Finally, in southern England a long-barrow at Avebury, Wiltshire covered an area of plough-marks some fifteen metres square. It was radiocarbon dated by material from underneath and within it to 3500–3200 BC (Fowler and Evans 1967). The coincidence of these dates is remarkable.

There is also a striking similarity between the dates for the appearance of the plough and the cart, and when the evidence is plotted in conjunction (Figure 6.9) it forms a consistent pattern. The plough and cart seem to have been developed somewhere in northern Mesopotamia by the early fourth millennium BC, and to have spread in not much more than 500 years as far as north-west Europe (Table 6.1), where it arrived around 3500 BC.

169

Assuming a similar rate of spread to other parts of Europe, it would have reached the Aegean by around 3400 BC, and Iberia by 3200 BC.

This horizon has long been recognised as marking a major change in culture and settlement patterns. It marks the beginning of the Early Bronze Age in Transcaucasia, Anatolia, the Aegean and the Balkans; the Tripole–Usatovo transition in the Ukraine; the Baden culture in central Europe; the Middle Neolithic (Passage-grave) period in north-west Europe, and the Chalcolithic of south-west Europe. There is thus reason to believe that the introduction of this traction complex, and perhaps other features, was of major importance in European culture-history; and that its spread to other areas may have been equally significant.

Animals for riding and transport

The fourth millennium also saw the domestication of four or five species of animals which, although hunted in earlier periods, had not been economical to domesticate. These, however, were animals which could be ridden, or used as pack- or draught-animals, and included equids and camels. Their suitability as transport animals helps to explain their independent but near-contemporary domestication from Egypt and Arabia to the Ukraine and Turkmenia.

The equids. The genus *Equus* entered the Old World in the Late Pliocene, and the modern distribution of species is the result of geographical speciation during the Pleistocene. This produced four main groups within the desert-steppe belt: zebras in sub-Saharan Africa, asses in north Africa, half asses (hemiones) or onagers in the Near East, and true horses in Eurasia.

The horse (*Equus caballus*) was widespread in the steppe-tundras of the last glaciation, and survived in small numbers in forested areas in the Holocene; but its main habitat was the steppe belt from the Ukraine to Mongolia. The contexts of the earliest horse domestication were the sedentary cattle-keeping but non-agricultural communities of the middle Dnepr, neighbours of agricultural Tripole groups in the parallel river valleys further west in the late fifth and fourth millennia BC. These sites of the Sredni Stog group of the Dnepr–Donets culture contain Tripole B imports. At one of these, Dereivka, south of Kiev, a large number of bones of a small variety of horse have been recovered, and dated by radiocarbon to around 4400 BC (Telegin 1971). These have been widely accepted as indicative of an early stage of domestication, and features of material culture interpreted as riding equipment. The keeping of horses spread from this area only in the mid-fourth millennium, at around the time when the traction complex was becoming widespread. The percentage of horses in Tripole C assemblages shows a leap from 5 per cent to 15 per cent over the previous period (Figure 6.10), at the same time that sheep became more common than cattle both

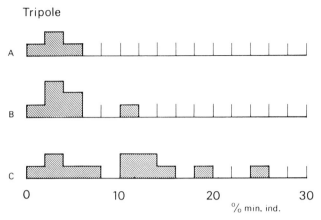

6.10 Percentages of horse (minimum numbers of individuals) in faunal assemblages of the three phases of the Tripole culture (data from Murray 1970). [In fact, the increase probably reflects Tripole expansion into the steppes, and thus mostly hunted animals – not the spread of domesticated horses.]

among Tripole groups and the successors of the Sredni Stog group. This coincided with a widespread colonisation of the true steppe area in the interfluves between the major river valleys, and formed part of the radical economic changes behind the emergence of the Pit-Grave culture in this area.

Horses spread more slowly into forested Europe than did the traction complex, but became widespread in the later third millennium. They are evidenced in large numbers on the Island of Csepel below Budapest in the Beaker period, when they also seem to have reached Ireland (Nobis 1971; van Wijngaarden-Bakker 1975). At the same time they spread down into the Near East through the Caucasus and eastern Anatolia, down to the Levant and Mesopotamia. Riders on horseback are shown on terracotta plaques of the Old Babylonian period, and though difficult to distinguish from the native onagers, horses are well documented by the later third millennium, though the expense of keeping them in a sub-tropical environment restricted their ownership.

The onager (*Equus hemionus*) was a widely hunted species in the Near East during the early Neolithic. Lightly built and fast-moving, it is not easy to domesticate and is often shown muzzled in Mesopotamian representations. It was probably first used in the steppes of Assyria or Khuzestan in the later fourth millennium BC, before the spread of the horse, and is most probably the equid shown on proto-Elamite tablets (Scheil 1923). In Early Dynastic times during the third millennium they (or their hybrids) were applied as draught animals to the solid-wheeled battle-cars with two or four wheels of the kind shown in the Agrab model or on the Standard of Ur. They were harnessed in the same way as cattle, and controlled by means of a nose ring: but it took four animals to pull even the two-wheeled cars. Terracotta

6.11 Pottery model of donkey with panniers, broken from the rim of a vessel. From Cyprus, EB III (late third millennium BC); (Ashmolean Museum).

plaques show that equids were ridden at least by the later third millennium.

The southwards spread of the horse displaced the onager from most of its uses, including that of traction animal. The vehicles with which it was used, however, underwent a more rapid development to make them more suitable for equids. This probably took place in northern Mesopotamia, Anatolia and northern Iran: an early stage is shown by the use of the cross-bar wheel with a central splat and two struts on a seal from Tepe Hissar, and true spoked wheels are known from Cappadocia from the end of the third millennium (Moorey 1968). In Mesopotamia in the early second millennium, traction equids were still controlled by a nose ring: but on the Eurasian steppes the new light vehicles were joined to more sophisticated traditions of horsemanship using the bit. Horse bits and spoked wheels are together evidenced in eastern Europe shortly after 2000 BC in sites of the Mad'arovce and Otomani cultures, where bone cheek-pieces and clay models of four-spoke wheels have been found in Hungary, Slovakia and Moravia (Tihelka 1954; Bona 1960; Vizdal 1972). The spoke-wheeled cart spread equally rapidly eastwards across the steppes, and it is represented in a drawing on a pot of the Timber-Grave culture, and on rock engravings in Kirgizia and Kazakhstan (Cherednichenko 1976). It was probably by this route that spoke-wheeled vehicles reached China.

The third equid to be domesticated at this time was the ass or donkey (*Equus asinus*). Its natural distribution is from Algeria to Sinai and possibly into the Levant. The advantage of the species is its docility and low dietary needs, making it a most economical animal especially in the Near East and Mediterranean. It thus provided a natural complement to the horse in this region. It was known as a domesticated animal for pack use in the EBA of Palestine around 3000 BC and in Egypt from the early third millennium BC onwards. It was used in Cyprus in the later third millennium as a pack animal, as shown in EB III figurines (Figure 6.11). Especially when crossed with the horse to produce the mule, the vigorous but infertile inter-specific hybrid, it was perhaps the most important form of bulk, long-distance transport, and must have formed the basis for the expanding overland trade networks of the later third and second millennia, such as the well-documented route linking Aššur with the *karum* of Kaniš. In this role, it was of even greater economic importance than the horse itself.

The camels. Like the equids, camels also spread through the Old World in the Pleistocene, though they did not penetrate so far or split into geographical species to the same extent. While all belong to the species *Camelus dromedarius*, they fall into two regional populations which were probably independently domesticated. The more primitive woolly, two-humped or 'Bactrian' camel is adapted to the cooler steppe and mountain fringe of Eurasia, and the more advanced, single-humped dromedary or 'Arabian' camel to the more arid areas of Arabia and north Africa. The advantage of the camel as a transport animal is that it can carry twice as much as a donkey, faster, for less frequent feeding and watering (Bulliet 1975).

The one-hump camel was probably domesticated from at least the early third millennium, and is possibly shown loaded on a pot from the cemetery of Abusir-el-Melek in lower Egypt; while the two-humped form is shown on a contemporary bronze pick from Khurab in southern Iran (Zeuner 1963). The two-hump form seems to have been part of the traction complex, being controlled by a nose ring and shown pulling vehicles in central Asia, for instance on third-millennium cart models with solid wheels and a camel's head from Turkmenia, or on rock drawings showing camels pulling spoke-wheeled carts from the region of Minusinsk (Bulliet 1975, 153, 185; Figure 7.6). Camel bones are known from the Andronovo and Timber-Grave cultures, and camel-hair was claimed at Maikop. The one-hump form, traditionally controlled by a noseband, became more common in the first millennium as Arab groups opened up the desert trade routes.

With the equids and the camels, five independent but parallel episodes of domestication took place during the fourth millennium, partly in direct association with the traction complex, and partly in adjoining parts of the semi-arid zone. Asses and camels in north Africa, onagers in the Near East itself, and horses and camels in the Eurasian steppe and semi-desert zone, all contributed to a more general transportation complex able to deal with a wide range of conditions. Within this area, individual animals spread and replaced or complemented the others, as well as expanding beyond this nuclear area into many parts of the Old World. Together they produced a revolutionary increase in transport potential.

Milk and wool

Milk. Basic to the economics of keeping animals for exploitation in the ways discussed earlier in this article is the use of milk. If animals are being used for purposes other than meat, they are too valuable a resource to slaughter simply when required for food. While surplus males may be eaten, larger numbers of females are needed for breeding stock. To carry the numbers of beasts required for a working population and a breeding population, some continuously usable food-product is really necessary – milk or in some cases blood.

Milk has several advantages. From a dietary point of view, it supplies the amino-acid lysine which is missing in cereal-based food. It contains fat, protein and sugar in a balanced form, and is a useful source of calcium. Being liquid, it is easily handled, and can be converted into a variety of storable products. These qualities, together with its almost universal association with domesticated livestock at the present time, have led many writers to assume that milking was practised from the earliest Neolithic onwards.

But the matter is not so simple. In the first place, animals which are not specially bred for the purpose do not produce large quantities of surplus milk; and moreover may not readily surrender it to the herdsman. Nor are human populations physiologically well adapted to use, as adults, the specific form of sugar which milk contains. Indeed, most adults suffer an unpleasant, even dangerous, reaction to drinking milk – 'a bloated feeling, flatulence, belching, cramps and a watery, explosive diarrhoea' (Kretchmer 1972, 72). Realisation that Euroamerican populations are unusual in their tolerance to milk as adults has come only recently. Tests with American negroes first showed that the adult ability to digest milk is not present in mankind as a whole (Bayless and Rosenzweig 1966), and tests of populations around the world showed how restricted that ability is (McCracken 1971). This realisation made sense of the evidence being assembled on the distribution of the milking habit itself (Simoons 1969; 1970). It was so long in being recognised because of the concentration of research and medical skills among the populations most tolerant of milk – European and American whites. In the present context, it is of fundamental importance.

Milk has three components: fat, protein, and milk-sugar, known as lactose. This last is a disaccharide, composed of glucose and galactose, and is synthesised only in the mammary gland. It is broken down in the small intestine by the enzyme lactase, which splits the disaccharide into glucose – which is used directly – and galactose, which is metabolised by the liver. In the absence of lactase, the lactose remains undigested and is fermented by the bacteria of the colon. It is this which causes the explosive diarrhoea.

174

The cause of lactose intolerance is thus lactase deficiency (Kretchmer 1972).

In all mammals except human lactose-tolerant populations, the production of lactase is at a maximum shortly after birth and ceases after infancy – in man, from two to four years of age. This represents the normal situation, and fits the pattern of other temporarily produced enzymes. Lactase production is not stimulated to any extent by the continued ingestion of lactose. Lactose-tolerance is transmitted genetically, and indeed is a dominant trait, although incompletely so. American black populations are approximately 70 per cent intolerant in comparison with ancestral West African populations, who at the present time are 98 per cent intolerant. Lactose-intolerance is particularly high among Chinese, Thais, agricultural West Africans (though not nomadic groups like the Fulani), South Americans and New Guineans, of those tested. In short, lactose-tolerance is the result of a relatively recent evolutionary episode, and adult milk-drinking a late and restricted feature of human diet (Kretchmer 1972; Simoons 1969).

The elaborate preparation of milk products may have been necessary because of a limited tolerance of lactose. Fermented products such as yogurt and cheese have a lower lactose content than fresh milk (McCracken 1971), and it is a general pattern in the Mediterranean that most of the milk is processed in this way. Low levels of tolerance are common today in Greece and south Italy, and such processing is analogous to the preparation of bitter manioc for consumption in South America.

The well-known Chinese aversion to milk, often cited as an example of an irrational food preference, is part of a more widespread phenomenon with a basic biological explanation. The geographical distribution of the practice of milking (Simoons 1970, 702) shows a continuous area from Morocco to eastern India (with non-milking enclaves there suggesting a recent expansion of the practice), extending southwards in east Africa but not penetrating into south-east Asia and Oceania. It comprises those areas connected via the steppe corridor and the Sahara, the arid belt across Africa and Eurasia. In the centre of this area are the mountains of the Near East and surrounding steppes. The distribution suggests a mid-Holocene origin for the practice, somewhere in this central area, and it seems likely that milking and milk-consumption form another aspect of the complex of secondary uses and products which has been outlined above; indeed, it was probably a precondition for these developments.

The limited tolerance of human populations to milk is only one side of the problem: the reluctance or inability of the cow to provide it is the other. For a modern perspective on this we may turn to the pastoral groups studied by ethnographers (Cranstone 1969). These illustrate the difficulties faced by people who do not have the highly bred milch animals of north-west Europe. The problem is to allow the animals to accumulate their milk, and to persuade them to let it down to a human milker. Cows are often separated from their calves during the day, to prevent their taking milk. However, they

6.12 *Cylinder-seal and drawing of its impression, showing reed-built byres with calves and milk-jugs, with a frieze of adult animals above. The seal itself is surmounted by a silver ram. From Iraq, Uruk period (late fourth millennium* BC); *(Ashmolean Museum).*

176

6.13 Inlaid scene of milking, forming part of the frieze of the temple to Nin-Hursag built by A-an-ni-pa-da at El 'Ubeid, Iraq. Early Dynastic (mid-third millennium BC); (by permission of the Trustees of the British Museum).

or some surrogate need to be present at the milking, to stimulate lactation and to activate the milk ejection reflex (Amoroso and Jewell 1963). The action of letting down the milk is a true reflex, involving the release by the pituitary gland of the hormone oxytocin which stimulates contraction of the muscles which press on the milk storage sacs. This reflex may be activated by stimulation either of the teat and mammary gland, or (because of the role of oxytocin in initiating uterine contractions) the vagina and cervix. It is thus a common custom among present and ancient pastoralists to blow, often using a special tube, into the rectum or vagina of the animal during milking. The milker is thus positioned behind the animal, rather than at the side as is otherwise more convenient. Instruments for this purpose have been identified archaeologically, for instance in the Baden culture (Banner 1956) and in south Russia (Galkin 1975).

These features were once widespread, not only among specialised pastoralists but in all the groups which practised milking. Uruk period seals show the adult cattle returning to huts where the young have been stalled during the day (Figure 6.12). From the Early Dynastic III period comes the famous relief from the temple of Nin-Hursag at El Ubeid, built by A-an-ni-pad-da, second king of the first dynasty of Ur. This shows in great detail the actual milking – from the back, with the aid of an insufflator – and the processing of the milk (Figure 6.13). The small udders on these early cows suggest that they were not highly bred for milk, and such stimulation would be essential. The milking position behind the animal is also shown in an Early Dynastic inlay from Kish; and it was still in use in Minoan times, as shown by a sealing (Figure 6.14) from the Archives Deposit at Knossos (Evans 1935). Goats are also shown being milked on Early Dynastic cylinder-seals. In Egypt a hobbled cow is shown being milked in the presence of a calf in the tomb of Ti in the Old Kingdom (Klebs 1915, 63). Milking is apparently shown on some central Saharan rock drawings from Tassili and the Fezzan, but their date is difficult to determine and there is no evidence that they are earlier than the third millennium BC (Simoons 1971; Clark 1976).

The biochemical and iconographic evidence thus suggests that although milking was known by the time of the first representations in early urban

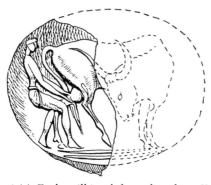

6.14 Early milking: left, *sealing from Knossos, Crete, Late Bronze Age (later second millennium), showing milking from behind (Evans 1935(4), fig. 534);* right, *shell inlay from Kish, Iraq,* ED III *(mid-second millennium) (Ashmolean Museum).*

contexts in the Near East, it was not of much greater antiquity. Is there any other evidence which would date the adoption and spread of the practice? One suggestion comes from pottery. It has long been noted that the Bronze Age sees a radical change in the kinds of vessels which constitute typical assemblages. Specifically, the open bowls which dominated Neolithic assemblages were supplemented by a range of drinking and pouring vessels, and a variety of pails (Figure 6.15). In the Mediterranean, the jugs and cups have been attributed to the discovery of wine (Renfrew 1971, 282), and this may be the case, but the changes affect a much wider area than that feature could explain. They clearly reflect some dietary innovation occurring in southern, central and northern Europe within a similar time range. Some types of Bronze Age pottery, like the Appenine 'milk boilers' or the Cypriot 'milk bowls' have already been characterised as being for such use. It seems likely that the widespread adoption of shapes appropriate for the manipulation of liquids is connected with the spread of the milking habit and the use of milk products. This would explain the often uncanny resemblances between distant areas, which have usually been used to argue for major migrations. The massive array of parallels assembled by Kalicz between the Baden culture and Anatolian Early Bronze Age cultures, for instance, finds an acceptable explanation here [though see Chapters 8, 15 and 16]. Parallels between EBA Bulgaria and Cyprus become comprehensible. The universal appearance of strapwork-ornamented bucket-shaped pots, from one end of Europe to the other, becomes less surprising; while the *Fischbuttengefäss* which appears in central Europe with the Baden culture has long been explained in Ghassulian contexts in Palestine as a churn.

Such lactic products, if such they were, probably had initially some ritual and social significance, especially if they included the intoxicating products of fermentation such as kumish. Precisely such an association is demonstrated in the Baden culture cemeteries of Hungary, where the two cart

CENTRAL EUROPE   BALKANS   CYPRUS

N-W. EUROPE   BALKANS   ITALY

6.15 *Pottery forms concerned with the manipulation of liquids and associated with the spread of the secondary products complex. [The lower ones may be for milk-processing, the upper ones – many with metal models – more probably for alcoholic drinks.]*

burials at Alsónémedi were accompanied by identical assemblages consisting of a finely made pottery jug, cup, dipper and bipartite bowl. From the grave which produced the Szigetszentmárton cart model (Figure 6.2a) came a precisely similar combination; and that model was itself a cup! The association of drinking and driving evidently began at an early stage in their history. These coincidences strengthen the view that we are dealing with an interdependent complex of features, which spread to a large extent in association.

Wool. The textile-fibre which became most important in the Old World, wool, was not present in the first four to five millennia after the initial domestication of the sheep. Vegetable fibres formed the basis of the earliest textiles, as in the New World, where cotton (*Gossypium*) fibre was developed by agricultural groups to supplement the older tradition of skin and leather clothing. Flax (*Linum usitatissimum*) was the most common Old World vegetable fibre, and already woven into elaborately patterned linen textiles before the emergence of wool. This persisted in some hot countries even after wool became common elsewhere: Egyptian Old Kingdom sheep were commonly of non-woolly types. Wool sheep were not introduced into Egypt until the Middle Kingdom.

The date at which wool sheep developed is being made more precise by microscopic examination of prehistoric fibres (Ryder 1969). These have already suggested that claims of an early date for woollen fibres (as at Çatal Hüyük) are mistaken. As with milking and paired-draught traction, the earliest evidence comes with the beginning of a literary and pictorial record during urbanisation in Mesopotamia. While such evidence gives only a *terminus ante quem*, the replacement of linen by woollen textiles can be traced in some detail from waterlogged contexts in Europe, and these show that the transition had not occurred there before the mid-third millennium BC. It seems most likely, therefore, that it had developed not long before the first indications in the Near East. Examination of further samples will make this more precise.

The wild sheep has a brown, hairy coat with short, woolly underhair. It was the development of underhair at the expense of the coarser outer hairs or kemps which produced the wool sheep. This was probably deliberately selected, in cold environments where the tendency was already present in wild populations. Lighter colours of fleece were also sought, though early sheep were probably more pigmented than today's breeds.

By the time of the Uruk pictographs (Falkenstein 1936) there were over thirty signs representing sheep. Pictorial evidence from the Proto-literate period indicates that both hairy and woolly sheep were known, as well as the fat-tailed breed. Sheep which are shown as being milked belong to the spiral-horned variant of the wool sheep (Zeuner 1963, 173; Amoroso and Jewell 1963). Early Dynastic sculptures and cylinder-seals not infrequently show woolly sheep alongside hairy ones, while Old Babylonian shearing lists indicate the organisation of wool collection (Kraus 1966, 47) and the importance of the spring shearing in the agricultural calendar. The wool would at this stage have been plucked, as it was naturally moulted, and somewhat finer wool obtained as many of the coarser hairs were left behind.

Marked changes in the exploitation of sheep appear in Europe in the third millennium. In Hungary, sheep increase as a percentage of bones on sites to 40 per cent or more, in comparison to figures of around 10 per cent in the preceding period (Bökönyi 1974, figs 1 and 2). A similar change occurs in the Early Bronze Age in the Alpine region and in Greece (Halstead 1981). In addition, the withers height increases dramatically, and there are higher percentages of mature and old animals. Horns also increase in size, though individuals without horns are common. These Bronze Age sheep must have resembled the still-surviving Soay breed.

These changes become comprehensible when attention is paid to the textiles preserved in the Swiss lake villages (Vogt 1937). Of the fourth- and early-third-millennium examples, all are linen, with leather being used for garments requiring greater robustness. Wool appears in the late third millennium. The proliferation of Early Bronze Age pin types represents the adoption of fastenings suitable to the loose woollen weaves which were introduced in this period, replacing the buttoned leather clothing of the Neolithic. The extensively preserved Bronze Age costumes from Danish coffin burials (Hald 1950) indicate the types of garment produced.

One factor which favoured the expansion of textile production was the change to a predominant male role in agriculture, leaving the women free to spin and weave (see below). As medieval economic historians have long been aware, woollen commodities are among the most basic items of inter-regional trade, and are usually the first manufactured goods to be traded on a large scale. Exports in developing areas shift from basic subsistence items like grain to manufactured products. This process can be observed in Meso-potamia during the course of the third millennium, and the development of such trade may have had an important role in extending the urban network. The role which wool and textiles played in the economies of the second millennium is clear from the textual evidence, both in Mesopotamia, Anatolia, and in Crete (Killen 1964).

The economics of secondary products exploitation

When animals are raised purely for meat, it is economic to slaughter them while they are relatively young. For instance, the same amount of fodder (33,000kg of hay-equivalent) would raise seven calves to two years as would be needed to take three of them to three and a half years; and the former strategy yields 40 per cent more meat (Lotka 1956, 120). The increase in live weight for the first two years is roughly proportional to the amount of feed consumed, but after that age the live weight increases more slowly while the feed consumption stays constant (ibid., 133). It is therefore advantageous to crop the population at this point (or even earlier, when there are seasonal fodder shortages), leaving only breeding stock, mostly females. Even the breeding stock, however, would not be kept beyond the age of reproduction.

Milking is a highly efficient mode of exploitation, giving four or five times the amount of protein and energy from the same amount of feed as would exploitation for meat. The use of cattle for beef recovers about 3.5 per cent of the energy which they have consumed in feed: with modern breeds the use for milk recovers 18 per cent (ibid., 136). Vitamins and salts (like calcium compounds) which are present only in small quantities in muscular tissue are abundant in milk. The kill-off strategy must be thus adjusted to maximise the number of lactating animals, by increasing the proportion of mature females. Male animals may either be mostly slaughtered very early (even at birth in a documented example from medieval Ireland: Amoroso and Jewell 1963, 135), or else kept for a longer period as an insured meat supply in extreme environments. Thus the Karimojong of Uganda, although dependent largely on milk (Dyson-Hudson and Dyson-Hudson 1969), may have only 12 per cent of lactating animals in their herds because of the high proportion of males (40 per cent), the long maturation period for cattle (three and a half to four years), the long period between calves (fourteen months), and the short lactation period (eight months or less). Female animals kept for milk are usually retained for long periods: an Estonian herd recorded in 1651 had half its cows over seven years and a third over ten years old (Slicher van Bath 1963, 287).

Animals used for traction are usually castrated males which at the age of three to four years are almost fully-grown, and have been trained as draught-animals since the age of two or three. The numbers of animals which must be maintained depends on the total amount of work during the year, and the extent to which it has to be done simultaneously. In India (especially the Central region), a short wet-season makes it imperative that each peasant should have a pair of bullocks to get his cultivation completed in time, since it must be done at once when the rains come (Clark and Haswell 1964, 55): this need underlies the maintenance of large numbers of scavenging cows as breeding stock, even though their milk yields are poor (Harris 1966). In medieval Europe there was increasing pressure on working livestock because of the expanding arable, even though plough teams were shared by the community (Warriner 1939).

The interpretation of kill-off patterns in a prehistoric European cattle population has been considered by Higham and Message for the TRB Middle Neolithic settlement of Troldebjerg in Langeland, Denmark (1969). On the basis of metacarpals, radii and mandibles, they reconstructed a pattern with low mortality in animals of both sexes up to two or three years of age, differential slaughter of castrated males from that age up to four years, with about a sixth of all animals surviving beyond that point. This argues against a pure meat economy, but does not suggest very highly developed exploitation of secondary products. It suggests small numbers of milch cows, and the possibility of a few traction-animals. The pattern conforms to Boessneck's observations (1956, 34) from Bavarian Neolithic settlements, that half the animals slaughtered were young to subadult. The handful of systematic investigations which have so far been made on this material, however, needs to be multiplied many times before comparative patterns can be defined. [Recent publications (Davis 1987; 1993; Benecke 1994a; 1994b) have continued to refine the picture presented here.]

For sheep, Payne (1973) has reported early results from his continuing investigation into comparative patterns of mortality. He has suggested model life-tables for different types of exploitation (ibid., figs 1–3). For meat, similar considerations apply as to cattle: the optimum period for cropping surplus stock is between one and a half and two and a half years, with males preferentially slaughtered at this point. Milk production makes it advantageous to keep at least half of the female animals beyond five years, and some even up to ten. With wool production, males become equally valuable at these ages also, so that there is a roughly symmetrical distribution with a high proportion of both sexes being kept up to six years and beyond. Historical samples studied by Payne show animals being carried up to eight years, as does a Bronze Age sample from the west Anatolian site of Beycesultan: by contrast, the sheep from the Early Neolithic site of Nea Nikomedia in north Greece were all killed before four years of age, many in their first year (Payne, pers. comm.). Ducos has suggested that kill-off patterns characteristic of secondary product utilisation began in Palestine with the Ghassulian (1973, 84). Halstead (1981) has investigated these suggestions in Neolithic Greece and concludes that secondary products were not a feature of early stock economies there. The evidence from osteological studies thus supports the contention that domestic animals before the fourth and third millennia BC were exploited only for their meat, and that the spread of secondary products utilisation brought about major changes in animal husbandry.

INTERACTIONS AND EFFECTS

A general model

The evidence reviewed above suggests that a number of major innovations occurred in the Near East and adjacent areas in the middle or later fourth millennium BC; and that these innovations spread and interacted with each other so as to cause major economic changes during the course of the third millennium. This revolution in animal husbandry involved using old domesticates in new ways, and in domesticating a new range of species. It resembled the previous phase of Near Eastern domestication in the eighth and seventh millennia in that different parts of the area, evolving in parallel with local resources, each contributed to a package of compatible elements with widespread application. A general explanation may therefore be suggested.

These developments were not accidentally coincident. They represented a variety of similar responses to a common problem, the pattern of population growth and territorial expansion which had been initiated by the beginnings of animal and plant domestication in that area some four thousand years before. Such problems became especially acute with the need to penetrate increasingly marginal environments in a landscape containing sharp contrasts in climate and terrain within short distances. They were partly dependent on biological changes both in man, in the case of tolerance to lactose, and his stock, for instance with wool. They involved an increased scale of investment in animal husbandry, and together they produced a new phase of man–animal relationships (Figure 6.16).

An increase in the scale of animal keeping was the basic feature. The population of domestic animals had to contain both breeding stock and working or production stock, as well as any beasts kept solely for meat. The maintenance of such an increased population was greatly facilitated by the practice of milking. It was this which made other uses possible, by allowing the continuous cropping of a subsistence product from a standing herd.

As agricultural communities expanded to the edges of the Fertile Crescent, they encountered extensive semi-arid areas which supported large mobile animal populations. Because of the uncertainty it involved, in areas without alternative resources, hunting was not a viable economy. With a product like milk which could be continuously obtained, and especially with the added mobility given by draught- and riding-animals, such areas could be exploited by pastoralism. Because of the easier alternative methods of increasing subsistence, especially by small-scale irrigation, this pattern was slow to evolve. The evolution of lactose-tolerant populations removed an important brake on the development of such systems, which could themselves develop techniques of milk processing (initially for storage) which rendered it usable by non-tolerant populations. The adaptation could thus spread more rapidly than its genetic basis.

Where did this process of adaptation take place? It is probably misleading to look for any closely defined region of origin, but it would appear that the process was occurring during the late Ubaid period in the second half of the fifth millennium BC and first half of the fourth, in northern Iraq, Syria and Palestine. The Ghassulian culture in Palestine shows a ceramic inventory including vessels for pouring and manipulating liquids, including the famous 'butter churn', and the suggestion of a mortality pattern among its livestock of the kind indicating secondary products has already been noted. Equally suggestive are the large numbers of sites which appear at this period in the arid areas of south Palestine and Sinai (Rothenberg 1970),

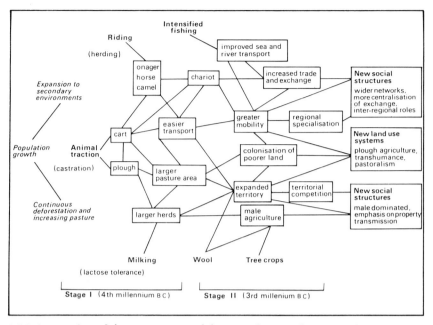

6.16 *Interaction of the components of the secondary products complex in western Eurasia through time. [This diagram has been much misunderstood, and is perhaps misleading in trying to combine chronology and causality in a single representation. Note, in any case, that it is not regionally specific: it offers a general picture of western Eurasia as a whole.]*

indicative of methods of coping with such dry environments, and important also in the acquisition of raw materials like copper. Indeed, the formation of populations in the dryer interstices would have had an important effect on patterns of trade and contact (Sherratt 1976).

The application of certain features of this system was not restricted, however, to semi-arid areas. The use of draught-animals, especially, had revolutionary implications for cultivation in better-watered areas. Not only did the cart improve transport on the farm, but the innovation of a 'mechanical hoe', the plough, increased the farmer's ability to prepare his land by a factor of up to four or more. (For the economics of this, see Clark and Haswell 1964, 55.) This both increased the productivity of good land, and made economical the preparation of land from which a poorer yield might be expected. It seems likely that the plough played a critical role in the cultivation of tree crops which began at this period (Zohary and Spiegel-Roy 1975). An intensification of agricultural production was thus a parallel development to the expansion of pastoral populations. Furthermore, the large-scale production of wool, an animal product suitable for manu-factures, provided a greatly increased potential for trade. It was the juxta-position of contrasting environmental zones which produced in the Near East such innovating co-action (Figure 6.17; cf. Clarke 1968, 355).

185

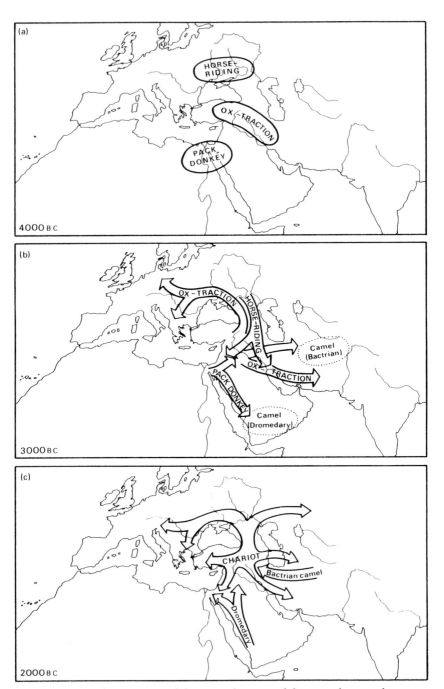

6.17 *Origins and interaction of the main elements of the secondary products complex: (a) 4000 BC, primary developments; (b) 3000 BC, inter-regional exchange and spread; (c) 2000 BC, continuing exchange and interaction. [In (b), I would now take ox-traction through Anatolia as well as the Pontic steppes, as in Fig. 0.5; and in (c) I would take the chariot through the Balkans rather than the Caucasus, as described in Chapter 7.]*

186

This agricultural revolution was well under way by the later fourth millennium in Mesopotamia and Khuzestan, where the massive increase in population on the alluvium created an extensive demand for raw materials. Ramifying trade links spread advanced techniques into the hinterlands, while the increasingly urbanised populations of the lowlands began the manufacture of woollen textiles. At the same time, semi-dependent pastoral populations continued to grow in the areas where grain-growing was unprofitable.

The links between these differentiating subsistence specialisations, intensive cultivation and mobile pastoralism, were probably deeper than simple trading relationships. Such diversity opens up the possibility of poly-ethnic and symbiotic social systems (Barth 1969), with a fluctuating balance between sedentarisation and nomadisation, or long-term flows of population between economies with different patterns of fertility and mortality – notably across ethnic boundaries (Barth 1964, ch. 9). Such a complex system, despite its inbuilt homeostatic features, has the potential for violent change when there are rapid shifts in the balance of power: the relationship between villager or town-dweller and nomad was always ambivalent. The degree of interdependence involved in a closely adjusted timetable for stubble grazing and use of winter pastures always contained the potential for conflict.

The dual economy of plough and pastoralism was characteristic of areas of ecological diversity. Thus in mountain areas the pastoral sector was occupied by transhumant groups which were directly analogous to the nomads of the arid plains. This pattern became characteristic not only of the Zagros and the Taurus but also of the Tertiary fold mountains of southern Europe, where it was also a creation of the third millennium.

In more arid areas, pastoralism spread without the plough. While plough cultivation spread along with the rest of the secondary products complex both to Europe and to India, it did not reach into Africa further than the upper Nile. Pastoralism, involving milking, was common in the Sahara probably by the later fourth and almost certainly by the third millennium BC, and with the third-millennium desiccation some of these populations were forced southwards (Clark 1976). The continuing penetration into east Africa took a ploughless and cartless pastoralism down the tropical grassland corridor, as cattle replaced the native wild ungulates. Cattle were much less efficient than these animals, some of which (like the eland) were potentially herdable; and indeed it was their plentiful provision of milk, urine and dung – which in the native antelopes were sparse and concentrated – that made the introduced animals so valuable a resource (Kyle 1972).

On the Eurasian steppes, pastoralism did not become divorced from traction and the plough was used in oasis situations. On the other hand, the well-known Chinese intolerance to lactose inhibited the development of a pastoral sector and thus a ready supply of draught-animals, which may explain the occurrence of draw-spades and plough-like instruments pulled by human traction (Leser 1931). In India, Harris (1966) has argued that the very large numbers of animals needed for ploughing with the sharp onset of the monsoon necessitates a large population of generally poorly nourished cattle. He has also suggested that the prohibition on pork in large parts of the Near East stems from the need to devote resources to animals giving secondary benefits of milk or traction.

The spread of the secondary products complex, then, offered new opportunities to populations in many areas of the Old World. Many of the characteristic features of the present-day ethnographic pattern can be traced back to this dispersal.

Changes in agricultural systems and settlement patterns

The changes which the secondary products revolution brought to pre-historic Europe and the Near East are best demonstrated by the major changes in settlement pattern which are characteristic of the fourth and third millennia BC. Before looking at the archaeological evidence, however, a brief comment on models of early agricultural economies is needed.

It has often been assumed that the earliest agriculture was some form of shifting cultivation, involving a 'slash and burn' system of temporary clearings which were allowed to revert to woodland after a few years of cropping. Such systems are widely known from agriculturally less developed areas in the tropics and in peripheral parts of Europe. Ester Boserup (1965) has suggested a general model of agricultural change in which the fallowing cycle is progressively reduced as population pressure forces intensification of production. Plough agriculture would thus be a threshold of development separating temporary from permanent cultivation.

The archaeological evidence from Europe and the Near East, however, does not support such a scheme, and suggests that it may be misleading to apply directly a model based largely on cultivation in the tropics to the situation in temperate and sub-tropical regions. In these areas, cultivation began by being concentrated in small areas of high-yielding land which did not require a long fallowing cycle. Only later did cultivation spread to poorer soils where longer fallows were required. In temperate Europe, slash and burn systems are characteristic of the poor soils under coniferous forest in Finland and the Carpathians (Balassa 1972) which were among the last to be settled agriculturally. The introduction of the scratch-plough to Europe made it economical to cultivate a wider range of soils than before, and thus to extend the area of cultivation.

In the Near East and Europe, present evidence suggests an early stage of spatially restricted, fairly intensive cultivation of areas of high productivity (Allan 1972), followed by an expansion of the cultivated area either through irrigation or by tackling more extensive areas of less productive land. The earliest cultivation systems in the Near East seem to have resembled the floodwater-farming of the American south-west (Bryan 1929), and to have concentrated on naturally watered mudflats by lakes, rivers and springs. Expansion in the sixth millennium took place by small-scale irrigation by water-spreading on alluvial fans, marking the beginning of the Early Chalcolithic pattern (Oates and Oates 1976). Forms of settlement reflect a continuing interest in localised resources, with substantial and long-lived settlements like Jericho and Çatal Hüyük existing at an early stage and tell sites continuing to be characteristic. Despite this stability, however, many of these early agricultural sites continued to obtain their animal protein by hunting or loose herding. Gazelle were still the animal staple at Jericho, while frescoes of cattle at Çatal Hüyük and onagers at Umm Dabagiyeh show that there was little incentive to full domestication in open areas supporting large herds.

In central Europe, it has been usual to see the first Neolithic communities as slash and burn agriculturalists with shifting cultivation and settlement (*Wanderbauerntum*). This idea was supported by tropical and boreal-forest analogies, by the existence of temporary clearance phases in pollen diagrams, and by inference from the fact that the settlements did not form tells. This would conform with expectations on the Boserup (1965) model. However, close study of Early Neolithic settlement, especially in Poland and in the Netherlands and adjacent parts of Germany (Kruk 1973; Modderman 1970), has demonstrated the stability and longevity of such sites. The absence of tell formation relates more to differences in building material than to the character of agriculture, and individual locations were continuously occupied for comparable spans of time, up to 1000 years in some cases.

Moreover, the locations chosen for such sites show a marked preference for high-quality loessic soils, and within these for waterside positions. In Little Poland, where the topography has sufficient relief to show locational preferences with particular clarity, it is clear that these valley-bottom locations offered access only to a relatively narrow area of land along the rivers. The distribution of such sites is conspicuously linear throughout central Europe, and the exploited zone was spatially very restricted although of maximum productivity. Such limited clearances in the primary forest would have offered very limited grazing. Cattle must have been kept only in small numbers and probably partly stall-fed in the characteristic long-houses.

The economy would thus have resembled a garden system not unlike the horticulture or semi-agriculture of the south-eastern parts of pre-contact North America. While some comparison may be made with hoe cultivation in the tropics, this temperate hoe cultivation has no true analogy in the Old World, where it represents an extinct economic type which has everywhere been replaced by plough cultivation.

189

These early agricultural systems were characterised by a highly selective pattern of land use, in which population was concentrated in a few zones of high productivity, and relatively small areas of land were intensively cultivated. The system allowed the maintenance of large herds only where there were significant tracts of naturally open countryside accessible from the 'oases' of settlement. Grazing was increasingly problematic as such systems penetrated into European forest environments. The lack of large-scale forest clearance is reflected in a toolkit lacking large, wide-bladed axe forms.

The effect of the spread of plough cultivation was to produce major alterations in the structure and distribution of settlement. By contrast to the limited areas along rivers which the earliest settlers opened up in the forest, the wider areas opened up by third-millennium groups would have provided the necessary grazing for the animals needed to till them, and the new system operated on an extensive rather than a localised, intensive basis. The sites chosen for settlement were less long-lived, and more rapid turnover of cultivated area would have left sufficient fallow for a more balanced form of mixed agriculture in which the pastoral component was able to grow continuously with the progress of deforestation. The appearance [or, rather, intensification of activity] at a similar date from England to Russia of mines and quarries to produce material for effective flint and stone axes for forest clearance is eloquent testimony to this new scale of attack on the woodland (Sherratt 1976).

An increase in the animal component of agriculture which was thus made possible would have introduced for the first time problems of over-wintering numbers of stock, but would also have provided manure in useful quantities. For the first time a balanced crop–livestock husbandry came into being, with different requirements and patterns of land use. In central and northern Europe, on the loess lands and the North European Plain, functionally undifferentiated villages of longhouses were replaced by the variety of sites which are characteristic of the TRB and related cultures. [This was initially because of the integration of indigenous populations, as described in Chapter 13, using more extensive methods of cultivation in which the plough was increasingly advantageous; but the real shift in settlement patterns did not occur until Corded Ware: see Chapter 16.]

The main expansion of hoe agriculture had taken place on medium (silt-grade) soils like loess. The main expansion of agriculture based on the scratch-plough in the later third and second millennia took place on lighter land, especially on sandy soils which were less able to withstand prolonged cultivation. The vast numbers of round-barrows in areas like central Jutland, for instance, bear tribute to the speed with which Late Neolithic and Early Bronze Age farmers effectively reduced large areas of precariously wooded glacial outwash-sands to infertile heathland. The occurrence of Bronze Age tumuli under forest in many parts of Europe show that, once exhausted, such land was often never recolonised. This cycle of expansion

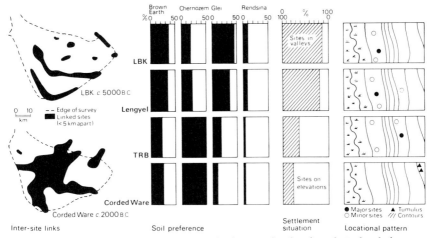

6.18 *The development of settlement in the loess uplands of Little Poland, from 5000 to 2000 BC: locational preferences and contact networks. Note the similarities between the first and last pairs, and the shift between Lengyel and TRB (data from Kruk 1973). [This major shift in fact pre-dates my plough horizon, and owes more to fusion with native groups, as discussed in Chapter 13.]*

reached its limits in the later second millennium, when heavier types of ard capable of turning a sod were developed as settlement spread to the still little-used heavy clay and alluvial soils.

The move from a pattern of concentrated and localised agricultural exploitation to a wider use of the terrain for light plough cultivation and extensive grazing had a marked effect on settlement patterns further south. It is a notable feature of the later fourth millennium BC that the pattern of tell sites established over the previous two millennia underwent substantial modifications over a wide area, from Transcausasia to the Balkans. Instead of long-lived tell sites in the valleys near to water, valley-edge or spur sites appear and settlements are found in upland locations. The tell sites which do continue are usually larger, frequently fortified, and with greater intervening distances (Sherratt 1976). The disappearance of large, nucleated Neolithic sites is also evidenced from the Tavoliere of Apulia, where the large ditched settlements have been documented by aerial photography. The shift of population to the plain edge and surrounding mountains in the Bronze Age indicates the relative advantage of a milk-based pastoral economy over intensive lowland cereal cultivation. The model has a wide predictive value throughout the Mediterranean, especially where extensive upland areas suitable for transhumance surround lowland plains.

In the Near East, these processes lay behind the increasingly urbanised character of settlement. Population expanded in the fourth millennium BC in areas like the terraces of the Konya Plain or the alluvium of lowland Mesopotamia. In the latter case, the use of the plough was part of the irrigation-based system which made possible a fivefold increase in the number of sites during the Uruk period. Subsequent development involved an increasing concentration of population in a few defended centres. Whether such defences were erected against potentially hostile pastoralist populations in the drier areas between the irrigated farming areas, or against the other cities of the region, such concentrations of agrarian population were made possible by use of the ox-drawn cart for local transport.

Longer-distance transport links were also made possible by the domestication of equids as transport-animals. The fertile but stoneless and metalless alluvial basin of the Euphrates and Tigris generated an enormous demand for raw materials. The size of the hinterland over which effective trade links existed has been demonstrated to extend for up to 1000km in each direction. To the south-east, the discovery of Proto-Elamite tablets at Tepe Yahya demonstrates links from Khuzestan to Kirman as early as the later fourth millennium; while at the same time the site of Habuba el-Kabireh in northern Syria indicates links along the Euphrates to southern Iraq (Lamberg-Karlovsky and Lamberg-Karlovsky 1971; Strommenger 1976). In the third millennium the importance of east-central Anatolia to Mesopotamia is shown both by the military expeditions of Sargon and the Anatolian origin of gold from the royal graves at Ur (Maxwell-Hyslop 1977). By the second millennium the overland trade routes northwards from Aššur and westwards from Mari were major distribution lines for bulk supplies both of raw materials like metals and manufactured products like textiles. These would have been impossible without the use of transport-animals.

While the Mesoamerican evidence shows that animal-traction is not a necessary precondition for the development of urban communities, the rarity and much later appearance of towns in the New World suggests that while a variety of settlement systems may eventually reach an urban form, the higher energy of Old World systems greatly accelerated movement along this trajectory.

Pastoralism and linguistic change [See also Chapter 19]

The secondary products revolution had large-scale effects in the semi-arid areas of the Old World. The Eurasian steppes in particular saw important changes in the distribution and density of population.

Previously, in the fifth and early fourth millennia, population had been largely concentrated in the valleys of the major rivers flowing into the Black Sea. Agricultural settlements of the Tripole culture were confined to the forest steppe parts, with cattle-keeping, fishing and collecting groups of the Dnepr–Donets culture along the rivers in the true steppes.

With the arrival of the cart and traction complex and the spread of the horse, both groups began to make a greater use of the drier interfluves; and sheep became the predominant domestic animal. The effect of new transport possibilities, and probably also milking, was to create on the steppes an economy with sufficient mobility to be able to exploit effectively the previously neglected zone stretching eastwards into central Asia; though at this stage such pastoralism was probably 'transhumant' rather than 'nomadic'.

This set of economic changes precipitated the formation of a new cultural group on the basis of the previous riverine groups and under strong technological influence from the Caucasus. A characteristic of this group was the erection of burial mounds covering graves in increasingly elaborate pits and wood-lined chambers – the Pit-Grave, Catacomb-Grave and Timber-Grave phases of expanding steppe culture. These herding and farming groups penetrated eastwards along the Eurasian steppe belt as far as the Volga–Ural interfluve in the early third millennium, and (using spoke-wheeled vehicles) as far as the Altai in the early second.

Some backwash of this expansion was also felt in Europe. Wool sheep and the horse, along with tumuli and alloy metallurgy, spread westwards from 3000 onwards and spoke-wheeled vehicles followed at the end of the third millennium. The opening-up of the European forests, and especially the creation of large areas of heathland on sandy soils, allowed a wider network of contacts and facilitated the penetration of steppe elements into the temperate forest area.

It is instructive to compare the effects of horses and wheeled vehicles to the spread of imported Spanish horses among the tribes in the Plains area of north America (Roe 1955). As well as tempting a variety of formerly settled riverine groups to colonise the prairies and create the classic Plains Indian cultures of popular image, it also gave the opportunity for mounted Athebascan sheep-herders – like the Navajo – to spread over a thousand kilometres from the home area of their language group.

The spread of settlement in the semi-arid corridors of the Old World had important implications for linguistic distribution there. The expansion of population in east Europe and central Asia provided the opportunity for the spread and differentiation of a previously localised language group which now occupies a major area of Eurasia. The dispersal of these Indo-European languages was paralleled by the similar expansion and differentiation of the Semito-Hamitic group in the Near East and north Africa.

Philologists have long contended that the extensive resemblances in form and vocabulary between geographically removed languages like Latin and Sanskrit imply a common ancestral *Ursprache* which differentiated after dispersal: and that, moreover, since such resemblances rapidly decay, it must have taken place relatively recently. An often quoted estimate for such a dispersal (Robins 1964) is 3000 BC – to some extent a circular argument from the archaeology, but consistent with observed rates of change (Swadesh 1968). The eastward movements of population onto the steppes in the third millennium BC linked east Europe with the Pontic and Trans-Caspian regions as far as the Tarim Basin and the Iranian Plateau, and there seems no doubt that it was such relatively rapid movements in the semi-arid zone which gave Indo-European its geographical range. This is also consistent with the first appearance of specifically Indo-Iranian names in northern Syria and Mesopotamia in the second millennium BC.

The extent to which Indo-European languages were already present in the forested parts of Europe is uncertain. Nevertheless there are good philological grounds for inferring some westwards spread of Indo-European languages in the second millennium BC, and this could well have taken place in the context of the changes in settlement and economy documented in a previous section.

Social structure

Besides the large-scale effects of the secondary products revolution in creating new forms of subsistence economy, its effects on the texture of social relations was equally important. By its major alterations in the allocation of subsistence roles between the sexes, it created new social structures and patterns of organisation, and by giving a new importance to the transmission of land it necessitated new mechanisms of inheritance.

The arguments for associations of this kind are inevitably based on cross-cultural surveys, and especially the *Area Files* of the Institute of Human Relations and the *Ethnographic Atlas* (Murdock 1967) abstracted from them. Interpretations of such material in historical terms is especially dangerous: but the archaeological perspective given above on the spread of features such as the plough allows a time dimension to be fitted to the recurrent patterns of association which have become clear from statistical analysis of this data. Such considerations allow a sketch of the kinds of society which may have been characteristic of temperate hoe-based horticulture.

In common with some of the systems based on the intensive collecting of localised subsistence products on a sedentary basis, agriculture involved the transmission of property consisting of facilities such as fields and houses. It is therefore usually associated with continuing kin-based corporations such as lineages, often with a specifically unilineal mode of inheritance (Harner 1970). The mode of inheritance is strongly influenced by patterns of residence: in an uxorilocal system, where the husband joins the wife's community on marriage, transmission is likely to follow the female line. Residence systems, in turn, reflect the relative importance of the sexes in subsistence pursuits. In simple hoe agriculture, the major subsistence contribution comes from female labour in sowing, weeding and harvesting. There have been some suggestions that a clear worldwide association occurs between simple hoe-based agricultural economies and matrilineal inheritance, and that this association would be even stronger were it not for the effect of recent influences (Keesing 1975). Societies based on matrilineal lineages are thus likely to have been typical of early agricultural communities in the Old World. This pattern is characteristic of aboriginal societies in the woodlands of the American south-east which have been identified as the closest parallels to pre-plough agriculturalists in Europe (Driver 1961).

Both plough agriculture and pastoralism, by contrast, show a strong association with male dominance in subsistence activities, virilocal residence, and patrilineal descent. This pattern is often reinforced by the kinds of warfare which are common when large quantities of livestock are present. On a world sample, two-thirds of plough agriculturalists and two-thirds of pastoralists have purely patrilineal inheritance. Moreover, such societies are likely to evolve beyond the lineage mode of production to be composed of larger non-localised clans or to become stratified as scarcity of land becomes increasingly important.

Changes in the sexual allocation of tasks affected non-agricultural production. The decline of the female role in agriculture released labour from the fields to the home, making possible an expansion in spinning, weaving and textile production. This increase in scale made economical the use of more elaborate forms of loom. Archaeologically, traces of weaving equipment become much more prominent in the third millennium (e.g. Trump 1960).

Besides reallocating productive roles between the sexes, plough agriculture introduced new principles to the transmission of property. Greater flexibility of land use and the ability to use wider holdings gave a new importance to the acquisition and devolution of land. The advantages of 'marrying out' came to be balanced by the advantages of keeping land within the descent group, retaining resources within the productive unit. Marriage would thus tend to become an important move in the determination of patterns of land-holding, and a focus of interest to the descent group as a whole (Goody 1969). Such a concern leads to arranged marriages in which women, as carriers of property, have to be appropriately matched to maintain the status of the family. These features are likely to be more pronounced the greater the scarcity of land and the more intensive its use.

Goody (1976) has recently contrasted the kinds of property transmission characteristic of plough-less Africa with those commonly found among the plough-based agriculturalists of Eurasia. He characterises the contrast as the difference between homogeneous devolution, where property is transmitted between members of the same sex and there is no community of property on marriage, and diverging devolution, where children of both sexes inherit and marriage establishes a joint fund. In the former case, typical of African hoe cultivators, property reverts to the lineage of a deceased person, and is not passed to his or her offspring: in the latter, typical of Eurasian plough cultivation, marriage produces successive recombinations of holdings in each generation. Diverging devolution is characteristic of societies where land forms a major heritable commodity, and is associated with a particular emphasis on marriage and control over the choice of mate.

In examining a worldwide sample from the *Ethnographic Atlas* (Murdock 1967), Goody found diverging devolution to be characteristic of over half of the societies of Eurasia, including the most populous, but to occur in only a twentieth of the African examples; and moreover that the earliest Eurasian law codes show this contrast to reach back to the second millennium BC. Features which showed a high correlation with diverging devolution were advanced and plough agriculture, male farming, in-marriage, monogamy, prohibited pre-marital sex, and kinship terminologies separated siblings from cousins. Such features are often associated with stratified and state societies. Goody (1976, 25) suggests that the increase in production made possible by the plough had major implications for inter-personal relations: 'For differentiation arose even at village level and the scene was set for the development of relationships such as lord and serf, landlord and tenant, which exist in Eurasia but not in Africa.'

In so far as forms of society are determined by the organisation required for work and the types of property which are passed between generations, we may apply these insights to the historic situation in Eurasia. The secondary products revolution produced an economy dominated by men, who played a dominant role in handling large livestock either as herds or in ploughing. Women became increasingly relegated to the domestic sphere. Where the absolute amount of cultivable land was relatively restricted, as in the Near East and the Mediterranean, ownership of land became increasingly subject to competition. Differences in access to land became the basis of growing inequalities, while the transmission and coalition of property became a major preoccupation of the landed classes.

In inland Europe, the archaeological evidence indicates that land was still relatively plentiful as the Bronze Age farmers continued to clear primary forest on somewhat less fertile soils. These features were probably not pre-cipitated, therefore, until the end of the second millennium when organised field systems were laid out, heavier forms of plough were developed, and extensive indications of status differences appeared. Second-millennium Europe may thus have exemplified a second extinct economy of the tem-perate zone – an extensive light-plough cultivation with a predominantly male role in agriculture, but without the highly differentiated social order where groups struggled to maintain their status by the vertical transmission of property. The 'rich' graves with prestige items at this time probably repre-sent a 'big-man' system rather than true chiefdoms (Sahlins 1963). Essen-tially a transient type, such societies have not survived to reach the pages of the *Ethnographic Atlas* (Murdock 1967); only the extreme contrast between tropical matrilineal shifting hoe cultivators with homogeneous devolution, and the more northerly patrilineal intensive plough cultivators with stratified societies and diverging devolution, suggests the possibility of structurally intermediate ancestral forms.

CONCLUSION

Eduard Hahn's perceptive remark quoted at the beginning of this section still stands as a fundamental observation about the origins of western society. The progress of archaeological research, however, has provided a time-depth which allows a further definition of the processes involved. As the beginnings of agriculture and domestication have been traced further back into the post-glacial period, so the major developments of the fourth and third millennia BC have emerged as a second burst of economic innovation with far-reaching consequences.

The spread of the plough was arguably the most important development in Old World prehistory after the adoption of cereal cultivation itself. It firmly tied together the arable and pastoral sectors of husbandry in an interdependent system, and it fundamentally affected the character of settlement and the structure of society. Use of the plough was only part of a wider set of changes, however, which marked a new phase in man–animal relationships, involving larger numbers of domestic animals, the domestication of new species, and new uses for long-domesticated ones.

The use of animals for traction purposes seems to have begun in Mesopotamia, and involved first the familiar ox and then the onager, spreading to include the Bactrian camel in the lands east of the Zagros. Riding was developed on the steppe-plains north of the Caucasus and the Black Sea, as the horse was domesticated. Pack-transport began in the lands around the head of the Red Sea with the domestication of the ass, and then of the dromedary. The production of wool was probably a development in the sheep populations of the Taurus–Zagros arc. These innovations spread and interacted, some animals changing role or adding new ones. Basic to all of them was probably the beginning of milking, giving a continuously available form of animal food and making economical the keeping of large numbers of animals which could be put to a variety of uses.

The focus of all these developments was the Near East, in different parts of which the various elements emerged and spread. The key to this productivity lay in large part in the diversity of adjacent environments which this area offers. The arid belt of the Old World crosses north Africa and swings north-east into central Asia: but it is interrupted in its course by the great chain of Tertiary fold-mountains running from the Alps to the Himalayas, which catch the rain-bearing winds of winter. This intersection of desert, mountain and sea provides an intimate mixture of zones with different stresses and opportunities, maximising the possibilities of innovation and providing a theatre in which interaction and cross-fertilisation can take place.

The impact of the secondary products revolution was felt principally in that part of the agricultural zone of the Old World characterised by cereal crops, rather than the tropical part where root-crops were cultivated. Its

197

innovations spread rapidly along the arid corridors and penetrated into more temperate regions. The axis of Old World development from Europe to India came into being as a result. These influences penetrated only slowly and incompletely into east Asia. There an alternative system of protein capture based on fish (especially in rice-paddies) and on the pig was already supporting a relatively dense population, and the expanded pastoral sector which the secondary products revolution required could not easily be brought about. For this reason, the civilisation of China was in many respects comparable to those civilisations of the New World where domestic animals played a minor role.

Beyond the zone of cultivation, the practice of milking allowed the in-filling of arid areas by animal-based groups, and produced a secondary impact on the hunting peoples of the northern forests. The milking of reindeer by Lapp populations is a notable example. In Africa, milking may have spread relatively early from its south-west Asian focus, but pastoralism was imposed on existing systems of tropical hoe cultivation. It did not achieve the organic linkage with cultivation that was characteristic of Eurasia, and animals were not used as sources of energy.

The effects of the secondary products revolution thus spread widely both to north and south of the main axis, affecting much of the Old World. Many of the cultures recorded ethnographically therefore were, like the historical societies of Eurasia, products of the second half of the post-glacial period.

As David Clarke showed in 'Mesolithic Europe: the economic basis' (1976), archaeological data are most effectively used in the context of wider ethnographic comparison; not by taking recent groups as direct analogies of prehistoric ones, but by analysing both in the perspective of evolutionary change. The societies which flourished in temperate and sub-tropical Eurasia in the Early Holocene form an important extinct phylum of human culture, which cannot be directly compared to any surviving groups. Their character was completely altered by the secondary products revolution, which created many of the basic features of the modern world.

7

The Secondary Exploitation of Animals in the Old World

(1983, Revised)

In the historical and ethnographic record, western Eurasia appears as a mosaic of pastoral and mixed-farming groups in which livestock has played a major role. Specialised forms of animal husbandry have been adapted to a wide range of geographical and economic conditions, from steppe nomadism to large-scale commercial livestock rearing. In the perspective of prehistory, however, this picture is a relatively recent one. Many of the features which now appear basic to Old World farming only became widespread three or four millennia after the beginning of farming. In Chapter 6, I drew together archaeological and archaeo-zoological evidence for the early use of secondary products and applications of domestic animals in the Old World. The purpose of this chapter is to present some additional information which confirms and modifies these conclusions, and also to sketch the outlines of a general model of the development of animal husbandry from c.6000 to 2000 BC. Many of the innovations considered here seem to have emerged in restricted parts of the Near East, and to have been exchanged and disseminated as part of the process leading to urbanisation. Important interactions also occurred with the steppe belt, where new ways of life appeared at this time, and the new features which were introduced to

This chapter was intended to update the information given in the previous chapter, and I have taken the opportunity to allow it to continue this role by adding new material up to 1995, and entirely rewriting the section on the horse. As well as citing new information, this paper (originally written by invitation for a World Archaeology *volume on pastoralism) modifies it in two respects: in recognising that milk-drinking, while secondary, may have emerged during the first spread of farming (thus satisfying Bogucki 1984); and in emphasising the importance of the Urban Revolution in Mesopotamia as the context in which the features of secondary farming were integrated and dispersed. The new picture of horse domestication fits very well with that point of view. As so often, Roger Moorey provided invaluable guidance on Near Eastern matters.*

7.1 Ard marks of the
Early Neolithic
C/Middle Neolithic I
period under a long
barrow at Snave, near
Dreslette, Denmark.
Drawn by Claus
Madsen (Fyns Stifts-
museum): published
in C. Madsen and
H. Thrane,
'Sydvestfynske dysser
og yngre stenalders
bebyggelse' Fynske
Minder 1982, 17–42:
Odense 1983 [from
Sherratt 1987b].

temperate Europe caused a revolutionary change in the character of agriculture and social systems there. Despite the fragmentary nature of present
evidence, therefore, it is useful to consider this phenomenon as a whole,
since its elements are clearly inter-connected. The dating of these features
will first be discussed in a European context, and then considered as part
of the pattern of development in the Near East. [The sections on horse-
domestication, riding and chariotry have been amalgamated and substantially rewritten.]

USE OF THE SCRATCH-PLOUGH (ARD)

The best evidence so far for the regular use of the plough in agriculture
comes from the discovery of actual plough-marks on old land surfaces, and
the recent multiplication of such discoveries offers the hope that this will
lead to a more precise definition of the date at which animal traction was
first applied to cultivation. The most impressive corpus of early plough-
marks comes from Denmark, where they have recently been comprehensively reviewed by Henrik Thrane (1982; [1989: see Introduction]). Among
those dated to the end of the EN and the beginning of the MN (c.3500 BC)
is the splendid example from Snave near Dreslette, where 175 square metres
of criss-cross furrows have been exposed under a long dolmen-mound
(Figure 7.1). These examples can be dated by a series of radiocarbon de-
terminations on material of these phases to c.3700–3300 BC (see e.g. Bakker
1979, 141–5; [Midgley 1992, 205–20]). These fit well with the date of
c.3500 BC for furrows in the surface below the South Street longbarrow[1]
(Avebury) and the other evidence considered in the previous chapter.

Further welcome evidence comes from the circum-Alpine region. In the
Valle d'Aosta, from phase II of the site of Saint-Martin-de-Corléans in the

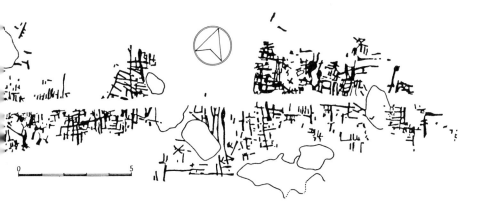

0   5

suburbs of Aosta in northern Italy, an area of plough-marks has been exposed on a ritual site beneath Neolithic cist-graves (Mezzena 1981). The furrows are bracketed by radiocarbon dates calibrating to 3600–3000 BC. These show an impressive congruence with the Scandinavian dates. Slightly later, with a calibrated radiocarbon date of c.3000 BC, is the site of Castaneda at the mouth of the Calanca valley in Graubünden, Switzerland, where another large area of criss-cross furrows has been exposed beneath an Iron Age cemetery (Zindel and Deluns 1980). Another Swiss site, Chur-Welschdörfli, yielded furrows sandwiched between Lutzengüetle (late Neo-lithic) and Early Bronze Age layers, and so dating to the later fourth or third millennium BC. Although the occurrence of such finds is naturally dependent on the preservation of old land-surfaces, the existence of such conditions under monuments dating to before 3500 BC (e.g. earthen longbarrows) offers some control on this kind of evidence;[2] and the emerging pattern of dates both for plough-marks, stelai and figurines from several parts of Europe seems to be a convincing one.

As well as the contemporary iconographic evidence for paired draught in the form of the pottery models discussed in the preceding chapter, the copper models of yoked oxen from Bytyń near Poznan in Poland (Piggott 1968; Figure 7.2) also date to around 3500 BC on the evidence of the associated flat copper axes. Since the figures were made by a more sophisticated method of casting (probably lost-wax) than was practised in Europe at that time, it is possible that they were imports from a more advanced area such as Anatolia [and recent evidence confirms this].[3] The possibility of such contacts is suggested by a series of remarkable pottery vessels from Olden-burg, north-west Germany (Figure 7.3), which was clearly based on a metal prototype (Bakker 1979, 123; [Körner and Laux 1980, Abb. 33–8]). This evidence of long-distance contacts is important for the apparently rapid

7.2 Copper models of yoked oxen from Bytyń, central Poland, reportedly found (in the 19th century) with flat copper axes of Copper Age type (Poznań Archaeological Museum) [new photo, courtesy Lech Krzyżaniak].

spread of yoked traction at this time. [Two further finds have filled out the pattern of evidence for traction in the later fourth millennium BC. The first is a painted pottery figurine of a yoked ox (not dissimilar to the Bytyń representation) found in a transitional EH I–II context (c.3000 BC) at Tsoungiza near Nemea in the northern Peloponnese, Greece (Pullen 1992). The second is from Bronocice, southern Poland, in the Baden-influenced phase V (c.3000–2700 BC, some centuries after phase III with its pot bearing the drawing of a wagon that was noted in the previous chapter: Figure 6.3). It is a bovid horn-core with marks of rope-compression, suggesting that the draught-pole of ploughs and wheeled vehicles was attached to a horn-yoke (Milisauskas and Kruk 1991). It is contemporary with the assemblage of cattle bones from a Bernburg context at Schalkenburg, central Germany, half of which belonged to animals over five years old, and many of which showed pathologies of the hip joints suggesting their use as traction animals (Müller 1985).] There is thus good agreement among the various lines of evidence for paired draught (plough-marks, models, drawings of yoked oxen, carts and ploughs, paired-bovid burials and osteological evidence) to date its introduction to c.3500 BC, coinciding with a major horizon of change in European settlement patterns.

202

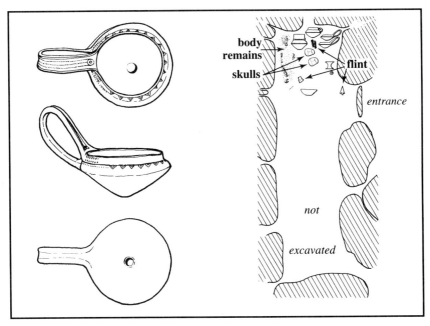

OLDENDORF II

7.3 Handled pottery vessels copying metal original (note skeuomorphic rivet) from rectangular dolmens near Oldenburg, Lower Saxony, Germany: Middle Neolithic, c.3200 BC, after Körner and Laux 1980 [new drawing].

THE SPREAD OF WOOL-SHEEP IN EUROPE[4]

The basic problem in assessing the change from textiles based on plant fibres (linen and bast) to those made of wool is one of differential preservation. Vegetable fibres survive only in alkaline contexts such as the calcareous muds of Neolithic Switzerland, while woollen fibres survive only in acid contexts such as the oligotrophic peat-bogs of northern Europe (although carbonisation may preserve exceptional examples of both). The great abundance of textile finds from Switzerland in the period from 4000 to 3000 BC (Vogt 1937) shows that linen was widely used in the Neolithic. After this time, in the Corded Ware and Early Bronze Age periods, the sharp decline in textile remains suggests that linen had been largely replaced by wool, which would not be preserved in such environments. On the other hand, there is abundant evidence from northern Europe (especially in Denmark and adjacent areas: Hald 1950) that woollen cloth was the major textile in use during the Bronze Age, from c.2000 BC onwards. The problem is thus to identify the point in the third millennium at which the change-over occurred.

An important find in this context is the 'Spitzes Hoch' tumulus at Latdorf near Bernburg in central Germany, excavated by Klopfleisch in 1880. It

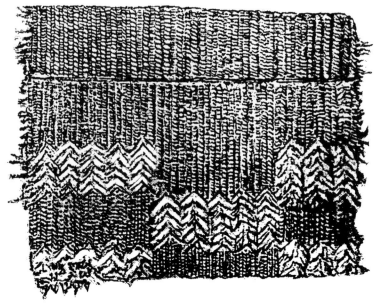

7.4 *Drawing by the excavator, Klopfleisch, of a fragment of patterned (linen) cloth – now destroyed – from the Spitzes Hoch tumulus, Latdorf (Kr. Bernburg), central Germany. The accuracy of this drawing was doubted by Schlabow (1959), who knew of no Neolithic analogy for the technique; but this seems no reason to dismiss it.*

contained a collective burial with Bernburg (later TRB, c.3000 BC) pots and copper beads, within a circular stone setting covered by oak planks. The burning of this wooden covering had carbonised nearly sixty textile fragments, many decorated (Figure 7.4), which – though not all preserved – have been examined by Schlabow (1959). These he described as being of 'erstaunlicher Feinheit', and consisting of 'feine, langhaarige Schafwolle' – finer than wool from the Bronze Age. However, Dr M. L. Ryder (*in litt.*, April 1981) informs me that he examined some of this supposedly Neolithic 'wool' in 1964, and is of the opinion that it is flax; and carbonised flax-seeds occurred in the grave (Vogt 1937, 43). It seems most likely, therefore, that this late-fourth-millennium sample is linen, like contemporary Swiss textiles.

The earliest European find of woollen fibres is the wrapping from the handle of a flint dagger, found in its leather sheath in a peat-bog at Wiepenkathen in northern Germany (Cassau 1935). This fabric is particularly interesting, since it consisted of woollen threads that had originally been interwoven with others, presumably linen, that had not survived the acid conditions. This is neatly paralleled by a contemporary Swiss find (Ruoff 1981), in which the converse obtained: linen fibres interwoven with now vanished ones, presumably of wool. The Wiepenkathen dagger can be dated typologically (Lomborg 1973) to the earliest phase of the Late Neolithic 'Dagger Period', beginning around 2400 BC. Moreover, a find of carbonised wool from Clairvaux-les-lacs Station III, French Jura ('plusieurs poils de laine de mouton': Hundt and Körber-Grohne in Pétrequin 1986, 240f and fig. 7 no. 4) dates to c.2900 BC. [Winiger (1995, 172) notes that the sudden paucity of linen remains in the Corded-Ware levels at Zürich-Mozartstraße may indicate the introduction of wool.] It seems reasonable, therefore, to suggest that wool was introduced [on a small scale] to north-central Europe some time in the early to middle third millennium (probably in a Corded-Ware context), and was used in conjunction with linen until it became the dominant textile fibre in the second millennium [or even later, in the far west of Europe]. [These conclusions are in agreement with recent expert discussions of the subject (Barber 1991; Bender-Jørgensen 1986; 1992) which describe an extended transition from textiles based almost entirely on plant-based fibres to wool-textiles during the third and early second millennia. The recent find of the Alpine Iceman, dating to the final centuries of the fourth millennium, shows that even an individual wealthy enough to carry a copper axe was dressed at this time entirely in skin clothing and a woven straw cape; indeed Winiger (1995) questions whether linen was used for large items of clothing at all, and suggests that most Bronze Age clothing was essentially a direct translation of skin garments into textile. If so, then the introduction of wool marked a fundamental transformation of this aspect of material culture.]

THE ANTIQUITY OF DAIRYING

One of the most important questions about prehistoric economies is the origins of milking. It cannot be assumed that this was practised from the beginning of domestication; although it was probably considerably older than the first iconological evidence for the practice, which appears only in Uruk contexts in the fourth millennium BC. The answer can come only from a large number of studies using age- and sex-specific mortality estimates [and probably only unambiguously from residue-analysis: for comments on faunal studies see Introduction, esp. Note 15]; and although many more such studies are required, some initial results relevant to the early use of milk in Europe will be noted here [see also Hesse 1982; 1984; Davis 1984 for the Near East].

Sakellaridis (1979) has provided detailed data on faunal assemblages from Neolithic Switzerland, and although sample sizes are small, some interesting patterns emerge. In the Pfyn and Cortaillod cultures (4000–3500 BC), 40 to 80 per cent of the cattle survived to maturity, of which the majority were female. The lack of adult males confirms that they were not kept as draught animals, but the high proportion of adult females implies the possibility of milking as well as breeding stock. This pattern occurs as early as the Roessen levels at Eschen-Lutzengüetle (fifth millennium), where over 80 per cent of cattle were more than two to three years old. A similar pattern was also noted for ovicaprids: Cortaillod populations also contain 20–60 per cent of adult animals, mostly female. This argues against their use for wool, as predicted, but leaves open the possibility that goats in particular were used for milking. (Incidentally, sheep were regularly used as milk animals in northern Europe until the Industrial Revolution, as in southern Europe today.) It is thus not impossible that milking was being practised in Europe by 4000 BC, or even earlier, though the use of milk in Neolithic Europe seems to be a local rather than a general feature.

[One piece of evidence that has been drawn into the discussion is the occurrence of perforated pottery vessels or 'sieves', interpreted as cheese-presses, which occur from *Bandkeramik* times onwards (Bogucki 1984; 1986). This is but one amongst many possible interpretations of their function; and though it is not unthinkable that the cattle or sheep of the first farming groups in central and northern Europe were being milked by this time – some two or three thousand years after the initial domestication of these species – the quantities produced must have been rather small, given the essentially horticultural nature of the farming system and the very small areas of forest which had been cleared. It would also be surprising in view of the fact that *Bandkeramik* domestic animals were principally cattle rather than sheep (see below), perhaps because of the necessity of reliance on leaf-fodder. It must of course be admitted that milking, being neither a specific technology (like the traction complex) nor dependent on highly specific strains of livestock (like wool-bearing sheep), could well have emerged in-dependently over large areas of Eurasia, and been practised already in Neolithic Europe. Possible though this is, however, 'milking' is now too easily attributed to early farming cultures in Europe, and care should be taken not to retroject too far the large-scale image of 'temperate dairying' as it has been practised in north-west Europe in historical times (e.g. Legge 1981). McCormick (1992) has pointed out that age-profiles for prehistoric cattle indicating the slaughter of very young calves, often taken as diagnostic for a concentration on milk production, are in fact the very reverse: for in primitive breeds (in Ireland lasting down to recent times, and in England down to the medieval period) the presence of the calf is essential for the mother to let down her milk (Chapter 6), so that the high incidence of young calves in bone assemblages would *not* imply dairying but meat production. On this interpretation of the kill-off patterns from early Ireland, a true 'dairying' economy of the kind known historically only appeared in Early Christian times, in the mid-first millennium AD. As with many archae-ological problems, recent images are misleading: prehistoric practices were very different from modern ones and hard to imagine from recent models.

Milk (and especially cow's milk) was not in prehistory the universal commodity it has now become, and milk products – which were mostly from sheep or goats – would always have had a special place in prehistoric economies and diets – in many respects a (pre-monetary) 'cash-crop', like

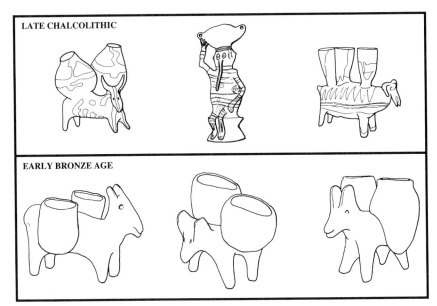

7.5 Upper row, *Chalcolithic (early fourth millennium) figurines from sanctuaries in the southern Levant: (a) ram or bull with churns (En-Gedi); (b) woman with churn (Gilat); (c) ram with cornets (Gilat);* lower row, *Early Bronze Age (later fourth millennium) figurines from the southern Levant; (d) donkey with vessels (Bat-Yam); (e) donkey with vessels (Giv'atoyim); (f) donkey with large vessels (Tel Azor tomb 10) [new drawing].*

olive oil, wine and wool.[5] This is certainly the impression given by the Ghassulian and EB I figurines from the southern Levant, showing rams and donkeys with pots (i.e. containers for liquid) and a woman with a churn (see below, and Figure 7.5). The later fourth-millennium pictographic tablets from Uruk (Green 1980) deal mainly with sheep and goats, and it is evident that goats were the principal providers of milk, and that sheep were of interest principally for their wool. Cattle seem to have been kept in very small numbers.[6] The search for the beginning of milk utilisation should probably therefore concentrate on the ovicaprids, and the first extensive milk production may indeed turn out to coincide with the introduction of wool-sheep and the major shift to secondary products in the later fourth millennium. The cattle-raising cultures of the Neolithic and Copper Age were probably largely meat-oriented, though milking may have played a more important part in temperate Europe than elsewhere.]

How does this fit with other indications of the antiquity of dairying? In Chapter 6, I discussed the relevance of the restricted adult tolerance of lactose in human populations. The ability to digest milk, made possible by persistence of the production of the enzyme lactase into adulthood, is very low or absent in Mongoloid, New World, Melanesian, Australoid and Khoisan populations. In the Near East it is generally low, with the exception of the Bedouin of Saudi Arabia. Likewise in Africa, most Negroid populations except pastoralists like the Fulani, Hima and Tussi are intolerant to lactose. Roughly half of the inhabitants of Mediterranean countries are intolerant, and the only populations in which the majority of adults can digest milk are those of north-west Europe. Although the practice of milking has some correspondence with the distribution of lactose-tolerant individuals, it does not depend on the existence of high levels of lactose tolerance in the population. The use of milk products such as yoghurt and cheese (in which the lactose is broken down into simpler sugars) is thus likely to have preceded the ability to drink milk directly.

Two selective factors are thus likely to have been responsible for the present distribution of lactose tolerance. One is the advantage, under extreme conditions on desert margins with few alternative food sources, of being able to consume large amounts of fresh milk. [Such niches may have only been occupied fairly recently.] This does not explain the high levels of tolerance in northern Europe, however, and an ingenious hypothesis to account for this has been put forward by Flatz and Rotthauwe (1977). This relates lactose to the promotion of calcium absorption where there is a deficiency of vitamin D, when it is beneficial in preventing rickets. The development of lactose tolerance would thus parallel the selective advantage for de-pigmentation in areas of low sunlight (since vitamin D is produced in the body by UV radiation). With a cereal-based diet, and little vitamin D from fish and liver, agricultural populations in Europe would have been prone to calcium deficiency and consequent bone deformations. If milk was available, there would be a selective advantage for the prolongation of lactase activity into adult life, which would allow milk to be consumed directly, thus helping to prevent rickets.[7]

We may therefore suggest that milking may have been practised in Europe on a small scale by Neolithic populations, and that selective pressure in favour of milk-drinking became increasingly important with the northwards spread of agriculture. The limited opportunities for grazing in the primary forest would have inhibited the development of large herds, but the ability to keep small quantities of domestic livestock for milk would have been valuable in small scattered communities. Enlargement of the pastoral sector, and the development of larger-scale dairying, would have depended on the progress of forest clearance and in particular the change from small-scale horticulture to a larger scale of agriculture (Figure 8.4). It is in this context that the arrival of the plough and wool-sheep were important and mutually reinforcing.

TRANSPORT AND TRADE IN THE FOURTH AND THIRD MILLENNIA BC: THE NEAR EAST

Having surveyed the European evidence for secondary exploitation, we may now turn to the Near East, and in particular to transport animals which spread only marginally into prehistoric Europe. [We shall then look at evidence for the horse, a transport animal which spread from the steppe belt both into Temperate Europe and to the Near East.]

Non-caballine equids

As with the use of paired draught, the use of pack animals can be illuminated from the evidence of figurines (Figure 7.5). A group of terracottas from southern Palestine is the first known indication of the use of pack animals, and particularly the ass or donkey, *Equus asinus* [Epstein 1985; Ovadia 1992]. The earliest of them [which show rams rather than donkeys] are from the Ghassulian (Late Chalcolithic) period, of the late fifth or earlier fourth millennium BC, while others [including donkeys] come from EB I contexts, equivalent to the Egyptian late Pre- and Protodynastic periods of the later fourth millennium. From Ghassulian contexts, and especially ritual centres, come a bovid carrying 'churns' from En-gedi (Ussishkin 1980, 35), a ram with conical vessels on its back, and a woman with a 'churn' on her head, from Gilat (Alon 1976). [A small donkey figure from Giv'atoyim, with two globular containers (pots? leather bottles? baskets?) high on its back (Kaplan 1969), originally thought to be Chalcolithic is now considered to be EB I (Ovadia 1992, 20).] The best representation of a pack donkey comes from an EB I tomb at Tel Azor (not far from Tel Aviv), along with a copper dagger and a predynastic Egyptian palette (Druks and Tsaferis 1970). It carries two tall containers. A somewhat similar figure of a donkey, broken from the rim of a vessel, comes from Cyprus and belongs to the EB III period at the end of the third millennium (Figure 6.11).

The context of these early figurines from Palestine is interesting: the Late Chalcolithic Ghassulian culture saw a major expansion in the Negev and Sinai, associated with an expansion of trade and metallurgical activity (Rothenberg 1970), and the formation of links across the arid part of southern Palestine with the cultures of Predynastic Egypt, where metal objects appear in the Gerzean (Naqada II). These routes became increasingly important during the period of formation of the Egyptian state. Loaded donkeys appear on the rock drawings of Upper Egypt (Winckler 1939), and in Protodynastic representations of trade or tribute scenes. Egyptian interest in the Levant is indicated by the occurrence of traded objects (and even the *serekh* of Narmer on a sherd from Tel 'Erany), and this sphere of influence in southern Palestine parallels the interaction zone around the early Mesopotamian states, indicated for example by the occurrence of proto-Elamite tablets on the Iranian plateau. These Egyptian land routes based on pack transport were superseded from the fifth dynasty onwards by the development of effective maritime transport and bulk trade by sea (Marfoe 1987; [Esse 1991]). The scope of these earlier contacts was clearly dependent on the existence of domestic donkeys used as pack animals.

Faunal evidence shows that the donkey was present in both Palestine and

Upper Egypt from the fourth millennium onwards, and the evidence of the figurines suggests that it came to be important locally among transhumant groups in southern Palestine, perhaps first in transporting milk and milk-products, and in carrying rare materials from distant extraction sites. The growing demand from expanding populations in the Nile valley, however, gave it a broader significance within the expanding network of trade routes. [Since the first real evidence for use of the donkey (Ovadia 1993), whether in the form of figurines or an increase in the numbers of bones on sites, dates to EB I (later fourth millennium), it seems that it was this larger geopolitical context which was responsible for promoting it as a transport animal, and for spreading it all around the Fertile Crescent – though the domestication process could well have begun in the preceding Chalcolithic, and both rams and bovids were perhaps then being used as pack animals (Figure 7.5). The Chalcolithic way of life is hard to describe by ethnographic analogy: an intensive floodwater horticulture (apparently not yet using the plough: Levy 1992, 74), and in places also arboriculture (olive) with extensive trans-humance, keeping sheep both for milk and wool – fragments of woollen textile, as well as the remains of a loom, accompanied the spectacular Nahal Mishmar hoard of Chalcolithic metalwork, which also had olive, date and pomegranate remains (Bar-Adon 1980). It is a good example of an 'extinct' way of life with no recent analogies. Both ploughing and a more intensive pastoralism seem to have accompanied the urbanisation of EB I, sparked off by Egyptian intervention (Horwitz and Tchernov 1989; Smith and Horwitz 1984; Esse 1991), and it was in this context that the domestic donkey spread rapidly all round the Fertile Crescent: primarily as a beast of burden but soon, too, as a ridden animal – whose style of riding was transferred to the horse when it arrived from further north. It must have been especially useful on overland routes which articulated with the Euphrates supply routes from the Uruk colonies. Perhaps crossed with other equids (horse or onager), it was also an important traction animal in the warfare of third-millennium Sumer.] This spread of innovations in transport (for example the use of the sail, which also came into wider use during this time) took features formerly important in local niches and gave them an international role in the expanding relations between early complex societies and their peripheries.

The donkey was introduced to the Aegean during the third millennium, occurring both at Lerna V and in Troy IV (Gejvall 1969; 1946), and is thus likely to have spread widely through the Near East during this period. Tracing this spread is complicated, however, by the difficulty of distinguish-ing donkey from the remains of other equids which were present in this region. A further complicating element is the probability of hybridisation between the various equids. These complexities have been comprehensively assessed by Juris Zarins (1976) in a work which is a fundamental source of information on this question. Central to his thesis is his contention that the onager (*Equus hemionus*), although hunted, was unlikely to have been

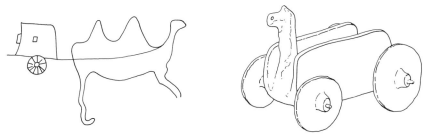

7.6 *The camel as draught animal:* left, *as a rock-engraving, drawing a spoked-wheel vehicle, from the Minusinsk depression, eastern Siberia (after Bulliet);* right, *on a clay model from Altyn Depe, Namazga* IV *period (after Masson); [new drawing].*

domesticated in the same sense as the donkey (cf. Littauer and Crouwel 1979). However, onager-like equids such as those shown in teams of four pulling battle-cars on the 'Standard of Ur' might well represent hybrids, either with donkeys or perhaps with horses (see below). The use of the onager, therefore, seems to be secondary to the use of other equids, and may represent local attempts to extend the stock of a rare and valuable imported species by the developing techniques of hybridisation with a locally abundant equid.

Camels

Returning briefly to the early stages of urbanisation in the fourth millennium, it is possible to suggest that the domestication of the camel closely paralleled that of the donkey, but in a complementary area. Two species are involved, the Bactrian (*Camelus bactrianus*) and the Arabian camel or dromedary (*C. dromedarius*). Although there is no unambiguous evidence for the domestic status of either animal before the second millennium, indications of the presence of the camel on settlements, together with the long overland routes which came into use in the later fourth and third millennia on the Iranian plateau, suggest that it was already in use as a transport animal. Tosi (1974) has suggested an early focus of use at sites like Shar-i Sokhta in Seistan, where its bones, dung and hair have been identified; and this area shows close cultural links with Turkmenia, where figurines suggest that it may have been used initially as a traction animal (Figure 7.6; Masson and Sarianidi 1972, plate 36; Bulliet 1975). Seistan is linked southwards to the area of Kerman and the Makran, where there are now further indications of the Bactrian camel (Compagnoni and Tosi 1978) [and as far as the Indus valley by the third millennium: Zarins 1979].

On the other side of the Gulf, the Oman peninsula was part of the same interaction-sphere (probably the historical *Magan*); and there are fourth-millennium camel bones at Hili and Umm an-Nar, while representations on grave-stones show that the species present was the dromedary (Ripinski 1975; Zarins 1978). The camel also occurs at Bahrein (*Dilmun*). It is thus

211

possible that domestication of the two species occurred in the developing zone of long-distance trade contacts on opposite sides of the Gulf, linked to the growing urban areas of Mesopotamia and the Indus. While the initial focus of camel domestication may have been in some localised area of Iran, it achieved a major significance within the expanding network of fourth- and third-millennium trade-routes. These routes did not extend at this time to western Arabia, and the relatively slow spread of the dromedary may reflect the undeveloped nature of this hinterland until the end of the second and first millennia BC, with the development of the Arabian incense trade [Artzy 1994].

The Bactrian camel, however, seems to have undergone a major dispersal as a transport animal in the third millennium: camel bones occur on Harappan sites (Ratnagar 1981, 173), and by the second millennium on Andronovo sites in central Asia, where they may be linked to drawings of camels pulling carts in the Minusinsk depression (Bulliet 1975; Figure 7.6). They may even have penetrated by way of the steppes into eastern Europe in the late fourth and third millennia: fabrics identified as camel-hair have been noted at Maikop in the northern Caucasus (see Chapter 18), and camel bones have been found in barrows on the Pontic steppes and at Gurbaneşti east of Bucharest in Romania (Rosetti 1959, 802). It is clear that the steppes acted as an important secondary axis of dispersal, as with other secondary forms of animal exploitation. The fourth and third millennia thus saw the emergence and dispersal of three major means of animal transport: wheeled vehicles, pack transport and riding; and these techniques, and the domestic species on which they were based, spread and interacted both within the Near East and on its steppe hinterland.

THE DOMESTICATION AND SPREAD OF THE HORSE [New]

[Information on the early history of the horse is now much more abundant than when Chapter 6, or even the present chapter, was first written; and this new account, replacing the original sections on the horse, may serve as a guide to these subsequent developments – for although they modify the detail, in many ways they relate horse domestication more closely to the other elements of the secondary products complex.[8]

Domestication

Horses survived into the Holocene even in forested parts of Europe, and were apparently hunted in Neolithic France (e.g. Carnac, Roucadour – Chasséen) and Germany (e.g. Dümmersee – early TRB), though apparently not in Britain after the Late Glacial, as recent radiocarbon dates have shown.[9] These local populations, which would have benefited to some extent from human opening of the woodlands by early farmers, seem to have made a discernible contribution to European early domestic populations in the third millennium, and the horse (like cattle and pigs, but unlike sheep) seems to have undergone several geographically distinct domestication episodes, within a finite period in the fourth and third millennia. These cannot be considered 'independent', however, but are better seen within the context of the large-scale cultural interactions at this time.

It was on the steppes (Figure 7.7) that human populations had known and made use of the horse for longest; while few sites in forested Europe before 3000 BC have yielded more than a few per cent of horse bones, the Copper Age cultures of the Ukraine include sites where they form the largest proportion of animal bones. Of these, the site of Dereivka near Kiev (now published in English: Telegin 1986) has tended to dominate discussion as further techniques have been applied to its study, and their conclusions are generalised to other contemporary sites. Dereivka is a small habitation site dating to c.4000 BC, with the remains of two houses, overlooking a tributary of the Dnepr. The pottery included vessels with cord-impressions, typical of the later phase of the Sredni Stog culture. Three-quarters of the faunal remains are horse, which would have provided a high proportion of the food; the other domestic animals were cattle, sheep and pig. Horses from this site had been claimed as domestic by Bibikova (e.g. 1975), and this view was accepted by Nobis (1971) and by Bökönyi (1978), principally on account of the contrast with earlier horses from the region – in fact mainly Pleistocene ones, since Mesolithic examples were not available. A further line of argument was cultural: on the eastern part of the site there were ritual animal burials, including the skull and legbones of a horse (a seven to eight year-old stallion) and foreparts of two dogs – all, perhaps, originally stuffed, as the Iron Age Scythians are known to have done, in the manner of 'head and hooves' burials (Piggott 1983, 91–2). A nearby pit contained a boar figurine, long blade, and perforated antler fragments of a type thought to represent bridle-bit cheek-pieces (Piggott 1983, fig. 44: but see below), of which the site has yielded six single examples. It is, of course, crucial that the stallion burial is contemporary with the rest of the site, and doubts have been widely expressed about this possibility: direct radiocarbon measurements on it would decide.[10]

Two recent analyses of the faunal remains, by different methods, have given what appear to be contradictory results. The first was a detailed study of the mortality statistics, carried out by Marsha Levine (1990), and compared with other assemblages which she has personally studied. Her conclusion was that the age-profile of the Dereivka horses was characteristic of a population exploited by hunting. An alternative approach was attempted by David Anthony and Dorcas Brown: an SEM examination of the wear surfaces on the second premolar teeth of the ritually buried horse has demonstrated a pattern of attrition consistent with use of a bit – which did not, however, occur on other specimens (Anthony and Brown 1991). If this specimen is indeed contemporary with the site as a whole, rather than being

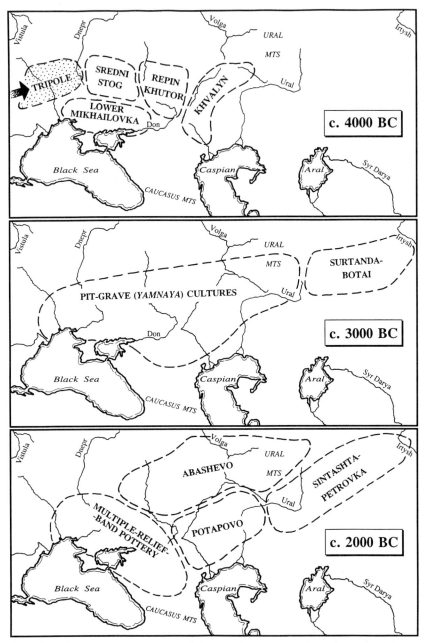

7.7 *The principal cultural groups of the Pontic steppes and northern Kazakhstan at millennial intervals, 4000–2000 BC [new drawing].*

a later intrusion, it would suggest that at least one horse at this time was a domesticated (or at least tamed) animal used for riding. In this case it might be hypothesised that ridden horses were used in hunting, on the principle 'it takes one to catch one'. Alternatively, the stallion is intrusive and Sredni Stog-period Dereivka is simply a horse-hunting site. Similar considerations would apply to contemporary sites of the Khvalynsk culture on the Volga, such as Sezzhee.

Another candidate which has attracted recent attention as an early centre of horse domestication has been the site of Botai near Petropavlovsk in northern Kazakhstan (Zaibert 1993), for this large village of circular, semi-subterranean huts also has a faunal assemblage consisting very largely of horse, and would be a plausible candidate for the eastern origin favoured by Marija Gimbutas. The relative chronology is now becoming clearer, how-ever, thanks to a dating programme undertaken by the Oxford Radiocarbon Accelerator Unit, and Botai now appears to post-date Sredni Stog, and to be largely contemporary with the Pit-Grave culture in the later fourth millennium. Although some horses have been claimed to show bit-wear, the great majority are wild; so this might exemplify a mode of 'horse-catching' which has no recent analogue in its combination of domestication and hunt-ing of a single species. Where domestic animals are not used for secondary products, the hunting of horses can make use of pasture which is beyond the range of cattle, because of their water requirements, slow movement and inability to graze under snow. In a wider context, however, this seems to be a fairly marginal phenomenon, rather than an evolutionary step towards horse-rearing and pastoralism.

The long experience of steppe tribes with the hunting of horses, even if it shows no inbuilt tendency to domestication, would have provided an opportunity when new motives impinged on this area. This took place after 3500 BC, when the Maikop culture of the northern Caucasus was formed under influence from the Uruk colonial expansion (Chapter 18), and in turn created the conditions for the formation of the Pit-Grave culture.[11] This included the use of wheeled vehicles (apparently four-wheelers, rather than a mixture of wagons and carts: Izbitzer 1993), and probably wool-bearing breeds of sheep whose wool may have been used for felt.[12] As well as the use of cattle as draught animals, new species of transport animal such as the camel (see above) and donkey may have been encountered. These would have provided new models of animal utilisation, which may have been the stimulus for the domestication of animals used for riding (see below). This would have provided the mobility needed to make effective use of the extensive interfluvial pastures. Domestication of the horse would initially have been the outcome of culture-contact, but soon became integral to a new way of life. The expansionist character of this cultural grouping, whose tumuli dot the steppe interfluves eastward to the Urals and also penetrated westwards in enclaves as far as the Hungarian Plain (Chapter 11), is well known; but unfortunately its often insubstantial settlement sites have not yielded large animal-bone assemblages which have attracted detailed analysis. Only Mikhailovka has provided an assemblage, so far subjected only to species identification, in which horses form 10 to 15 per cent of a spectrum of predominantly domestic animals (mostly cattle and sheep). There is thus no direct osteological evidence to demonstrate that the horse was domesticated at this point, though it remains an outstanding probability that it was so, as is indicated by the spread of domestic horses to adjacent areas, both within and beyond its natural distribution.

Spread of the horse in the Near East

The onager was widely distributed in western Asia and had long been hunted, and the donkey spread rapidly in the late fourth millennium as a pack animal. The potential presence of three different species of equid (and six possible hybrids) thus makes osteological (and even iconological) identification of horses difficult; but there is sufficient evidence to be reasonably confident of the presence of the horse in the third millennium, and perhaps the late fourth (Littauer and Crouwel 1979, 23–30). Since the survival of relict Pleistocene populations is not everywhere excluded (e.g. for Anatolia), simple presence is insufficient to demonstrate domestication. There is unambiguous evidence of the presence of horses and the use of equids for riding from the later third millennium (Moorey 1970), and the accumulation of indications suggests an earlier third-millennium spread of domesticated stock, though in very small numbers. An equid humerus from Late Chalcolithic Shiqmim (identified metrically as horse) with an associated date of 3240 BC has a claim to be the earliest (Grigson 1993), as would contemporary horse bones claimed from Tal-i Iblis in south-central Iran. Their cases are respectively strengthened by EB horse-bones from Arad and Aphek, and by a bone inlay portraying a horse from Susa; but some ambiguity remains because of the small numbers of specimens and alternative species of equid. The clearest indications of the presence of horses are in eastern Anatolia (Bökönyi 1991). It is possible that the consistent representation of horse in late-fourth- and third-millennium sites in the upper Euphrates valley in Turkey – like Arslantepe, fundamentally affected by the Uruk expansion[13] – is a reflection of the importance of a route along which these animals were imported. The early Near Eastern horses seem to have been ridden only incidentally (Moorey 1970), since this activity is not the focus of elite iconography, which rather concentrates on the military uses of equids as draught animals. Current opinion is that the equids shown pulling battle-cars are not the notoriously untamable onager, nor just an ass, but rather a hybrid – either mule/hinny or a donkey–onager cross. (Such hybrids were occasionally used as draught animals in ploughing, according to textual evidence.) If that is so, then the principal reason for importing horses from a northern breeding pool (via the

Caucasus and eastern Anatolia?) may well have been to provide hybrid pack-animals, and increasingly also draught-animals for military use, in the context of the growing conflicts between early states (see below, in connection with the chariot). In this perspective, the beginning of horse domestication in the area immediately north of the Caucasus could have been intimately connected with the northward penetration of the secondary products complex, and the use of the donkey – initially as a pack animal but used experimentally both for riding and draught. Horse-domestication and riding may therefore be less independent of the main secondary products complex than it is currently presented in archaeo-zoological discussions (e.g. papers in Hänsel and Zimmer 1994).

Riding and horse-control

Horses only became draught animals in their own right when a light, wheeled vehicle had been invented (see below). The representational evidence provides the answer to the old question as to whether early domestic horses were ridden: yes, they were. With such small horses, however, the seat may have been unusual to modern eyes – perhaps more like the 'back seat' (over the pelvic girdle) that is appropriate on a donkey, or a very forward seat like that of American Indians on their mustangs. The former method of riding was used in the Near East in the third and second millennia, at first using a nose-ring instead of a bit (Littauer and Crouwel 1979, fig. 37); the latter may have been usual further north. These two styles would have been the manner of riding until the first millennium BC, when horses were first ridden for military purposes. In the meantime, however, over the course of the second millennium, chariotry had been developed, and with it an array of control techniques using bridle-bits and other harness attachments. The combination of this developed type of bridle, together with larger breeds of horse, made possible the military use of the ridden horse as it was employed by the nomads of the steppes, and the use of cavalry as it developed amongst the Iron Age civilisations of the east Mediterranean. Earlier riding styles should not be confused with these more advanced forms of control.

The question then arises as to how early ridden horses were controlled, outside the Near East where the use of a nose-ring was transferred from cattle. Here another shift in perception has taken place, in connection with the interpretation of various pieces of perforated antler taken to represent elements of harness. Antler objects interpreted as the cheek-pieces to bridle-bits (and in some cases found in position in burials) are known from the steppe area and eastern Europe in the early second millennium onwards; bronze bits are known from the Near East after 1600, and in temperate Europe after 1300 (Potratz 1966; Hüttel 1981). Both of these sets of bits fall into two broad types: the vertical bar (*Stangenknebel*) or the disk (*Plattenknebel*), the latter sometimes with spikes (and in Near Eastern metal forms sometimes explicitly imitating a wheel). Temperate European

(Urnfield) ones are largely of the bar type, and were preceded during the earlier second millennium by an often highly decorated series of antler examples, known both from temperate Europe and the western steppes (see below, Figure 7.8). It is these objects which have encouraged the interpretation of the perforated antler pieces from Dereivka and elsewhere as primitive bridle-bits. But the second-millennium examples were used in connection with the chariot, i.e. most probably for *driving*, when the horse must be controlled without other physical contact; so they are not really necessary for controlling a ridden horse, except in the kind of disciplined cavalry movement which took over from chariotry at the end of the second millennium, and for which increasingly elaborate bits were designed. The horse could thus have been initially controlled in a rather simple way by a rope noseband; and decorative impressions on pottery indicate an extensive knowledge of cordage and presumably ropes, probably made from hemp (cf. also Chapters 15 and 16).

The spread of horse-riding in Europe

Horses seem to have come into use in Europe at approximately the same time as they spread into the Near East: the first half of the third millennium. Since horse populations survived in temperate Europe, including the Carpathian Basin, the sporadic occurrence of horse bones in early Copper Age (Tiszapolgár) contexts in Hungary need not be explained by the import of exotic animals in exchange for copper. Instead, their first regular occurrence in assemblages of the Baden culture may be taken as a token of a new interest in horses of local origin. Since the latter part of this culture coincides with the arrival of small enclaves of Pit-Grave burial within its east Hungarian distribution at the end of the fourth millennium and the beginning of the third (Chapter 11), these facts may well be related; and this event can plausibly be seen as the stimulus for local domestication.

In a recent survey of the European evidence, Norbert Benecke (1994) has pointed to the appearance of horses in greater numbers, and with more morphological variability, in the late TRB Bernburg culture in central Germany, and in the contemporary Cham culture in Bavaria – both situated on the main westward contact-routes from the Carpathian Basin, and dated to c.3000 BC. In the Bernburg culture, this coincides with the introduction of a larger (probably wool-bearing) breed of sheep, which also occurs in Poland and Hungary (Müller 1994). The central European horses show a degree of continuity with earlier populations there, and are therefore plausibly interpreted as a local intake from indigenous wild stock (either here or in the Carpathian Basin), under the influence of new practices in adjacent regions. Scandinavian horses seem to be of central European rather than local type (Benecke 1994, 135), and were apparently introduced from there. The first plentiful occurrence in Denmark is in pits at the late TRB (MN III–V, i.e. parallel to Corded Ware) site of Lindskov in central Jutland

(Davidsen 1978, 142). The first burial with a horse-skull occurs in a Corded Ware context at Borgstedt in north-west Germany (Bauch 1988).[14] There is also a similar Bell-Beaker burial from Moravia, while the well-known Hungarian Bell-Beaker site of Csepel Haros (Bökönyi 1978) seems to have been a specialised breeding centre, potentially supplying the adjacent Bell-Beaker network with the central-European type of horses (see Chapter 15).

These occurrences suggest successive westward extensions of the domesticated horse, presumably as a riding-animal, reaching western Europe (the British Isles, France, Iberia) in the Bell-Beaker period of the later third millennium (van Wijngaarden-Bakker 1974, 345–7 for horses at Newgrange). Uerpmann (1990) has emphasised that Spanish populations were derived from local wild stock; indeed, he views the domestication process as having begun not in east Europe but in the far west of Europe in the third millennium. Underlying this are the twin ideas of direct Near Eastern influence in the Spanish Chalcolithic fortified sites ('colonies') like Los Millares, in contact with the area where donkeys were already domesticated, and of a Bell-Beaker expansion from the Iberian peninsula. Whilst the model of a knock-on effect from donkey domestication is attractive, this particular reconstruction does not seem to me to be tenable on archaeological grounds (cf. Renfrew 1967a); and he does, in any case, note as an exception the striking increase in stature in Bavarian horses of the Cham culture (later fourth millennium BC), which he attributes to eastern immigration from the lower Danube (1990, 139–42), postulated as an alternative centre of local domestication. This multi-centric model of several unrelated domestication-episodes of small relict populations seems to me implausible; the reconstruction of a single, large-scale episode of horse domestication on the Pontic steppes in the later fourth millennium, whose effects were felt in eastern and central Europe in the later fourth millennium and in western Europe in the third millennium, seems more persuasive than any postulated alternative. (And my suggestion that Pontic horse domestication might indirectly reflect earlier experience with the donkey would preserve the structural coherence of Uerpmann's proposal.) Whatever the spatial logic, however, the chronological pattern is clear: domesticated horses and local domestication only began to spread into forested temperate Europe as the plough came into general use in these areas, and more extensive patterns of cultivation began, making it possible to keep larger quantities of livestock (cf. Fig. 8.4).[15]

The origin of the chariot

During the third millennium, solid-wheeled wooden wagons continued to be placed in some elite graves under tumuli on the Pontic steppes. The more elaborate design of these sunken chambers, with a side-chamber for the burial, gives them the name 'Catacomb-Graves', and they are especially numerous along the lower reaches of the Ingul and Dnepr.[16] This focus of elaboration suggests the possibility of coastal links with the Caucasus and perhaps northern Anatolia. (Links from north-west Anatolia to the lower and middle Danube, bringing amongst other things knowledge of faience and tin-bronze, were established at this time: Sherratt 1993, 22–4.) On the Anatolian plateau, ox-carts decorated with a variety of bronze openwork mountings were in use by eminent personages at sites such as Alaca Hüyük. Over the same period, Mesopotamian city-states came into conflict both with each other and with the secondary states springing up in their immediate periphery. (Some of the latter, like Ebla, may already have established merchant colonies in central Anatolia.) As well as the four-wheeled 'battle-car' pulled by four equids (controlled by a nose-ring), several experiments had been made in northern Mesopotamia and Syria with military vehicles having two solid wheels – one type used as a moving platform, the other straddled as if riding an animal (Littauer and Crouwel 1979, 37). There was clearly a military incentive to develop a fast two-wheeler; but the solutions involved solid, heavy carpentry. Attempts were made to lighten them, by use of the cross-bar wheel (evolved from a tripartite disc-wheel with lunate openings and strengthening-bars); and some solid two-wheeled vehicles – with rather implausible reconstructions – have been claimed from Catacomb-Grave contexts (e.g. Marievka mound 11, Zaporozhye region: Pustovalov 1994, fig. 11). From this background a completely new, light, horse-drawn vehicle emerged and set a new standard in fast personal transport: the chariot (Moorey 1986).

The first evidence of spoke-wheeled vehicles occurs in the early second millennium. Establishing claims of priority is an unprofitable exercise since the evidence takes such different forms: what is more striking is the simultaneity (with current levels of resolution) of their appearance over a triangle from central Anatolia to Hungary to the southern Urals. Two different interpretative emphases are possible. Looking at Anatolian seal-impressions from the late third and early second millennia, with their images of deities or royal personages on vehicles with cross-bar or spoked wheels, drawn by four and then two equids, Littauer and Crouwel (1979, 68–71) have seen an evolutionary sequence. Piggott (1983, 103), following Childe, has stressed the fundamental contrast between the light, bentwood 'tension structure' of the chariot, by comparison with the heavy 'compression structure' of the cart, and looks for its origin in non-urban communities with experience of horses: the steppes. Which origin is more plausible? It may be possible to compromise, and suggest a relationship between the two; but first, chronology.

In the Carpathian Basin the first part of the third millennium saw the absorption of the enclaves of intrusive steppe population in the east, and new links with the Adriatic through Bosnia and Slovenia; while the second part saw the effects of a wider linkage along the Danube, and up into central Germany. The radical change of pace, including the rapid development of the Transylvanian bronze industry, nevertheless took place at the beginning

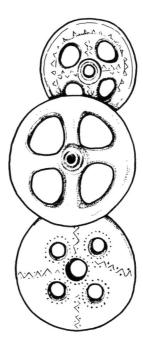

7.8 Evidence for the chariot in the Carpathian Basin, early second millennium BC: left, antler cheek-piece of bridle-bit (Százhalombatta), length 9cm, diameter 1.3 (top) to 2cm (base); right, models of spoked wheels (various sites); (from Sherratt 1987e, after Kovacs and Tihelka).

of the second millennium, with the appearance of fortified centres along the key Carpathian passes, and plentiful evidence for horse-driving in the shape of models of spoked wheels and items of antler horse-gear, pre-eminently bar-shaped cheek-pieces, often elaborately decorated with a compass-drawn ornament that was soon transferred to gold- and bronzework (Figure 7.8). In Hungary this is principally associated with a group of cultures conveniently designated as Otomani; in Moldavia it is equally typical of Monteoru: both of them, on a major trade route from the Black Sea, are characterised by fortifications and chariotry (Sherratt 1993, fig. 7).

It is now clear from new radiocarbon dates that the series of steppe cultures which succeeded the Catacomb-Graves and their contemporaries also came into existence right at the beginning of the second millennium: west to east, from the Pontic steppes to beyond the Urals, the *Mnogovalikovaya*, Timber-Grave (Potapovo phase), and Andronovo cultures (Figure 7.7). These bordered in the west on the Monteoru and Otomani cultures of Romania and Hungary, and in the east were in process of eastward expansion across the steppes – south of a line of forest cultures (Seima-Turbino-Samussk) which had their own sophisticated socketed bronze metallurgy, probably of east Asian origin. The originality of these steppe communities has been emphasised by the recognition of a series of circular ditched fortifications along the border of the steppe and forest (e.g. Arkaim and Sintashta: Zdanovich 1988; Gening, Zdanovich and Gening 1992) between the upper Ural and Tobol rivers east of Magnitogorsk. These amazing structures, with concentric rings of c.60 trapezoidal houses in a (consciously?) wheel-like array, 150m in diameter, are now known from some fifteen examples in this area, and may well be much more common in the steppe zone than has hitherto been recognised. They are associated with a flourishing metallurgy. This cultural florescence argues for new structures of trade and contact at this time, and such sites recall contemporary fortified sites in Slovakia like Barca. Associated with the Sintashta settlement is a series of cemeteries, including a large 'temple-mound' and its associated shafts with timber-lined chambers, five of which contained the remains of two-wheeled vehicles, circular antler cheek-pieces of bridle-bits, and head-and-hooves burials of horses. In one of these, the impression of the lower part of the wheel was preserved where it had been sunk beneath the floor-level, and indicated a ten- or twelve-spoked wheel. It should be emphasised that little is known of the vehicle-type of steppe chariots apart from the wheels (i.e. the impression of a multiple-spoke wheel at the eastern end of the distribution, clay models of four-spoke wheels at the western end). Two enigmatic representations on pots, of the early and mid-second millennium respectively (Piggott 1983, 93–4), suggest light, minimal (and thus probably bentwood) structures. It seems likely that the light vehicle we recognise as the chariot had its critical development in the steppe zone, in association with the development of the bridle and bit (and perhaps also a yoke specifically adapted to equine needs by the development of yoke-saddles). It is in this context that the distinctive style of compass-drawn ornament is likely to have spread, over the area from the Pontic steppes to Alalakh (and later to Mycenae). Did the typical compass-drawn *Wellenbandmuster*, so often found on harness-related equipment (Figure 7.8), represent the spinning, bouncing wheels of the light chariot?[17]

This is not, however, to argue for an 'independent invention', carried south by Aryan hordes. It can reasonably be argued that such a vehicle only emerged under southern influence. The impetus to develop a fast two-wheeler for personal transport was an urban rather than a rural necessity, and has no obvious precursors in the large four-wheel wagons of the Pit-Grave tradition. The use of equids for traction, too, was a southern practice. Its appearance on the northern shore of the Black Sea can only be understood in terms of the growing links with Anatolia, which was itself increasingly linked to Syria and northern Mesopotamia. The establishment of merchant settlements at cities on the Anatolian plateau, as far north as the Black Sea, has been established from documentary sources; and it is likely that links established from north-west Anatolia to the Danube were now supplemented by coastal connections around the whole of the western perimeter of the Black Sea. One of the commodities in demand, as well as metals, is likely to have been horses; and whereas earlier supplies may have been obtained via the Caucasus, this western route now offered an alternative. If later second-millennium evidence is anything to go by, this no doubt also included experienced trainers.[18] It was in this connection that horse and fighting-vehicle might have come together, and a new means of transport invented on the steppes: a combination of spoked wheels (perhaps already developed in Anatolia), bentwood construction, and most especially horse-training and new methods of control. Shortly after 2000 BC, in the Old Assyrian *karum* towns of central Anatolia, representations of vehicles with pairs of four-spoked wheels appear on cylinder-seals from Kültepe (*Kaniš*) near Kayseri; while from Acemhüyük (south of Tuzgölü, the great Salt Lake) comes a set of bronze model wheels with four spokes (Littauer and Crouwel 1979; 1986). In representations, the Anatolian early second-millennium two-wheelers look cumbersome and rectangular, pulled by pairs of badly-drawn equids with nose-rings and bearing heavy yokes probably without yoke-saddles. More sophisticated machines only appeared a century or so later. The earlier examples look like the first attempts to use horse (rather than hybrid) traction, in a tradition not pre-adapted for such use, by imitation of an outside model. It is significant, therefore, that these central Anatolian developments are effectively contemporary with the first evidence of spoke-wheel vehicles and antler bit-elements on the Pontic and trans-Ural steppes, and in the Carpathian Basin.[19] It seems best to regard this area as a huge interaction-sphere, in which Anatolia provided the need, and the western steppe zone the solution. Its genesis must go back to the closing centuries of the third millennium.

The creation of the chariot thus exemplifies a theme which has run throughout this discussion of early uses of the horse – the intimate relationship between the two sides of the Black Sea: Anatolia and the Caucasus on the one hand (linked since the Uruk expansion to the Near Eastern heartland), and on the other the broad belt of open country running unhindered eastward to the Altai, where mastery of the horse is the key to success. It also exemplifies a model which seems very widely applicable: an *interactionist* interpretation, based on a particular conjunction of circumstances, rather than a gradualist one of local, evolutionary change.]

THE SECONDARY EXPLOITATION

CONCLUSION: THE ORIGINS AND SPREAD OF SECONDARY ANIMAL EXPLOITATION

Previous sections have reviewed evidence for the widespread appearance of secondary uses and products in the fourth millennium BC. How far back may these innovations be traced, and what were their areas of origin?

The earliest forms of cereal cultivation in the Near East were closely tied to restricted areas of seasonally moist soil (Chapter 3), requiring minimum soil preparation. Neolithic sites first proliferated in the scattered environments where such cultivation could take place. Expansion beyond those limits took place in the Early Chalcolithic (later seventh and sixth millennia BC), particularly in two sorts of location. Samarran cultivators on the fans of eastern Iraq (on or beyond the 200mm isohyet) pioneered the use of water-spreading by constructing channels across braided streams (Oates and Oates 1976). At the same time, Hassuna farmers expanded on the brown steppe soils of northern Iraq (within the 200mm isohyet). The latter area offered few opportunities for irrigation; and while precipitation at that time may have been higher, it is likely that greater soil preparation would have been necessary for cereal-growing. Since cattle were at that time becoming widespread on lowland sites, the preconditions for traction cultivation were present. Although the first representations of ploughs occur in southern Mesopotamia only in the fourth millennium (Chapter 6), it is likely that (as with irrigation) ploughs were first developed within Greater Mesopotamia in the preceding millennia. These considerations would point to an origin in northern Iraq in the period from the late seventh, sixth or fifth millennia.

Although this innovation was probably a basic element in the spread of irrigation-cultivation on the alluvial plain of Mesopotamia, it may not have been widely used outside the lowland area. At this stage it is likely to have been a localised feature of cultivation systems where sufficient numbers of cattle were available; and there were still sharp contrasts in the type of animal husbandry practised in different regions. For instance, faunal assemblages from the Kermanshah region of western Iran show that down to the fifth millennium BC the animal economy there was based on meat, primarily juvenile goat and gazelle (Davis 1982). During the Late Chalcolithic (fifth millennium BC), at the same time as major agricultural expansion was taking place in the Ubaid period, there was a further development of animal economies on the fringes of Mesopotamia. In Kermanshah the economy diversified, with the appearance of cattle and an increase in sheep, which now became more important than goats (Davis 1982). Moreover, the sheep were now kept to a greater age, and it is likely that wool was being extensively used for the first time. Wool-sheep may have been present in this area from an earlier date, since the Sarab figurine (Bökönyi 1974, fig. 44) seems to indicate the V-shaped staples of hairy medium wool (M. L. Ryder,

224

pers. comm.). Wool-bearing sheep probably spread from the Zagros to the lowland steppe and semi-desert margins where significant changes were taking place in the fifth millennium. In southern Palestine and Sinai the colonisation of new areas in the Ghassulian was associated with a similar increase in the importance of sheep, and the infilling of the area between Palestine and Egypt was important in linking the Nile valley with developments in western Asia.

The spread of new features within the Fertile Crescent created some of the conditions for the urbanisation which took place in the fourth millennium. The conjunction of expanding populations on the alluvium using irrigation and plough agriculture, with the opportunities for long-distance trade, resulted in attempts to secure direct supplies of metal, stone and wood. The growing influence of Mesopotamia and Egypt affected a wide hinterland, as trading partners and colonies were established in resource-rich areas of Palestine, Syria, Anatolia and Iran, using both river-transport on the Nile and Euphrates and land routes with donkeys (Palestine) and camels (Iran). The sledge, probably used since the invention of the plough, was transformed by the Sumerians into the wagon or cart by the addition of wheels, as shown in the Uruk pictograms (Piggott 1968); and equids were used as traction animals for the first time to pull battle-cars in the Early Dynastic period. In the larger-scale economies of lowland Mesopotamia it became possible to support a specialised pastoral sector in the interstices of the irrigated land. Herds of dairy-cattle were kept in marshy areas (as shown by dairying scenes in reed huts), while wool-flocks were maintained partly by stubble-grazing. Animal-keeping thus began to move (like the cultivation of tree-crops) from the sphere of subsistence to that of commodity production, and manufacturing industry based on wool provided textiles for export. Secondary products had become an essential part of the urban economy.

The development of economies based on secondary animal exploitation thus began as a mosaic of individual innovations, mostly in the semi-arid areas of the Near East, initially as a response to the problem of adapting early forms of farming to new types of environment, especially to the opportunities of open landscapes where it was possible to maintain larger quantities of livestock. These innovations came together during the period of rapid economic change leading to the rise of urban communities, and were disseminated by the expansion of trade-routes linking the early states with their resource-rich hinterlands. The process opened up a wider hinterland, from Anatolia through the Caucasus to Iran, in which local communities – Troy, Maikop, Altyn Depe – were developed by wider contacts. The introduction of these new elements to the Pontic steppes created a major area of secondary development and dispersal, carrying new elements both into central Asia and into eastern Europe. In the forested conditions of temperate Europe, livestock-keeping had been restricted in scale by lack of grazing; but the introduction of the plough initiated a more extensive type of agriculture that could support a larger pastoral component. The Carpathian Basin acted as an important centre of dispersal within Europe, and its links to the North European Plain had carried advanced forms of stock-raising to the Atlantic seaboard by the third millennium BC.

NOTES

1. [Note that this type of 'short' longbarrow is a later fourth-millennium type, and not an example of the earliest unchambered longbarrows discussed in Chapters 13 and 14.]

2. [Thrane (1989, 118) makes the same point: 'In view of the number of unchambered long-barrow excavations during the last decades it is worth noting that none of these have produced ard-marks.' It is noteworthy that the other set of ploughmarks from Poland besides those from Sarnowo, the set from Łupawa 15 in Pomerania (Jankowska 1980), belong to a group contemporary with Wiórek or Danish EN C/MN I.]

3. [The two ox-figures and six flat axes were found last century, in 1873, and though the findspot is fairly precisely known there is no record of their archaeological context. The question of their association thus arises: could the ox-figures be much later, as Klavs Randsborg (pers. comm.) has suggested? As part of a recent study (Pieczyński 1985) the objects were analysed in Warsaw (and two of the axes also in Heidelberg). The axes show a number of impurities typical of the *Fahlerz* ores used in the northern Carpathians in the later fourth millennium (see Chapter 4): 0.5–1.0% of arsenic, 0.02–0.04% of antimony, smaller amounts (0.01–0.03%) of silver and nickel. The oxen show 4.0% and 2.3% of arsenic respectively (amongst other impurities, representing 0.3% and 0.7% respectively, not reported), which would suggest deliberate arsenical alloying. Since this composition was not used after the third millennium, this confirms the date of the oxen as pre-Bronze Age; and by comparison with the axes the higher arsenic values of the ox-figures suggest a different but broadly contemporary origin. (This is supported by their technology: lost-wax casting was not introduced to this area before the Bronze Age, or used for animal figures before the Hallstatt period.) Where did the ox-figures originate? The lost-wax casting method would suggest EBA Anatolia or the Levant at this date, and the examples illustrated by Littauer and Crouwel (1973), such as the one from Alaca Hüyük near Ankara (their No. 4, pl. xxxvii) now in the Boston Museum of Fine Arts, illustrate the genre to which the Bytyń figures might belong – specifically, paired cattle pulling wagons. The most likely interpretation still seems to me that they are imports from Anatolia (and perhaps specifically from the lower Kızıl Irmak region, famous for its EBA metal figures), at the time of the introduction of ox-traction for wheeled vehicles and ploughs. Such a phenomenon would suggest something of the impact and scale of connections implied by the new traction usage and technology.]

4. [The evidence for prehistoric textiles has now been magnificently summarised in a classic work by E. J. W. Barber (1991).]

5. [All crops are cash crops, but some more so than others: the ones mentioned here are those in which value is added by secondary production (oil-pressing, cheese-making) before distribution and consumption, rather than in the home (cooking).]

6. [The pictographs distinguish between the different containers used for goats', sheep's, and cows' milk (Green 1980, fig. 3).]

7. [The most sophisticated discusssion of the inter-related processes of natural and cultural selection is by Durham (1991, chapter 5). He discusses (1991, 242 and 252) my original suggestion, following Simoons, and integrates it with the vitamin D hypothesis: 'the genes responsible for adult lactose absorption have evolved to high frequencies in populations that (1) have a long-standing tradition of dairying and fresh milk consumption, and (2) live in environments of low ultraviolet radiation where vitamin D and metabolic calcium are chronically deficient' (279); 'I submit that the memes of dairying and the genes of adult lactose absorption *coevolved* as a function of latitude' (282).]

8. [Historians of the subject may wish to compare the two versions! The accounts differ in the following respects: (1) in being more sceptical about early-fourth-millennium domestication on the steppes, and preferring a mid-fourth-millennium date; (2) ceasing to rely on the evidence of antler 'cheek-pieces' before the undoubted second-millennium examples; (3) acknowledging the survival and contribution of local horse populations in forested Europe; (4) seeing the chariot as the outcome of steppe technology and Near Eastern military needs; and thus, in general, seeing horse-usage on the steppes as being *more* intimately related to Near Eastern developments. In revising this section, I greatly benefited from participating in the conference *Die Indogermanen und das Pferd* in Berlin in 1992, now published as Hänsel and Zimmer (1994); and also from discussions with Viktor Trifonov and Marsha Levine.]

9. [They are distinguished by size and robusticity: the eastern (open-country) populations were larger, and this distinction between 'eastern' and 'western' horses was still evident in European domestic populations into the early medieval period. Uerpmann (1990) has divided European wild horses into geographical subspecies: *Equus ferus ferus* for the steppe population, *E. ferus sylvestris* for the north-west European forest population, *E. ferus lusitanicus* for the Iberian population, and *E. ferus scythicus* for a postulated Balkan-Anatolian population. These would all represent 'tarpan' populations, rather than Przewalski horses (*E. ferus przewalskii*), typical for central Asia. (There is, of course, no justification for a separate species, *E. caballus*, for domestic populations.) It also appears that there was some geographical overlap between the distribution of wild horses and that of other equids, e.g. *Equus hydruntinus* (a now extinct ass, surviving into the Holocene in the Carpathian Basin), and also with *Equus hemionus*, the onager, further east.]

10. Date now released: (KI-5488) 2380 ± 120 bc = 3300–2650 cal BC, i.e. post-Sredni Stog.

11. [On this model, the area of genesis of the Pit-Grave culture would be in the Pre-Kuban area, north of Krasnodar, in the late Maikop period (parallel to the formation of Novotitarovka); that would be my prediction for the area of initial horse domestication, too.]

12. [Traces of coloured cloths with geometrical patterns have been observed in a number of Pit-Grave burials, e.g. Tri Brata (see discussion in Ecsedy 1979, 38–9).]

13. [And also serving as way-stations to the Caucasus, whose metallurgical repertoire shows the influence of precisely the forms discovered at Arslantepe (see Chapter 18).]

14. [The interesting grave at Großhöflein-Föllik in the Austrian Burgenland (Pittioni 1954, 247), within a stone setting, contained the burial of an adult woman and child, together with a 20-year-old mare and foal, cow and a calf, nanny-goat and a kid, ewe and a lamb, and also another 4-year-old mare and the skull of another 20-year-old. It was formerly thought to belong to the late-third-millennium Guntramsdorf-Draßburg group (loosely described as 'Corded Ware' by Pittioni), but is now considered to belong to the early second-millennium Mad'arovce culture, chariot-using and closely related to its east-Hungarian neighbour, Otomani.]

15. [The arguments set out in the preceding section now throw doubt on the interpretation of a set of antler objects which were interpreted by Lichardus (1980) as the cheek-pieces of bits. The whole subject of pre-Bronze Age bridle-bits has been recently reviewed by Dietz (1992), who comprehensively and critically reviews the evidence for perforated antler tines and concludes that all of them are better interpreted as toggles or in ways unconnected with horse harnessing, and not essentially different from the perforated antler tines common in Neolithic lake-villages. As described above, however, this does not invalidate the reconstruction of horse domestication; it merely removes a potentially convenient (but actually misleading) artefactual marker for its spread.]

16. [These tombs are especially interesting for the numbers of graves with specialist metal-casting equipment, probably making use of local ores. Some fortified sites are known (the upper levels of Mikhailovka, the Bayda fortress on an island in the Dnepr); and a remarkable circular temple-mound has been excavated at Molochansk on the Ingul (Pustovalov 1994).]

17. [Following this line of thought: may that also be the origin of that archetypal Aryan symbol, the *swastika* (four spokes, felloe omitted, with trailing lines suggesting movement)? The layout of the Arkaim settlement, with its outer circle of houses arranged in four circumcurrent 'wings', offers a plausible origin.]
18. [No doubt speaking Indo-Aryan (eastern Indo-European) languages: see Chapter 19.]
19. [Within the steppe region, the outlines of two regional schools of chariotry may perhaps be discerned: a western one (extending into the Carpathian Basin) using four-spoked wheels and bar-bits; and a more easterly one, represented for instance at Sintashta, with multiple-spoked wheels and circular bits. There was considerable mixing and hybridisation between them. Both contributed to the development of Near Eastern chariotry (Moorey 1986), via both the central Anatolian and Caucasian routes, with the latter tradition extending eastwards and eventually reaching China.]

8

Wool, Wheels and Ploughmarks: Local Developments or Outside Introductions in Neolithic Europe?

(Submitted 1985, published 1987)

In the 1982 issue of the *Bulletin* of the Institute of Archaeology, Dr J. C. Chapman devoted an article entitled 'The Secondary Products Revolution and the Limitations of the Neolithic' (Chapman 1983) to a critical discussion of ideas which I had put forward in two papers, in 1980 and 1981.[1] This short note is intended to remove some of the misconceptions in Chapman's review. The following observations refer to points raised by Chapman: page references are to his article.

The cart (p. 111). The appearance of the wagon and cart in Europe is one of the clearest examples of an introduced technology (Childe 1951; Piggott 1979). There is no evidence for wheeled vehicles in Europe before the mid-fourth millennium BC[2] (the beginning of the Baden and Ezero cultures). Claims of an earlier origin in the Balkans are based solely on finds of clay discs taken to represent model wheels. Since it is often hard to distinguish the clay wheels of model vehicles from clay spindle whorls, perforated clay discs can only be taken as evidence for use of the wheel when models of the vehicles themselves are present. This is the case in the Early Dynastic period in southern Mesopotamia, but such models are completely absent from the Balkan Neolithic and Copper Age, though they do appear with the Baden

---

This was published in the Bulletin *of the Institute of Archaeology (University of London), and was a reply to a review-article there by John Chapman, in which he offered an autonomist view of European development in the later Neolithic – which dated the appearance of the light plough to what I have called (Chapter 5) the mature Neolithic – and sought an origin for transhumance in continuity from Palaeolithic hunting practices. (Publication of this reply was delayed by the appearance of a special edition of the* Bulletin, *celebrating the opening of the Institute in Regent's Park in 1937.) John and I still disagree on this, but usually over a drink. Indeed, the principal interpretative change signalled in this paper is to attribute the dietary change which is reflected in jugs, cups, etc. to the arrival in Europe, not of milk, but alcohol (see Chapter 15).*

culture. There is no reason to consider the 'model wheels' claimed for Gumelnitsa as other than spindle whorls, and quite irrelevant to the problem of wheeled vehicles (Piggott 1983, 17).

The plough (p. 112). The earliest representations of ploughs are those in the Uruk IV pictographs. I speculated (Chapter 3) that the light plough may have come into use some two millennia earlier in the Hassuna-Halaf period in the moist steppe areas on the edges of the Mesopotamian Plain, in parallel with the development of simple irrigation in Samarran contexts on valley-edge fans. The recent find of ploughmarks in a Susa A context (c.5000 BC) in Khuzestan (Wright et al. 1980) fits very happily with this suggestion. This firm evidence from the Near East contrasts with the absence of comparable indications in Europe before the fourth millennium BC. The 'territorial evidence supported by certain technological data' is hardly enough to persuade one otherwise.

The evidence from buried soil-surfaces preserved under settlement-remains, earthworks or peat is, of course, crucial and is by no means confined to the period after 3500 BC which is when plentiful traces of ploughing appear. These contexts can provide evidence for a variety of soil-preparation practices besides the use of the traction-plough, and need to be scrutinised carefully for such traces. Convincing ploughmarks made with the light plough (ard) in temperate Europe take the form of the criss-cross furrows that result from cross-ploughing. The earliest and best example is the 175 square metres preserved under a long barrow with three megalithic chambers of EN C/MN I date (c.3500 BC) at Snave near Dreslette on Fyn (Figure 7.1; Thrane 1982). These criss-cross furrows are the earliest unambiguous ard-marks in Europe. Other possible traces of cultivation may be earlier, and one candidate for such an interpretation is the parallel traces of cultivation beneath Barrow 8 of the longbarrow cemetery at Sarnowo in Kujavia. The Sarnowo furrows are wide, unidirectional[3] channels about 20cm apart (Dąbrowski 1971). Their chronological position is bracketed by an underlying pit with a radiocarbon date calibrating to c.4500 BC and the overlying barrow, which dates to the mid-fourth millennium BC. It has usually been assumed that these are ard-marks made by animal traction: but it is also possible that Neolithic gardening techniques included features such as 'lazy beds' (cultivation ridges) which would also leave parallel traces. Such ridged cultivation is characteristic of intensive horticultural systems without animal traction in many parts of the world, and it seems highly likely that various intensive forms of cultivation would have appeared by this stage in the European Neolithic. One might guess at the possibility of hoe-based cultivation in the Mediterranean and central Europe, with a zone of spade-based cultivation in the north. Some hint of this is present in the design of European ards of the second millennium: the sole- and crook-ard in the south and the bow- or spade-ard in the north, loosely based on the design of the hoe and spade respectively.[4] Spade-based cultivation may have continued in widespread use in parallel with traction cultivation, and may have been prevalent in areas such as Ireland (Caulfield 1978).

The example of 'ploughmarks' quoted by Chapman from a time before my postulated introduction of the ard, however, raises problems as to whether they have anything to do with agriculture at all. A rectangular enclosure some 150m long by 5m wide at Březno in north-west Bohemia is dated to the Early Eneolithic (i.e. late TRB, c.3600 BC – and only briefly ante-dating my ard horizon) and is distantly related to the Kujavian longbarrow (Pleinerová 1980; 1981). It was probably originally covered by a low mound. Within this, and parallel to its long axis, are short, discontinuous shallow ditches or furrows. These are not the accidentally preserved remains of an old land surface beneath the barrow, but – as their orientation shows – part of its construction. Whether they are traces of internal divisions or some more regular preparation of the surface is not clear, but they are in no way comparable to the convincing series of Bronze Age and later Neolithic criss-cross ploughmarks such as those from Denmark. They may have some connection with the Sarnowo furrows, but they do not prove ploughing.

Also quite irrelevant to this problem is the so-called 'rope-traction ard' from Satrupholmer Moor, Angeln (Steensberg 1973), which is actually a common form of Ertebølle canoe-paddle, closely comparable to the recent find of an elaborately decorated example from the underwater site of Tybrind Vig off Zealand (Andersen 1983; conveniently illustrated in Jensen 1982, fig. 18). The two holes in the Satrup one are probably for repair (Søren Andersen, pers. comm.). The unlikely scenario of precocious plough-ing around a lake in Schleswig Holstein can thus be replaced by the more plausible idea of canoeing across it.[5]

One more type of evidence should be noted, since it has sometimes been used to argue for an earlier use of ox-traction for ploughing. This is the morphology of cattle bones from the early fifth-millennium BC site of Vădastra on the lower Danube in Romania (Gheție and Mateesco 1973; Mateesco 1975). On the basis of deformation in the epiphyses of the humerus and femur, it was suggested that the forelimbs of subadult animals had been subjected to vertical compression as the result of carrying loads. While this phenomenon deserves further study, it cannot by itself be taken as evidence of the use of bovines for traction.

In short: all the evidence confirms the antiquity of ploughing in the Near East, and its much later appearance in Europe – most probably in the mid-fourth millennium BC.

Milking and alcohol (pp. 112, 116). My views on this subject have progressed considerably since 1981, and are summarised in Chapter 7. I would no longer directly associate the emergence of lactose tolerance with the horizon of drinking-vessels which characterises later-fourth- and early-third-millennium pottery assemblages in Europe, on which more below. Further data on lactose tolerance show that it is present only in relatively low frequencies in Mediterranean and Near Eastern populations, though much higher in northern Europe (Piazza et al. 1981). For this reason it is very unlikely to have been associated with the initial spread of farming populations (*contra* Chapman, p. 116). Flatz and Rotthauwe (1977), however, have provided a plausible evolutionary mechanism for its appearance in temperate European populations some time after the spread of agriculture to northern Europe. They point to a selective advantage given by the ability to drink unprocessed milk in the prevention of rickets. This calcium-deficiency disease is characteristic of areas of low sunlight and thus low levels of vitamin D production. Although rickets must have been an endemic problem in northern latitudes,[6] a cereal-based diet, deficient in vitamin D, would create a particular problem in this respect. Since milking was an advantageous way of using the rich pasture grasses that would have colonised abandoned fields in temperate Europe, lactose tolerance had a selective advantage among north European farming populations and could indeed have emerged during Neolithic times [cf. Bogucki 1984], although it probably reached present frequencies only much later. The implication of all this is that milk was probably not drunk directly in early times in any case, but only used in the form of yoghurt, koumish and cheese. This added complication was no doubt one factor in the relatively late emergence of milk-based pastoralism in the Near East (Davis 1984).

The interpretation of European fourth- and third-millennium pottery assemblages with an emphasis on drinking equipment is an interesting question on which I have done further work (Sherratt 1987). These new forms contrast with the wide, shallow vessels that dominate Balkan Neolithic and Copper Age assemblages, and which in view of the above discussion may well have held milk products, as Chapman quite rightly notes. The horizon of drinking vessels from Troy II via Baden and Globular Amphorae to Corded Ware and Bell-beakers, however, continues to demand explanation. Professor Renfrew (1972) originally asserted the importance of the introduction of wine (see below on tree crops) in explaining the appearance of this assemblage in the Aegean. This is most probably the case in that area, but would not explain the very similar vessels in the Baden culture, since the wild grape *Vitis sylvestris* – although present in temperate Europe – does not contain enough sugar to ferment, and cultivated vines were not grown in central Europe before the Roman period. Chapman is almost certainly right, however, in pointing to the range of alcoholic beverages potentially available by this time: mead, beer and (as I originally suggested) koumish. This wider range of sugars and carbohydrates was itself partly due to the complex of economic changes which I have described,[7] while the male ethos of social drinking was closely related to the social effects of an enlarged pastoral sector. What thus seems to appear in common over large areas of Europe is a social practice (itself arguably Anatolian and Near Eastern in origin) rather than a particular beverage: though the sophisti-

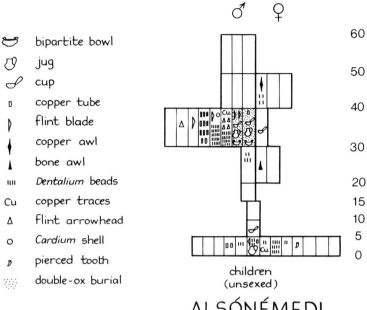

bipartite bowl
jug
cup
copper tube
flint blade
copper awl
bone awl
Dentalium beads
Cu   copper traces
Δ   flint arrowhead
o   Cardium shell
ꝑ   pierced tooth
⠿   double-ox burial

♂ ♀

60
50
40
30
20
15
10
5
0

children
(unsexed)

ALSÓNÉMEDI
Baden Culture

8.1 Grave goods with burials in the Baden culture cemetery of Alsónémedi, Hungary, arranged according to age and sex. From Sherratt (1976); data from J. Korek, 'Ein Gräberfeld der Badener Kultur bei Alsónémedi', Acta Archaeologica Acad. Sci. Hung. I, 35–91 (1951). [Note the association of drinking sets with paired cattle burials (cow and calf): see also Figs 8.2 and 15.4.]

cated, sunshine-rich areas of the east Mediterranean, with their wine and silver drinking-vessels, seem to have exercised a powerful stylistic influence over neighbouring parts of Europe. Both drinking vessels and wheeled vehicles rapidly became symbols of the elite. The combination of equipment for drinking and driving in the rich Baden culture graves of the Alsónémedi cemetery c.3500 BC is the precursor of a tradition of ostentatious burial that was to last throughout prehistory (Figures 8.1 and 8.2; also 15.4).

Wool (p. 113). It is hard to understand Chapman's comments on this subject. Textile experts (Ryder 1983; Barber 1991) are agreed that wool was a late introduction to Europe – as, incidentally, to Egypt: it first became widespread in the Near East c.4000 BC[8] and appeared in Europe c.3000 BC (Chapter 7). Of course there were loom-made textiles before this time, but these were of plant fibres – linen, nettle or lime bast. The absence of flax seeds in botanical samples from particular sites is scarcely surprising, and in no way contradicts this point. There is no reason to suppose that Balkan Neolithic loom-weights, spindle whorls and textile-like designs on pottery reflect anything other than the production of linen textiles, of the kind plentifully preserved in Swiss lake-villages. [The absence, not only of wool

ALSÓNÉMEDI

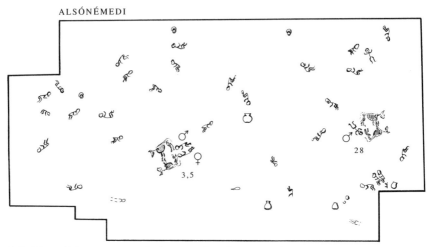

8.2 *Plan of the cemetery of Alsónémedi (schematic: after Banner 1956, redrawn). The paired-cattle burials, accompanying graves 3&5 and 28, are represented conventionally [new drawing].*

but even of other textiles known at the time, was a striking feature of the complete set of clothing preserved with the late fourth-millennium 'Iceman' of the Hauslabjoch, who was dressed entirely in leather and fur, underneath a grass cloak: Spindler 1994, 132–47.]

Tree crops (p. 113). The economically important tree crops of southern Europe and western Asia were dates, figs, grapes and olives. Their domestication is a feature of the fourth millennium BC, or perhaps a little earlier in Mesopotamia (dates) and its surrounding hilly flanks (grapes). Vine and olive were particularly significant as sources of liquid commodities that could be grown as 'cash crops' and widely traded. The various members of the *Prunus* family mentioned by Chapman, which flourish in the forest-steppe margins and light woodland, are hardly comparable in importance.

Transhumance (p. 114). Chapman's position is summed up in his sentence: 'The importance of upland grazing had been recognised and exploited since the Palaeolithic; there was no reason for this long-term adaptation to cease before the Bronze Age.' This Higgsian view of the world can surely no longer be maintained. Late Pleistocene hunting groups undoubtedly moved between upland and lowland grazing areas; but postglacial afforestation intervened between this and the transhumant grazing system linked to Roman and later urban markets for animal products. These two phenomena reflect different historical situations, not two ends of a continuous process. Upland pastures had to be created from the woodland, and this was a slow process. Some small-scale flock movements in marginal areas no doubt took place in the Neolithic: but the rationale for large-scale sheep rearing only became available with wool – and only assumed any importance in the late Bronze and Iron Ages (cf. Figure 2.2). Lewthwaite (e.g. 1981) has convincingly demonstrated the subtleties of this process in the west Mediterranean.

Mining and quarrying (p. 114). There is more justification here for Chapman's strictures, in that the single sentence at issue (Chapter 6) conflated a number of points. Mining began, in an area from western Russia to Britain and from Poland to the Balkans, around 4000 BC. The context in which this took place was the shift from a *Bandkeramik* type of wedge technology exemplified by stone 'shoelast adzes' to a true axe technology in flint, classically represented by north European thin- and thick-butted forms but also characteristic of later Gumelnitsa (e.g. Berciu 1961, 419, fig. 197; Păunescu 1970, 297, fig. 33). In the North European Plain this clearly reflects the need to clear forests in newly-colonised areas, and this may be true on a smaller scale even in Bulgaria (cf. the analysis of Detev's Plovdiv site maps in Sherratt 1976, fig. S10). Its coincidence with the beginning of copper-mining, however, reminds us that it may equally be related to the significance of stone axes as a medium of exchange, and it occurred at the same time as the movements of Wolhynian flint blades and early domestic horses noted above. All this preceded my postulated arrival of the plough.

This new axe technology, however, provided the means for the greatly increased scale of forest clearance in the mid-fourth millennium which was associated with the beginnings of plough cultivation and the expanded role of livestock which went with it. This is most eloquently shown in pollen diagrams from long-occupied areas such as the Aldenhovener Platte, where a pollen diagram prepared by A. J. Kalis (Kalis 1988; Lüning and Kalis 1988) shows a dramatic increase in open country during the fourth millennium BC, by contrast with the tiny impact of earlier farming. The same effect is apparent in Denmark in the so-called B-Landnam (Troels-Smith 1953) of the Danish Middle Neolithic, with its permanent clearances and plentiful occurrence of *Plantago lanceolata*. The massive increase in the scale of flint mining which accompanied this major assault on the forests is well demonstrated in the area supplied by the largest of the Polish flint-mining complexes, Krzemionki (Lech and Leligdowicz 1980, fig. 23). In the TRB period, the overwhelming preponderance of its distinctive axes occur within 100km of the source (Figure 8.3, above). In Globular Amphora contexts, after 3400 BC, the volume of production had undergone a massive expansion, reflected in a fivefold increase in its distribution radius, with large numbers occurring up to 400km away, in Kujavia (Figure 8.3, below).

Once again, it is the largely forested nature of Neolithic Europe which has to be borne in mind when discussing changes in subsistence economy. The first farming systems were very small in scale and occupied only a tiny fraction of the landscape, as a glance at any of Sielmann's (1971) maps will reveal. The importance of the plough in temperate Europe was that it first made larger areas of cleared land an advantage, so creating the necessary preconditions for any form of specialised animal husbandry [cf. Figure 2.1].

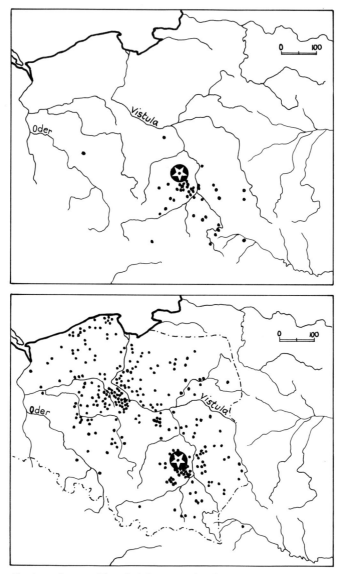

8.3 *Distribution of axes of banded flint in Poland, around the mining centre (starred) of Krzemionki Opatowskie: above,* in the TRB *period (4000–3400 BC); below,* in the Globular Amphora period (3400–2800 BC). Redrawn after Lech and Leligdowicz (1980). A massive increase in the scale of forest clearance is indicated.*

This completes a review of the substantive points offered by Chapman, and his other opinions are perhaps best discussed in a more general context. A main aim of my 1981 article was to demonstrate that the European evidence cannot be considered in isolation; the Near East and its temperate European hinterland must be discussed from the fourth millennium onwards as a potentially interacting system in which innovations appeared in Europe in 'package' form, having had a longer developmental history further east (Figure 0.4). This conception is not novel: indeed it precisely characterises our present view of the origins and spread of farming itself. What I am in effect postulating is a second generation of pastoral and agricultural techniques, originating in the dry areas which make up a large part of western Asia and the adjacent steppes, and appearing in different parts of an area stretching from the Pontus to Arabia. Since these individual innovations were widely applicable within this zone, they rapidly spread[9] and interacted to produce a more differentiated pattern of agriculture than the relatively archaic, small-scale systems which continued to characterise forested Europe where pasture had to be won step by step from the forest.

It is not surprising, therefore, that experiments in animal-keeping began earlier in the east than in Europe, whose relative isolation ('the autonomy of the south-east European Copper Age' in Colin Renfrew's expressive phrase) meant that even in fairly open areas such as eastern Hungary, many of these innovations remained unknown. For this reason, European horticulture – like European metallurgy – pursued its own course, no doubt developing more intensive hoe or spade cultivation in some areas, slash and burn systems in others. Lacking a complementary package of new livestock and pastoral techniques, however, Europe in the Copper Age did not undergo the cumulative and sustained pattern of interactive growth that characterised this period in the Near East. The isolated elements that did spread to the more open areas of Europe – like horses in Hungary – made no further headway. Only when the full package was assembled could fundamental, systemic changes occur. Basic to all the others in temperate Europe was the use of the plough, with its logic of extending the area under cultivation, even at the cost of lower yields per hectare, and sustaining a larger pastoral sector on the fallow. This pastoral sector then provided the traction animals for cultivation. It was this linkage that built in a cumulative advantage to forest clearance, and made possible the expansion of livestock rearing and the integration of new practices. It is no accident, therefore, that both wool-sheep and horses seem to have spread across Europe in the wake of the plough and the accelerated rate of forest clearance.[10] The complementary nature of the various elements makes it a classic case of what Dr Joseph Needham (1970) has called 'package transmission'.

The incentive to adopt new techniques was no doubt building up in European farming communities, as a result of the filling-up of optimal zones for simple cultivation, the deleterious effects on many of these landscapes of two thousand years of previous cultivation, and the continuing growth of population (Figure 8.4). But the historical process which brought about the transfer of these innovations had no necessary relation to the long-term ecological dynamic which made them desirable. Innovations do not always magically appear when they are needed: there is an element of contingency which is essential to a true understanding of any historical situation.

SMALL-SCALE CULTIVATION

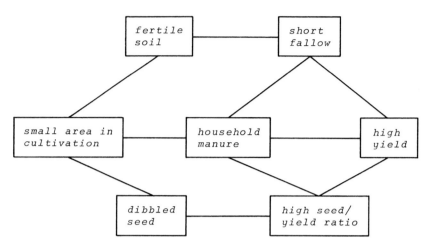

LARGE-SCALE CULTIVATION

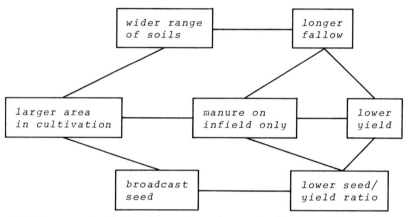

8.4 The contrasting logics of intensive and extensive farming with a pre-industrial technology: above, small-area, intensive cultivation ('horticulture'); below, extensive farming, which may be either swidden or plough-based (cf. Fig. 2.1). A long-term trend from horticulture to a greater reliance on swidden may have made the plough such an attractive innovation in fourth-millennium Europe [Sherratt, 1980, unpublished].

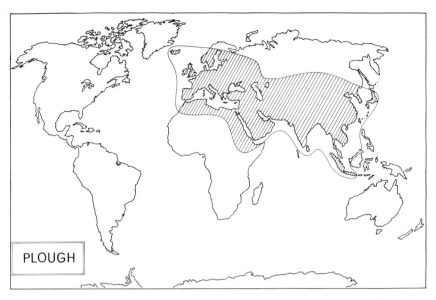

PLOUGH

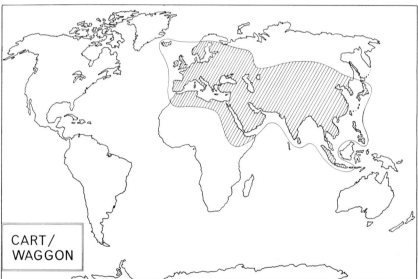

CART/
WAGGON

8.5 Distribution of the plough (above) *and wheeled vehicles* (below), *before the expansion of western technology c.*AD *1600: adapted from maps in E. Werth,* Grabstock, Hacke und Pflug, Ludwigsburg *1954. This congruence suggests that both should be considered as aspects of a 'traction complex', which spread out from a single nuclear area, rather than as parallel developments in several places, like irrigation.*

Whereas the basic options of labour intensification (irrigation, terracing, land reclamation) are widely available, those involving a specific technology or gene-pool (plough cultivation, woolly sheep) are not. How else to explain the limited distribution of plough and cart in a narrow belt of the Old World before AD 1500? (Werth 1954; Figure 8.5). These features can only be modelled by a process of contagious spread, to explain the coherent distribution area of plough cultivation on a global scale. [This spatial association between plough and cart, echoing the chronological association of their introduction to Europe, strengthens the idea of a *traction complex*, with its own technology, ideology, and attitude to domestic livestock.]

The factors which controlled the spread of these features in Europe were no different in principle from those governing other innovations. In so far as some of these leave less ambiguous traces than does prehistoric farming, they may help us to reconstruct the processes at work. Copper metallurgy provides an obvious example. The tradition of copper-working which developed in south-east Europe during the Copper Age was quite idiosyncratic and unrelated to contemporary Near Eastern industries (Renfrew 1969): its pure copper and simple casting techniques allied to an extensive use of forging distinguish it from the more efficient and sophisticated systems based on alloying and the bivalve mould. These latter innovations appeared in Europe in the third millennium BC, as a result of new contacts with the Caucasus and Anatolia (Chernykh 1978; Chapter 4) – a set of events ultimately linked to the expansion of long-distance trading networks around the rapidly urbanising areas of Mesopotamia. An isolated and independent tradition of copper-working, with an archaic technology, was brought into contact with a wider pool of experience. If this model is acceptable for metallurgical development, then why not for agriculture and pastoralism?

The contrast between this conception and Chapman's view of plough cultivation and woolly sheep appearing spontaneously among the inhabitants of Neolithic Europe is one that is probably not resolvable by reference to the ambiguous evidence for these features which survives in the archaeological record. It relates to more abstract expectations about the way the world works, and how it has done in the past. Neolithic Europe was an altogether more curious and interesting place than a homogenised image of 'prehistoric farming' would suggest; and not to see the contrasts is to blur the picture. What I have tried to show is that a piecemeal approach is inadequate to understand the nature of the problem, and unhelpful in making the most of the evidence available. Which conception prevails in the light of future evidence and debate I am content to leave to the test of time.

NOTES

1. I have dealt only with the main points raised by Chapman, and have not attempted to correct errors of transcription or to question his somewhat curious phraseology. I hope that this brief statement will clarify some of the issues involved.

2. Since I do not quote individual radiocarbon dates in this article, I have used calibrated dates and date-ranges throughout in order to avoid confusion. Terms such as 'Neolithic' and 'Copper Age' are used in a general sense, since local usages are inconsistent. My use of 'Copper Age' would not include Baden.

3. Dr Magdalena Midgely points out to me that recent excavation of a further area of the old land surface has revealed criss-cross marks as well as unidirectional furrows (Gabałówna 1970; Wiklak 1980). They would thus seem to represent genuine plough-marks. By analogy with other areas, they would date to the later part of the possible time-bracket. [The often-quoted radiocarbon date of 3620 ± 60 bc (Bakker et al. 1969, 7), it must be emphasised, is a single determination from a pit preceding the barrow (and most probably also the furrows).]

4. Though hypothetical in Europe, this relationship between hoe and plough design can be documented for Egypt both from tomb-paintings and actual objects. Neolithic soil-preparation practices are illuminatingly discussed in Schultz-Klinken (1976), partly summarised in Lüning (1980).

5. The idea of a rope-traction ard as a precursor of the true plough but pulled by human muscle-power is a pervasive one. Recent ploughs drawn by human traction are confined to the rather special circumstances of south-east Asian paddy-farming or irrigation horticulture. The basic advantage of the plough is to apply a new source of energy; and students are no substitute for draught oxen (*pace* Lüning and Meurers-Balke 1980, fig. 22!).

6. It is not without significance that this condition occurred already among Neanderthal populations, the first permanent occupants of the tundra zone; indeed, it was this condition, in one of the classic early finds of a Neanderthal skeleton, that gave rise to his persistent portrayal as a shambling idiot.

7. Alcohol may not have been widely known in Neolithic Europe – though no doubt their knowledge of hallucinogenic mushrooms was considerable, as was that of their Mesolithic predecessors.

8. Textile remains are more frequently preserved in the dry conditions of the Near East; a good example are the pieces of cloth from the Nahal Mishmar caves (Bar-Adon 1980), dated to the fourth millennium BC. Of the 45 samples tested, 37 were of linen, eight of wool. Remains of a loom were also found.

9. The scale of long-distance connections which existed in the Near East at least from the beginning of the Holocene is well demonstrated by the length of the obsidian exchange networks in Neolithic times. Obsidian distribution in forested Europe never achieved such distances.

10. There were, of course, already great contrasts in the extent of deforestation, especially from east to west. While the plough seems to have been rapidly accepted in most areas, wool-sheep may be much later in areas such as the British Isles.

9

Two New Finds of Wooden Wheels from Later Neolithic and Early Bronze Age Europe

(1986)

The purpose of this note is to draw attention to two recent finds of wooden wheels, one of which extends the area of Pontic vehicle burials into Balkan Europe and the other takes examples of Neolithic wheels in Europe back to a still earlier period. While the former find suggests the importance of the Pit-Grave culture in transmitting innovations from the Caucasus around the northern shore of the Black Sea c.3000 BC, the latter suggests the possibility of an earlier derivation for European wheeled vehicles, possibly via Anatolia.[1]

PLACHIDOL, NEAR TOLBUKHIN, NORTH-EAST BULGARIA
(PANAYOTOV AND DERGACHOV 1984, 107–9)

The site is a cemetery of six tumuli belonging to the intrusive 'ochre grave' group, and was excavated in 1979. Tumulus I was 7.30m high and 50–5m in diameter. Seven metres south of the centre of the mound, at a depth of 4.90m, was a rectangular pit (Figure 9.1) orientated east–west; apparently not the original central burial of the tumulus but dug into a subsequent extension. The pit (Grave 1) contained the crouched inhumation burial of an adult female (c.25 years) facing north. The skeleton lay on a mass of

---

Stuart Piggott's magisterial book on wheeled vehicles (1983) provided (as Gordon Childe foresaw it would) the best demonstration of the transmission of advanced technology from the Near East to Europe, which no one has seriously questioned. Since the wheel appears in Europe at the same time as the first evidence for ploughing, it strengthens the idea of a 'traction complex' as being an introduction there. This brief note added two pieces of new material to Piggott's corpus; and I have included some photographs which I took of a simple cart still in use in Portugal in 1990. Piggott's book has been a lasting influence, not just as a source-book but as a model for the way in which technology must be seen in a cultural and social context.

PLACHIDOL Tumulus I Grave 1

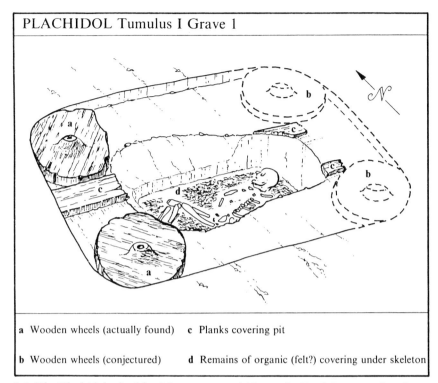

a Wooden wheels (actually found)   c Planks covering pit

b Wooden wheels (conjectured)   d Remains of organic (felt?) covering under skeleton

9.1 The Plachidol wheel-burial, as excavated (drawn by Keith Bennett after the plan and section by Panayotov and Dergachev).

plant material covering the bottom of the pit, and had red ochre sprinkled on its head and feet. There were no grave goods.

The pit was surrounded by a ledge, 50–90cm wide and 10–15cm deep, on which wooden beams were placed lengthwise over the pit to roof it. The eastern end of this ledge was partly destroyed, but in the two corners of the western end of this ledge lay a pair of solid wooden disc-wheels. They appear to be made of single pieces of wood, and have a diameter of 75cm. Each wheel has an integral nave projecting on both sides with a circular hole for the axle: no other details are given. The circular hole indicates that the wheels rotated about a fixed axle and were held in place by a linchpin: the normal type for this period (Figure 9.2, bottom).

Tumulus I was the largest of the group, and had originally been crowned by a stone anthropomorphic sculpture. Although the excavation report mentions no other burial in this tumulus, the anthropological report (Jordanov and Michailova 1984) lists four more (two adult males and an adult female). Tumulus II contained nine burials (four of children), all with red ochre, but rare grave goods; two adults each had a copper ring and flint flake. It had also originally been marked by an anthropomorphic sculpture. Tumuli III, IV and V each contained only a single burial of an adult male with

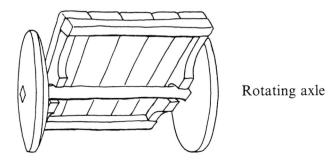

Rotating axle

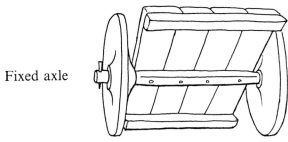

Fixed axle

9.2 Alternative principles of construction for wheeled vehicles: above, wheels fixed to a rotating axle; below, removable wheels held on a fixed axle by linchpins. The cart shown at the top can be lifted bodily off its axle (cf. Fig. 9.3); the one below can be jacked up for the removal of individual wheels. With a fixed axle, the wheels can rotate independently of one another.

artificially deformed skull, with ochre but no grave-goods. Tumulus VI was not excavated.

The Plachidol ochre-grave Tumulus cemetery is one of ten known from Bulgaria, preponderantly in the north-east. Approximately twice this number are known from Romania (mostly in Moldavia and the Dobrudja); and many hundreds are known from eastern Hungary (Ecsedy 1979). While excavations of some dozen tumuli in Hungary have repeatedly revealed square, plank-roofed chambers with ochre burials and few grave goods, none has so far revealed traces of a wheeled vehicle. All these tumuli are outliers – in areas which are themselves steppe enclaves – of the great mass of Pit-Grave tumuli on the Pontic steppes (Häusler 1971). They are most reasonably interpreted as culturally autonomous groups penetrating from the Pontic steppes into open areas within the territories of their western neighbours. Intruders and indigenes maintained their own traditions of burial side by side. The burials in the Plachidol tumuli closely resemble those known from the Pontic steppes; the arrangement in Tumulus I Grave 1 is precisely paralleled by burials such as that in the famous Tri Brata and neighbouring Arkhara tumuli near Elista on the Kalmyk Steppe (Piggott 1983, figs 23–5). This was the most elaborate form of interment in the Pit-Grave culture, and no doubt indicates elite status. The fact that the Plachidol I wheel-burial was that of a woman is thus particularly interesting.

Some forty radiocarbon dates are available from Pit-Grave tumuli in the southern Ukraine, covering the later fourth and earlier third millennia BC. Dates for tumuli in Romania and Hungary all fall in the later part of this period. These dates are parallel to those of the Baden and Ezero cultures, in Hungary and Bulgaria respectively, confirming the contemporary existence of these groups side by side. A date of c.3000 BC would thus be appropriate for the Plachidol cemetery.

ZÜRICH, SWITZERLAND; 'AKAD.' SITE, NEAR TO 'PRESSEHAUS' (RUOFF 1978; WOYTOWITSCH 1985)

Investigations by U. Ruoff on urban rescue sites at the edge of Lake Zürich have revealed a series of waterlogged occupations belonging to the later third millennium BC. At the 'Pressehaus' site (Ruoff 1978; Piggott 1983, 51) excavated in 1976 a pair of wheels and their connecting axle were discovered stuck in the mud with a third nearby, near to the palisaded perimeter of a Corded Ware settlement. These wheels were of a more complex construction, and on a different principle of attachment to the axle, from the other solid, tripartite or single-piece disc wheels known from third-millennium contexts in Europe (van der Waals 1964). The two (or perhaps three, since the upper parts were truncated) planks of which the wheel was composed were held together by three battens with a trapezoid section let into the outer face of the wheel. Moreover, the wheels, which lacked naves, had a square hole which acted as a mortice for the axle to which they were thus firmly fixed. The whole element of wheels plus axle thus turned as a unit – the axle had a circular section (apart from its morticed ends) and the body of the vehicle sat directly on top of it (Figure 9.2, top).

After this find, fragments of a similar wheel (along with a wooden yoke) were then noticed among old finds from Vinelz on the Bielersee, also probably of Corded Ware date. Radiocarbon estimates on Corded Ware contexts in Switzerland fall into the range of 2800–2600 BC. (They are thus broadly contemporary with, or slightly later than, the Plachidol find.) Wheels with this square mortice-hole are characteristic of the circum-Alpine area in the Bronze Age; a solid, single-piece example of Late Bronze Age date came from Castione dei Merchesi in northern Italy, and it is also a feature of contemporary crossbar wheels from this area (Woytowitsch 1985, figs 7, 36).

The form, however, goes back earlier than the Corded Ware period. Another small but identifiable fragment has been recognised from a Chalcolithic context at Egolzwyl 2 (Lucerne), and from the type-site of Auvernier

(Ruy-Chatru) on Lake Neuchâtel. Now another find from Zürich makes this the oldest surviving example of a wooden wheel from Europe, contemporary with the classic Baden culture cart-models of Budakalász and Alsónémedi in western Hungary. Excavations by U. Ruoff on an early Horgen site 'Akad.', near to the 'Pressehaus' site, brought to light a single-piece solid disc wheel, which nevertheless still had the characteristics of being naveless and having a square hole for an axle rotating with the wheel. The wheel itself is 55cm in maximum diameter – it has suffered some lateral compression – and just over 5cm thick at the centre. Like the others from this area it is of *Acer* (probably field maple) wood. Radiocarbon estimates for the Horgen culture range from 3400–3000 BC, while those for the earlier part of the closely related SOM culture in northern France suggest a beginning around 3500 BC (Howell 1983, 52).

This date thus takes finds of wooden wheels back to the widespread horizon of indications of the use of paired draught indicated in central Europe by paired-ox burials, figures of yoked oxen and wagon-models, and in northern Europe by plough-marks.[2] Although no wooden wheels are yet known from northern Europe before the Corded Ware period, this find suggests that earlier examples may be found, taking the innovation back into TRB (Middle Neolithic) times. This strengthens the suggestion that the 'traction complex' of plough and wheeled vehicle appeared as a unity in fourth-millennium Europe (Sherratt 1981; 1983; 1986).

Although the occurrence of wheel-finds at this date was thus predictable, these examples (with their contrasting typology) raise afresh the question of the route of their transmission to Europe. Links via the Pontic steppes to the Caucasus are evident not only from the distribution of the burials of the Pit-Grave culture but also from the introduction of Caucasian types of bronze axes and chisels using arsenical copper and the two-piece mould (Chernykh 1978). But these appear in Central Europe and the Balkans only after 3000 BC; and while wheeled vehicles were clearly an integral part of the Pit-Grave complex, they were apparently already in use in both Baden and Horgen contexts at the time of its arrival. Since all the analogies for Baden pottery – mostly skeuomorphic echoes of metal vessels – point to Anatolia (Kalicz 1963), this would provide a plausible source for wheeled vehicles of the mid-fourth millennium.

One point of typology remains: were the square-hole, naveless wheels, fixed to a rotating axle, characteristic of the 'first wave' of possibly Anatolian-derived wheeled vehicles, continuing to be used through into the Bronze Age in the relative backwater of Switzerland; or were they a specific adaptation to circum-Alpine conditions? Examples of fixed wheels in the Near East are sporadic, and belong to the second millennium or later: all the third-millennium finds have round-hole, freely rotating wheels with or without naves (Littauer and Crouwel 1979, 13–14). But we have no idea of the nature of fourth-millennium Near Eastern wheels, since the only evidence is from

9.3 below and right, *simple cart with rotating axle and fixed wheels (in this example made of iron, though traditionally of wood), on sale in a village market, Minho, northern Portugal;* top, *similar cart drawn by two cows, with elaborately carved wooden yoke, Minho, northern Portugal. (Photos: author, 1990, fieldwork with F. Queiroga.)*

Uruk pictographs rather than finds or detailed representations. It is thus possible that the earliest wheels were generally fixed to the axle.

However, functional differences between two types should not be forgotten. With a fixed axle and freely rotating wheels, a damaged wheel can easily be removed. When the vehicle is stuck in mud, however, this procedure is difficult. With a rotating axle, the body of the cart can simply be lifted off the bogged-down wheels and axle. Since this is arguably what actually happened in the case of the Zürich Pressehaus example, it may be the explanation for its preferred use in circum-Alpine lakeside settlements. The alternative design would have been preferable on the steppes, and on the dry plains of lowland Europe.[3]

NOTES

1. Both finds form interesting footnotes to the comprehensive survey of European wheeled vehicles published by Professor Stuart Piggott (1983). Since 1985 was Professor Piggott's 75th year, this note is affectionately dedicated in celebration of it.

2. This horizon includes, of course, the wagon-models of Budakalász, Szigetszentmárton (both in Hungary) and Radošina (Slovakia), as well as the drawing on a pot from Bronocice (Little Poland). Professor Piggott's dating of this horizon (1983, 44–5) needs to be corrected; or rather, returned to the date which he originally suggested fifteen years before (1968, 304). Since Lengyel and Tiszapolgár run parallel in western and eastern Hungary respectively, there is no need to compress Bodrogkeresztúr (itself parallel to late Lengyel) into the third millennium bc. He was thus originally correct in dating the onset of Baden to c.2700 bc. Bronocice IV and V correspond to *late* Baden; Bronocice III with its cart-drawing parallels classic Baden (like Budakalász), and has four associated radiocarbon dates of 2740–2570 (Kruk and Milisauskas 1981). The Radošina model, in a Boleraz (proto-Baden) context, is the earliest example and would just precede them at c.28/2700 bc.

3. With characteristic perception, Mrs M. A. Littauer (*in litt*. Jan 1986) provides a further dimension to this argument. If wheeled vehicles developed from sledges with captive rollers (as the pictographs hint), then a fixed wheel/revolving axle would be a logical design for the earliest carts. It would require less sophisticated carpentry and would be less vulnerable to wear than a wheel whose nave was carefully cut to rotate on a fixed axle. The fixed axle, allowing the wheels to revolve differentially, was particularly advantageous for *four*-wheeled vehicles, especially where used in battle (as in Mesopotamia). The bias towards prestige vehicles (usually four-wheelers with fixed axles) in graves and artistic representations may mask the widespread contemporary use of a less sophisticated design, the two-wheeler with rotating axle. Such a primitive but robust design has survived down to recent times in areas less sophisticated technologically or with a more abrasive environment (Portugal, Fig. 9.3, Anatolia, Mongolia). I am very grateful to Mrs Littauer for these and many other helpful observations. [For more recent surveys of early wheel finds, and technical discussion, see Hayen 1983; Schovsbo 1983; Häusler 1984; various articles in Treue 1986; Winiger 1987 (with a convenient illustration of the Vinelz yoke shortly after discovery, fig. 20 on p. 107); Höneisen 1989. What appear to be 15–20m of cart-rut occur under the extension to a long mound covering multiple cists of probable mid-fourth-millennium date at Flintbek in NW Germany (Zich 1992; information from J. Hoika); some mid-third-millennium trackways in the same region seem to be associated with the use of wheeled vehicles, to judge by the growing numbers of broken wheels and axles associated with them. Winiger (1987, 100), quoting a conversation with the excavator, Ulrich Ruoff, notes that the chronological attribution of the Zürich-'Akad.' wheel, stratified *between* early Horgen and Corded-Ware deposits, is uncertain; Winiger himself would prefer a Corded-Ware date for the introduction of the wheel to Switzerland. His interpretation of the rotating axle as a technological advance, however, is less compelling than Mrs Littauer's suggestion above.]

Section IV

PATTERNS ON THE GROUND

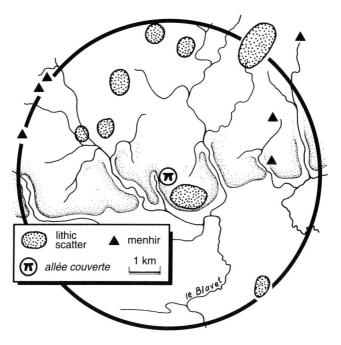

The relationship between a central monument, occupation areas, and outlying standing stones, near to the Late Neolithic dolerite quarries at Plussulien, central Brittany, c.3200 BC (after C.-T. Le Roux, based on fieldwork by M. F. Le Provost).

The wider area of archaeological theory ... treats processes with space- and time-scales for which there is no social terminology, or patterns which nowhere survive within the sample of recent human behaviour. Archaeology in essence, then, is the discipline with the theory and practice for the recovery of unobservable hominid behaviour patterns from indirect traces in bad samples.

DAVID L. CLARKE (1973)

The ideas discussed above are only of use if they help to make sense of patterns on the ground. For my doctoral thesis, I had travelled widely in Turkey and south-east Europe, and in setting up a fieldwork programme I wanted to create a trade-off between the robustness of the prehistoric record in the south-east (Balkan tells) and the sophistication of data-recovery (museum coverage, survey work) in the north-west. The optimum solution was Hungary, which had the additional advantages of being axially placed in relation both to the Danube route from Anatolia and the steppe zone stretching eastwards beyond the Pontic region and the Caucasus to the Urals and beyond.

The Archaeological Topography of Hungary programme provided precisely the opportunity I sought: although conceived as a project to register sites rather than to reconstruct settlement patterns, its collaborative team combined vast experience with uniquely long periods of time engaged in survey. In eastern Hungary, in particular, the combination of durable and typologically distinctive ceramics, and a heavily-tilled landscape of open, collectively farmed fields, provided an unparalleled opportunity to reconstruct prehistoric settlement patterns with a resolution never before achieved. It was Nándor Kalicz who made this work possible, though sadly his health prevented an active collaboration in the field (and also the late Sándor Bökönyi who gave continuous support). Nevertheless, the experience of working with István Torma and György and Julia Goldman, and getting to know István Ecsedy and Pál Raczky, remains a great pleasure; and among the British team were Sue and Steve Shennan, John O'Shea, John Howell, Nick Starling, Brendan Grimley, Basil and Mary Turton, Mark and Jenny Robinson, and Sue Sherratt, following earlier visits with Paul Halstead, Colin Ridler, Neil Roberts and Fred Hamond. The Archaeological Topography, and the survey and sondage work undertaken to calibrate it, permitted a detailed set of observations on the spatial and distributional characteristics of settlement (pottery + house-building materials) within something like 200–500 year intervals. These demonstrated gradual drift, sharp shifts and a fluctuating pattern of concentration and dispersal, that can be linked to changes in the internal organisation of settlements and their cemeteries, as well as to changing patterns of supply and flow in materials and artefacts. Equally importantly, they demonstrated both the validity of the proposed model of early farming, and the magnitude of the shift which coincided with the first evidence of animal traction. Such patterns stimulated the construction of more detailed models of regional development and environmental change, and confirmed suggestions of a co-existence between two populations – one indigenous and one intrusive from the steppes – at the beginning of the third millennium.

My conditions of employment at Oxford do not permit fieldwork other than in periods of annual leave. When my growing family began to demand a holiday rather than forced labour, some compromise was required; and I began instead to investigate spatial and morphological patterning within the 500 known megalithic monuments of the Morbihan, on the southern coast of Brittany, of which nineteenth-century plans and drawings in Oxford and elsewhere provide an invaluable record. The parallelism with Hungary was remarkable: over a precisely comparable period of time (though beginning somewhat later), an exceptionally well-preserved and recorded series of Neolithic sites revealed a remarkable density of occupation, and permitted a diachronic study. The only difference was that these were not settlements, but tombs. Such a contrast, and the more general exclusiveness between substantial sites and substantial burial-monuments in Neolithic Europe, points to the arbitrariness of our ethnocentric distinction between rational, secular domesticity and religious, ritualistic disposal of the dead. Both types of site provide permanent inscriptions on the landscape – one emphasising the presence of the living, the other of the departed. For their Neolithic constructors, houses were as 'ritual' as tombs – and tombs sometimes as domestic as houses. This fundamental realisation, together with Ian Hodder's illuminating writings on the subject, led to the reconsiderations of European megalithism which complete this section.

Mobile Resources:
Settlement and Exchange
in Early Agricultural Europe
(1982)

Interpretations of the archaeological record in social terms have usually been undertaken within an implicit evolutionary framework. The most successful of these studies have been those concerned with the Near East and Mesoamerica. In these areas the rapid onset of social inequality following the adoption of agriculture has suggested that stages of increasing social complexity are a normal succession in agricultural communities. In Europe, however, this approach has been less fruitful. One of the notable features of the European prehistoric sequence is the relatively late appearance of complex societies associated with an urban base. Yet the first farming communities appeared in Europe in the seventh millennium BC, and the long intervening period cannot be adequately described by a simple evolutionary succession of increasingly ranked societies. Archaeologists have used technological criteria to divide this time into Neolithic, Copper and Bronze Ages on the basis of surviving artefacts; but although the use of metal is clearly relevant to the question of social change, the dynamics of such a process cannot be inferred from the artefacts alone. It is necessary to try and reconstruct the total flow of produce between different areas, since it is this pattern that determines how particular

---

The objective of this article was to break down the artificial distinction between 'subsistence and settlement' and 'trade and exchange', by suggesting that the movement of livestock was an important part of prehistoric economies, especially at certain phases of development. To avoid constant recourse to external causes, it took as its dominant metaphor the idea of (ecological) succession, in an attempt to look at purely autonomous reasons for change: the evolving role of livestock in a newly Neolithicised region. It was originally prepared for the 45th Annual Meeting of the Society for American Archaeology in Philadelphia (1980), in a symposium masterminded with characteristic flair by Colin Renfrew, and described by Shanks and Tilley (1987, 37) as 'in many respects the culmination of the programme of functionalist social archaeology in Britain'.

areas develop in terms of the opportunities open to them at different times.

Gordon Childe attributed the egalitarian nature of early farming communities to the primitive character of agriculture and the lack of a surplus for trade (1951). This view can be criticised on several grounds, not least the clear evidence that Neolithic groups were capable of acquiring substantial quantities of materials from considerable distances (Chapter 4). Because of the importance of regional interaction in determining the course of economic and social development, it is worthwhile to examine the nature of such Neolithic exchange networks and their social contexts. This chapter proposes a fundamental reason for large-scale regional exchange in Early Old World agricultural societies, and investigates the social structures in which it was embedded. It uses detailed evidence from an area of central Europe to explore the usefulness of this model in explaining a wide range of archaeological observations.

THE POTENTIAL FOR EXCHANGE IN EARLY AGRICULTURAL SOCIETIES

In discussions of exchange in simple agricultural societies, attention has usually focused on the movement of hard stones for axes and cutting tools (Chapter 4; cf. Hughes 1973). In a stimulating article in 1965, however, Kent Flannery discussed the development of early agricultural communities in the Zagros in terms of inter-zonal exchanges both of mineral resources and of new domesticates. The movement of domesticated species was seen as an aspect of social contact and trade rather than just a biogeographic dispersal. That domestic livestock were an important item of trade among early agriculturalists should not be surprising in view of their prominence in New Guinea exchange cycles (Rappaport 1968, 105); but archaeologists have usually considered them under the heading of 'subsistence' rather than of 'exchange'. While the role of horses as trade items (by analogy with their spread in North America) has recently been raised in unpublished work by Stephen Shennan and John O'Shea in connection with Beaker and early Bronze Age trade networks in Europe (cf. Schüle 1969), the significance of livestock as an item of Neolithic trade has not been systematically explored.

The role of cattle in this context is likely to have been particularly important. The earliest Neolithic economies were based on sheep, which spread as part of the primary agricultural complex from a restricted mountain habitat. Cattle, on the other hand, were a widespread native animal in the areas to which agriculture was introduced, and were probably domesticated independently in a number of lowland foci (Herre and Röhrs 1977). These included northern Mesopotamia, central Anatolia and parts of southern Europe. Domesticated cattle were supplied from these areas to surrounding regions. The continuing significance of lowland cattle-breeding centres is well known from the historical period: Thessaly and Boeotia exported animals in Homeric times, while classical Attica brought cattle by ship from as far away as Macedonia, North Africa and Scythia (Semple 1932, 318). The movement of livestock is thus likely to be of major importance in explaining regional exchange systems in prehistory.

One site which may be illuminated by being considered in this light is Çatal Hüyük in central Anatolia (Mellaart 1967; Todd 1976). Large herds of wild cattle (aurochsen) flourished in the seventh millennium in this well-watered part of the alluvial Konya Plain, and their skulls are a prominent feature of the numerous shrines found at the site. The capture or handling of an aurochs bull is actually shown in wall paintings. Cattle formed over ninety per cent of the faunal remains recovered from the site, and the stature of the animals decreased in the upper levels. Since domestic cattle arguably appeared in this region for the first time at Çatal Hüyük, it is likely that the site had a major role in the domestication of these animals (Perkins 1969).

The site also had a key role in relation to its surrounding region, since it is notable for the extraordinary quantity and variety of imported materials: some thirty-five different foreign minerals have been identified, including rocks for axes, grinding stones, pigments and beads, as well as several varieties of flint and very large quantities of obsidian (Todd 1976, 126; cf. Jacobs 1969, 27–54). The last is particularly notable, as it was obtained from the Acigöl source, which is 200km away to the north-east. This trading florescence was a temporary one, however, as the site had no immediate successor of comparable size or importance – James Mellaart has called it a 'supernova'. A possible explanation for this brief concentration of wealth is the role of the site as a source of domestic cattle during the phase of agricultural expansion, when it supplied sites proliferating in the nearby upland basins and was thus able to acquire abundant supplies of highland resources.

Despite the flow of traded items at Çatal Hüyük, it did not form part of a site hierarchy in the same way as (for instance) the Protoliterate communities of the Mesopotamian Plain (Adams and Nissen 1972). Although only a fraction of the site has been excavated, the buildings are remarkably uniform and there is no differentiation of large elite or public buildings: the numerous shrines form part of domestic complexes. Whatever the precise social organisation of the site or the character of the trade that supported it, there is little indication of ranking of the kind discussed elsewhere in this volume. The site thus raises in acute form the question of the nature of exchange in Neolithic communities and the social structures associated with it. It suggests that early agricultural communities were on occasion capable of operating large-scale exchanges in the absence of developed hierarchies, and that such societies may have undergone cycles of increasing complexity and devolution that defy characterisation as stages in an unilinear progression.

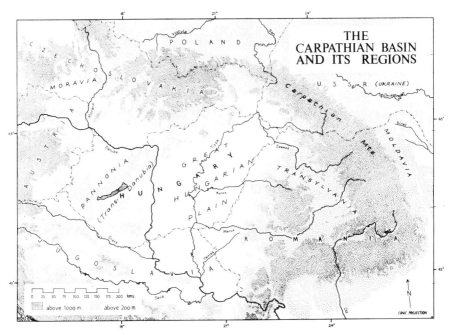

10.1 *The Carpathian Basin and its regions, showing the Great Hungarian Plain (Nagy Alföld); [from Sherratt 1983b].*

Another area where a phenomenon of this kind may have taken place is the Great Hungarian Plain. Its marshy depressions and open, steppe character provided a similar habitat for numerous herds of cattle in the postglacial period. Early farming groups (as in Thessaly) concentrated chiefly on raising sheep, though domestic cattle were known and aurochsen occasionally hunted. During the fifth millennium BC, however, cattle became the principal form of domestic livestock, and there is evidence in one area for interbreeding with wild herds and probably an intake of the latter for domestication. What is particularly interesting is that this period saw a notable increase in 'wealth' (in terms of both imported materials and local craft products), an elaboration of ritual, and a significant change in the character of settlements, with the emergence of large aggregated sites in between phases of dispersed settlement.

The rest of this chapter consists of an examination of the relationships between these changes, at both a local and a regional level. It uses some of the preliminary results of intensive survey work around Szeghalom in the Körös depression[1] to describe patterns of settlement and material culture in the centre of the Plain. It then uses a colonisation model to examine changes in the role of this area within the larger regional system of the Carpathian Basin.

	Settlement	Subsistence	Material culture	Exchange	Cemeteries
TISZAPOLGÁR & BODROGKERESZTÚR (late 5th / early 4th mill.)	Dispersed; small coherent settlements (not ditched); stable pattern	Domestic cattle predominate; cereals, etc.	Plain pottery, without local styles; no figurines; "battle axes"; (copper axes and daggers + gold ornaments on edge of Plain	Some obsidian, greenstone, etc.; occasional extra-Carpathian imports (esp. on edge of Plain)	Large formal cemeteries (for whole community or several sites)
SZAKÁLHÁT & TISZA (early 5th mill.)	Large aggregated settlements (defence?); often burnt; stable pattern	Domestic cattle predominate; wild cattle locally important; cereals etc.	Elaborately decorated pottery and cult objects in local styles; textiles	Large quantity and variety of imported materials – obsidian, flint, greenstone, grinders, etc.; imported fine pottery	Small formal groups of graves (households or lineages)
KÖRÖS & AVK (6th mill.)	Dispersed; linear shoreline settlements; fluid pattern	Domestic sheep predominate; fishing important; cereals etc.	Basic craft skills; decoration not regionally specific	Obsidian becoming important; some greenstone and grinders	No formal cemeteries

(a)

10.2 *Summary of evidence for settlement and exchange in the central part of the Great Hungarian Plain, 6000–3500 BC, divided into three major phases: (a) descriptive summary; (b) schematic settlement-forms, at the level of the individual house, settlement, and settlement-cluster. Compare the detailed survey results in Chapter 11 below. [Re-arranged.]*

SETTLEMENT AND ECONOMY IN THE CENTRAL PART OF THE GREAT HUNGARIAN PLAIN

The Great Hungarian Plain is an alluvial basin with extensive areas of fertile land along its broad floodplains (Figure 10.1).[2] Although it has a steppe climate, irrigation was not necessary in preindustrial times, and there are no sharp contrasts in productive potential as in the Mesopotamian Plain. The landscape was undegraded at the time under discussion, and cultivation systems based on the hoe or digging stick can be inferred for the whole of the period before c.3000 BC. The contrasts discussed here thus emerged from a relatively uniform environmental and technological base. The principal changes are summarised in Figure 10.2.

The earliest agrarian communities of the Körös culture,[3] spreading into the Carpathian Basin from the south along the major rivers, took the form of linear settlements up to a kilometre or more in length, along the levees of old watercourses. Such sites were composed of individual household clusters – consisting of postbuilt rectangular houses with their associated pits – arranged at intervals of 50 metres or so along the riverbank. They yield evidence of cereal cultivation, the keeping of domestic livestock

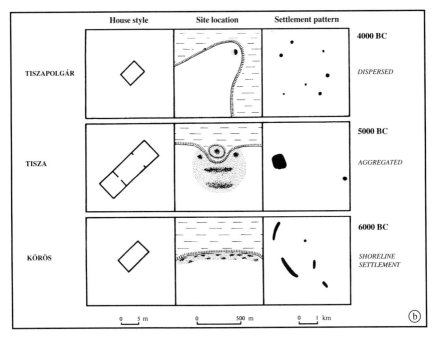

House style	Site location	Settlement pattern	
TISZAPOLGÁR			4000 BC *DISPERSED*
TISZA			5000 BC *AGGREGATED*
KÖRÖS			6000 BC *SHORELINE SETTLEMENT*
0 — 5 m	0 — 500 m	0 — 1 km	(b)

(mainly sheep), hunting of deer and wild cattle (Bökönyi 1974), and plentiful indications of fishing in the form of fish remains and net-sinkers. Large quantities of locally produced coarse pottery are present. The finer pottery is undecorated, and there are no marked local stylistic groupings. There are some clay figurines, but they are not elaborate. By the end of this period obsidian was reaching the area from the edge of the Plain to the north (Tokaj), though the chipped stone industry lacks the variety of materials used in later periods, and stone axes are rare. Burials were placed within the settlements, not unusually in rubbish pits with other animal bone, and no formal cemetery areas have been recognised.

The linear arrangement of settlement and the very large number of sites probably indicate frequent minor shifts of individual household clusters within the general area of exploitation over a relatively long span of time, rather than a high density of large contemporary settlements. The absence of cemeteries may imply that descent was not important in defining group membership. This pattern suggests considerable fluidity of pioneer settlement, freely growing and proliferating without constraint. Such adventitious colonisation at a low overall population density in a productive environment would not have created competition and would have made unnecessary the development of wider networks of alliance.

This pattern persisted with only minor modifications throughout the sixth millennium, during which the wave of population advance passed on through the Carpathian Basin to the other parts of the central European loess belt. Broad cultural affinities were maintained between these proliferating *Bandkeramik* populations further north and their contemporaries in eastern Hungary, who are distinguished as the Alföld variant (AVK).

A major change occurred in the Great Hungarian Plain around the beginning of the fifth millennium BC, affecting both settlement patterns and material culture. This corresponds to the beginning of the Szakálhát and Tisza cultures.[4] Although the same parts of the Plain continued to be occupied, settlement became increasingly aggregated. Far fewer sites are known, but on further investigation these turn out to be very large (of the order of 500m × 500m) and to consist of parallel lines of household-clusters, often centred on a slight prominence with natural defences or suggestions of artificial ditches.[5] True tells first appeared at this time. All sites have substantial accumulations of settlement debris consisting of several layers of mud-walled buildings, sometimes simultaneously burnt over large parts of the site. The subsistence base of these settlements contained no new species, but cattle now predominated heavily over sheep among the domestic livestock, while the hunting of aurochsen made a substantial contribution in the eastern part of the area. Fishing was now with harpoon rather than net, perhaps indicating that animal protein came mainly from meat.

The pottery includes a high proportion of elaborately decorated wares with painted and incised ornament often imitating textile patterns. These divide clearly into specific local styles in different parts of the Plain and surrounding areas.[6] Figurines and anthropomorphic vessels are similarly elaborate, as are decorated household fittings. Equally striking are the quantity and variety of imported materials. Many new types of flint make their appearance, along with large quantities of obsidian (see Chapter 12). Massive fragments of tabular flint up to 20cm long show the size of the raw materials that were acquired. Saddle querns and grindstones are frequent finds, while greenstone axes occur in very large numbers. All these materials were imported from beyond the alluvial plain. Finely decorated pottery was also widely traded. Although burials occur in small formal groups within the settlement area, and male and female graves were differentiated by their orientation, large quantities of objects were not deposited with the dead.

The emergence of large, rich 'supersites' some 10km or so apart indicates a greater stability and constraint on settlement coincident with the expansion of trading activity. The overall density of settlement was still relatively low, since there are few smaller settlements between the 'supersites'. Such sites, therefore, do not appear to form the upper level of a hierarchy, but rather a general tendency to aggregation of settlement. The two factors most likely to have promoted aggregation are an enlargement of the resident co-operative (e.g. animal-breeding) unit, or more likely the need for defence – though the threat was not sufficiently severe to require enclosing earthworks (as in the Bronze Age). The sites probably consisted of an aggregation of compounds with livestock enclosures and kitchen gardens in between (cf. Brookfield and Hart 1971, fig. 9.1. A4). The burials, which seem to have taken place in the context of the domestic or lineage group rather than of the whole community, also suggest a loose aggregation of lineage groups rather than fusion into a single integrated unit. The evidence of ritual activities in the form of figurines and cult fittings also has a domestic context.

The pattern which succeeded this one in the later fifth millennium (Tiszapolgár culture) reversed many aspects of the picture, at least in the central area of the Plain. While the same parts of the area continued to be occupied, settlement reverted to a dispersed pattern. The sites themselves were more integrated than before, however, and consist of a concentration of huts and other facilities within a more or less circular area having a modal diameter of 50–100m. They do not appear to have been ditched. Many tells continued to be occupied, though the layers are thinner and rarely burnt (Bognár-Kutzián 1972). The domesticates included no new species (with the exception of occasional bones of horse, which appeared in appreciable numbers only in the third millennium), and domestic cattle remained the most common animal. By the beginning of the fourth millennium cattle remains are almost entirely from domestic stock (Bökönyi 1974). The pottery is predominantly plain, with decoration consisting for the most part of knobs and perforations rather than elaborate patterns. Figurines are absent. The pottery is remarkably uniform over the whole of the Plain and does not divide into clear regional styles as in the preceding periods. Larger formal cemetery areas outside the settlements appear for the first time in this period, with graves arranged in rows and differentiated both by sex and by relative quantities of grave goods. The larger and richer excavated examples, however, come from outside the central area of the Plain. Stone continued to be imported for tools, but not in the quantity and variety of the preceding phase. New materials and products – long flint blades, and axes and simple ornaments of copper – are known from this period, but few seem to have reached the centre of the Plain.

The large number of substantial sites indicates that this period was stable and prosperous, and there is no evidence for declining fertility, even though materials from outside the Plain were not imported in such quantity. Conditions seem to have been more peaceful than in the preceding phase, since settlement was able to disperse and there is less evidence of destruction. Both the layout of Tiszapolgár sites and the existence of community cemeteries indicate a more organised composition of local groups, probably structured by descent.

The early fourth millennium BC (Bodrogkeresztúr culture) saw for the first time a major shift in the area under occupation in the central part of the Plain, with relative depopulation (or less visible settlement) in the parts previously settled most intensively. A truly radical break occurred in the later fourth millennium (Baden culture), with the settlement of new micro-areas and the construction of large burial mounds in the previously

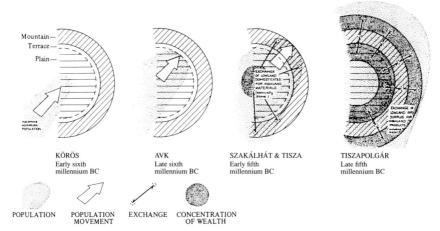

10.3 *A model of agrarian colonisation and changing patterns of exchange in relation to new opportunities, as exemplified by the eastern part of the Carpathian Basin, 6000–4000* BC. *[The diagram does not show long-distance inter-regional exchange, which becomes significant in the final period.]*

inhabited ones. Faunal remains show a shift to sheep (now probably for secondary products), while other parts of central Europe provide evidence for the use of paired draught animals and the plough. This major transformation is beyond the scope of the present discussion.

THE CARPATHIAN BASIN AS A REGIONAL SYSTEM

These developments can only be understood in a regional setting (Figures 10.3, 10.4). The earliest settlers in the sixth millennium formed part of a river-based network, spreading from the south and largely confined to the Plain itself. Contemporary settlements in adjacent areas occupied similar environments, and there was little penetration of surrounding uplands. Small quantities of necessary materials were imported, but early populations had a high degree of self-sufficiency.

The changes of the early fifth millennium coincided with the first major penetration of the uplands (Kalicz and Makkay 1977). Sites with clear cultural affinities to those on the Hungarian Plain are known not only from the valleys reaching up into the mountains but also up to 900m in the limestone caves of the Bükk mountains themselves. The existence of groups with direct access to highland materials and the resources on the edge of the Plain[7] opened new possibilities for the supply of desirable materials to lowland areas. The appearance of large quantities of imported materials there suggests that contemporary alterations in settlement and material culture may be a part of a change in organisation to take advantage of these opportunities. The new pattern of relationships was a relatively short-lived

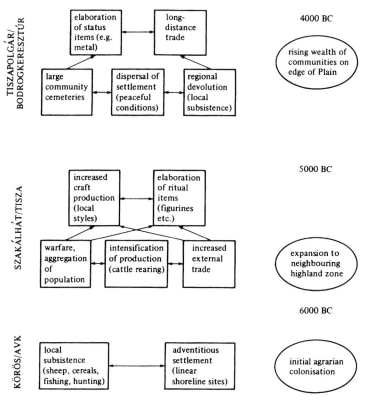

10.4 *Descriptive model of the inter-relationships between the succession of settlement and exchange systems in the eastern part of the Carpathian Basin, 6000–3500 BC. (Similar models would apply, for instance, to the Konya Plain, central Turkey 7000–5000 BC, or parts of northern Europe 4000–2000 BC.)*

episode, however, for many of its elements disappeared in the succeeding phase; though even so it lasted for several hundred years.

The sources of imported materials on one lowland site are considered in Chapter 12, and can be seen to lie in a broad arc some 100 to 150km away in the surrounding uplands to the north and east (cf. Comşa 1967). Such resources could only have been mobilised if the intensification of lowland production were articulated within a regional system of exchange. The first requirement of such a system would have been the existence of an exportable lowland resource (cf. Godelier 1977, 141–5). While the archaeological record gives no direct evidence of what this was, it can be argued that cattle were the most important lowland product. The movement of surplus grain over such distances is unlikely in primitive conditions of transport, and in any case would give the central area no advantage over the peripheries. Textiles of plant fibres are a possibility, especially in view of the characteristic geometrical designs on pottery, though as flax grows well in surrounding areas (Illés and Halász 1926) its production is unlikely to have been a monopoly of the lowlands. Similar considerations apply to salt, which is known to have played an important role in the acquisition of stone resources by groups in alluvial lowlands in New Guinea (Godelier 1977). Fine pottery was manufactured both in the lowlands and in the area of the Bükk mountains, and traded in both directions.

The most likely commodities for specialised production in the Plain, therefore, are cattle and cattle products. The well-watered, open plains were a natural breeding-ground for cattle, both wild and domestic. Faunal remains from the Plain show a predominance (fifty to seventy-five per cent) of cattle at this period, with very high proportions of wild forms especially in the eastern part. In this area (around Berettyóújfalu) the intergradation of sizes and mixture of morphological characteristics between domestic and wild forms is taken by Bökönyi (1962) as evidence of local domestication. The open character of the Plain environment (Kosse 1979) would have provided a valuable reservoir of livestock as population moved into the wooded areas on the fringes of the Carpathian Basin. The demand for cattle among these expanding populations could have been met by breeding cattle for export in much of the central Plain, and by actually domesticating new stock in the eastern part, where wild herds were extensive. If the practice of milking was a later introduction, as has been suggested (Chapter 6), then it is the animals themselves rather than their secondary products that are likely to have been of importance. Such an export could literally move itself over the required distances. Since the initial clearings in forested areas would have been small,[8] herds in the wooded fringes and uplands would have taken some time to become self-sustaining. As it would in any case have been difficult to maintain large herds (which would only be able to expand after several generations of forest clearances), there was probably a continuing dependence on lowland supplies, both as breeding stock and as meat on the hoof.

If this interpretation is correct, then it suggests that the changes in settlement pattern and material culture in the Great Hungarian Plain in the early fifth millennium represented the intensification of one aspect of local production and the consumption of a wider range of goods through participation in regional exchange. The use of livestock as a commodity moved it from the subsistence sphere into that of negotiable wealth. The effect on settlement patterns was to concentrate population into larger and more permanent social units that could handle and protect a valuable and mobile resource.

The trade in livestock was the main means of acquiring necessary materials from the surrounding highland zone. These complementary exchanges also provided the opportunity for the distribution of other goods based on craft skills at a village level, such as fine pottery and textiles (cf. Jacobs 1969). The increase in the volume of traded goods thus coincided with the greatest diversity of local pottery styles and most elaborate types of decoration: it was advantageous to make local products sufficiently distinctive to break into the flourishing regional exchange system. (This is equally true of highland areas: it is the limestone mountains of the Bükk – without volcanic rocks for axes etc. – that are most notable for their fine pottery.) Such local specialisation disappeared in the following period.

One feature that was characteristic of the whole region during the early fifth millennium, and disappeared in the following phase, was the production of elaborate cult items, especially figurines. These include some of the finest examples of Neolithic art (e.g. Gimbutas 1974, figs 102–9). Ritual activity was clearly an important feature of the social system, and its significance in this context is considered in the next section.

In the later fifth millennium, a somewhat different pattern can be discerned. Some measure of local devolution (reflected in the dispersion of settlement and decline in imports) seems to have taken place within the central area of the Plain, but this was balanced by the rising wealth of areas nearer to the edge of the Plain (Figure 10.3). Metal objects (copper shafthole axes and daggers, gold ornaments) now supplemented those of stone as status items (Bognár-Kutzián 1972), and their distribution in the late fifth millennium is clearly restricted to sites immediately adjacent to the highlands or within 100km along the major rivers (Tisza and Maros).[9] This most probably reflects the decline in importance of the central region as a cattle-breeding area and supplier of a major commodity. Groups on the Plain margins, however, were able to acquire objects such as fine flint blades (and perhaps also the first horses) from expanding populations on the other side of the Carpathians; and some of these objects travelled over longer distances than the commodities used in earlier intra-Carpathian exchanges (Chapter 4).

THE SOCIAL CONTEXT OF EXCHANGE

Discussion of the archaeological evidence for fifth-millennium exchange has emphasised the lack of discernible hierarchies, the general conditions of insecurity, and the increasing concern with ritual. A model of this exchange must encompass these three interdependent elements. Dalton (1977) has characterised exchange in acephalous (egalitarian)[10] societies as one aspect of alliance. Since the largest political unit was the local descent group, relations were horizontal – fluctuating coalitions and enmities between a multitude of similar small groups. Alliance allowed peace and therefore social and economic relationships. Such alliances were both initiated and maintained by exchanges of women, valuables and trade items; relations outside this network took the form of raiding, abduction and capture. Power within the group consisted in control over marriageable women, both directly and through valuables used as bridewealth and exchange items, and through access to ritual formulae for ceremonial.

Where relations between neighbouring groups were minimal, as in the phase of early settlement in the sixth millennium, such networks of alliance were little developed. The intensification of economic activity in the fifth millennium, however, was accompanied by increased competition between groups and a strengthening of control within them. Since alliances would have taken the form of chains linking different resource areas, rather than clusters in a coherent block of territory, individual settlements or groups are likely to have had potentially hostile relations with at least some of their neighbours. Defensive aggregation was the logical settlement pattern for an open plain. Control within the community, however, was a problem common to all. This control may have been accomplished by ritual and ideological means rather than by more overt expressions of power. The elaboration of cult objects at this period indicates the existence of ritual codes shared by all the communities of the area. Relations within groups could thus have been regulated by ritual; those between groups by selective alliance.

The pivotal points in both of these sets of relationships are likely to have been the men, especially senior males and lineage heads. The evidence for this comes from grave associations of goods which are likely to have played the role of primitive valuables. The late *Bandkeramik* cemetery at Nitra in Slovakia (Pavúk 1972) exhibits a striking pattern in which both stone axes and ornaments of imported *Spondylus* shell occur in all but one case in the graves of older males (Figure 4.8). Some forty per cent of men over twenty years old were buried with such items, and they occur in increasing proportion to age. Moreover, the greater longevity of males makes it likely that the age of marriage for men was high, so that powerful seniors could monopolise the women of marriageable age, probably by control of bride-wealth valuables. Such valuables, which would have included the main prestige items of intergroup exchange like axes, obsidian blades, ornaments, fine pottery and cattle, are likely to have circulated in their own economic sphere and to have been exchanged only between eligible males (cf. Godelier 1977, 231 n. 29). The social system of these later Neolithic groups can thus be reconstructed as one dominated by senior men, who controlled both the movement of goods and the formation of alliances through the exchange of marriage partners.

This picture of autonomous communities linked only by alliance and the attendant circulation of valuables, with ritual as an important medium of internal control, does not fit the pattern of the following Tiszapolgár and Bodrogkeresztúr periods. The evidence of insecurity diminishes, the volume of traded valuables declines, and the evidence of cult activity disappears. The large number of distinctive pottery types gives way to uniformity, suggesting that the pottery was no longer a competitive prestige item. At the same time, specific status-linked items appear, like shafthole axes and daggers of stone and copper, and ornaments of gold.[11] These are less common than the stone axes and shell ornaments at Nitra (occurring only in fifteen per cent of adult male graves at Tiszapolgár II (Figure 4.8), and arguably indicate a new level of status differentiation. These items may also occur with younger adult men, especially the daggers. The cemeteries are larger, representing whole communities rather than household or lineage groups, and contain greater quantities of grave goods. (The cemeteries themselves may now have served as foci for groups of scattered settlements.) Family authority and ritual regulation seem to be giving way to wider structures in which a greater element of relative ranking and hierarchisation was possible. In regional terms, wealth was being spatially concentrated, with communities on the edge of the Plain or on main waterways becoming conspicuously richer than those in the centre. These communities had access for the first time to items of extra-regional trade.

The contrast with the preceding period should not be overdrawn: an ethnographic equivalent might be the difference between highland New Guinea and the more advanced parts of coastal and island Melanesia – both within the ethos of the Big Man rather than the Polynesian chief (Sahlins 1963). Nevertheless, European societies had entered the era of inequality.

Conclusions

The model presented here has important implications for the interpretation of early agricultural societies in many parts of the Old World. Although Çatal Hüyük is probably unique in that the whole region seems to have been focused on a single site, the early spread of domestic cattle is likely to have had a similar effect in promoting regional exchange systems linking nodal lowland areas and their hinterlands, for instance during the Halaf period in northern Mesopotamia, and somewhat later in highland Iran. Such nodes may also have existed in south-east Europe, for instance in Thessaly, the Marica Basin and the lower Danube.[12]

A comparable, though attenuated, process may also have occurred even where initial agricultural occupation took place in forested areas, as in much of central and northern Europe. In these areas there is a clear distinction between primary settlement, usually on loess, and secondary expansion, which occurred up to 1000 years later. By this time there would have been a marked contrast between the already cleared and partly exhausted landscapes of initial settlement (where animals could be reared in quantity), and the small clearings round newly founded sites (cf. Kruk 1980). It is thus significant that enclosures often interpreted as cattle-pounds should appear by late *Bandkeramik* times, for example in the Rhineland; and that larger, centrally placed enclosures of a more elaborate kind should be associated with expanding settlement in the subsequent Michelsberg period (Boelicke 1976/7). [These enclosures may have a defensive purpose: for trade and warfare are two sides of the same coin.] Such enclosures are increasingly being recognised as characteristic elements of the late fourth- and third-millennium settlement patterns in north-west Europe, as forest cover was being opened up, and have analogies in many parts of the continent, from Les Matignons in the Charente to Dölauer Heide in central Germany.[13] They are likely to have served as centres for the concentration of surplus animals from the surrounding area, and their dispersal to outlying communities. These seasonal cattle fairs would have been occasions for general trade, as well as the observance of ritual. Such sites are of particular significance in northern Europe (including Britain), where expansion into forested environments was a large-scale process that continued into the period when animals were used for traction and secondary products.

The model is equally significant for understanding the social structure of early agricultural groups. The idea of self-sufficient groups 'budding off' and immediately achieving independence is probably true only in large uniform areas. In many cases there was probably an initial phase of continuing dependence and linkage. Where colonisation linked zones with complementary resources, regional exchange systems could develop that were capable of handling impressive quantities of goods. Such exchanges could be handled by transactions between acephalous groups linked only by alliance in conditions of general insecurity. A characteristic of such systems was the elaboration of many kinds of competing prestige items within the range of utilitarian artefacts. Since objects such as stone axes were used as social tokens (for example as bridewealth), they were probably produced in quantities beyond practical necessity. Although the importation of stone axes no doubt raised the productivity of the Hungarian Plain, demand was stimulated by social rather than technological factors. These societies appear 'wealthy' to the archaeologist in the sense that many sites produce quantities of stone tools, decorated pottery, ritual items, etc.

As regional differences in animal-raising potential became evened out with continuing forest clearance, the former structure, based on complementary exchanges in a regional system, began to break down. Contrasts emerged between areas whose wealth was purely agricultural and those which had both agricultural and mineral wealth. In the latter, competition was increasingly focused on rarer and rarer prestige goods, especially metal objects. These usually take the form of prestige symbols (for example battle axes and sceptres) rather than commonly used items (for example work axes). Exchanges between these richer nuclei brought exotic materials over longer distances than before, and greater inequalities in access to imported materials are evident within the richer areas. These are well exemplified in the contemporary cemeteries of Tibava and Lučky (Bognár-Kutzián 1972) in the north-east of the Carpathian Basin (with both local stone and metal artefacts and imported materials from across the Carpathians) and at Varna (Todorova 1978) on the Black Sea coast of Bulgaria (with local copper and ?Anatolian gold).[14] Both areas have relatively undeveloped hinterlands where such prestige items are not found. These societies appear 'wealthy' to the archaeologist in the sense that a few sites produce spectacular quantities of specifically status items. Although many of these items are weapons, conditions appear to have been more peaceful than in the previous phase of acephalous communities linked by alliance.

A very similar succession seems to be behind later Neolithic developments in north-west Europe. The communities of 'middle Neolithic' megalith-builders, with their emphasis on ritual rather than rank, have many of the attributes of central European acephalous communities in the period of intensive regional trade. The main difference lay in the availability of draught animals for tillage and construction. The significance of middle Neolithic defended enclosures has already been noted. Ritual played a prominent part in social control, and burial took place in communal lineage ossuaries. Explicit symbols of rank are absent, but there was an elaboration of everyday items – decorated pottery, stone axes, flint leaf-points – for use as valuables. The succeeding 'late Neolithic' pattern of Corded Ware and Bell Beakers was characterised by dispersed settlement without defensive and ritual elements, at the same time as the emergence of status-linked weaponry – battle axes, daggers and archery equipment, and rare ornaments. Long-distance trade (as opposed to the regional axe trade) brought increasingly rare materials into circulation, especially metals. This fits the pattern of rank competition. The last area to adopt the new pattern was the British Isles, where archaic structures (with a strongly ritual aspect) continued to be elaborated, producing sites like Avebury and Stonehenge long after comparable forms had disappeared from continental settlement patterns.

The element that transformed European economies in the early Bronze Age was the arrival (along with the horse) of woolly sheep (Chapter 6), that first provided a cash crop and the basis for a larger scale of textile production.[15] In this way, well-populated areas with extensive grazing were able to enrich themselves despite the lack of local metal sources. The chalklands and sands of Wessex and Jutland were able to develop a complementary relationship with the Irish/Welsh and Harz metal sources respectively, and to intensify regional differences in wealth. Bronze (and textiles?) became a 'fetishised commodity' (Godelier 1977, 152) that could now be accumulated, with some of the characteristics of primitive *money* (cf. Douglas 1958; Dalton 1977) as opposed to primitive *valuables*. Competition was still largely for goods, and not linked to ownership of land. The rapid expansion of this extensive, land-hungry economy reached its ecological limits in the later second millennium, when land became a scarce good. Laid-out fields mark the beginning of formal landholding systems in which true social stratification could occur (Bradley 1980), creating the preconditions for interaction with the expanding Mediterranean world.[16]

The contrast between European and Near Eastern developmental trajectories from the fifth millennium onwards thus lay in the way such landholding inequalities were linked to the operation of regional exchange systems from an early date in areas like the Mesopotamian Plain. The conjunction of increasingly large-scale exchange with competition for access to high-yielding irrigated land caused inequalities between descent groups to build up into a truly stratified pattern from the fourth millennium onwards. The greater uniformity of the temperate European landscape deferred the emergence of such rigid forms of inequality for another 3000 years.

NOTES

1. Systematic surveys have been carried out by the Archaeological Institute of the Hungarian Academy of Sciences as part of the Archaeological Topography programme in Co. Békés (*Békés Megye Régészeti Topográfiája: A Szeghalmi Járás*, 1982). This was the basis for further fieldwork by a joint Hungarian–British team directed by Dr I. Torma and the author (see following chapters).
2. For a less schematic view of the topography, see maps in the following chapter.
3. For a general archaeological background see Kalicz (1970) and Tringham (1971).
4. Szakálhát and Tisza are successive phases, closely related in both material culture and settlement pattern. For other contemporary groups in the Great Hungarian Plain see n. 6.
5. Many examples are well known in the archaeological literature: Hódmezövásárhely-Kökénydomb, H.-Gorzsa, Szegvár-Tüzköves, Battonya-Gödrösök, Szeghalom-Kovacshalom, Dévaványa-Sártó.
6. E.g. Szilmeg, Esztár and Bükk in the Szakálhát phase; Herpály and Csöszhalom in the Tisza phase.
7. Well exemplified in the settlement of Boldogkőváralya-Tekeres Patak (Co. Abaúj-Borsod-Zemplén), a site of the Bükk culture which included several workshops for flint and obsidian, including a cache of 567 blades as well as cores and lumps of raw material (Kalicz and Makkay, 1977, 68–9).
8. It is likely that many animals were partly stall-fed on leaf-fodder in the early stages of settlement in forested areas, as suggested for Neolithic Denmark and Switzerland on the basis of pollen diagrams and finds of excrement and leaf-fodder in settlements (see Guyan 1971, 151–4). If early Neolithic animals were not kept for milk, this would involve the fattening of individuals for slaughter, like the 'family pig' of recent times.
9. Access to rivers for canoe transport became an important element in determining settlement patterns from this time onwards, and is especially notable in the Bodrogkeresztúr and EBA periods.
10. Dalton's term is 'stateless': but this is too inclusive since it is not intended to describe the various kinds of ranked society (best attested by archaeology) that preceded the state.
11. A similar contrast may be observed at this time further north, in Czechoslovakia and Poland, between the earlier and later phases of the 'Lengyel culture'. The early phase has many local styles of painted pottery, figurines, intensive use of local resources (salt pans), regional exchange (obsidian) and defended or enclosed sites (Kyjovice-Těšetice, Hluboke Mašůvsky, Křepice); the later phase has plain pottery, no figurines, long-distance contacts (metal, flint, pottery types) and 'rich' graves (Jordanów, Brześć Kujawski).
12. For the west Mediterranean, Jim Lewthwaite has discussed the importance of sheep as traded items in the Cardial interaction area. As in central Europe, cattle seem to have increased in importance in the fifth and fourth millennia, and the large enclosed site of Passo di Corvo in Apulia – contemporary with the Tisza sites discussed above – is likely to have had an important role in this respect. The expansion of sheep-herding (for secondary products) in the third millennium is again associated with large defended sites, especially on limestone plateaux.

13. The existence of earthworks and earth or stone monuments is sometimes taken as evidence of the central direction of labour: but this is to underestimate the capacity of egalitarian societies to mobilise labour for communal projects (L. Groube, pers. comm.). The existence of settlement networks with enclosed, centrally placed sites is not evidence for social hierarchisation, but is often characteristic of developed egalitarian societies with a strongly ritual focus (cf. the fifth-millennium Moravian Painted Ware sites in n. 11).

14. The importance of Varna is closely linked to its potential for coastal trade. The composition of the goldwork, with its high values for platinum, is almost unparalleled in Europe (Hartmann 1978). Although little is known of late Chalcolithic northern Anatolia, this source seems very likely. The objects were *manufactured* locally, however, in the Balkan Copper Age tradition.

15. In the east Mediterranean this was combined with another cash crop, the olive, to produce high-quality manufactured commodities for the international maritime trade. This was the economic basis of the Aegean palace system.

16. In sub-Saharan Africa, complex societies developed in the absence of intensive agriculture and its attendant landholding systems: hence the critical role played by competition for prestige goods at the time of the early states (Goody 1969, 25ff.). Such systems are thus only partly analogous to those of first-millennium Europe.

11

The Development of Neolithic and Copper Age Settlement in the Great Hungarian Plain

(1983, 1984)

I: THE REGIONAL SETTING

The purpose of this chapter is to describe the succession of patterns which characterise the first four millennia of agricultural settlement in the Great Hungarian Plain. It consists of two parts: a regional description and analysis of the distribution of known Neolithic and Copper Age sites in Eastern Hungary, and a more detailed consideration of the patterns of site location as they have been revealed by recent survey work in the Körös basin.[1] The aim is to relate the evidence from a planned survey programme to the development of prehistoric settlement in the region as a whole.

The area chosen has particular advantages for a study of this kind. The archaeological study of the region has a continuous history from the early nineteenth century when finds were first systematically recorded. The cultural sequence is well known from numerous excavations, including deeply-stratified tell settlements. The Neolithic and Copper Age cultures have been well described in a series of monographs which contain comprehensive lists of known sites. The environmental setting of these distributions, consisting of an alluvial plain with surrounding terraces and uplands, has been systematically mapped and described. The large areas of relatively uniform landscape simplify the problem of analysis and general-

---

Fieldwork in Hungary was designed to track changes in object-distributions and settlement-patterns over thousands of years, from c.6000 down to 2000 BC, in order to see how long-term social processes worked out on the ground in a nodal area of central Europe. This long chapter, originally published in two parts, attempts a systematic presentation of these patterns, zooming in from a regional to a local perspective. The contrasting patterns of site-distribution in the survey area are a unique record of fluctuating (and slowly evolving) forms of spatial organisation over long periods of time, with a comprehensiveness and degree of resolution unequalled anywhere.

isation. The sample of sites at a regional level is thus both large and well dated, and its geographical context is well known.

In addition, a central part of the region has been selected for planned investigation in the programme of the Archaeological Topography of Hungary.[2] This county-by-county survey consists not only of the systematic recording of known finds but also of active fieldwork directed to an assessment of the density of archaeological sites in the area. For the first time it has been possible to appreciate the numbers of prehistoric settlements and the regularities of their distribution at a local level. This both revolutionises the interpretation of distribution patterns on a regional scale, and must itself be interpreted in the wider context of regional development. A major theme of this article is thus the interplay between different types of sample of the spatial patterning, and the way in which each contributes to a comprehensive view.

The information from the topographic survey of Co. Békés was the basis for a co-operative research programme between the Ashmolean Museum of the University of Oxford and the Archaeological Institute of the Hungarian Academy of Sciences. This was concerned with the closer definition of the distribution and structure of Neolithic and Copper Age settlement by an integrated programme of surface collecting, geophysical survey and sampling by excavations.[3] The present chapter provides a background to this programme of fieldwork, which takes the analysis offered here down to the level of individual communities and their components. The complementary study of traded materials is discussed in Chapter 12.

EASTERN HUNGARY WITHIN THE CARPATHIAN BASIN[4]

The Carpathian Basin (Figures 10.1, 11.1) occupies a critical position in European prehistory. As a major lowland area on the middle course of the Danube, it is connected by natural routes with the Mediterranean, the Pontic steppes and the loess-lands of central Europe. It was important both in the initial spread of agriculture from the east Mediterranean in the sixth millennium BC,[5] and also in the transmission of elements from the steppe belt from the third millennium onwards. Its largely enclosed character, ringed on all sides by mountains rising to over 1000m, nevertheless made it the focus of a distinctive series of cultures which had a continuing influence on surrounding areas.

The Basin itself is a downfaulted median mass formed during the Tertiary mountain-building phase that produced the Alps and the Carpathians.[6] Its sinking surface has been covered by the erosion products of the surrounding uplands. During the Miocene and Pliocene it was occupied by the sea, and marine limestones were deposited. These, mantled during the Pleistocene by loess, form the predominant landscape in the area to the west of the Danube – the historical Pannonia. The eastern part, affected by continuing tectonic

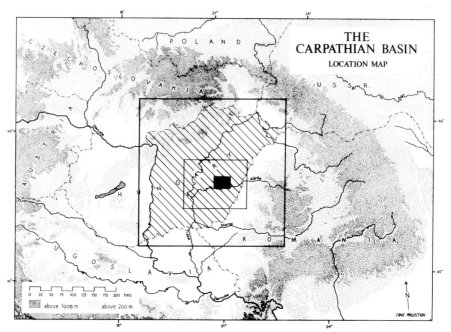

11.1 The Carpathian Basin, showing the areas covered by detailed maps. Hatched area: eastern Hungary (regional distribution maps, Figs 11.3–4, 11.8–9); rectangular outlined area: the Körös-Berettyó region (Figs 11.10, 11.12–13, 11.16); rectangular filled area: the Szeghalom survey (Figs 11.18–27) [from Sherratt 1984a].

depression, has been filled by alluvial deposits of various kinds to produce a level plain with only minor changes in relief – the Great Hungarian Plain (*Nagy Alföld*).

This contrast is accentuated by a climatic difference, the eastern part having the low rainfall and high evaporation characteristic of the Pontic steppe belt further east. While the western part forms a southern projection of the central European loess region, the eastern part has an individual character resulting from the combination of a concentration of surface water from the surrounding mountains with a yearly precipitation in the Plain of less than 600mm. The slow drainage from its level surface has created a mosaic of marshy floodplains and dry interfluves, in which minor differences in relief have a marked effect in creating suitable conditions for early settlement.

The alluvial plain, covering an area of 100,000km^2, is surrounded first by a narrow terrace of marine limestones, and then by the ring of fold mountains, rich in the hard stone and metal ores sought by early man. The upland and lowland areas thus formed a complementary unity in their respective mineral and agricultural resources.

In cultural terms, the western part of the Carpathian Basin has always had strong links via Moravia with the central European loess area, begin-

272

TISZAPOLGÁR   HATVAN

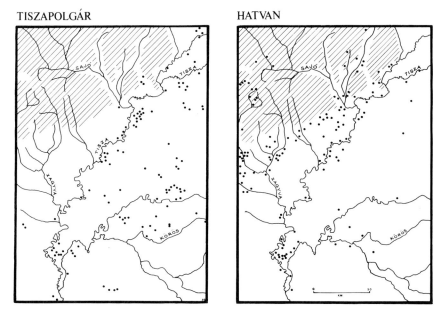

*11.2 The contrasting distribution of settlement in north-east Hungary in the Early
Copper Age (Tiszapolgár culture) and Early Bronze Age (Hatvan culture).
Compiled from Bognár-Kutzián (1972) and Kalicz (1968).*

ning with the formation there of the Neolithic *Bandkeramik* complex which
spread throughout central Europe. This pattern may also be discerned in the
later Neolithic and Copper Age Lengyel culture, and was still evident in
the Bronze Age. The eastern part of the Carpathian Basin, lacking an easy
northern outlet, followed a rather different course, with more evident
southern links. It formed the northern margin of early Neolithic cultures of
Balkan/Near Eastern character, and later in the Neolithic it again marked
the furthest extension of settlement types including tells. It was increasingly
integrated within the central European sphere, however, first by the
strengthening of links with the Ukraine and southern Poland across the
north-eastern Carpathians and secondly by the infilling of the sandy area
between the Tisza and the Danube which allowed the first cultural unification of the Carpathian Basin in the Baden period.

From this time onwards the eastern part of the Carpathian Basin began
to play a major innovating role in central European prehistory. The focus
of settlement shifted from the central areas of the Plain to the fringes of
surrounding uplands (Figure 11.2). This marks the beginning of a new
pattern characteristic of the Bronze Age, in which a powerful centre of
political and cultural development emerged in the north-eastern part of the
Carpathian Basin. The advanced social organisation and metallurgical skills
associated with the rise of the Otomani culture had a major impact on
surrounding regions.

THE EVOLUTION OF THE EAST HUNGARIAN LANDSCAPE

Geomorphology

The surface of the Great Hungarian Plain took its present shape within the Quaternary epoch. Infilling by rivers during the Pleistocene period contributed up to 300m of alluvial deposit. This accumulation created the basic units of relief (Figure 11.3), which relate to the main bodies of water entering the region (Pécsi 1970). The largest of these was the Danube, which in the Pleistocene flowed south-westwards in a number of braided channels to create a major fan now lying between the present courses of the Danube and Tisza. From the north-east, the waters from the catchment now drained by the Tisza, Szamos and their northern tributaries converged to form another fan in the area now known as the Nyírség.[7] These fans lie at 150–120m above sea-level, having been extensively mantled by blown sand during the closing phases of the Pleistocene and the early Holocene. The Maros, draining southern Transylvania and entering the Plain from the south-east, also built up a large loess-covered fan at 110–90m. A row of piedmont fans produced by smaller rivers along the edge of the Tertiary terrace completes the picture. Together, all these fans enclose a central triangular depression – the Körös region – forming a water and sediment basin some 5–10m below the level of the surrounding Plain, within which loessic sediments were redeposited.

At the beginning of the Holocene, this area received water from all the surrounding territories (Papp 1969), the greatest volume being supplied by the palaeo-Szamos + Tisza, which flowed along the southern margin of the Nyírség in a valley now occupied by a small creek called the Ér. This major river, flowing across the area in a south-westerly direction, built up a substantial series of raised beds at about 85m, with backswamps on either side. Its frequently changing course created a tangle of old channels outlined by levees, coalescing to form a discontinuous flat-topped ridge or terrace known as the Dévaványa Plain.

At the end of the pre-boreal phase, this situation was abruptly altered. Sinkage of the northern margin of the Plain diverted the Tisza and Szamos across the northern part of the Nyírség through the chain of depressions now marked by the Szatmár basin and the Rétköz. This water then found its way southwards, at first through the Hortobágy and then along the present valley of the upper Tisza, separating the outlier known as Great Cumania (*Nagykunság*) from the main body of the north Alföld fans. At about the same time the Maros also moved southwards to occupy its present course. These two diversions reduced the hydrographic importance of the Körös region and interrupted the process of infilling. The rivers draining into it were now smaller, and the sediments which continued to accumulate there became generally finer. The Dévaványa Plain was left in a fossilised form, as the Berettyó and Rapid Körös spread respectively into the back-

11.3 The development of the landscape of eastern Hungary during the Quaternary (after Pécsi and others).

swamps on either side, where their slow drainage created the bog-like conditions of the Great (*Nagy-*) and the Little (*Kis-*) *Sárrét* (literally 'bog-meadow'). Water from the Tisza and Szamos still occasionally found its way into this region as overspill in times of flood, following both the Ér valley and the Hortobágy.

The floods of the Tisza and its tributaries occur in two peaks, one in early spring and a larger one in early summer, the former caused by snowmelt and the latter by rainfall. At these times the water occupied large parts of the Körös area, depositing a black organic meadow-clay that contrasts with the yellow loessic deposits of the ridges. The river-courses themselves were in any case highly unstable, with extensive meanders and ox-bow lakes reflecting frequent changes of course. Regulation of the Tisza during the nineteenth century reduced its length by approximately one third, and all the rivers of the Plain are now constrained by massive dykes. This canalisation, by restricting the flood areas and altering the water-table, had extensive secondary effects on sedimentation and soil-formation.

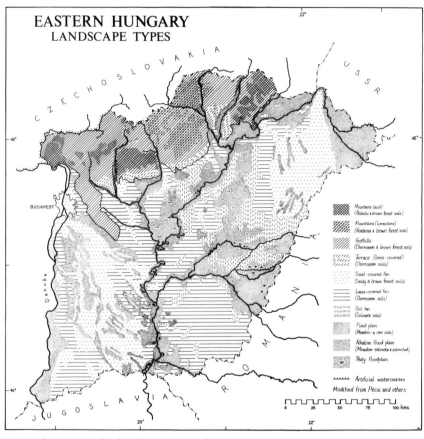

11.4 The geomorphic landscape units of eastern Hungary and their associated soils.

Soils and vegetation

The soils of eastern Hungary are closely related to the relief (Figure 11.4). The whole of the lowland area is dominated by processes producing steppe soils (Somogyi 1964); only where the hills on the edge of the Plain rise to over 200m, and in the north-eastern area where there is an increase in rainfall and summer moisture, do forest soils occur. Skeletal sandy soils occur on the Danube fan and the Nyírség. Over the rest of the region, varieties of chernozem are the rule except where modified by groundwater conditions. There is a graduated sequence from true chernozem on the loess-covered fans to the alluvial and marsh soils of the floodplains. In between lie meadow chernozems, and the saline soils – solonetz and solonchak – that occur under a steppe climate where salt-charged groundwater evaporates at the surface. These soils are particularly important since they occupy a position intermediate between the dry soils of the interfluves and those of the low floodplain, where inundation inhibited cultivation and permanent settlement.

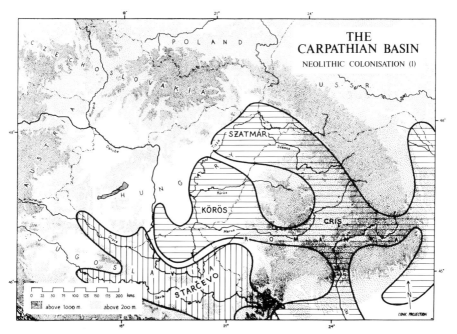

11.5 Initial spread of farming into the Carpathian Basin in the Early Neolithic, showing the 'western stream' (Starčevo) and the 'eastern stream' (Körös-Criş).

Most of the Great Hungarian Plain is covered by vegetation classified as forest steppe. Considerable areas, notably on the chernozem-covered inter-fluves, are unlikely to have undergone extensive afforestation during the Holocene. Riparian forests, however, are likely to have been characteristic of the floodplain margins and wet depressions. The extent of forest cover on the lower terrace now characterised by solonetz soils is problematic, but a mosaic of light forest and more open areas is most likely.

The landscape of the Great Hungarian Plain, therefore, as it presented itself to early settlers, offered a range of environments each with its attend-ant problems, from aridity to inundation. This fine balance of advantage made the choice of settlement-location a critical one, and the distribution of prehistoric sites is thus an important source of information on the ecological requirements of early farmers.

THE CULTURAL SUCCESSION AND THE STRUCTURE OF REGIONAL CONTACTS

The well-investigated succession of Neolithic and Copper Age cultures and the growing number of radiocarbon dates provide a firm framework for the interpretation of the settlement-evidence. The classification of these groups will be briefly reviewed in this section before presenting the details of their distributions.

277

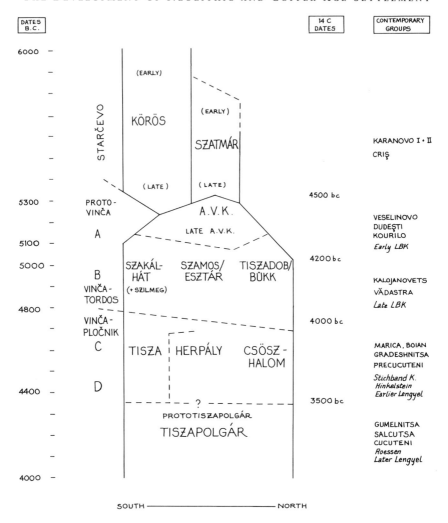

DATES B.C.			14 C DATES	CONTEMPORARY GROUPS

THE NEOLITHIC AND EARLY COPPER AGE
CHRONOLOGY OF EASTERN HUNGARY

11.6 *The cultural succession in eastern Hungary, showing contemporary groups in the Balkans and west-central Europe.*

The Neolithic period

The earliest agricultural communities in eastern Hungary (Figure 11.5) belong to the Körös culture (= Romanian Criş culture), long recognised as part of the Balkan early Neolithic complex (Kutzián 1944). Its sites occur in the southern part of the Plain and are characterised by plentiful pinched and rusticated pottery with chaff tempering. Radiocarbon dates take it back to the early sixth millennium BC (Figure 11.6). The origins of this culture have

278

usually been sought in the Starčevo culture of Jugoslavia, but since material closely resembling the Körös assemblage occurs as far east as Moldavia, on the border of the USSR, a primary dispersal centre in Transylvania seems more probable. The recent discovery here of a pre-Körös phase of painted pottery with strong analogies in northern Bulgaria (Comşa 1974) indicates the possibility of an eastern stream of Neolithic population, parallel to that of Starčevo further west, which would have provided the basis for such a Körös dispersal. In this case, the eastern part of the Carpathian Basin would have been the meeting point for two streams of incoming Neolithic population as shown in Figure 11.5. True Starčevo sites occur in the southern part of western Hungary, where they are represented by recent finds at Lánycsók· and Becsehely (Kalicz 1980).

A further element in this picture is the recently-defined Szatmár group in the north-east part of the Carpathian Basin with a material culture basically similar to that of Körös (Kalicz and Makkay 1977). It can plausibly be interpreted as a further movement from Transylvania around the northern margin of the Bihor Mountains. Far fewer sites are known than for Körös, and it probably arrived somewhat later (Figure 11.5).

Around 5300 BC major changes took place within the Carpathian Basin. Eastern Hungary became the focus of a new group centred in the Great Hungarian Plain, while western Hungary was occupied for the first time by agricultural groups expanding from the former Starčevo area. These changes must be seen as part of a wider reorganisation throughout south-east Europe, reflected in new cultural groupings such as Vinča and Veselinovo. The south part of the Carpathian Basin formed part of the zone characterised by dark, burnished pottery ornamented by channelling; in the south-east (from Serbia along the Maros to Transylvania) it is represented by the Vinča culture, and in the south-west (along the Sava and Drava) by the related Sopot group. To the north of this zone, incised, linear ornament was characteristic – the so-called LBK or *Linienbandkeramik* – which divides into two regional groups. Within the previously occupied area of the Great Hungarian Plain, the group known as AVK (*Alföldi Vonaldíszes Kerámia* = Alföld Linear Pottery) developed from local Körös and Szatmár populations under strong Vinča influence (Kalicz and Makkay 1977). In the hitherto un-occupied area west of the Danube a new group, the west Hungarian branch of pan-European LBK, made its appearance as the first stage in a major movement of agricultural expansion.

These two groups in the east and west of the Carpathian Basin thus emerged in parallel, with a common background in the earlier agricultural communities of the Balkans. Although imports demonstrate a continuing contact between them, they continued on independent lines of development. In terms of European prehistory, the western group was the more significant: for it was this group that carried agriculture into Moravia and northwards beyond the Carpathians to the whole of the central European loess belt from

France to the Ukraine. Expansion in eastern Hungary took place along the valleys reaching up into the mountain foreland to produce important peripheral groups in the karstic landscapes of north-east Hungary and Slovakia, but major expansion was blocked. While western Hungary maintained an important role as intermediary between the Balkans and central Europe, eastern Hungary continued an introverted development in which Balkan elements became increasingly pronounced.

The changes marked by the appearance of AVK and earliest western *Bandkeramik* seem to have been relatively rapid (Figure 11.6), for by c.5200 BC the cultural uniformity of eastern Hungary had given way to a series of regional pottery styles (Bognár-Kutzián 1966; Kalicz and Makkay 1977) with further Vinča influence in the south and a lively focus of trade and stylistic innovation in the north. This pattern was more stable, lasting for some 300 to 400 years. On the lower and middle Tisza and along the Körös, the Szakálhát group is distinguished by pottery ornamented with paint outlined by incised decoration. To the north of this the Esztár group occupied a wide territory on the Nyírség, Szamos and upper Berettyó, in which pottery with dark painted ornament was used. Various smaller groups emerged on the fringes of the northern mountains: Szilmeg in the Bükk foothills, Tiszadob in the Sajó valley, and Bükk in the mountains themselves, with exceptionally fine incised and occasionally painted pottery. All these groups are distinguished by their characteristic finewares, which occur in smaller quantities as imports in each others' areas. This small-scale cultural distinctiveness is probably related to a degree of economic differentiation, and the trade between mountain and plain in obsidian and other hard stones was greatly expanded. Bükk sherds and obsidian from the Tokaj and neighbouring sources occur on Vinča sites in Serbia and southern Transylvania, a distance of 400km.

Around 4800 BC another horizon of stylistic cultural change can be observed in many parts of the Balkans, for instance in the transition from Vinča-Tordos to Vinča-Pločnik. At this time the Great Hungarian Plain saw the emergence of Late Neolithic groups represented by the Tisza and Herpály-Csőszhalom groups (Bognár-Kutzián 1966). Decorated Tisza fine pottery, with its intricate incised, textile-like patterns is characteristic of the southern area and shows continuity from the Szakálhát group. The northern part of the Plain – with the exception of the mountain fringes, where settlement was abandoned – was occupied by the Herpály-Csőszhalom group, with painted finewares. This replaced the multitude of smaller groups on the northern edge of the Plain, and is found in the former Esztár area. Small differences in the colour-combinations distinguish Herpály from Csőszhalom, but together they differ from Tisza not only in their pottery but also in their settlement-pattern and in the occurrence of small numbers of simple copper objects, for instance at Herpály. Since both these groups shared a common set of domestic pottery, the sharp frontier between Tisza and Herpály finewares may indicate a genuine social boundary that is particularly interesting because of the differences in settlement-types, in which true tells are confined to the north and east. These groups were long-lived, persisting for perhaps a 300 to 400 year span. During this period the elaborately-decorated finewares declined, with the final phase of Tisza being distinguished as the Gorzsa group.

The Copper Age

A new pattern marks the beginning of the Copper Age[8] around 4400 BC, when a much more uniform culture developed over eastern Hungary and neighbouring parts of Transylvania (Bognár-Kutzián 1972). This was the Tiszapolgár culture, which has a new range of shapes (especially pedestalled forms with decorative lugs), but lacks the element of painted decoration. The larger cemeteries of this period provide evidence of the first heavy copper objects and also goldwork. These indicate the rising wealth of areas on the edge of the Plain, with access both to the highland metal sources and to trade routes, which for the first time crossed the Carpathians to bring commodities such as blades of Ukrainian flint into circulation. This new, outward-looking pattern reduced the importance of the hitherto wealthy central area.

By 4000 BC this pattern may be perceived with even greater clarity in the succeeding Bodrogkeresztúr culture (Patay 1974). The scale of copper pro-duction was greatly expanded, with copper axes occurring in graves up to 200km from the copper sources. This metalwork and even pottery occur north of the Carpathians in Little Poland, while cultural mixing with late Salcutsa groups on the Lower Danube testifies to the increased importance of links in this direction also (Roman 1971).

The most radical break in the prehistory of this region occurred around 3500 BC. The appearance of the Baden culture, with its roots in the Lengyel tradition of western Hungary and Czechoslovakia, marks the integration of eastern Hungary into a wider grouping including the whole of the Carpathian Basin (Banner 1956). The pottery assemblage was transformed by a new range of types including pails, jugs and cups that testify to funda-mental changes in eating habits, with an increased importance of liquids. This occurs over a wide area of south-east and central Europe. The first evidence for the cart, and probably also the plough, appears at this time (Chapter 6).

Another important development of this period was the appearance of large numbers of tumuli (some up to 70m in diameter and 10m high) con-taining burials covered by planks and hides, with the body in a characteristic supine position, with knees drawn up, and the skull painted with stripes of red ochre. They have few grave-goods, but occasionally ear- [or hair-] rings of silver. Such burials have close analogies on the Pontic steppes, and other examples are known from the Lower Danube. They have plausibly been in

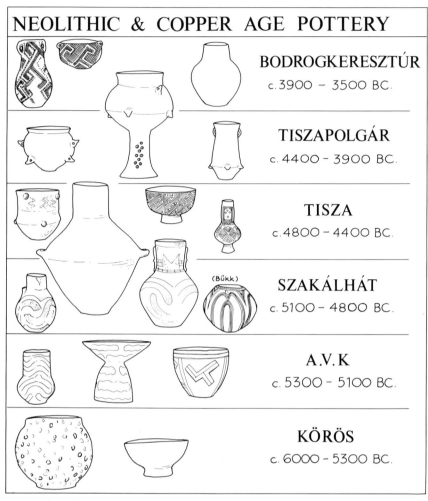

NEOLITHIC & COPPER AGE POTTERY

BODROGKERESZTÚR
c. 3900 – 3500 BC.

TISZAPOLGÁR
c. 4400 – 3900 BC.

TISZA
c. 4800 – 4400 BC.

(Bükk)

SZAKÁLHÁT
c. 5100 – 4800 BC.

A.V.K
c. 5300 – 5100 BC.

KÖRÖS
c. 6000 – 5300 BC.

11.7 Selected pottery types characteristic of the main phases of the Neolithic and Copper Ages in eastern Hungary.

terpreted as evidence for an intrusive steppe population, maintaining a cultural distinctiveness alongside native groups (Ecsedy 1979).

The Early Bronze Age

By 2800 BC these populations had fused to form the Early Bronze Age groups of this area, broadly divided between a north-eastern (Nyírség) group and a central (Makó) group (Kalicz 1968). Innovations at this time include improved techniques of copperworking such as the two-piece mould and the new types it made possible, and also the advent of horse-breeding on a large scale. Trade in metal items, and also warfare increased in significance, reaching their full development in the Nagyrév, Hatvan, Otomani and Perjámos cultures. These occupy discrete territories, the first on the

Danube and middle Tisza, the second and third in northern and north-eastern Hungary, and the last on the Maros. These are more than simply ceramic styles, and the burial evidence indicates that they may be consciously distinguished cultural groups (O'Shea 1978). Sites of this period show significant new features such as large cemeteries with several hundred graves (especially in the south, on the major rivers at the Maros confluence) and the reappearance of tell sites, which now had a fortified character. These are especially common on the margins of the Basin (though flat sites fortified with ring ditches are known from the Körös region). The Otomani culture in particular shows a new level of centralisation, and its sites have produced evidence of bronze- and gold-working, early ironwork, chariotry and stone-built fortifications (Vladár 1973).

THE REGIONAL DISTRIBUTION OF SETTLEMENT

The agricultural occupation of eastern Hungary in the periods described in the preceding section may be followed in the series of distribution maps presented in Sherratt (1983b).[9] What is essential to such comparisons, however, is an appreciation of how this archaeological record has been built up and how it must be supplemented by future research. The characteristics of this record will therefore be briefly reviewed before discussion of the distributions.

History of research

Hungary has a long tradition of archaeological research, with the oldest national museum in Europe, founded in 1802. As well as this national focus, local museums and amateur societies have been active from the later nineteenth century onwards. By the time of the International Congress of Prehistoric Anthropology and Archaeology in Budapest in 1876, organised by Flóris Rómer (1878), commissions with local correspondents were investigating the problems of obsidian distribution, tell settlements, tumuli and hillforts. County archaeological maps were exhibited at the Congress. The Tisza/Körös region was well represented, with reports on excavations at the Bronze Age tell of Nagyrév and finds from the important Tisza culture sites of Szegvár-Tüzköves and Békésszentandrás (Rómer 1878). Before the First World War excavations had taken place at the eponymous sites of Lengyel (1880s), Tiszapolgár (1900s) and the crucial Bronze Age tell at Tószeg (1906–13).

Investigations in the Interwar years clarified the Neolithic cultural succession (Tompa 1929; 1937) and saw extensive regional fieldwork – notably by Janos Banner (1942) in the Szeged-Hódmezövásárhely area and by Jenö Hillebrand (1937) in the Bükk mountains. Kutzián summarised the Körös culture, and since the Second World War further monographs in the series *Archaeologia Hungarica* have described the assemblages and known

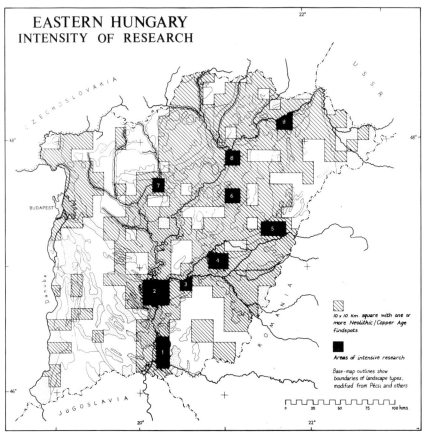

11.8 *The intensity of field research in eastern Hungary before the commencement of the* Archaeological Topography of Hungary, *showing the distribution of reported Neolithic and Copper Age finds, and individual surveys or projects.*
Key: (1) Banner – Hodmezövásárhely; (2) Kalicz – Tiszazug; (3) Banner – Szarvas; (4) Bereczky – Dévaványa; (5) Makkay – Derecske; (6) Korek, Gazdapusztai and Mesterházy – Hortobágy; (7) Kalicz – Tarnabod; (8) Bognár-Kutzián – Polgár; (9) Kalicz – Nyiregyháza.

findspots of the Körös, AVK, Tiszapolgár, Baden and EBA cultures (Kalicz and Makkay 1977; Bognár-Kutzián 1972; Banner 1956; Kalicz 1968), while Bodrogkeresztúr has been summarised in a major article (Patay 1974). Only the Tisza-Herpály-Csöszhalom complex remains without monographic treatment. Excavations on tell settlements have taken place at Herpály, Tapé-Lebö, Szegvár-Tüzköves, Battonya-Parázstanya and Vésztö Mágor, as well as the settlement and cemetery at Aszód and at many Körös sites.[10]

At the same time regional surveys have been conducted, first by Kalicz in the Tiszazug (1957), by Bognár-Kutzián in connection with the major excavation of the Tiszapolgar cemetery (Bognár-Kutzián 1963), and by Makkay near Derecske (Makkay 1957). These pioneer projects have led to a current interest in the discovery and registration of sites, fuelled by the need to identify priorities in rescue work on the part of local institutions in many areas. This work has been organised and given central direction by the Hungarian Academy in the programme of the Archaeological Topography of Hungary (*Magyarország Régészeti Topográfiája*), a county-by-county survey of finds, sites, and monuments. Although the initial volumes have been concerned with western Hungary (Co. Veszprém, Co. Komárom), a major programme on the northern part of Co. Békés (covering the Körös area from the Romanian border to Szarvas) is nearing completion (e.g. Ecsedy et al. 1982). This work is unique in its scale and sustained intensity, and has multiplied the number of known prehistoric sites by a factor of ten.

These planned surveys represent a new threshold in the discovery of prehistoric settlement-patterns which complements the overall picture built up by chance finds and selective recording. They can be used to calibrate existing maps by demonstrating the arbitrary character of existing records and indicating the real nature of changes in the number, character and location of sites. But they must also be interpreted in the light of conclusions gained from wider studies about the role and significance of the areas in question within the region as a whole. Both levels of analysis are needed to make sense of the information.

On a practical point, it is difficult (and misleading) to mix the two kinds of information on a single small-scale map. It is better to realise that traditional distribution-maps indicate only the occurrence of sites in a given area, but not their relative density: this can only be assessed from full survey data.[11] For this reason, findspots from the recent Topographic Survey have not been plotted on the small-scale regional maps. Figure 11.8 shows a first attempt to map the intensity of research which underlies the following distributions. [Maps of Körös, AVK, Tiszapolgár, Bodrogkeresztúr and Baden distributions are not reproduced here.]

The Körös and Szatmár cultures

The first Neolithic communities show a strongly constrained distribution with a riverine emphasis and little or no expansion into the side valleys or onto the fans. The Körös and Szatmár distributions are very similar in this respect, and their complementary character, with a boundary on the middle Tisza, is consistent with a convergence along the Tisza from south and north respectively. Although the apparent clusters of settlement are largely related to the intensity of fieldwork (e.g. around Hódmezővásárhely and in the Tiszazug), there appears to be a real difference between the density of Körös sites and those of Szatmár. The very high density of Körös sites is remarkable, and contrasts in this respect also with Starčevo (Kalicz 1980). Where the floodplain is narrow, the sites show a linear arrangement on bluffs overlooking the valley; where the floodplain is broader they occur on the small islands of higher ground within it. In places (as around Hódmezövásárhely) the pattern of sites may relate to an earlier course of the Tisza. The only exception to the general riverine distribution is the group of sites on the Maros fan around Orosháza, which may indicate more extensive penetration of this region. By comparison with the following period, there is a notable absence of sites on the broad, flat floodplains of the Hortobágy and the middle Tisza.

Excavated evidence of the Körös economy demonstrates a substantial seasonal contribution from fishing, shellfish-gathering and fowling, as well as the cultivation of grain and the keeping of domestic livestock, mainly sheep (Bökönyi 1974). Clay weights, probably net-sinkers, are common finds.

The Alföld Linear Pottery (AVK) culture

This period was probably shorter than the others considered here, and is contemporary with the earliest phases of the Vinča culture (sites not known), which extended up to the Maros confluence. The basic pattern resembles that of Körös, with some additional movement along the side-valleys up into the Jászság and along the Sajó, with an initial penetration into the foothills. (It is likely that some of the sites of the Tiszadob group shown in the following map began before the end of this period.) A complementary expansion occurred on the floodplain to the north of the middle Tisza, and in the now highly saline lands of the Hortobágy. The distribution was still predominantly riverine, with no settlement of the northern fan on the Hajdúság and Nyírség.

The economy is less well known, but there are indications that there was less reliance on wild resources and a greater emphasis on cattle and perhaps cereals. Net-sinkers no longer occur.

Szakálhát and its contemporaries (Figure 11.9)

This period saw a general expansion in the north, encompassing the Jászság, the northern foothills and limestone mountains, and the Nyírség with its surrounding floodplains – the upper Tisza depressions and the upper Berettyó. Some expansion is also observable in the south, on the east bank of the Tisza (e.g. around Szentes) and lower Körös, and also around the marshy depressions on the Maros fan around Battonya. Many tell sites were founded in this period, e.g. Vésztö Mágor. There was no penetration of the Danube-Tisza interfluve, and the sites in the Hortobágy appear to have been abandoned.

The emergence of the Nyírség and its surrounding areas created a north-eastern focus marked by Esztár pottery. The lower foothills of the Bükk mountains are picked out by the curious small concentration of the Szilmeg group, extending to the opposite bank of the Tisza. The mountains themselves, and the adjacent valleys of the Sajó and the Hernád, were the focus

11.9 Mapping at the scale of cultural distributions: Late Neolithic (late sixth/early fifth millennia BC) findspots of Szakálhát, Szilmeg, Bükk and Esztár material (data from Kalicz and Makkay 1977); findspots of contemporary Zseliz and Vinča material not shown. (For distributions of material from other periods plotted at this scale, but not reproduced here, see Sherratt 1983b.)

of the distinctive Tiszadob and the Bükk groups, which are also represented on the Rétköz and the northern Nyírség.

Bükk sites (both on terraces and in the plentiful caves) occur in the greatest number in the limestone mountains of the Bükk itself and the North Borsod Karst. The absence of sites in the acid Mátra mountains is conspicuous. They are, however, frequent in the foothills of the Cserehát and around the fringes of the volcanic mountains of the Zemplén range, where raw materials are likely to have been the motive for settlement. The presence of sites in the deep, well-watered upland valleys of the northern karstic mountains indicates an emphasis other than cereal-growing. Animal remains from the Domica cave across the border in Slovakia indicate a high proportion of hunted species, with predominance of sheep among the domestic stock. Within the cave, lines of postholes outline rectangular pens

287

some three by four metres, while smaller camp-sites occur nearby next to springs. These indicate the importance of animal-keeping, perhaps on a transhumant basis, though carbonised cereals and grinders indicate the consumption of grain. The village-like open sites at lower altitudes had an economy similar to that of sites in the Plain, based on cattle-keeping (Lichardus 1974).

An important element in the economy of the region was trade, both in raw materials and manufactured products.[12] Although the limestone areas themselves have no hard rocks, the andesites and rhyolites of the Bükk foothills and the Zemplén mountains, along with the obsidian deposits of the latter (especially around Erdöhorváti) were both exploited and widely traded. Hoards of blades in local siliceous rock are known from Barca and Boldogkőváralja – the latter apparently an obsidian workshop also – and there is a group of nine axes from Domica (Kalicz and Makkay 1977; Lichardus 1974; see Figure 12.10). Bükk groups were active both in the direct exploitation of these resources and as middlemen in their distribution both northwards and southwards. Another traded commodity was pottery – apparently manufactured from terra rossa in the caves themselves. This was superbly decorated with fine parallel lines and was traded over a similar area as obsidian, as far as Serbia, Transylvania and southern Poland. The economy of these sites cannot be understood in terms of local self-sufficiency.

In the Plain to the south the prosperity of this period is emphasised both by the number and size of sites and by their evident ability to acquire highland products and materials. The emphasis on cattle has prompted speculation that this formed an important traded commodity in its own right (Chapter 10).

Tisza–Herpály–Csöszhalom

The sites of this period have not been systematically mapped, but from the known distribution a great similarity to that of the preceding groups may be inferred, the main difference being the lack of sites in the northern mountain fringe. Continuity in the main cultural boundary, from Szakálhát/Esztár to Tisza/Herpály–Csöszhalom is very striking, with a proliferation of sites in the upper Berettyó region, which continued as a major focus of settlement. Large numbers of tell sites (including Herpály itself: Korek and Patay 1956) are known from this area. The tell at Csöszhalom near Polgár (Bognár-Kutzián 1958) can be seen as part of the northern wing of this group on the other side of the Nyírség.

In the Tisza province further south two types of settlement are known (Kalicz 1965): a zone of 'pit settlements' on the middle Tisza and a zone on the Lower Tisza and Körös where very large aggregated sites up to a kilometre across are common.[13] Such sites are usually near to important river links, and may reflect the advantages of congregation at nodal points of trade. (This seems to be the case in the Vinča area, as at Vinča itself.) The smaller size of Herpály tells may thus reflect a different organisation of trading activity in a zone with more immediate access to highland resources.

The lowland economy continued to be dominated by cattle-raising, with high proportions of large animals of aurochs size on sites of the Herpály–Csöszhalom group (Bökönyi 1974). Lowland sites continued to import large quantities of highland materials. The lack of sites in the mountains appears to indicate that control of these resources now lay with adjacent lowland groups, and that the regional economy no longer supported a fringe of specialised middleman-trading combined with herding. Examples of spectacular long-distance trading in pottery or obsidian are less frequent.

The Tiszapolgár culture

The map of Tiszapolgár settlement shows a pattern (emphasised by the loss of the mountain fringe) that was still essentially riverine. The territory on and around the Nyírség remained the main area of interest outside the river valleys. Contemporary Lengyel groups again occupied the north-west of the area (sites not shown) on the upper Galga and Zagyva, forming a link westwards from the Jászság. One or two Tiszapolgár sites are known from the eastern fringes of the Danube-Tisza Interfluve, but there was no real penetration of this area. The Körös-Berettyó area was well populated, while Makkay's survey of the Derecske region (1957) indicated a large number of sites between the upper Berettyó and the Nyírség. The Polgár area is similarly highlighted by Bognár-Kutzián's work, while the Tiszazug again shows the plentiful sites from Kalicz' survey. Two areas of settlement, indicating the possibility of further sites, are picked out on the Maros fan, around Orosháza and Battonya.

Although they have not been differentiated on the map, large cemetery sites are known. The Tiszapolgár-Basatanya cemetery contained over sixty graves of this period and was not directly associated with an adjacent settlement (Bognár-Kutzián 1963). Such cemeteries seem to have had a distinctive role in the settlement pattern, perhaps serving as the common focus for several small hamlets.

Subsistence evidence shows a continuing emphasis on cattle, though now without the large, aurochs-sized specimens that have been interpreted as evidence of hunting and local domestication. A new traded commodity, however, was the heavy copper axe, mostly in the form of simple axe-hammers. The distribution of these finds (Schubert 1965) is notably restricted to the edge of the Plain, mostly outside Hungary: one group occurs in the north-east, for instance as grave-goods at Lučky and Tibava in Slovakia, another group is at the foot of the Rézhegység (Copper mountains) along the headwaters of the Berettyó in Romania, and a third lies in the portion of the Plain in northern Jugoslavia (Bognár-Kutzián

289

1972). The central area of the Plain, although well populated, was not rich in metal goods.

Bodrogkeresztúr

The map of this period is more complicated, since it attempts to differentiate settlements and cemeteries, and also records stray finds of copper axes. Characteristically, rather few settlements have been recognised, though eight times as many cemeteries are known and an equal number of stray axes – many themselves probably derived from destroyed graves. Cemeteries clearly continued to be important in the settlement pattern, and the Tiszapolgár-Basatanya cemetery contained nearly 100 graves of this period. The small number of settlement-sites is partly related to the difficulty of recognising Bodrogkeresztúr pottery, only a small proportion of which is decorated. The distribution of sites defined on the occurrence of pottery (less than half the number of comparable Tiszapolgár sites) can usefully be supplemented by findspots of types of copper axes known to belong to this period. This information amplifies, but does not radically change, the basic pattern shown by settlements and cemeteries.

While the riverine axis continued to be important, a scatter of sites occurs on the fans, notably on the Nyírség and less obviously on the Maros fan (though this may be due to the poorer representation of metal finds in the central part of the Plain). Some increase in activity is evident on the Danube-Tisza Interfluve, while the important linking area between the Jászság and the Danube bend was absorbed from Lengyel into the Bodrogkeresztúr grouping, emphasising the increasing significance of east–west links. Small numbers of finds reappear at this period in the northern mountains and the intermontane valleys behind, and there is evidence for some occupation in the Hortobágy again. The most striking contrast with the preceding distribution is in the Körös-Berettyó area, previously well settled but now apparently deserted, which contrasts with the evident continuity of the Szeged-Hódmezövásárhely area.

On a regional scale, there is a large measure of continuity from Tiszapolgár to Bodrogkeresztúr, both in terms of way of life (continuity in ceramic forms, similar subsistence pattern) and in the continuity of particular sites such as the Tiszapolgár cemetery. The distribution of copper objects, too, shows a similar pattern but on an expanded scale (Schubert 1965). The greatest densities are on the northern Nyírség and the upper Tisza, probably representing the east Slovakian centre exemplified in the previous period by Tibava; the southern Nyírség, upper Berettyó and north-east Maros fan, again the western fringe of a Transylvanian group; and in the area of the Danube bend, reflecting west Slovakian sources. A few strays from Serbian sources complete the picture in the south. Relatively few copper objects reached the central part of eastern Hungary, Tiszazug and the lower Körös.

Baden and Early Bronze Age

Banner's map of sites belonging to the Baden complex was published in his monograph of 1956, and has a serious gap in its coverage of lowland eastern Hungary. A recently-published map of the adjacent area of Romania (Roman and Németi 1978) gives a better impression of the numbers of sites now known. Together, these two maps indicate the growing importance of the areas on the edges of the Plain. In particular, intermontane valleys such as those of the Hernád and Sajó now supported a substantial population, both in their lower reaches and along their headwaters in Slovakia. This substantial upland expansion brought to an end the dominance of the Plain. There is some suggestion of an emphasis on cattle in the upland valleys and on sheep in the lowlands (Bökönyi 1974). Sites (including the well-known cemetery of Alsónémedi) appeared at this time on the Danube-Tisza Interfluve in larger numbers, and opened further westward links.

Bronze Age sites have been accurately mapped only for certain cultures (e.g. Kalicz 1968), but the general pattern follows strongly from Baden and shows the continuing importance of the basin-edge as opposed to the centre of the Plain. The magnitude of this contrast is well summarised in Figure 11.2, which compares the Tiszapolgár distribution with that of Hatvan. The main EBA concentration is along the northern margin of the Plain, and picks out the line of the terrace between the Jászság and the Hernád-Sajó confluence. Many of these sites are tells, including the eponymous examples of Hatvan and Füzesabony. This line (now followed by the main Budapest–Miskolc road) was an important route of contact and trade, especially as horses were now bred in large numbers and bone harness-pieces are not uncommon finds.

The role of trade is also significant in explaining the continuing importance of the major rivers within the Plain. Positions on the river itself, rather than just with access to the soils of the floodplain margin, were especially sought. The Tisza and the Maros, with their potential for long-distance trade by dugout canoe, were more important than the Körös in this context. It is significant that the name of the eponymous EBA site on the central Tisza, Nagyrév, actually means 'Great port'. The concentration of large cemeteries at the Maros confluence (Szöreg, Deszk, Ószentivan, etc.) is also notable, and imported items such as copper ornaments and fossil shell beads are conspicuous items in the graves (O'Shea 1978).

The large volumes of bronze goods in circulation are indicated by stray finds and hoards, whose distributions form a special topic that will not be considered here (though see maps in Bóna 1975; Mozsolics 1967 and 1973; Hänsel 1968). The overall pattern of metal supply, however, was dominated by two groups of sources: a north Transylvanian group (perhaps including the Rézhegység) serving north-east Hungary and adjacent parts of Romania, and a west Slovakian group serving western Hungary and penetrating as far as the lower Tisza and Maros, probably through the Nagyrév and succeeding Vatya groups of the Danube-Tisza Interfluve.

Fortification is a noteworthy aspect of EBA settlement, especially around the fringes of the Carpathian Basin – though by the time of the Vatya culture there was also a ring of 'hillforts' around the territory of this culture in the strategic linking area between the Danube and Tisza. The most striking examples of defensive works are the major fortified centres at Barca and Spišsky Štvrtok in the montane valleys of Slovakia, which have notable concentrations of wealth (Vladár 1973); but many of the lower-order tell- and flat-sites throughout the region were protected by concentric ditches.

CONCLUSIONS

Systematic comparison of the patterns of finds over the 4000 years from the Neolithic to the Early Bronze Age demonstrates a considerable measure of continuity in the areas chosen for settlement, but also important variations both in the central area of the Plain and on the margins of the occupied area.

The rivers played a primary role, first in the initial dispersal of population, secondly through their association with well-watered environments, and increasingly because of the role of the waterways in trade. Year-round settlement in the floodplain itself was precluded by the spring and early summer floods; yet the broad interfluvial areas with their low rainfall were equally unsuitable for early agriculture. Early settlement was therefore concentrated on the lower terrace or intermediate zone, overlooking the floodplain, either beside the major rivers or on raised areas with the basins defined by the larger fans. Along the active river-courses, this gave settlement a linear character, as in the Tiszazug; elsewhere clusters of settlement occurred where sites occupied the margins of small islands rising from the floodplain, as in the area around Hódmezövásárhely or the Dévaványa Plain.

Some settlement took place within the Maros fan and the Nyírség, but occupation here was less continuous and confined to favourable depressions. Very little penetration of the Danube-Tisza Interfluve took place until Baden times. The upland fringe experienced a brief, specialised occupation in the Bükk period, after which settlement was again largely confined to the plains. Permanent occupation was pushed up the river valleys penetrating into the highlands during the Baden period, initiating a general movement of population from the central part of the Carpathian Basin to the edges, particularly along the northern and eastern terrace margins where the main concentration of Bronze Age tell sites occurs.

The area of the Körös-Berettyó depression, for which more detailed evidence is available, was thus a core area of Neolithic settlement which gradually lost its importance in the later periods. The marked local shift in population at the time of Bodrogkeresztúr raises the possibility that significant ecological change took place in this extensive lowland area at this time; but the long-term decline of this area must also be related to its structural position in the context of the expanding margin of settlement in the Carpathian Basin as a whole.

The detailed settlement-patterns which can be reconstructed from planned surveys such as that in the northern part of Co. Békés make it possible to examine the relative densities of settlement over this period and to follow these changes in terms of the location of particular sites. The broad geographical treatment of this section can thus be refined to deal with the behaviour of individual communities.

II: Site Survey and Settlement Dynamics

Scales of study

In the first half of this chapter, the distribution of settlement in the four thousand years following the introduction of agriculture in eastern Hungary was discussed at a regional level. From the maps presented, based on the accumulated record of chance finds, excavations and small-scale surface surveys, it was possible to define changes in the areas selected for occupation by early farming groups and fluctuations in the margin of settlement at different periods. A major shift in the emphasis of settlement, from the centre of the Plain to its periphery, was noted in the mid-fourth millennium BC.

To complement this picture, a more detailed view is required of the development of settlement at a local level. This is necessary both to calibrate the accuracy of the relatively coarse-grain mapping attempted in Part I, and to reveal the fine structure of settlement development. This might include localised shifts in the areas occupied at different times, and changes in the numbers and size of sites. The nature of such changes may be expected to reveal some of the underlying reasons for alterations in settlement pattern: environmental, social and historical factors.

Fortunately, a unique combination of circumstances makes it possible to provide such evidence. The level surface of the Great Hungarian Plain has suffered minimal erosion by comparison with many parts of central and western Europe, where much of the Neolithic landscape has been truncated and partly removed. The low rainfall of the area minimises the destruction of surface-scatters of pottery, which occur in profusion there on Neolithic sites. Uniform patterns of land-use based on collective farms provide extensive areas of ploughed land for the recovery of such material, which can be related to the succession of cultures summarised in Figure 11.6. These opportunities have been seized by Hungarian archaeologists as part of the programme of the Archaeological Topography of Hungary (*Magyarország Régészeti Topográfiája*) undertaken by the Institute of Archaeology of the

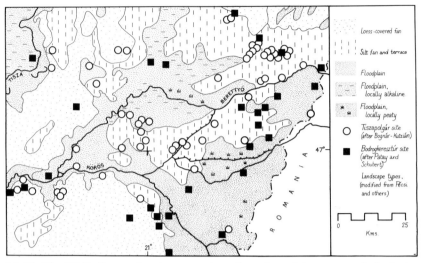

11.10 The Körös-Berettyó region: an enlarged portion of the geomorphological map (Fig. 11.4) with known sites of the Tiszapolgár (after Bognár-Kutzián 1972) and Bodrogkeresztúr cultures (including both settlements and cemeteries, after Patay 1974, and stray finds of contemporary copper axe-adzes, after Schubert 1965). The positions of findspots at this scale are approximate.

Hungarian Academy of Sciences in conjunction with local museums. The recent publication of volume 6 in this series (Ecsedy et al. 1982) is the first of several volumes in preparation covering the northern part of Co. Békés. Because of the relative scarcity of standing monuments in Hungary, this work has not simply taken the form of a description of finds and buildings, but an active search over one of the largest areas of prehistoric landscape yet surveyed. The parishes covered in volume 6, comprising the administrative district (*járás*) of Szeghalom, total some 1220 square kilometres; and within these, approximately 500 Neolithic and Copper Age sites have been recognised. This survey work thus provides information whose extent and fineness of resolution are unparalleled elsewhere in Neolithic Europe. The position of this unique sample in relation to the regional distribution maps discussed is indicated in Figure 11.1.

As a link with the type of evidence discussed in Part I, an enlarged portion of the geomorphological map used as a base for the regional distributions is presented in Figure 11.10. It shows the Körös/Berettyó region with sites from two successive periods (Tiszapolgár and Bodrogkeresztúr) taken from monographs published before the results of the Topographic Survey were available. As can be seen by comparison with the more detailed environmental map of the same area presented later (Figure 11.13), the natural units are indicated in a highly generalised form. Nevertheless, the broad pattern of association between sites of the Tiszapolgár period and the tongue of redeposited loess across the centre of the map – the Dévaványa

Plain – is clearly evident. What is also striking is the contrast between this pattern and the following distribution of Bodrogkeresztúr sites. Although there is some continuity in the types of environment chosen for settlement, it is notable that the later sites avoid the major parts of the area settled in the previous period. What seems to be occurring is a small-scale displacement of population to previously unoccupied parts of the area, mostly to rather similar sorts of soil but also to new sorts of location within the floodplain.

How does this evidence compare with that of the detailed surveys? The area of the Szeghalom survey is confined to the central area of the map, where there are large numbers of Tiszapolgár sites but little indication of Bodrogkeresztúr occupation. We shall see that this pattern is strikingly confirmed by the survey evidence (see below, Figures 11.21, 11.22): but it is important to note that the significance of this localised abandonment can only be appreciated within the context of its wider setting: the shift is a limited one of the order of c.25km, and it is possible to predict that similar detailed surveys, for instance in the area of Co. Hajdú-Bihar to the east, would recover larger numbers of Bodrogkeresztúr sites. The levels of analysis represented by regional mapping and local survey are thus complementary to one another, and neither is sufficient in isolation from the other.

THE GEOMORPHOLOGICAL SETTING OF THE KÖRÖS-BERETTYÓ REGION

Before presenting the detailed site distribution maps it is necessary to refine the generalised description of this region given in Part I. The triangular depression drained by the Berettyó and Körös rivers is defined by the three major Pleistocene loess-covered fans to north, west and south (Figures 11.10–13). The depression has a general slope from east to west (Figure 11.11): at the Romanian border the relatively steep gradient reflects the outwash fans of small rivers like the Rapid Körös which descends from the

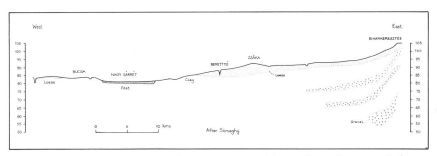

11.11 *East–west section across the Körös-Berettyó basin, from the outwash fans on the Romanian border to the east (Biharkeresztes), through the tongue of early Holocene redeposited loess (Zsáka), to the northern backswamp (Nagy Sárrét). Vertical scale in metres above sea-level. Adapted from Sümeghy.*

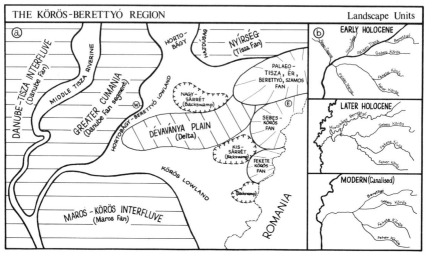

11.12 (a) Landscape units of the Körös-Berettyó region. E and W mark the ends of the section shown in Fig. 11.11; (b) changes in the drainage pattern of the Körös-Berettyó basin during the Postglacial period.

Bihar massif, and also the somewhat larger fan built up by the palaeo-Tisza, when (together with the waters of the Szamos and Berettyó) it flowed across this area in the Pleistocene and early Holocene. The major element of relief within the depression is the deltaic formation (the Dévaványa Plain) built up by this body of water as it crossed the area in a series of raised beds. With the tectonic diversion of the Tisza and Szamos in the early Holocene, the smaller volume of water entering the depression was diverted to either side of the ridge, forming peaty backswamps to the north and south of it. These landscape elements are shown in schematic form in Figure 11.12a.

The frequently shifting courses of these lowland rivers, and their extensive flooding, led to a major programme of canalisation in the nineteenth century: the course of the rapid Körös through the southern backswamp (*Kis-Sárrét*) was straightened, and a new channel was created for the Berettyó. This took it across the Dévaványa Plain instead of through the northern backswamp (*Nagy-Sárrét*), where it had previously joined the Hortobágy to flow along the edge of the Cumanian fan segment. The lower course of the Körös was also shortened, by cutting through meander-loops (Figure 11.12b).

The full complexity of the situation can be appreciated from the more detailed map of surface geology shown in Figure 11.13. While the surrounding loess-covered fans form a relatively uniform environment, the Körös-Berettyó basin has a mosaic character with islands of various sizes rising from the floodplain. With the exception of limited areas of sand on the small fans to the east, and isolated patches of true loess, these islands are essentially the levees of the early Holocene river-system. They are composed of

296

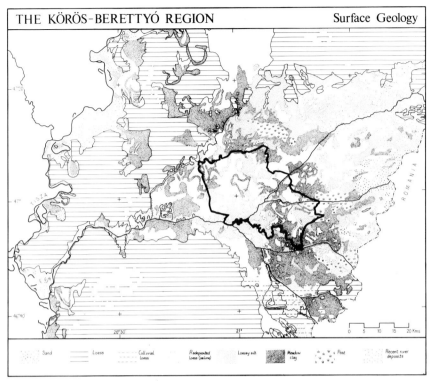

THE KÖRÖS-BERETTYÓ REGION   Surface Geology

| Sand | Loess | Colluvial loess | Redeposited loess (saline) | Loessy silt | Meadow clay | Peat | Recent river deposits |

11.13 Surface geology of the Körös-Berettyó region, after Magyarország Földtani Térképe *(1:300,000), showing the position of the Szeghalom region mapped in Figs 11.18–27.*

redeposited loess. In some parts these form an extensive, more or less level terrace with well-defined palaeochannels; in others they are broken into a multitude of small promontories and creeks. Beyond the chain of larger islands, smaller and more isolated hillocks break through the alluvium.

Before the regulation of the rivers, these islands of higher ground within the depression were literally insulated by the spring and early summer floods, as can be seen from historical maps.[14] Besides the permanently wet areas of the backswamps where peat accumulated, the floodplain can be further subdivided into the larger basins where loessy silt continued to be seasonally deposited in the later Holocene, and the shallower basins and creeks where a finer deposit of black meadow-clay was laid down. Occasional floods of exceptional strength sometimes reached the level of the early Holocene terrace itself, so that settlements there sought the highest elevations available – even where the advantage was no more than an additional metre above the surrounding area. After the regulation, the rivers were confined by dykes within which somewhat coarser silts have accumulated.

How far is the present pattern of surface geology a valid basis for interpreting prehistoric settlement distributions? In so far as the shift in river-courses in the early Holocene reduced the flow of water and sediment through the depression, leaving the chain of levees in 'fossil' form, no major changes have occurred within this early Holocene terrace. Floodplain deposits, however, have continued to accumulate in the lower-lying areas. Some idea of the extent of alluvial accumulation may be gained from the distribution map of tumuli (Figure 11.16), mainly dating to the third millennium BC, whose significance is discussed in a later section. Their importance here is that – unlike sherd-scatters – they can be recognised on the surface even where alluviation has occurred. While the major concentration of tumuli occurs on islands (and inaccuracies of mapping have undoubtedly caused minor displacements around their edges), there are significant groups of these monuments within the area of meadow-clay – for example on the northern margin of the *Nagy Sárrét*. The implication of this is that the accumulation of meadow-clay and peat in the later Holocene, particularly around the backswamp areas, has mantled lower-lying areas of the early Holocene land-surface which may have been settled in Neolithic times. Geological slit-trenches dug as part of the excavation programme at Sártó[15] confirm that significant accumulation of meadow-clay has also occurred in the palaeochannels between the islands. Since the data from the Szeghalom survey are mainly concerned with the higher parts of the early Holocene terrace, this problem does not seriously distort the picture of prehistoric settlement there. As the permanent sites are often located on the higher levees on the edges of the islands (e.g. Figure 11.15), however, some evidence of seasonal activities within the adjacent floodplain may be inaccessible to surface investigation. This factor has been considered in designing the excavation programme, and has led to the discovery of previously unsuspected pits at the edge of the floodplain by the Körös settlement at Réhely-Dülö.

The soils of this region at the present time correspond largely with the surface geology. They range from chernozems on the loess-covered fans to the meadow- and raw-soils of the floodplain. The characteristic soils of the islands are varieties of solonetz, whose saline character results from the high watertable and net upward movement of salt-charged water during the summer months. These are especially developed on the broad, flat islands in the centre of the Dévaványa Plain. The acutely saline character of these soils is a natural result of their position just above the floodplain and the high temperatures and low rainfall of eastern Hungary (Szabolcs 1971; 1974). It is likely that salination posed a problem for prehistoric agriculture.

The position of the parishes represented in the survey data given in Figures 11.17–25 is shown on Figure 11.13. As noted above, this area coincides with the largest extent of early Holocene terrace in the central part of the Dévaványa Plain. It also includes some of the lower-lying land to the north, on the southern margin of the *Nagy Sárrét*, and extends south-eastwards to the edge of the *Kis Sárrét*. On its north-western part, therefore, it includes an area of broad, flat islands separated by well-defined palaeo-channels, south of which is an extensive area of loessy silt characteristic of the Körös lowland. To the east the islands are smaller, and separated by broader inlets filled with meadow-clay. As well as the marked contrast between the early Holocene terrace and the floodplain, therefore, the difference in character between the eastern and western ends of the area is significant in terms of prehistoric settlement.

THE SZEGHALOM SURVEY AND ITS RESULTS

In historic times large parts of the area, and especially the expanses of solonetz soils, have been pastureland. In the postwar period, following the collectivisation of agriculture and the mechanisation of farming, a major campaign to extend the area of arable has been undertaken for the culti-vation of maize and sunflowers. Since soil salinity was a major obstacle, this necessarily included a programme of amelioration which took the form of digging large quarries – the so-called 'digo-pits' – into the non-saline loess. The saline topsoil was pushed to one side, and the (archaeologically sterile) loess was spread over the surrounding area.

During the 1950s these operations were watched by the village school-master in Dévaványa, Dr Imre Bereczki. He noted the very frequent remains of prehistoric sites, and made an extensive collection of Neolithic and Copper Age pottery and other artefacts. This first revealed the potential of this area for systematic archaeological work. The finds came to the attention of Professor Gyula Gazdapusztai of the University of Szeged, who organised the first programme of recording and survey in 1968. The execution of this work was then incorporated within the framework of the Archaeological Topography of Hungary, centrally organised by the Archaeological Institute of the Hungarian Academy of Sciences in Budapest, with the co-operation of local museums. The intention was to make a complete inventory of archaeological sites in Co. Békés. A field-by-field survey has so far been conducted in the administrative divisions of Szeghalom (published in 1982: Ecsedy et al. 1982) and Szarvas (Dénes et al. 1989; cf. also Bökönyi 1992). Since 1979, under an agreement for scientific co-operation between the Ashmolean Museum and the Institute, further work has taken place to use this information for the reconstruction of prehistoric settlement patterns and to carry out a programme of fieldwork based upon it.

The sites are identifiable on the surface from the scatter of pottery, lithic artefacts and lumps of burnt daub which occur in great profusion. The large scale of arable farming makes it possible to define the sizes of these scatters with some precision. These sites are listed and described in the published volumes of the Topography (in Hungarian), and limits are assigned to each site. Since many of these have multi-period occupations, however, it has

299

been necessary in using this data for settlement-pattern studies to return to the original field-reports and make use of observations on the extent of occupation at particular periods within the life of a site.[16] It is these reconstructed limits which have been used in plotting Figures 11.17–25.

Not all the area is under arable, although the long period over which the survey was conducted made it possible to make repeated visits in relation to changing patterns of land use. Where land was continuously under pasture – usually the highly saline *puszta* areas – it is often possible to recover sherds under the dry conditions of late summer and autumn, and identify the positions of sites even though their extent cannot be precisely defined. Other limiting factors include the fragmented pattern of land-use and built-up area around the villages themselves. Since modern settlement is highly nucleated, the proportion of such land is relatively small; there is one major village or town for each of the parishes included. The effects of one of these (Dévaványa) will be noted below, where it coincides with an area of preferred prehistoric settlement.

The existence of numerous soil-improvement quarries (digo-pits) has already been noted. These are easily recognisable as rounded rectangular hollows some 100 by 50m. Finds from the area of the quarry occur in the dumped topsoil on its perimeter: since archaeological levels occur in the saline soil layer, finds have not been strewn across the fields with the non-saline loess. Their effect on the size of sherd-scatters has thus been minimal.

Bearing in mind the limitations noted in the previous section due to the continuing alluviation of the floodplain, therefore, the extent and character of settlement in the prehistoric period can be reconstructed with some accuracy. The robust patterns and internal consistency evident in the period-by-period distribution maps are themselves testimony to the amount of information which can be recovered. While not every site can be considered to have been accurately defined, the regularities in size, morphology and distribution are a true reflection of the changing character of settlement in this region.

An example: north-west Dévaványa

In the programme of joint British/Hungarian fieldwork, certain sites known from the survey have been selected for more intensive investigation. Most of these have so far been in the north-western part of the parish of Dévaványa. The initial aim has been to define the limits of sites more accurately, and as an example a worksheet from the first season's work at the large late Neolithic site at Sártó is presented in Figure 11.14. This shows a series of transects with 4 by 4m collecting grids over an area of c.2000 by 500m. Finds of diagnostic pottery types are plotted, indicating the growth and reorganisation of this major settlement. (Further work has been conducted in later seasons, including an extensive fluxgate survey and selective excavation: Sherratt 1984c.)

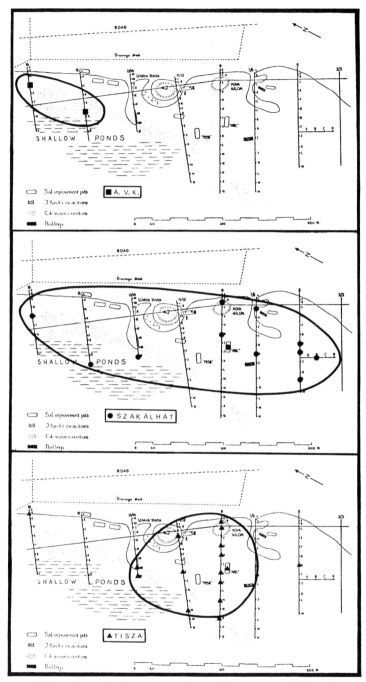

11.14 Worksheets from the first season of British/Hungarian fieldwork at Sártó, in the parish of Dévaványa, showing the gridded transects and finds of diagnostic pottery from three periods. [See Sherratt 1984c for a full plan of Sártó and survey results.]

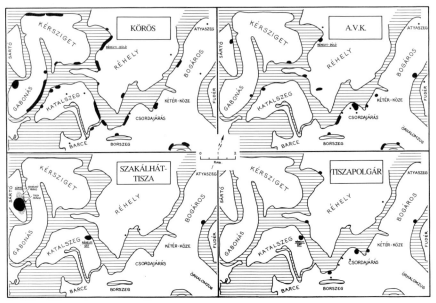

11.15 *The* NW *corner of the parish of Dévaványa, showing the site of Sártó and contemporary settlements in relation to the early Holocene terrace (open) and floodplain (hatched). Sites where intensive survey and excavation have taken place are named. After* Magyarország Régészeti Topográfiája *vol. 6, and British/Hungarian fieldwork.*

The context of this site in terms of the environmental setting and settlement history of the area from 6000–4000 BC is shown in Figure 11.15. Practically without exception, the sites are located on the edge of the early Holocene terrace, overlooking the floodplain; there is little trace of Neolithic occupation on the interfluves. Each period, however, has a characteristic pattern of site density and morphology, from the linear shoreline settlements of Körös to the aggregated pattern of Szakálhát and Tisza and the small, dispersed sites of Tiszapolgár. While these patterns are repeated elsewhere, the density of such early sites in this area is characteristic only of the western part of the Szeghalom survey, and later sites are less well represented here. These larger patterns will now be described in chronological order, following the sequence of cultures defined in Part I.

Körös (6000–5300 BC?): Figure 11.19

The maps in Figures 11.18–27 cover the four large parishes of Dévaványa, Szeghalom, Körösladány and Vésztö, together amounting to 68,400 hectares. Within this area, 125 Körös sites have been defined. The actual number of findspots is somewhat artificial, however, since some of the smaller adjacent sites might be considered as parts of a single linear scatter, and elongated shapes have been defined only where there is positive evidence for a continuous spread of material. Nevertheless, the extent and

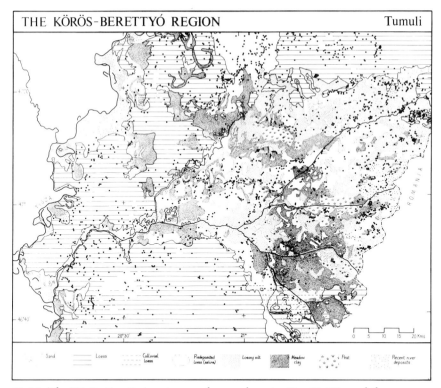

THE KÖRÖS-BERETTYÓ REGION   Tumuli

Sand   Loess   Colluvial Loess   Redeposited Loess (saline)   Loessy silt   Meadow clay   Peat   Recent river deposits

*11.16 The Körös-Berettyó region: surface geology (as Fig. 11.13), and the
positions of early third-millennium tumuli (after Viragh 1979). Owing to
inaccuracies of re-scaling, the positions are approximate.*

density of occupation evidence is striking, and represents a vast quantity of
sherd material and settlement debris.

This material is found over a large part of the area represented in the
map. The major unoccupied areas are to the south-west, in the basin of
loessic silt to the south of Dévaványa, and in the similar basin which lies in
the north-central area east of Atyaszeg (cf. Figure 11.13: both of these
floodplain areas contain small islands, however, which were subsequently
settled). The broad band of settlement from north-west to south-east
represents the main extent of the chain of larger islands. Within this, there
is a greater density of material in the north-western part. This not only
contains two-thirds of the findspots, but the sites themselves are more
substantial. True linear 'shoreline sites' (up to 2km in length) only occur in
this part.

After the scattered dot-distributions of chance finds of this culture
mapped at a regional level, this density of sites strikes the observer with the
force of a revelation. It highlights the arbitrary nature of the sample which
is available from sources other than planned survey. For the first time it is
possible to appreciate what the archaeological record may hold in the way

303

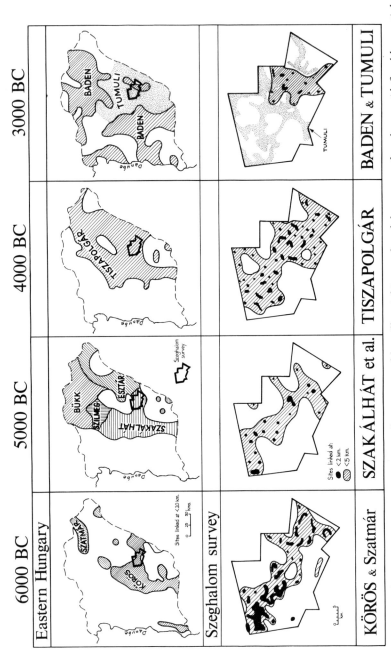

11.17 Summary diagram giving successive snapshots, at roughly millennial intervals, of the extent of settlement (defined by spatial proximity linkage) at two scales: above, in eastern Hungary as a whole (see Fig. 11.9 and other maps in Sherratt 1983b: sites linked at <20km) and below, in the Szeghalom survey area (see Figs 11.19–27: sites linked at <2 and <5km). Note the gradual south-eastward shift in settlement, from the larger interfluvial areas in the NW to the more interrupted expanses of terrace in the SE, probably in response to increasing salination of the earliest-settled areas. In the final snapshot, settlement is confined to the SE sector, and Pit-Grave tumuli occupy the more saline areas. On a regional scale, settlement has expanded into the dry sandy area of the Danube-Tisza interfluve, and the upland areas around the Basin.

304

of prehistoric sites. However, it would be wrong to infer from this evidence that there was a particularly high density of population at any one time during this phase of the Neolithic. The period in question may be a relatively long one, since although its end is well defined, there are too few radio-carbon dates to be sure of its beginning. It may last for more than 500 years.[17] Although the sites contain substantial evidence of occupation in the form of massive pits and large quantities of burnt daub, there is no certainty that even the area defined as belonging to a single settlement site was in simultaneous occupation. The linear scatters may represent a pattern of settlement drift over several generations, with the smaller sites being similar but less long-lived. Equally, however, the smaller sites may represent seasonal stations subsidiary to the major scatters.

These problems can only be resolved by intensive fieldwork and excavation, and some relevant points from current work may be noted here. For instance, it is clear that the scatters do not represent a continuous, built-up area. Geophysical survey has demonstrated the existence of discrete clusters of structures, some 50m or so apart, separated by areas with no structures (and a low density of finds) that probably represent the areas where horti-culture took place. While cereal-cultivation is demonstrated by plentiful finds of carbonised seed-remains, the large numbers of fish-remains and net-sinkers, as well as bones of wild mammals and birds, indicate that seasonally-available wild resources were an important component of the diet. The position of the settlements immediately on the low bluffs over-looking the floodplain is consistent with this dual emphasis on cereals and fish.

Although the larger settlements (and perhaps the majority of finds) probably represent permanent, sedentary occupation on a year-round basis, it is likely that there was a considerable degree of long-term fluidity in settle-ment location, and that the pattern shown here is a palimpsest of many generations.

AVK (5300–5100 BC): *Figure 11.20*

The pattern shown by sites of the Alföld Linear Pottery culture (*Alföldi Vonaldíszes Kerámia* = AVK) continues many aspects of its predecessor. Some 95 sites are represented, and although the same considerations of site definition apply as in the Körös period, the conditions which produced a proliferation of sites seem to have continued. The overall distribution of sites is very similar, with a centre of gravity in the north-west and a con-tinuing presence in the south-east, though with some abandonment of the small sites on the far eastern edge. Some extension of settlement is evident, however, on the small islands in the basins of Dévaványa and Atyaszeg.

The timespan covered by this period is shorter, of the order of two to three hundred years, strengthening the argument for a relatively dispersed character of contemporary settlement. While the absence of linear sites might be explained by the lack of time for settlement drift to occur, more detailed observation of AVK sites suggests that their morphology was rather different from that typical of Körös. Such sites are often set back somewhat from the terrace edge, and the component units form small clusters rather than lines. This may be linked with a decline in the importance of fish, since net-sinkers are no longer such common finds, and perhaps a greater concentration on cereals. Seen in the context of the succeeding distribution patterns, that of AVK clearly belongs to a primary phase of settlement, before fundamentally new properties emerged in the settlement system.

Szakálhát (5100–4800 BC): Figure 11.21

After the widely-strewn evidence of settlement from the preceding periods, a major change is evident with Szakálhát. Only 29 sites are known, but these range from massive, 2km long, concentrations to small groups of sherds. Although the central axis of the islands remained in occupation, the peripheries were all abandoned. A process of settlement aggregation seems to have been operating, in which previously dispersed populations came together in larger units.

The outstanding example is the case of Sártó discussed above, which is the large site in the north-west corner. At this stage it was a relatively elongated area, parallel to the shoreline and covering approximately 1800 by 400 metres. Fluxgate surveys carried out in recent field seasons demonstrate that like earlier Neolithic sites, such aggregated sites also have a compound character and are composed of individual concentrations of structures, separated by 50m or so of postulated garden areas. Although this is the only site of its kind in this area which has been investigated in detail, the cluster of apparently separate sites in the east-central portion (including Kovácshalom in the parish of Szeghalom) may turn out to represent a similar aggregation in a somewhat less even topographic setting where the clusters occupy separate hillocks. (Sártó itself is centred on a small eminence which may have a special role in the site layout.) It is also just possible that a third site, that of Simasziget near the town of Dévaványa in the west centre of the area, may be larger than it appears because of the character of land-use on the edge of the town. In this case there might be some regularity in the spacing of these 'supersites', which would occur some 10–15km apart: though at the moment this can only be speculation. Not all sites were of this character, however, and some formed small compact units that grew up into minor tell-like mounds. A typical example is Réhelyi Gát, 4km from Sártó (Figure 11.15). Two or three such sites occur in the vicinity of the major aggregated settlements.

A notable feature of the aggregated sites is their great wealth of imported materials. As well as large quantities of obsidian and other stonework, sherds of Bükk and Vădastra pottery testify to cultural contacts over a range of 200km. This aspect is discussed more fully in Chapter 12.

Tisza (4800–4400 BC): Figure 11.22

The process of aggregation became more pronounced in this period, with the number of sites falling to nineteen, mainly by loss of the smaller peripheral stations. The three main nuclei established in the previous period continued, and the limitations on site definitions continue to apply. At Sártó, intensive survey (Figure 11.14) has shown that the site changed in shape to a more compact form, shortening and extending backwards from the shoreline;[18] Simasziget remains as a possible further nucleus; while the Kovácshalom complex continued to occupy several adjacent sites. The main subsidiary tell-like sites also continued.

The quantities of material items recovered from surface collection and excavation at Sártó demonstrate the continuing wealth of the 'supersites', which were able to pull in supplies of hard rocks and flakeable stone from a 150km radius on the periphery of the Carpathian Basin. Such supplies must have been moved by boat, and it is possible that the course of the Hortobágy-Berettyó ran closer to the site than at present, perhaps even along the Sártó channel.

The process of aggregation characteristic of Szakálhát and Tisza seems to have lasted for a period of the order of 700 years. The main sites were probably occupied throughout that time, absorbing a successively greater proportion of the population of the smaller settlements. It is not clear that any decline in population occurred, since it has been argued that the more abundant sites of earlier periods were a reflection of the fluidity of settlement rather than the effect of a large contemporary population. The small number of large, stable sites in the period of aggregation thus probably gives a more accurate impression of the size of the Neolithic population at a single moment in time.

It may be inferred that large areas of land went out of use in this phase, since it is unlikely that territories of the order of 10km in radius (the areas in between major sites) were exploited even for grazing. Crops were probably grown only in the immediate vicinity of the sites (or even within them, in the extensive 'empty' areas). Models involving nucleation within well-defined territories are probably inappropriate for the low population densities and small scale of agriculture of the Neolithic, which allowed great variability in the disposition of settlement. Social factors are likely to have been more important then ecological ones in determining these patterns: people wished to live together in large groups and as far from their neighbours as possible, and the large settlements may have been sited at locations advantageous for external contacts. The conditions underlying this pattern therefore probably included both insecurity and the importance of exchange networks linking this area with the expanding periphery (Chapter 10).

Tiszapolgár (4400–3900 BC): Figure 11.23

The conditions which gave rise to settlement aggregation were abruptly reversed in the Tiszapolgár period. Small sites became the rule, and these were widely dispersed over the area available for settlement. Some 106 sites are known, few larger than a few hundred metres in diameter and most averaging around 100m.[19] From the intensive survey investigations, these sites seem to represent small hamlets of a few houses: unlike the settlements of previous periods, they do not have a compound character with individual clusters of structures and empty areas.

Before this period there is no evidence for a differentiation of settlements and cemeteries: burials occurred within the settlements in small groups associated with the component units. Now, however, at a time of small, dispersed settlements, formal cemeteries seem to have assumed a particular importance. In the case of the best-known example, Tiszapolgár-Basatanya (Bognár-Kutzián 1963), there seems to have been no nearby settlement, and these fairly large cemeteries (c.50–100 graves) may have served more than one settlement site. No cemeteries have been identified as such within the survey area, but it is possible that some at least of the findspots may represent sites of this kind. The implications of this important shift in settlement-pattern and contemporary burial practice must be considered as part of the general problem of Neolithic and Copper Age social structures.

The distribution of Tiszapolgár sites extends over the whole survey area with the exception of the small peripheral islands. There is a roughly equal emphasis on the eastern and western halves of the area, with a slight preponderance in the east. Many of the sites in the western part are small stations with a few sherds, though there are also many more substantial sites. Even the larger ones, however, do not produce the striking quantities of imported materials noted for the preceding phase.

Bodrogkeresztúr (3900–3500 BC): Figure 11.24

In contrast to the plentiful remains of settlement in earlier periods, those of Bodrogkeresztúr are sparse in the extreme. Only a dozen findspots, each represented by no more than a few sherds, have been identified. The period in question is not notably shorter than the others (c.400 years), and though the pottery assemblage is less diagnostic because of the relatively small percentage of decorated sherds, it seems likely the small number of insubstantial sites is a genuine reflection of a sharp fall in population in this area.

This result accords with earlier discussion (cf. Figure 11.10) of the indications from stray finds: the survey area is located in the middle of a zone of abandonment, from which population moved to a number of nearby locations – mostly previously unoccupied. A large group of such sites occurs at a somewhat higher elevation further east, and others appear on the edges of the Pleistocene fans or on the small islands in the floodplain. Displacement of population thus seems to account for the lack of local finds. Since it is noteworthy that the main focus of earlier settlement was on soils most prone to salinity, this factor deserves to be considered as a major cause of this change.

Boleráz and Baden (3500–2900 BC): Figure 11.25; Tumuli, Figure 11.26

The reappearance of more substantial settlement traces in the Boleráz and Baden periods was restricted to one quarter of the total area. Some 24 sites are known, all from the eastern part around Szeghalom. Their average size is rather small (the majority being less than that for Tiszapolgár), with only half a dozen extending for more than 100m. It is again possible that some findspots represent cemeteries, though Baden cemeteries elsewhere were generally quite small. Since the recolonisation of the area after its effective abandonment in Bodrogkeresztúr did not necessarily take place right at the beginning of Boleráz (only a quarter of the sites belong to this phase), the effective span of this period may be rather less than the five to six hundred years suggested for Boleráz and Baden as a whole. Even so, the amount of settlement material is not great by comparison with that which occurs in this area from the Neolithic and earlier Copper Age.

The restricted distribution of Boleráz and Baden sites (Figure 11.25) should be compared with the occurrence of tumuli (Figure 11.26). Recent work on these burial mounds (Ecsedy 1979), which has included the excavation of Barcé-halom in the parish of Dévaványa, has pointed to a date contemporary with Baden. It is immediately apparent from the maps that the two distributions are complementary, and should be considered together. The tumuli fall into two groups, separated by a gap representing the intervening Boleráz and Baden settlements. The major group in the northwest largely coincides with the area of particularly dense settlement in Neolithic times, on the larger and flatter islands of the parish of Dévaványa. Unlike the earlier sites, however, their locations are not tied to the shorelines. Although they do occur along levees on the edge of the islands, they are more commonly found on prominent spots further inland: it is the advantage in height which is being sought. Partly as a consequence of this, they tend to form chains along the more prominent ridges.

Because such tumuli have often been used as landmarks on cadastral maps, a more comprehensive record can be compiled of the distribution of these monuments (Viragh 1979). Plotted on a base-map of surface geology (Figure 11.16), they reveal a general pattern of which the Szeghalom survey examples form a part. Dense concentrations occur in the Hortobágy, on the Berettyó and Körös fans near the Romanian border, and along the Dévaványa Plain. They also occur as a general scatter on the loess-covered Pleistocene fans.

The interpretation of these apparently contemporary tumuli and Baden settlements has been a matter of controversy. The material culture and burial rite of the tumuli differ from those of Baden and stand in stark contrast to them. Moreover, the Baden culture extends beyond the limit of the tumuli in western Hungary, and the tumuli occur eastwards to the Pontic steppe which is their centre of distribution. It thus seems likely that small populations of eastern origin penetrated around and within established groups in the eastern Carpathian Basin: and this interpretation is strengthened by the spatial exclusiveness of the two distributions. If this is so, then the tumulus-building groups seem to have sought relatively open terrain (presumably for stock-raising), either on the chernozems of the Pleistocene fans or in those parts of the Körös Basin with a long history of settlement and clearance of woodland but which were now perhaps unsuitable for agriculture. If the reasons for Bodrogkeresztúr abandonment were connected with the effects of salination, this penetration could be seen as the occupation of empty niches around contemporary farming populations. Since there is evidence in Baden contexts elsewhere for the use of animal traction and thus probably of the plough, farmers may themselves have been able to open new areas for cultivation, as was noted in Part I for the edges of the Carpathian Basin.

Early Bronze Age (2900–2000 BC): Figure 11.27

Only forty-one sites are known from this long period, and many of these are very small. The area of occupation corresponds closely to that of the preceding Baden and Boleráz period, although there is little continuity in the location of individual sites. Only a few, small sites occur within the former area of tumulus distribution, and the western part of the area was effectively abandoned in favour of the east. The phase of land-use represented by the tumuli was evidently a relatively short interlude in the settlement history of the region.

Seven of the EBA sites can be attributed to the earlier part of the period (Makó-Nyírség) and eleven to the later part (Otomani), of which four are fortified. The latter take the form of circular ditched enclosures some 60–80m in diameter, and 10–15km apart. These densities are very low when compared with the large numbers of such sites known, e.g. from Co. Hajdú-Bihar (e.g. Bóna 1975, Verbreitungskarten I and II), and the area continued to be of relatively minor importance in the Middle Bronze Age.

Implications of the survey data

Besides demonstrating the very large number of Neolithic and Copper Age sites in this area, the Szeghalom survey has also revealed marked contrasts in the numbers, distribution, sizes, and shapes of settlements in different periods. These provide raw material for the analysis of community size, locational preferences and major demographic shifts. They do not, however, provide any easy answer about the detailed course of population change during the prehistoric period. Archaeologists have often used counts of the number of sites in successive periods as an indication of the changing density of settlement and thus of population levels. The survey results demonstrate the dangers of this approach. In many cases a change in the number of sites is accompanied by changes in their size, so that what is being measured is effectively the relative aggregation or dispersal of population rather than the numbers of people involved. Only in those cases where a fall in the number of sites coincides with a steady or declining average size of site can population decline be suggested. In fact, the calculation of relative population densities in different periods within a given area depends on a complex equation, many of whose variables (such as the average length of site occupation) remain unknown. Without a major programme of excavation and site-dating, therefore, estimates of the actual course of population change remain subject to wide margins of error. It is more useful at the moment to discuss the phenomena of settlement aggregation and dispersal or settlement displacement in their own terms, without attempting to translate this information into relative sizes of population.

CONCLUSION

Settlement dynamics

It is clear that there is no single trend over the long period of agrarian settlement recorded in the site-distribution patterns of the Szeghalom area. General similarities persisted through successive periods – Körös and AVK, or Szakálhát and Tisza – but the trends were reversed by factors operating on a local, regional or even a pan-European level (Figure 11.17).

The first 1000 years were characterised by a profusion of settlement sites. Although some of these sites cover extensive areas, they were occupied at a low density and may not have persisted for more than a few years. Although there were consistent changes in the internal layout and organisation of sites, this initial phase of relatively fluid settlement lasted until c.5100 BC.

There then followed a period of 700 years in which population tended to aggregate into larger, more stable units. Some of these sites were spectacularly large, although still occupied at a low density. The trend towards a concentration of settlement is evident throughout the late Neolithic of central Europe (cf. Starling 1984). This phase seems to represent a peak in the material prosperity of this area.

Around 4400 BC a fundamental change in the organisation of settlement took place. Smaller unitary settlements were dispersed widely across the landscape. Elsewhere, it is known that cemeteries came to play a prominent role in the settlement pattern and social fabric (Chapter 5). By this period, the area was probably less wealthy than the zone nearer to the edge of the Plain where finds of copper objects occur. The pattern of dispersed sites and cemeteries continued to be typical of many parts of eastern Hungary for the next 300 years; but in this area it was interrupted by a phase of relative abandonment. It would appear from this that local ecological factors were responsible, and the correlation with areas of high salinity at the present day suggests that this may be relevant.

By some time around 3500 BC a new pattern had emerged, that was to be characteristic of the next thousand years. The focus of settlement shifted eastwards, at the same time as the Carpathian Basin as a whole saw a major movement into the surrounding uplands. For part of this time, the zone apparently abandoned for agricultural settlement was occupied by groups coming from outside the area, who constructed large numbers of burial mounds and apparently existed side by side with local groups. From the general distribution of tumuli in the lowland area, it appears that these local agricultural groups occupied only small enclaves within it (Figure 11.16). By 2900 BC the phase of tumulus-building was apparently over, and the agricultural areas were characterised by small defended villages occupying an area that was now marginal to the main zone of Bronze Age occupation further east.

The factors responsible for these alterations of settlement pattern thus represent a conjunction of widespread social changes, environmental processes and historical opportunities, through which the area rose to prominence and was then progressively reduced in importance (Chapter 10).

Implications

Few areas of Europe possess the combined advantages for surface survey of the central part of the Great Hungarian Plain. Nevertheless, much progress has been made in recent years through programmes of planned survey and excavation (e.g. Kruk 1980), and the number of comparable bodies of data may be expected to grow rapidly in the next few years. These need to be combined with systematic mapping of all finds on a regional basis, so that more intensive work can be planned to answer questions arising from what is already known. Where systematic fieldwork has taken place, it has revealed the often astonishing abundance of prehistoric sites and the magnitude of changes in the sizes and abundance of sites over long periods of time. Work such as that described here is important because it demonstrates some of the properties of this record, and its potential for reconstructing fundamental information about the nature of prehistoric communities.[20]

NOTES

1. This was originally published in two parts, in vols 1 and 2 respectively, of the *Oxford Journal of Archaeology*. Some of the regional maps have been omitted in this present version.
2. Magyarország Régészeti Topográfiája: Vols 1–4, Co. Veszprém (1966–72); Vol. 5, Co. Komárom (1979); Vol. 6, Co. Békés (Dénes et al. 1989).

3. The programme of Hungarian-British fieldwork was directed jointly by Dr István Torma and the author.

4. The natural physiographic unit is the Carpathian Basin, consisting of Pannonia in the west, the Great Hungarian Plain in the centre and Transylvania in the east. This was also a political entity until 1920, when it was divided between Hungary, Romania and Jugoslavia. Since recent research has been organised within these national boundaries, the term 'eastern Hungary' is used here to describe the territory of the present Hungarian state east of the Danube.

5. Calibrated radiocarbon dates are used throughout, using the table provided in Clark (1975). Uncorrected radiocarbon dates are indicated as bc.

6. For a convenient introduction to Hungarian geography, see Pécsi and Sárfalvi (1964). The environmental background and its changes are usefully discussed from an archaeological standpoint in Kosse (1979).

7. For the names of these physiographic units and their location, see Sherratt 1982b, Fig. 11.5.

8. The Hungarian divisions of the later Neolithic and Copper Age do not directly correspond to other east European systems, where the term 'Chalcolithic' or 'Eneolithic' is used. Hungarian usage of the term 'Copper Age' rightly stresses the important changes that begin with Tiszapolgár, but by including Baden (as Late Copper Age) it fails to indicate the radically new aspects of the latter.

9. A comparison of Körös and AVK distributions with various elements of the landscape (climate, vegetation, hydrology, geology, soils) is given in Kosse (1979), which includes a statistical analysis of the occurrence of sites in different zones. While this usefully complements the approach adopted here, it is limited to small-scale maps and uses the stylistic groups rather than a regional framework as the units of analysis. For further comments on the statistical methods, see the review in *Proceedings of the Prehistoric Society*, 46 (1980).

10. For references to recent work, see especially Kalicz (1970) and the yearly reports in *Mitteilungen des Archaeologischen Instituts* (Budapest). An unpublished study of the Tisza culture has been written by J. Korek, *A Tiszai Kultúra* (Budapest 1973).

11. A more serious problem is the interpretation of negative evidence: the blank areas on distribution maps. Where sites are known for some periods and not others, it is reasonable to assume that this absence is significant. Where no prehistoric sites of any period are known, judgement must be suspended until the region has been actively investigated. The interpretation of distribution maps is therefore only one point in the cycle of archaeological research, reaching preliminary conclusions and posing questions for future fieldwork.

12. It is worth noting the presence in the uplands of a macrolithic industry ('Grobgerätiges Mesolithikum' or Eger-Avas culture) usually taken to be of Mesolithic date and sometimes seen as a source of the Szatmár and AVK populations (e.g. Kalicz 1980). Its dating, however, is uncertain, and such tools have occasionally been found in association with pottery (Dobosi 1976). It is possible that these actually indicate Neolithic extraction sites, and are thus similar to the Lengfeld, Campignian, Montmorencian and Hackpen Hill industries in western Europe.

13. These include some of the most famous Late Neolithic sites in Hungary, many of which are on present or former courses of important rivers, e.g. Hódmezövásárhely-Kökenydomb (Tisza), Szegvár-Tüzköves (Tisza), Szarvas-Pepikert = Békésszentandrás (Körös), Dévaványa-Sártó (Hortobágy-Berettyó), Szeghalom-Kovacshalom (Sebes Körös) and Battonya-Parásztanya (Száraz-Ér).

14. E.g. Mátyás Huszár (1822) *Hydrographia depressae regionis fluviatilis Crisiorum Magni, Albi, Nigri, Velocis, Parvi, Fl. Berettyó cum ramificationibus ... horumque omnium illustrata inundationis topographia.*

15. In 1981 a test-trench 50m from the terrace edge at Sártó demonstrated that a scatter of Neolithic artefacts from the settlement, directly overlying redeposited loess of the early Holocene, was covered by 75cm of meadow-clay.

16. The extent to which surface pottery is attributable to particular cultural groups depends on the proportions of diagnostic pieces such as decorated sherds or distinctive knobs, handles, etc. For some periods the fabric is immediately recognisable (e.g. Körös chaff-tempered ware). The following table offers a rough, order-of-magnitude guide to the proportion of diagnostic pieces:
    Körös: almost all
    AVK: more than a quarter
    Szakálhát: less than a quarter
    Tisza: less than a quarter
    Tiszapolgár: about half
    Bodrogkeresztúr: perhaps a twentieth
    Boleráz, Baden and EBA: about half
    Changes of fabric, e.g. from chaff- to sand- and grog-tempering, allow a further proportion to be classified as 'Neolithic', 'Copper Age' or 'Bronze Age', and others as merely 'Prehistoric'. A relatively small proportion of the total number of sites can only be attributed to these gross periods: 85 Neolithic, 5 Copper Age, 23 Bronze Age, 95 Prehistoric. Most of these are small finds in the vicinity of larger, attributed sites.
17. Many of the sites, however, may belong to a relatively late phase within it, since excavations at Réhely Dülö in 1980 produced Körös material in association with proto-Vinča pottery.
18. In 1981 a fluxgate survey carried out by Mr Basil Turton covered an area of 40,000m². This indicates a pattern of magnetic anomalies (shown by excavation to represent burnt houses) spaced about 50m apart.
19. The dimensions of these settlements may be slightly exaggerated, since comparison of the extent of the surface pottery scatter with the limits of features revealed by the fluxgate survey at Póhalom in 1980 showed that the pottery spread beyond the indications of structures.
20. It is a pleasure to acknowledge the advice and help of Hungarian colleagues: Nándor Kalicz, János Makkay, István Torma and György Goldman – none of whom should, however, be held responsible for any errors or deficiencies of this article. The maps are the work of Nick Griffiths. Fieldwork in Hungary has been supported by the British Academy, University of Oxford, the Leverhulme Trust and the National Geographic Society.

The following 10 maps show the distribution of sites of successive periods in the parishes of Dévaványa, Szeghalom, Körösladány and Vesztö (see Fig. 11.13 for location), with limits of occupation reconstructed from MRT vol. 6 and field notes.

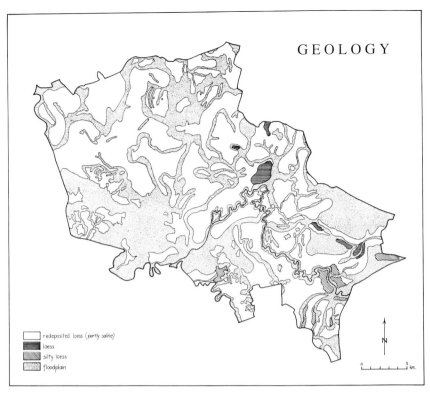

11.18 Surface geology (as Fig. 11.13) [new map].

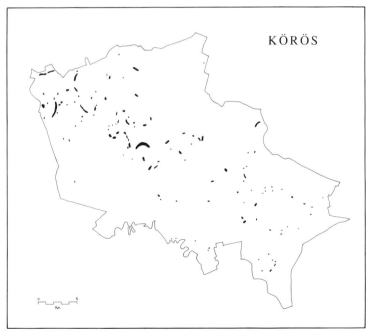

11.19 The distribution of Körös culture sites.

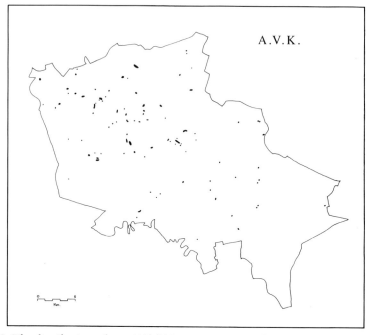

11.20 The distribution of AVK (Alföld Linear Pottery) culture sites.

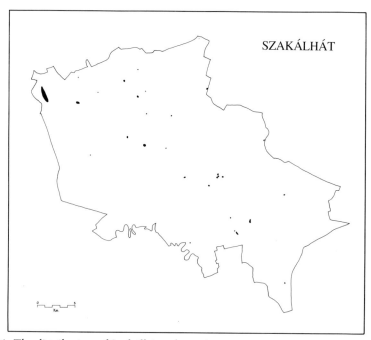

11.21 The distribution of Szakálhát culture sites.

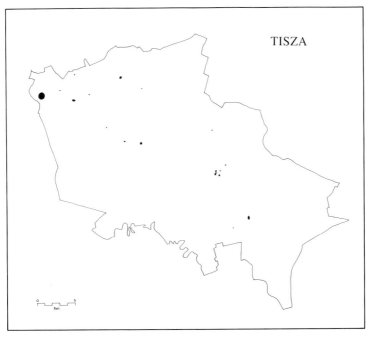

11.22 The distribution of Tisza culture sites.

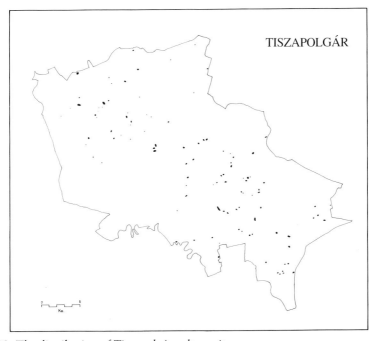

11.23 The distribution of Tiszapolgár culture sites.

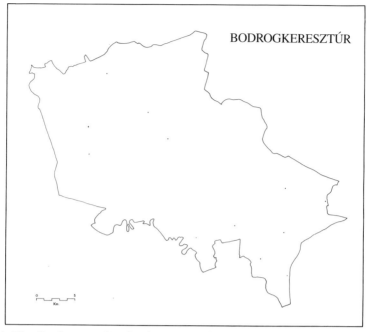

11.24 The distribution of Bodrogkeresztúr culture sites.

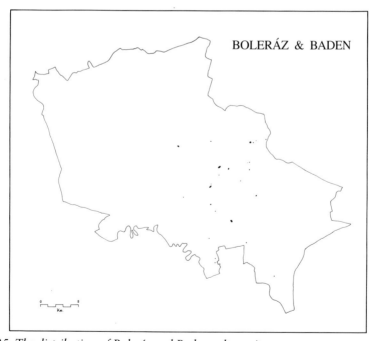

11.25 The distribution of Boleráz and Baden culture sites.

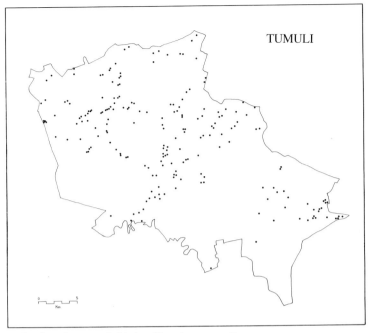

11.26 *The distribution of third-millennium tumuli.*

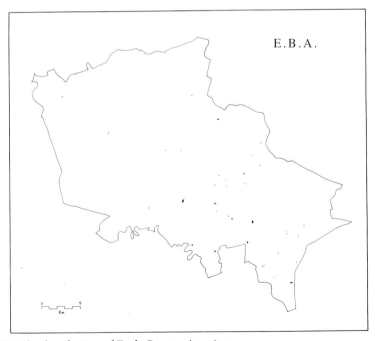

11.27 *The distribution of Early Bronze Age sites.*

12

Neolithic Exchange Systems in Central Europe, 6000–3500 BC

(1987)

The results of identification programmes dealing with flint, hard rocks and obsidian have long since exploded the idea that the Neolithic period was characterised by self-sufficiency and an absence of trade (Chapter 4; Willms 1982). Exploration of the range of items traded by Neolithic communities has revealed a bewildering diversity of exchange systems covering impressive distances and often involving large volumes of material. At the same time, the application of radiocarbon chronologies and acceptance of the implications of recalibration have emphasised just how large a span of time we are dealing with – something like 4000 years between the introduction of agriculture and the regular use of tin–bronze in central Europe. It would thus be quite false to try and force the evidence for traded materials into a single model of 'Neolithic trade': the diversity of evidence truly reflects the major contrasts that must have existed in social and economic organisation during these millennia.

The large, relatively uniform alluvial plain of eastern Hungary provides a natural laboratory for the study of lithic exchange systems, being practically devoid of stone resources but surrounded by mountain and piedmont areas with a wealth of stones (including obsidian) and metal ores. The flint and chert sources of Hungary are described elsewhere [Bíró 1988; cf. also Kaczanowska 1985]: in general they are of rather poor quality by com-

---

The very different patterns of settlement and social organisation defined in previous chapters for the three millennia following the introduction of farming have correspondingly contrasting patterns in the circulation of material goods: broadly, the frugality of a pioneer phase, the bulk circulation of materials in the mature Neolithic, and the appearance of conspicuously exotic types of flint in the Copper Age. This account of materials collected as part of the British-Hungarian project was made possible by raw material identifications undertaken by Mrs C. Takács-Bíró of the Hungarian Geological Institute, and first presented at the Fourth International Flint Symposium in Brighton, 1983.

parison with siliceous materials from Jurassic and Cretaceous deposits north of the Carpathians. The acquisition of cutting materials of any kind thus required special procurement, while the acquisition of high-quality materials for specific purposes involved particular effort. The sequence of stone sources used in this area is thus an effective index of changing needs and the scale of the sustaining area upon which local communities were able to draw. That this area was able to acquire stone at all is significant; that it did so in certain periods in enormous quantities or from great distances is particularly interesting. However, these patterns only make sense when seen in the context of complementary flows of other materials and the social setting in which they took place. (For discussion see Chapter 10.)

The proportions of various types of flaked stone materials at three neighbouring sites of the period under consideration in Co. Békés, eastern Hungary is given in Figure 12.2. These assemblages are characteristic of their respective periods, and similar observations (though not cast in quantitative form) have been made on other contemporary sites in this region. The assemblages represent three distinctive systems: an early, pioneer phase following the first introduction of agriculture; a phase of regional interaction in the Late Neolithic; and a phase of inter-regional exchange in the Early Copper Age.

THE PIONEER PHASE

The quantities of chipped stone material found on early Neolithic sites in the centre of the Plain are not large, and the pieces themselves are generally small. Partly worked cores were imported, but these and their debitage are rare and good flint was carefully conserved – in one case the flakes and debris from a knapping operation were carefully collected and stored in a vessel (Kaczanowska, Kozłowski and Makkay 1981). At first, stone supplies came mainly from the south; but as agricultural communities reached the obsidian sources of the Zemplén mountains in the north, this material came into widespread use. At Méhtelek, a site of the Szatmár group near Szatmár (Satu Mare) on the Hungarian–Romanian border, it formed up to 80 per cent of the chipped stone, the remainder being a great variety of other stones. It was traded both to surrounding Mesolithic groups in Moravia and Little Poland (Kalicz and Makkay 1977b, 17) and southwards to the agricultural communities of the Plain. At one of these, the site of Réhely–Dülö (Körös culture), some 170km from the sources, it was the dominant material (Figure 12.2). The rest of the assemblage was made of small quantities of less useful jasper, probably from river pebbles. Supplies of obsidian were limited and perhaps sporadic. There was great variability in the size of blades, and extensive reworking shows an intensive utilisation of the material available.

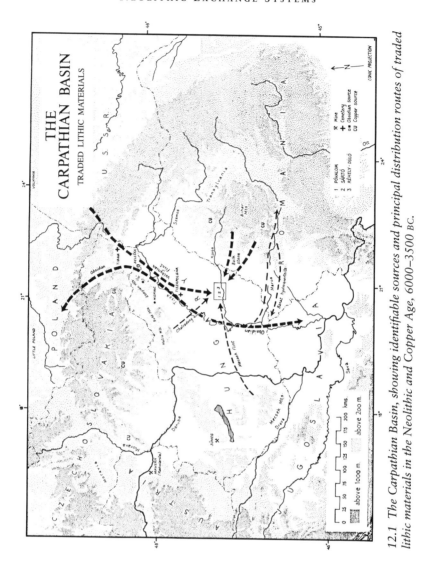

12.1 The Carpathian Basin, showing identifiable sources and principal distribution routes of traded lithic materials in the Neolithic and Copper Age, 6000–3500 BC.

REGIONAL INTERACTION

Within a few hundred years, however, this situation had been transformed: by c.5000 BC large, prosperous lowland sites had established intensive relations with an expanding periphery that was actively supplying quantities of desirable rocks from the highland fringe. The amounts of material recovered from settlements of this period are impressive: surface investigations at the Late Neolithic site of Sártó (Szálkahát and Tisza cultures), a settlement some 500m in diameter, have yielded over fifty greenstone axes and more than 45kg of grinding stones, for instance (Figures 12.3, 12.4). The

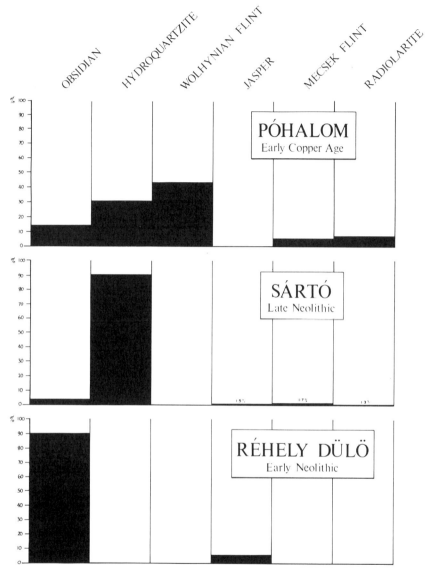

12.2 Changing proportions of imported materials on three sites in the centre of the Great Hungarian Plain from 6000 to 4000 BC. The histograms give the percentages by weight of different raw materials in the flaked stone assemblages from three adjacent sites, representing the Körös, Tisza and Tiszapolgár periods respectively. Note that this diagram shows only relative proportions: the absolute quantity of obsidian, for instance, greatly expands in the Late Neolithic, and falls away again in the Early Copper Age.

12.3 Types of imported materials at Sártó (Dévaványa parish, Co. Békés) in the Late Neolithic (Szakálhát and Tisza periods): axes of volcanic and metamorphic rocks, including trapezoid (left) and shoelast (right) forms.

12.4 As 12.3: saddle quern (length: 37.5cm; weight: 8.73kg).

flaked stone assemblage is dominated by large quantities of limnic hydro-quartzite, imported in the form of tabular pre-cores weighing up to 1.35kg (Figure 12.5). It is not a high-quality material, but its usage was prodigal – large cores and quantities of debitage are found in abundance, as well as tools such as knives, scrapers and sickles (Figure 12.6). Supplies were clearly plentiful and reliable. Jasper was also used in small amounts, but more significant is the sporadic appearance of small quantities of longer-distance imports such as the type of flint found in the Mecsek mountains of south-west Hungary, and of the radiolarite which occurs at a number of sources on the southern fringes of the Carpathians and which was exploited by Lengyel groups in western Hungary, Austria and Slovakia (see Chapter

12.5 As 12.3: tabular pre-core of hydroquartzite (weight: 1.35kg).

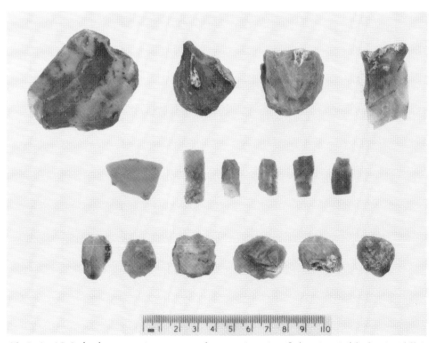

12.6 As 12.3: hydroquartzite cores and core-trimming flakes (top), blades (middle) and scrapers (below) – one blade with sickle-gloss.

12.7 As 12.3: obsidian cores and core-trimming flakes (top), blades (middle) and scrapers (below).

4). Obsidian, although proportionally far less than the abundant hydro-quartzite, was nevertheless available in large quantities: it occurs as large cores, little smaller than the 'bombs' (ejecta) of the original raw material, and as regular blades, implements and debitage (Figure 12.7). With the obsidian at this site should also be mentioned a number of sherds of the fine, decorated Bükk pottery which was made in the areas around the obsidian sources to the north (Figure 12.8).

Sites such as Sártó, which are conspicuous for their size and wealth, probably represent the upper tier of a settlement hierarchy, being surrounded by smaller settlements (Makkay 1982; Chapter 11). The major sites occur at something like 30km intervals, and are located at points along the major rivers (notably the Körös and lower Tisza), which must have played a major role in the distribution of such items. However, within these sites there is remarkably little evidence for social differentiation in the form of rich households or well-equipped graves, or of material items distinctive of an elite. Nevertheless, imported materials came in regular flows: their movement was well organised and not just a sporadic windfall.

Where were these materials coming from? Figure 12.9 represents a first attempt to define the supply radii for some of them. Two areas in particular

12.8 As 12.3: sherds of imported fine pottery of the Bükk culture, incised and incrusted with red paint.

stand out: first the edges of the Bihar Massif, to the east, along the upper reaches of the various branches of the Körös River in Romania; and secondly the north Hungarian mountains, linked either along the Tisza and lower Körös or more directly along the flood-course of the Hortobágy. Both areas are known as sources of cherts. Comşa (1967; 1976) has described sources for cherts widely used in Neolithic times in the region of Crişana (Ér Valley), at Iozaşel (on the White Körös) and in the Banat (Poiana Ruscăi mountains near Bega), while small shafts for limnic hydroquartzite are known near Miskolc in north-east Hungary (Vértes 1964, 210). Axes of volcanic and metamorphic rocks could have either a northern or an eastern origin, but in the days before wheeled vehicles and pack animals the bulky products like grinding-stones are likely to have been transported directly by boat from the nearest eastern source. Direct access at certain seasons is a possibility here, though the distances are impressive: 100km or more.

Higher-value items – obsidian and decorated pottery – came from the north over a slightly longer distance. Their bulk was smaller, but in the case of pottery more fragile. The northern mountains form an interesting study of the relationship between settlement and the exploitation of raw materials (Figure 12.10). The mountains fall into three blocks: Matra, Bükk and

327

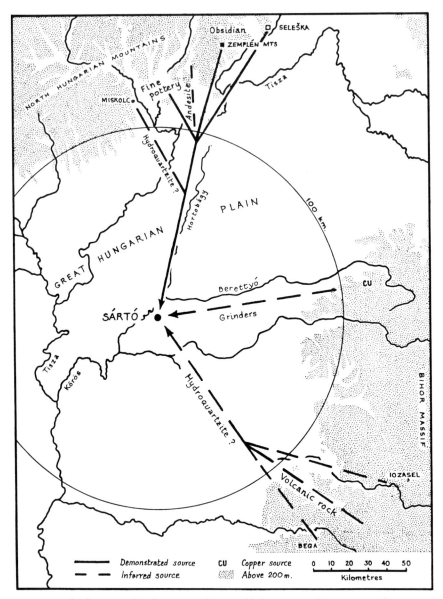

12.9 *Supply distances for the major classes of lithic material at Sártó in the Late Neolithic, c.5000 BC.*

Zemplén. The Bükk, in the middle, is the exception – it is limestone, and has plentiful caves. Zemplén, on the other hand, is volcanic and metamorphic, supplying a variety of rocks of which the most important was obsidian. Other siliceous rocks also occur there. Two main sources of obsidian have been distinguished analytically (Williams-Thorpe 1978; Williams-Thorpe et al. 1984): one, which was the major supplier throughout prehistory, and the

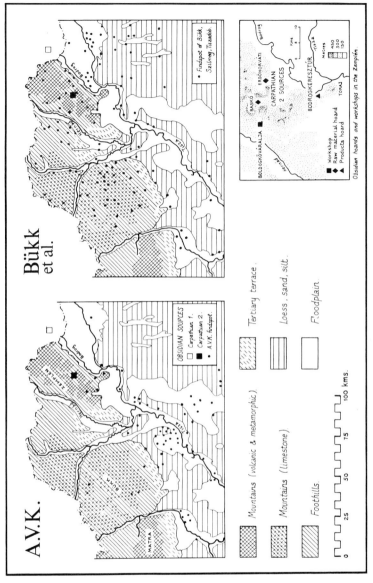

12.10 Colonisation of the North Hungarian Mountains, 5300–4800 BC (AVK and Szakálhát/Bükk periods), in relation to lithic sources. Obsidian sources in the Zemplén ('Carpathian 2' source) became important in the Bükk period: detail map, bottom right. Base-map cf. Fig. 11.4: distributions after Kalicz and Makkay (1977), obsidian sources after Williams-Thorpe.

sole Carpathian source for most of it, is just over the Czech border at Seleška (Szöllöske), in a fairly low-lying position. But just at the period under discussion, smaller secondary sources within the Zemplén mountains were opened up and specialised workshop settlements with hoards and production-debris are known from the valleys leading down from them (Figure 12.10, detail map). What is even more remarkable is the extent of settlement in the Bükk mountains themselves. Occupation traces occur up to 900m above sea level in the limestone caves that are famous for their Palaeolithic assemblages. This upland occupation lasted only for a short time from c.5000–4800 BC, and much of the area was then abandoned. The sites seem to be tied in with the extensive trading opportunities of the period. Remains from the caves show traces of hunting, sheep herding, and evidence for pottery-making, as well as hoards both of axes and blades (Lichardus 1974). It seems that, as well as being concerned with the direct exploitation of sources in the Zemplén and nearby, these groups were also acting as middlemen in the dispersal of this range of materials and were also perhaps engaged in forms of secondary specialisation such as the manufacture of specially fine pottery or the transhumant movement of sheep. The most easily recognisable product, obsidian, found its way 400km down river to Transylvania and Jugoslavia, and also (along with some pottery) across the Carpathians for 200km into Little Poland.

The pattern of trade, then, was one of intensive localised movement of highland products to adjacent lowlands, with one or two more special items moving from one side of the Basin to the other, and occasionally just into the area over the mountains from important sources. The asymmetry of this reconstruction, in which durable items of many kinds were moving into the Plain, strongly suggests the counter-movement of some balancing exportable commodity, of which cattle is the most probable (Chapter 10). The cultural pattern at this period is one of fragmentation, with a multitude of small groupings defined by their fine pottery, suggesting a rather localised scale of interaction in which middleman positions could be exploited, since there was no elite participation in longer-distance trade by which intervening areas could be bypassed. This, then, is what I have defined as a regional network, and marks the first climax of trade activity within the Carpathian Basin.

INTER-REGIONAL EXCHANGE

We now move to a very different situation. This is defined in the Hungarian sequence as the beginning of the Copper Age (c.4500 BC), although populations in surrounding areas were still stone-using and indeed in Poland this period saw the development of open shaft-mining and specialist flint-workshops. Technological labels – Neolithic, Eneolithic or Copper Age – are less important than the recognition that a major change had occurred in social organisation and the character of trade.

In the examples presented here, this period is represented by the Early Copper Age site of Póhalom (Tiszapolgár culture). The absolute quantities are no longer as impressive as those of the preceding period, and the sites have no obvious hierarchy; but the component of long-distance imports is substantial. Hydroquartzite continues as an everyday material for small cutting tools, and obsidian is also present; there are also significant numbers of pieces of Mecsek flint and radiolarite. But almost half of the chipped stone industry, including the larger and longer blades, is made of a Cretaceous flint which has been identified as coming from deposits in Wolhynia (the region east of L'vov on the upper Dnestr: Kaczanowska 1981; 1985). This was capable of being made into the longer blades which were thought particularly desirable (see below). Such supplies were obtained on a regular basis for some hundreds of years: Wolhynian flint makes up to 60 per cent of assemblages of the succeeding Bodrogkeresztur period (c.3900 BC).

DISCUSSION

The three types of exchange systems characterised above form only a part of the history of trade in lithic materials, which continued to circulate alongside copper for a further 1000 years. This latter period saw the development of the Sümeg flint mines in western Hungary and the major development of bulk production and distribution in the flint-mining areas of the North European Plain (Lech 1987; Schild 1987). The enlarged scale of flint production must be related to the increasing population and accelerated rate of forest clearance linked to the introduction of plough agriculture and more extensive types of farming (Kruk 1980; Chapter 6).

In northern Europe the need for stone axes in forest clearance was marked by the development of effective upright axes with a long cutting edge and rectangular cross-section (Montelius' 'thin-butted' and 'thick-butted' types) that have no counterparts further south. These were produced in very large quantities from mined flint. However, towards the end of the third millennium there was a shift in north European flint production away from axes and towards large cutting implements – especially daggers but also knives and sickles. This is associated with the very widespread distribution of specialised products such as the daggers of Grand Pressigny flint, whose use as equipment for warrior males shows continuity with the first copper daggers in north-west Europe, as demonstrated by Beaker grave-goods in the Netherlands (Lanting, Mook and van der Waals 1973, 45). In some respects, therefore, this change in northern Europe recapitulates the type of transition described here for central Europe about 1000 years earlier. The mass circulation of everyday items gave way to a concentration on specific exotic materials and types with a more explicit symbolism of social status. It is significant that the regular use of copper occurs in this context in both areas. Materials such as obsidian seem to have been incapable of carrying such a message: as with *Spondylus* shell, its main period of use occurs in earlier Neolithic contexts at a lower level of social differentiation.

The interpretation of studies of lithic material sources thus inevitably leads not only to a consideration of the other items circulating in exchange networks, but also to attempts at evaluating the social significance of the materials in question and how they were manipulated by the individuals concerned (Douglas and Isherwood 1980). The complementary evidence from settlements and graves provides a starting-point for the analysis of how such commodities were used by Neolithic populations. The study of lithic artefacts thus remains a challenging area of archaeological research, but one which cannot be isolated from more general consideration of the archaeological record, and indeed of ethnography as well.

13

The Genesis of Megaliths:
Monumentality, Ethnicity and
Social Complexity in
Neolithic North-West Europe
(1990)

Houses for the living,
Dolmens for the dead:
Are these distinctions 'on the ground'
Or only 'in the head'?

And whose head is it anyway:
The 'writer' of the 'text' –
Or just the archaeologist's
Who stumbled on it next?

I'll break my skull on megaliths
And join the pile of bones;
And then perhaps I'll empathise
With builders of the stones.

(Old folk song)

Monumental architecture was one of Gordon Childe's ten criteria of urban civilisation; and monument building is still employed by evolutionary archaeologists as an important index of social complexity. It is misleading,

---

On the western and northern edges of the central European loess corridor, lying next to the sea, a very different pattern of Neolithic land-occupation occurred from that in Hungary – inscribing the landscape not with settlements but tombs. Chapter 5 suggested that the answer lay in a fusion between Mesolithic indigenes and incoming Neolithic groups; this chapter, written for a World Archaeology *special issue on monumentality, describes the physical setting and chronology of the process. The account was much influenced by the work of Richard Bradley (who solicited it) and Ian Hodder. It demonstrates that local manifestations can only be understood in the context of interactions over very large areas; and it shows how a setting within such large physical and cultural structures influences the 'personality' of a region.*

however, to approach all monumentality with the same model in mind. Although megalithic monuments were constructed for two millennia in Atlantic Europe, they belong to a relatively early phase of the development of farming economies there. Unlike the architectural achievements of early Mesopotamia or Mesoamerica, they were the products of societies able to mobilise relatively unskilled labour rather than specialist craftsmanship; and their experiments, while impressive, gave rise to no wider architectural tradition. They thus belong more to the spread of farming than to the onset of urbanism.

In Childe's view, the whole European megalithic phenomenon was itself an indirect reflection of contemporary oriental civilisation, carried as part of a mortuary cult by seaborne missionaries along the Atlantic coastlands. While radiocarbon chronologies have severed this diffusionist link, mega-lithic monuments still retain some of the glamour of this earlier association; they have thus been treated as indicative of new forms of social organis-ation, or indications of territorial consciousness as the result of a shortage of land (Renfrew 1976; Chapman 1981; Hodder 1984). In consequence they have continued to be seen as something additional to the processes leading to the appearance of farming in north-west Europe, marking out their users as in some sense more 'advanced' than their neighbours. It would be a mistake, however, to draw too sharp a line between early constructions in earth and stone and the substantial timber buildings of contemporary Neolithic groups in central Europe; or to see the effort devoted to 'religious' structures as fundamentally different in character from that devoted to 'domestic' structures elsewhere. By considering the genesis of megalithic monuments in this wider context, I hope to avoid the teleological overtones of an evolutionary view which sees them simply as a stage in the rise of social complexity, emerging as a local response to problems of population pressure. Instead of examining their evolutionary credentials, therefore, this paper explores the initial role of monuments in the spread of farming to the outer parts of Europe.

The areas under consideration here – western France, Britain, northern Germany, northern Poland, and southern Scandinavia – form an arc around the central European loess belt along which farming spread from 5500 BC onwards, and to which it was initially confined. In each of these areas, dense hunting and fishing (Mesolithic) populations existed for a long period after the arrival of the first farming groups on the loess. It will be argued that this relationship was critical in explaining the beginnings of monumentality in each area; and the argument will be pursued in greater detail in relation to western France and the North European Plain.

It is useful to divide European earthen and megalithic burial monuments into two major cycles: the first, which is that considered here, lasted from c.4500 to 3500 BC; the second, which I prefer to distinguish by the term 'neo-megalithic', began c.3500 and lasted in some areas down to 2500 or even 2000 BC. These two cycles were different in character, those of the second cycle being associated with use of plough agriculture and rather different types of settlement pattern, as well as with the spread of mega-lithism to new areas. In the following sketch I shall deal only with the first cycle, and attempt to defend the view that the variety of early monumental forms was an essential part of the interaction between natives and new-comers, and was not due to more generalised factors such as a scarcity of land.

EARLY FARMING AND THE CREATION OF COMMUNITY

The spread of farming to Europe took two forms. In the Balkans and central Europe, the 'west Asiatic package' was imported wholesale, with cereal farming (horticulture), livestock keeping, pottery, and villages of substantial houses. This pattern spread, largely through migration, along the central European loess corridor. In the central and west Mediterranean, a second pattern prevailed: cereals were less important, and there was initially no radical alteration of settlement patterns or replacement of population. Individual elements of the farming technocomplex were selectively inte-grated within an existing way of life. This latter pattern was also typical of the later spread of farming among 'sub-Neolithic' groups in the far north and east of Europe.

Around the margins of the area occupied by immigrant farmers in central Europe, a more complex set of interactions between incoming and native groups took place, associated with the transfer not just of the more easily transmissible features such as pottery and livestock, but of cereal cultivation as well. In the circum-Alpine area, the nucleated village pattern was trans-ferred to native groups around the margins of morainic lakes, to produce the characteristic pattern of 'lake-villages'. Here the spread of horticulture to a new ecological setting was directly associated with a pattern of village life and its community structure. On the western and northern margins, how-ever, this simple correlation did not occur. The spread of cereal cultivation was associated, not with substantial timber villages, but with what can be considered as their monumental surrogates: mounds and megaliths. This pattern should thus be seen as the first stage in the transformation of indigenous foragers into indigenous farmers; and monumental tombs appear to have been an essential element in that transformation.

This interpretation of the role of the first monuments in north-west Europe rests on two arguments. The first is inductive: the mutually exclusive occurrence of substantial villages and non-domestic ('funerary') structures in the archaeological record of Neolithic Europe. The second is deductive: the need for an organisational framework (involving both material culture and social relations) appropriate to the new requirements of cereal cultivation.

The first point is very widely applicable to the study of Neolithic (and earlier Bronze Age) settlement patterns: indeed, it is almost an axiom of archaeological research that substantial settlement traces and funerary monuments seem mutually exclusive (e.g. Kowalczyk 1970, 161 on TRB Poland; Scarre 1983, 330 on later Neolithic southern France). A comparison of Neolithic north-west Europe with the central European loess zone is especially instructive. The absence of burial monuments in central Europe is not due simply to the lack of stone in this area. While both cemeteries and earth-built structures such as enclosures are not uncommon features in Neolithic central Europe, their combination in the form of monumental burials scarcely exists. Instead, substantial settlements fill the archaeological record. In western Europe, conversely, the burial monuments are often all that we have in the absence of intensive survey or lucky accident; especially in the earlier period, settlement traces are scattered and unimpressive. This marked contrast is not accidental: it corresponds to a fundamental difference in the structure of settlement. Whereas the village was the basic settlement unit and primary community of Neolithic central Europe (whether in the form of a Balkan tell or a looser aggregation of substantial timber longhouses in the loess zone), early Neolithic settlement in western Europe was insubstantial and dispersed. The element of permanence seems to have been provided not by the settlements themselves, but by monumental tombs and enclosures.

The second point explains why such monumentality was necessary. The requirements of cereal cultivation would have necessitated a more radical social reorganisation of hunting and foraging communities than the keeping of small quantities of domestic livestock. It required a continuing commitment to particular places, and to a social and ecological transformation of the landscape. Larger labour teams (of perhaps twenty to fifty men) would be required for certain operations in the farming cycle, and cultivation required constant hoeing and weeding. These placed a premium on the recruitment of a labour force, and thus on control both of female labour and female reproductive capacity. In place of the demographic flux characteristic of foraging societies, it was necessary to create stable lineages whose depth could provide a dependable pool of labour through the widened cone of kinship. In the immigrant Neolithic societies of central Europe, this continuity was assured through the existence of the village community as a residential unit, cross-cut by family ties and made up of individual households occupying substantial longhouses, whose construction (like forest clearing and harvesting) involved the co-operation of several households. To reproduce this social mechanism in the absence of large, stable residential units required the invention of some equivalent ritual mark of continuity and common descent. The monumental tomb was the surrogate for the living village (Sherratt 1984, 129; Hodder 1984, 54): a permanent house and household of the dead amongst the insubstantial huts scattered within its territory. Often reconstructed and enlarged, such monuments served their communities for many generations: as the burial places of founding ancestors, as communal ossuaries, and as a continuing focus for ritual.

The adoption of monumental tombs seems thus to be characteristic of areas which were already fairly densely occupied by Mesolithic groups, who adopted Neolithic horticulture on the central European model, but who did not not take over the village-based settlement pattern with which it had previously been associated. Instead, tombs formed the basis for their symbolic construction of community (cf. Cohen 1985). It can thus be argued that these tombs, like the architectural elaboration and permanence of *Bandkeramik* and tell settlements, were as basic a feature of early cereal cultivation as the hoe and the axe: the material infrastructure of the organisation of labour was as crucial in the establishment of horticulture as the more obvious elements of technology (Thomas 1988). Moreover, the advantages of this form of organisation were not limited to the cultivation of cereals; and once established, could be applied to other modes of subsistence (such as marine fishing) where the recruitment of a more extensive labour force gave a competitive advantage.

MEGALITHIC MORPHOLOGY AND ITS DEVELOPMENT IN NORTH-WEST EUROPE

In many parts of northern and western Europe, a general sequence of structural types may be observed (sometimes even within the same monument); and since it occurs in widely separated areas at different times, it seems to be a general trend rather than evidence of direct contact. The earliest forms of burial monument are frequently long mounds of earth and timber, often trapezoidal in shape. Stone then replaces timber for revetments and internal structures, still often in long mounds; round forms then become more frequent, and the chambers increase in size. These phases may overlap, or occur in spatially discrete areas, and there is no simple succession: types may continue to co-exist and be consciously elaborated in opposition to each other, older forms may be revived or accommodated to new ones; so that individual cases must therefore be explained in their context. Yet there is an underlying regularity, which demands explanation.

From the perspective indicated above, it is significant that the sequence begins with monuments that have explicit similarities with contemporary houses in the loess belt, and then progressively diverges from this pattern. Following an idea of Gordon Childe (1949) and suggestions by Stuart Piggott in relation to unchambered long-barrows (1966), this argument has been persuasively developed by Ian Hodder (1984), who points out the many analogies between the houses of the later *Bandkeramik* tradition and the first monumental tombs of the western and northern Neolithic, from the middle Vistula to the Charente. In the metaphor of the longhouse, therefore, a diverse array of cultures in western and northern Europe would have symbolised their adoption not only of a new mode of subsistence but the organisation necessary to sustain it.

The transformation of these timber surrogates into stone was a consequence both of the local occurrence of stone in the new territories beyond the loesslands, and of the need for more permanent monuments (just as the church in a medieval village was often the only building of stone). Moreover, the use of extravagantly large stones ('megaliths' *sensu stricto*) in their construction suggests a further element. In a society where labour was the most important commodity, moving large stones symbolised the size of the workforce which could be assembled at any one time – an epideictic demonstration of demographic strength and co-ordinated effort. The monuments developed a meaning in their own right, as well as an inherited typological continuity from their skeuomorphic origins. These constructional changes in early monuments were also accompanied by an enlargement of their use. Early long-mounds often cover individuals (who probably represent members of founding lineages rather than 'chiefs'); chambered megalithic tombs received greater numbers of individual remains (and often operated as a 'bone bank' in the wider circulation of human relics); and many of these 'tombs' continued to receive offerings and act as foci for non-monumental burials long after they themselves ceased to be used for interment.

It would be wrong, however, to see these changes simply as a linear sequence or as a prescriptive necessity. The longhouse model, already monumentalised, was apparently the common stimulus to megalithism in each of the areas concerned; but due weight must also be given to the role of indigenous inhabitants in this process, for this is basic to the overall distributional argument (which must also take into account areas such as Iberia, remote from the central European loesslands), and to the strong local continuity generally evident between Mesoliths and megaliths. Detailed local distributional studies can here suggest an answer, for there is often a spatial contrast between the first long, unchambered forms on the one hand, and the round or chambered forms on the other. The former often avoid Mesolithic concentrations, the latter often coincide with them (see detailed examples below). It looks as if the early long forms, with a central European background, provoked a conscious reaction from native groups, perhaps associated with a different conceptual or cosmological framework. Some elements of megalithic design, such as the round mounds and chambers, may therefore be an indigenous contribution to the process – an idea that goes back at least to Montelius (1899, 41–6). If the chambers and circular forms reflect native house-types or concepts of space, the proliferation of such types would mark the widespread adoption of monumentality and its associated social structures by indigenous communities; and various

338

degrees of fusion or incorporation of one group by the other might then occur.

This reconstruction implies the participation of both incoming and native elements in the process by which agriculture reached the outer parts of northern and western Europe, and the monumentalism which accompanied it. The model could apply equally to western France, the British Isles, and the North European Plain and Scandinavia – all of which combined substantial indigenous populations with potential contacts to adjacent parts of the loesslands. Their similarities of sequence would in this view result from a common background and similar influences, rather than from any coastwise contacts as were envisaged in the traditional picture. That these remarkably parallel developments took place independently in each area is indicated by the fact that while monumentality in western France began c.4600 BC, it only appeared in Denmark c.3800 BC. While the situation in Britain is less clearly established (and will not be discussed here), a date of c.4200–4000 BC is a plausible estimate. The process of expansion would thus have occurred in a clockwise progression, successively but independently, in three separate areas around the north-west margins of the loess.

THE GENESIS OF MEGALITHS: FRANCE

One recent revelation of French archaeology has been the extent of Impressed Ware influence from the west Mediterranean (Joussaume 1986), which by the later sixth millennium reached west-central France as far north as the Vendée and along the northern margins of the Massif Central (Figure 13.1). Although this has led some (west!) French archaeologists to assert its importance for subsequent developments, the early date of its appearance (c.5300 BC) has rather served to emphasise that local monumentality in fact only began with the onset of influences from the Paris Basin and the loesslands, some 700 years later. The widespread distribution of pottery related to Impressed Ware, and the minimal changes in *genre de vie* which accompanied it, suggest the dissemination of easily accommodated novelties such as pottery and domestic livestock among existing networks of native Mesolithic contact, and it is doubtful whether any cultivation of cereals is implied. Domestic livestock and a local variety of simple pottery also appeared in parts of Brittany during this time, and the well-known shell middens with cist burials from Hoëdic and Téviec in the Morbihan date to this period. Since some twenty metres of the contemporary coastline have been lost in the postglacial eustatic rise in sea-level (in contrast to northern Denmark where it has been preserved through isostatic uplift), these sites must stand *pars pro toto* for a considerable concentration of indigenous coastal settlement in that region.

The second revelation of recent work has been the extent of *Bandkeramik* settlement – ultimately of central European origin – in the Paris

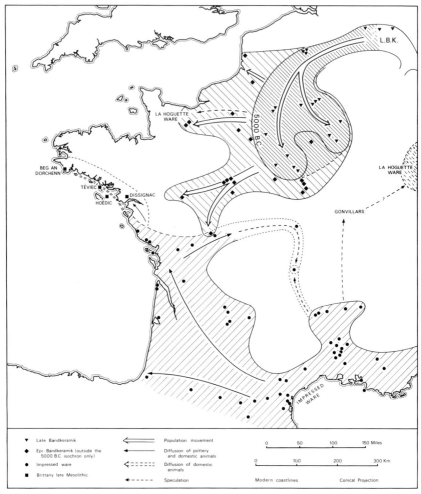

13.1 Neolithic France, 5000–4700 BC, showing initial Impressed Ware spread from the south, and Linear Bandkeramik (LBK) intrusion into the Paris Basin and beyond. Data from Constantin, Joussaume, Roussot-Larroque, Lichardus-Itten, L'Helgouach.

Basin and adjoining areas at the western end of the loess zone by c.5200 BC, and the extent to which *epi-Bandkeramik* influences penetrated into the western margins (Constantin 1985). In the period from c.5000–4700 BC, sites belonging to successive *epi-Bandkeramik* groups expanded westwards in three salients, following the loess plains: along the Somme through Picardy; into Normandy, reaching the Plain of Caen; and south-westwards across the Plain of Beauce into the middle Loire and towards the Gate of Poitou (see Figure 13.2). The pottery of these groups began to diverge strongly from the mainstream *Bandkeramik* tradition and its successors in the Rhineland: it carried comb-impressed ornament and had a distinctive

340

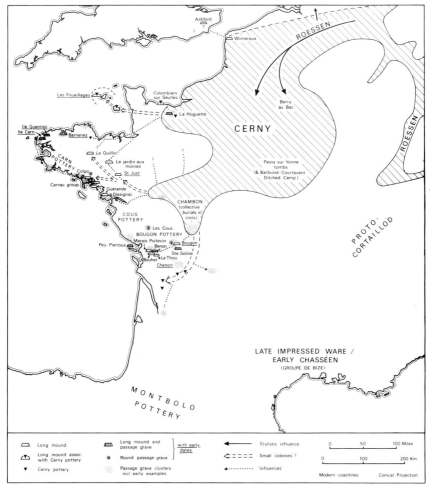

13.2 *Neolithic France, 4700–4300 BC, showing interaction between Paris Basin (Cerny) group and indigenous populations in the west, with early monuments. Data from Constantin, Joussaume, Burnez, Mohen, Giot, L'Helgouach, Le Roux, Kinnes.*

bone filler – features which may perhaps indicate a native contribution to the tradition. Although western finds are mainly pottery (often recovered from beneath later monuments), sites of these groups in the Paris Basin show typical late *Bandkeramik* trapezoidal house-plans (e.g. Maisse, Essonne).

This far-reaching extension of the central European farming tradition, albeit receptive to western elements, was carried further and into more intimate admixture with indigenous groups in the following phase, that of Cerny, which corresponds chronologically to middle Roessen in the Rhineland (Figure 13.3). Late Roessen influence then gradually brought

B.C. (cal)	WESTERN FRANCE	RHINELAND	DENMARK	CENTRAL GERMANY	CENTRAL POLAND	B.C. (cal)
	S.O.M. (Late Neo.)	WARTBERG	MIDDLE NEO. I	WALTERNIEN--BURG/BERNBURG	LUBOŃ	
3500	(Middle Neo.)	M I C H E L S B E R G V	FUCHSBERG	SALZMÜNDE	WIÓREK	3500
	CHAS-SÉEN	IV	EARLY NEO. 'C'		PIKUTKOWO	
		III	VOLLING-OXIE	BAAL-BERGE	SARNOWO *	
4000	CASTELLIC, SOUC'H	II	E R	GATERSLEBEN & "LATE ROESSEN"	BRZEŚĆ KUJAWSKI	4000
	(Early Neo.)	I	T			
	CARN	POST-ROESSEN	E			
4500	COUS (CHAMBON)		B			4500
	BOUGON * / CERNY	ROESSEN	Ø	ROESSEN	LENGYEL	
	(Augy-Ste Pallaye)	GROSSGARTACH	L			
	EPI-BANDKERAMIK (Villeneuve St. Germain)		L	STICHBANDKERAMIK		
5000	IMPRESSED WARE	HINKELSTEIN	L			5000
	LATE LINIENBANDKERAMIK		E	LATE LINIENBANDKERAMIK		

13.3 Schematic chronological chart of the cultural succession in western and northern Europe, on a calibrated radiocarbon timescale. Asterisks mark the beginning of monument building: note the later onset of monumentality in the north.

back the Paris Basin into the Rhineland orbit, while western Cerny groups (e.g. Chambon) formed part of an emerging western complex including Bougon, Cous and Carn wares. This phase, from roughly 4700–4300 BC, saw the genesis of a new pattern of western farming. The complex inter-digitation of newcomers and natives took place along three principal routes: in Normandy and the adjacent Channel Islands; in the areas around the mouth of the Loire; and in the *départements* of Charente, Charente mari-time and Deux-Sèvres (Figure 13.2). Two basic forms of monumental tombs resulted from these contacts: long-mounds covering burials in a timber or stone-lined space without external access; and stone-built chamber-tombs with an entrance passage giving continued access from outside (passage-graves). I shall argue that the former show a direct con-nection with contemporary longhouses, and that the latter are best seen as a native reaction; (but it should be noted that tombs enclosed by a circular ditch and approached by a long passage formed by parallel ditches occur in a Cerny context in the Paris Basin at Passy-sur-Yonne, so that an explanation in terms of this origin is also possible for the circular passage-graves).

It is in Normandy and the Channel Islands that Cerny influences seem to be most direct, and in which its pottery is most plentiful; here, too, that the long-mound tradition seems initially to be the dominant one (Hibbs 1983). Indeed, longhouse villages may have existed not far away at this time, on the rich loess soils of eastern Normandy. Important examples of long mounds from western Normandy and the Islands are Les Fouaillages on Guernsey (Kinnes 1982), with its stone-edged triangular or trapezoid mound covering several cists, and the long-mound currently under excavation by Kinnes and Chancerel at Colombiers sur Seulles near Caen. Les Fouaillages dates to c.4600 BC; slightly later, on radiocarbon evidence, is the long (though not trapezoid) cairn of La Hoguette near Caen, with its dozen dry-stone passage-graves with round chambers, indicating affinities to the early passage-graves of Brittany (L'Helgouach and Le Roux 1986).

Long-mounds (often defined by a peristalith and enclosing cists) occur in eastern Brittany and the Carnac region, and at the mouth of the Loire – in the two latter cases adjacent to clusters of monuments including early passage-graves (Figure 13.2). Pottery from the long-mounds hints at Cerny connections along the Loire. Further round the coast of Brittany to the north-west, where no long-mounds are known, are mid-fifth-millennium multiple passage-graves such as Barnenez with its trapezoidal mound, and the trapezoidal cairn (later enclosed in a circular blocking-mound) of Ile Carn. These are mostly of drystone construction, though some of the chambers are truly megalithic. These funerary monuments are associated with the plain Carn ware, which shows similarities with those from Bougon and Cous further south and together define an emerging 'Atlantic' cultural province with a stong indigenous background.

A crucial complex of monuments near the southern salient is that at Bougon (Deux-Sèvres), with long trapezoidal mounds (one enclosing small cists) and simple chambered tombs in round mounds, all from the mid-fifth millennium, as well as later and more developed forms. At nearby St Soline, multiple passage-graves occur in a trapezoidal mound; while nearer the coast in the Forest of Benon and at Bouhet there are numerous long-mounds, one at the latter covering a timber structure (Joussaume 1986). All the diversity of early western megalithic forms is here present within a small compass – unfortunately without the degree of chronological resolution necessary to establish typological priorities, but clearly in a context where influences from the western loesslands were interacting with native traditions. The situation can best be described as one of morphological flux in which long-mounds and stone-built passage-graves appeared in varying combinations. Long-mounds seem to initiate the sequence, and to provide a continuing influence, although small passage-graves (often combined in composite monuments of various shapes) seem to have been more adaptable to local needs.

How can these developments be summarised? The pattern of monument-building seems to have crystallised on the margins of loess-based settlement with its longhouse villages, at a time when cereal cultivation was being adopted within a more dispersed pattern of settlement by native Mesolithic populations in surrounding areas. In each area, and arguably at the beginning of the process, early monuments took the form of trapezoidal long-mounds covering wooden structures or small stone cists. Several are associated with pottery ultimately of *Bandkeramik* tradition, and contemporary with Roessen in west-central Europe. It is not improbable that they were erected by colonists from the loess zone; but it is equally possible that they were built by natives in contact with longhouse village settlements. The two are not exclusive, since recruitment of a labour force would be an important initial objective of early settlers, and the two groups were not strangers to each other. Whichever was the case, these longhouse-like models initiated a period of rapid monumental innovation.

It appears that the external input was stronger nearer to the main loess extension in the north (Normandy), and the native element stronger in the south (Brittany and west-central France). Passage-graves were particularly characteristic of areas where relatively dense Mesolithic settlement can be inferred, especially on the coasts. Their basic design, a round chamber in a round mound, may be a direct reference to indigenous house types; and the provision of a passage for continued access after interment may suggest a different attitude to the dead: but the frequent grouping of passage-graves in trapezoidal mounds shows an accommodation to the exterior appearance of the long-mound model. Passage-graves – at first drystone structures with corbelled chambers, often several grouped together as a single monument, then increasingly megalithic and with single, larger chambers with internal subdivisions – became the most frequent form of monument in western France, and it seems as if the initial loessland stimulus was largely absorbed in the native reaction. The long-mound tradition did, however, survive in certain enclaves, and was the basis for further developments on this theme in the Middle Neolithic. I shall return to this in a later section.

THE GENESIS OF MEGALITHS: NORTHERN EUROPE

The major reservoirs of *Bandkeramik* population in north-central Europe were the loess-covered basins along the major northward-draining rivers: Vistula, Oder, Elbe and Rhine. Some penetration of farming populations beyond the loess, especially along the Oder and Vistula, took pioneer *Bandkeramik* groups into the zone of glacial-meltwater valleys (*Urstromtäler*) in Poland and eastern Germany, where they established longhouse village settlements on small patches of fine-grained soils in Kujavia, west Pomerania and the Uckermark. To the north of these lay the glacial outwash sands and moraines of the North European Plain, and the shallow coastlands of the Baltic with the Jutland peninsula and islands. Mesolithic groups occupied many of the more productive habitats in this area,

344

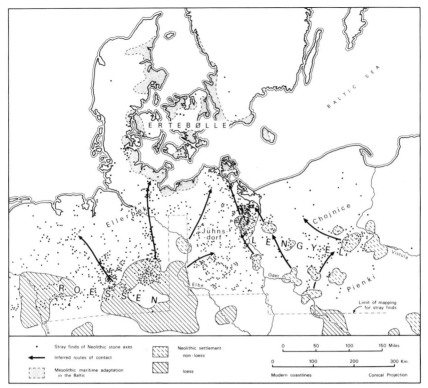

13.4 *Northern Europe, 4700–4000* BC, *showing imports from* Bandkeramik *successor-groups (Roessen and Lengyel) to Mesolithic communities in the North European Plain; the west Baltic maritime Mesolithic (Ertebølle culture) is emphasised. Data from van der Waals, Brandt, Schwabedissen, Gramsch, Kozlowski, Fischer, Jennbert.*

especially by lakes and rivers but particularly on the west Baltic coastlands where shellmounds and fishing stations demonstrate the importance of littoral and marine resources.

On the loesslands, later *Bandkeramik* was succeeded in the west by Roessen and further east by Lengyel, with its closer links to the Carpathian Basin and south-east Europe. The outposts of central European farming along the Oder and Vistula retained their southern contacts, while inter-acting with local native populations as shown by finds of imported pottery and stone shafthole axes in later Mesolithic contexts in the surrounding area (Figure 13.4). Pottery making, and perhaps some domestic livestock, was widely adopted as part of the indigenous way of life, seen most notably in the Ertebølle culture of southern Scandinavia. These coastal Mesolithic groups achieved a considerable degree of social complexity, largely asso-ciated with specialised marine fishing. This stable co-existence lasted for more than half a millennium, during which no major structural trans-formation took place (Figure 13.4).

In the pioneer phase of *Bandkeramik* colonisation, the domestic structures were clusters of longhouses, generally 25–30m in length, grouped in villages or in hamlets strung out along rivercourses. In the subsequent phase (Roessen or Lengyel), beginning around 4800 BC, a new pattern emerged, with single, larger longhouses, often associated with enclosures or stockades. Some of these longhouses were truly vast, reaching 45–50m at sites like Inden 1 or Biskupin 18a, and a massive >65m (the full length was not preserved) at Bochum-Hiltrop (Müller-Karpe 1968, Tafel 234). By late Roessen times in the western part of this area, such massive longhouses show a tendency to fragment into a series of smaller, square buildings, as at Berry-au-Bac or the Goldberg. These changes reflect adjustments to the size and composition of the domestic unit as settlement proliferated within the loess belt and began tentatively to spread beyond it.

During the early fourth millennium, signs of a fusion between groups occupying the loess areas of the North European Plain and their native neighbours became evident, indicated archaeologically in the development of the TRB (Funnel-neck beaker) cultures. This blanket term is an unfortunate one, since it carries over some outdated overtones of 'nordic influence' from an earlier phase of prehistoric studies: but it correctly identifies the process of convergence which was taking place between the northern loesslands and surrounding territories, at a time of general inter-regional contact, realignment of exchange networks and cultural fusion contemporary with the developments of the south-east European Copper Age. This resulted in the formation of a series of regional groupings, broadly following the earlier pattern of Roessen and Lengyel cultures, such as Michelsberg in the Rhineland and Baalberge on the Elbe. These, however, show a quite new form of settlement pattern at a local level; for the domestic sites were generally much less substantial, and instead the non-domestic sites such as earthwork enclosures and burials became more emphasised. The former are more common in the Rhineland, the latter on the Elbe, where they sometimes took the form of stone cists in small mounds (Fischer 1956).

Baalberge sites, spreading from the Middle Elbe, occurred in small clusters in the morainic lakelands of Mecklenburg to the north, where they seem initially to have avoided centres of native population (Preuss 1966). In the north-west corner of Germany, in Lower Saxony and Schleswig-Holstein, there seems to have been a greater degree of admixture between local Mesolithic communities and the immediate successors of Roessen just to the south; lakeside and coastal settlements from this period show a more extensive use of pottery and may have imported cereals from their southern neighbours. Neither of these processes of localised interaction, however, produced a major shift towards agriculture with fundamental demographic consequences. Hunting and fishing remained the basis of the economy: the settlements of these marginal groups consisted for the most part of insubstantial groups of round or D-shaped huts, and there were as yet no monumental tombs. A similar situation existed in the Rhine delta, where Swifterbant and Hazendonk groups continued until Middle Neolithic times (beginning c.3500 BC) to maintain a comparable relationship with Michelsberg populations upstream on the loess.

A somewhat different pattern characterised this process further east in Poland, in the region centred on the *Urstromtal* of the middle Vistula and Noteć, the area known as Kujavia. Here the older pattern of trapezoidal longhouses on scattered enclaves of fine-grained blackearth soils lasted somewhat longer than in the west; and in their immediate hinterland, within the morainic zone, there appeared a pottery assemblage which broadly resembles Baalberge and is named after the site of Sarnowo (Kośko 1980). The initial phases of this assemblage seem to overlap with the final phase of Lengyel nearby (e.g. at Brześć Kujawski), but the two groups are spatially discrete; they might thus be considered as communities peripheral to the Lengyel villages, but intermarrying with native groups. Their domestic sites were insubstantial. This close juxtaposition and inter-relationship between Sarnowo and final Lengyel explains the appearance of the monumental tombs which characterise this group: the 'Kujavian graves'. These elongated trapezoidal mounds, outlined by morainic boulders and covering single burials sometimes with wooden structures, are direct copies in earth and stone of contemporary timber houses (Midgley 1985). The significance of these tombs is that they seem to have provided a model of monumentality which answered the needs of pioneer farming groups, establishing themselves in new territories and drawing in native populations, over a large part of northern Europe. What is noteworthy about this pattern was the way it served both to incorporate native populations and to maintain cultural links with the loesslands to the south.

The distribution of these forms of long funerary monuments in northern Europe forms an interesting pattern: they occur predominantly in the zone of glacial outwash sands, running across the North European Plain north of the loess but south of the young-moraine and coastal belt with its continuing concentrations of Mesolithic settlement (Midgley 1985; Figure 13.5). The latter areas were to become the heartlands of Nordic megalith-building, in the period after 3700 BC; but this later development can only be understood in relation to an earlier spread of long, unchambered forms. Unchambered long-mounds, often in groups, form the principal type of Neolithic monu-ment in Kujavia, Pomerania and central Meckenburg, where the very large numbers of such mounds, and the absence of later forms of megalithic tombs, suggest that they remained the predominant form of monument down to the later fourth millennium BC. Similar structures, the so-called *kammerlose Hünenbetten*, are found further west, along the lower Elbe, in the Altmark and the Sachsenwald (Sprockhoff 1938). Northwards again, they occur in central and northern Jutland, where the best excavated

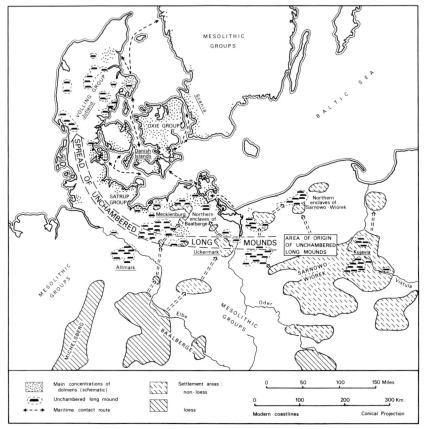

13.5 Northern Europe, 4000–3500 BC, showing interaction between central European (Michelsberg, Baalberge, Sarnowo-Wiórek) groups and indigenous populations in the North European Plain, with early monuments. Data from Preuß, Sprockhoff, Schuldt, Kozłowski, Midgley, Madsen, Aner. [Long-mounds are shown as originating in central Poland before spreading westwards because of the unique survival of the long-house model there into the period of long-mound genesis; note also the common drinking-set: Figs 16.4, 16.5.]

examples are to be found, dated to c.3800 BC (Madsen 1979). These north German and Danish monuments again seem to fit themselves into the interstices of existing distributions, and should perhaps be seen as a series of small-scale migrations, travelling from east to west, and absorbing local populations into the new pattern at each stage; but maintaining their exchange networks with the south.

This pattern is evident in western Denmark, where the first unchambered long-mounds occur in Jutland – an inland area less densely settled by Mesolithic populations – in association with pottery of the Volling group (Madsen 1986). A particularly noteworthy feature is the occurrence in Jutland of perforated copper discs, imported via Poland from Copper Age groups in the Carpathian Basin. The import of copper axes is also reflected in the design of thin-butted flint axes, whose flat sides show the influence of copper forms. Such a small-scale intrusion of southerners, building monuments of earth and timber as well as introducing various exotic items, would help to explain the burst of megalith-building which took place in the following few centuries, principally in eastern Denmark and Mecklenburg. The first Neolithic groups in this area were associated with a somewhat different set of flintwork and pottery types: point-butted axes (unaffected by copper models), flake-axes of Ertebølle ancestry, and pottery of the Oxie or A-group that links the Danish Islands both to Mecklenburg and Scania. These features demonstrate a considerable degree of continuity from Ertebølle and related Mesolithic groups. While ecological changes may have played some part in destabilising native coastal populations (Rowley-Conwy 1984), the major impetus for change seems to have been the arrival of a foreign cultural model in adjacent parts of north Germany and Jutland.

The megalithic forms characteristic of areas with a strong Mesolithic background are the *dolmens* (Danish: *dysser*), i.e. closed megalithic chambers made from glacial erratic blocks, set either in round or in long (usually rectangular) mounds. Although the dolmen chambers have no passages, and are thus not accessible from outside, they do nevertheless show some resemblance to the size and shape of the small huts in contemporary use. The long chambered mounds (*langdysser*) occur both on the east Danish islands and in Jutland, around and including the area where unchambered forms first appeared; the round mounds (*runddysser*) are largely confined to eastern Denmark, which has the greatest density of dolmens (Bekmose 1978). The megalithic chamber is thus principally associated with areas outside the initial long-mound area; but the two ideas were rapidly combined (at Bygholm Nørremark in central Jutland, for instance, a trapezoid mound, overlying wooden buildings and graves and outlined by a post-bedding trench, was subsequently covered by a rectangular long-mound with a peristalith and megalithic chamber, showing the local replacement of an early timber form by a chambered, megalithic version: Madsen 1979).

As in France, therefore, there seems to be a spatial polarity between the intrusive monumentalised longhouse and the development of alternative megalithic forms in areas where substantial populations already existed. The initial stimulus thus gave rise to complex reaction and interaction, producing a range of monuments with overlapping characteristics, but with a continuing set of cultural differences. This polarity is also reflected in other ways, for instance between the rich grave goods which accompanied burials in Jutland, and the votive deposits of similar materials (amber, stone axes) which occur in the Islands. (These contrasts were to re-emerge in later phases of prehistory, for instance with the spread of Corded Ware.) The continuing external connections between the intrusive long-mound groups and central Europe would have been responsible for introducing new features such as the collared flask (already known in Poland: Knøll 1981) and other features which came to characterise the Early Neolithic C phase in Denmark (see Chapters 15 and 16).

It is even more difficult in these circumstances to distinguish clearly between 'natives' and 'newcomers', since the whole process is characterised by the gradual breakdown of this distinction, through intermarriage and incorporation. Nevertheless, it is possible to perceive different mechanisms by which farming was spread northwards: small-scale colonisation from the loesslands, shifts of marginal groups into areas of intervening opportunity, *in situ* acculturation of indigenous populations, together with isolated pockets of resistance, where hunting groups seem to have continued to exist alongside farmers. These form a complex mosaic, sometimes maintaining a degree of cultural discreteness, but at the same time participating in exchange networks that in some cases extended far back into central Europe.

ALTERNATIVE IDEOLOGIES AND THE RHETORIC OF TOMBS

In discussing the French evidence, it was suggested that the contrasting designs of long mounds and passage graves, tentatively attributed to a background in incoming and native groups respectively, might have some deeper ideological significance. This view receives some support from the subsequent history of megaliths in this area during the Middle Neolithic period of the French sequence (4300–3500 BC), though the exciting possibilities arising from current French excavations can only be briefly alluded to here.

In this period, the morphological variety of early passage-graves had settled down into regional varieties of a basic model with a single passage and square, internally divided chamber or transepts, set either in a round mound or axially in a long one (L'Helgouach and Le Roux 1986). But there is now evidence that in parts of the Morbihan, and probably also the Charente maritime, long-mounds with cists or inaccessible chambers were still being built at this time. (Long-mounds may also have been constructed in the Paris Basin at this period, as indicated by the recent excavation of a Middle Neolithic trapezoidal mound covering a stone cist at Maisse, Essonne.) The long-mounds of the Carnac region – which include both 'normal'-sized mounds and the gigantic examples known as Carnac mounds – are associated with a style of pottery (Castellic ware), and also items such as stone rings, which have a background in the Paris Basin and the central European tradition, as opposed to the plainwares of the Atlantic group which demonstrate growing links to the Chasséen culture of southern France (Giot, L'Helgouach and Monnier 1979, 218–25). The contrast between long-mounds and passage-graves extends to a different attitude to burial and the role of the dead, which in the case of long-mounds is associated with closed cists and external indicators in the form of decorated menhirs, and in the case of passage-graves is associated with accessible chambers which are decorated on the inside; and the contrast extends even to a consistent difference in orientation, which is to the east in the case of the former and south-east in the latter.

The co-existence of these two patterns, with their respective links to wider cultural entities generated by the early spread of farming, suggests the possibility of competition and tension between them in these parts of western France. The hypertrophied growth of long-barrows into Carnac mounds (of which there are over a dozen in the Carnac-Locmariaquer area) is perhaps best seen in the context of an ideological struggle between these two competing patterns, in which elements of central European origin were consciously stressed and elaborated in opposition to those of native origin. It is all the more interesting, therefore, that recent work by L'Helgouach and Le Roux has demonstrated that at some time around 3800 BC a massive phase of iconoclasm occurred in the area around Locmariaquer, which involved the pulling down of major sculptured standing stones, and their incorporation (usually as capstones) in a new generation of large passage-graves with large, undivided, rectangular chambers in round-mounds: and that in at least four cases these were directly adjacent to (and presumably intended to replace) Carnac mounds (Le Roux 1985). The largest of these later Middle Neolithic passage-graves is Gavrinis, with its profusion of intricately carved ornament and sensitive astronomical alignments. This revolutionary shift of ideological dominance seems to have coincided with a new wave of southern, Chasséen, influence (both in western France and the Paris Basin), associated with the arrival of elements such as *vase supports*. (It is tempting to interpret these as items of cult apparatus, such as narcotic burners, which have often accompanied revivalist religious movements in more recent ethnography – an interpretation which would also explain the remarkable character of the Gavrinis engravings as entoptic images produced under the influence of drugs: Bradley 1989 and Chapters 15 and 16.) Whatever interpretation is preferred, it is clear that these monuments must be considered in the context of potentially conflicting religious beliefs and practices; and that the most elaborate examples must be seen not as the culmination of a single evolutionary series, but as increasingly emphatic dialectical contributions to a megalithic debate.

COMPARISONS

Whereas farming had spread across the loess without substantial opposition from native groups, its appearance in the north and west required an accommodation to already established ways of life in a different set of environments. The greater degree of settlement mobility required in these circumstances, and the smaller groups needed for a greater diversity of tasks, made substantial timber villages inappropriate. The first steps were apparently taken by peripheral loessland communities, 'going native' in many aspects of their everyday life as they moved into the new territories. But colonising groups, needing to recruit a labour force – or native groups, wishing to compete with them – required a focus for this process; and for the major ceremonies associated with the remembrance of ancestors they chose monumental versions of timber longhouses still in use in the heartlands of Neolithic settlement. Where these models were available close by, as in Normandy, the long burial mounds were present from the beginning. In northern Europe, monumentalised forms seem to have spread from the edges of the eastern loesslands after a first generation of farmers had already moved north. In somewhat different circumstances, the same solution prevailed. In both areas, moreover, this move provoked a reaction: partly an imitation, partly something distinctively different; but monumental and megalithic.

A similar interpretation could be applied to Britain. The western end of the loess corridor reaches the Channel at Boulogne, and the nearby long-mound at Wimereux is only forty miles away from an English example such as Ashford in Kent. Unchambered earthen long-mounds occupy the chalk Downs of Wessex; circular mounds with cist-burials underlie several trapezoid Cotswold chamber-tombs, which fuse the characteristics of both. Trapezoid chambered long-mounds were introduced to Ireland; round passage-graves were the reaction. The actors changed, but momentum was conserved.

These three areas of megalithic proliferation – western France, Britain, and northern Europe – seem to have acted out such scenarios independently, from different starting points on the loess periphery. They began to do so, moreover, at different times: France during the Neolithic, northern Europe during what in central Europe was already the Copper Age. The complexity of northern Europe is partly due to the long-distance links with central Europe which were present from the very beginning; the ideological conflicts of the west were partly due to the continuing strength of native tradition and the absence of this homogenising influence. Even so, however, we begin to discern different patterns of reaction and external alliance in each of these areas, rather than a static typology of 'cultures'; and such regional differences of origin persisted, to emerge again at subsequent points in prehistory. Behind the general regularities of European development lay the roots of later nationalisms. Is it inappropriate in these circumstances to speak of ethnicity?

EPILOGUE

Megaliths are perhaps the most durable structures ever erected by prehistoric societies, and they have survived down to recent times in vast numbers: perhaps 10,000 in the North European Plain and Scandinavia, more than 500 in a single French *département*. They have dominated the European archaeological imagination since the sixteenth century. Recent excavation work in central Europe, however, has done something to redress the balance of differential survival. From the less impressive evidence of postholes, the older farming societies of the loesslands have been shown to have had their own forms of monumentality – megaxyles rather than megaliths – which were as fundamental to the organisation of agrarian society on the loesslands as megaliths were in the wilder landscapes of outer Europe. Basic to this interpretation is the idea that houses are not just 'machines for living in', as architects once misguidedly asserted, but parts of the social system itself. Neolithic villages provided not only shelter, but the means of creating and perpetuating social relationships. Tombs, similarly, were not just machines for the disposal of the dead, but could on occasion assume some of the sorts of roles otherwise played by domestic constructions

The building of long mortuary mounds was both a continuation of earlier symbols of community and a monumental focus around which new groups were established. The idiom of monumentality was apparently then adopted by a wider range of indigenous groups as the basis for their own assimilation of cereal cultivation and the construction of an appropriate cultural and social framework for a farming existence – sometimes in conscious opposition to intrusive communities. These monuments were subsequently elaborated and transformed in western and northern Europe throughout the Neolithic, responding both to changing demographic and social circumstances, and to the possibilities of further interpretation established by their own material existence. Megalith building became the metaphor within which social conflicts and ideological competition were played out. In this sense, megaliths were as much a cause as a consequence of social complexity.

14

Instruments of Conversion?
The Role of Megaliths in the
Mesolithic–Neolithic Transition
in North-West Europe

(1995)

Megalithic monuments were one of the first prehistoric phenomena to be recognised by archaeologists, and their durability ensured that they became objects of antiquarian curiosity even before the emergence of a scientific study of prehistory. By the later nineteenth century they had been recognised in many parts of Europe, and even beyond. Unlike more specific categories of artefact, however, it soon became apparent that they were not diagnostic of a single period or culture. Like other types of prehistoric site, such as 'earthworks' or 'hillforts', they represent a category of construction which came into existence at different times and for different purposes. Like 'hillforts', however, they are nevertheless typical of certain areas and phases of prehistory, and demand an interpretation which is both general and specific: general, in terms of their common social and technological characteristics, and specific, in terms of the concrete historical circumstances which gave rise to them. In their more general properties, European megaliths may usefully be compared with similar constructions from other periods and times; but in their specific characteristics they must be set in a context that includes the whole range of prehistoric domestic, mortuary and ceremonial constructions, both in stone, earth and timber.

Although the use of large blocks as constructional elements may in certain circumstances have an ergonomic rationale (depending on the nature of the rock employed), the use of massive, relatively unaltered stones is more

---

This chapter presents excerpts from a paper originally given in Mannheim in 1992, at a conference on Vergleichende Studien zur Megalithik: Forschungsstand und ethnoarchäologische Perspektiven. *It takes the arguments of the preceding chapter one step further, in reviving (though in a very different way) Childe's conception of megaliths as rhetorical devices – arguments in stone – concerned with the propagation of a set of interests and incorporation of people within an ideological and organisational framework. While treating the emergence of megalithism as a process, it combines function with intention and genealogy.*

typical of pre-urban societies than urban ones. Among urban societies, the constructional components are adapted to the design of the building, whose plan exists independently in an abstract conception of (usually straight) lines and spaces. Where massive blocks are employed in such a context (as with Mycenaean 'cyclopean' walling or Inka fitted-block construction), they are usually replicated elements modified to fit together, or else carefully shaped obelisks or colossi. The use of largely unaltered blocks, where the shape of the blocks themselves in part determines the nature of the construction, is more typical of pre-urban societies – whose architecture (like other aspects of their culture – chipped stone rather than moulded metal, for instance) is literally less 'artificial'. Hence the major effort is devoted to transporting the blocks rather than to altering their shape, and the resulting constructions grow more organically from the nature of the raw material. They thus employ 'natural metaphors' of size, permanence, etc. (perhaps in conscious opposition to secular buildings of earth and timber); and they also embody the symbolism of undifferentiated communal effort involved in hauling the huge blocks. The monuments themselves are thus often emblematic of the unity of the group, and possess a special, sacred character that is inherent in the nature of their construction. The term 'monument' (from Latin *monere*, 'remind', 'warn') is specifically appropriate where a particular form of building is not employed for domestic purposes, but is used to impress an ideal on those who see and use it. It is typical of megalithic architecture that its use is confined to such a single class of constructions, and not used more generally as a technology for building everyday structures. The point is aptly made by comic-strip cartoons of Stone Age life (whether in the context of dinosaurs or Gaulish tribes) where a typical Stone Age family is shown living in a dolmen-like dwelling – the reverse of archaeological reality.

In many instances, therefore, the context in which megalithic construction is employed is that of burial. It is misleading, however, to describe such structures simply as 'funerary monuments', since they are not just vehicles for disposing of dead bodies, and many contemporary societies (such as those of Neolithic south-east and central Europe) made no use of above-ground containers for corpses.[1] Nor are they 'monuments' in the sense of memorials to specific individuals. Rather, it is the dead themselves who are employed as a metaphor in the same way as the architecture. The co-incidence with burial is a tactical one, and megalithic architecture may be employed in ceremonial contexts beyond the funerary, while human bones may be deposited or used in other places than the megalithic 'graves'. The association comes through a common identification of death and megalithic architecture with the realm of the 'other', perhaps a world in which the community of the ancestors retains a powerful existence, to which access may be gained by appropriate ritual action at particular times in the context of the monuments. (The incorporation of astronomical alignments may suggest that such ceremonies had a regular calendrical occurrence, calculated by phases of the heavenly bodies.) It is a not uncommon ethnographic observation that such ceremonies may employ mind-altering drugs which are consumed by certain individuals in the context of such ceremonies, and whose effects are interpreted in terms of communication with this 'other world' (Reichel-Dolmatoff 1975; Chapter 16).

Such comments would apply fairly generally to the class of constructions which are termed 'megalithic', in many parts of the world. This chapter is concerned, however, with the specific appearance and development of megalithism in Neolithic north-west Europe; and its purpose is to suggest a set of circumstances in which such phenomena may have made their appearance. Megalithism in Neolithic Europe is typical of certain areas, especially the West and North, and also has certain manifestations in the Mediterranean. It is not a universal feature of Neolithic societies, although it seems to have been a latent property which could be called into existence in certain circumstances. In the most general terms, it was associated with a permanent occupation of the soil which was typical of (though not necessarily restricted to) the practice of farming; in this sense, the megalithic monuments have some functional equivalence to the 'monumentality' of domestic settlements in south-east Europe and the Near East, where Neolithic occupation is often marked by the partly deliberate accumulation of a *tell* or settlement-mound: a visible symbol of the existence of the farming community. Such symbolism of the permanent occupation of a particular spot is not restricted to farmers, for the (surely deliberate) accumulation of shell-mounds by sedentary fishers and foragers such as the Ertebølle communities of the western Baltic or late Mesolithic groups in Portugal may be considered as part of a similar phenomenon. The particular forms of many European megaliths – in widely separated areas – has a more specific set of references, however, in that certain classes of monument echo the constructional characteristics of houses (either dwelling-houses, or, perhaps more likely, club-houses). This is particularly explicit in forms such as the *allées couvertes* of northern France, or the dolmens of the western Caucasus, and relates not just to the natural idiom of building sheltered spaces but to the organisational and ideological importance of the house and household among the acephalous farming communities of the Neolithic, who in other circumstances expressed the same values in female figurines and clay models of hearths and homes. A final feature which distinguishes these groups is the emphasis on the communal. While later burial monuments such as Bronze and Iron Age tumulus burials were sometimes equipped as 'houses of the dead', buried below ground for prominent deceased individuals (for instance Ukrainian Timber-Graves or the Hallstatt *Fürstengräber*), Neolithic burial monuments in northern and western Europe were typically structures for collective burial. Indeed, they increasingly stressed this communal and continuing, corporate character through their provision of ossuaries in prominent and accessible structures above ground, in which human remains were regularly deposited (often rearranged in categories that cross-cut those of the individual skeleton), and at which regular offerings were made to the dead.

The distinctive character of Neolithic megalithism in Europe is thus its highly visible symbolism of the living community, through the medium of monumental constructions for the dead. Truly 'megalithic' monuments formed part of a spectrum of such constructions, which otherwise used earth, timber and smaller stones; and the beginnings of monumentalism must be sought in the transformation of the repertoire of domestic and funerary structures in other materials. The first element of this transformation was the monumentalisation of forms already used for other purposes, in which domestic metaphors were applied to the creation of more permanent representations of such structures, themselves useless as domestic dwellings, which were intended to stand for many generations – many times the expected lifespan of the average peasant house (which in effect was probably a single generation). The second element was the use of large stones to produce an enclosed, three-dimensional space to which continuing access was possible for the purposes of ritual and ceremony. In some of the areas in which such megalithic chambers were constructed (and especially in the far west, in areas such as Brittany and the British Isles), a further phase of megalithic construction saw the building of open monuments (like the Breton alignments, or British henges and stone circles) which provided ritual spaces that were enclosed but not roofed, and in which the 'ceremonial' aspect was more prominent than the funerary. This whole process occupied a period of more than two millennia.

Megalithism, therefore, was a set of monumentalised messages. Neolithic communities in certain parts of Europe apparently felt the need to build permanent statements about the nature of their society. Some of these (like the larger passage-graves) were on a scale which suggests that their messages were intended to be read very widely within their region: veritable beacons in stone. Whatever its original motivation, megalith building came to embody messages which were directed to more than the local group. The question which I would like to raise is therefore: to whom were those messages addressed?

Symbols of community

A characteristic of the first farming societies, as Ian Hodder has emphasised (1984; 1990), is their investment in domestic structures. These went far beyond the mere requirements of shelter, and can be seen both as ideological statements and media of social organisation and control, owing their prominence to the role which they played as part of the cultural infrastructure of a horticultural society without specialised social institutions and mechanisms for maintaining unity and order. The house as an architectural and social unit was one part of a larger entity, the settlement, which provided the face-to-face community and the permanent, ongoing unit of organisation. The first farming settlements in the Near East – like Jericho, Tell Abu Hureyra or Çatalhöyük – were often spectacularly vast, and this concentration of population and facilities was a necessary phase in the emergence of Old World farming as a way of life. Having achieved a viable model, these settlements were then replicated or modularised on a smaller scale, in the form of the *tell* settlement as it spread into Balkan Europe in the sixth millennium BC. That such tells were not simply dwelling units, but embodied organisational and even cosmological principles, is shown by the careful order and astronomical orientation with which some of them were originally laid out (e.g. Polyanitsa, Bulgaria). The physical representation of community, on the ground (in the form of a prominent settlement and constituent houses), was a fundamental feature of Neolithic social organisation. This 'package' of farming practices, domestic technologies (pottery, weaving) and social infrastructure was introduced to Europe as the basis of the first agricultural communities.

Where farming was introduced by population expansion (the 'demographic wave of advance'), as it was in south-east and central Europe, this package maintained its coherence. Even where some accommodation was necessary to ecological circumstances, and a degree of pioneer simplification occurred (for instance in central Europe, with the relatively dispersed settlement patterns of Körös and LBK), nevertheless the tendency to nucleation reasserted itself, and the later phases of the Neolithic in those areas (Tisza and Roessen) once more show aggregated forms of settlement (Sherratt 1982; Starling 1985). The houses remained large, rectilinear structures throughout; and where large villages were not present, there was nevertheless some effort to construct impressive ceremonial facilities, such as *Kreisgrabenanlagen*, near to the domestic structures (Burgess et al. 1988). These permanent marks on the ground were characteristic of the primary horticultural community which formed the basis of Neolithic social organisation.[2]

The first phase of European farming, therefore, down to c.4500 BC, was characterised by a congruence between the social community and the physical setting of everyday life. This was possible because of the primarily horticultural emphasis of early farming, in which livestock played a subordinate role. As economies began to differentiate (both in time and space), however, and livestock rearing and hunting came to play a larger part in the economy, potential tensions and contradictions developed between the village and its domestic structures as the basis of social organisation and the need for greater flexibility in settlement patterns. In the early-settled loess areas of central Europe, this was primarily because of the needs of the expanding cattle-keeping sector of the economy; on the fringes of the loess-lands, in western France and on the North European Plain, the opportunities for hunting and foraging (in environments already exploited in this way by indigenous Mesolithic groups) offered a comparable alternative. Over much of the continent in the later fifth millennium, therefore, a diversity of new forms of settlement made their appearance. Because the social relations formerly embodied in the physical form of the village settlement still remained important, however, some symbolic continuation of this focal point remained necessary when the individual households split away from their former collectivity. The new forms of settlement pattern thus typically included an emphasis on tombs and cemeteries, making explicit the relations formerly expressed in proximity of residence. Rituals, including burial, which had formerly taken place within the context of the settlement (either close to the houses themselves or in nearby small cemeteries), now came to be associated with special locations that were not necessarily places of habitation. These provided symbols of a community which no longer had a permanent physical existence on the ground.

WHY MONUMENTS?

The application of this model to the beginnings of European megalithism has been set out in the preceding chapter, which emphasised the essential complementarity between substantial house construction and the building of monumental tombs in the archaeological record of Neolithic Europe. The first farming groups in central Europe, the LBK and succeeding Roessen and Lengyel groups, occupied substantial, timber-built villages – a temperate European adaptation of the pattern of *tell* settlement in the Near East. Their architectural investment was in domestic structures. Major monuments were generated when this complex of village-farming reached the outer edges of Europe, and was adapted and changed to the different circumstances of the Atlantic and the North European Plain. It was in this outer arc – in Iberia, western France, Britain and Scandinavia – that the first centres of megalithism were established. The stages by which this was accomplished are defined below, but in general the process could be defined as a splitting-up of the ideal pattern of domestic co-residence, the physical community which had been the basis of early Neolithic social organisation from Jericho to the Paris Basin, in the different conditions of outer Europe, where cereal farming was perhaps less important and settlement patterns more mobile; and what was absent from the early Neolithic of these areas were precisely the large, timber, domestic structures. The underlying reason for the appearance of megaliths, then, was the transformation of the primary horticultural community, as it had been constructed in the Near East at the beginning of farming. Non-domestic structures, and especially funerary ones, supplied the focal symbolism formerly provided by domestic architecture.

The formative phases of this process are now becoming clearer. The predecessors of the truly megalithic structures which survive so well in the archaeological record were the equally monumental but less robust (and archaeologically less visible) structures of earth and timber, which were built by a variety of groups of ultimately *Bandkeramik* origin on the margins of their main loessland distribution, and in some cases within it.[3] Timber mortuary houses were monumentalised by the addition of a long earthen mound, typically trapezoidal in shape. Where appropriate, as in the North European Plain, these mounds were edged with large stones, to increase the impressiveness and permanence of the structure; and in western France the timber internal structures might be replaced by small stone cists. Such early earthen or stone-edged long-barrows did not cover communal burials, and the graves were not accessible after the erection of the mound. Structures of this kind, which occurred independently in western France, southern Britain and Kujavia at different times between 4500 and 4000 BC, are particularly associated with a rapid dispersal of small groups beyond the loessland frontiers. These groups did not replicate the domestic longhouse architecture of the farming villages in which they originated, but echoed the shape and significance of houses in the plan and appearance of the tombs. They might be considered as part of a small-scale colonisation movement, which carried farming groups from the margins of the loesslands as far as Brittany, western Britain and Denmark; but there is also some evidence of a cultural contribution from (and hence probably interbreeding with) the indigenous populations of those areas.

It is this context of a breakup of the primary horticultural communities of the loesslands which explains the significance of monument building. From a more general perspective, these earthen long-barrows are simply one aspect of the greater emphasis on burial and funerary elaboration which took place in several parts of Europe in the later fourth and early third millennia BC. It was precisely at this time in Hungary and Bulgaria, for instance, that large formal cemeteries with rich grave-goods, like Tiszapolgár or the more famous example of Varna, made their appearance. These, too, were associated with the breakup of primary horticultural communities in the form of large villages.[4] But such funerary elaboration in central and eastern Europe did not take the form of monumentality. Elaborate burials, yes; but not funerary *monuments*. What was absent was the *architectural* aspect: these groups in the older Neolithic heartlands did not transfer the domestic metaphor to their tombs. The specific feature of prehistoric megalithism in western and northern Europe which requires explanation, therefore, is precisely its monumentality – its architectural character. This in turn raises the question: to whom were its messages addressed? In the case of Varna and Tiszapolgár, we can say that the messages of the burial – whatever they might have been – were primarily addressed to those at the graveside: members of the immediate social group assembled for the burial. In this they resemble many later funerary practices in prehistoric Europe. Megalithic monuments, however, have the added dimension of durable visibility. Whom were they meant to impress, and to whom was their rhetoric directed? Was it simply the womenfolk and junior members of their own lineages, as neo-Marxists have claimed (Tilley 1984)? Was it their contemporaries and farming neighbours, as Lord Renfrew's territorial model would imply (Renfrew 1976)? Or was it a wider circle of spectators?

The critical difference between eastern and western Europe at this time was the existence of indigenous, Mesolithic populations. It is generally agreed that the expansion of *Bandkeramik* cultures across the loesslands is best regarded as a spread of population – a slow 'migration' (in the sense of a demographic expansion in space through the proliferation of new settlements on the edge of an existing distribution). By contrast, the spread of farming to outer Europe was more a process of adoption, by which indigenous groups absorbed farming technologies from their neighbours. David Clarke likened the preceding demographic pattern of Mesolithic Europe to a huge doughnut – a ring doughnut, dense on the edge but empty in the middle (Clarke 1976, 462–8). The first phase of farming spread filled in the centre; the second phase converted the edge. It was in the second phase that farming appeared in rich Mesolithic environments on coasts and lakelands, like morainic northern Europe or morainic Switzerland – the heartlands of hunting, fishing and foraging communities. In the Alpine foreland, this involved replicating the village communities of the loess, in the form of the rectangular timber houses of Egolzwil and Cortaillod, on the reedswamps around the lakes. In western Europe, with its more extensive Mesolithic populations sustained by seafood, it involved the emergence of monumentality. Why?

INSTRUMENTS OF CONVERSION?

The clue comes in the word *conversion*. Mesolithic societies were *converted* into Neolithic ones. We can use this word in two senses – in a general way, to describe an economic change from foraging to farming; or in a religious context, to describe a change in belief from Christianity to Islam, for instance. Prehistoric archaeologists usually use it in the first sense. I want to explore the second one, and to suggest that the messages of megaliths were at least in part directed *outwards*, to Mesolithic communities, when farming groups began to settle in landscapes that were already occupied. The idea which I want to pursue is an old one: it was an essential part of the model of diffusion, as presented for instance by Gordon Childe. Megalithic monuments, in this view, were part of a religion, propagated by megalithic missionaries. Agriculture had already reached western Europe, when groups of ideologically committed Egyptians (rather like those tiresome American evangelists) set out in boats to convert the Neolithic pagans of Portugal, Brittany and Ireland. This interpretation is now clearly unworkable in the way that Childe envisaged it (which to a large extent derives from his knowledge of the Phoenicians); but it does contain one element of possible truth which has been lost sight of in later models. That is this element of *conversion*. This term seems to capture something of the monumental rhetoric of megalithism.

One assumption of Childe's model that is no longer appropriate is his perception of the spread of farming and the spread of monumentality as two different processes.[5] Whilst megaliths in the strict sense of large-stone constructions are indeed a somewhat later feature, it has been demonstrated that in western France, the British Isles and northern Europe, monumental earth-and-timber structures (non-megalithic long-mounds) lay right at the beginning of Neolithic sequences. Monumentality was thus a fundamental aspect of the spread of farming practices into outer Europe. It was not some optional luxury, grafted on to the primary process: it was part of the process itself (Thomas 1988). Why were such efforts necessary? There are many instances in European and World prehistory of the adoption of farming by native populations. The Cardial/Impressed Ware groups of the Mediterranean, for instance, or the Pit-and-Comb Ware groups of eastern Europe; on a wider scene, the makers of Wavy-line Ware in north Africa or Woodland groups in north America. In these cases, however, the process of adopting farming was often slow and partial; many of these groups are best described as sub-Neolithic, since they adopted pottery (for their own purposes) and livestock, but often without cereal cultivation as a major element, and without major changes in settlement patterns or probably in social organisation either. The early Neolithic in western and northern Europe, on the other hand, seems to be rather different from these: it was a 'full' Neolithic, with the whole range of characteristics taken over in a single stage. Mesolithic communities in north-west Europe not only acquired crops and livestock from their Neolithic neighbours, but they also 'adopted' new forms of social organisation, and indeed new forms of architectural construction, as well as new technologies of potting and perhaps textile-making. The appearance of funerary architecture seems to be a specific feature of this process. Did it therefore involve an active propagation of organisation and ideas – a 'conversion' process in Gordon Childe's sense, as well as just a conversion from foraging to farming? Was it, in a way, more like the process of Hellenisation or Romanisation, in which an impressive architecture was used as a kind of propaganda?

It may be useful to think about the problem in this way. The most important 'commodity' in Neolithic societies was labour. Land was not in short supply; and the most essential items of external trade were the flint and hard stone supplies which were needed to make labour more effective. Recruitment of a labour force was the key to success. In spreading across the loesslands, *Bandkeramik* groups were fuelled by internal demographic growth. Culturally, there seems to have been very little intermixture with indigenous groups. The cultural network and the mating network were largely congruent. At the western end of the loesslands, however, this strategy began to change. In the Paris Basin, in particular, the formation of 'epi-Bandkeramik' groups was characterised by the addition of cultural elements from an existing repertoire, and with Cerny the difficulties of classification highlight a dual relationship with the Bandkeramik tradition, and with other, local groups of native or southern origin (Scarre 1992). It looks as if the earlier exclusiveness of mating networks was breaking down. The central European farming pattern was being propagated westwards, not just by internal demographic growth, but by external recruitment and incorporation. In short, it was the beginning of a process of conversion – the 'reformatting' (to use a computing metaphor) of an existing demographic pool. This process was therefore an active, social one, involving a set of changes in relationships, rather than just the passive adoption of a set of new practices. This incorporation was itself an active process, involving persuasion, propaganda, and competition for recruits. A successful strategy would be immediately rewarded by rapid growth. But how was such a strategy discovered?

FROM EARTH-AND-TIMBER MONUMENTS TO MEGALITHS

The solution that I would like to suggest is one that arises from the morphology of the monuments themselves. The two classes into which the early monuments fall – unchambered long-mounds, and truly megalithic structures with chambers (often in conical mounds) – represent different strategies on the part of their builders. The former were simply surrogates for houses, and were constructed – as the foci of residentially more dispersed communities – by descendants of the Neolithic villagers who had colonised the loesslands. Once created, however, the idiom of monumentality had a potential for employment in other ways. The latter types of monument, the chambered megaliths, were a further development of monumentalism through a strategy of incorporation, and reflect the distribution of older, native populations. This explains the distributional contrast between the two forms of monument. The earliest monumental structures, in the form of long-mounds covering timber mortuary structures, seem to be typical of the areas just within the loessland centres of epi-Bandkeramik, Lengyel and Roessen villages, or in between (or just inside) these areas on the one hand, and the coastal concentrations of Mesolithic population on the other. This is the case in the apparently independent episodes of long-mound creation in western and northern France, and in northern Poland (Figures 13.2 and 13.5). It was in old coastal heartlands of Mesolithic population, however, that megalithism – in the strict sense of stone-built monuments – reached its greatest development. The first type of monument, the 'unchambered' long-mounds, seem to be characteristic of a rapid movement into areas where

Mesolithic groups were less dense, and perhaps less highly organised in a social sense; the second type of monument, the megalithic chambered tombs, seem to be typical of the phase in which farming moved into the optimal ecological zones of Mesolithic settlement, with dense populations and probably more highly organised social networks – perhaps even an existing lineage structure.

The second phase of this process thus involved the evolution of a truly megalithic architecture, instead of the earth-covered timber or small stone structures which had characterised the first generation of monuments. This process of lithicisation seems to have occurred independently in the coastal regions of western France, western Britain, and also of Scandinavia and northern Germany – resulting respectively in the appearance of French passage-graves, British portal-dolmens and chambered cairns, and Nordic *dysser*. It can therefore be seen as symptomatic of a general development in the role of the monuments. The most striking feature was the employment of large stone slabs as constructional elements for internal as well as external features. This change in building technique from timber to stone was functionally linked to an equally fundamental architectural change: from unchambered to chambered structures, and often from long mounds to round ones. The earlier mounds usually covered small cists for individual burials; the later megalithic structures emphasised an accessible chamber for the continuous addition of burials.[6] The emphasis moved from exterior symbols (like those on the decorated menhirs which accompanied long barrows in Brittany) to interior symbols such as the various kinds of passage-grave art, visible to those admitted to ceremonies inside the structures. From being simply a monumentalised burial, the use of stone allowed the creation of an enclosed ritual space. What took place within these spaces may also be relevant to the process of recruitment, for if recent suggestions of the ritual employment of hallucinogens are correct, this may have been a powerful inducement to belief in the cosmology represented by the tombs.

It is particularly noteworthy that the areas where megalithic construction (*sensu stricto*) developed and most rapidly proliferated from its antecedent long mounds were areas of relatively dense Mesolithic population – in Brittany, western Britain and Zealand (as also in Portugal). The two facts seem to be connected. Various different scenarios could be envisaged: the building of new forms of stone monuments could be seen as an indigenous imitation of the new forms of monumentality as native groups adopted farming,[7] or as an adaptation by colonising groups to new circumstances where native populations existed in greater numbers. In the first case, the change indicates a shift of initiative from immigrant groups to indigenous communities, imitating the monumentality but changing its ideology. In the second case, there was a single, continuous process, but with a greater emphasis on the incorporation of native populations. The two scenarios are not necessarily exclusive, in that both processes could operate simultaneously, perhaps with a different balance in different areas; and neither are they necessarily distinguishable archaeologically. In both cases, however, the process involved the propagation of a new form of social structure – the kinds of trans-generational (lineage) groups necessary for the organisation of work in a farming economy.

If this model is correct, it suggests that the incorporation of native populations was a *continuing* process. If so, then the proliferation and growing elaboration of megalithic monuments is itself an index of the scale of the process. Bursts of monument-building would thus correspond to phases of demographic intake. Monuments such as Gavrinis or Newgrange would mark the local climaxes of this process, where the reservoirs of native population still provided scope for growth through incorporation. The complexity of these outstanding megalithic structures could thus reflect a sort of social stratification, between original, founding members of the group, and lineages which had joined more recently. The great conical mounds would symbolise in a physical way the conical clan structures that resulted.[8] Social ranking could build up much more rapidly in these circumstances than on the loesslands; and in this sense the megalithic communities of the far west may indeed have been more 'complex' than their contemporaries in central Europe.

MESOLITHIC SURVIVAL

One implication of this idea is that Mesolithic populations survived alongside the first farming groups in outer Europe for very much longer than is often supposed. It suggests that there was not an instantaneous, mass conversion of native groups, but rather a continuous and long-drawn-out propaganda campaign. This suggestion in not inherently implausible. Earlier Neolithic groups in western and northern Europe occupied only relatively small areas of the total landmass. There is no ecological reason why Mesolithic groups should not have survived in the areas between: and there are several indications that they did, even though such populations are inherently less visible archaeologically and harder to date. An interesting further implication is therefore to revive the possibility of another old idea, that of a 'primary' and a 'secondary' Neolithic (Piggott 1954; Briard and L'Helgouach 1957). This idea was abandoned when it became clear that 'secondary' features were largely later than 'primary' ones; but there is no inherent contradiction here, if the process of Mesolithic incorporation is seen as a continuing and accelerating one, rather than an instantaneous conversion. Especially after 3500 BC, when we can envisage some use of the light plough and a spatial expansion of agricultural activity, we might expect a further intake of surviving indigenous groups with a Mesolithic way of life which had survived on poorer soils beyond the earlier frontiers of farming.

One index of the absorption of indigenous populations is the appearance

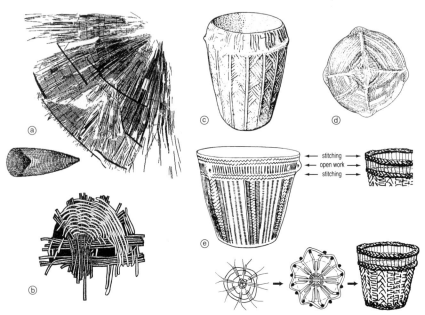

14.1 *Skeuomorphic echoes: the shape and decoration of later Neolithic pottery from NW Europe and its derivation from stake-frame basketry: (a) Mesolithic fish-trap, Netherlands; (b) basket from late Neolithic lake-village, Charavignes, Switzerland; (c) Grooved-Ware flat-based pot, southern England; (d) late Neolithic round-based pot, Ireland; (e) TRB Middle Neolithic 'flowerpot', Netherlands, with construction diagram for corresponding basket shape; [new drawing, after Louwe-Kooijmans, Egloff, Thomas, Herity, Bakker].*

of new cultural elements which were not part of the repertoire of the incoming *Bandkeramik*-derived tradition. These arguments have been applied to flintwork (Newell 1972), to suggest that the assemblages of the westernmost (Younger) *Bandkeramik* populations contain Oldesloe elements, in contrast to the 'purer' assemblages from more central areas of the loesslands. This interpretation is reinforced by the appearance in the same contexts of a category of pottery, Limburg Ware, which is equally without parallel in more central regions, but which is based on shapes which resemble organic containers. It is suggested that these, and the comparable La Hoguette wares (Lüning 1989), represent the ceramicisation of indigenous container forms as a result of contacts with the native groups. These form part of a general pattern of new ceramic features on the western margins of the *Bandkeramik* distribution, and suggest that an admixture with native populations was taking place in a small way from the beginning. It is thus particularly interesting that the ceramic assemblages of many later Neolithic groups in north-west Europe – for instance Grooved Ware in Britain and the Middle Neolithic phase of Nordic TRB – contain many angular and bucket-like shapes with skeuomorphic decoration that has its origins in stake-frame basketry (Figure 14.1). This technique had been used for many millennia by Mesolithic groups in northern Europe for the construction of fish-traps, and it contrasts with the south-east European/ Near Eastern tradition of coiled basketry whose shapes are echoed in the forms and decoration of *Bandkeramik* pottery. While this argument cannot be pursued further here, it is symptomatic of the continuing contribution made by the indigenous populations of outer Europe to the formation of the Neolithic cultures associated with megalith building.

I suggest that the elaboration of passage graves is a functional concomitant of this process, which is reflected in the renewed vitality of the megalithic tradition in outlying areas such as Ireland and Orkney in the period after 3500 BC. The position of Irish passage-grave cemeteries in particular, on a line of hills across the centre of the country, is surely indicative of the way in which their messages were directed outwards to populations who could see them from afar. They emphasise that the adoption of farming and its associated belief systems was as much an ideological conversion as a calculation of economic benefit, and that monu-mentalised messages could play a crucial role in its propagation.

[This cline, from the largely immigrant populations of the loesslands to the largely indigenous populations of the far west, is reflected in the tension between quadrilateral and circular structures: ultimately, the farmer's timber longhouse and the hunter's tent (Figure 14.2). Quadrilateral struc-tures continuously dominate in continental Europe, from the Passy long-mounds to the *allées couvertes*; circular ones in the west, increasingly dominant with time as further indigenous groups were absorbed. In between was a zone of ambiguity, where the two models competed, hybridised or passed decisively from one to the other. Even at the very end of the tradition of megalithic construction, when the technique was used not for tombs but for open, ceremonial monuments, the same duality was evident: on the one hand, Carnac, whose alignments take the form of hypertrophied trapezoidal longhouses; and, on the other, Stonehenge, whose great ring-beam echoes that of a circular timber house. The insularity of the British round-house tradition was still evident in the Iron Age.]

CONCLUSION

Let me briefly try to summarise what I have been trying to say. European megalithic architecture can be seen as the conjunction of two processes. The first was the long-term trend towards the splitting up and adaptation of the primary horticultural community, centred on Ian Hodder's (1991) *domus*, with its background in the Neolithic origins of Old World farming. The second was the outcome of specific circumstances in northern and western Europe, where foragers were converted to farming as a total package of economic, social and ideological practices. This phenomenon, precisely because it was so radical, took the form of an extended process of con-

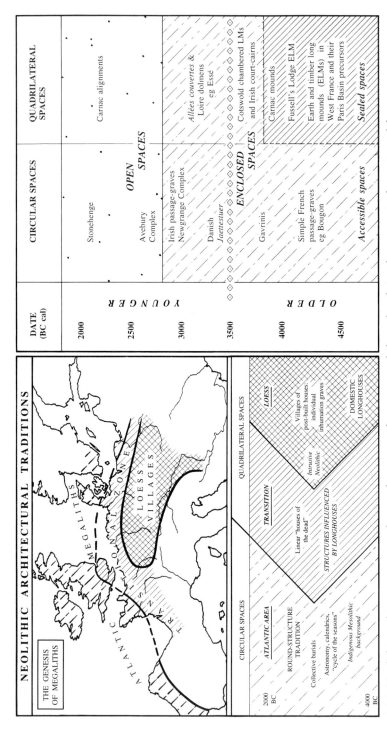

14.2 *Neolithic architecture, east and west: the contrast between quadrilateral and circular spaces in domestic and funerary structures, from the mid-sixth to the third millennium* BC; *[new drawing].*

version, taking millennia to complete. Megalithic architecture was part of the rhetoric of this process; and its successive elaboration in different areas was part of a deliberate strategy (or at least a feedback system with similar effects) to extend the labour supply in areas where this was still possible.[9]

It is possible to distinguish two phases in the genesis of megalithism. The first lay largely *within* the village-based Neolithic cultures which had colonised the loessland corridor from east-central Europe to central Germany and the Paris Basin. While villages remained the foci of the settlement pattern in the Carpathian Basin after 4500 BC, increasingly taking nucleated, tell-like forms of the kind already established in south-east Europe, the settlement patterns of the northern loesslands evolved in the opposite direction. Instead of the clear sequence of village plans which had characterised the preceding millennium or more, a bewildering variety of non-domestic structures began to appear. Because the loesslands themselves have been under continuous cultivation ever since, the earth and timber mounds which formed a prominent part of this new landscape have been subject to heavy destruction, and are only just being recognised archae-ologically (e.g. Passy). Paradoxically, therefore, their forms are better known from outlying examples in areas off the loess (e.g. Kujavia, Normandy), and often adjacent to the centres of later, truly megalithic developments (Schleswig-Holstein, Jutland, Charente, Brittany). These examples indicate that a pattern which had its origin within the older areas of Neolithic occupation was instrumental in the process of spread beyond them. This phase of monumentality was generated by the splitting up of older forms of community.

The second phase, which took place where this process of expansion came into contact with the heartlands of continuing Mesolithic settlement, marks a transformation of this monumentality into an instrument of incorporation: a 'conversion' of existing peoples, ideologies and social structures. The incorporation is symbolised by the change from an emphasis on the external longhouse form, covering a completed burial, to a structure that could be periodically entered and its contents 'updated'. This mor-phological change took different forms in different areas, as the same underlying processes were played out in different contexts; but the parallelisms are striking (and it is not surprising that they were formerly attributed to direct contacts by migration or diffusion). The success of this cultural mutation is indicated by the rapid growth of large and complex examples, increasingly of truly megalithic construction, as Mesolithic populations were successfully incorporated.

It was the existence of the monumentalised longhouse model, therefore, that determined the mode of Mesolithic incorporation in these areas. On other parts of the loessland frontier, such as the Ukraine, there was no such convergence on a monumental solution: Tripole/Cucuteni farming villages became successively larger and better defended, whilst the indigenous population developed along quite different lines into the sequence of pottery-using and livestock-rearing sub-Neolithic groups that increasingly specialised in pastoralism. Rather than incorporation, there was a successive differentiation. The Neolithic cultures of western and northern Europe, on the other hand, created a unique synthesis of an ultimately Near Eastern form of social organisation centred on a transformed *domus*, and an indigenous population with its own distinctive forms of culture and subsistence base. Metaphorically, therefore, Childe was right: it was, indeed, a meeting of the indigenous and the exotic; but it was the density of the existing, native population which made it such a spectacular phenomenon. Childe was also right that this pattern of investment in the physical symbolism of the domestic community was in the end replaced by its eastern, steppe-land alternative with its origins on the steppes: the more mobile, dispersed, and probably livestock-centred pattern of individual warrior-burials that is typical of the Pit-Grave culture, Corded Ware and Bell-Beakers – an economy, cosmology and settlement pattern within which the accumulated skills of megalithic construction had no role.

This coincidence of culture-historical and demographic factors explains why Atlantic Europe is the classic area of megaliths. In other parts of Europe, north Africa and the Near East – and indeed in other parts of the world – some of these factors have recurred. Stone-using, or simple metal-using societies have experienced the break-up of formerly concentrated communities, and have used monumentalised house-forms, typically employed as tombs, as surrogate foci for the creation of community identities.[10] The phenomenon of megalithism is associated not with a particular kind of economy, but rather with a social process in space. Such monuments were everywhere 'houses of the holy', associating the sacred with specific times and places. What is remarkable about the European examples, however, is the degree to which this pattern was elaborated, to an extent that rivalled the monumental efforts of contemporary civilisations. It was the position of western Europe, close enough to the nuclear centres of agriculture and urban life to be affected by them, but sufficiently distant not to be directly incorporated into the developing world-systems of the time, that allowed this unique cultural experiment to flourish.

NOTES

1. For this reason it is no more accurate to speak of 'passage-tombs' than 'passage-graves', and the latter has priority as a technical term.
2. In the central and west Mediterranean, this pattern was not immediately replicated. Instead, various features of the package were individually absorbed by indigenous coastal communities, principally the more easily transferable elements of pottery and small quantities of domestic livestock, which appeared in the Impressed Ware culture in sites (often caves) which show continuity from the preceding Mesolithic. With time, however, the full package was absorbed and more formally organised settlements appeared, usually accompanied by the technologically advanced forms of painted pottery which were

produced in village communities. This pattern persisted until the spread of the plough in the later fourth millennium, when various megalithic phenomena began to appear in the Mediterranean region.

3. These various episodes of monumentalisation, for instance in the Paris Basin (Passy: Cerny culture) or central Germany (Latdorf: Baalberge culture), seem to have taken place quite independently, and at different times (up to five centuries apart), reflecting similar processes of change on the basis of a common cultural background. The most impressive examples, however, are those just beyond the margins of the loesslands, like Kujavian long-mounds such as Sarnowo. It is in this last case that the most literal copying of domestic longhouses took place, since these elaborate dwellings were still in use amongst contemporary final Lengyel groups nearby (e.g. Brześć Kujawski), at a time when such structures were no longer being built in central Germany and the western loesslands.

4. Though Tiszapolgár is associated with a scattered pattern of *small* tell settlements.

5. Even quite recently, it was believed that megaliths began at a 'mature' stage of the Neolithic in northern and western Europe: a stage of crystallisation, when populations were sufficiently dense to require territorial markers – what geographers would describe as a 'packing phenomenon'.

6. Outside Scandinavia, the beginnings of megalithic architecture and collective burial were effectively simultaneous; in the Nordic region the first megalithic forms (*dysser*) were mainly individual burials. The addition of a passage for continuous access developed some centuries later, at the beginning of the Danish Middle Neolithic c.3500 BC, in the form of the Nordic passage-grave (*Jaettestue*).

7. On the analogy, perhaps, of those 'rituals of resistance' and 'cargo cults' with which native populations more recently attempted to counter foreign political and ideological influences.

8. Do we not, after all, describe hierarchical social structures of the kind which characterised the early Egyptian state as 'pyramidal'? Are not the Pyramids themselves social metaphors in stone?

9. There are many gaps in this argument, especially as it relates to Iberia. Did long-mounds of ultimately loessland inspiration penetrate beyond the Garonne, to stimulate the onset of monumentality in north-east Spain? (Note how recently long-mounds have been recognised in such well-known areas as the Paris Basin!)

10. This more general explanation would therefore apply to the varied examples of megalithic construction which appeared in different parts of Europe and surrounding areas in the third millennium BC and afterwards. The Levantine 'dolmens', for instance, date principally to Early Bronze IV, at the end of the third millennium, and are related to the splitting up of the kinds of large, nucleated communities established there in the period of Early Bronze Age urbanism. A similar explanation may lie behind the 'dolmens' of the northern Caucasus, in relation to their complementarity with more nucleated forms of settlement and social organisation. These are chronologically and culturally parallel to non-megalithic burial monuments in the form of the Catacomb-Graves of the adjacent Pontic steppe region, and emphasise the fact that the availability of raw material ultimately determines the expression of monumental forms, and whether they are constructed of earth or stone.

INVISIBLE FLOWS: LANGUAGES, CULTURE AND DRUGS

The golden bowls from the Vulchetrun treasure, c.1600 BC
(National Museum of Bulgaria, Sofia; drawing by T. Taylor).

'O for a beaker, full of the warm south …'

JOHN KEATS
Ode to a Nightingale (1818)

The last section looked at built structure: fixtures in the landscape, whether settlements or tombs. This section looks at the less tangible parts of the archaeological record, concerned with flows of items – some of which get caught in 'artefact-traps' on sites, but many of which escape entirely: language and music (totally lost, in the absence of writing), organic consumables (rare, apart from fortuitous residues) and precious metals (mostly recycled, unless deliberately placed in tombs or hoards). These aspects must be reconstructed, or the archaeological image enhanced, if our picture of the past is not to remain an impoverished and misleading caricature of what life was like.

Both linguistic and genetic distributions as they are known at the present day or in the recent past offer tantalising patterns; and both need to be explained historically, by postulating previous stages of the pattern. With genetic information, there is some hope that palaeo-DNA studies will one day reveal past patterns of variability; but direct evidence of ancient languages can never be pushed beyond the urban, literate societies of early historical times. It remains the classic case of attempting to reconstruct diachronic patterns from synchronic ones, using both the properties of the phenomenon itself, and surrogate evidence of related phenomena, to infer past states of the system. Given its inherent problems, it is not surprising that there is so little unanimity about such reconstructions; but as a methodology it is more common in archaeological arguments than might be supposed. Discussion of 'hunter-gatherer' or 'pastoralist' societies implies precisely such a retrojection of recently-observed categories: an essential step in constructing a narrative, but fraught with the dangers of anachronism (as Sections II and III above tried to show). A large part of the prehistorian's task must be the conscious testing of palaeo-ethnological models – reading the record in the light of prior expectations – and the reconstruction of extinct patterns.

One aspect of this which I have to some extent pioneered is the study of the use of psychotropic substances in prehistory (see now Goodman, Lovejoy and Sherratt 1995). Historical Europe was undoubtedly a realm of 'drinking cultures', just as North America at the time of its discovery by Europeans was a realm of 'smoking cultures'. The archaeological record of European prehistory – together with one or two clues from the Ur-ethnographer, Herodotus – contains tantalising suggestions about the appearance of alcohol, and what might have preceded it. The importance of drinking in recent Europe, as of coca-consumption in aboriginal Colombia, is both social and economic: social, in that it structures and characterises the major occasions of social interaction, and economic in that constant supplies need to be assured. This concern with consumption in its literal sense is a model for the general turnover of material goods in use by human populations: the consumption of woollen textiles, say, or metal tableware; and it is an important aspect of the way in which theory in the social sciences has changed over the last two decades.

Whereas the comparison of static distribution-patterns (like sites) against largely permanent backgrounds (like environmental zones) leads to a concern with regular, localised movements in the winning of daily bread, a concern with rarer types of consumable materials throws the emphasis on to flows of materials along transport arteries. These networks, especially the longer-distance ones carrying relatively precious materials, are often the routes by which new consumption practices, technologies and languages have spread across the continent. They are crucial to understanding why certain regions stand out from others because of their wealth; and especially to understanding the emergence of asymmetric patterns of exchange, in which certain areas yield up their valuable raw materials in order to import the 'added value' of manufactured products from other regions.

15

Cups that Cheered: The Introduction of Alcohol to Prehistoric Europe[1]

(1987)

The study of pottery forms a large part of the work of the archaeologist: most of the entities with which we populate prehistoric Europe are named after their pots. Unlike many other expressive elements of material culture, such as clothing, it has survived in large enough quantities to permit some attempt to study it as a system of communication. Even so, it is only part of the language of cuisine: the symbolism of the containers is closely connected with the significance of their contents. Whatever prestige attached to pottery is likely to have been derived from the special nature of what was consumed from it rather than from any inherent value in the pots themselves: their elaboration was simply appropriate for the value of what was provided in them. While the pots may have been admired, it was on their contents that the hospitality was judged.

The diagnostic feature of the Bell-Beaker complex is its eponymous vessel, the decorated drinking cup. The purpose of this chapter is to suggest that the association between such a container and an international style of ostentation is not fortuitous; and indeed that it forms part of a wider pattern which may be discerned throughout the continent of Europe. Discussion of this assertion in the following chapter falls into four sections, of differing character: the first concerns chronology, the second deals with the arrival of

---

This chapter was written, shortly after having given the Munro Lectures in Edinburgh on 'Drinking and Driving', for a conference in Oxford on the Bell-Beaker culture. Having analysed the Early Bronze Age pottery from Sitagroi (and studied with David Clarke, authority on British Bell-Beakers), I was well aware of a horizon of drinking-vessels that in Hungary was explicitly associated with carts and cart-burials (Chapter 8), and associated with massive changes in settlement-patterns (Chapter 11). Was alcohol, too, an introduction? And if so, was the use of animal traction equally a cultural (rather than just a subsistence) innovation? (This piece was originally printed without its bibliography, and with the illustrations misnumbered; it appears here for the first time intact.)

technological innovations in later Neolithic Europe, the third looks briefly at the sociology of stimulants, and the fourth tries to apply these ideas to the detail of the archaeological record.

EUROPE IN THE FOURTH AND THIRD MILLENNIA BC

Europe at the beginning of the fourth millennium was a land of contrasts. Although in its south-eastern part there were village communities whose ancestors had been farmers there for two thousand years, on the north-western margin of the continent the appearance of stone tombs in small clearings marked a relatively recent shift to an agricultural way of life by peoples who had previously lived by fishing, foraging and fowling. Along the Atlantic coastlands, the convergent development of megalithic architecture picked out a zone of communities, with varied backgrounds but often located in the heartlands of earlier, Mesolithic population, which formed a distinctive development on the western edge of Europe. Although the later Iberian (e.g. Millaran) builders of collective tombs were to acquire some skills from contacts along the Mediterranean in a more advanced phase of their development,[2] the origin of European megaliths was essentially a local one. Nothing points up more clearly the contrast between our present picture of European prehistory and that presented by Gordon Childe than the interpretation of the megalithic monuments and their makers. Far from being recent immigrants or converts to Near Eastern religions, the megalithic communities of western Europe can now be seen as equally if not more isolated, archaic and rural than the peasants of the central European loess – themselves unsophisticated by the standards of the early-settled regions of the south-east.

Even the Balkan and Carpathian areas, technically and perhaps socially the most advanced regions of the European landmass, had a curiously isolated appearance by comparison with the technological *koine* which existed over much of the contemporary Near East (Renfrew 1969). Its copper and gold metallurgy, although typologically distinctive, was nevertheless still based on unalloyed metal shaped by single-mould casting and hammering. After the close links with Anatolia indicated by the material culture of its pioneer farmers, Balkan and Carpathian Europe seem to have pursued their own, independent course; while in the adjacent central European loess belt the pioneer unity of *Bandkeramik* similarly gave way to more localised groupings. These tendencies towards disunity, however, were beginning to be reversed; and the core of this process was the Carpathian Basin. The cultures of the Copper Age seem to show new properties not possessed by their predecessors. The appearance of display gear in metal, especially shafthole axes, was paralleled not only by new forms of flint-working (notably long flint dagger-blades: see Chapter 12) which had to be brought from great distances, but also by new conventions of displaying

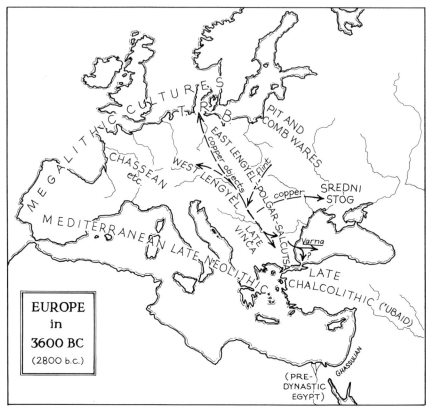

15.1 Europe in the period of long-distance connections ('linkup phase') c.3800–3600 BC.

wealth or status at death – the appearance of rich, differentiated cemeteries like that of Tiszapolgár (Bognár-Kutzián 1963). This pattern of individual ostentation, and the long-distance trade needed to support it, was the motor for spreading innovations like the domestic horses from the Pontic steppes which appeared in Hungary at this time (Bökönyi 1978).

Such developments were reaching their climax around 3700/3600 BC, in what might be termed the *Linkup* phase (Figure 15.1). It is marked by three related phenomena:

1. the extension of trade routes carrying copper from the Carpathian Basin (already reaching the Russian steppes, perhaps in exchange for horses) to the newly emerged farming communities of Denmark in the TRB C period (Bygholm, Salten, etc.: Randsborg 1979);

2. a pattern of stylistic convergence among adjacent cultures, forming a chain from Bulgaria to Poland and characterised by frayed boundaries and mixed groups (Bodrogkeresztúr/Sălcutsa IV; Lengyel-Polgar);

3. the emergence of certain inter-cultural ceramic types, notably those concerned with serving food or drink.

378

15.2 Inter-regional pottery forms for serving liquids, early fourth millennium BC: *eastern group (two-handled). Left, Silesia (Jordanów); centre, Slovakia (Lengyel V); right, Bulgaria (Sălcutsa IV). Various scales and sources.*

All three are aspects of a process of increasing connection between regions, in which the movement of rare commodities like metals was associated with a degree of cultural convergence, beginning with common conventions for ritually important activities. The first represents an interesting example of directional drift in commodities between two demographically important centres of settlement, along an axis that was to be of crucial importance in later prehistory. The second probably relates to new patterns of mobility in mating networks and the formation of kinship links of greater geographical scope (Chapter 5). The third, most relevant for present purposes, offers in embryo a phenomenon not dissimilar to that later represented by the Bell-Beakers themselves.

Two inter-regional pottery types present themselves: an 'eastern' form and a 'western' one.[3] (To these may be added the Funnel-beaker drinking set considered in the following chapter: Figures 16.14 and 16.15.) The eastern type is the two-handled vessel that distinguishes the latest phase (IV in Berciu's terminology) of Gumelnitsa and Sălcutsa, appears in eastern Hungary with the distinctive *Scheibenhenkeln* of later Bodrogkeresztúr (Hunyadihalom), and is known from later Lengyel-Polgar contexts in southern and central Poland, such as the copper-rich graves of Jordanów (Figure 15.2). The western type has a single handle, and appears in the form of a cup or tankard among the constituent groups of the later Lengyel complex: the Balaton group in Hungary, Aichbuhl and Schussenried in Bohemia and the east Alpine foreland, Baalberge in central Germany (Figure 15.3). If material culture is fossilised behaviour, it may be possible to infer

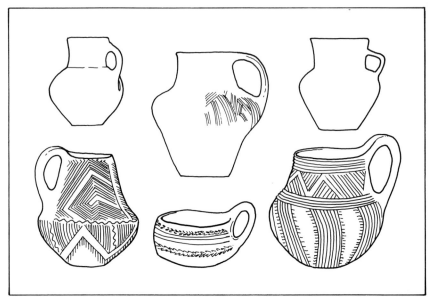

15.3 Inter-regional pottery forms for serving liquids, early fourth millennium BC:
western group (one-handled). Top row, right and left, central Germany
(Baalberge); top row, centre, Bavaria (Wallerfing); bottom row, Slovakia
(Furchenstichkeramik). Various scales and sources.

the appearance of conventions of hospitality or at least the social dispensing
of liquids (e.g. from the Schussenried jug) among the interacting groups
around the Carpathian Basin.[4] It may not be coincidence that one of the
more distinctive (and again, eponymous) shapes among the pottery of the
first northern farmers, the funnel-necked beaker, should appear at this time
in an area demonstrably linked to that of the Carpathian Basin by trade in
copper. Contemporary early farming cultures in Atlantic Europe had no
such distinctive drinking vessel: they were 'bowl cultures'.

This pattern of growing connections within and around central Europe,
centred on the prosperous, copper-using groups of the Carpathian Basin but
reaching out to include both steppe groups to the east and new farming
communities in the North European Plain, was the nucleus from which
more extensive networks of trading and cultural contact were to develop.

In the next phase, lasting from 3500–3000 BC, this network was
decisively linked to that of the urbanising Near East by way of Anatolia and
the Aegean: its mnemonic is thus the *Aegeo-Anatolian* phase. These influences are unambiguous in Balkan and Carpathian Europe, but their echoes
can be traced into central Germany and Poland. An important feature of
internal development was the unification of the 'eastern' (Bodrogkeresztúr)
and 'western' (Lengyel) wings of the Danubian province into a single entity,
the Baden culture.[5] Baden pottery shows little continuity with that of either
group (though perhaps owing more to Lengyel than to Bodrogkeresztúr),

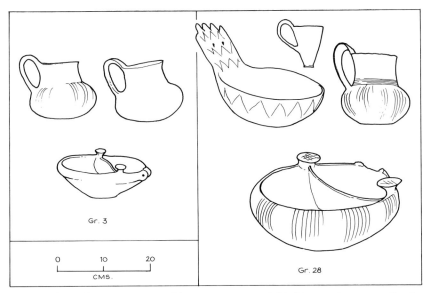

15.4 Baden culture grave assemblages consisting of drinking equipment, reflecting metal prototypes: pottery from the two male burials accompanied by paired cattle in the cemetery of Alsónémedi, Hungary (cf. Figs 8.1, 8.2). Drawn from photographs in J. Banner, Die Péceler Kultur, *1956.*

but instead it is characterised by an entirely new assemblage of forms and decorative syntax. The shapes include many-handled vessels for dispensing and consuming liquids, often combined in graves as a 'service' or set of vessels of complementary types (like our decanter and glasses), either for personal enjoyment (Figure 15.4) or social entertainment (Figure 15.5), and also occurring in domestic assemblages (Figure 15.6). The stylistic and

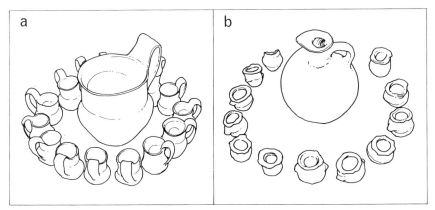

*15.5 Two contemporary pottery drinking-sets, inspired by metal forms, in central Europe and the Aegean: right, Baden culture assemblage from Dřetovice near Brandýs, Czech Republic (*Pravěk Československa, *1960, p. 138 and Plate 17); Early Cycladic grave assemblage from SE Naxos (from Renfrew 1972, Plate 16).*

381

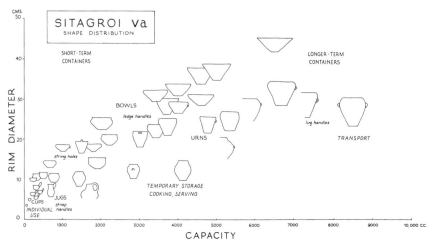

15.6 The pottery assemblage from the 'burnt house' at Sitagroi, Macedonia (Phase Va, mid-third millennium BC), arranged according to volume and rim-diameter: note the jug/cup complex at the personal end of the scale; [from Sherratt 1986a].

morphological features of this assemblage, such as the use of strap-handles, omphalos bases and channelled decoration, are indicative of the impact of metal prototypes. Nándor Kalicz long ago (1963, 42–52) assembled an impressive list of features of Baden pottery which have their origins in the type of precious metal vessels then existing in Anatolia. This metal impact is very clear in the Beycesultan sequence, and I have described it (Sherratt 1986a) in the north Aegean at Sitagroi, with the appearance of these metal-related features in phase IV there. The same is true for Ezero (with specific parallels at Troy) and also Cernavoda III and Baden (Chrpovsky 1973). Its impact can be traced less directly further north, in some Salzmünde types in central Germany, and more generally thereafter with Bernburg and early Globular Amphorae, which have the rounded, southern shapes of the Baden 'metal style' as opposed to the angular, Nordic profiles of Walternienburg [which I suspect go back to the tradition of stake-frame basket forms: Chapter 14; cf. also Chapter 16].

To summarise the pattern of this phase, therefore, we can see the establishment, in the Carpathian Basin and south-east Europe (with some echoes further north), of a major cultural block with close stylistic connections to the adjacent areas of the Aegean and Anatolia. This style is typically expressed in sets of drinking vessels, whose forms were inspired by metal originals.

Our next phase is more complex, and involves eastwards contact with the area to the north of the Black Sea. For this reason I have called it the *Steppe* phase (3000–2500 BC); and it falls into two parts. A striking feature of its earlier part is the expansion of the Globular Amphora complex (Wiślánski 1970; Nagel 1985), over an area from south Denmark to Kiev (Figure 15.8).

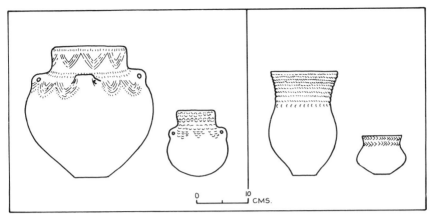

15.7 Pottery characteristic of the two successive major inter-regional complexes of the North European Plain, 3400–2400 BC: left, Globular Amphora culture (eastern Poland); right, Corded Ware culture (western Poland).

Its essential feature is the liquid-container, the eponymous globular amphora (Figure 15.7 left). A comparable form of vessel occurs in the areas more immediately influenced by Aegean prototypes, including both the Baden area and Italy. It is sometimes accompanied, in a true drinking set, by handled cups; but this is not true everywhere. The Globular Amphora culture picked up, on its 'eastern front', the practice of impressing pottery with cord decoration which was already practised by Pontic Steppe groups (Telegin 1973; Merpert 1974); and its burial practices were an eclectic mixture of southern paired-ox burials, western megalithic cists, and eastern tumuli. At about the same time, there was a short, temporary fashion for cord decoration in the Balkans (e.g. at Mikhalich and Sitagroi Va; for a general survey see Roman 1974), and what seems to be an actual steppe intrusion of ochre-grave (= Pit-Grave, '*Kurgan*' or tumulus-building) groups into the Lower Danube and eastern Hungary from the Pontic steppes (Ecsedy 1979). This was the time when two-piece mould casting and arsenical alloying started in south-east Europe. The Globular Amphora diaspora had its own impact on TRB, most clearly seen in MN IV in Denmark (E2 in the Netherlands), when the cord decoration was imitated rather laboriously in local *tvaerstik* – stab and drag ornament (Bakker 1979).

As a second stage of this process, the Corded Ware complex (Behrens and Schlette 1969, *Schnurkeramik Symposium Halle* 1979) crystallised around a further set of international (and typically male) equipment. This consisted essentially of the shafthole stone 'battle-axe', the flint dagger, and the cord-decorated beaker (a large drinking cup with wrapped-round decoration) often associated with a larger liquid-container, the globular amphora – and usually occurring with single burials in the tumuli that now became the standard form of burial monument (Figure 15.7 right). The core area of the Corded Ware complex lay to the west of that of Globular

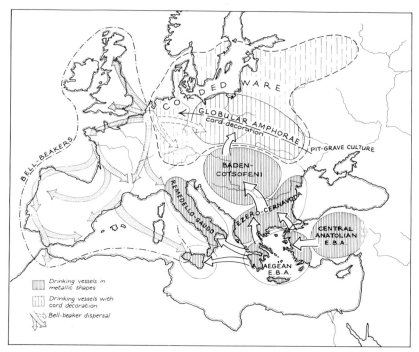

15.8 Map showing the spread of the drinking-vessel complex in Europe in its three regional manifestations: SE *Europe with vessels of shapes inspired by metal originals;* N *Europe with a more rustic style incorporating cord decoration; and Atlantic Europe with various groups of the Bell-Beaker culture. (Bell-Beaker arrows distinguish between* AOC *Beakers – hatched; Maritime Beakers – stippled; and Beaker groups appearing in former Corded Ware areas – blank, broken outline.) Drawn by Pat Jacobs.*

Amphorae (Figure 15.8), but Corded Ware took over the western periphery of the latter, and expanded widely beyond it to the east.[6] The western wing of this complex extended from Switzerland to Scandinavia; the eastern wing as far as Moscow and beyond. I leave on one side whether this was a population (e.g. acculturated remnant hunters), a specialised minority (e.g. pastoralists), or merely a set of symbols indicative of social convergence on a common formula: for the moment I merely want to clarify the spatio-temporal pattern.

The last part of this process (Figure 15.8), at the far western end, was the formation of a further international complex with maritime and riverine links to western and south-western Europe: hence its designation as the *Maritime* phase (2500–2000 BC). The Bell-Beaker sequence (Clarke 1976; Harrison 1980), beginning with AOC (All-over-Cord) beakers in the North Sea basin, was initially close to the Corded Ware model; it substituted archery equipment for battle axes, but continued the daggers, single burial under a tumulus, and especially the emphasis on a cord-decorated drinking vessel. This was followed by the 'Maritime' or 'Pan-European' phase, in which the cord ornament was translated into zones of comb-stamped decoration and Beakers spread even more widely, perhaps meshing with pre-existing maritime trade networks to bring northern novelties to the west Mediterranean in exchange for copper. The scale of this Bell-Beaker diaspora was to exceed even that of Globular Amphorae and Corded Ware; from Scotland to Sicily, Cornwall to Moravia. Nevertheless, its position peripheral to a continuing Baden-like core should still be noted, as should the continuing irradiation of this periphery by metal-inspired forms: the so-called *Begleitkeramik*. This interaction – in which Nagyrév jugs and cups spread into the loesslands and the north Alpine foreland, while decorated beakers spread into central Europe from the west – was also marked by the transfer of technological sophistication to the periphery: copper (and then copper-alloy) daggers began to replace flint ones in Bell-Beaker graves (Burgess and Shennan 1976; Shennan 1977).

Comparing this sequence of maps, one may discern a pattern unfolding over the course of a millennium, and consisting of the following features: the establishment of a Carpathian/Balkan bridgehead of Aegeo-Anatolian styles; two successive diasporas in the North European Plain – one in the east, one in the west – creating a chain of common conventions from the steppes to the Rhineland; and finally a more selective linking-up of the main centres within the great arc of western Europe. The whole process thus took the form of an anti-clockwise movement around the European landmass, coming full circle in the Mediterranean: Italy in general, and Sicily in particular, received impulses from both directions – from the east, originating in the Aegean, and from the west, along the Beaker sea-lanes (hence that unique phenomenon, a painted Bell-Beaker).

Each of these major, inter-regional cultural complexes had at its heart a set of distinctive drinking vessels, usually closely associated – in the typical burial formula, and putatively therefore in the minds of their users – with an equally distinctive kit of personal weaponry, and more generally (as we shall consider in the next section) with another important novelty: the use of the horse.

EUROPE IN TRANSITION: SOME KEY INNOVATIONS

These very large-scale phenomena demand equally large-scale explanations; so let us consider some of the major changes that were taking place at this time or just before (Figure 0.6), which were the results of a second generation of revolutionary changes within Old World farming practices.[7] These changes have been discussed in the preceding chapters; and together they produced a fundamental alteration in social organisation, sexual roles and settlement patterns. Horses arrived early in the open steppes of eastern Hungary, but for another millennium spread no further into a continent still largely forested. The existence of the plough, demonstrable from c.3500 BC onwards, was the main incentive for an accelerated pace of forest clearance, and prepared the way in northern and western Europe for other innovations requiring open country, such as horse-rearing, or the keeping of sheep in sufficient numbers for wool. I have argued that the introduction of the light plough (ard), as part of a larger 'traction complex' that also included wheeled vehicles, can be dated to the beginning of the 'Aegeo-Anatolian' phase that followed the great Copper Age linkup; that is, Baden in Hungary and earliest Middle Neolithic in Denmark. The association between the traction complex and new features of ceramic style in central and south-east Europe (including the coincidence of drinking sets and paired-ox burials in the Alsónémedi cemetery) suggests a common origin; and perhaps, there-fore, a similar route of spread via Anatolia. Animal traction was clearly a very significant innovation, and I envisage the plough as spreading along the Mediterranean at the same time as it did along the central European axis, to be present in Millaran Spain (along with bastion fortifications) just as it is known to have been in Middle Neolithic Denmark or the British Isles. The same would probably be true of wheeled vehicles, the other application of animal traction. This is the horizon c.3500 BC in calendar years, maybe a couple of hundred years later in the west Mediterranean, which corresponds to radical changes in settlement pattern and organisation in many areas, though its full impact was only to become evident when the full suite of innovations was present to make use of the new conditions. One continuing effect, however, was a relative enlargement of the pastoral sector, and a concomitant enhancement of male domination of the system of production. This continued a trend first evident in the Carpatho-Balkan Copper Age, but now much more widely occurring and especially marked in the North European Plain as settlement rapidly expanded onto the easily-deforested outwash sands in the Corded Ware period.

Links with more open areas to the east, both through the Carpathian Basin and across the North European Plain, continued to have a crucial effect on the development of forested temperate Europe. Domestic horses had both an origin and a continuing reservoir on the Pontic Steppes; and I suspect that wool-sheep may have arrived in central and northern Europe by the same route a little later, to replace the existing hairy varieties that had come in with the Neolithic. The use of horses for riding can be traced by the occurrence of their bones on settlements and in graves, and seems to have been carried successively further west and south on our series of flor-escences, first with Corded Ware and then with Bell-Beakers. Their associ-ation with early Mediterranean Bell-Beakers, in Iberia, Italy, and now on Majorca, is striking.[8] The keeping of horses for riding must at this stage have been confined to a limited elite, since they would have been very expensive to maintain on the limited areas of grazing then available. Nevertheless, they must have been an impressive sight to communities which had never seen ridden horses before, and must have conferred great prestige on their owners: probably the same people who figure prominently in the graves as possessors of fine stone or copper weaponry and drinking equipment. They would have been desirable items of trade; and, as a means of transport themselves, would have facilitated travel and the distribution of other high-value items. They would also have had an important role in more open areas in the enlarged scale of flock- and herd-management.

Since linen was the universal fibre of the Neolithic (locally supplemented by nettle or esparto grass), the introduction of wool-bearing sheep meant the appearance of a new, prestige commodity that could be made into a wider range of garments, potentially more colourful than before.[9] Although it was later to become a major item of trade, wool is likely to have been a rather rare, elite commodity for many centuries after its first appearance, and perhaps even longer in heavily forested regions. The introduction of wool sheep is rather harder to date than that of the horse, and must be inferred from a mixture of different types of evidence including metrical data on sheep bones, the transition from buttons to pins, and on the very infrequent finds of the fibres and their textiles. The combined evidence for the first use of wool suggests a date in the later part of the 'steppe' phase, and a slow spread westwards: perhaps later Baden in Hungary, later Corded Ware in Germany, middle Beaker in the far west. The geometrical, zone-filling motifs of mature beakers suggest an obvious inspiration from textiles – perhaps garments like the woven belts[10] on the Swiss/north Italian statue-menhirs; while more elaborate clothing might be one reason for the shift from crouched to laid-out burials, to display their finery in the grave. Woollen textiles are therefore likely to have been carried to new areas over the Beaker network, although an independent spread along the Mediterranean was probably taking place at the same time.

To summarise: the spread of the 'drinking complex' – a common emphasis on sets of vessels, often combined in graves, which in several cases are so distinctive stylistically as to have given their name to whole cultures – took place during a period of unusually rapid social, cultural and economic change. During this time, Europe was opened up – both literally, in terms of the further deforestation of its landscapes, and metaphorically, in terms of its new contacts and social opportunities. Fundamental to this process was the increasing importance of livestock, and the emergence of male warrior elites whose sub-culture was portrayed in the characteristic combination of weaponry[11] and drinking vessels in their graves. Their distinctiveness was enhanced by their possession of horses, and probably of woollen clothing. The progress of metallurgy, keeping pace with the need for metal equipment for fighting and display, was shortly to cross the technological threshold which allows us to speak of the Bronze Age.

The pattern that we have so far recognised is encouragingly congruent: the introduction of major innovations in animal husbandry, and the new lifestyles associated with them, do seem to coincide with the main currents of cultural change as they can be reconstructed from the ceramic inventories of the groups concerned. But can we be more specific? What was the significance of Corded Ware, or Bell-Beakers? Can these features be tied together as comprehensible elements of social practice? To say more will involve us in a brief excursion.

SYMPOSIA: DRINKING TOGETHER

Our timetable – in conferences or at work – is structured by drinking-events. The day is punctuated by social occasions which differ from one another in their scale, character and appropriate beverage. In England, 11 o'clock means coffee-time; water would satisfy our thirst, yet hospitality would be lacking were that to be the only drink provided. A mild stimulant is required. Symmetrically, the British provide tea at 4 o'clock. At lunchtime it is a common practice to drink a glass of beer; a more formal, evening dinner would be accompanied by wine. None of these is strictly necessary for physical well-being. What they do is to partition the day into units, separated by events at which graded levels of social interaction take place[12] – each stage and level marked by its appropriate drink (cf. Douglas 1975; 1982).

So too with the containers (Vintners 1933). I expect my wine in a glass, and of a different shape from that in which I would drink my beer. It may even be specifically appropriate for the type of wine, whether it is imported from the Rhineland, Champagne or Portugal. The hot beverages are more appropriately presented in pottery; the tea, especially, in good china with an unnecessary saucer. If it is not a social occasion – travelling, for instance, by train – I may be content with a plastic beaker; and if I relax at the end of the day with a private drink of cocoa, it is taken unpretentiously, in a mug.

Each of these modest stimulants thus has its own container, its own etiquette, its own ritual. Other rituals surround such mild narcotics as tobacco, consumed by smoking.[13] Each of the non-alcoholic drinks, interestingly, has its origin in a different part of the world (Hobhouse 1985) and only arrived in Britain in the sixteenth century;[14] and, moreover, each was part of a tradition of social entertainment in its area of origin: for instance tea in China and Japan, with its ritualised 'tea ceremony'. This beverage brought with it its own material culture, the porcelain 'china' tea-service, subtly transformed for western use. Coffee performs a similar role in Arabia, and more widely in the Near East: anyone who has excavated in the Arab world is familiar with the seemingly endless sequence of cups of coffee, without which formal negotiation is impossible. Cocoa – *kakao* – was the elite drink of the Maya and the Aztecs. Tobacco, in American Indian culture, was equally social and communal: the pipe of peace, passed around the fire. So too were the rather stronger narcotics: cannabis in the Islamic world, and opium (which we associate with south-east Asia, but is only so characteristic of this area because we promoted it there). All of these drugs started off in well-defined and controlled social occasions – rare, special and essentially communal. It is only with the atomisation of society that has followed industrialisation that public use has given way to private use, and hence to uncontrolled indulgence, abuse and addiction. Originally they were social lubricants, agents of hospitality. So too was alcohol.

They are also, of course, symbols. Don't ask for alcohol in Riyad; don't smoke cannabis in the streets of Oxford. In the Arab world, cannabis – and later coffee to complement it, as a social drink – symbolised the victory of Islam and camel-riding desert pastoralists, with their brass drinking-vessels, over the populations which they conquered: the Christian, wheel-going, wine-drinking, silver-vessel-using town dwellers. The place of wine in Near Eastern and especially Christian ritual needs no exposition: *Hic est calix novum testamentum in sanguine meo* (Luke 22: 20) – the blood of the New Testament shed for the forgiveness of sins, the chalice, the cup of sacrifice; an image that goes back to libations poured from animal-head rhyta in the early Bronze Age. These are powerful symbols, and people have died for misusing them. Alcohol is especially suggestive, with its potential for euphoria and ecstasy: one thinks of course of the cult of Dionysus, but do not forget the Vulgate version of the 23rd Psalm: *calix meus inebrians est* – my chalice inebriateth me. [These arguments are developed further in Sherratt 1995.]

So all of these stimulants, and most especially alcohol, are likely to have had strict social contexts and profound symbolic and social implications when they were first introduced. Let us concentrate first on alcohol, and try to tie it in with some archaeology. Alcohol depends on sugar, transformed by the fungus *Saccharomyces cerevisiae* (otherwise known as yeast) through the process of anaerobic glycosis (otherwise known as fermentation). When was it discovered? Not, I suspect, in the early Neolithic. All the encyclopedia entries on alcohol start by saying that it began way back in prehistory: I am not so sure. I think it is more like horses, ploughs and woolly sheep – a second-generation development of the farming tradition, with its origins in the south. The sugars available to prehistoric man were glucose, fructose, maltose and lactose, available from honey, fruits, sprouting grain and milk respectively, to produce mead, wine, beer and koumish. Few of these sources of sugar were abundant in primeval temperate Europe, and our own sugar-saturated environment is a poor guide to the conditions that obtained then. Fermentation is constantly happening accidentally now – in some long-forgotten bag of fruit in the kitchen – but only because of the highly selected, sugar-rich varieties of fruit that are now so easily available on the super-market shelves. Wild fruits, and this includes the wild grape *Vitis sylvestris*, simply do not have enough sugar to ferment. Given that the process also includes lengthy preparation in closed containers with the appropriate

15.9 Drinking scenes: above, *beer-drinkers using straws, on an Early Dynastic (mid-third millennium) cylinder-seal impression from Mesopotamia;* below, *a wine-drinker from a Hallstatt-period (6th-century BC) situla from Kuffarn, Austria [from Sherratt 1985].*

variety of yeast, I think it entirely probable that alcohol was not invented in Neolithic Europe.

That is not to say that they were completely without stimulants; seeds of the opium poppy, *Papaver somniferum*, are well known from *Bandkeramik* contexts in Germany, from Neolithic Switzerland, and from the later Neolithic levels of La Cueva de Los Murcielágos in Granada (see next chapter). While it is unlikely that opium was highly prepared and smoked, it is quite possible that it might have been chewed or infused (Merlin 1984). Birch-bark chewing gum, itself mildly narcotic, is incidentally also known from a lakeside site in southern Germany.

So where was alcohol discovered? The most likely origin, I suspect (Figure 0.3), is in the tree crops cultivated from the fourth millennium onwards in the east Mediterranean and around Mesopotamia (Zohary and Spiegel-Roy 1975). The date palm, both in its fruits and its sap, is one of the most concentrated natural sources of sugar (Werth 1954, 233–41; Samuelson 1898). Cultivated vines, *Vitis vinifera*, carry both sufficient sugar and natural yeasts. Mediterranean polyculture, as practised in the east Mediterranean, was closely associated (as Colin Renfrew pointed out long ago) with the elite consumption of wine (Sereni 1981), reflected in a whole range of pouring and drinking vessels which significantly all have metal prototypes (Renfrew 1972). The *depas amphikypellon* at Troy, the 'sauceboat' in Early Helladic Greece, and the 'teapot' in EM Crete, are all regional variants of craftsman-made, elite drinking vessels surely concerned with the consumption of wine.

The introduction of alcoholic drinks, with their properties of intoxication and the generation of conviviality – a socially accepted alteration of consciousness – is a major event for any society (Malcolm 1971). The religious and elite overtones of wine in later European and Near Eastern societies point to its fundamental social importance, and its use in prehistoric times is likely to have been accompanied by cult and ceremony (Lutz 1922; Kossack 1964; Goody 1982). The preparation of alcoholic drinks required investment and the ability to concentrate surplus for conspicuous consumption, as did also the manufacture of appropriately ostentatious vessels. Such privileges may have been available only to the few. Such a socially visible form of enjoyment and display is highly likely to be emulated by elite groups in contact with those already practising alcohol consumption: the recent history of North American Indians in contact with white settlers offers an instructive, if more concentrated example – interestingly paralleled by the adoption of the horse in the same context.

Now look at the chronological relationship of the various culturally emphasised drinking vessels that we have been considering in later Neolithic or Copper Age Europe. East Mediterranean developments (wine and precious metal vessels), and their Balkan/Carpathian imitations, were clearly at the beginning of the sequence Baden, Globular Amphorae, Corded Ware, Bell-Beakers. Are we not witnessing the spread of the 'alcohol cult',[15] the socially desirable use of intoxicating drink with elite and perhaps religious significance?

But think again about the Baden case. Here is a set of drinking equipment, clearly equivalent to that in use in the Aegean, copying similar metal models. Yet Baden is already beyond the limits of viticulture (just as it was beyond the area of advanced technology in which metal vessels could be produced). Cultivated vines were not grown in central Europe before the later Iron Age or the Roman period; and wild ones do not ferment. So what we must be witnessing is a *substitution*, the development of a local alcoholic

391

drink as substitute for wine, most probably mead. I think this is a pattern that we can see time and time again, on a global basis. Alcohol ultimately became very widespread, but largely by imitation of introduced drinks (as I shall argue below in the case of koumish). In the same way, the prestige technologies associated with the serving of alcoholic drinks were also imitated. Looking ahead, through later European prehistory, we can see how the technology caught up with its imitations: first precious metal drinking vessels, then bronze ones, and finally bulk imported wine and then viticulture itself, under the Romans (see Chapter 17). What we see in north-west Europe is a long-drawn-out series of substitutes, both for the drink and for its original Mediterranean style of serving.

We can appreciate, then, why in the third millennium there should be a series of international drinking sets, spreading between dominant groups in different areas as part of a complex of new subsistence technology and as parts of new modes of social interaction. What we are actually looking at is the origin of a tradition of alcohol-based hospitality that we will see later on, in the Classical world, as the *symposium*:[16] more than just a drinking party or a forum for philosophical discussion (for that is what it became, and why we use the word today), but originally a fundamental social mechanism, the 'feast of merit', the gathering of a following of warrior-companions, like the *Männerbund* of early Germanic history (Murray 1982; 1983; Quiller 1981). As Morton Fried (1967, 178) recalls, ranked societies are particularly characterised by their frequent 'intercommunity activities, most notably feasts, parties, ceremonies and other ceremonies predicated on organised hospitality'. It is a common and fundamental feature of later pre- and protohistoric societies in Europe. As kinship networks became larger and less linked to immediate communities, so the possibilities of creating and organising an armed body of supporters became greater, and the emphasis on warrior feasting and hospitality became more pronounced.[17] It is the genesis of this fundamentally new social fabric that we are witnessing in the third millennium, behind the spread of drinking equipment and weaponry which is the elusive characteristic of the beaker complex that we are trying to tie down. And the social lubricant of this process was, I believe, alcohol: that is what the beakers were for, and why their decoration was so elaborate.

'WHAT BEER THE BEAKER FOLK WERE WONT TO BREW'[18]

The question of what kind of drink might have been consumed from Bell-Beakers is an old one, which can be taken further only by combining evidence, argument and speculation. Since sources of sugar were relatively restricted, the possibilities are likewise limited. Beer is clearly a possibility, and will be discussed further below. We may set aside koumish, which requires large quantities of surplus milk (especially the sugar-rich mares' milk) and is unlikely to have been produced in forested temperate Europe at this date. Likewise tree-sap and native fruits or berries: there are few temperate equivalents to the sugar-rich palms, and although birch-sap can be tapped (like maple syrup in North America) it is not very sweet. Fruit wines require added sugar (for example from honey) and are best considered as types of flavoured mead (Gayre 1948). Beer or mead are thus the best candidates.

On a global scale, only a fraction of cereal-cultivators convert their grain into beer. In temperate North America, for example, no alcoholic beverages were produced in pre-contact times despite the extensive cultivation of maize, even though this grain was used further south (in Mexico and Peru) to make beer (Hatt 1953, 158). It is unlikely, therefore, that beer-making (and leavened bread) was part of the original way in which domesticated grains were utilised (Braidwood et al. 1953). Early cereal-based diets are more likely to have used parched and cracked grains for porridge ('grits'), or – if ground – for coarse, unleavened bread (Mauritzio 1932; 1933; Forbes 1954; 1955). For fermentation, conversion from starch to sugar is neces-sary; and various methods have been used. The most primitive is to chew the grain, making use of the enzyme ptyalin (amylase) in the saliva – a widespread technique, used both with grains and roots (and also to make *kava* from *Piper methysticum* in Polynesia). In the rice-growing area of south and east Asia, a fermenting fungus (*Aspergillus oryzae*) is used, that accomplishes both saccharification and fermentation. The most common method today in Eurasia and Africa is malting, using the naturally produced enzyme diastase which occurs during sprouting. This last method may not be as ancient as the first beer production in Europe, however: finds of sprouting grain are not known to me before the Roman period (though there may be many reasons for this), and the chewing method may have been the original one in Europe (with malting confined to the Near East). It has certain echoes in folklore: bear-spittle was used to induce fermentation in one episode in the Finnish *Kalevala* epic.

A good deal is known about the production of beer in the ancient civilisations of Egypt and Mesopotamia (Lutz 1922; Oppenheim 1950; Forbes 1954). Written evidence indicates that beer was made in both areas from the beginning of the historic period, and brewing-vats are shown in Predynastic Egyptian figurines. Not only barley was used, but also emmer. Dry malt-loaves (sometimes spiced) were often made as a durable com-modity that could be converted into either bread or beer. The yeasts, perhaps originally gained from making palm-wine, survived in the brewing-vats, or from the remains of a previous mash; and the mixture could be strengthened by the addition of honey or date-juice. The grains were not de-husked, and the beer was either strained or drunk through straws. The first illustration of such straws occurs in the Protoliterate (Jamdat Nasr) period, around 3200 BC, and the custom was still encountered by Xenophon (*Anabasis* IV, 5, 26) in Asia Minor in 400 BC. By this time it was probably a rather rustic survival: in lowland areas a 'strong drink' (*shekhar*), largely made from dates, had become more common.

Perhaps surprisingly, beer was not produced in the Aegean in Classical times, and the only tentative indication of its earlier use is an MM III jug from Knossos with what resemble barley-ears moulded in relief. It is not clear, therefore, whether the production of beer was a widespread early habit that was ousted in the Aegean by wine, or whether – as is perhaps more likely – we are dealing with two quite separate regional traditions that grew up independently in the Near East and Europe, and may have used quite different methods. The beer of Egypt was sufficiently unfamiliar to the Greeks to be thought worthy of remark by Herodotus (*Histories*, II, 26); while the god Dionysus was said to have fled to Greece from Mesopotamia in disgust at its inhabitants' liking for beer. On the other hand, the Greeks and Romans also associated beer with the Celts: Pliny (*Natural History* XIV, 29) recorded that the natives of western Europe (principally Gaul and Spain) intoxicated themselves with a drink made from corn and water, while Dionysius of Halicarnassus (*Roman Antiquities* XIII, 10) snobbishly noted that 'the Gauls at that time had no knowledge of wine ... but used a foul-smelling liquor made from barley rotted in water'. The Latin word for beer, *cerevisia* (Spanish *cerveza*), is relatively late and is itself a compound of the Latin for cereal plus a Celtic element meaning 'water' and surviving today in the word 'whisky'. Tacitus (*Germania* XXIII) records the use of beer amongst the Germans, and both he and other writers mention the use of wheat as well as barley to make beer in the north.

We can also turn to the kinds of cereals grown in later prehistoric Europe to see if they contain any clues. The most useful survey (for northern Europe) is by Hopf (1983), and the results are somewhat surprising. Modern brewers prefer the hulled form of two-row barley (*Hordeum distichum*); but there was no two-row barley in prehistoric Europe, only the six-row form (*H. hexastichum*); and the naked form, in contrast to the Near East at this time, was the predominant one down to the Urnfield period. Since the naked form has no advantage for brewing, it seems unlikely that its major use was for beer, whose production on any scale may have been one of the many innovations of Urnfield times. Thus the oft-cited general trend towards barley in the later Neolithic and Early Bronze Age is unlikely to be related to beer-making, and most probably it simply reflects the spread to secondary soils. There are some indications, in fact, that emmer was the cereal used for brewing in northern Europe: we shall return to this point after considering the evidence for mead. Tentatively, however, we may conclude that beer as such probably only gained its prominence in continental Europe in the Late Bronze Age or Iron Age, and may only have become predominant in the Middle Ages, by which time it consumed 20–30 per cent of the total cereal crop.

We may next consider honey and its product, mead (Gayre 1948). Honey was the most concentrated source of sugar in prehistoric temperate Europe, and no doubt a valuable and much-traded commodity (Forbes 1957). Quite how much was available, however, is an important question. 'The collection of wild honey must have been a laborious business involving movement over wide areas' (Clark 1942, 210); and Eva Crane (1983) has usefully summarised the ways in which the natural production of honey can be increased by human intervention. One system of domestic bee-keeping existed among the ancient civilisations, and is shown on Egyptian Old Kingdom reliefs. It was based on the use of a horizontal hive, of the type known ethnographically from many parts of Africa, and in Egypt used in stacks of several hives. Horizontal hives (in a pottery form still used in the Cyclades) are known from Classical times in Greece, and wood or wicker ones are described in Roman Italy by Columella. This ancient type of formal bee-keeping, typical of unforested areas and characterised by the horizontal hive, did not spread to temperate, Transalpine Europe. Instead, the tradition of forest bee-keeping – managing wild populations in living trees – lasted down to historic times. It is known from England in the Middle Ages, and remained the sole method in the Slav lands (in competition with the bears) down to fairly recent times. The erection of artificial beehives, in the form of vertical logs mimicking the trees, is known from the early centuries AD on the north German heathlands, and may be older if the more doubtful example from an Urnfield context near Berlin is accepted as a beehive. The first wicker skep – the typical Medieval form of west European beehive – again dates to the early centuries AD, at Feddersen Wierde. (All references in Crane 1983.) The keeping of domestic bees, therefore, although of some antiquity in the Mediterranean, was largely a development of the historical era in temperate Europe. The quantities of honey available to earlier Bronze Age populations are likely to have been neither large nor easily increased; honey would have been a prestige commodity. Although in Bronze Age Greece mead may have been a major competitor of wine, and even preceded it in general use (as some of the myths indicate: Zafiropulo 1966), it must have been much more restricted further north. The supply of honey in temperate Europe is not likely to have sustained a mass production of mead, which even in the Middle Ages was four times as valuable as ale.

Not surprisingly, therefore, the first evidence for a pure mead in temperate Europe dates to the Iron Age, and comes from the Hallstatt princely wagon-burial dated to around 500 BC at Hochdorf near Stuttgart (Körber-Grohne 1985). In an imported bronze cauldron set in one corner of the grave-chamber was an organic deposit consisting largely of pollen grains and beeswax. The 'tide-mark' on the vessel indicates a capacity of c.350 litres, and the mass of pollen indicates a 15–60 per cent honey content: a very high-quality mead. Some sixty different plants were represented in the pollen, covering a wide variety of ecotopes including heathland with wild thyme, pastures, meadows and bean-fields: several honeys of different origin (perhaps four or five by comparison with modern samples) would have been used. This clearly represents, like the elaborate material fittings of the tomb, a very considerable concentration of wealth. It also testifies to a rather open landscape, with many communities of honey-bees, using fields and pasture: looking towards the Medieval pattern rather than typical of the conditions of earlier prehistory.

The most direct indicator of the kind of honey known in Beaker times is the material from a spilled S4 Beaker in a cist-burial on Ashgrove Farm, Methilhill, Fife, associated with a fine metal dagger (Clarke 1970, fig. 1016; Dickson 1978). Pollen samples from a mass of leaves and moss next to the recumbent vessel gave a pollen spectrum matching the smaller quantities still adhering to the vessel wall, and presumably reflecting its original contents. It is dominated by small-leaved lime (*Tilia cordata*) at 54 per cent, followed by meadowsweet (*Filipendula* cf. *ulmaria*) at 15 per cent, and with *Calluna* heather and ribwort plantain (*P. lanceolata*) around 7 per cent each. Perhaps two honeys were used; certainly several ecotopes are represented: lime-forest (i.e. mixed oak forest selectively sampled by the bees), and much smaller areas of pasture and heath – a very different picture from Hochdorf. Interestingly, the find lies at least 100km north of the boundary of *T. cordata* at that time, and must reflect a honey traded from northern England. The meadowsweet (*medesweete* = mead-sweet) seems likely to have been added as a flavouring, and is known from other Bronze Age finds. Since the contents of the vessel as a whole were not examined, it would be wrong to conclude that this was necessarily a pure mead; we can only be certain that (no doubt fermented) honey was a component.

The best guide to the nature of Bronze Age brews is still the famous birch-bark container from an oak-coffin burial in the tumulus at Egtved, Denmark (Thomsen 1922, 184). The residue in this vessel had three components: 1. honey, indicated by pollen of lime, meadowsweet and clover; 2. fruits and leaves used for flavouring, notably *Vaccinium* (probably cranberry) fruits, and leaves of sweet gale (see below, note 22); and 3. cereal grains, identified as wheat (and therefore most probably emmer). Precisely the same mixture was found in the Danish Juellinge find of the Roman Iron Age. This is a mead, an ale, and a fruit wine all in one!

Such a mixture was almost certainly more typical of early temperate European alcoholic drinks than the 'pure' forms which probably began to appear during the first millennium BC. Before that, all sources of sugar were pressed into service, and techniques of alcohol were probably much less effective than those in use at that time in the Near East. The answer to the question of what drink was consumed from Bell-Beakers cannot be given in a single word. Alcohol was a precious substance, hard-won (no doubt with much ritual and mystique) from a temperate environment, and often adulterated with other things. Its effects would have been a remarkable experience, perhaps not available to society at large, and monopolised by the powerful.

A FINAL CLEW

It remains to explain one important thread in the argument which I have just discussed, the significance of which occurred to me only after writing this text in 1986. The thread is, of course, the strand of twisted cord that linked the societies of the North European Plain, from the Pontic steppes to the British Isles, and was a fundamental feature of the first generation of Bell-Beaker, the All-over-Cord type (Figure 15.10). Why was cord decoration so prominent, albeit temporarily, in that area? Can we follow the logic of our explanation further? I believe that we can.

Cord ornament started earliest on the steppes, in Sredni Stog and Pit-Graves (Telegin 1973; Merpert 1974). It was also widespread in east Asia from quite early Neolithic times (the Sheng-wen horizon in China and Jōmon in Japan: both terms mean 'corded ware'); but not in the northern forest belt of Eurasia, where rather similar, coarse, impressed pottery was nevertheless decorated only with pit-and-comb ornament, not cord impressions. Cord decoration spread west with Globular Amphorae, and then with Corded Ware, and it was painstakingly imitated as false cord and stamped comb decoration. Why? Think about the steppes. The drinking complex – jugs and cups related to metal forms, or even distinctive drinking vessels of any type – did not penetrate until very late; not till Greek colonial

15.10 Cord impressions on a cord-impressed (AOC) Bell-Beaker from Cassington, Oxfordshire (Clarke 730); (Ashmolean Museum); [new photograph].

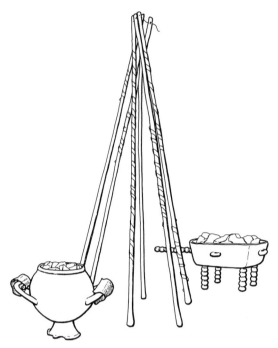

15.11 Equipment for inhaling cannabis smoke from Barrow 2 at Pazyryk, Altai Mountains, Siberia (late 5th/early 4th century BC: bronze 'censers' with charcoal and hemp seeds, and wooden framework for small tent (after Rudenko 1970); [new drawing].

influence in Scythian times. That is probably when the steppe tribes invented koumish – like mead, a local wine substitute. So how did they amuse themselves? The answer is in Herodotus, supported by the archaeology of the Pazyryk tombs (Figure 15.11):

> On a framework of tree sticks, meeting at the top, they stretch pieces of woollen cloth. Inside this tent they put a dish with hot stones on it. Then they take some hemp seed, creep into the tent, and throw the seed on the hot stones. At once it begins to smoke, giving off a vapour unsurpassed by any vapour bath one could find in Greece. The Scythians enjoy it so much that they howl with pleasure.[19]

Poor Herodotus: he thought it was an alternative to washing. Years before, the inhabitants of the steppes had discovered the joys of the native hemp plant, *Cannabis sativa*, that they cultivated for its fibres, and converted it into a socially approved intoxicant (Merlin 1972). I think that those people were the Sredni Stog group, and that they celebrated its importance by imprinting it on their pottery.[20] They passed on their knowledge, and their cultigen,[21] to their neighbours, the eastern wing of the Globular Amphora culture, who incorporated it in the complex of male-associated paraphernalia inspired by the southern alcoholic tradition. They may even have mixed them in some amazing combination[22] – the trick, apparently, is to heat the hemp leaves in butter – and passed on their secret to their Corded Ware successors. Did the All-over-Cord beaker, like those Late Bronze Age Cypriot opium jugs in the shape of a poppy, actively advertise its contents through its ceramic form and decoration? It is an attractive thought.

Cord decoration remained typical of northern Bronze Age pottery well into the second millennium. Hemp was probably ousted, as a fibre by wool, and as an intoxicant by better brews of alcohol, perhaps beer. It survived on the steppes, of course, and it was passed on, via the Persians, to the Arabs. The rest you know. But what of Beakers? Hemp seems to have remained a northern plant, until it was introduced into the Mediterranean from Anatolia by Hellenistic Greeks and Romans, who wanted it for ropes. As Bell-Beakers spread south, they left their cord decoration (and presumably their hemp) behind them. For a short time its memory was kept alive by imitative comb decoration, but then incised panels, drawing their inspiration from woollen textiles, took over. And the Beakers themselves diminished in size as they spread further south. I like to think that alcohol's long journey, through remote northern regions where it was adulterated by other infusions, was coming to an end. In the west Mediterranean, the alcoholic tradition found once again sunshine, and sugar, and strength (Walker 1985). It was like coming home.

Epilogue: das Glockenbechersymposion[23]

The specific interpretation offered above may or may not be true. The general point remains: beakers were for drinking, and most probably for drinking alcohol. This form of (usually male) entertainment has been a characteristic feature of European culture ever since, and is still a familiar part of the pattern of social life. It is basic to an understanding of our everyday modes of interaction.

The fabric of social relations is held together by knots of hospitality: social occasions at which the participants come together in larger numbers than usual to display their achievements, to compete with their neighbours, choose their partners and cement their alliances. The character of a culture takes its tone from these events. That we can understand these aspects of Beaker society – far better than we can think ourselves into the ways of their megalithic predecessors – is because these motives are still with us. Our cups still cheer; our conferences are still symposia.

Notes

1. On the subject of drinking, it is hard to avoid literary allusions: hence both the title, and the quotation which introduces this section. William Cowper's interest was in temperance: the 'cups / That cheer but not inebriate' (*A Winter Evening*; 1785) were part of the

new, middle-class tea ceremony. John Keats' intentions (*Ode to a Nightingale*; 1818) were alcoholic, but misguided. His beaker 'full of the warm south, / Full of the true, the blushful Hippocrene, / With beaded bubbles winking at the brim, / And purple-stained mouth' could have been no more than a mirage – for the Hippocrene was in fact a spring, the 'horse's spring' supposedly created where the foot of Pegasus struck Mount Helicon in Boeotia. Although the well was sacred to the Muses and said to be the inspiration of poets, Keats may have found red wine more effective in his quest, 'That I may drink, and leave the world unseen.'

2. The Millaran *Küppelgräber* seem to represent a somewhat different phenomenon from the other, truly megalithic burial monuments which occur from Iberia, through Brittany and Britain to Scandinavia and north Germany. The former are distinctive not only in their more sophisticated architecture and the quality and quantity of their grave-goods, but also in their association with large, nucleated settlements (like Los Millares itself). The more northerly megalithic tombs, while they may in certain phases be associated with ritual enclosures, seem to be in some way an *alternative* to nucleated settlement on the pattern of central and southern Europe. The social units represented by the two sorts of megalithic collective tombs, and the social organisation and ideology underlying them, may thus have been very different.

3. Whether this development was a purely European phenomenon, or whether there was already some connection with the Late Chalcolithic cultures of Anatolia (where handled jugs and cups were prominent features of pottery assemblages) is unclear: unfortunately this phase is not yet represented in well-excavated levels in the central Bulgarian tells (e.g. Dipsiska Mogila, Ezero, which has a hiatus at this point). Neighbouring areas, including both Greece and Moldavia, seem more conservative in their culture at this time, and their assemblages continue to be dominated by painted pottery, figurines, and other archaic elements. The Carpathian Basin (and, on a smaller scale, areas like Thrace) had the combined advantages of dense populations, copper and gold sources, and open land for stock-raising. This area thus became the focus of European developments; and it is possible that already by this stage it had links to Anatolia. The rich finds at the cemetery of Varna suggest that the Danube/Black Sea trade route to northern or western Anatolia was already in use. These latter areas, however, are very poorly known at this period.

4. Since they are open, handled shapes, then the alternative explanation, that they were containers for traded organic commodities, seems less likely (although some later inter-regional shapes, like the TRB collared flask, almost certainly were).

5. One reason for this is a large-scale internal redistribution of population (probably con-sequent on use of the plough), which produced a move to the foothills and interfluves, filling in the Danube-Tisza interfluve which formerly separated these blocs. On a large scale, this is typical of the shift from riverine to interfluvial patterns of settlement, and the changed topology of interaction which it brought about.

6. Although the Corded Ware complex seems to have spread initially in areas formerly influenced by the Globular Amphora complex, the two complexes existed in parallel for some centuries in distributions which were to a large extent mutually exclusive (Kruk 1980). The Globular Amphora 'heartland' in Kujavia and the middle Vistula resisted the pattern of Corded Ware expansion (which engulfed surrounding areas) down to the emergence of the Chłopice-Vesele group.

7. For the evidence behind these assertions, see previous chapters.

8. The use of domesticated horses in the west Mediterranean seems to show a striking association with the Bell-Beaker culture, even if they then became very rare before be-coming more common in the Bronze Age. The association with Beakers was first pointed out for Spain by Schüle (1969), confirmed for Italy by the site of Sesto Fiorentino near Florence, and now for Majorca at Ferrandell-Oleza by Waldren. The same picture seems also to apply to Ireland, and probably the British Isles as a whole. I thank Lawrence Barfield and Bill Waldren for their comments on these finds.

9. Wool has a very high affinity for dyes, and takes the colour well and evenly; linen has a

very poor affinity (worse than cotton) and its structure prevents an even penetration of dyestuffs. I am much indebted to Mrs Beatrice Clayre (Beatrice Blance) for confirming this point and providing me with a photocopy of *From Fibre to Fabric* (1946), a handbook printed for the staff of G. and R. Wills.

10. It is, of course, significant that we describe Bell-Beaker ornament as being organised in zones, using the Greek word *zone* meaning a belt. The association of belts and warrior prowess is an old-established one. The elite troop of Greek soldiers are the *Evzones*, the 'well-belted ones'; and the various colours of belt ('Black Belt' etc.) are still used to denote grades of attainment in the martial art of judo. The bone belt-fastener is a characteristic feature of rich male Corded Ware and Bell-Beaker graves (Clarke 1970, 265 and 299, fig. 144), and the tangless buckle survives today in English heraldry in the insignia of the Order of the Garter. The belts on the Aosta statue-menhirs are particularly emphasised and decorated with (possibly woven) geometric motifs. They may have been worn with leather armour, or possibly quilted clothing, to give the characteristic lozenge-shaped decoration found also on later Bell-Beaker pottery (and onto which the Clandon lozenge would perhaps fit?).

11. It is possible to define different regional traditions in weapon use (or, more often, display). The axe was characteristic of central Europe, supplemented by the dagger (perhaps for younger males, as hinted by the grave finds); in western Europe the bow and arrow was more common, with the dagger being somewhat rarer – perhaps equivalent to the axe further east. Several of the characteristic features of the 'Beaker complex' relate to archery (and perhaps to leather armour). Daggers became the standard personal weapons of the early Bronze Age throughout Europe, supplemented in the later phase by pole arms: halberd and spear.

12. As Mary Douglas has remarked (Douglas and Isherwood 1980): 'The ultimate object of consumption activity is to enter a social universe whose processes consist of matching goods to classes of social occasions.'

13. Tobacco is a particularly privileged substance, with its own social conventions: if I cadge a cigarette, it is polite also to accept a light for it – to light one's own in such circumstances is to deny the essentially social character of the transaction by treating one's partner as a machine.

14. Tea, coffee and drinking-chocolate all arrived in London in 1657; but coffee was already being drunk in Balliol College, Oxford, twenty years before; while Oxford had its first coffee-house (the 'Angel') in 1650.

15. Direct comparison with the drug-based cults of the New World such as Mescalinism (the Peyote Cult) in North America is misleading, since this was related to the breakdown of native cultures in the post-contact period. Indeed, in some aspects this cult mimics the Christian Eucharist, and it forms part of an ideology of accommodation to Western culture, after the rebellion of the Ghost Dance. What is interesting, however, is the way in which the use of the peyote cactus did not spread into the Great Basin, because of the existing use there of Jimsonweed. There may be some analogy here with the apparent failure of the drinking complex to spread on the Pontic steppes in the third millennium BC. (For discussion of hallucinogenic substances and their cult significance see Furst 1976; Harner 1973; and La Barre 1972.)

16. See Athenaeus for extended descriptions of feasting, and especially drinking (Book XI), in the Graeco-Roman world. The book itself is cast in the form of an after-dinner discussion, and its various participants introduce quotations from older writers and information from their own experience to provide an extensive 'ethnotaxonomy' of drinks and drinking-culture in the Ancient World.

17. Cf. C. A. Wilson (1973, 331) on early Medieval England: 'Mead was a warrior's drink, the drink of the aristocracy both Celtic and Saxon. Not for nothing was the great hall of the Saxon palace called the mead hall. In the highland zone mead drinking had a special significance. The bodyguard who surrounded a Celtic chief or princeling consumed his mead, but in recompense fought his battles, a service known as "paying for mead". When 300 Celtic warriors met the English at Catraeth in the late sixth century, "the pale mead

was their feast and their poison"; for all except one gave their lives in battle in payment for their mead.'

18. The quote is from Stuart Piggott's famous *Ballade* to Gordon Childe, written in 1935:
    All secrets of the past are here laid bare –
    What beer the Beaker Folk were wont to brew,
    The answer to a Lausitz maiden's prayer
    The recipe for Maglemose fish glue ...
    You'll find them all in footnotes in *The Dawn*.
    The reference is to a footnote on what became p. 223 of the seventh edition of *The Dawn* (Childe 1957), where millet grains are reported from a Beaker in Portugal (International Institute of Anthropology Congress 1930, Portugal, 356).
19. Herodotus, *Histories* IV, 75.
20. It is worth noting that the early use of cord-impressed pottery in China – the so-called Sheng-wen horizon – was associated with an early use of hemp and an appreciation (explicit in the early historical records) of its narcotic properties.
21. The first certain identification of hemp in Europe is in the Hallstatt-period *Fürstengrab* of Hochdorf near Stuttgart, dated to c.500 BC. The report on the organic remains (Körber-Grohne 1985) is the most thorough summary of data on the question of the introduction of *Cannabis sativa*. It corrects the list of finds reported by Willerding (1970) and removes as uncertain all the claimed pre-Iron Age occurrences; and it provides a pioneering set of criteria for microscopic identification. These now need to be systematically applied to the well-preserved fibres from Swiss lake-village textiles, usually identified macroscopically as linen. My suspicion is that hemp was introduced to Europe in the third millennium, but largely died out and only became common again under Scythian influence.
22. This may seem far-fetched; but do we not even today flavour our beer with lupulin from another member of the Cannabiaceae: the hop, *Humulus lupulus*, a close relative of hemp? Other historically recorded European beer-flavouring plants were the sweet gale, *Myrica gale*, and members of the genera *Salvia*, *Artemisia* and *Laurus*: see Behre 1984; Hartley 1954; 1964. There are records also of *Tamarix germanica* and *Vitex agrius-castus* among the ancient Germans, and yarrow, *Achilloea millefolium* (a plant with medicinal properties) in Iceland. In ancient Egypt, lupin, *Lupinus termis*, and skirret, *Sium sisarum*, were apparently used: Lutz 1922. In Mesopotamia the work of the brewer in the Akkadian period 'consisted mainly in the grating of aromatic substances and their mixing into liquid or fatty carriers for the preservation of their specific smell or taste' (Oppenheim 1950, 9). The method of heating hemp-leaves in butter to make a *ganga*-drink was used in Pakistan early this century.
23. Forgive the *double entendre*: I have argued that Bell-Beakers were symbolic of hospi-tality; and a major conference on the Bell-Beaker culture took place in Oberried in 1974 – the *Glockenbechersymposion* – at which David Clarke gave a famous paper.

16

Sacred and Profane Substances: The Ritual Use of Narcotics in Later Neolithic Europe[1]

(1991)

The opposite of sacred is secular;[2] the concept of profanity is dependent on the pre-existence of a division between them. Just as dirt is matter out of place, so profanity is part of the sacred which has escaped from its proper context, into the realm of the secular. It is this structure which underlies our colloquial usage of the word 'profanity' to mean an oath or swear-word: for even the trivial emphatic 'bloody' began life as a religious invocation ('by Our Lady').[3] It is a religious utterance made in a secular context. The fact that we no longer see it in this light is a consequence of the way it has lost its religious force and has been dulled by repetition.[4] In current usage the term 'profanity' has almost lost its distinctive meaning, and the words 'profane' and 'secular' are practically interchangeable. In understanding pre-industrial Europe, we need to regain our sensitivity to such distinctions.

Like other categories of cultural classification, the distinction between sacred and secular begins by partitioning the world into paired opposites, and so can generate further qualities from the mixture of the two (Leach 1976; Douglas 1966). Profanity is a form of pollution resulting from this mixture: the sacred-out-of-context as opposed to the sacred-in-context. But what distinguishes the sacred/profane distinction from the merely inappropriate collision of categories – putting one's feet on the dining-table,

---

The conclusions of the last chapter raise the question: what came before alcohol? Surely not sobriety! In recognising the central significance of consumption-events involving psychotropic substances, this approach offered suggestive interpretations for some of the most prominent artefacts in the archaeological record. (The prediction concerning Grooved Ware was magnificently fulfilled recently by the discovery of henbane (Hyoscyamus niger) seeds in a pot at Balfarg, Scotland.) This particular account was prepared for another Oxford conference, under the title 'Sacred and Profane'; and I used the opportunity to explore the contrast between megalithic and succeeding cultures in terms of what I would now call 'shamanic' and 'hospitable' uses of psychotropic substances – the domestication of ecstasy.

for instance – is the degree of supernatural power inherent in the sacred. Where the power which attaches to sacred things has to be restricted to its proper places, the *fana* or shrines, it is important that it should be confined within these limits; taken outside this conceptual boundary, the sacred becomes literally pro-fane. Within such a religious system, profanity is a particularly powerful form of pollution. This does not mean that it never happens; but when it does, it has important consequences.[5] Unless traditional values are reasserted, the sacred can be allowed to atrophy; or it can be actively subverted, and used to new ends. In this case it may be an important lever of social change, as I shall try to exemplify later in this chapter.

When the sacred has spatial boundaries, it also has temporal ones. Sacred time is periodic, punctuated by appropriate ritual observance and visits to sacred places (Leach 1961, 124–36). Objects used at these times will pass into the category of sacred things, after which they have to be treated in a special way – as with the consecration of the host in the Christian Eucharist. With food, this is usually consumption within the context of the sacred; that is, within particular spatial and temporal limits. Theological arguments over the reservation of the sacrament hinge upon this point: to what extent can the power of consecrated elements be carried over from the ritual meal of which they form part? This dilemma is more acute where the ritual involves an inedible residue, as in the case of animal sacrifice where the bones and offal are left over. Consumption by fire, or by burial, is often an appropriate response.[6] Neolithic 'ritual pits' may find an explanation in this context, as an appropriate way of disposing of inedible remains of sacrificial meals by returning them to the earth. In the same way, pottery containers used in ritual may be deliberately smashed: they belong to the world of periodic time.

In prehistoric communities the distinction between sacred and secular power is unlikely to have been a sharp one; priestly and elite activities are unlikely to have been strongly differentiated, as they often are in literate societies. Nevertheless, the basic opposition, sacred:secular, was undoubtedly present, and is likely to have been congruent with structures of social power, although potentially in several different ways. Thus the various 'elites' recognised by processual archaeologists can also be seen as social categories with preferential access to supernatural force, whether they are recognisable by megalithic monuments or by burial with such apparently secular items as drinking-cups and copper daggers. The profound changes in the later Neolithic of north-west Europe, indicated by the shift from the former set of artefacts to the latter, have often been seen as a process of secularisation: in caricature, as the replacement of communities of religious devotees by groups of boozy warriors. Yet such a crude contrast is undoubtedly an oversimplification, however disguised in structuralist or Marxist clothing. The purpose of this chapter is to review some of the phenomena which cross-cut this division, and to trace some of the common 'super-natural' elements in the construction of social power in the two periods. Having identified this continuity, however, I shall return to the contrast; for it suggests that 'profanity' is a concept which makes sense in one sort of religious universe but not in another.

THE ANTHROPOLOGY OF INTOXICATION

Archaeologists, by the very nature of their raw material, tend to place undue emphasis on durable artefacts. Anthropologists and historians, observing their societies in the round, have given equal emphasis to perishable, organic items as distinguishing characteristics of cultures and social groups: and the subtle languages of clothing and cuisine have both been illuminated by structural analysis (e.g. Douglas 1975; 1982; 1987). Following this lead, archaeologists have to follow such indirect clues as pin types and pot shapes, supplemented occasionally by the analysis of organic clothing or food residues. This often requires an imaginative leap: but our vision of pre-historic Europe is likely to be more misleading if we ignore these clues than if we mis-identify their detail. That is the justification for this essay in speculation.

In approaching any pre-industrial society, there are many features of the modern world which we must leave behind. The loudest noise in Medieval Europe was the sound of church bells; the brightest colours were the clothes of the rulers and the vestments of the priests. The sweetest taste was honey; the sharpest spice was, for most people, something like wild mint. Neolithic Europe had even fewer sensual stimulants, and it is hard for us to imagine how powerful would be the impact of even modest innovations in this mon-otonous sensory spectrum. Conversely, there would have been an extensive knowlege of the various mood-altering substances which occur in the natural flora, and which survive today in the attenuated form of 'herbal remedies'. Temperate Europe, however, was not rich in such herbs, which are more abundant in Mediterranean and sub-tropical areas where sun-shine, seasonal aridity and competition factors produce a greater variety of stimulating and aromatic chemical substances in plants. There was thus considerable potential for the spread of even mild stimulants, and of methods of preparation which enhanced their effectiveness.

The acts of eating and drinking, however, like the wearing of clothes, are not simply private responses to individual needs. In societies other than the present capitalist world of takeaway junk food and TV dinners, such con-sumption is a public affair whose structure and organisation say much about the social relationships of those involved. Special foods are for special occasions, and the composition of the social grouping at such times is of special significance, providing opportunities for exercises either in inclusive-ness or exclusiveness. This is true both for overtly religious feasting and for forms of conviviality which while not explicitly 'sacred' are nevertheless episodic and meaning-laden. While we cannot predict the precise form that such consumption ceremonies will take, we might expect the archaeological record to be particularly eloquent about such phenomena, since the equipment for the occasion is likely to be the focus of unusual elaboration and the residues especially copious. With care, one might hope to discern various cycles of feasting, from domestic celebration to communal occasions requiring the large-scale slaughter/sacrifice of animals[7] and the brewing of drinks.

Eating and drinking themselves, however, are only a part of the spectrum of expressive consumption behaviour. Organic substances are also used for cleansing and scenting, and so can form part of purification ceremonies – often, though not necessarily, combined with occasions for feasting. Although it appears common sense to modern western observers that cleansing is achieved by washing, it may equally be carried out by fumigation. The northern steam-bath and sweat-house has its counterpart in the smoke-bath and fumigation-tent; and both may use scented media to enhance the effect. In more concentrated form, these may be available as perfume and incense – the close relationship between them indicated by the name perfume (*par fume*, 'by smoke'). These bodily applications in turn grade into other categories such as cosmetics and paints, and the use of ornaments and special clothing. All are likely to be combined in periodic special occasions, as aspects of ritual.

Expressive behaviour of this kind is especially significant in such rituals if it is accompanied by changes of mood and metabolism. Of particular importance on such occasions, therefore, is the consumption (either by ingestion or inhalation) of substances which have psychoactive effects, inducing excitement, inebriation, hypnosis, phantasy or euphoria (to use conventional pharmacological categories). The quantities of the stimulant may be small, but if the sensation is an unusual one it will have a corresponding effect, which may be enhanced by fasting or breathing control. Such experiences are likely to be deliberately sought in the course of ceremony or religious ritual, when they can be interpreted within a cosmological scheme and perhaps seen as a means of access to other worlds. Such shamanistic rites must go back to an early phase of prehistory, perhaps shortly after the emergence of *Homo sapiens sapiens*; and the emergence of a written record provides ample evidence of the employment of drugs in this way: the ritual use of *Nymphaea caerula* as part of the Osiris cult is known from Dynastic Egypt, just as the Inkas used *coca* leaves and the Aztecs considered hallucinogenic mushrooms to be *teonanacatl*, the flesh of God; the Aryans of the *Rig Veda* drank the intoxicating *soma* as a divine beverage; while Herodotus described the Scythians' practice of inhaling *Cannabis* smoke in communal (male) ceremonies (Emboden 1979). Wine was the gift to Greece of Dionysus, praised in the *dithyramb* before drinking at the

406

symposion; and the Christian whose 'cup runneth over' echoes the cry of the psalmist: 'My chalice inebriateth me'. Any account of prehistoric Europe which omits a consideration of such substances is likely to be incomplete.

NARCOTIC ARCHAEOLOGY

There are two avenues of discovery which may potentially lead to the kind of information which is needed. One is palaeobotany, which can demonstrate the occurrence of plants producing narcotic[8] substances; though this is not in itself sufficient to show that they were used as such. The other type of evidence, less direct but more abundant, is material culture, principally pottery. Certain distinctive and widely distributed artefacts can find an explanation in this context.

Palaeobotanical evidence for prehistoric narcotics

Although many plants contain substances with psychoactive properties, two in particular stand out as possibilities for narcotic use: the opium poppy (*Papaver somniferum*) and the hemp plant (*Cannabis sativa*). The former was a member of the native European flora (perhaps with a southern or Mediterranean distribution), while the other has an eastern and Steppe distribution. Both were grown and utilised in Neolithic times.

The evidence for the early history of opium has been reviewed by Merlin (1984). Poppies occur as weeds in fields of cereals, and their seeds are nutritious and tasty, so that they may initially have been cultivated for this purpose. The complex of narcotic alkaloids (morphine, codeine, papaverine, etc.) known collectively as opium occurs most abundantly in the sap of the unripe seed-head (capsule), from which it may be extracted in dilute form by soaking and in a stronger form by puncturing or scoring the surface of the capsule. Dilute forms of opium were used medicinally in the ancient world to assuage a variety of conditions and as an analgesic, as noted by Galen in the second century AD. Earlier literary and iconic references show that it was often used in religious contexts in the first and also the second millennia BC.

Poppy seeds were identified as early as 1878 among material from the Swiss Neolithic lake villages; and more recently they have been identified among the earliest *Bandkeramik* assemblages in the Rhineland. They have also been found in Neolithic caves in Spain. The very wet and very dry sites preserve capsules as well as seeds. As with other early cultigens, the taxonomy of early cultivated forms is complex, but indisputably domesticated forms may be identified (as with the non-shattering rachis in cereals) by loss of the ability to seed themselves. In the case of poppies, this is the closure of the dehiscent ring of pores around the head of the capsule, through which the seeds are ejected by jactitation. This condition has been identified in prehistoric specimens. The general view is that the opium poppy was domesticated in the West Mediterranean, perhaps as early as Impressed Ware times, and spread from there to other parts of Europe.

The most explicit indication of its cultural significance in Neolithic times comes from discoveries in a burial-cave fifty metres above the bed of a ravine at Albuñol near the coast of Granada in southern Spain. This site, the Cueva de los Murciélagos ('Bat Cave') was explored and largely destroyed by digging for bat-guano and minerals in the mid-nineteenth century; but the finds were published by Gongora (1868) and have recently been restudied and radiocarbon-dated to c.4200 BC (Giner 1980; see especially plate 1, p. 147[9]). A large number of burials was reported to have been found, accompanied by globular bags of esparto grass (*Stipa tenacissima*) with a variety of items inside them, including large numbers of opium-poppy capsules. This find suggests that poppy-heads had a symbolic significance beyond the simple use of their seeds as a source of food, and that this symbolism was particularly appropriate as an accompaniment for the dead.

The case for cannabis is similar. Its use in the Iron Age, from western Europe to China, is established by the abundant finds from the Hochdorf Hallstatt D wagon-burial, from Herodotus' famous account of the Scythians (whose accuracy has been confirmed by the Pazyryk finds), and from references in Han medical texts (Chapter 15). The plant has been sporadically noted in earlier contexts, and there are two finds from the early third millennium which establish its probable use as a narcotic at that time in eastern Europe (Ecsedy 1979, 45). The first is from a Pit-Grave (Kurgan) burial of the later third millennium BC at Gurbaneşti near Bucharest in Romania, where a 'pipe cup' containing charred hemp-seeds accompanied one of the burials in the tumulus.[10] The second is a more or less contemporary burial belonging to the north Caucasian Early Bronze Age, where a similar 'pipe-cup' with hemp-seeds in it came to light.[11] The appearance of these items coincides with the rise of the Pit-Grave culture on the steppes, and its westward penetration to Romania, Bulgaria and Hungary. This agrees with the botanical data for a steppe distribution of *Cannabis sativa*, and its spread from this region as a cultivated plant into Europe and China.

In both these cases, the plants were known to early farmers in Europe, and some familiarity with their narcotic properties may be presumed. The varieties with a stronger narcotic content probably evolved later (perhaps by conscious selection?), but even a weak narcotic effect would have been appreciated in Neolithic times. The early varieties may well have gone out of use when other psychoactive substances such as alcohol came into widespread use, to reappear when stronger forms were available and perhaps also had the social *cachet* of exotic, introduced novelties. Their social history is thus likely to be a complex one. Various other plants with similar weak narcotic properties may also have been used in prehistoric times, though their use has been forgotten since they did not evolve more potent varieties.

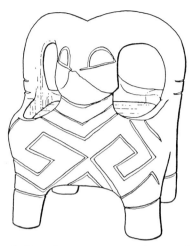

16.1 *Pottery 'altar' (probably a lamp or aromatic-burner) from a deposit of pottery vessels in the Vinča-period copper mine at Rudna Glava, Serbia; height 20cm (after Jovanović).*

Such narcotic substances could have been used in several different ways: either by inhaling fumes or by ingestion in solid or liquid form. All of these methods may have been used, before the Industrial Revolution provided the means of preparing chemically pure forms; but there are suggestions from the archaeological record (see below) that burning was the original mode of narcotic use, and that it survived in peripheral parts of Europe when infusion had become more common. It is likely that the context of consumption by whatever method was a ritual one, and the particular mode of use was probably dependent on the prevailing symbolism of burning, eating and drinking, and its significance as a means of purification, communion, or whatever. (The causation is complex, for such significance could be recursively affected by the appearance of new psychoactive substances with a single mode of use, as I shall argue for alcohol.) Such 'religious' uses would no doubt have included 'medicinal' uses as well, since it would be artificial to separate physical healing from ritual observance.

The ceramic evidence: 1. smoke inhalation

Among the ceramic items of the Balkan Neolithic, and especially common in the fifth millennium BC, is a group of objects which have long been described as 'ritual' and discussed in the context of figurines and models of houses, ovens and shrines. These objects are usually described as 'altars' (Figure 16.1), and consist of a small dish on three or four feet. They often incorporate representational elements such as animal-heads at the extremities, and they are usually richly decorated in the manner of contemporary fine pottery. It has been suggested that they are lamps (Nandris 1973), but this 'common-sense' interpretation may conceal an expressive

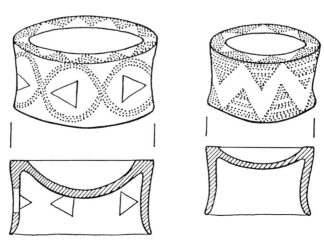

16.2 Pottery 'vase-supports' (probably braziers; perhaps for opium?) of the Chasséen period from the ceremonial site of Er Lannic, Morbihan, Brittany; height c.10cm (after Le Rouzic). Some 160 vessels of this kind were recovered from the site, an enclosure of standing stones.

dimension beyond simple functionality, which is suggested by their elaborate form and decoration. Fire and smoke have a particular potential for symbolic meaning (and can be enhanced by the burning of simple aromatic substances such as pine resin);[12] such vessels may have combined the characteristics of lamps and incense-burners (*thymiateria*), rather than simply providing illumination. They are sufficiently common to suggest a context in domestic ritual. However, fragments of such elaborate vessels have been found in the Vinča-period copper mine of Rudna Glava in north-east Jugoslavia (Jovanović 1982), which might suggest that an element of (propitiatory?) ritual may have accompanied the extraction of metal ores.

Such items do no more than suggest the widespread symbolic importance of small braziers in the minor rituals of households or work-groups of a variety of cultures in Neolithic south-east Europe; but a more specific significance may attach to various classes of 'inter-cultural' braziers which appeared later on in the Neolithic. One of these is the so-called *vase-support* (Figure 16.2): a characteristic artefact of Middle Neolithic France in the early fourth millennium BC, associated with the spread of the Chassey culture – a convergent grouping of heterogeneous megalithic and non-megalithic societies, from the Midi to Brittany and the Paris Basin. They are associated with a particular style of pottery decoration, which seems to have spread from south to north. Again, they are shallow, bowl-like containers of limited capacity, set within a cylindrical or cubic stand, and almost invariably carrying profuse decoration; and some of the bowls carry traces of burning. The suggestion that these were stands for round-bottomed bowls is less convincing than the interpretation expressed in their alternative name: *brûle-parfums*. These objects occur in caves in the south, and in ditched enclosures in the Paris Basin, and they occur not infrequently in megaliths in the west. In Brittany, they occur in vast numbers on the sacred site within an arc of standing stones (*cromlech*) on the hilltop (now an island) of Er Lannic, opposite the great passage grave of Gavrinis in the Morbihan.

Their use in group ritual, within sacred contexts in space and perhaps in time, seems rather clear; and their inter-regional distribution suggests that they were associated with a cult which spread from south to north over a large area of western Europe, uniting groups of different ultimate origins – Impressed Ware in the south, *Bandkeramik* in the north, indigenous in the west. Were they also, therefore, associated with the use of a particular substance, perhaps with psychoactive properties, which was the focus[13] of a specific ritual? There are many ethnographic examples of the spread of cults centred on the use of narcotics, of which the north American *peyote* cult (based on an intoxicating cactus) in the historic period is perhaps the best known, though tobacco provides an older example of a widespread New World ritual narcotic (cf. Hopewell stone smoking-pipes). Is it coincidence that the appearance of the apparatus of a southern cult should occur in northern France at the same time as Breton megalithic art reached its psychedelic climax in the entoptic forms and hallucinogenic images of the Gavrinis carvings (Bradley 1989; Chapter 13)? Since the palaeobotanical evidence suggests a west Mediterranean focus for the use of *Papaver somniferum*, this would seem to constitute a *prima facie* case for the ritual use of opium as a narcotic.

Such 'inter-cultural' artefacts, suggestive of the cult use of narcotics, appear on an even wider scale in the later Neolithic. One of the clearest examples, commonly interpreted as a brazier, is the polypod bowl, often with a radiating star or 'sunburst' design of incised or cord-impressed ornament within it, which occurs in several parts of eastern Europe in the early third millennium BC (Figure 16.3). Its occurrence has recently been usefully reviewed by Ingrid Burger (1980). The earliest examples occur on the Pontic steppes, in the fortified settlements of the Mihailovka culture. It spread westwards to the Carpathian Basin, where it is particularly characteristic of Vučedol, and then into southern Germany and Czechoslovakia where it occurs in Cham and Řivnáč contexts, and it survives in EBA contexts (Čaka, Nagyrev) in the Carpathian Basin. This westward progression parallels the spread of the system of decorative elements based on cord-impressions (although this also occurs beyond the distribution of the braziers, as we shall see below). The point to note is its retention of highly specific characteristics of form and decoration over a thousand miles and half a dozen cultures, spreading from the steppes into temperate Europe. This, too, is suggestive of a cult context: and in view of the palaeobotanical evidence discussed above for the use of *Cannabis sativa*, is strongly suggestive of its interpretation as a ritual hemp-burner (perhaps in conjunction with a small tent of the kind described by Herodotus).[14]

411

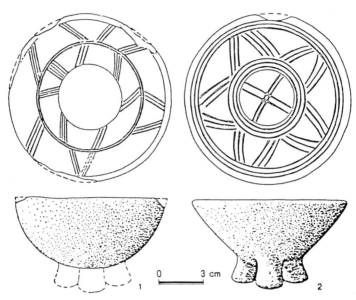

16.3 *Pottery polypod bowls (Fußschalen – braziers, perhaps for cannabis?) from eastern and central Europe: left, Mihailovka period, Ukraine; right, Vučedol period, Slovenia; heights are 11 to 14cm. The design has been interpreted as a solar symbol (after Gimbutas).*

The ceramic evidence: 2. eating and drinking

Bearing in mind these indications for the possible reflection in material culture of the social use of psychoactive substances by burning, let us turn to other means of consumption, by ingestion. The elaboration of particular sets of eating and drinking equipment may indicate a comparable role for the ritual uses of food and drink, and its sanctification in ceremony. Some of these recipes, especially by the late Neolithic, may have involved special ingredients.

It is important to bear in mind that *all* assemblages of pottery containers are likely to reflect a culinary syntax, more or less elaborate, and that such an elaboration of cuisine is one of the characteristics of farming societies. A perception of this kind of difference lies behind our classification of Ertebølle (with its simple repertoire of large point-based pots) as Mesolithic, and TRB (with its variety of bowls and amphorae) as Neolithic, despite the fact that both are formally ceramic, used polished stone axes, and had not dissimilar subsistence economies.[15] With increasing elaboration of cuisine, one might expect an increasing differentiation of pottery according to the contexts in which its contents were consumed. Neolithic pottery assemblages, however, have traditionally been analysed on the assumption that coherent styles represent either the different periods or regional variability, with some allowance for a functional contrast between coarse and fine wares. This minimal model is often enough to produce a sufficiently

412

coherent ceramic sequence for the purposes of dating and correlation. Increasingly, however, this model is causing confusion: the data are not patterned in this simple way; and this kind of complexity is especially evident in the assemblages of the later Neolithic.

In Britain, for instance, it is apparent that Grooved Ware has a totally different pattern of variability from that predicted on the expectation of tight regional or chronological groups; the various sub-styles are distributed without regard to the geographical zonation of other classes of artefacts such as stone axes, and, moreover, Grooved Ware occurs on its own in specific contexts such as monuments or isolated pits, without other wares known to have been in contemporary use. In this respect its deposition resembles that of metalwork, which is notoriously difficult to integrate into conventional ceramic sequences. Although it is not in itself of intrinsic value (as could be argued, for example, with the finer types of Bell-Beaker), Grooved Ware seems to have had a special quality which set it aside from everyday containers. It can therefore be suggested that this quality lies in the context in which it was used, and that this is likely to have been some form of ceremonial meal with sacred connotations, taken at central cult places throughout the length of Britain. If this is so, then what was consumed at such a meal may also have some sacramental significance, and may have involved more than everyday ingredients: something more sugary, spicy, or exciting (even narcotic) than was encountered in secular existence. There is at present no evidence to suggest what it might have been.

The taxonomic problems of later Neolithic pottery are not peculiar to Britain; and a particularly knotty example is presented by central Germany. Baalberge, Salzmünde, Walternienburg, Bernburg, Globular Amphorae, Corded Ware: all these 'cultures' are represented in a single settlement cell within a span of 500 years (Bakker 1979). There is certainly a chronological dimension: the list is roughly in sequence. There is also a spatial dimension: Walternienburg has the angular shapes of the Nordic area, Bernburg the rounded shapes of the south, Globular Amphorae (with their cord-decoration) relate to the east. But there is no simple partition of units in time and space, as distribution maps (Behrens 1973) make clear. Some, such as Salzmünde, have a more restricted, central, distribution within the loess heartland of central Germany;[16] the others occur more generally within it. Why such rapid alterations of style and decoration, in a series of apparently competing configurations? The answer is likely to lie in competing forms of ceremonial, even cult, use of the most distinctive types of vessel, which together in their particular assemblages formed the appropriate containers for the ritual consumption of their own, liturgically appropriate, food and drink.[17] The complexity of the ceramic sequence records a competing variety of possible approaches to the sacred.

How can we make sense of this? At the risk of reductionism, I want to suggest that all of these could have involved psychoactive substances,

16.4 Pottery assemblage of TRB *(EN)* C *consisting of a lugged amphora, collared flask (perhaps for infused opium?) and a funnel-beaker, from a grave under a long-barrow at Tovstrup, Denmark: heights are c.30, 15 and 9cm respectively; (after Knöll). This 3-piece set is especially characteristic of Jutland.*

including both the narcotics postulated above, and also alcohol, in various permutations. I have suggested that early narcotics (both in temperate Europe and on the steppes) were consumed by smoking. During the fourth and third millennia BC, ceramic assemblages in all parts of Europe were transformed by the appearance of distinctive drinking-cups and vessels for manipulating liquids. This is particularly striking in the case of the metallic style of pottery drinking-sets of the Baden culture, which echo the silver drinking vessels of the kind preserved in the Troy II treasure – whose influence (in the form of globular shapes, strap handles, channelling, omphalos bases, etc.) can be traced northwards into the Carpathian Basin and adjoining areas (Chapter 17). More rustic forms of standardised drinking vessels came to characterise the areas further north and west, most spectacularly in the case of the Bell-Beaker complex. For reasons which I have set out elsewhere, I believe that what this reflects is the impact of alcohol on prehistoric Europe.[18] These arguments indicate a southern origin, originally based on the fermentation of sugar-rich fruits, and adapted further north to other sources of sugar and flavouring – honey, milk, grain, and wild temperate fruits. Thus while wine was known in the Aegean, substitute concoctions took over further north.

The first 'inter-cultural' drinking-sets were the jugs and cups which are characteristic of 'Aeneolithic' assemblages c.4000–3500 BC: the phase which saw the beginning of the various TRB cultures in northern Europe,

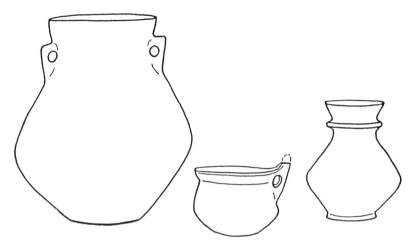

16.5 *Pottery assemblage of early* TRB *consisting of a lugged amphora, collared flask and a handled cup, from a grave at Chruszczów Kolonia, near Lublin, Poland; heights are 18, 9 and 6cm respectively; (after Knöll). This combination is characteristic for south-eastern* TRB, *occurring e.g. in graves under long-barrows.*

and the first imports there of Carpathian copper. Indeed, it can be argued that what gives the variety of local versions of TRB their distinctive character is essentially the appearance of a particular drinking complex. Consider the name: TRB, *Trichterrandbecher*, Funnel-necked Beaker culture – the first of a long line of 'beaker' cultures which superseded the older 'bowl' cultures. The various cultures (such as Danish Early Neolithic, Baalberge, and Polish TRB groups) which are grouped together under this label have diverse origins, but their common feature (at least in the formative phase) is their equipment for handling liquids. This is not just the eponymous drinking-vessel (which is principally characteristic of the Nordic area, and whose place further south is taken by handled cups of central European type), but the formalised *set* of vessels (Figures 16.4 and 16.5) consisting of the beaker or cup, long-necked flask or amphora, and the smaller, round flask with a distinctive collar (Knöll 1976; 1981). This assemblage occurs together in graves (with individual burials) over an area from southern Poland to Scandinavia, in a consistently replicated set of associations – not unlike the combination of cut-glass decanter, water jug, and tumbler or thistle-glass for Scotch whisky (cf. Piggott 1959) – providing a complementary set of vessels appropriate for ritual consumption. It seems to represent a local adaptation of the south-east European drinking sets which I have related to the intro-duction of wine and other alcoholic substitutes.

What, then, was the elixir (cf. whisky = *Uisge bheath*, 'water of life')? Invert the TRB decanter, the collared flask. Is it not absurdly like a poppy-head? Does this not give us a clue? Are we again dealing with opium, this time in soluble form? Far-fetched as the suggestion may seem, it has a well-documented prehistoric analogy. For precisely such an interpretation was

16.6 *Selection of pottery vessels from the mortuary house at Tustrup, Jutland: pedestalled conical bowls ('fruitstands') and pottery spoons, some with sockets for wooden handles; height of the tallest vessel is c.28cm; (after Kjaerum). These elaborate vessels (for communal consumption of some special food?) are characteristic of* TRB (MN) *I, and especially of such ritual sites.*

suggested by Robert Merrillees (1962) for a common type of Late Bronze Age flask or juglet, the base-ring *bilbil* manufactured in Cyprus and widely exported to the adjacent lands of Egypt and the Levant. Analyses of organic residues from several such vessels has recently been undertaken by Dr John Evans, of the North London Polytechnic: and in two cases he has been able to confirm that the contents did, indeed, include opium. Reading the record, even upside down, may sometimes reveal a hidden iconography. If this reading is correct, and it can potentially be tested by the same methods of organic chemistry, then it fits perfectly with the reconstruction offered above: the use of traditional intoxicants in new medium, as the result of an introduced model: consumption by mouth in liquid form. The full set of ritual equipment for its consumption – containers for the concentrated elixir, the dilutant, and the cup – became the hallmark of TRB.[19]

Could this model be further extended? In the previous chapter I suggested that precisely this phenomenon was involved in the spread of cord-decoration, from a steppe origin: the cord was hemp, *Cannabis*, and in northern Europe the cannabinol was infused rather than smoked, as it was in its area of origin (and as it was to be again, in a further phase of steppe influence associated with the spread of 'sunburst' braziers). By the time of the emergence of the Corded Ware beaker it may well have been combined with alcohol itself (as we still do in the case of the close relative of *Cannabis*, the hop, *Humulus lupulus*, to make bitter beer). In this case, too, the cord

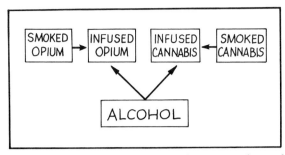

16.7 Postulated relationships between various indigenous and introduced narcotics and intoxicants in later Neolithic Europe. The arrangement is roughly geographical: horizontally E to W, and vertically N to S.

decoration would be a hidden iconography, continued in early Bell-Beakers.

Small wonder, then, that the central German ceramic sequence shows such a frenetic proliferation of ritual pots, for this area was the crossroads of these various intoxicating currents, and its successive ideological transformations had potentially powerful lubrication.[20] After the early TRB (Baalberge) phase, elaborate Walternienburg bowls take the prominent place of jugs and cups; and a similar development took place in contemporary Middle Neolithic Denmark, with the appearance of forms such as the distinctive conical bowls on stands found with pottery spoons in mortuary houses such as Tustrup and Ferslev (Figure 16.6). These seem to indicate more solid sustenance as the core of the consumption event: a food, rather than a drink.[21] This seems to be a particularly north-west European feature (as with Grooved Ware in Britain and Late Neolithic pottery in Ireland),[22] and may represent a native reaction to the earlier foreign drinking practice; and this north-western pattern spread to central Germany with the Nordic influences evident in Walternienburg.[23] The competing southern and eastern influences evident in Bernburg and Globular Amphorae, on the other hand, continued the emphasis on drinking vessels and amphorae with their associated cord decoration: alcohol and, if you believe it, infused cannabis. This pattern was again to spread northwards and westwards in a new form, that of Corded Ware and Bell-Beakers.

It is possible, therefore, to summarise a large part of the ceramic variability of later Neolithic Europe in terms of different ceremonial pottery sets, each probably appropriate for a specific type of food or drink, with the suggestion that psychoactive substances played a part in each of them. The various oppositions which I have identified are diagrammed in Figure 16.7.

THE SOCIAL CONTEXT OF DRINKING

To place these typological changes in a social setting, we must turn to the very different types of archaeological context in which they are found; for there is a profound contrast between the communal pot-smashing of Nordic

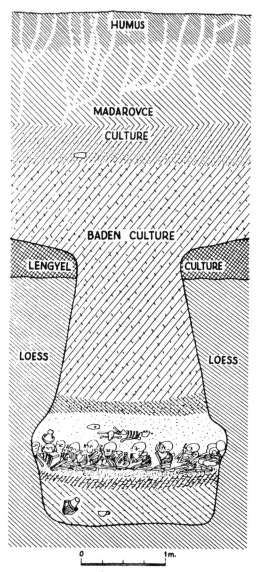

*16.8 The 'death-pit' at Nitriansky Hrádok-Zámeček, Slovakia (after Točik).
For description, see text. Note the lugged amphorae in channelled ware, and
the handled cup. The amphora/cup combination occurs in contemporary
'rich' graves with paired cattle burials in western Hungary.*

Middle Neolithic, for instance, and the individual graves with Corded Ware
beakers which succeeded them in large parts of northern Europe.

First, central Europe: in the Carpathian Basin in the later fourth and third
millennia there is a clear association between drinking equipment and other
indicators of 'wealth' in individual burials such as the flat-grave cemeteries
of the Baden culture. Thus, for example, in the Alsónémedi cemetery in

Hungary the two male graves (one accompanied by a younger female) which contained assemblages consisting of a bowl, jug and cup, also contained copper ornaments and were accompanied by burials of paired cattle.[24] In common with others of my generation, I have been prone to describe such assemblages as an 'elite drinking set' (e.g. Chapters 8 and 15). While justifiable etymologically, this usage carries a secular, even military, connotation which may be inappropriate for the societies under consideration. It is appropriate, therefore, to draw attention to another find which illustrates a ritual dimension to their use.

The site in question also belongs to the Baden culture, and was encountered by chance during excavation of the important EBA fortified hilltop settlement of Nitriansky Hrádok in western Slovakia (Točik 1981, 25). It is a truly remarkable discovery (Figure 16.8): a bell-shaped pit, four metres deep and widening out to a chamber some 2.75 metres in diameter, within which lay several layers of sequential deposit that must have been made on a single occasion.[25] In the lowermost layer, thrown in with the fill, are a two-lugged amphora and a one-handled drinking cup. This deposit is sealed by a layer of burnt material. Above it is a deeper layer, within which ten skeletons are disposed around the perimeter of the chamber, each kneeling (on a layer of clean earth) but with the bodies upright, the arms uplifted and with the hands held before the face. The posture of each of the individuals is similar, and must be a ritual gesture rather than an attempt to avoid asphyxiation, since each one has maintained the same pose in alignment with the others as the pit was filled over them. Above them, in the same layer, lies the articulated skeleton of a dog; and at the same level is a perforated stone 'battle-axe' and another amphora. A final layer of burnt material seals the chamber, and the shaft is filled with soil.

Of its many significant features, two must be singled out. The ten individuals must have been interred willingly; there are no signs of struggle or disorder.[26] Equally, however, they must have been stupefied, and perhaps also poisoned: truly *der Trunk des Abschieds*.[27] The stupefient was presumably contained in the amphorae, and drunk from the cup: a sacrament of death. Both the substance which it contained, and the beliefs of those who drank from it, must have been extremely powerful to carry out such a ceremony. It is hard to generalise from the unique, but this was surely the realm of sacrifice and the sacred.[28] The use in this ceremony of vessels which are otherwise associated with 'elite' graves suggests that preferential access to the sacred through intoxication was one of the elements employed in the construction of social power.

This element lies behind the appearance of drinking sets in early TRB in northern Europe. After this brief appearance, however, drinking vessels north of the Carpathians were not thereafter associated with individual burials until the Corded Ware period. As with the Danish Middle Neolithic and Walternienburg bowls, drinking vessels in the Bernburg and Globular

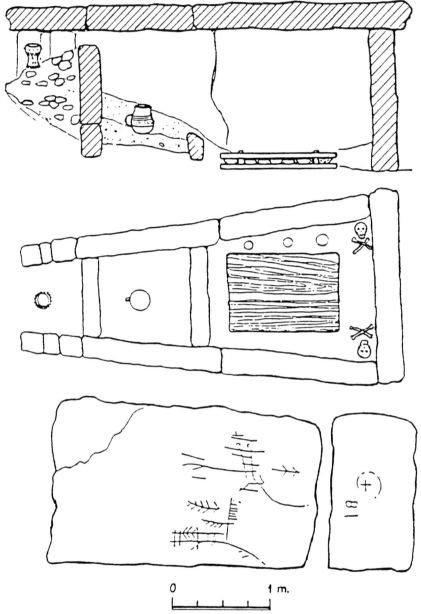

16.9 *Long cist of the Bernburg period at Nietleben, central Germany (after Sprockhoff, from Kruse). For description, see text. Note the large handled cup and pottery drum.*

Amphora cultures seem to have a communal rather than individual context. Similarly, some of the features of the Alsónémedi cemetery occur in the context of communal burials in stone cists of the Globular Amphora culture, which sometimes also contain burials of domestic animals including paired cattle: sacrifice again seems to play an important role. The communal character of drinking vessels at this time can be illustrated by the Bernburg tomb at Nietleben, in the Saalkreis of central Germany (Figure 16.9). This is a trapezoid stone cist of the general class of *Hessische Steinkisten*, with incised drawings on its covering-stone that may resemble the cart-drawings from the famous example at Lohne (Züschen). It dates to c.3200 BC, approximately contemporary with the Nitriansky Hradok death-pit. It is in three parts. In the larger, innermost section, defined by a low cross-slab, lie two opposed skulls and crossbones, one in each of the end corners. In the centre of the chamber is a low wooden structure of two tabular planks separated by timbers, beside which stand three small pots. In the second, smaller compartment is a single, centrally placed pot: a globular, one-handled cup or *Bernburger Tasse*. An upright slab closes off the narrower end, and defines a small vestibule half filled with deposit, on top of which, again centrally placed, stands a pottery drum (Sprockhoff 1938, 109).

The tomb itself falls into a class of later Neolithic stone monuments, including the *allées couvertes*, which evoke communal cult-houses.[29] This is not the burial of an individual; the cup does not appear as an item of personal equipment but as a more generalised symbol forming part of a larger conceptual unity. Although the vessel form is ultimately a foreign, southern, one, it is incorporated into a local context. The cup is sealed in the tomb as part of the interment ritual; outside, but covered by its roof, is a musical instrument, the *Tontrommel*,[30] which was a characteristic part of the elaboration of pottery forms indicative of communal ritual, which began in Salzmünde and continued to be a feature of central Germany until the beginning of Corded Ware. As part of the ceremonies, therefore, we should imagine the artificial production of loud noise, probably for a large audience (including both the living and the dead) during the performance of communal and mortuary rituals.[31]

In the North European Plain, therefore, the second half of the fourth millenium BC was characterised by investment in communal ceremony, frequently involving the dead, which in the east took the form of drinking rituals and in the west – perhaps in conscious reaction – took the form of eating rituals. Features of southern origin (not only the drinking complex but also paired traction for wheeled vehicles and the plough, as well as the circulation of imported items of copperwork) were absorbed into local contexts and interpreted in terms of the ideology of common ceremony and burial.

The radical break with this pattern occurred with Corded Ware. In the new pattern of individual burial, adult males were often interred with a specific kit: the stone battle-axe and a drinking set consisting of a cord-decorated beaker and an amphora.[32] No continuing offerings were made at the tomb, which was not a focus of ceremonial in the same way as earlier burial monuments. Nor are there comparable ceremonial centres separate from the tombs where drinking ceremonies could have taken place:

the ritual cycle was apparently constructed in an entirely different way. This pattern was propagated westwards with Bell-Beakers (the battle-axes being replaced by daggers and archery equipment, the beaker no longer accompanied by an amphora), to intrude on other communal, monument-building societies in the British Isles, Brittany and Iberia.

THE PROFANITY OF BEAKERS

What interpretation can be placed on this change in ritual eating and drinking, from an initial pattern of shrine-centred cult to a more personal association? It is important to note that this devolution of drinking paralleled a devolution in settlement and in burial itself, from the centralised villages, ceremonial centres or mortuary shrines of the later TRB groups to the scattered hamlets and tumuli of Corded Ware (Starling 1985). The new pattern was more fluid, and less permanent. The settlements were less substantial and less long-lasting; the tombs were less durable, no longer built of large stones to last for eternity. The general dispersal of settlement units was accompanied by a change from collective graves (often megalithic in construction) to single graves (often under smaller, round, mounds). Centralised ritual observance thus gave way to practices associated with particular individuals in smaller (family?) units. The 'sacred places' were de-emphasised: earthwork enclosures and mortuary shrines went out of use (some megaliths being deliberately sealed), and burial became a different type of event. Stone structures above ground were replaced by pits below ground;[33] the bodies were buried once and for all, rather than being de-fleshed and remaining accessible in a built structure. Personal possessions, including drinking equipment and weapons, were stressed for the first time and buried with individuals. The shift from an elaboration of monuments to a concern for items of personal equipment is indicative of a change in emphasis from collective representation, often associated with remembrance of group ancestors, to a society more oriented towards personal possession and perhaps to more specific lines of ancestry. The changed context of drinking was thus congruent with a larger social transformation.

The occurrence of personal drinking equipment does not mean that substances such as alcohol were generally available, but rather that from being a prerogative of individuals acting on behalf of the community, in a shamanic or priestly role, their consumption became a hallmark of some more general status category, probably that of older males in positions of familial authority. (Even today, among the Tuva Mongols, the drinking of alcohol is only permitted to males over forty!) Instead of being part of communal ceremony by stable and long-lasting groups, drinking could be used tactically through hospitality and the formation of horizontal relations among a more fluid pattern of communities: a class of event whose best-known representative is the Greek *symposion* (Chapter 15).

Despite this structural transformation, what continued was the consumption of psychoactive substances in a socially constituted context. Differential access to the sacred through intoxicating experiences could be seen as part of the ritual definition of authority in both cases; it was simply deployed in a different way. It is possible, therefore, that the ideological resources available for the construction of social power at the transition from TRB to Corded Ware were to a large extent already present in existing ritual systems. Seen in this way, the devolution of drinking was not a process of secularisation, but of profanation: the escape of a sacred medium from its place in the established shrines, and its successful propagation in new loci. It was a redeployment of the religious properties associated with drinking rituals and more generally with the consumption of psychoactive substances.

Such a redeployment of the resources of the sacred is a characteristic feature of certain types of social change, as Edmund Leach has pointed out in the contrast between what he calls 'icons of orthodoxy' and 'icons of subversion' (Leach 1983). Leach argues that superficially similar sets of beliefs and symbols can be used in radically different ways. He draws attention to two contrasting theologies in the early history of the Christian church, before and after its adoption as a state religion. 'One of these can serve to support the legitimacy of an established hierarchical political authority, the other is appropriate for an under-privileged minority seeking justification for rebellion against established authority' (Leach 1983, 84). These theologies are based on different conceptions of the relationship between God and Man, through the mediation either of sacrifice or of direct inspiration. In the former:

> The mediator is a human being, the priest of the sacrifice, who acts on behalf of a lay congregation. The sacrificial rite is viewed as an 'offering' to the Deity, and the priest, who stands in a superior position to his congregation, is in a suppliant status *vis à vis* the Deity ... In the second pattern it is God who takes the initiative by offering grace to the faithful. The individual devotee is directly inspired. The charisma is a direct gift from God which is in no way dependent on the efficacy of a mediating human priest. (*Ibid.*, 67)

This model neatly summarises a continuing duality within the Christian church, in which the second mode was to reappear with the Reformation; but it can also be applied more generally in the sociology of religion: Leach points to analogies between his second pattern and protest movements such as the cargo cults of Melanesia, the Ghost Dance, and the Taiping rebels of nineteenth-century China. Viewed in this light, the transition from TRB to Corded Ware has certain formal analogies with the Protestant Reformation in the same area 4500 years later: the shift from a hierarchical model with a mediating priesthood and elaborate shrines intended to last in perpetuity, to an emphasis on personal salvation, individual responsibility, architectural and liturgical simplification, often with a millenarian perspective of impending cosmic change. It was also, of course, marked by a shift from a female imagery – expressed in devotion to the Virgin Mary – to an exclusively male imagery consistent with a strengthening of patriarchal authority.

The parallel should not be pressed beyond its usefulness, but it is a provocative analogy for the formal contrast between earlier and later Neolithic Europe. Investment in sacred places and sharply defined sacred events was characteristic of megalithic and monument-building societies with their plentiful traces of 'ritual' activity in the form of enclosures, astronomical alignments, esoteric paraphernalia, pits and sacrificial offerings – the residues of public ceremonies. TRB and Grooved Ware belong to this category. Its perspective was one of cyclical change within eternal changelessness, in which access to the sacred was constrained to specific times and places. These would have provided the rhythms within which everyday life was organised, including the slaughter of livestock and the exchange of goods and marriage partners. This pattern was subverted by one in which the sacred was no longer tied to ritual cycles and specially constructed shrines. The perspective of time was shorter, and did not require such permanent monuments; while the burial-mounds (and perhaps also the patterns of exchange) were organised in terms of particular events, rather than being accommodated to a predetermined cycle.[34] Opportunity and mobility replaced predictable regularity. This attitude began in northern Europe with Corded Ware, and penetrated, initially as a minority ideology, into areas such as Denmark.[35] The older pattern survived longer in the west, where a similar pattern of penetration was repeated with Bell-Beakers.

This way of thinking about the problem is particularly instructive because it situates ideological change within a social and economic context. Leach instances the rise of a new economic class, 'a self-identifiable community which can readily be led to perceive itself as alienated from the interests of the paramount political power' (Leach 1983, 71). This description accords well with the situation that can be reconstructed in the later Neolithic of northern Europe. The increasing areas of pasture opened up by deforestation, following the introduction of plough[36] agriculture, made possible more flexible economic and social arrangements involving a larger role for animal-keeping. It was to those parts of the population involved in herding activities that such a revolutionary ideology would have made its appeal. The transfer of legitimacy and social power to such nascent political groupings, however, required the capture of means of access to the supernatural, and its liberation from the established *fana*: the profanation (but not secularisation) of psychoactive substances, and especially alcoholic drink.

True or not, this parable offers a model for the relationship between economic, social and ideological change. Ritual is not an autonomous domain, obeying only the laws of structural symmetry; it can be, and is, one of the levers by which groups within society attain ascendance and temporal power. Nor is its metaphorical content arbitrary, for the images of family relationships and 'female' values are important in constructing wider concepts of community and social order on a consensual basis, while warrior images and 'male' values are important in breaking up and realigning such groupings, with the more explicit threat of force. Each produces its own ritual and iconography, sometimes (perhaps even typically) by the transformation or partial inversion of its predecessor. While the first pattern is perhaps easier to recognise as more formally 'religious', it would be a mistake to categorise the second as simply 'secular'.

Is it, then, 'profane'? Yes, from the point of view of a stable orthodoxy, with shrines and sacrifices; but not from the point of view of the subversives, for whom the concept has no meaning in a world scheme which is structured on different principles, and in which shrines as such do not exist. Profanation as a process, therefore, is characteristic of the transition from one type of system to the other, which then redefines the world in its own terms.

Treason doth never prosper; where's the reason?
If it do prosper, none dare call it treason.

Successful profanity, like successful treason, rewrites its own history.

[On a visit to the Soviet Union in July 1990, two strands of this argument came together in an unexpected way. Discussing *Prehistoric narcotics* above, I mentioned finds of *Cannabis sativa* from 'pipe-cups' in the Early Bronze Age of eastern Europe, without knowing quite what this term implied. Later on in the same section, I singled out polypod bowls or braziers as a typical inter-cultural form of the kind likely to have been associated with narcotics. I was therefore delighted to learn that the term *kurilnitsa*, which had been translated as 'pipe-cup', was in fact the common Russian term used to describe such footed bowls, and that they are interpreted as small braziers. The connection between these two lines of evidence has, in fact, been completed. These forms begin, in the Pontic steppe region, in the period from c.4000 to 3600 BC. This is the period when cord-impressed ornament appears, for the first time, on the Pontic steppes, before spreading westwards with Globular Amphorae. This considerably strengthens the arguments, presented in Chapter 15, for an association between corded ornament and the use of *Cannabis* as a fibre-plant and potentially as a narcotic.]

[In the *Proceedings of the Society of Antiquaries of Scotland* for 1993 is the information which answers my question in the section on *The ceramic evidence: 2. eating and drinking* above, concerning Grooved Ware – which

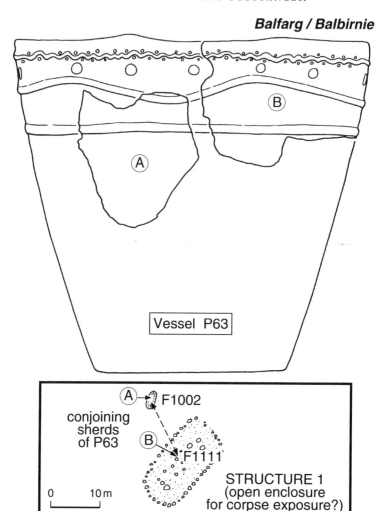

Balfarg / Balbirnie

Vessel P63

conjoining
sherds
of P63

A—F1002

B

F1111

STRUCTURE 1
(open enclosure
for corpse exposure?)

0   10 m

CONTEXTS OF DISCOVERY

16.10 The Grooved Ware vessel from Balfarg/Balbirnie with preserved food-residues; the plan shows the features inside and outside Structure 1 (an open timber enclosure) which yielded sherds of this vessel [new drawing, after Barclay and Russell-White 1993].

I suggested should contain something 'more sugary, spicy or exciting (even narcotic) than was encountered in secular existence'. A botanical report by B. Moffatt (in Barclay and Russell-White 1993, 108–10) on the carbonised residue preserved in a pot from Balfarg Riding School, Glenrothes, Fife (Figure 16.10) describes it as representing a porridge-like substance prepared from barley and oats, sweetened with honey (minute droplets of beeswax were observed) and flavoured with meadowsweet (*Filipendula ulmaria*), with other potherbs such as fat hen (*Chenopodium album*), and some species of *Brassica* and one of the Umbelliferae (probably as a condiment), and a little flax (perhaps as oil). The cereals were identifiable from seeds, the other herbs from pollen. One further plant was indicated both by seed remains and pollen, in some quantity: henbane, *Hyoscyamus niger*. Sweet, spicy and narcotic: using a classic 'Saturnian herb', long associated with witchcraft. Was this also the food dispensed from the TRB 'fruitstand'? A further article is in preparation ...]

NOTES

1. I use the term 'narcotic' to cover a range of psychoactive substances including some which are more correctly described as stimulants. Despite the fact that the technical meanings of the two words are in fact quite opposite (i.e. sleep-inducing *versus* arousing), their usage is now irremediably confused – largely for bureaucratic and legal reasons! I have avoided the word 'drug', which is best applied to the refined substances. The opening remarks of this paper were prepared for general discussion at the conference; the paper itself was written afterwards. I must thank the organisers and editors for their invitation to contribute, and especially Paul Garwood for his perceptive comments on the text.

2. The literal meaning of secular is 'lasting for an age' (cf. *in saecula saeculorum*, 'for ever and ever'): the idea of continuity is opposed to periodic or cyclical occurrence, as in the term 'secular trend' (i.e. a continuous, long-term process). The sacred, on the other hand, is characterised by regular, periodic, rites and festivals, usually on an annual cycle.

3. As did the now extinct Shakespearian exclamation 'Zwounds!' ('by God's Wounds'). Such expressions imply a Catholic theology, which is one reason why they have atrophied in a largely Protestant context. The difference between Catholic and Protestant theologies in this respect is an example of a more fundamental contrast in religious attitudes, to which I shall return at the conclusion of this paper; for in this more abstract form it has a surprising relevance to Neolithic Europe.

4. A similar pattern can be discerned in words for other emotionally charged but culturally regulated activities, such as sex. The first unexpurgated edition of D. H. Lawrence's *Lady Chatterley's Lover* contained, if I remember rightly, a preface by Richard Hoggart in which he neatly exemplified the change of role in the word for which that text was then chiefly famous. A soldier, returning from service abroad, was reported as saying: 'Three effing months in effing Africa and what do I effing-well find? My wife engaged in illicit cohabitation with another man.' I quote from memory. The whole point of Lawrence's novel was to reassert the sanctity of the sexual act and to rescue its terminology from casual profanation, as many eminent witnesses pointed out at the trial of its publisher, Penguin Books, in 1960.

5. Note, for example, the political dimension (and hence the historical significance) of events such as the 'Profanation of the Eleusinian Mysteries' by Alcibiades in 415 BC.

6. There is an analogy here in Catholic practice in the appropriate treatment of the consecrated wafer if the communicant fails to digest it; a regurgitated wafer should be burnt. (I have a similar attitude to the Christmas tree after it has been ritually decorated and is then unceremoniously taken down after Twelfth Night – it seems inappropriate just to consign it to the dustbin, so I usually burn it.)

7. The killing of animals has always been an act of social significance. In hunting and foraging societies, the meat is typically shared among the group, while gathered products are consumed by individual family units. In many farming and pastoral societies, the relative rarity with which domestic livestock was slaughtered (by comparison with the more regular flow of vegetable- and secondary-products) has often made it a principal event within the periodic observances of the ritual cycle. In some societies, all slaughter is sacrifice, and can only take place within the context of the sacred, after appropriate kinds

of purification. This is likely to have been one of the activities which took place at Neolithic ceremonial centres. (It is worth remembering that a 'sacrificial stone knife' was discovered within a niche within one of the altars in the Tarxien temple in Malta.) Such structures could perhaps be envisaged as elaborate abattoirs, much as certain Near Eastern Bronze Age temples contain metallurgical debris and must have operated as foundries: their categorisation as 'religious' structures should not exclude a range of activities which we would now think of as purely mundane.

8. As noted before, I use the word in its colloquial sense, to include all psychoactive substances, including stimulants, inebriants, etc. – in fact, the complex mixtures of organic compounds which occur naturally in plants often combine several of these properties.
9. The date, on esparto grass, is 5400 ± 80 BP (CSIC–246).
10. The seeds, being the most resistant, form the carbonised residue – the flowers and leaves, which have the greatest concentration of cannabinol, having been burnt away. Unfortunately the 'pipe-cup' was not illustrated.
11. I am grateful to Istvan Ecsedy for pointing out these finds, whose significance he drew attention to in 1979.
12. Substances such as birch-bark resin were also chewed, as indicated by an Alpine lake-village find with toothmarks!
13. *Focus* = 'hearth'; the metaphor is not accidental.
14. Finally, and beyond the chronological scope of this paper, one should note the occurrence of comparable artefacts in earlier Bronze Age contexts in Britain: the 'Aldbourne cups' – some with perforated sides – and related 'grape-cups' or 'incense cups' that are associated with 'rich' burials of the Wessex culture in Britain (e.g. Gerloff 1975). These have long been interpreted as small braziers for aromatic substances (though I am not aware of any suggestion of a narcotic use), and apparently represent a more localised cult/elite practice than the 'inter-cultural' forms discussed above, which seem to relate to the first spread of specific types of narcotic use over long distances.
15. Thomas Harriot observed just such a point-based cooking pot in Virginia in 1590: 'Their woemen know how to make earthen vessels with special Cuninge and that so large and fine, that our potters with [their] wheels can make no better ... After they have put them uppon an heape of erthe to stay them from fallinge, they putt wood under[,] which being kindled ... they or their woemen fill the vessel with water, and put in fruite, flesh and fish, and let all boil together like a gallimaufrye which the Spaniarde call, olla podrida.' This he contrasts favourably with the complexity of contemporary European cooking, which he considers responsible for 'many kynes of diseases which wee fall into by sumtwous and unseasonable blanketts, continually devisinge new sawces, and provocation of gluttonye to satisfie our insatiable appetite' (D. B. Quinn, *The Roanoke Voyages*, London: The Hakluyt Society, Ser. II, Vol. 104, 1955). This neatly summarises both the polarity between 'primitive' and 'civilised' cuisine, and also the strain of iconoclastic utopianism (usually espoused by a rising bourgeoisie) which can potentially challenge this elite cultural elaboration and seeks a return to the purity of the primitive. Modern organically grown wholefoods are a good example of this in practice. For the anthropological significance of this polarity, see the final section of this article.
16. The Saale-Mittelelbegebiet (Starling 1985).
17. Although such vessels are often associated with tombs, they should not be considered as 'tomb pottery' in the sense of being specially made for burial (like Greek vases for Etruscan tombs!); rather, they occur as *offerings*, usually in the forecourt, and should thus be seen as ritual food containers in the context of a feast that included the dead. Such vessels may be poorly represented on settlement sites, except those larger or centrally placed sites where communal ceremonies took place.
18. This article should be considered as complementary to the present paper, and I have tried to avoid repeating its arguments. It is shortly to be reprinted without the many editorial alterations and deficiencies which marred its publication in 1987.
19. Compare the flagon, cruets and chalice of the Christian communion-set. Other pieces of standardised 'ritual' equipment, in a modern, secular context, would include the silver

cocaine-spoons, made by expensive jewellers and occasionally worn as neck ornaments by the smart set; or even the standardised shape of the Coca-Cola bottle (which now contains neither *coca* nor *kola*, though originally it was made of both these stimulants). Psychoactive substances, whether sacred or profane, create their own material culture.

20. The symbolic significance of intoxicants in relation to specific, competing ideological systems is well exemplified in the contrast between Judaeo-Christian wine and Islamic cannabis.

21. This probably excludes alcohol, but might still contain opium, cannabis, or other psycho-active herbs. A similar transformation from drink to food is indicated in the British Early Bronze Age by the shift from Bell-Beakers to Food Vessels, which Professor Hawkes has suggested might contain a substance such as frumenty.

22. Both, incidentally, skeuomorphs of organic containers – made perhaps of leather on a withy framework – which may have their origin in native (ultimately Mesolithic?) vessels. This is pursued further in Sherratt (in prep.).

23. The collared flask, however, continued its inter-cultural spread westwards, to appear in the TRB West Group in the Netherlands and in SOM contexts in northern France shortly after it disappeared from Denmark (Huysecom 1986).

24. Symbolising, if not actually accompanying, wheeled vehicles of the kind represented in the Szigetszentmárton and Budakalász models, which were themselves handled cups.

25. This pit is No. 107, and was excavated in 1952. Another pit, No. 119, apparently similar and containing 19–25 skeletons, was found in 1949 but not recorded in detail. Other remains of the Baden culture on the hill included the ovens and hearths of a domestic settlement, and many storage pits. Two smaller pits also contained double graves, one that of two infants, one of an infant and an adult.

26. An alternative, but rather less likely, explanation is that they were mummified. For other mass 'ritual' burials, though in an explicitly elite context, see Woolley's account of the 'death pits' at Ur, and more generally such royal graves with slaughtered retainers as the Shang royal tombs at Anyang.

27. The parting drink, or cup of farewell; the final song of Mahler's *Das Lied von der Erde*, translating a Chinese poem, uses it as a symbol of release from earthly cares.

28. I cannot resist the observation that such a sacrifice would be the structural inverse of the Christian Eucharist, whose cup offers life and the grace procured by the sacrifice of the Crucifixion. What both rites have in common, however, is a union of the themes of drinking and sacrifice.

29. See my forthcoming article on Neo-megalithism (Sherratt in prep.) for a justification of this statement. In France, such structures are associated with a specifically female iconography (breasts, 'guardian goddesses').

30. See the article *Trommel* in J. Filip (ed.) *Enzyklopädisches Handbuch zur Ur- und Frühgeschichte Europas*, 2, 1494 (Prague 1969), and further references therein, especially Seewald and Mildenberger.

31. Loud noise may be associated with events in the other world: cf. the 'Last Trump'.

32. The occurrence of drinking vessels in graves and their use in communal ritual are not, of course, mutually exclusive: priests in medieval times were sometimes buried with a token chalice of non-precious metal, often of lead.

33. The classic Corded Ware (Single Grave) sequence is a progression from earth graves to tumuli: 'Under-graves' (*Untergräber*); 'Ground-graves' (*Bodengräber*); 'Over-graves' (*Obergräber*) in the body of the barrow: i.e. from simple pits to a new, though simpler, form of monumentality.

34. There is a direct analogy here with the change in the concept of time which came about with the Reformation: the other-worldly, ritual time of the Medieval church was challenged by the bourgeois concern for commodified time and opportunistic trade. Usury was condemned by the church as 'selling time'. See Jacques Le Goff, *Time, Work and Culture in the Middle Ages* (Chicago, 1980), esp. pp. 59–61. Perhaps bronze hoards fit into an 'opportunistic' pattern, rather than a 'cyclical' one (unlike Neolithic 'ritual' deposits of pots and axe 'hoards'?).

35. There is not space here to go into detail, but there is considerable evidence that the Corded Ware 'culture' began in Jutland while the final phases of TRB (V and perhaps IV) dominated in the Danish Islands. (Denmark often shows this regional pattern, as it did with EN longbarrows: Sherratt 1990.) While there is a similar chronological overlap in the Netherlands between Corded Ware and TRB phases F and G, the contrast is contextual rather than regional. After c.2700 BC (in the 'Ground-grave' phase) the Corded Ware pattern became the single dominant one in both areas. A similar pattern of limited penetration, ideological competition and recruitment, and finally total subversion, can be reconstructed for Bell-Beakers in Britain. It was at this point that many of the monumental tombs were blocked and symbolically sealed.

36. Like such symbols as drinking and the use of wheeled vehicles, the plough in northern and western Europe was initially absorbed into traditional social structures, and was associated during the MN period of TRB with a settlement system based on stable and long-lasting patterns of land use associated with large settlements or megaliths and ritual enclosures, of the kind established by the initial, horticultural, communities. Only with the ideological transition to Corded Ware was the potential fluidity of the new economy unleashed. ('Religion' retarding 'progress', as Gordon Childe would have described it!)

17

Metal Vessels in Bronze Age Europe and the Context of Vulchetrun
(with T. Taylor)
(1984, published 1989)

METAL VESSELS AND THEIR SOCIAL SETTING IN BRONZE AGE EUROPE

One of the recurring themes of Bronze Age archaeology is the occurrence of drinking equipment. This theme was present from its very inception: the beginning of the Bronze Age in the Aegean is defined by the arrival of a pottery assemblage containing handled jugs and cups (with good prototypes in metal), while contemporary third-millennium cultures further north are distinguished by 'Globular Amphorae', 'Corded Ware beakers' and 'Bell-Beakers'. This interest in the social uses of alcohol – whether mead, beer, koumish or wine – was to continue throughout later prehistory, and is presumably related to the importance of hospitality and competitive feasting in Bronze Age society: a ritualised practice of communal drinking that was to emerge in the literary record of archaic and classical Greek times as the *symposium*.

Throughout the Bronze and Iron Ages, the style of such entertainment in

This chapter was put together with Tim Taylor for a conference in Amsterdam, and is reproduced here in abbreviated form. Tim had just examined the Vulchetrun treasure in Sofia, and concluded that it was a conflation of two assemblages of different dates (see technical details in the original publication). Isolation of an earlier part produced a convincing local context, reflected in mid-second-millennium ceramic forms, and so providing evidence of contemporary goldsmithing techniques and contacts with craft workshops in neighbouring areas; it also illustrated a 'drinking set' or 'symposium kit' of the kind otherwise known only from the Troy treasures or the Mycenae Shaft-Graves. This interest in alcohol and ostentation parallels my colleague Michael Vickers' work on the relationship between pottery design and precious metalwork in the classical period, and has a common inspiration in the work of our Oxford predecessors Arthur Evans and J. L. Myres, and their pupil V. G. Childe.

Europe was set by Aegean practice – a land of exotic fruits, wine and sun-shine, and also the most advanced area in terms of economy and technology. Basic to this style was the use of metal – especially precious metal – vessels, which were frequently copied in pottery. This theme can be traced from the treasures of Troy II, through the Shaft-Graves of Mycenae, to the metal prototypes that lie behind the typological proliferation of archaic and classical Greek vases. The set of mixing, serving and drinking vessels defines a 'wine ceremony' that may be compared with the oriental 'tea ceremony' and the appropriate set of equipment which accompanied its diffusion in eighteenth-century Europe.

Europe beyond the Mediterranean initially lacked both the practice of viticulture and the technological expertise for making metal vessels. The spread of wine, first by large-scale import and then by local production, is a story that belongs to the later first millennium BC. Nevertheless, the style of temperate European drinking equipment in the second and early first millennia owed much to Mediterranean models; and the technological development of European sheet-metal industries can usefully be considered in the light of this relationship. The three maps which accompany this article are an attempt to chart the spread of sheet metalworking techniques as applied to the manufacture of drinking vessels; and although presented only as summary sketches, they effectively demonstrate a zonation of techno-logical sophistication and a progressive northwards spread of technical capability. These patterns are useful both as illustrations of the socio-economic context of European metalworking, and as a means of defining possible areas of origin for the often enigmatic and unaccompanied examples of Bronze Age goldwork. They provide a necessary background to the interpretation of the Treasure of Vulchetrun (or at least a part of it) and the other recently discovered pieces related to it that form the subject of this chapter (see now also Vulpe and Mihăilescu-Bîrliba 1985).

The use both of copper and gold has a long history in Europe before the beginning of the Bronze Age. Although the manufacture of sheet bronze did not appear in temperate Europe until the Late Bronze Age in the later second millennium, beaten goldwork was already present in the Copper Age and was extensively represented by the time of the Varna cemetery (c.4500 BC), even in quite large pieces. Significantly, however, it was not made into vessels, although it was in fact applied in powdered form as a paint in the manner of contemporary graphite-painting on large, open bowls. Sheet-metal vessels first appeared in southern Europe at the same time as the first evidence for the production of wine in the Early Bronze Age, as part of the life-style of a new elite.

The initial use of sheet-metal for vessels probably began with gold and silver in Anatolia or the northern Levant, represented in the fourth millen-nium BC by the bowl from a tomb at Tell Farah North, Israel; and expertise in decorated metalwork was undoubtedly promoted in the urban craft centres of fourth-millennium Mesopotamia in the Uruk period, even though examples of the products are rare, in the absence of rich graves (for a peripheral exception see Maikop in the northern Caucasus: Chapter 17). The technique was used to make spouted bowls (e.g. at Tepe Gawra) in the later Protoliterate period, although the first extensive sample of the products of this technology in Mesopotamia comes from Early Dynastic tombs such as the royal cemetery at Ur. By this time the technology was also represented in adjacent areas, for instance at Alaca Hüyük and Troy where both gold, silver and copper-alloy sheet-metalwork occur. Such products were at this date closely related to the existence of craft workshops in palaces or early urban centres, which were also capable of using other advanced gold-working techniques such as filigree or granulation. Beaten gold and silver vessels slowly made their appearance among the 'barbarian' societies of temperate Europe during the second millennium, but it was another eight hundred years before their Late Bronze Age successors acquired the techniques of sheet bronzework for vessels and armour, which had continued to be restricted to the palace workshops of the Aegean.

This disparity reflects two factors. In the first place, there is the technological aspect: the malleability of gold makes the manufacture of sheet and the raising of vessel shapes much easier than with bronze, whose brittleness requires constant annealing. Secondly the attractiveness, incorruptibility and scarceness of gold made it a natural first choice of a restricted elite, perhaps anxious that their sumptuary prerogative should not be diluted by the greater availability of comparable forms in baser metal. A similar sequence can be seen underlying the succession from precious metal to bronze coinages in the first millennium BC, and a similar principle is evident

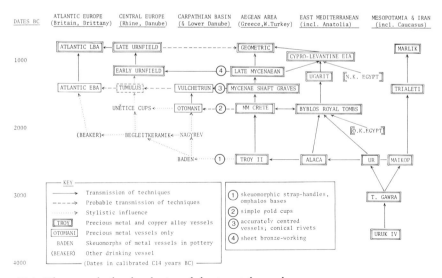

17.1 *The spread of technologies of sheet-metal vessels.*

433

in the trend from highly decorated, individual weapons to more uniform, mass-produced ones within the Bronze Age itself.

The technological history of Europe (Figure 17.1) during this period thus reflects the social background of a rising, and broadening, elite that set and maintained its style by reference to more sophisticated Mediterranean neighbours, from whom it occasionally imported finished models and absorbed techniques. These styles were set by wine-drinking, semi-urbanised communities in the Aegean (which were themselves on the fringe of more sophisticated societies in the Near East). Unable to import the substance, since wine was difficult to transport in bulk with Bronze Age organisation and technological capacities, the inhabitants of temperate Europe attempted to imitate the style; and many rustic brews must have been drunk from gold and silver vessels originally inspired by wine.

The technological and cultural history of metal vessels in Bronze Age Europe and the Near East can best be summarised in a series of maps, sketching the variety of regional traditions from the rare surviving examples of metal vessels, and from their skeuomorphic echoes in pottery.

Stage I: 3500–2000 BC (*Figure 17.2*)

During the later fourth and third millennia the only area of Europe to manufacture metal vessels was the Aegean, which lay at the western end of a belt of urbanising societies in contact with Mesopotamia. The Ur royal graves illustrate the skill of metropolitan craftsmen, while neighbouring areas show distinctive styles: decorated with animal figures in the Caucasus and Iran, or with plentiful channelling and fluting in central Anatolia – as shown both by the gold vessels of Alaca Hüyük and the Early Bronze Age pottery of Beycesultan, whose contrast with the preceding Late Chalcolithic 4 wares is marked by the appearance of thin, brilliantly polished and often fluted fabrics, indicating a close dependence on metal models. Egypt's skill in sheet goldwork (even gold leaf) is well known, though surprisingly few gold vessels have escaped the tomb-robbers to place alongside the plentiful copper examples from royal and aristocratic tombs. (For examples of Near Eastern metalwork see illustrations in Piggott 1961.)

These areas shared a common basic technology that was capable of producing sheet-metal, gold, silver and copper-alloy vessels (though some of the last were still produced by solid-casting). The westernmost assemblage demonstrating the whole of this range of competence is that represented by the seventeen vessels (two-thirds of silver, the rest either of electrum, or copper alloy) from Treasures A, B and S from Troy II, and other hoards from the Troad (Schmidt 1902; Bittel 1959); but precious metal vessels were also made on the other side of the Aegean, under strong west-Anatolian influence. Examples include gold vessels in the local 'sauceboat' shape, that were probably made in craft workshops attached to fortified centres such as Lerna, as well as small silver bowls in the Cyclades, and the possibly

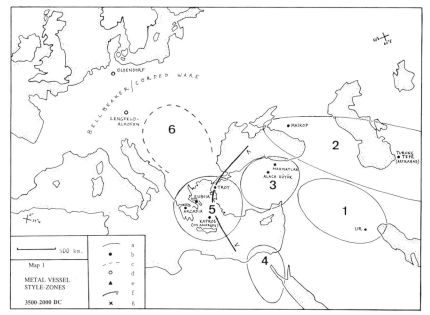

17.2 *Map of metal-vessel style zones, 3500–2000 BC: (1) Mesopotamian classic;
(2) Iranian figured; (3) central Anatolian channelled; (4) Egyptian sheet-goldwork
and bronze vessels; (5) Aegean plain; (6) Baden culture (pottery skeuomorphs).
There are other pottery skeuomorphs in the Levant. (a) boundaries of style-zones;
(b) finds of metal vessels; (c) style-zones defined on metallic skeuomorphs; (d) finds
of metallic skeuomorphs; (e) imports (metal vessel finds or skeuomorphs); (f) the
limit of sheet-metalworking in copper alloys; (g) sheet-metal finds other than
vessels.*

imported gold bowls from Euboia (Renfrew 1972; Buchholz and
Karageorghis nos 1072–82). Even so, Helladic goldwork was simpler than
that from western Anatolia: the sauceboats have riveted strap-handles
rather than tubular ones like the two-handled cups (depata) from Troy
(Childe 1924).

The appearance of tubular spouts on the pottery 'teapot' vessels from
Early Minoan Crete (Figure 17.3) is very suggestive of metal prototypes
(known in silver from the Levant in the next period) which may have been
in bronze or more likely in precious metal (Evans 1921, 79–82). The Cretan
case resembles that of the Levant itself in this period, when metal types can
be inferred from the pottery but are not so far represented by finds of metal
objects. More generalised skeuomorphs of metal features occur in northern
Greece and as far north as the Carpathian Basin. High-flung strap-handles
and omphalos bases (Figure 17.4) are characteristic of the Ezero and Baden
cultures (Kalicz 1963), which also have pottery examples of the suspension-
vase known in silver from the Troy treasure. Since there are no 'proto-
palaces' of the Lerna type in this area, it is unlikely that metal prototypes
would have been locally manufactured: probably, rare examples circulated

17.3 Pottery and metalwork: above, Early Minoan 'teapot' from Vasilike, Crete; below, early first-millennium BC bronze spouted vessels from Luristan: the tubular construction of the spout is characteristic of the metal form and skeuomorphic in pottery (Ashmolean Museum); [new photographs].

from further south. This is also likely to be the explanation for the very rare metal-derived shapes in pottery from TRB and related contexts further north, in Bavaria at Lengfeld-Alkofen and, more surprisingly, at Oldendorf (Kr. Lüneburg) in northern Germany (Sprockhoff 1952; Milojčić 1953: see Figure 7.3). These postulated examples of metal vessels circulating outside their zone of manufacture would interestingly prefigure the route over

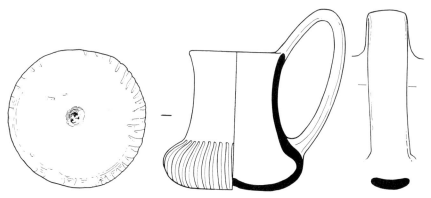

17.4 Baden handled cup with classic metal-skeuomorphic features: polished grey surface, strap-handle, omphalos base, channelling: from Vinča, Serbia (Ashmolean Museum); [new drawing].

which techniques of local production were to spread in the following millennium.

Stage II: 2000–1300 BC (*Figure 17.5*)

This span of time encompasses a series of changes, which for convenience have been conflated within a single map. The undoubted presence of precious metal vessels in the Near East is only sparsely represented in the archaeological record, mainly because of the rarity of ostentatious royal tombs. However, the geographically marginal site of Trialeti in the Caucasus (some of whose tombs date back to the previous millennium) shows the complexity that goldwork could attain (Schaeffer 1948, figs 288–92), and the numbers of bronze vessels from humbler tombs in the Luristan region by the end of the period show that they were no longer confined to a restricted elite. Although whole areas (including potentially very important ones like western Anatolia) are still definable only through pottery skeuomorphs, royal and aristocratic tombs in the Aegean and the Levant provide good examples of contemporary products in the east Mediterranean.

Among the earliest are the royal tombs at Byblos (Schaeffer 1948, fig. 63), with silver vessels – including a teapot – that resemble the massive silver treasure from a temple context at Tôd in upper Egypt, datable to c.1900 BC (Bisson de la Roque et al. 1953). This silverwork is either Levantine or – conceivably – Cretan, where local production of silver vessels is shown by the crinkly kantharos from Gournia and from skeuomorphic representation in Kamares ware (Evans 1921, 191–3). Cretan goldwork in a similar style is illustrated by the vessels of the 'Aigina' treasure, probably from northern Crete (Higgins 1979), while further connections between Byblos and the Aegean are demonstrated by the occurrence in both areas of a type of carinated, two-handled cauldron (Schaeffer 1948, fig. 78; cf. Catling 1964,

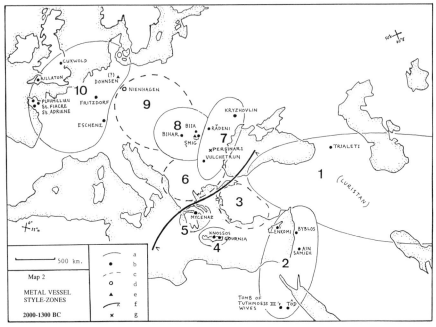

17.5 *Map of metal-vessel style zones, 2000–1300* BC: *(1) Near Eastern figured; (2) Aegean-related gold- and silver-work in the east Mediterranean; (3) west Anatolian (pottery skeuomorphs); (4) Cretan crinkly; (5) Mycenaean; (6) Balkan (pottery skeuomorphs); (7) west-Pontic zone of Vulchetrun-related vessels; (8) Otomani goldwork; (9) Únětice (pottery skeuomorphs); (10) west European* EBA *gold and silver cups. (Symbols as in Fig. 17.2)*

fig. 18, 5). These examples illustrate the increasing links between various parts of the east Mediterranean.

For the Aegean Late Bronze Age (Davis 1977) the best sample comes from the sixteenth-century Shaft-Graves at Mycenae, which contain gold vessels in both the Cretan tradition (cf. the cups from Vaphio) and in simpler shapes in the tradition of Middle Helladic pottery (e.g. the simple two-handled cups). The development of this school of metalworking can be followed at nearby Dendra where a tholos and chamber-tombs of the fourteenth century have produced technically more advanced pieces, giving evidence both of lathe-finishing in the manufacture of bowls, and of the application to vessels of the kinds of black inlay previously used on weapon-blades (Buchholz and Karageorghis 1973, no. 1108, cf. 1684). Bronzework is particularly plentiful at this time, both on the mainland and in Crete (Matthäus 1980), where a good example of a set of personal drinking equipment comes from the warrior-burial in tomb 14 at Zapher Papoura (Buchholz and Karageorghis 1973, fig. 33).

It is to this period that a bronze cup said to have been found at Dohnsen north of Hannover (Sprockhoff 1961) can be attributed; and a possible

17.6 *Hoard of Otomani culture gold cups from former County Bihar, (former) Hungary, c.1800 BC (after Mozsolics).*

indication of a somewhat earlier metal vessel import from the Aegean is the pottery pillar-handle (like those on the Vaphio cups) from Nienhagen in Saxony (Gimbutas 1965, 58). While some doubt must attach to both of these pieces (Harding 1985, 108), there is nothing inherently improbable in such rare long-distance imports, which are paralleled in the previous period at Oldendorf and by many instances in the first millennium.

In any case, the local production of precious metal (but not bronze) vessels had already begun in central and western Europe. The earliest are the gold vessels of the Hajdúsámson metalworking phase of the Otomani culture in the Carpathian Basin, dating to c.1800 BC and preceding the Shaft-Grave period in Greece. The Otomani area provided an advanced economic context (though not a palatial one), with its stone-built hillforts, skilful gold- and bronzework, and even experimental ironworking (Vládar 1973). Four one-handled gold cups or bowls, found in Co. Bihar, Hungary in 1922, have vertical channelling, and one has incised compass-based ornament of the kind known from contemporary bronzework (Mozsolics 1968, Tafeln 4–10; Figure 17.6). (Forms with elaborate toreutic shapes are suggested by contemporary pottery copies: Figure 17.7.) Probably slightly later is the example from Biia (Magyarbénye) with repoussé bosses and concentric circles, and incised lines of dots (Moszolics 1968, Tafel 12). Like the Bihar examples, the handles are formed of one piece with the rim of the vessel, and are not attached at their lower end. The double-spiral terminals of the two handles of the Biia vessel resemble gold bracelets of c.1600–1400 BC from Hungary. Probably of similar date is a hoard of sheet-gold ornaments from Șmig (Somogyom) (Mozsolics 1968, Tafeln 13–16) associated with part of a globular bronze bowl with a distinctive flat, outwards-rolled rim. As virtually the only sheet-bronze vessel in Europe before the Urnfield period, this bowl is likely to represent an import, even though it has no obvious correspondence with contemporary Aegean types and may well be an import from the Caucasus or Anatolia.

17.7 Pottery cup, Otomani culture, probably Berettyó Újfalu, Hungary (Ashmolean Museum); [new drawing].

The area between the Carpathian Basin and the Aegean was probably capable of producing gold vessels by at least the middle of the second millennium, and metallic 'kantharos' shapes in pottery (distantly related to Anatolian Middle Bronze Age and Middle Helladic ones, though not wheel-made) strongly hint at their presence (Bóna 1975). These shapes, especially the pottery of the Monteoru culture, provide the best analogies for the simpler pieces in the Vulchetrun treasure and related recent finds from Rădeni and Kryzovlin that are discussed below (Vulpe and Mihăilescu-Bîrliba 1985). If Vulchetrun is not a unity, as we suggest, then there is no difficulty in assigning these pieces to such a horizon. It would be later than the Bihar vessels but perhaps overlapping with the later products of the Otomani tradition. A postulated contemporaneity with the goldwork of the Shaft-Grave period would accord well with the generalised similarities between these pieces and the kantharoi from grave IV of circle A and the one from Kalamata in Messenia (Buchholz and Karageorghis 1973, no. 1086; Hartmann 1982, no. 4367; Figure 17.8). The gold vessels of the Vulchetrun group in the lower Danube and west Pontic area, with their riveted handles, are more confident and sophisticated pieces than the Otomani examples; and some contacts between goldsmiths working in the lower Danube and

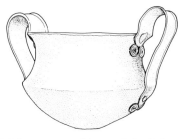

17.8 Mycenaean gold cups: left, *Kalamata;* right, *Mycenae, Shaft-Graves: [from Sherratt 1987e].*

those of the Late Bronze Age Aegean or western Anatolia is clearly shown by the Perşinari dagger, with its close analogies to the sword from Shaft-Grave delta of Circle B. The possibility of similar overseas connections with Anatolia is hinted at by the crinkly kantharos shapes in pottery, recalling the Shaft-Grave and Cretan examples in silver and marble, which may have a common background in Anatolian metalwork (as Childe suggested in 1956).

The next area with plentiful evidence of gold and silver vessels is western Europe, with its small, handled cups with carinated or sinuous profile. Their distribution ranges from Rillaton and Cuxwold in Britain to Eschenz in Switzerland (Gerloff 1975; Bill and Kinnes 1975; Taylor 1980), and they date to the period 1800–1400 BC. Although not directly evidenced in the Únětice and Tumulus cultures that lay between here and the Otomani examples, the characteristic Únětice pottery cup with its sharp carination and concave upper section is closely paralleled by the gold cup from Fritzdorf in the Rhineland (von Uslar 1955), which may well have travelled there from the Únětice area. The small gold and silver cups which are typical of later Breton and Wessex tumuli are echoed in amber and shale examples (Gerloff 1975), and in Denmark in the tree-trunk coffin burials there are small wooden cups ornamented with tin nails (e.g. Glob 1970; the associated horn spoons recall the sheet-gold example associated with the Ploumilliau gold cup: Eluère 1982). The two Breton silver examples, St Adrien and St Fiacre (Briard 1978), are notable as the first silver vessels known outside the Aegean. These small cups, in very diverse materials and occurring over a very wide area, are nevertheless remarkably uniform in conception; and the same idea was occasionally translated into pottery, as in the case of the Scottish handled 'food vessel' from Balcuick.

This evidence demonstrates a chronological cline in the spread of precious metal vessel production: crudely – Troy, Otomani, Wessex. In each case the idea of metal vessels was added to a local competence in the working of gold sheet (Copper Age in central Europe, Beaker in the west), and a local repertoire of prestige drinking vessels in pottery. In south-east Europe rather larger and more sophisticated gold vessels were produced

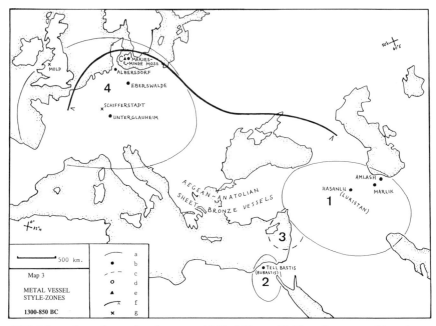

17.9 *Map of metal-vessel style zones, 1300–850 BC: (1) Near Eastern goldwork (Urartian-Assyrian-Babylonian); (2) Egyptian gold and silver vessels in oriental style; (3) Cypro-Levantine (bronzes and pottery skeuomorphs); (4) Urnfield goldwork. (Symbols as in Fig. 17.2)*

than in the north-west. The capacity to produce gold and silver vessels was not, however, paralleled by an ability to produce bronze ones, even though smaller pieces of sheet bronzework were used for ornaments in all these areas. The production of gold and silver vessels in this period thus seems to have devolved from a skill available only in palace workshops and craft centres to one more widely available to barbarian elites. Its spread took the form of successive steps, with each new area taking a general model from its predecessor but creating its own local form, often widely shared among neighbouring elites. (These metal forms probably explain some of the more widespread forms in pottery.) Although there are possible examples of individual vessels travelling along the northwards axis from the Aegean, the process of technological spread owed nothing to Mycenaean imports; it began before the Mycenaean period and was to continue after it. Only the typology of certain pieces of goldwork in the lower Danube area suggests some kind of contact, probably during the Shaft-Grave period.

Stage III: 1300–850 BC (*Figure 17.9*)

This period corresponds to a time of fundamental transition in the economic and social life of Europe and the Near East, as well as a major technological shift from bronze to iron in the southern part of the area. The new pattern well reflects the radical nature of these changes. Very little goldwork, and

442

no gold or silver vessels, are known from the Aegeo-Anatolian area where Mycenaean and Hittite civilisation collapsed and in which Geometric Greece and Phrygian Anatolia were emerging. This is consistent with the brown-painted, basket-like ornament on shapes which only indirectly reflect metal forms. Somewhat greater continuity in elite craftsmanship is probable in the Cypro-Levantine area (especially in the production of Egyptianising bronze tripods in Cyprus: Catling 1964 – though his dates are compressed: see Matthäus 1985), but precious metalwork is only well demonstrated in Egypt and northern Iran. In Egypt the important hoard dated by inscriptions to the late XIXth Dynasty from Tell Basta (ancient Bubastis) includes a silver jug with gold theriomorphic handles which strikingly anticipate Achaemenid forms (Simpson 1959). Further east, the undoubted wealth of the Assyrian, Urartian and Babylonian areas is best exemplified archaeologically from the site of Hasanlu in Iran, though otherwise known from representations in Assyrian reliefs. (Many of these features were to spread westwards with the orientalising movement in the eighth and seventh centuries.) Goldwork from the Marlik Tepe tombs included gold beakers with repoussé animal friezes (somewhat in the manner of the Ishtar Gate at Babylon) showing the links between Achaemenid metalwork and earlier Mesopotamian and Iranian traditions, and the continuity of (presumably) Bactrian gold sources. Bronze objects, including vessels, are known from this time in enormous numbers from looted Luristan tombs. The lack of precious metalwork in the Aegean/Anatolian area is striking, but the continuing production of sheet bronzework there indicates that metalsmiths were restricted by supplies of precious metal rather than by any lack of skill: and if gold or silver vessels were produced, they were too valuable to consign to the ground. Even the Gordion tombs are remarkable for their emphasis on bronzework alone, much of it of the highest order.

In temperate Europe quite a different situation obtained. Metalwork, both in bronze and gold, greatly expanded in the Late Bronze Age – especially in the Urnfield area of central Europe. Here several hoards of gold vessels are known (as well as more extraordinary sheet-gold creations, like the golden 'hats' of Schifferstadt and Ezelsdorf (which may actually be hats: Menghin and Schauer 1977) and for the first time bronze vessels made their appearance outside the Aegean. The technology of sheet bronzework is demonstrated by two sets of items from chieftains' graves: handled cups, and sheet-armour cuirasses (Sprockhoff 1930; Childe 1949; von Merhart 1969; Piggott 1959). By 1000 BC there was a full array of buckets, bowls and sieves, as well as the remarkable wheeled cauldrons (Piggott 1983).

Although the precise dating is disputed, this new technology appeared in Europe not at the peak of Mycenaean power but during and after the collapse of the palaces, in the later LH IIIb and IIIc periods. It is tempting to suggest that large-scale bronze sheetworking had been virtually a palace monopoly, and that the new conditions allowed experienced craftsmen to work for other patrons (not necessarily the richest) – especially further north where opportunities were expanding (Sandars 1983). (At the same time, techniques of solid-casting of swords and spearheads went south, to appear in the Aegean.) A major school of sheet-bronzeworking grew up in the long pre-eminent Carpathian area, whose products were widely distributed, going north as far as Denmark. A characteristic product (that seems to have taken the place of the large, two-handled bowl of Vulchetrun type as the container at the symposium), was the biconical bronze 'amphora' (von Merhart 1969, Tafel 48) that is echoed in pottery as the Villanovan urn. The continuing vitality of central European metallurgy, especially sheet bronzework like armour and vessels, contributed to the revival of these skills in Greece and Italy during the early first millennium.

Beyond the Urnfield area, in Atlantic Europe and Scandinavia, the traditions of cast bronzework continued, and were carried to new heights in the creation of 'belt-boxes' (*Hängebecken*), *lurer*, or Irish horns. Sheetbronzeworking was slower to penetrate, though it eventually spread from central Europe to start a local tradition of buckets and patch-built cauldrons (Hawkes and Smith 1957; Gerloff 1975). The only bronze cups known from the early first millennium in the British Isles, however, are cast ones (e.g. Welby) and despite the craftsmanship attested by the Mold gold cape or the abundance of Irish gold ornaments, there are no gold cups. Sheet-bronze cups were used in Denmark from the equivalent of the early Urnfield period (Thrane 1962). Even in Denmark the famous gold cups from the Mariesminde Mose hoard were probably imported from northern Germany, and only the handles added locally. Horns were probably the main ostentatious drinking vessels, and occasionally occur in Danish treetrunk-coffin burials; and they are known from the early Iron Age in central Europe by their bronze or gold mounts.

THE CONTEXT OF THE VULCHETRUN A-TYPE VESSELS

The Vulchetrun hoard came to light in 1924 near the village in Pleven district, N. Bulgaria, after which it is named.[1] It was not recovered under scientific conditions and part of it was dispersed on discovery. Of fourteen objects which were documented, thirteen arrived at the archaeological museum in Sofia. At least three of these remaining objects are incomplete. Only five of the objects from the hoard are of importance in this discussion – five vessels which appear to be elements of a drinking set (illustrated on p. 373 above); it will be necessary to justify the treatment of these separately from the other objects which form part of the hoard in its present state.

That the Vulchetrun hoard does not constitute a unity in either the technological, chronological or cultural sense of the word has already been argued by one of us (Taylor 1985, 131; 1986). The hoard is listed in Table 17.1: objects V_1–V_5 are grouped as Vulchetrun 'A', the rest as 'B'.[2] The fourteenth object reported at the time of the discovery can be given the number V_{14}; it may well have been the pair to one of the objects V_7–V_{11} if their function as cymbals is accepted (Minchev, pers. comm.). The obvious incongruousness of the forms and implied functions of the objects in the hoard immediately suggests that it represents a hotch-potch of objects hastily deposited at a time when some of them may already have been antique. It is not just on the basis of the various forms and implied functions that the objects can be separated, rather it is pre-eminently in terms of techniques and materials that a primary assemblage 'Vulchetrun A' can be distinguished from the remaining, and apparently later, set of material designated 'Vulchetrun B'. Vulchetrun B may itself be of heterogeneous origin and display various phases of construction.

Table 17.1 The Vulchetrun Hoard.

VULCHETRUN A

V_1 : a large double-handled bowl; gold (c.10% Ag) (Inv. No. 3192)

V_2 : a large single-handled vessel; gold (Inv. No. 3193)

V_3–V_5 : three small single-handled cups; gold (Inv. Nos 3194, 3195, 3204)

VULCHETRUN B

V_6 : a curious 'triple vessel' consisting of three tear-drop shaped bowls of gold, connected by tubing and a trident construction of electrum (Inv. No. 3203)

V_7–V_{11} : five small 'lids', two of which have an onion-shaped central boss surviving (Inv. No. 3198, 3199) and three of which have sections broken away and missing; (c.20% Ag) (Inv. Nos 3200, 3201, 3202); gold

V_{12}, V_{13} : two large 'lids', both with onion-shaped central bosses; gold, decorated with silver (Inv. Nos 3196, 3197)

On the basis of appearance alone, the objects, when viewed under uniform lighting conditions, seem to be made up of three different golds. The vessels V_1–V_5 appear to have the most 'neutral' gold colour with no detectable variation among them, whilst the 'lids' V_7–V_{13} are uniformly greener or more 'brassy'; the three teardrop-shaped dishes of the triple vessel V_6 are redder or more 'coppery'.

It is not only on grounds of a proposed variation in the materials used for different parts of the hoard that its basic disunity is proposed, however, but also from the evidence of different manufacturing technique. The five vessels V_1–V_5 are constructed in hammered gold plate, raised into open forms and finished with repoussé work. Their handles are joined back to their bodies with conical-headed rivets. These techniques demonstrate a fundamental dissimilarity between these vessels and the rest of the hoard, which are of much more complex construction: V_6, for instance, is joined with solder to a *cire perdue* cast electrum trident; V_7–V_{13} display complex polymetallism, being constructed of gold over cast bronze, and the two larger examples

V_{12}–V_{13} have been pattern-silvered within zones delimited by punched lines.[3] It is clear from this appraisal that the objects V_6–V_{13} display quite different and much more complex metal-working techniques than V_1–V_5. We suggest that manufacture within an urban context is likely for these complex objects. The closest parallel for the 'lids' seems to support this – a gold and silver banded 'lid' with a pomegranate-shaped central boss from Karmir Blur, Urartu, which carries an inscription dating it to the eighth century BC.[4] A similar date could be proposed for the triple vessel.

Essentially, the dating and provenance of V_6 to V_{13} need not concern us in this discussion as, whatever their origin, they clearly distinguish themselves from Vulchetrun A in terms of shape, function, fabric and construction: on the one hand we have complex polymetallism with casting, soldering and bonding, whilst on the other hand we have five pure sheet-gold vessels, hammered and riveted. Further, within the last five years, two new discoveries of sheet-gold vessels have been published which display the same technology and a range of similar forms. These represent the first true parallels to the Vulchetrun A drinking set to appear so far. They are the vessel found near Kryzhovlin in the Ukranian S. S. R. (Dzis-Rayko and Chernyakov 1981) and the five vessels found near Rădeni in the Neamṭ district of Romania (*Revista Muzeelor* 1981 (8); see now Vulpe and Mihăilescu-Bîrliba 1985). Figure 17.5 shows the distribution of the three findspots. We shall discuss each set of material in turn.

VULCHETRUN A

The assemblage put forward as Vulchetrun A comprises the five vessels V_1–V_5. They are made of gold of a similar colour, hammer-worked from sheet into open forms. The strap-handles are in all cases integral, rising from the lip in 'high-handle' form and curving back down onto the outside of the vessel to be held in place by three gold rivets apiece. In our illustrations (Figure 17.10, and p. 373 above) the handles of the large vessel V_1 have been reconstructed to what is considered to be their original height. The hoard was recovered in a crumpled state and only partial restoration has taken place; compare the photograph of the hoard as discovered (Mikov 1958, pl. 1) and as it is presently displayed (Venedikov and Gerassimov 1975, pl. 33). It seems sensible to assume that the form of the double handles originally followed that of the less damaged vessel V_2. This fits with the proposed reconstructions of the Kryzhovlin and Rădeni vessels (see below). Vessel V_1 weighs about 4.395kg; a rough volumetric calculation suggests that it could have conveniently held between 7 and 8 litres of liquid. Vessel V_2 weighs 0.919kg. Vessels V_3, V_4 and V_5, the three small cups, are nearly identical in shape and size and their rivets are made as smaller versions of the rivets on the two larger vessels; they weigh 123gm each. The cups would have held about 0.2 litres of liquid, according to how full they were. This

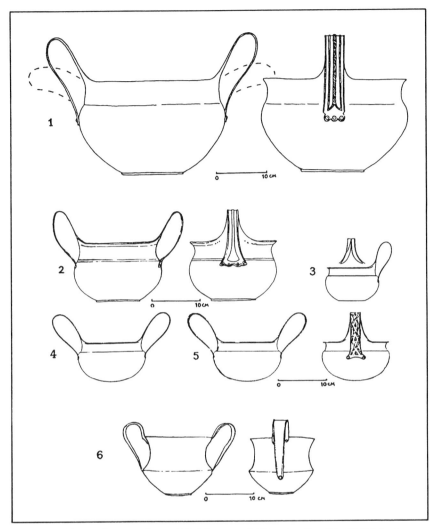

17.10 Gold vessels (to scale): (1) Vulchetrun; (2) Kryzhovlin; (3)–(5) Rădeni; (6) Mycenae, Shaft-Grave IV.

falls somewhere between two of the modern European standard wine measures – the glass, at between 0.115 and 0.125 litres, and the German 'Viertel' or quarter-litre glass (0.250 litre). The cups stand upright only when filled and would presumably have to have been hung up when not in use. On the inner surface of all three cups there is a small indentation; it occurs in the centre of the base and seems to have been caused by a tool with a compass-like point. It is not visible on the outside and is probably an index of a particular production method in which either the tool or the vessel was rotated to enable the vessel to be formed symmetrically.

All five of the vessels are decorated. The body of V_1 is plain with a distinct shoulder two-thirds of the way up. The handles are decorated in five parallel bands or ridges, pressed up out of the thick gold sheet. The central three bands link to form what Venedikov and Gerassimov have termed a 'fish-tail' terminus to either end to the handle (1975, 351). The central band, or spine, is patterned with diagonal slashes which appear to have been excised with a sharp graving tool,[5] the two edges of the handle are decorated with the same diagonal pattern but in much narrower bands, and probably punched. Vessel V_2 is decorated in exactly the same way, although lacking a shoulder. The three vessels V_3, V_4 and V_5 are decorated in a slightly different manner to the two large vessels. There are only three raised bands on the handles – the central band with diagonal slashes, with the outer bands, forming the edges, merely punch-dotted. The same 'fish-tail' termination is present, except that on the inside the ends, after dividing, become a continuous repoussé band around the vessel rim; immediately below this are two further bands so that three bands in all define the rim of each cup.

The bases of all five vessels have standing surfaces formed by regular upraised circular bands. On both V_1 and V_2 there are two such raised bands, organised concentrically (Mikov 1958, figs V and VIII). The small cups V_3–V_5 have a flattened basal plane with a single raised ring on which they stand (Mikov 1958, fig. XI).

KRYZHOVLIN

The Kryzhovlin bowl (Figure 17.10, 2) was discovered by chance in the Balta region, north of Odessa. No associated finds were recorded. It was published by Dzis-Rayko and Chernyakov in 1981 under the title 'A gold bowl of Vulchetrun type from the north-west Pontic region'. It weighs 765.59gm; its maximum diameter is 17.9cm. The handles of the vessel have undecorated 'fish-tail' termini (similar though not identical to Vulchetrun V_1) which were originally held in place on both sides with four rivets apiece; these rivets are rounded on their outer faces and hammered down against the inner surface of the vessel. Like V_1 the bowl has a distinct raised base. On Kryzhovlin this consists of two concentric rings beaten down to form a standing plane between which six rivets have been hammered (Dzis-Rayko and Chernyakov 1981, 153, fig. 3:3). A rough volumetric calculation suggests that the vessel could once have held around 2 to 2.5 litres of liquid.

RĂDENI

Information concerning a hoard of badly damaged vessels from near the village of Rădeni in Romanian Moldavia (Figure 17.10, 3–5) has been slow to emerge since its accidental discovery during farm work in 1965 or 1966 (Vulpe and Mihăilescu-Bîrliba 1985, 47). Three vessels reached Piatra Neamț museum in 1977 and appeared on the cover of *Revista Muzeelor*

1981 (8) but with little documentation. A fourth vessel passed, by way of a jeweller in Oradea, Transylvania, into the collection of the National Museum in Bucharest in 1971. A fifth passed from private hands into the Romanian National Bank between 1979 and 1980. It seems that the hoard had consisted of as many as eight small gold vessels which had been hung from a larger two-handled vessel by means of (?gold) wire (Vulpe and Mihăilescu-Bîrliba 1985, 48). The five vessels, R_1–R_5, which can be documented are listed in Table 17.2.

Table 17.2 The Rădeni Hoard.

R_1 (Figure 17.10, 5) Piatra Neamţ Inv. No. 5548: a two-handled gold vessel with distinct shoulder and decorative engraving on the handles; weight 458.6gm; the strap-handles are integral, rising from the rim to be fixed back against the body using two rivets apiece. The base is formed by two concentric rings with six rivets hammered flat between them, very similar to the base of the Kryzhovlin vessel.

R_2 Piatra Neamţ Inv. No. 5549: a two-handled gold vessel with distinct shoulder and 'fish tail' decoration; weight 243.10gm; the strap-handles are integral, two rivets apiece; the base appears to be defined by a single raised ring but without rivets.

R_3 (Figure 17.10, 3) Piatra Neamţ Inv. No. 5550: a single-handled gold vessel with distinct shoulder and 'fish tail' decoration; weight 203.7gm; the handle is integral, with two rivets; there is a distinct circular pressed-out base (see Vulpe and Mihăilescu-Bîrliba 1985, 52 and Abbildung 5:1e).

R_4 (Figure 17.10, 4) National Museum, Bucharest Inv. Nos B 32/1–9: (fragmentary) a two-handled gold vessel, similar to R_2, with 'fish tail' decoration; weight of fragments 198.17gm; two rivets per handle.

R_5 Romanian National Bank, Bucharest: (five fragments) a gold vessel with either one or two handles, integral with the rim and fixed with a row of three rivets; 'fish tail' termini to the handle(s) are clearly visible; weight of fragments 158.5gm.

The five vessels appear like a set of miniature variations on the Vulchetrun V_1 type, with high strap-handles and conical-ended rivets. A rough volumetric calculation suggests that they could have held between 0.2 and 0.25 litres, a little more than the three cups V_3–V_5. They seem to have been constructed from at least two types of sheet; Vulpe and Mihăilescu-Bîrliba note that R_1 and R_5 appear to be much 'redder' than the other vessels.

The vessels from Vulchetrun, Kryzhovlin and Rădeni display a large number of shared traits. Despite their different sizes, they have forms and decorations which appear as variations on a theme. They were all constructed from sheet-gold and using similar workshop techniques. They occur in the extra-Carpathian zone which links the Steppe to the Lower Danube Basin (Figure 17.5, zone 7), but, given their close similarity, the distances between their respective findspots is remarkable – as the crow flies, about 250km between Rădeni and Kryzhovlin, about 400km between Rădeni and Vulchetrun and about 650km between Kryzhovlin and Vulchetrun.

It seems reasonable that a similar date should be sought for the production of all of the vessels; however, the fact that no associated material was documented at any of the three findspots which might have helped in suggesting a date (for the depositions at least), makes this endeavour a hard one.[6] The history of scholarship concerning Vulchetrun is long and complex (see Bonev 1977). During the last sixty years various datings ranging from the late third millennium BC to AD 700 have been put forward. Because the hoard has been considered a unity, the postulated dates have had to accommodate both components. Furthermore, no close parallels were known until recently for any of the objects in the hoard; thus specialists tended to ascribe the 'treasure' to the period with which they were most familiar.

The most favoured time-bracket has always been between the thirteenth century BC and the eighth century BC. We hope to demonstrate here that this is absolutely the *least* likely period within the entire date range in which to countenance the production of gold vessels of the type described. We consider that the distinction of more than one techno-cultural complex within the Vulchetrun hoard marks a major step forward in the attempt to understand the material. Ridding ourselves of the 'lids' with their bizarre technology and unknown function immediately removes all the arguments for dating the Vulchetrun A component on the basis of the curvilinear meanders on the 'lids' (general parallels for which can be found in many periods – they formed the basis of Filov and Kazarov's medieval ascription). Arguments based on the form of the bronze components to the 'lids' (Mikov 1958; Venedikov and Gerassimov 1975, 27f., pl. 36; Bonev 1984, figs 8–11; Taylor 1986, fig. 1) are also spurious, as these are both incomplete and of a very different form to that supposed by most authors.

Given the lack of associated material at Kryzhovlin and Rădeni, and the problematic material 'associated' with Vulchetrun A, we are left with four indirect means of proposing a cultural and chronological context for the phenomenon of the Vulchetrun A-type vessels. These are contextual analysis, formal analysis, functional analysis and technological analysis.

The absence of material associated with the gold vessels itself suggests a certain depositional and cultural mode. All the finds were uncovered in a crumpled state (at Rădeni apparently deliberately crushed); none of the finds was part of a burial; likewise none was found within, or in any close association with, any known prehistoric settlement. Although, strictly, the Vulchetrun hoard must be ruled out of this discussion (having argued above that the vessels in it were incorporated into a secondary deposition), the finds from Rădeni give enough support to the idea that the original eight small vessels there may have formed part of a hoard in which a large two-handled vessel of V_1 type may have been the centrepiece. Such deposition of drinking equipment seems to have been widespread during the period after 2000 BC in Europe (Figure 17.5) with a number of hoards from the Otomani area (zone 8) and individual pieces in central western Europe (zone 10). After 1300 BC no such depositions are known from south-east Europe, the Aegean or Anatolia (Figure 17.9) until the appearance of the Kazicheni gold vessel ('Sofia treasure') in the eighth or seventh century BC. Indeed, the lack of goldwork from eastern Europe at a time when it is plentifully represented in the Urnfield area further west (e.g. Menghin and Schauer 1977) suggests that alluvial gold in the Carpathian area may have been coming to an end after three thousand years of exploitation from the Copper Age onwards. Later goldwork of the Classical and Hellenistic periods was mostly made from mined gold, probably from the area of Mount Pangaion where ancient authors describe it (see Unger and Schütz 1982).

In the absence of datable contexts for finds of gold vessels of Vulchetrun A-type, further clues may be sought in the local pottery shapes. Double-handled vessels resembling the Vulchetrun large vessel (V_1), with two high strap-handles rising from the rim and joining at the shoulder, are found in a broad arc of related cultures stretching from the Balkans to the North Pontic area, and including the Tei, Monteoru and Costişa cultures. Particularly close parallels occur in the Classic phase of the Monteoru culture (1800–1500 BC) – notable also for the abundance of small sheet-goldwork in the form of hair-rings (Zaharia 1959). The parallels extend to the presence of a median ridge along the strap-handles in the manner of the Vulchetrun, Rădeni and Kryzhovlin examples (e.g. Gimbutas 1965, fig. 152, 2). Even in pottery, such vessels were valuable and significant enough to accompany individuals to their graves, as in cemetery 4 at Sărata-Monteoru itself (ibid., fig. 153).

From the point of view of function, the Vulchetrun A–Kryzhovlin–Rădeni group fits very well into the Bronze Age 'symposium' category. We have already outlined the form taken by the development of this elite custom or pastime in the commentary on the maps (above). If we consider these finds as the remains of elite drinking sets, then we can imagine them originally consisting of a central, communal, liquid-holding vessel – Vulchetrun V_1, Kryzhovlin and the inferred V_1-type vessel from Rădeni – for use with a number of individual drinking cups holding roughly the same volume as a modern large wine glass – Vulchetrun V_3–V_5 and Rădeni R_1–$R_{(8)}$. In such chance finds it is by no means unreasonable to postulate similar small drinking cups for use with the Kryzhovlin vessel. The vessel V_2 probably represents an elaboration on the basic drinking ceremony (perhaps like the later role of the rhyton in relation to the crater and phiale, or as a 'loving cup' for communal use). It is interesting to note that the small vessels from the Rădeni hoard were apparently discovered hanging with wire from the now missing larger vessel, as the balance of the Vulchetrun A drinking cups (referred to above) suggests that they too would have to have been hung from something if they were not to roll around and become damaged; the central vessel V_1 would present the ideal choice. Pingel has calculated that V_1 would have weighed around 15kg when full and therefore would have been kept in a fixed position (1982, 176).

The analysis of depositional context, form and function do no more than suggest a general milieu for the production and use of drinking vessels of the Vulchetrun A-type. We have suggested that the period from 2000–1300 BC is the only viable one in which to place them. Within this long period, however, it is only technological analysis that can tie down the date of production further.

We will attempt to argue for a date between 1600 and 1400 BC for the vessels of the Vulchetrun-A–Kryzhovlin–Rădeni group. The Vulchetrun A-type vessels display a technology which, although practised locally, owes much to the type of metalworking known from the Mycenaean Shaft-Grave and Palace periods; therefore they must date to the period in which contact between the Aegean and those areas around the Black Sea where they were made was at its height.[7]

The techniques with which we are dealing are much more sophisticated than those of the native Otomani goldworking tradition, and bear little direct debt to it. They might well be seen as in response to the influence of Trojan or Mycenaean contacts with the Black Sea coastlands. It is in the Shaft-Grave period that these stylistic links are most obvious, as long recognised in the compass-decorated bonework (mostly horse-gear) with a Carpathian background, and more demonstrably in the occurrence of Baltic amber in Greece – though this followed an Italian rather than a Balkan route (Harding 1984, 79f; Bouzek 1985). Metals may have been the motive for such contacts (a trade perhaps later marked by the copper ox-hide ingots off the Gulf of Burgas and inland, and the double axes of apparently Mycenaean type from Bulgaria, Romania and the Ukraine (Panayotov 1980; Buchholz 1983), since Carpatho-Balkan copper and Bohemian tin was potentially available to Trojan or early Mycenaean traders. The influence of such contacts on local goldworking traditions is best exemplified in the Perşinari dagger with its Shaft-Grave parallels (e.g. circle B grave Delta), and the nearby Măcin gold daggers, from the Lower Danube Basin (Figure 17.5; and see Gimbutas 1965, pl. 8b, 1; Mozsolics 1965/66, Tafel 1, 1 and 2). These imply a much closer relationship during the sixteenth century BC between these areas than possible imports in other areas (e.g. Dohnsen) can suggest.

It is in this context that the Vulchetrun A-type vessels should be viewed. We suggest that the following developments took place in south-east European metal vessel production as a result of the influence of palace workshops (in terms either of emulation following imported models or of the actual movement of craftsmen). None of the following traits is characteristic of the Otomani sheet-gold vessel horizons, but all of them are found in Aegaeo-Anatolian (including Cretan-Mycenaean) metalworking and in the Vulchetrun-A–Kryzhovlin–Rădeni group:

1. The raising of sheet vessels with regular circular cross-section in the horizontal plane: this is lacking in the early second-millennium gold vessels of the Otomani group, and was achieved – perhaps independently – in the Atlantic Early Bronze Age (Fritzdorf, Rillaton) at a date approximately contemporary with the Shaft-Grave goldwork and the suggested date of Vulchetrun A.

2. The sharp shouldering or carination of the vessel body: again apparently developed independently in the west (Fritzdorf), it is unknown in the Otomani group. The shoulder, which brings the vessel over into a closed form, is much more difficult to achieve while retaining a regular horizontal section, than it is when raising an open shape.

3. The use of the classic 'kantharos' form with two strap-handles: this form, which probably originated in Anatolia or Crete (Gournia; and the imported silver kantharoi from Tôd, dating to c.2000 BC; Davis 1977, figs 52 and 53) is well known in the Mycenaean world. The example from Mycenae Shaft-Grave IV is illustrated for comparative purposes here (fig. 4:6); it is similar in scale to the Rădeni and Kryzhovlin vessels, but the shoulder is set much lower. The twin-handled bowls in the Otomani region may owe something to early Cretan types, but if so then they have not retained the shoulders or riveted-back handles and are unlikely to have served as a starting-point for the Vulchetrun A-type vessels.

4. Concentric ring bases and raised circular bases: these are typical of early Cypro-Levantine production (Tôd, Ain Samieh) and are characteristic of all Cretan-Mycenaean non-footed sheet-metal vessels. The slightly raised sub-circular bases which occur on some Otomani vessels (Bihar) might be related, but the competent concentric basal rings of the Vulchetrun A-type vessels seem unlikely to represent a development from these; rather, they are more likely to follow Aegean models directly. Compare the raised base of Rădeni R_3 (Vulpe and Mihăilescu-Bîrliba 1985, fig. 5:1d, 1e) with Cretan-Mycenaean examples.

5. The use of high strap-handles and conical rivets: nearly all the handles of the Mycenaean metal vessels are attached at both ends, using rivets; only a few of the 'teacups' have handles which are integral with the rim at one end (e.g. Ayios Ioannis). Neither riveting nor high strap-handles are used at all in the Otomani goldwork; while in the west the separately made handles are held in place both top and bottom by flat, rhomboidal, 'washer-rivets' which are a feature peculiar to this group.

If taken together, these traits suggest that there was an important link between the production of the Aegean workshops and the Vulchetrun A–Kryzhovlin–Rădeni group. These similarities effectively rule out a pre-Mycenaean date (cf. Pingel 1982). There is only one important divergence from the tradition represented at Mycenae. As mentioned above, few Mycenaean vessels have integral handles, and those that do are not of the kantharos type which, we suggested, provided the basic model for the V_1 type. The vessels of the Hajdúsámson period (2000–1800 BC) all have such integral handles, joined at the rim and open at the bottom. Because of the strong general influence of early Mycenaean techniques and overall lack of similarity with the Otomani tradition, the Vulchetrun A-type vessels are clearly of Mycenaean date; nevertheless, the integral handles may indeed reflect continuation of this single feature from Otomani goldwork.

Vulpe and Mihăilescu-Bîrliba suggest that the Rădeni and Kryzhovlin vessels were made in the same workshop (1985, 57) but this is perhaps to over-interpret their clear similarity as a group. The differences among the Vulchetrun A-type vessels, with rivets from two to four per handle, sizes from fractions of litres to several litres, and the various ways in which the 'fish tail' motifs have been rendered, all suggest a common style rather than the production of a single atelier. The very fact that, after appearing to be unique for so many years, Vulchetrun now has parallels, should suggest both that more vessels are to be found and that more vessels *have* been found during the period of 3500 years or so since the deposition of such hoards. The full documentation of eleven vessels from three widely dispersed findspots, unmarked by any burial monument, in three separate countries after so long a period seems to provide ample grounds for the belief that many more existed, probably with a sequence of internal developments.

These considerations require there to be a zone of common contact around the western margin of the Black Sea over which a common form of luxury symposium set was in use, and that this zone was in contact with the Aegean world. This is exactly what Dzis-Rayko and Chernyakov feel to be a prerequisite for the production of their bowl (1981, 157f) and believe it to exist between the fifteenth and thirteenth centuries BC. This is indeed a possibility. We believe, however, that the vessels should date a little earlier, to the sixteenth to fifteenth centuries BC, because this is the period of most obvious Mycenaean influence (Perşinari) and because of the continuation of the Otomani goldsmithing tradition of raising the handles directly from the lip.

In conclusion, the arguments presented for the various technical and chronological phases in the production of sheet-metal vessels from 3000 to 850 BC lead to a much clearer understanding of the place of the Vulchetrun vessels and their relatives within a broader European pattern. The view that such vessels were used for the presentation and distribution of alcoholic drinks in a formalised social context sheds light on the function of many types of ceramic vessels which survive from areas and periods when precious metal has failed, for one reason or another, to be well represented in the archaeological record. From 3000 BC down to the end of the Aegean palaces we can see how important the axial position of western Anatolia, Greece and the Mediterranean islands was in mediating the transmission of techniques and fashions often originating in the urban centres of the Near East. It is the effective collapse of this network which divided gold and silver vessel-working into isolated oriental and occidental schools.

It is unnecessary for present purposes to pursue this story in subsequent periods: the effect of the Mediterranean revival and the orientalising movement, the spread of further types of Mediterranean buckets, amphorae and jugs along the central European axis (e.g. Stjernquist 1967; Schaaff and Taylor 1975; Werner 1954; Eggers 1951), and the arrival of wine itself through the agency of the Greeks and Romans. The theme is a continuing one. Whether the vessels of Vulchetrun held wine or mead, beer or koumish, they were part of an aristocratic 'golden age' of alcoholic hospitality.

The goldwork of the Vulchetrun group would thus represent a metal-working tradition influenced by the advanced workshop practices of the Aegean palaces, and perhaps acting as intermediary between these and the more distant workshops of temperate Europe. Such contacts between the west Pontic area and Mycenaean Greece did not outlast the Mycenaean period itself; but they interestingly prefigure the future pattern of Archaic and Classical Greek colonisation and its introduction of the set of vessels which were to characterise the second golden age of Thrace, that of Panagyurishte.

NOTES

1. Vulchetrun is romanised from the village name ВЪЛЧИТРЪН following Venedikov and Gerassimov's 1975 English transliteration. Other romanisations in the literature include VБLČI TRБN (Ebert), Vulchi Trun (Hoddinott), Vălcitrăn (Matthäus) and V'lči-Tr'n (Harding).
2. Observations carried out by T. F. Taylor in May 1985 with the permission and guidance of the Antiquities department. We would particularly like to thank Prof. Venedikov and Dr Lazov for their help.
3. These punch-marks are made by a different tool from those on V_3–V_5.
4. This inscription is of the King Argishti I who came to the throne in the second quarter of the eighth century BC (Piotrovsky 1959, pl. 42). Although not argued in detail here, a referral of V_7–V_{13} to an urban and possibly Urartian production context seems to us to be reasonable; their incorporation and deposition with a set of locally made antique drinking vessels does not seem inherently unlikely. Filov and Kazarov's medieval ascription (cited Wilke 1925) is also worthy of consideration in this respect. The incorporation of a chance discovery of gold vessels (Vulchetrun A) into a later church treasure (Vulchetrun B) is an attractive scenario.
5. These are dissimilar in detail to those on V_{12} and V_{13}. Both the tool and the technique differ.

6. None of the finds was excavated scientifically, and important material may have gone unrecognised and/or missing.
7. The Troy II treasures form the best source for third-millennium metal vessels in the Aegean; the Mycenae Shaft-Graves the best for the second millennium. Both were probably typical of both sides of the Aegean in their respective periods and it would be a mistake to attribute similarities specifically to either.

18

Troy, Maikop, Altyn Depe: Early Bronze Age Urbanism and its Periphery

(1991)

The early history of the Old World was centred upon the Near East: a unique conjunction of environments created by the intersection of the Arid Zone and the chain of recent mountains which runs from the Alps to the Himalayas. The complex geography of this region, with its intimate mixture of mountains, deserts and oases, contrasts with the more uniform zones which surround it – forest, steppe and desert. It was in the Near East that farming began, that irrigation and plough agriculture developed, and in which urban civilisation appeared. The northern boundary of this nuclear zone is interrupted by the Black Sea and the Caspian, so that three land bridges mark the points of contact between the Near Eastern core area and the northern zones: western Anatolia, the Caucasus, and Turkmenia. Anatolia is the point of contact with forested Europe, the Caucasus overlooks the steppes, and Turkmenia the desert. Each of these has played a special historical role, on the frontier of Near Eastern farming and urbanism.

Three famous sites mark these meeting-points in the fourth and third

---

This chapter was written for a conference at Novorossiysk, where the northern flanks of the Caucasus meet the Black Sea, on the subject of the Maikop princely burials – the easternmost phenomena discussed in Childe's Dawn. Participants then travelled to St Petersburg to view the material in the Hermitage: thirty-two surprisingly comfortable hours by train. Culturally, this area forms a bridge between Greater Mesopotamia and the steppes (just as Troy and Anatolia do with the Balkans); and it provides an opportunity to relate the well-understood Tripole sequence of painted pottery styles – perhaps the longest and most finely-divided such sequence in prehistory – to the uncertainties of the Near Eastern sequence as urbanism crystallised and colonial contacts were set up for the first time. Thanks are due to Professor V. M. Masson, the excavator of Altyn Depe, who organised the conference; and to Dr Roger Moorey, Donald Matthews and Professor Michael Roaf for their Mesopotamian insights.

millennia BC, when urban civilisations first had contacts with their northern neighbours: Troy, Maikop and Altyn Depe. Each of them marks the edge of the area of cultural and technological sophistication shown, for instance, by elite craft production of metal vessels, complex jewellery and lost-wax casting, or by the production of wheelmade pottery. Beyond them lay simpler societies – whether in Bulgaria, where precious-metal vessels were imitated in hand-made pottery by Early Bronze Age farmers, who could reproduce the new design of bronze axes using two-piece moulds, but not the more advanced skills of palace metalsmiths; on the Pontic steppes, where emerging pastoral tribes adopted the use of wheeled vehicles in a distinctive new culture; or in the deserts of the Kyzyl Kum, where a foraging existence continued relatively unchanged. At each of these points there was contact and interaction with northern neighbours: but each marked a boundary. Each of these sites, therefore, sits on the frontier between socially more complex societies, with dense local populations already organised in hierarchical forms and linked by long-distance trade, and an outer periphery of less complex societies which were still 'tribal' in their organisation, technology and attitudes to wealth. Each of these sites, moreover, has provided a unique archaeological treasure-house of urban craft skills, in the hoards of objects from Troy II, the wealth of the Maikop and Novosvobodnaya burials, and the priestly quarter of Altyn Depe. Such frontier sites have therefore revealed aspects of elite culture which are often unmatched by contemporary sites in the urban heartlands of Mesopotamia.

From this point of view, therefore, these sites are very similar; but in their concrete aspects they are very different. Troy is a stronghold destroyed by fire, preserving its metal finds by chance. Altyn Depe is an urban settlement, whose wealth was concentrated in its religious complex: a massive mud-brick temple. Maikop is not even a settlement, but a spectacularly rich group of tombs, the only deliberate deposit of material wealth. In this respect it is the first of a long line of 'barbarian' societies which have flourished on the edges of urban civilisations, and are characterised (like the Scythians in the same area in the first millennium) by the ostentatious display of material goods in the context of burial. If these are 'complex societies', they are all complex in different ways; and by comparing and contrasting, we can sharpen the concept.

URBAN CORES AND HIGHLAND PERIPHERIES

The common background to all of these sites, however, was the new scale of urban production, trade and transport which developed in the fourth and third millennia BC. The dense mass of consumers in hierarchically organised societies, concentrated in the alluvial basins and sustained by irrigation farming, made possible a division of labour in which raw materials were moved over long distances to supply urban manufacturers and craft centres.

River transport was fundamental in moving bulk products, but these arteries were linked to overland routes (using newly domesticated transport animals such as the donkey and camel) which could carry high-value materials over long distances.

In the fourth millennium the urban heartlands were confined to a relatively restricted area of Sumer and Elam, but in the third millennium a number of different core areas appeared, with competition for access to routes and resources. The fourth-millennium situation is especially interesting, however, since there are fewer analogies for this situation in later history: a single dominant core area with long feeder routes reaching widely into surrounding territories. During this time (Late Uruk), a set of colonies (like Habuba Kabira and Jebel Aruda on the Euphrates in Syria) were established on the main riverine transport routes at points where they articulated with overland routes reaching deep into the highlands (Algaze 1989). The ramifications spread out as far as the Levant (perceptible in Gerzean Egypt, the Nagada II period), and also in eastern Anatolia, for instance in the Keban region (Frangipane et al. 1993). Another linked region, with evidence of writing, seals and trading activity, was Godin Tepe in Kermanshah on the Hamadan route to the plateau, and so to the Anarak copper sources and lapis lazuli supplies from Badakhshan (Young 1986). This is a truly vast area, already interacting over almost the whole range of the Bronze Age world system: but it was a relatively simple structure with only one major core area, albeit divided into many independent political units.

By the early third millennium, the proto-Elamite area centred on Susa was already competing, and controlling not only the Zagros but a further set of overland routes across the Persian Plateau, with tablets in its own writing system from Hissar, Tepe Yahya and Shah-i-Sokhta. These areas developed their own manufacturing capacity, in lapis lazuli, chlorite and steatite; and it was in this context that sites like Altyn Depe achieved prominence perhaps as a supplier of turquoise. Sumer in the Early Dynastic period received these materials and products by sea along the Gulf, and obtained its copper from Oman. By the mid-third millennium, new polities were also developing on the western supply routes at key points such as Ebla, with their own hinterlands in Anatolia (at sites like the yet unlocated Purušhanda). This demand led to the development of urban centres in Anatolia, as far west as the Aegean coasts. Akkadian Mesopotamia continued to look west – in the famous campaigns to Cedar Forest and Silver Mountain – and also by sea to the newer civilisation of the Indus, which channelled highland materials through its own territory (Marfoe 1987). These maritime links became increasingly important, and at the end of the third millennium led to the renewed importance of southern Mesopotamia in the Ur III period. Such, in crude outline (Figure 18.1), is the economic history of the period under consideration.

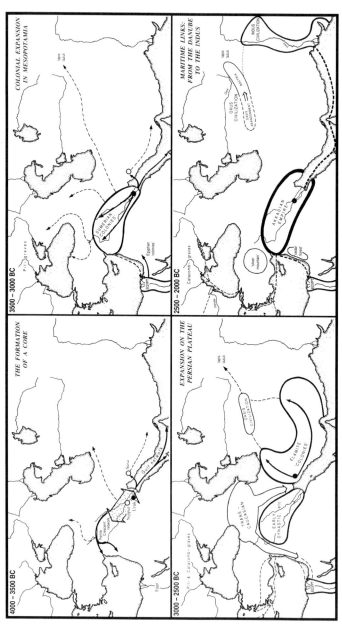

18.1 *Summary maps of Near Eastern culture history by successive half-millennia, 4000–2000 BC: (a) early fourth millennium – regional integration; (b) later fourth millennium – first cities and Uruk colonial settlements; (c) early third millennium – colonial settlements on the Iranian plateau, and expansion of Transcaucasian influence; (d) proliferation of secondary states and their temporary incorporation in the Akkadian Empire (clusters of secondary states in the Levant and central Anatolia labelled after the military propaganda of Sargon of Agade!). Boundaries are schematic.*

Where, then, do our sites fit into it? At the western end, the spectacular finds at Troy belong to the later third millennium, when Syria was an important consuming area in its own right. Out east, the high point of Turkmenian prosperity was the urban period of Namazga V in the later third millennium, when it was also part of a network of secondary states including Harappan India. What about Maikop?

THE CONTEXT OF MAIKOP

The traditional dating of the Maikop complex, suggested by Iessen, placed it c.2500–2400 BC, at a time which would broadly correspond to the context of Troy II and Altyn Depe, and thus to a developed stage of the Near Eastern economic system. This would provide some obvious analogies for vessels of precious metal, which are known from sites in Iran and Afghanistan. An obvious starting point for such comparisons is the Asterabad treasure, discovered in the 1840s at the site now known as Tureng Tepe on the south-east Caspian (published in the English journal *Archaeologia* in 1844 and never seen since), which contained not only silver and gold vessels but also copper objects such as a transverse axe-adze, bident, and poker-butt spearhead with analogies in the Maikop complex. The assemblage also contained objects like an alabaster vase (known from examples in sites like Shahdad), metalwork such as 'trumpets' and spouted jars like those from the hill of treasures in Tepe Hissar III, and an iconography on the metal vessels which would connect them with later third-millennium products of Bactrian or neo-Sumerian workshops. Other similar 'treasures' have appeared in recent years: the Kosh Tepe/Fullol hoard, recovered in Kabul market, with metal vases decorated with Namazga V motifs; the Quetta hoard, again with precious metal vessels, a bull's head like Altyn Depe, and again the alabaster vessels like Shahdad. All of these are closely related to the intensive trade in lapis lazuli across the Persian Plateau (Maxwell-Hyslop 1982; Amiet 1986). The date of these various hoards seems to cluster in the Ur III period, shortly before 2000 BC. At first glance, therefore, it is tempting to relate the florescence of Maikop to an advanced stage of Near Eastern economic development, roughly coeval with Altyn Depe and slightly later than Troy II.

However, as Andreeva has already indicated (1977; 1979), the Maikop finds do not belong to this period. The best analogies for the most distinctive features, the iconography of the silver vessels and the gold bull figures, are to be found in the art of the Late Uruk period, at least a millennium earlier. (See Figure 18.2 and accompanying note.) This would also agree with other evidence: ceramic parallels in the F phase of the Amuq sequence, the hoard of poker-butt spearheads (and solid-hilted swords) recovered from level VIA at Arslantepe near Malatya (Frangipane and Palmieri 1983), as well as the parallels for the Krasnogvardeskoe cylinder-seal (Nekhaev 1986) in Late

BC Cal	HUNGARY	MOLDAVIA	L. DNEPR	N. CAUCASUS	W. CAUCASUS	C. CAUCASUS	TR. CAUCASUS	ARSLANTEPE	GAWRA	NINEVEH	GODIN	MESOPOTAMIA
2500												
2600	Vučedol-Zók	Late Corded Ware (Budzhak)	Catacomb	North Caucasian	Dolmens	North Caucasian	Early Trialeti					EARLY DYNASTIC III
2700												EARLY DYNASTIC II
2800	Late Baden	Corded Ware	Late Pit-grave	Novo-Titarovka II	Dolmens	Late Kura-Arax	Late Kura-Arax					
2900												
3000	Classic Baden	Globular Amphorae	Early Pit-grave	Novo-Titarovka I	Dolmens	Late Kura-Arax	Late Kura-Arax	VI B	VII A		IV	EARLY DYNASTIC I
3100									VII B	V		
3200						Late Maikop			VII C			JEMDAT NASR
3300	Boleraz	(Local Tripole Groups) Tripole C 2	Late Eneolithic Groups	Late Eneolithic Groups	Novo-svobodnaya						(gap)	
3400								VI A	VIII			LATE URUK
3500									IX		V	
3600	Bodrog II	Tripole C 1	Sredni Stog II	Konstantinovka		Early Maikop	Early Kura-Arax		XA	IV	VI	
3700								VII	XI			
3800											VII	
3900	Bodrog I	Tripole B 2										
4000				Svobodnoe					XII	III		EARLY URUK
4100	Tiszapolgar	Tripole B 1	Sredni Stog I									
4200						Nalchik	Shulaveri-Shomu Tepe		XIII			
4300												
4400			Mariupol						XIV			
4500	Tisza	Tripole A										
4600												TERMINAL UBAID
4700												

18.2 Comparative cultural and stratigraphic sequences from east-central Europe, the steppes, the Caucasus and Greater Mesopotamia, on a calibrated radiocarbon timescale. Note that the Gavra sequence might be relatively older than indicated here (M. Roaf, pers. comm.). The relative sequences in the Balkan, steppe, Caucasian and Near Eastern regions have been plotted according to a calibrated radiocarbon chronology. Individual sequences have been compiled, with minor modifications, from Dergachev and Manzura, Trifonov, and Vértesalji, to whom I should record my thanks and apologies. (Note that other interpretations of the Gavra sequence would place it earlier, taking levels XII and below back to 'Ubaid.) The aim of the exercise is to demonstrate that accepted parallelisms are perfectly compatible with a calibrated radiocarbon chronology, provided it is consistently applied. Traditional chronologies for the Near East have been based on historical sources for the third millennium, with speculative dates for earlier units such as Jemdet Nasr and Uruk. However, it is now increasingly recognised (Algaze 1989; Hassan and Robinson 1987; Nissen 1987; Oates 1987; Vértesalji 1987; 1988; Young 1986; Weiss 1986) that these periods can only be dated by radiocarbon, and that such dates – fewer in number than for comparable phases in prehistoric Europe – require calibration. One implication of this is the much greater length of time required for Uruk: dates even for terminal 'Ubaid indicate that this period lasts only into the mid-fifth millennium. Early Uruk may well begin before 4000 BC; Late Uruk before 3500 BC. Many more samples are required to make these estimates more precise. Nevertheless, there is no conflict between these dates and calibrated radiocarbon dating of the Tripole-Cucuteni sequence; and the Caucasian cultures fit well between the two. What is perhaps alarming are the great spans of time now occupied by these units, and how limited is our sample of archaeological material from this time; but this is a fact which must now be faced.

Uruk cylinder seals (though probably not with the stamp-seals with similar motifs from Tepe Gawra, which are probably rather older). These indications are unanimous in placing the Maikop complex in a much earlier cultural context, and thus in the formative initial phase of Near Eastern urban economies and trading networks – a conclusion that was already hinted at in 1920 by Rostovtzeff.

The absence of comparable metal vessels from Mesopotamia itself at this period can be attributed to the lack of aristocratic tombs before the Royal Cemetery at Ur in the Early Dynastic III period. For this reason there are no vessels of precious metal which can provide a direct comparison, although the rich iconography of contemporary seals and sealings provides a wealth of detailed analogies. In this respect, the situation closely resembles that of the Scythian tombs three millennia later, which have yielded examples of craftsmanship in precious metal which are unknown from classical Greece itself. Nevertheless, there are many points of comparison between the Maikop vessels and Late Uruk representational art as preserved especially on seals and on other objects of stone: animal scenes without human figures, especially rows of beasts, sometimes with mixtures of different species. In matters of detail, it is easy to find points of comparison for bulls, lions, boars, caprids, vegetation; and the style and treatment are closely similar, e.g. the bulls' horns, tails and hooves, and the pig's bifurcate tail (Figure 18.3). As well as metropolitan examples, we can find good comparisons on impressions and sealings from the 'colonial' sites such as Habuba Kabira and Godin Tepe. Nevertheless, the mountains on the Maikop vessels, and the portrayal of horses, argue against the importation of these vessels from Mesopotamia, and indicate the existence of local workshops (either in the northern Caucasus or perhaps Transcaucasia) which were capable of producing such advanced craft metalwork, and absorbing elements of metropolitan iconography (and perhaps of religious belief).

This conclusion is of major historical importance, both in the pattern of inter-regional connections and in the social and cultural history of the period: for Maikop appears as the world's first 'barbarian' society, generated on the fringe of the area of initial urban expansion, and preserving in its ostentatious tombs a sample of the kind of elite equipment so far unknown from the urban heartlands at this time. The Caucasus was involved right from the beginning in the process of urban expansion in the Uruk period and the social changes consequent upon it. Moreover, the mountain chief-doms of the northern Caucasus played an important role in transmitting elements of culture and technology to the steppe region, leading to the genesis of the Pit-Grave complex which fundamentally affected societies further west. The Maikop region thus forms a crucial link between the historical events of the Near East and the slower transformation of pre-historic Europe.

The concentration of rich tombs in a relatively limited period confirms

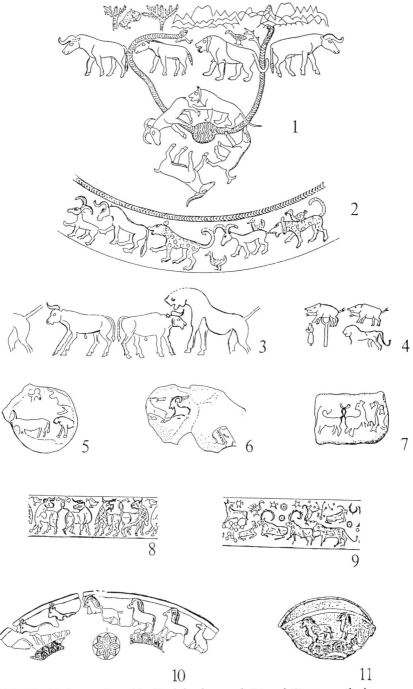

18.3 *The Maikop style and its Uruk background: (1) and (2), transcribed scenes from the two figured silver vessels from the Maikop royal tomb; (3)–(11), icon-ological analogies in greater Mesopotamia. These include both Late Uruk sealings from 'colonial' sites – (3) Nineveh, (4) Habuba Kabira, (5)–(9) Godin Tepe – and also later parallels (10) and (11) on a silver vessel from Early Dynastic Ur (after Rostovtseff, Collon, Young, Müller-Karpe).*

the impression that these political developments were a temporary phase in the historical situation, and the absence of tin alloys in this region in the third millennium (when they had come into widespread use in the Near East) suggests that no long-term economic articulation took place. The picture that emerges, therefore, is of the Caucasus as a peripheral region rather suddenly penetrated by outside influences – most probably motivated by the desire for precious metals – and not thereafter closely involved in the international trading system which grew up and circulated high-value materials such as lapis lazuli and precious metals among the major urban centres of the Bronze Age world. Like the Shaft-Graves of Mycenae, it had a burst of imported wealth; but unlike them, it did not develop into a palatial bureaucracy.

DIFFERENT SORTS OF PERIPHERY: DEFINITIONS AND COMPARISONS

The terms 'core' and 'periphery' can be used in a variety of situations. In a very general way, we may contrast the Neolithic societies of south-east Europe using painted pottery with the simpler Neolithic societies of the north-west, which were both later in adopting agriculture and simpler in their economic organisation. In this sense, Europe had an 'inner' and an 'outer' zonation from the beginning. On the other hand, in describing the industrial world, economic historians use the words in a more technical sense, to contrast manufacturing areas with suppliers of food or raw materials. Here there is a structural relationship between the two areas, which are inter-dependent zones of the same economic system (Kohl 1989). What sort of contrasts can we draw for the Ancient World?

It is clear that certain elements of advanced technology were able to spread from the urban area of the Bronze Age world into agrarian societies beyond: wheeled vehicles are the classic example, as well as alloyed copper metallurgy with the use of the bivalve mould. On the other hand certain advanced technologies remained limited to urban contexts: either because their production needed craft skills, like the metal vessels and jewellery of the Troy treasure, or because they represented economies of scale – for instance the use of the potters' wheel in the mass production of ceramics. Technologies which required large investments, such as the construction of sailing ships, or the production of oil and wine on a large scale, were therefore restricted to urban economies. Other features which distinguished 'urban' from 'barbarian' economies were the use of precious metals as a medium of exchange in standardised equivalents, as opposed to the circulation of copper artefacts and their dedication in votive hoards. Only the more advanced economies were capable of organising long-distance trade for the purpose of sustaining manufacturing industries.

Within the Near Eastern zone, a characteristic sequence can be recognised in which areas that were at first only important as suppliers of raw materials to the urban heartlands developed their own social hierarchies, belief-systems and manufacturing capacity, to become independent core areas or 'secondary states'. Syria or highland Iran are good examples of this process. The formation of such secondary cores required certain pre-conditions, such as an appropriate position within the network of economic relations, access to raw materials for manufacture, and outlets through adequate transport systems to export their goods. The Aegean demonstrates a process of increasing integration with such an international system during the Bronze Age, when it was successively promoted from being a supplier of silver to an independent producer of textiles, wine and olive oil in bulk shipments from the Cretan and Greek mainland palaces to the east Mediterranean.

In Balkan and Carpathian Europe, however, this economic linkage did not occur. The impact of Early Bronze Age craft centres in western Anatolia can be traced in the Baden, Cernavoda III and Ezero cultures, where it is especially marked in the pottery, which has new, 'Anatolian' types such as drinking vessels in metallic shapes. These new features are found, together with paired cattle or representations of wheeled vehicles, in 'elite' graves in cemeteries such as Budakalász or Alsónémedi. A selective integration of exotic features formed the basis of an economically independent Late Copper Age/Bronze Age culture. This contrasts with the Aegean during the same period, where very specific supply routes, probably related to silver, replicated Anatolian complexity on a small scale on the opposite side of the Aegean: sites like Lerna, with bastion fortifications, central buildings, craft workshops, seals, and soon with wheelmade pottery. The Aegean became proto-urban, climaxing in the Minoan palaces and secondary state formation.

By way of complete contrast, we may turn to Bronze Age Turkmenia with its highly urban, irrigation-based, temple centres like Altyn Depe (Masson 1976), which had continuing economic relations with neighbouring Kel'teminar groups in the Kyzyl Kum, where (as Vinogradov's work has shown: Tosi 1974) turquoise was actually mined and traded southwards. What is striking in this case is the lack even of any cultural influence on a neighbouring supply area at a much lower level of economic and cultural development: Kel'teminar remained a dispersed hunting and foraging economy, collecting and mining the turquoise on a seasonal basis. One is reminded of the south-east Asian forest hunters who supplied camphor to the Chinese in the historic period. There was no cultural convergence between urban economies and their suppliers, as there was on the north-west frontier of Bronze Age urbanism; when Kel'teminar populations were ultimately subsumed into a wider cultural grouping, it was with the ex-panding Andronovo culture complex of the steppes (Tazabag'yab variant) rather than by being incorporated in the urban networks of the south.

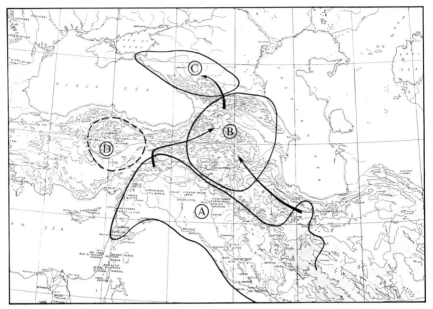

18.4 *Map of the major cultural regions in the later fourth millennium* BC: *(A) Late Uruk (plotted from the distribution of bevel-rim bowls); (B) the Kura-Arax culture (after Munchaev); (C) the Maikop complex; (D) the central Anatolian* EBA *culture area (after Mellaart).*

THE ROLE OF THE CAUCASUS IN THE EARLY BRONZE AGE

Having surveyed both its historical context and some comparative examples, we may now return to consider the nature of the Maikop phenomenon. It is no surprise that major new developments should occur at the time of Late Uruk expansion, with trade networks which were capable of moving high-value materials like lapis lazuli from Badakhshan to Egypt, and feeding the growing economies of lowland Mesopotamia. The founding of deliberate colonial settlements on the upper Euphrates and the Great Khorasan Road is reflected in the occurrence of typical Late Uruk bevel-rim bowls both in the Keban region (Arslantepe, Tepecik: Frangipane and Palmieri 1983) and in north-west Iran (Tepe Qabrestan). Both routes gave access to Transcaucasia, either via Erzurum or through Azerbaizhan. Discoveries by I. G. Narimanov at Leila Tepe on the Karabagh steppe may demonstrate the importance of the latter route (Kohl in Algaze 1989, 593); though both are likely to have been important in the introduction of new technologies and ideas. (See Figure 18.4.)

The result of these contacts was to transform the Eneolithic cultures of Transcaucasia into a successful and independent bloc of highland peoples, the Kura-Arax culture, which resisted incorporation into lowland polities but absorbed many of the characteristics of contemporary urban civilisation. The prominence of wheeled vehicles in the archaeological record of this and neighbouring areas suggests that animal traction and the adoption of plough agriculture was the subsistence basis for this florescence; the elaboration of domestic hearth structures and the absence of specialised temple buildings suggests that this did not reproduce a classic, lowland 'urban' pattern; but the occurrence of advanced metallurgy and wheelmade pottery argues for some degree of economic specialisation and elite culture. The richness of metal sources in this area offers an explanation for the wealth of the region, as well as its role in the exchange of domestic animals and plants which was a feature of this period (horse, donkey, ?camel, vine). Difficulties of transport prevented this area from following a comparable path of development to that which took place in the Aegean, or even in central Anatolia; a powerful state did not develop until the first millennium (Urartu), although the Kura-Arax culture did spread during the later part of the Early Bronze Age into both highland Iran and down to the Levant (Khirbet Kerak complex) – perhaps in part as a result of the breakdown of more complex economic and social organisation in those regions.

There is abundant evidence of the penetration at an early stage of elements of Kura-Arax culture through the main passes in the Great Caucasus into the upper Terek headwaters from its northern focus in the Kvemo Kartli area. The ecological contrast between the northern and southern slopes would have provided an incentive for the exchange of local products (e.g. horses: see Chapter 7). This penetration must be accounted the primary stimulus in the transformation of north Caucasian Eneolithic groups, and the consequent spread of advanced features from the south. However, the settlement pattern and social organisation of this region started from a completely different base, since local groups formed part of the Circumpontic steppe network with links to Eneolithic cultures on the Volga, Don and Dnepr. A basic feature of this region was the elaboration of funerary monuments rather than settlement sites as focal points in the social landscape – a common feature of the breakup of the primary Neolithic village community in many areas of Europe at this time. The feature which distinguishes the Maikop complex, therefore, is the occurrence of elements of elite culture in kurgan burials, which are especially richly furnished in the Kuban region with its metal sources and wide steppe hinterland. Its location allowed it to absorb features of ultimately urban origin, and to develop its own leading position in relation to steppe neighbours. This provided both a channel whereby metallurgy and animal traction was transmitted northwards, and provided a model for emerging steppe elites.

The northern Caucasus thus maintained its independence from the Kura-Arax bloc to the south, and became instead an independent core area in relation to the steppes. One reason for this is the plentiful occurrence of a variety of metal sources in the southern Caucasus: there was no incentive for southern traders to penetrate further to gain additional supplies in the north Caucasus (while horses came to be supplied from the western end of the Black Sea: see Chapter 7). Instead, Caucasian metal replaced Balkan-Carpathian metal supplies in the steppe region, and the Caucasian copper-working tradition (using two-piece moulds and arsenical alloying) exerted a technological influence on the development of south-east European metal-working across a chain of steppe cultures (Chernykh 1983). Until this time, the northern Caucasus was effectively part of the steppe zone of prehistoric Europe. Its culture, in the Early and Middle Bronze Age, is characterised by the elaboration of specific cultural features, such as metal or stone battle axes, hammer-head pins and dress ornaments, smoking rituals (perhaps involving cannabis, burnt in a *kurilnitsa*) and wagon burials in kurgans, which link the northern Caucasus and the steppes into a single cultural zone, and differentiate it from Transcaucasia.

The early part of this transformation coincided with the arrival of Anatolian influence in south-east Europe, and the emergence of the Ezero–Cernavoda III–Boleráz complex, which independently introduced wheeled vehicles and metal-influenced pottery drinking-vessels to this region. At the same time the Tripole culture, maintaining a more traditional culture, broke up into regional groupings under the influence of its neighbours. These developments are discussed in other chapters in this volume: but these western groups also contributed to the emerging steppe complex, before being in turn influenced by the spread of the Pit-Grave culture. Some aspects of these interchanges may have been important in the differentiation of the Novosvobodnaya group, although parallel causes (such as the influence of metal types on dark burnished pottery) and local traditions (cist burial) should not be neglected.

The Maikop phenomenon, therefore, marks a crucial formative stage in the emergence of an independent northern focus and way of life. It indicates an early impact from the south, and an important role in transmitting secondary farming to the steppes, and it is the beginning of a metallurgical tradition which was to act as a model for the Balkans and the Urals. It may also have been an intermediary in providing northern special products to its southern neighbours, just as Scandinavia was linked to central Germany from the Bronze Age to the Roman period; but it was never an integral part of Near Eastern trading networks on a large scale. It was not, therefore, to be a focus of political development or a proto-state. No doubt the northern Caucasus, with its variety of metal sources, was to be as diverse ethnically and politically in prehistory as it has been in more recent times. Complex, yes: but not a complex society in the sense of Troy or Altyn Depe.

19

The Archaeology of Indo-European:
An Alternative View
(with E. S. Sherratt)
(1988)

The study of linguistic prehistory is an important but inherently frustrating exercise: linguistic evidence is by definition the product of later, literate cultures, while languages have no direct correlates in the record of pre-historic archaeology. Any attempt at writing the prehistory of languages must therefore attempt to build a bridge between the detailed, technical reconstruction of linguistic relationships on the one hand and more general-ised, archaeologically-based models of cultural change on the other. By extrapolating each of these incomplete sources of evidence onto a problem of common interest, we may hope to define patterns which are compatible both with linguistic and archaeological arguments.

In conducting such an exercise, however, the properties of the different types of evidence have to be borne firmly in mind. There are unlikely to be any simple equations between the entities used by linguists and pre-historians, not least because of the differences in timescale involved. The advantage of archaeology is that it can range much further backwards in time to address questions not yet asked by linguists; while linguistic

---

Before 1987, it was commonly assumed that Indo-European languages had spread, perhaps by small migrations, around 3000 BC; most prehistoric archaeologists simply avoided the problem. In 1987–8, they spoke of little else. The book which broke the silence, and which put what Jim Mallory called 'a pigeon among the cats', was Colin Renfrew's Language and Archaeology *with its assertion that the Neolithic colonists of Europe spoke (proto-)Indo-European languages. The authors of this piece had respectively reviewed this volume and Jim Mallory's* In Search of the Indo-Europeans (AGS in Current Anthropology 1988; ESS in Antiquaries Journal 1989), *and together wrote this alternative scenario for an* Antiquity *special section. Both authors agree on the importance of socio-linguistic models of convergence; ESS (as a trained linguist) is perhaps more sceptical as to whether the question of 'Indo-European origins' is a scientifically soluble problem or a myth of Romantic-period Europe.*

arguments may force on the attention of archaeologists some features of later periods which prehistorians are prone to ignore.

Thus archaeologists may justifiably point out that the 'billiard ball' model used for instance by Gamkrelidze and Ivanov (1985b), which assumes that early Indo-European languages were originally placed in a tight cluster that was then scattered across the map to their present positions, is incompatible with a modern view of European prehistory which sees large, stable cultural groupings evolving *in situ* for many millennia. On the other hand, such phylogenetic models derived from linguistic comparison cannot simply be scaled up by archaeologists to cover a greater time depth, since the very definition of a proto-Indo-European entity is based on surviving languages and historical evidence and may only be valid for a relatively late point in time.

This short chapter, stimulated by Colin Renfrew's pioneering essay in relating modern archaeology to linguistics (1987), attempts to define possible phases in the evolution of Indo-European, and to suggest models appropriate to the different stages of this process.

Since we can only know languages which were spoken in recent times or which were written down by already complex societies, it is clear that much of the previously existing diversity of languages must be missing from our sample. This includes not only entire language-groups overlaid by dispersals such as that of Indo-European, but also languages within Indo-European (or even whole branches of it) which have not been written down or given rise to living successors. In addition, the time-depth for which relationships can be reconstructed from surviving and historically documented languages must have a limit. As languages drift apart and differentiate from a common ancestor, they must inevitably pass a point beyond which their common origin is no longer evident in terms of their taxonomic similarity (either lexical or structural) or in regular phonetic and semantic correspondences. Because of the absence of a 'fossil record', the relationships which are easiest to reconstruct from comparative study of surviving specimens are those resulting from relatively recent divergence. For both these reasons, language trees may be misleading models with which to approach 'deep' prehistory, since they inevitably give prominence to the products of recent differentiation and dispersal at the expense of older events.

A further problem is that the process of linguistic reconstruction, focusing back on postulated common ancestral forms, inevitably produces a model that emphasises divergence as the principal form of language change – even though *convergence* may be an equally common phenomenon. It would be misleading, therefore, to see the 'family tree' structure as any simple representation of the historical process: it can only be a partial model. It could be argued that convergence, by processes such as pidginisation or creolisation, would become an increasingly important feature of language change in the historical circumstances of increasing inter-regional trade which characterises the Bronze Age.

All these points can be summarised in the observation that linguistic comparison is intended to throw light on the relationships between *known* languages; it cannot reconstruct the *totality* of an earlier linguistic situation, and in any case linguistic relationships differentially preserve more information about *recent* events than more ancient ones. These points have long been recognised by linguists (e.g. Robins 1964, 323).

Archaeology has the advantage of being able to work forwards rather than backwards. We can therefore set out certain expectations about the long-term context of linguistic change, and see at what point they meet the retrospective models produced by linguistic comparison.

The emergence of relatively discrete linguistic communities may well be a fairly recent feature of human evolution, perhaps specifically associated with *Homo sapiens sapiens*; though even Upper Palaeolithic 'languages' may rather have taken the form of open dialectal chains in which each community could understand the speech of its near neighbours but not more distant ones. The beginning of farming is likely to have had a significant effect on the form of linguistic patterning, as a more dense network of sedentary communities gave rise to more circumscribed language groups than were previously prevalent. It is therefore at this point that the development of distinct language families of the sort known in historic times is most likely to have taken place.[1]

The patterns of language distribution resulting from the spread of farming would then have depended on the balance between two processes: 'demic diffusion' and indigenous adoption. At one extreme, where the spread of farming was associated with the expansion of a particular population group, a pattern of linguistic dispersal would result – an initially more uniform pattern, breaking down with time into more differentiated but related languages. At the other extreme, however, where farming spread through its adoption by existing native populations, no transfer of language need have been involved. A pattern of increased diversity, resulting from the crystallisation of local dialects into separate languages, might be expected.[2]

The pattern of uniform linguistic dispersal would have predominated wherever farming carried human populations into new environments; either empty areas (as in the Pacific) or into new zones within already occupied areas (as in western Asia and sub-Saharan Africa). Such a pattern could also be generated by secondary expansions associated with the spread of specialised forms of farming into hitherto under-utilised environments, such as pastoralism (as in central Asia or North Africa).

After the establishment of farming populations, regional patterns would again have depended on the balance between opposing tendencies: the continuing differentiation following initial dispersal, and integration resulting from the needs of trade and political expansion. The patterns of

473

phylogenetic relationship deduced from linguistic comparison could in theory relate to any of the mechanisms which produced uniformity followed by differentiation; though in practice it is the latest one which is likely to produce the dominant surviving pattern in a given region.

We may now attempt to apply these arguments to prehistoric Europe. Here both modes of agricultural spread seem to be represented: demic diffusion by the Balkan Neolithic and its central European *Bandkeramik* extension; the adoption of farming by the west Mediterranean Cardial Ware group and most of the cultures in Atlantic Europe and the North European Plain. In the light of the principles discussed above, and by analogy with the ethnographic examples, there would have been considerable continuity in western and northern Europe; while the spread of early farmers belonging to the *Bandkeramik* complex in central Europe could well have been associated with a 'Polynesian' pattern of initial linguistic uniformity, followed by fragmentation. These central European Neolithic languages are likely to have belonged to a larger family, including for instance the contemporary languages spoken in the Balkans and Anatolia.

However, given the early date of the agricultural dispersal in Europe, it is most unlikely that this language group would have survived in recognisable form down to historical times, and the resemblance between any surviving members of this group would be radically different from the very specific correspondences between existing languages of the Indo-European group. There is thus no reason to equate the initial spread of farming with the phenomenon reconstructed by linguists on the basis of comparisons between them, and indeed there are specific reasons why this is improbable.[3] This does not rule out some deeper affinity between Neolithic Balkan languages and historical Indo-European ones (cf. Diakonov 1985): but it implies that there are other events which must be invoked in order to explain the historical pattern of languages – there is no simple answer to the puzzle.

At the other end of the prehistoric timescale, however, there are some very plausible correspondences which can be postulated (e.g. Clarke 1965, fig. 73) between the expansion of members of the Late Bronze Age 'Urnfield' group (c.1400–700 BC) and the spread of Italic and Celtic languages (and others which have not survived as spoken languages). This would imply the continuing existence at this time in western Europe of other language groups: perhaps the descendants of indigenous (non-Indo-European) Mesolithic and western Neolithic languages, or perhaps branches of Indo-European now extinct. Yet such a late extension of the Indo-European area into western Europe could only have been the final stage of the story: Indo-European languages are known to have been spoken in Anatolia at least a thousand years earlier, and there must have been important intervening steps in the spread of this group, perhaps associated with the massive eastwards expansion which carried Indo-European languages to India. It is important, therefore, to look more closely at eastern Europe and the role of the steppes.

The farming systems of the early Neolithic were very limited in character by comparison with those of later prehistory: cultivation systems were based on the hoe rather than the plough, animals were exploited primarily for meat rather than for secondary products, and transport animals and the associated technology of wheeled vehicles were not yet used (see Section III). The extent to which dry areas could be utilised was thus severely limited. During the fourth and third millennia BC, however, a second generation of farming technologies appeared in the Near East and surrounding areas, leading to greater opportunities for mobile forms of exploitation such as pastoralism. This revolutionised the scope of farming economies in western Eurasia, and provides an economic context for a post-Neolithic spread of Indo-European languages.

This is most evident in the east, where an important consequence of these innovations was the extensive occupation of the Eurasian steppe and semi-desert areas, using horses, camels and vehicles as well as new breeds of wool-bearing sheep and perhaps also the light plough. Although this must not be confused with the emergence of true nomadic pastoralism, which was a feature of the first millennium BC, it resulted in an eastwards movement of population across the central Asian steppes, and links as far as China (reflected in the transmission of wheeled vehicles) by the second millennium BC. This infilling of the steppe zone (represented archaeologically by the spread of the Pit-Grave and Andronovo cultures of the third and second millennia BC) can be associated primarily with the spread of eastern Indo-European languages – the Indo-Iranian or 'Aryan' group which gave the Indo-European family as a whole its impressive territorial extent.[4]

During the later first millennium BC, however, this eastwards pattern of flow was reversed, as groups speaking Turco-Tartar languages spread westwards to take over the steppe areas previously dominated by Indo-Europeans. This historical picture has lent plausibility to the idea that the steppes were the original homeland of common Indo-European, and thus the source of western (i.e. European) as well as eastern Indo-European languages.

This idea, which has a long history in Romantic conceptions of pre-history (Bernal 1987, chapter 5), has been given its clearest archaeological expression in recent times by Marija Gimbutas (e.g. 1961, map 9) who sees a westwards incursion of proto-Indo-Europeans from a homeland beyond the Volga as the beginning of the process of expansion across the Pontic Steppes and into Europe.

A modified version of this idea, based on the importance of the horse and its domestication by fourth-millennium groups north of the Black Sea (Mallory 1976; 1977; Telegin 1986; Anthony 1986), offers an intermediate position. This envisages a spread of Indo-European languages both east and west from the North Pontic area, associated with the spread of the horse. It is not clear, however, whether this offers an adequate explanation for the appearance of Indo-European languages in Greece, and in Anatolia where Indo-European languages are first evidenced. Since the economic changes of the fourth millennium affected a much wider area of the Old World, it may well be that the steppes provide an important component of the story, but not the whole answer.

The earliest recorded Indo-European languages are the second-millennium Anatolian ones, Hittite, Luwian and Palaic.[5] These form a separate sub-group within the Indo-European family which may have a collateral rather than directly ancestral relationship with other branches of Indo-European, and is not easily derived from these other groups. The already differentiated nature of these three recorded languages implies some greater time-depth to the existence of this group, and Gamkrelidze and Ivanov (1985a, 14) have adduced technical arguments such as correspondences with neighbouring Semitic and Kartvelian (Caucasian) languages to argue for a long-standing geographical proximity. They thus argue that Anatolia itself should be considered as a primary part of the Indo-European area: though they are reduced to some implausible long-distance folk movements around the Aral Sea in order to relate the Anatolian languages to other members of the Indo-European family.

While there is no necessary reason why Indo-European languages should be earliest in the area where they were first recorded (since this relates to the spread of writing systems from Mesopotamia), it would be wrong to overlook the possibility that this may, indeed, be the case. Given the important role which Anatolia has played in relation to adjacent areas of south-east Europe, Colin Renfrew is right to explore the significance of this area in the origin of Indo-European languages as a whole (Renfrew 1987). While the evidence of Hattic suggests that their presence in eastern Anatolia does not long predate the second millennium, it is entirely possible that western and central Anatolia may have formed part of the early area of distribution of ancestral Indo-European.

We are thus presented with not one but several puzzles, converging on the area around the Black Sea: Anatolia, the Balkans and the Pontic Steppes. Was Anatolia the centre of ancestral Indo-European languages? What was the relationship between these and the languages of the Balkan Neolithic? What relationship did they have with the languages which spread eastwards across the steppes in the third millennium? At what point can one postulate the unity of Indo-European speech reconstructed by comparative linguistics?

It is important at this stage to go beyond conventional definitions in order to provide a common vocabulary between linguists and archaeologists. Within a historical timescale we are justified in speaking of Indo-European languages. Moving into later prehistory, we may adopt the linguists' convention of using an asterisk to indicate reconstructed forms based on rules derived from surviving evidence: hence *proto-Indo-European (*PIE) to describe the common language reconstructed as underlying known examples of the family. Moving further back in time, one can postulate an ancestral language or group of languages which ultimately gave rise to *PIE and its successors (and no doubt to others now extinct). Although beyond the limits of reconstruction, its existence is a logical necessity; and we may recognise its hypothetical status by a double asterisk – hence **pre-proto-Indo-European (**PPIE).

We can now reformulate our questions in terms of a series of stages. Where did **PPIE emerge, and what was its connection with the origins of farming; where did *PIE appear, and what was responsible for its dispersal; and when did IE languages finally attain their present limits of distribution?

It would clearly be optimistic to attempt to answer even one of these, but there may be some advantage to tackling the group of questions as a whole. The solutions proposed below represent a scenario (or, if you like, a 'just so' story) of how the various components may fit together. They are presented in the form of three hypotheses.

1. The nuclear region of western Old World farming, the Near East, was large and internally diverse; and it gave rise to population expansion in several directions (Sherratt 1980, fig. 15.5). It is unlikely, therefore, that this dispersal was associated with the spread of a single language group,[6] and it probably gave rise to several major language families on the basis of ancestral groups situated around the edge of the nuclear region. The resulting pattern (Figure 19.1a) would have resembled the petals of a flower, radiating from the area where farming began.

Since literacy came early to this part of the world, it is likely that many of the language groups represented in this process lasted long enough to be represented in the historical record. Candidates would include the Indo-European, Afroasiatic, Caucasian,[7] and (perhaps) Dravidian language families. Each of these achieved a wide distribution and are represented by many individual successor languages, and it is logical to postulate that their **pre-proto-forms achieved prominence as a result of the primary spread of farming.

Since each of them would have undergone expansion at the same time, their main direction of propagation was outwards – away from the core area of farming.[8] (This reverses older assumptions by which Indo-Europeans traditionally came off steppes and Semites emerged from deserts.) The ancestors of the Caucasian languages found their exit blocked by the mountains and steppe belt beyond, but those ancestral to the Indo-European family were able to penetrate beyond Anatolia to the Balkans and central Europe before meeting the resistance of native peoples in western and northern Europe. Together, these Anatolian and Balkan languages would constitute the **PPIE group, predating the period of *PIE unity.[9] This stage is represented on the first map of Figure 19.2.

2. As noted previously, many hypotheses concerning *PIE origins converge on the Black Sea area, postulating a homeland in Anatolia (Gamkrelidze and Ivanov), the Balkans (Diakonov) or the steppes (Gimbutas). May all contain some element of truth?

The problem is essentially a topological one: how to generate a spatial pattern which is congruent both with the reconstructed relationships of the Indo-European family tree and also with the major cultural areas recognised by archaeology. Each of the models listed above can cope with one major branch of Indo-European but has difficulty with the others. A comprehensive model requires another flower-like pattern, with a common centre but scope for expansion in different directions. The epicentre of this nuclear region would lie in the Black Sea.

This difficulty becomes less insuperable if considered in the light of mechanisms of linguistic convergence. One of the phenomena noted by linguists in areas such as the Caribbean or Melanesia is the formation of pidgins and creoles in connection with the growth of trading networks, especially those based on coastal contacts. If we postulate a coastal *koine* around the shores of the Black Sea (and perhaps also the Aegean – the 'international spirit of the EBA': Renfrew 1967) in the third millennium, bringing together elements from **PPIE languages already existing in Anatolia and perhaps in the Balkans and west Pontic area, these requirements are fulfilled. After all, boats – both large and small – are attested in the protolexicon as well as horses and carts, and the wealth of Troy II indicates the potential scale of trading activity at this time. The actual area of this 'homeland' would not be large, but its circumference was considerable: enough to establish a wide range of potential contacts in many directions (Figure 19.1b). This stage is represented in the second map of Figure 19.2.

*19.1 Models of three stages of Indo-European expansion, based on the spatial arrangements of major language groups. Each expansion coincided with major economic and social changes. (A) represents the formation of four major language-families as a result of the expansion from different ancestral speech-communities within the nuclear area of Old World farming (interrupted circle); 1 represents **pre-proto-Indo-European. (B) represents the expansion and differentiation of different groups of Indo-European languages around the Black Sea: (1) Anatolian; (2) hypothetical circum-Pontic *proto-Indo-European; (3) earlier European languages derived from **PPIE; (4) *proto-Greek; (5) central European – ancestral to groups shown in (C); (6) north European – ancestral to Germanic, Baltic and Slav; (7) *proto-Indo-Iranian. (C) represents the expansion and differentiation of the central European group associated with Late Bronze Age Urnfields and with movement into Anatolia.*

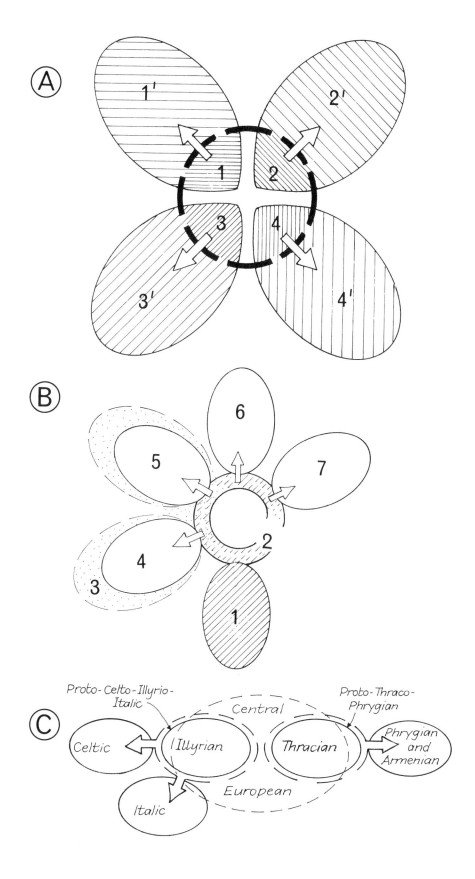

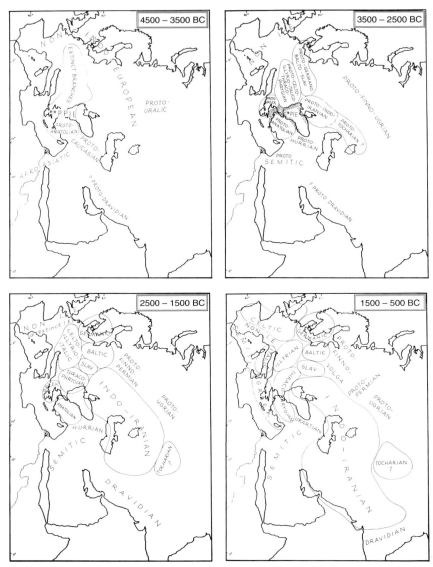

19.2 *Reconstructed distributions of the constituent groupings of Indo-European languages over four millennia (calibrated radiocarbon chronology). The boundaries are conventional. Stages in the differentiation of neighbouring language families are also shown. (See note 4 for Tocharian.)*

3. In thinking about the further propagation of Indo-European languages, the descendants of *PIE, it is important to bear in mind the potential complexity of factors operating in later prehistory. One of these is undoubtedly migration, even though it is unlikely to be the dominant mechanism that was once imagined. As an archaeological example, one might cite the westward penetration of Pit-Grave groups from the Pontic Steppes into dry areas of Romania and Hungary (Ecsedy 1979), and compare it with the southward penetration of Athabascan speakers in the dry areas of North America, taking the Navajo and Apache to the Southwest.

Trade is another, and perhaps more fundamental, factor. Just as Neolithic trade patterns took the form of multiple step, 'down the line' exchanges, so Bronze Age trade patterns show an increasing emphasis on directional trade (Figure 19.3). Whereas the former can be handled (as in highland New Guinea) through the use of bilingual speakers at each step in the chain, more direct forms of contact and trade increasingly require a common language. The spread of features of secondary farming like woolly sheep or horses would have involved the transmission of items of valuable livestock from one end of Europe to the other. The growth of the pastoral sector would in itself have provided opportunities for the monopolistic control of animal herds, potentially giving an advantage to particular ethnic groups in a way comparable to that involved in the spread of fish-weirs and Salish languages on the intermontane plateau of the American Northwest (Nelson 1973). Metals were increasingly traded in the form of prestige objects during the period in question; while less tangible influences may be discerned in the spread of cult practices involving alcohol or cannabis (Chapters 15 and 16). Each of these could have been accompanied by new forms of language, perhaps initially a special-purpose trade or elite language, used specifically in communicating within the context of extra-territorial exchanges.

The spread of Indo-European languages from a postulated Circumpontic area of *PIE would have involved all of these mechanisms, although in different contexts. The eastern wing of Indo-Iranian languages would have spread by expansion into a relatively empty zone.[10] Within Europe three main zones of development could be envisaged. In the south, *proto-Greek would have evolved in the context of EBA maritime contacts with north-west Anatolia which brought advanced metallurgy and Anatolian pottery forms to eastern Greece. In the centre, along the main Danube/Rhine axis in the area of the Baden culture, there would have developed a branch of central European languages ancestral to those which differentiated in the Urnfield period – Celtic, Italic, Illyrian, Thracian and Phrygian. Along the North European Plain a continuum of languages ancestral to Slav, Baltic and Germanic would have evolved in the context of the cultural contacts indicated by the distribution of Globular Amphora and Corded Ware elements. These processes are represented by the second and third maps of Figure 19.2, which should be compared with Figure 19.1b. With the exception of

481

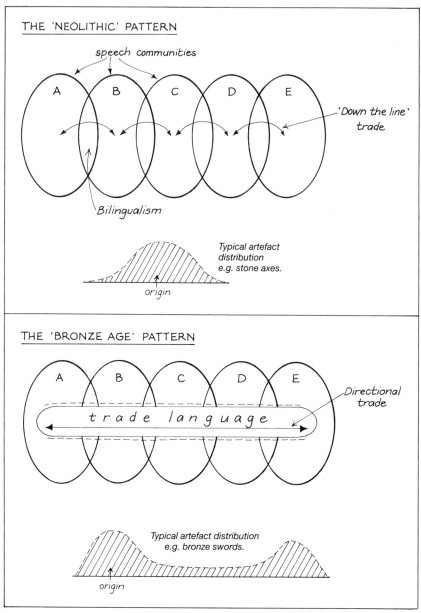

19.3 *Contrasting patterns of language and trade. Above, trade chain in many short steps, accomplished by bilingualism (e.g. New Guinea, Neolithic Europe). Below, directional trade necessitating a special trade language (e.g. Bronze Age Europe and the Near East).*

the eastern group, none of these should be envisaged as a simple equation between languages and archaeological cultures, resulting from a straight-forward migration in the old-fashioned sense: but each represents an axis of demonstrable cultural contact at the period in question. Moreover, this pattern is congruent with the major expectations derived from comparative linguistics.

These postulated stages of development take the story down to the threshold of historical times, when linguistic distributions can be reconstructed with greater certainty (fourth map of Figure 19.2). Besides the continuing ex-pansion of Indo-Iranian languages, the most notable feature is the further spread of languages from the central European zone, caused by Urnfield expansion and the contemporary recession and political collapse in the east Mediterranean. Thus Celtic[11] and Italic languages would have reached their historical positions at approximately the same time as Phrygian replaced the earlier, Anatolian languages in what is now western Turkey (Figure 19.1c). This phase marks the last major expansion of Indo-European languages before the great imperial conquests of the Achaemenid Persians, which began another chapter of the Indo-European story.

The attainment of a continuous distribution of Indo-European languages from Ireland to India in the first millennium BC created a continuum of related 'barbarian' societies across the Eurasian landmass, marked by several common features such as horse-gear and weaponry, aspects of funerary practice like wagon burial, and the influence of animal-style art. In the period before this continuity was severed by the arrival on the steppes of Turco-Tartar peoples from further east, there would have been the oppor-tunity for the transmission across this area of myths and religious motifs as well as features of material culture. It may be this period, rather than the time of proto-Indo-European unity, that is tantalisingly reflected in the evidence of comparative Indo-European mythology.[12]

Any attempt to grapple with a problem as intractable as that of Indo-European origins must essentially be an essay in controlled speculation. Nevertheless, it is permissible to describe some possible processes which fit with our current understanding of prehistoric cultural and social change.

An important part of this exercise is to go beyond the raw material of immediate observation to infer missing categories of evidence. Since many languages remain only as peripheral survivals,[13] a first step is to fill in a more realistic estimate of their original distributions. We may then go on to make allowance for extinct forms, and for ancestral groups beyond the limits of our direct evidence. In carrying out this exercise in relation to the evolution of Indo-European, we have set out a multi-stage model which takes account of the main currents of economic and social change in later prehistory as we perceive them (Figure 19.4).

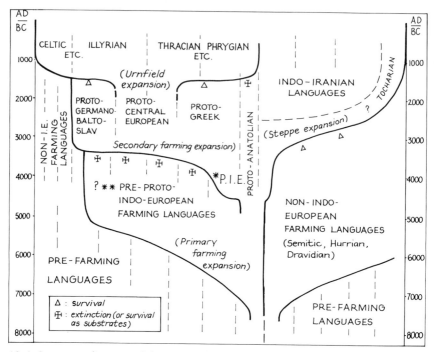

19.4 Summary diagram of the major phases of Indo-European expansion in prehistory, showing recorded languages and inferred ancestral groups and extinct branches. The diagram extends from NW Europe (left) to central and S Asia (right).

The reconstruction which we propose implies a relatively slow rate of spread over a period of 6000 years, made up of several advances into new areas which coincide with periods of economic innovation and consequent opportunities for expansion. It consists of successive overlays of new generations of Indo-European languages in radial patterns from a series of nuclear zones, moving outwards from an original centre, and reflecting the continuing importance of the Near East as a source of economic and cultural change. Such a sketch can only present a caricature of the complexities of the real process: but it may nevertheless be helpful as a first step in the controlled comparison of models of linguistic prehistory.

NOTES

1. Thus it may not be profitable to extend any kind of phylogenetic model much further back than c.10,000 BP, or to talk of a single 'common ancestor' for groups such as Indo-European and Afroasiatic.
2. The classic examples of a successful marriage between linguistics and archaeology are the dispersals of the Polynesian and Bantu language families. The reasons for this are twofold: first, the predominance in both cases of demic diffusion; and secondly the relatively recent date at which the dispersals occurred, so that the linguistic relationships are still clearly evident. It is instructive to compare these examples with the case of Melanesia, where agriculture appeared much earlier (as long ago as it did in Europe),

and where adoption probably predominated over demic diffusion. Although the pattern is perhaps exaggerated by the rugged terrain, New Guinea is notorious for its extreme linguistic diversity. There is no reason why this pattern should not be equally character-istic of Neolithic societies in other parts of the world, wherever these conditions applied.

3. These arise from the pattern of inter-relationships generated by this assumption (Renfrew 1987, fig. 7.7), which would predict a close genetic resemblance between Greek and Italian, for instance, or between the Slav and Indo-Iranian groups. This is not the case.

4. A complicating factor is the existence of Tocharian in Sinkiang. Two solutions are possible. One would see Tocharian as representative of the earliest phase of Indo-European steppe expansion, before the emergence of Indo-Iranian and its interaction with European neighbours (reflected for instance in satemisation): this is the option shown on the maps of Fig. 19.2. The alternative, and perhaps preferable, view is that it is a much later language connected with trade along the Silk Route – since the first written evidence is known from the first millennium AD. It might thus be considered as a creole.

5. Later ones, such as Phrygian and Armenian, are more recent and can be related to the period of expansion represented by the Urnfield phenomenon; their spread into Anatolia would have prefigured the Celtic expansion which brought Galatian.

6. This observation is likely to be a general one, since the world's major language groups do not show the simple, concentric patterns of distribution which such an equation would predict. The largest areas of linguistic uniformity, in Polynesia and sub-Saharan Africa, resulted from unidirectional expansion on the margins of a nuclear area.

7. The Caucasus is a complex refuge area with many different languages. Armenian is a branch of Indo-European (see n.5). The Caucasian languages proper form two groups, North Caucasian and South Caucasian, of which the former appears to be a descendant of Urartian and ultimately of Hurrian, which occupied a larger area in eastern Anatolia and Syria; the latter may be indigenous.

8. A more specific version of the hypothesis might envisage the Levant as the origin of the Afroasiatic family, north Syria/north Mesopotamia as the origin of the branch of Caucasian which gave rise ultimately to Hurrian and so to Urartian and Kartvelian, central and western Anatolia as the origin of the Indo-European family, and south-west Iran as the origin of the Dravidian family. While hypothetical, these equations are not entirely speculative, and deserve to be evaluated against competing hypotheses (cf. Mellaart 1975, ch. 11).

9. This might include the language later written in Crete in Linear A, and also the pre-Greek language whose toponyms survive in Greece and the Balkans.

10. The spread of Pit-Graves into Romania and Hungary would on this hypothesis represent a westward incursion of speakers of Indo-Iranian languages, prefiguring the later Scythian expansion into the same areas.

11. Perhaps in places (e.g. the British Isles) overlying extinct branches of northern zone Indo-European, if these had spread further in association with Bell-Beaker contacts. Since any such Beaker-related IE language would have had affinities with Germanic and the other northern zone languages, it cannot have been an early form of Celtic, whose affinities lie rather with Italic and the languages of the central European zone.

12. This would be the explanation for the common features described by Dumezil. It would be no accident, therefore, that Greece – no longer a member of this barbarian community – should be 'an embarrassing exception to the tripartite division of functions' (Kirk 1970, 210).

13. An obvious example is the 'Celtic fringe', or the survival of Romance languages (Romanian and Vlach) in south-east Europe. Other mountain relicts would include Illyrian, and the various Caucasian languages; while on a larger scale Iranian might be seen as a montane survival from a larger original area on the steppes.

A CONVERSATION WITH CHILDE

Childe at the UISPP *conference at Zürich, 1950, in Schaffhausen Museum with (left to right) Dame Kathleen Kenyon and Professors Richard Atkinson, Robert J. Braidwood, Stuart Piggott, Grahame Clark and Christopher Hawkes (photograph from Professor Stuart Piggott).*

Now I confess that my whole account may prove to be erroneous;
my formulae may be inadequate; my interpretations are perhaps
ill-founded; my chronological framework – and without such
one cannot speak of conjunctures – is frankly shaky.
Yet I submit the result was worth publishing.

V. GORDON CHILDE (1957)

The archaeological generation of which I form part can be justly proud of having helped to fill in a major missing element of the evidence of European prehistory with which Childe worked: the regional analysis of patterns on the ground, distilled from the much more abundant evidence of post-war fieldwork and excavation, which took place on a scale undreamed of before. It is not surprising that geography seemed to be a paradigm-discipline in this enterprise, even though that subject has now suffered a sharp decline in general academic esteem, especially in the USA. The need to build ecological and demographic realities into archaeological models of the past was one which it shared with contemporary history and other social sciences, and led to notable advances in understanding. In European prehistory, for instance, the altered conception of early farming – from rootless slash-and-burn *Wanderbauerntum* to a horticulture with a long-lasting commitment to particular places – represented a notable advance on Childe's under-standing.

Nevertheless, there was a price to pay: too great an attention to the forces of production led to a neglect of the forces of consumption: here Childe's Marxism and New (Processual) Archaeology shared a common blind spot. Stuart Piggott's sensitivity to the nuances of style in elite ostentation, for instance in matters of transport (1992), well illustrate this missing dimension; and it is the most positive contribution of Post-Processual Archaeology to have drawn attention to this aspect of the importance of the materiality of culture. While social evolution is difficult to demonstrate, cultural evolution is plain to see; and rather than seeking abstract and untestable social formulations of the nature of change, it may be more profitable to theorise the cultural record itself. (These thoughts, moreover, have now occurred to social anthropologists, too, making possible a degree of theoretical convergence.) Materiality, however, does not imply mere materialism, for material creations only make sense in the context of the social and the cognitive. Recognition of this fact helps to revive two aspects of Childe's account which had been neglected in the enthusiasm for local factors of demography, ecology and agrarian productivity: the diffusion of desirable forms of consumption (literal or metaphorical), and the cultural phenomena of substitution and skeuomorphism to which it gives rise.

By making use of these insights, it should be possible to combine the best of both approaches, and to overcome the dialectical conflicts built into the 'alternation of generations' between Enlightenment and Romantic models outlined in Section I; and in so doing it may be possible to retrieve a sense of overall direction and 'grand narrative', of the kind which I attempted to specify in my David Clarke Memorial Lecture for 1995 (Sherratt 1995b). Shorn of the Eurocentric bias which has so far accompanied all accounts of 'the rise of the West', such a grand narrative is no longer an account of the inevitability of European progress. Rather, it chronicles how, for a brief period following the discovery of the New World, the Atlantic coastlands acquired a centrality which made them masters of the global economy; a centrality, however, which they are now in the process of losing to the lands of the Far East and the Pacific Rim. Yet this shift in perspective brings Childe's question once more to the fore (Rowlands 1994). What was the origin of Europe's conception of liberty and freedom? Were these merely stages in the final disembedding of the economy from social constraints; or are they a precious inheritance to be preserved, as economic dominance shifts to a new continental configuration? The answers to these questions require an archaeological perspective, which arises from, and gives meaning to, our everyday preoccupations with stones and potsherds.

20

Gordon Childe:
Right or Wrong?

(1995)

Every prehistoric archaeologist has to come to terms with Childe.[1] The European prehistorian feels the need to measure his or her ideas against a classic like the *Dawn of Civilisation*, to see how far we have progressed; even prehistorians in areas outside Europe need to look back to the earlier phases of their discipline, which began in Europe, and in which Childe's synthesis forms a milestone. Nor (I think) is this just a matter of national, or at least anglophone, pride: even those continental scholars who regard modern British scholarship with suspicion can agree that Childe was a figure of European stature. Indeed, his chief critics are themselves English or English-speaking: from his own literary executor, Grahame Clark (1976: accusing him of being misled by Marx), to Colin Renfrew (1973: revolutionising his chronology) or to any aspiring young graduate student wanting to patronise an older and better exponent of his craft (e.g. Sherratt 1972, 477; Chapter 2). At the centenary of his birth, when most intellectuals are being subjected to revisionist critiques (or at least to scandalous revelations about their private lives), Childe remains a revered ancestor to a wide variety of schools of archaeology – many of which (like diffusionists, processualists, and post-processualists) are quite incompatible with one another, and indeed are mutually hostile.

The 1990s have seen no diminution of interest in Gordon Childe: a special issue of Australian Archaeology No. 30 in 1991 (including Sherratt 1991), an important conference in Melbourne (Gathercole, Irving and Melleuish 1995) and a London meeting (Harris 1994) all threw fresh light on his politics, early career and relations with Soviet archaeology. Yet this same half-decade saw the effective collapse of Marxism as the official political philosophy of a large part of Eurasia. When my old friend and fellow Childe-enthusiast Jacek Lech asked me to write something for a Polish conference on the contribution of Childe, these thoughts underlay what I wrote.

With such a reputation, not just within the subject but also outside it (since Childe is one of the few 'intellectual' archaeologists whose name is familiar beyond the discipline), it is often surprising to present-day students that his work now seems so old-fashioned. As a figure who achieved his major responsibility (the Directorship of the London University Institute of Archaeology) in the post-war era, and is still remembered – with great affection – by an active generation of pupils, he might be considered as a near-contemporary, marking the beginning of a 'modern' approach to prehistory. Yet much of his writing seems in many ways to be closer to the nineteenth rather than the twentieth century: his grand themes, archaic terminology (who dares talk of 'savages' nowadays?), his studied ignorance of the New World, curious ragbag anthropology with its stereotypes like the 'primitive metalsmith' – all these have an oddly antiquated ring.

In part, this is because the whole subject of prehistory is itself so young. As a product of Enlightenment rationalism, Romantic enthusiasm for exotic origins, and scientific Positivism with its belief in the value of observation and classification, it needed all these movements to create the kind of subject which exists today; and its scope and methods only became clearly recognised by some time around 1865, along with its name. For this chronological reason, prehistoric archaeology is 'out of phase' with other humanistic disciplines, and still enjoying its childhood (and juvenile tantrums) well into the twentieth century. It is easy to forget how recently we have acquired some quite fundamental information about the prehistoric past – like the use of the plough in the Neolithic – or how recently so much of our information (for instance about ecology and settlement patterns) has accumulated. To take an example: Childe's account of the Neolithic Revolution was written (like the classic Enlightenment evolutionary narratives of the eighteenth century) essentially from first principles, and without much real archaeology to put to it: the discovery of a pre-pottery Neolithic, at places like Jericho, came as a disturbing surprise. Whereas history and philology have been 'tempered' and matured by many changes of intellectual climate, archaeology is simultaneously acquiring both intellectual maturity and basic observations: 'learning on the job', as we might say. As a subject, it is still very much a teenager, with adult methods but immature ideas and emotions with which to approach its new-found wealth of observations. Childe helped to take archaeology out of its childhood – it makes a good pun in English, and one that was not neglected by Childe himself! – but now himself looks Childeish. It is a mark of how rapidly archaeology has progressed, by comparison with other historical disciplines, that something written in the 1950s now seems quite so outdated. So the conundrum of Childe is how he manages to be, at one and the same time, such a chronological zone-fossil for a past epoch in European prehistoriography and yet also a positive inspiration for a wide range of present-day workers in the field. The answer that I would like to suggest is that he first identified some

of the fundamental structures of prehistory by using the evidence of archaeology. Like some early scientist with a new optical instrument, he first put
names and definitions to what can be observed in prehistory, and described
what we can still recognise in the record. The details multiply and change,
but the structures survive, even when the interpretation changes. Some
aspects of Childe's vision were personal idiosyncracies; some were the
inevitable perceptions of the time; but above all these temporary aspects
there stands his recognition of the essential outlines of prehistory, in a way
that continues to be clarified by new information. I find this reassuring: it is
a demonstration that the past is real, and not just a fluctuating fantasy
which projects contemporary dreams and desires on to something essentially unknowable; though it is also something whose significance changes
with successive generations and new angles of vision. Childe remains
fascinating because his perceptions are at once so familiar and so strange.

To recognise his enduring contribution, it is therefore essential to
recognise those aspects of his imagination which were time-bound and
idiosyncratic. First, the personal aspect. It is not necessary to be an amateur
psychologist to discern the powerful influence of his father, Stephen Childe:
not by imitation, but by reaction. Stephen Childe was an Anglican clergy-
man, of catholic (ritualistic) tendency not greatly tempered by humanity
(Green 1981, 6–7). His congregation, at least, did not like him; and his son
must surely have found him as oppressive in childhood as he did when,
visiting his paternal home as an adult, he was not allowed to smoke his pipe.
His defences to this treatment were brilliance and radicalism. Not dissi-
pating his efforts in mere socialising (at which he had limited skills), he
concentrated a powerful intelligence on proving himself outstanding as an
academic. At the same time, he devoted himself, as soon as he had left home,
to radical and idealistic causes which questioned the basis of his family's
relatively privileged background. (His Marxism was, in a sense, a substitute
for his lost Anglican Christianity.) To a generation which takes youthful
revolt as a token of normality, this may seem nothing strange: in a British
colony at the time of World War I, however, it took the courage of con-
viction. Recent research on Childe's early political career in Australia has
revealed a picture that seems strikingly reminiscent of totalitarian regimes in
the Europe of more recent years: secret censorship and political persecution,
including debarment and dismissal from teaching positions (Mulvaney
1994). Childe hammered out his idealistic philosophy from experience and
opposition, not from the comfort of an armchair.

This oppositional attitude persisted throughout his life, even through
the time when he was a recognised international leader in his subject –
chosen, for example, to represent prehistoric archaeology among the sixty
scholars selected to address the Conference of Arts and Sciences organised
by Harvard University to celebrate its Tercentenary in 1936. As a Marxist
and communist sympathiser (though not a party member), Childe had

difficulties in the USA after World War II, in the era of McCarthyism: it is salutary to be reminded that intellectual intolerance (and a specific hostility to evolutionism and prehistory) has been an occasional characteristic of the 'land of the free', even as Morgan and Engels became the orthodoxy of the opposing power-bloc in the other hemisphere. Politicians recognise the importance of prehistory, which is why we must never let them take it out of the hands of an international and critical community of scholars. In Childe's case, this experience had the somewhat unexpected consequence of revealing with what affection he was regarded by his staff: 'when McCarthyism was rife in America ... the staff [of the Institute of Archaeology] all came to the conclusion that if there was any backlash on the Director, we would all go to jail with him': Rachel Maxwell-Hyslop, 1994. From an impeccably upper middle-class establishment, this was commitment indeed.

This personal and political background had two consequences for Childe's prehistory, one good and one bad (as far as archaeology was concerned). The first was a vision of social change which was to inform and underlie his writing of prehistory, giving it shape and relevance (Rowlands 1994). It was Childe's opposition to the inwardness of White Australia and the New Protectionism that later informed his search for a social dynamic in diffusionism, interchange and hybridisation: themes that constantly recur in his prehistoriography, and which have lost none of their relevance today. This goes a long way to explaining why Childe's vision has continued to occupy the attention of succeeding generations. It is a feature of Childe's writing that it combined an unsurpassed mastery of arcane detail (expressed in now legendary footnotes) with a sweep that is often described as Hegelian; and most particularly in a sustained commitment to making the often unpromising raw material of prehistory say something that is important about society. Criticisms of his work often focus upon the gap between these achievements: the lack of explicit methodologies and case studies that could convert a vision into working theories. It is important also to recognise the moral imperatives behind his writing, and his often metaphorical treatment of the subjects which he brought to prominence. The way that metal production in Bronze Age Europe escaped from the political control of courts and temples, which had characterised its development in the Near East, was not so much a narrow technological history as an attempt to translate Hegelian concerns with the origin of Western freedoms into the subject matter of prehistoric archaeology. Childe took archaeology seriously, because it mattered.

On the other hand, Childe's view of the prehistoric past was distorted by these experiences in what may be considered a negative way. Rationalism is easily combined with anti-clericalism; and reacting against an oppressive, Anglo-Catholic father figure did not make Childe sympathetic to religion, or subtle in his interpretation of it. He was, in short, against it. While I have no moral objection to this view (though I do not share it), it cannot be said to be an advantage in interpreting either the recent or the distant past – and especially not the cultures of theocentric Sumer in the Uruk period, or megalithic Pomerania. For Childe, religion was an incubus (or possibly even a succubus): a diversion of energy into a vain and fruitless activity that was essentially parasitic upon society. Religion was a dead hand upon development, a social pathology preventing progress – almost a disease. While he was sensitive to the nuances of secular symbolism (for instance the significance of buried grave-wealth), the social importance of religion, and hence the organisational (and thus local) role of megaliths, for instance, was neglected: he therefore saw megalithism as spreading like a contagious epidemic along the seashore of Atlantic Europe, rather than springing up as an expression of indigenous values among Mesolithic groups faced with longhouse-building Danubian newcomers. On a larger scale, he missed the long-term significance of the repeated shifts from communal to individual, *Wertrationalität* to *Zweckrationalität*, manifested in Uruk to Early Dynastic, TRB to Corded Ware, Bronze Age palatial civilisation to Iron Age mercantile city states in the east Mediterranean, communism to capitalism – in which his sympathies would not necessarily have been unidirectional. Childe's accounts need rewriting to give a more sympathetic and understanding (though still critical) role to religion – one of the most enduring, if constantly changing, modes of social integration. (Marxism is, after all, one of the great heretical movements of Christianity, with its own established churches and schisms.)

A second 'blind spot' was warfare (Flannery 1994). Again, not perhaps surprising in a pacifist and member of the No-conscription Fellowship (whilst a student at Oxford), and in an intellectual both temperamentally and philosophically opposed to war; but, as with anti-clericalism, perhaps an unhelpful sentiment in understanding the motivations and concerns of the Early Dynastic rulers of Mesopotamia or Egypt, or the nature of early states in general. His dislike of conflict extended to the internal divisions within society. Unlike his contemporaries in the CP Historians Group or *Past and Present* board (like Rodney Hilton, Christopher Hill, or Eric Hobsbawm), his models of social progress were consensual rather than conflictual. (Often, it was just religion that seems to have held things up!) Perhaps not surprisingly for a person of such likeable and unworldly views, he was an appallingly incompetent administrator; which is one reason why his successor as Director of the Institute was chosen for administrative ability rather than any intellectual spark. It is an experience from which that institution is only just recovering. Administrators can be hired; intellectuals like Childe are irreplaceable.

Childe's third 'blind spot' was luxury: pleasure in consumption. Not that he was personally frugal – he was known to enjoy champagne (reputedly in pints) in his London club, the Athenaeum – but because he disapproved of ostentation. This was a natural consequence both of his personality and his political philosophy, and fits with the attitudes discussed above. Like anti-clericalism and anti-war sentiments, hostility to ostentatious consumption forms part of a tradition of popular protest and radical rationalism in European culture (that goes back at least to the Anabaptists of Münster and beyond), which received more general acceptance in the French Revolution and the Enlightenment reaction to Baroque. Radicalism often carries with it a streak of puritanism, that is part of the natural rhetoric of social protest, and which has a certain tendency to present a moralistic view of history: for instance to interpret the past in terms of the present, and both in terms of rather puritan ideas of what is believed to be important in life. In the case of nineteenth-century philosophies which reflected the experience of the Industrial Revolution, like Marxism, the result has often tended towards a somewhat mechanistic materialism, a tendency to reduce things to calories in the belief that the bread is more essential than the butter; a trend still perpetuated in the 'cultural materialism' so dominant in American anthropology.[2] This attitude has only recently been questioned, as part of the post-modernist critique; and it is not surprising, therefore, that despite Childe's sophistication, he tended to share its assumptions. One of these was the emphasis on production rather than consumption,[3] and thus a stress on technology as instrumental rather than expressive – each step was an advance in the 'conquest' of 'nature', an instrument of domination rather than something to be enjoyed in itself. This rather stern moral attitude would condemn 'magic' as false consciousness, but approve of increased efficiency in changing the world; yet to approach prehistoric societies in this way is to espouse a naive anthropology, in the same way as neglecting religion.

Childe's explanations, therefore, tended to concern means rather than ends, mechanisms rather than motivations. His explanation for the Urban Revolution, for instance, was couched in terms of 'inventions' (plough, cart, sailing-boat, metallurgy), rather than in examining the contexts in which these innovations appeared, and the contemporary problems to which they might have been solutions. In the same way, he saw the need to import stone and metal resources to the alluvium, and the interactive growth of population and irrigation, largely in terms of the efficiency of subsistence farming. The achievement of a 'surplus', leading to the emergence of greater social and cultural complexity, was thus an accident rather than an objective. Childe's distrust of luxuries – it fits with the rather puritan streak in both Protestant rationalism and Marxism – helps to explain his emphasis on basic production rather than long-distance trade as the main determinant of economic growth. Yet it is the cultural significance of such exotic luxuries (embodying all the social propensities for ostentation and conspicuous consumption that Childe found so objectionable in his contemporaries) that is much discussed by anthropologists nowadays, in a way that his stark dichotomy of 'luxuries' versus 'neccessities' would not allow. Interestingly, it is the same deficiency that has been identified in the work of Immanuel Wallerstein on the medieval and early modern world-economy: and it is a general point of criticism of Childe's work to which I shall return.

Having paraded his deficiencies, to the extent that the reader might conclude that 'Childe was wrong', I want now strongly to assert the contrary viewpoint, that 'Childe was gloriously right'. I want to do so by discussing an aspect of my own work; and this involves situating my academic life in the rhythms of intellectual development since Childe. Childe was unique among his contemporaries, at least in Britain, in having a social model behind his interpretations. Others, like Grahame Clark, emphasised environmental reconstruction; but that was not a dynamic view, and certainly not a social dynamic. The rest were largely historicist in interpretation – a word I use to characterise the attitude summed up in the preface (dated 1936) to H. A. L. Fisher's *History of Europe*: 'Others, wiser and more learned than myself, claim to have discerned in history a plot, a rhythm, a predetermined pattern. Such harmonies are concealed from me ... I can see only ... the play of the contingent and the unforeseen.' (I quote from memory: it was our major history textbook at school.) Childe was a generalist and used models – even if to prove the uniqueness of the West, and to assert the culturally specific nature of human achievement ('Man makes himself'). It was intellectually subtle, but practically *sui generis* as a point of view even in history, and certainly within a lowbrow subject like archaeology.[4]

In the 1960s, and coming to prominence a decade after Childe's death, was the diverse series of movements together termed the 'New Archaeology'. Some were more subtle than others (notably that of my teacher David Clarke at Cambridge): but all had as common elements an emphasis on ecology and a more deterministic outlook than that of Childe. For American New Archaeology in particular,[5] the dynamic of cultural change was population growth; the mechanism was endogenous advance or adaptation rather than 'outside intervention' – all changes were local changes, and ultimately concerned with calories. ('Extrasystemic inputs' were mainly climatic perturbations.) In short, it was evolutionary rather than historical; its major metaphor was 'thresholds of change': continuous growth in one variable (usually population, or the ratio of population to resources) reached a point at which systemic change and restructuring was necessary. Each of these thresholds was a miniature revolution, but also a local manifestation of some more general change of category – from bands, to tribes to chiefdoms, or some such succession. The Enlightenment mission of New Archaeology was to clarify these categories. Noting a very widespread horizon of change across prehistoric Europe in 3500 BC, coincident more or less with the onset of urbanisation in Late Uruk Mesopotamia, I postulated a revolution. Its most tangible characteristic was its association with the first evidence for the plough and wheeled vehicles; but this was

quickly followed by the first evidence for wool and the spread of the domesticated horse beyond the steppes. In the Near East, this period saw the
domestication of the ass and the camel. Innovations in animal husbandry
were paralleled by changes in plant husbandry, such as the domestication of
tree-crops. All these added up, in my opinion, to a shift from the primary
product yielded by livestock – meat – to the various secondary products:
traction, use as a pack- or ridden animal, wool (and probably milk, too,
with the suggestion that the whole thing was made possible by the evolution
of lactose tolerance). In temperate areas it was made possible by growing
deforestation, creating grazing; in steppe areas it opened up otherwise
unusable pasturelands to exploitation; but its heartlands were the open
areas of the Near East, where the potential of animal domestication was first
realised. Hence the Secondary Products Revolution, a second generation of
innovations in agriculture which made possible the settlement of new areas
and the formation of new types of economy such as specialised pastoralism
(Chapter 6).

Not a bad generalisation, but note how it was conceptualised: as an ecological threshold, concerned with animal management, which made farming
more efficient at supporting a growing population. This reading of the
record tended to do two things. The first was to assume that logically related
features – like milking and wool-using – would probably occur together, and
was thus to align a rather varied range of phenomena into a single horizon.
The second was to 'edit out' other contemporary phenomena (not concerned with animal rearing) which might have been combined in a different
configuration: for instance in a 'transport revolution' involving cart, transport animals and boats with sails. The 'Secondary Products Revolution' was
presented, therefore, as a biological and deterministic change rather than as
a historical event; and the model was seen by some readers (because of
one of the diagrams rather than the text) as beginning with population
growth. Indeed, some revisionist (or rather, fundamentalist) critics of my
presentation (Chapman 1983; Barker 1985) took it further: whereas from
the beginning I had stressed its restricted Near Eastern origins and consequent spread to Europe, these commentators were happy to imagine use
of the plough and woolly breeds of sheep apparently appearing spontaneously, wherever they were necessary because of pressure on resources.
(Incidentally, they also attributed transhumant pastoralism not to a specialised exchange economy, but to a continuity from Palaeolithic hunting
patterns.) This accommodation to the fashionable 'continuity + threshold'
model, and complete rejection of anything that smacked of diffusionism,
stretched economic and environmental determinism to the limits of their
credibility, and beyond. In reaction, I emphasised the parallelism of the
Secondary Products Revolution with the Neolithic Revolution itself: the
conjunction and explosive dispersal of several different elements, each with
an older history in different parts of the Near East (Chapter 7). Thus while

individual elements might have older origins, it was their conjunction that provided the revolutionary effect.

But what was the revolution? It was, in fact, nothing other than Gordon Childe's Urban Revolution, perceived in terms of its spin-off and effects on outer, still prehistoric, Eurasia. Not to have seen it in this way from the beginning was excusable on my part, however, since Childe himself missed the major linking element: the plough, which in his writings he assumed to be a Bronze Age introduction in Europe. Yet he *had* worked out (and bequeathed to Stuart Piggott as a topic on which to write a classic book: 1983), a chronology for the spread of wheeled vehicles, involving a Mesopotamian beginning and an impact on south-east Europe with the Baden culture. With the current evidence of Neolithic plough-marks, putting the two elements (plough and cart) together as a 'yoked traction complex' becomes a particularly compelling model. This would have begun within the Taurus-Zagros arc, and only broken out of it at the time of Uruk colonial expansion in the mid-fourth millennium BC.[6] The Urban Revolution was thus the crucial agent of integration and dispersal, and crucially affected contemporary Europe at the same time as it transformed the Near East – as Childe quite correctly claimed. His perception of the structure of the long-term history of the Old World was in the long run to prove more plausible than the views of his ecologically better-informed critics. There is no doubt in my mind that the plough was 'diffused', in the sense that Childe gave to the word, and did not just magically appear whenever population passed a particular density threshold.[7]

What about his other classic examples of 'diffused' technologies? One of the realisations since his death has been the age and duration of the south-east European Copper Age, and the degree to which it developed in isolation from Near Eastern models (Renfrew 1969). This might seem to displace metallurgy from the role that he assigned to it, as an ultimate consequence of the Urban Revolution. Yet recent work at Troy and in south-east Hungary have suggested, within the context of a calibrated radiocarbon chronology, that the spread of tin bronze and the specific types associated with it (and also other technologies such as faience) came about as a result of contacts up the Danube around 2500 BC (summarised in Sherratt 1993b, 22f); and this in turn would lie behind the florescence of Aunjetitz metallurgy. It was arguably at this point that bronze became a useful metal, rather than simply a spectacular substitute for stone, as unalloyed copper had been. On this basis, Childe's interpretation might be summarised as 'right model, wrong evidence'! It was not copper metallurgy itself which followed his pattern, for copper-working had spread much earlier, but *advanced* forms of copper-alloy metallurgy which fit perfectly with his predictions. Copper Age metallurgy was playful by comparison (look at Varna and Nahal Mishmar), but Bronze Age metallurgy with its consistent suites of weapons was a serious international business.

In the same way, we may see the beginnings of the Baden culture itself as an earlier episode of such spin-off. I have suggested that the pottery container-forms which characterise that culture, such as handled jugs and cups, reflect the spread of an elite consumption of alcoholic drinks, originally from precious metal sets of serving-vessels, and beginning among urban elites in the Near East. Echoes of these practices would lie behind the subsequent importance of drinking vessels in the Corded Ware and Bell-Beaker complexes in northern and western Europe. These examples shift the emphasis from 'technology' to 'consumption habits'. The 'irradiation of barbarian Europe' (in Childe's famous phrase, caricaturing his own position – which lacked this sensitivity to consumption) took the form of acquiring new habits and lifestyles, new modes of ostentation and new media in which to create and in which to trade. These elements of style were at least as important (and often provided the motivation for) improvements in the efficiency of subsistence practices. The wagon, and even the plough (which often substitutes for it on Italian statue-menhirs: Figure 6.3) were prestige possessions and symbols of power, as were the first woollen clothes and metal weapons. Thus although the structure of Childe's model of the re-lationship between Europe and the Near East was correct, its nuances and 'feel' are somehow misleading. The innovations which spread were not practical improvements for everybody, which were immediately applied in workshops throughout the continent; more often, they were the rare and exotic tastes of the elite. History was less moral than he imagined.

What is becoming clear (to me, at any rate) is that there were many successive episodes of cultural transmission to Europe from the Near East, from the spread of the Neolithic to the arrival of Christianity: but these need to be grouped and classified by the social relations involved in the trans-mission. Some were the product of intimate trading relations; others were simply the gradual adoption of practices from further south. Childe's accounts tended to stress the former mechanism: his descriptions of the European Bronze Age suggest that the circulation of bronze objects in temperate Europe, and the progress in opening up new sources of metal, was 'rooted in the Aegean market' (Childe 1958, 166). In fact, his descriptions of Bronze Age Europe (as opposed to his descriptions of the Bronze Age of the Near East) increasingly appear to be anachronistic projections of a situation which only occurred in the first millennium BC: the colonisation of the west Mediterranean by Greeks and Phoenicians, and active commercial in-volvement north of the Alps, even the travelling smith. (In interpreting bronze hoards, his rationalism and anti-clericalism again led him astray: whereas he saw them as the stock-in-trade of a travelling smith, hidden for protection, we would now recognise a large number of them as votive offerings, transactions with the gods.) In short: Childe seems to have conflated the very different sets of conditions which existed in the late Neolithic/Copper Age, Bronze Age and Iron Age into effectively a single model of culture-contact, usually involving face-to-face relations and direct travel. His models need to be loosened up, elaborated, and made more specific to a whole range of very different conditions.

And so here I come to a remarkable paradox. Childe, who was by profession a European prehistorian, seems to have been consistently right about the Near East – although often quite wrong about Europe: megalithic missionaries, wandering bronzesmiths, even the whole chronology of the Neolithic and earlier Bronze Age.[8] Moreover, although within European prehistory his major field of research was Neolithic and Bronze Age, his detailed models often have more relevance to the Iron Age, about which he wrote very little.

Some clues to this paradox have been mentioned above: his highly literate, middle-class, urban background; his university training (classics); his antipathy to religion – which arguably is the most essential element in understanding the past. Childe did not really understand or empathise with the primitive: he came to Europe from Australia precisely to discover how such savagery had been left behind, and how civilisation had dawned. His views of the earlier stages of prehistory (although technically excellent when discussing relative chronologies and archaeological stratigraphies) are, really, a bit of a caricature.[9] One feels that, had Childe been asked (not un-reasonably, as a native Australian) about savages he had known, he might well have replied in the famous words of Sir James Frazer: 'Heaven forbid!'; for Childe, like Frazer, believed in the same progressive sequence of magic, then religion, then science. Childe's sympathies with prehistoric societies grew progressively with increasing complexity: fundamentally out of touch, in many ways, with the Palaeolithic and Neolithic; better in the Bronze Age (at least in the more civilised parts); most accurate in the period he knew best, the classical world of the first millennium BC. In fact, however, most of European prehistory consists of societies for which models derived from the Greeks and Phoenicians are fundamentally misleading (for surely those 'megalithic missionaries' in Childe's mind were Neolithic Phoenicians).[10] Whether or not it was accidental, his chronology compressed (as we now know) those bits of prehistory with which he was least sympathetic, and magnified the rest as a percentage of the whole. Thus time seemed to pass more quickly than it had done in prehistoric reality, and was made to appear more event-like than the slow, long-term processes that he was really study-ing – and more like the rapid changes of the period in which he was trained. In this respect, processualist archaeologists have made a genuine improve-ment in the interpretation of prehistoric Europe, going far beyond Childe; and it is this aspect which is perhaps the most important implication of the 'radiocarbon revolution': the slowness of change in Neolithic and earlier Bronze Age Europe, by comparison with the kaleidoscopic changes en-visaged by Childe, Milojčić, or Müller-Karpe.[11] What at first seemed to archaeologists to be like events were in reality slow transformations.

Part of the problem in Childe's conceptualisation of the Neolithic was precisely his rather literal and rationalist interpretation of technology. He separated science sharply from what he thought of as mumbo-jumbo: one was effective in changing the world, the other was mere illusion that was best discarded in the long term – error to be purified and burnt out.[12] An axe was an instrument for chopping down trees: any further cosmological or sexual symbolism it might have, and any social obligations which it might embody, were irrelevant to its 'real' purpose. Ornamentation and display were frivolous epiphenomena: 'the objects of Stone Age trade were always luxuries – if not merely shells or similar ornaments at least things that men could easily have done without' (Childe 1951, 35). This is not merely his puritan streak, but the voice of a man who does not himself indulge in the social display of ornaments and the symbols of wealth, and disapproves of those that do. It is not a good basis for understanding Neolithic motivations and the nature of Neolithic trade.[13]

Interestingly, the same prejudice is shared by one of the most influential and widely quoted left-wing theoreticians of world trade, Immanuel Wallerstein: 'long-distance trade was a trade in luxuries ... which depended on the political indulgence of the wealthy ... not really what we mean today by trade' (1974, 41f); again, the puritanism so often associated with radical critique. But as Jane Schneider has brilliantly pointed out (1977), this is thoroughly to misunderstand the nature of the pre-capitalist world, where the trade in 'useless luxuries' (like gold!) was often the major incentive for inter-regional relationships and the channel by which other commodities, ideas and techniques came to move. Such materials and contacts are as fundamental to an understanding of the evolution of the world economy as the inner meanings and symbolism of materials are to understanding the Stone Age trade in flint axes and shell ornaments. Wallerstein only allows the capitalist world-system to come into existence in the sixteenth century AD, with bulk exchanges of grain for manufactured goods; Childe saw it already in the sixteenth century BC, with Mycenaean entrepreneurship in the Alpine region: both operate with similar definitions but make arbitrary choices of threshold, early or late, within a continuous story.

What is missing in this debate is a terminology that recognises the different degrees of intervention between the 'inner' and 'outer' parts of the process: the core areas of change and the surrounding areas which are trans-formed in the process, and thus in turn affect the environment of the core itself. Following a suggestion of Jane Schneider (1977, 21), I have suggested a terminological distinction between *periphery* and *margin* (Sherratt 1993a; 1993b; 1994). In the classic definition of a periphery, there is a com-plementary (and exploitative) relationship whereby the periphery yields up its raw materials and imports the core's manufactures[14] – while trying, through import substitution, to rid itself of such dependency and become a core itself. (A process often resisted by the core, which may use imperial

501

expansion to prevent it.) Crudely adapting this definition to the ancient world, the 'core' represents already urban societies ('civilisations'), and the periphery represents the ring of chiefdoms which supply them and have a continuing relationship with them ('barbarians', like those directly in touch with the Phoenician and Greek colonies around the shores of the first-millennium Mediterranean). These latter societies are thus typically transitional between prehistoric illiteracy and urban literacy. The Hallstatt phenomenon would be a good example from prehistoric Europe; and the occurrence of *Prunkgräber* with southern imports is a convenient archaeological clue to the existence of such a situation (Mycenae Shaft-Graves, Thracian tumuli). But because of this transitional character, such societies form only small segments of the archaeological record; they are sandwiched between longer periods of preceding prehistory (which they typically bring to a close) and succeeding history. So for much longer periods than these phases of *direct* interaction, European societies have been *indirectly* affected by their civilised southern neighbours: and it is a mistake (as in the case of the supposed 'Mycenaean horizon' in Bronze Age Europe) to conceive of this in the same way as the emergence of barbarian societies in the Iron Age. Hence the usefulness of the term *margin*: precisely the element which is missing in Childe's models, but which encompasses at least three millennia of later European prehistory.

Within this sequence, bulk exchanges and direct commercial engagement with the 'civilised' world are fairly late features of European prehistory: in the Bronze Age affecting only Greece and perhaps peninsular Italy, and only reaching trans-Alpine Europe slowly in the Iron Age. Before that, it was the indirect ideological and technological influence (the two are not really opposites, but complements!) that penetrated into the temperate parts of the continent, carried often in quest of things which were remote, valuable and useless – like gold and amber – and bringing knowledge of new luxuries – like alcohol, wool and bronze. All this is far from a puritan view of progress, and man's enhanced mastery over the environment. The slow transformation of European culture and society can be crudely broken down into millennial phases. From 3500–2500 BC, innovations of general desirability spread across Europe over a broad front, creating new and enlarged cultural units: Baden, Pit-Grave, Globular Amphorae, Corded Ware, Bell-Beaker. Then from 2500–1500 BC, as bronze came to be used universally across Mediterranean and temperate Europe as a medium of exchange, more specific pathways and routes of trade emerged; while cultures themselves became both more uniform in essentials (bronze weapons and associated technologies) but more distinctive in idiosyncratic ways. From 1500–500 BC, Europe went from a peak of indirect exchanges with the Mediterranean, through a fundamental transition from bronze to iron (and thus a differentiation of currency-metal from utilitarian metal) that brought partial collapse to the urban world, before renewed expansion on a yet larger scale brought more intimate interaction between north and south, between temperate Europe and the Mediterranean. Only in the latter half of the third of these millennial phases do many of Childe's models even begin to work; and before that time, it is necessary to invent[15] an anthropology which is capable of understanding Europe's extinct cultures: but the effects of Near Eastern innovations were no less real for being transmitted indirectly.

What was so powerful that it was capable of causing this extended transformation in the continent of Europe? It was the qualitatively different nature of urban economies, and the contrast with surrounding non-urban ones, which created the conditions for such a patterning of spatial relationships. What is evident from archaeology is that the Urban Revolution produced more complex economic structures, not just in local terms (cities and their hinterlands) but in regional and global terms as well, because civilisations depended fundamentally on their barbarian peripheries, and together came to affect all the world's remaining populations; just as, four millennia previously, the appearance of farming in the same nuclear area had irrevocably altered the future history of Europe's hunting and gathering populations. It was these two revolutions which compare with the Industrial Revolution as the great turning points in the history of the human species; and it is to Gordon Childe that we owe their explicit recognition and the exploration of their conceptual consequences. It is tempting, then, to compare the continuing significance of these revolutions with those canonised by Karl Marx. With hindsight, the transitions from antiquity to feudalism and from feudalism to capitalism appear not as global shifts but as local episodes in the fortunes of Europe, created by shifts in the world-system from the Mediterranean to the Indian Ocean, and back to the Atlantic; transitions whose consequence was magnified in Marxian theory by their identification as precursors to the great future transition to socialism. Their revolutionary character, then, was established only through a retrospective eschatology. Childe was probably nearer the mark, in believing that aspects of capitalistic behaviour go back to the Bronze Age; though any starting-point is arbitrary, and the Stone Age would probably be more realistic. What is misleading is to associate capitalism with rationalism: its commodities are surely as fetishised as were Neolithic stone axes. It is a false perception of the past to make it the antithesis of the present, or to make the present the antithesis of the past. It is not in some intangible essence like 'rationality' or 'capitalism' that the answer to world history lies, but in the concrete transformations identified by Childe. Yet it would be equally misleading to mistake concreteness for mere materiality. The Neolithic and Urban Revolutions were, indeed, demographic and calorific thresholds: but they were also revolutions in cultural memory (houses, tombs, wall-paintings, writing), in which the material was merely a token for the ideal. It is the challenge to post-Childean archaeology, as to post-Marxist philosophy in general, to overcome the radical rhetoric of its intellectual origins and to paint a more nuanced picture: an account of material change that is not materialist in a reductionist way, and encompasses religious sacrifice as much as improvements in productivity. Consumption is always communication, not just the satisfaction of bodily needs.

Within the same structure, therefore, the interpretation can alter. Childe had a pioneer's clarity of vision: it is his sense of structure which can still inspire us as we continue to accumulate the detail. Today, however, we both know more and understand more than Childe could have done; and we no longer read him for revelation, as if he were a prophet rather than a fallible scientist. It is a hagiographic convention to ask what a great man would make of developments since his death: and Childe has already been invoked in this capacity – 'if Childe were alive today' (Trigger 1982). But he is not; he was a creature of his times, and should be celebrated as such. He will, however – like his mentor Marx – always be present, in ghostly form, for a dialogue with his pupils and successors: in Childe's case, likeable as well as stimulating, and still, perhaps, with carefully calculated eccentricities to startle the unprepared.

NOTES

1. Some of the thoughts in this essay were provoked by the publication of the 1992 London conference on Childe, published as Harris 1994, and reviewed by myself in the *TLS*, October 1995.
2. And in the assumption that there is a global food crisis in relation to present and projected population levels. There isn't: only a stark choice between growing food or cash-crops, for luxury consumption. It is humankind's desire for the latter, not simply its need for the former, that is the problem.
3. Perhaps it is just our different standpoints in the economic cycle that make us today see the problem differently from Childe: whether we see the ability to produce or the desire to consume as the more problematic. In times of poverty, production is the problem: in times of boom, the need to stimulate consumption. It is important to recognise to what extent our perceptions mirror the experience of our own times!
4. Childe's problem was that, as archaeology's lone intellectual, he didn't have anyone to talk to. His fellow historians on the CP Historians Group had such radically different ideas and timescales: Childe, remember, saw the origins of capitalism in the Bronze Age, the others took it as axiomatic that it began in the sixteenth century AD! Archaeologists and historians of the 1950s did not talk in terms of models, except in terms of Marxism, which was one of the few forms of historical generalisation. The patrician Grahame Clark, who might have been most sympathetic to such model-building, was certainly no Marxist (even though, in his own way, quite a rebel – and even known as 'corduroy Clark' whilst a graduate student, in reference to his informal style of dress: pers. comm. from the late Glyn Daniel). One reason why the New Archaeology really was so revolutionary was that it made explicit comparison and generalisation respectable. In Childe's day, that just wasn't done, at least in the humanities – which is why he generally didn't do it, and why it is such hard work trying to sort out what explicit models he actually held.
5. Reflected at Cambridge, England in the school of Eric Higgs (the 'palaeoeconomists') rather than David Clarke.
6. I do not accept the single Grn- radiocarbon date of 3620 ± 60 bc for Sarnowo as providing an estimate of the age of the ploughmarks under the barrow there.

7. Even though it should be added (in fairness) that this latter model may be appropriate for certain innovations like irrigation, in appropriate climatic conditions.
8. He consciously chose a short chronology (see Childe 1938), in the light of his views on diffusion, rather than simply failed to anticipate a timescale that was ultimately revealed by dendrochronology and calibrated radiocarbon.
9. Though it should be remembered quite what a revelation was the *Man the Hunter* conference (Lee and de Vore 1968), with its combination of archaeologists and anthropologists. Many stereotypes died at that conference, perhaps the most important one being that hunters have no spare time to build higher culture. Quite to the contrary: it is farmers and townsmen who work longer and longer hours.
10. Many of Childe's attitudes to European prehistory can be summarised in terms of the following equations:
    1. Neolithic = oriental = religion = bad
    2. Bronze Age = western = capitalism = good.
11. 'Prehistory' is, in this sense, different from 'history': though not in an etiological sense – that prehistory is 'determined' by process, but history is 'made' by individuals and events.
12. His famous example (1956, 171) was making a side-scraper: probably it was supposed to be done at full moon after fasting, imprecation and sacrifice; but all these aspects were irrelevant to its usefulness. Not merely were they (fortunately) lost to the archaeological record, but they were ultimately lost to the cumulative tradition of technology: 'futile accessories, expressive of ideological delusions ... Error expunged, knowledge stands out all the clearer ...' The vehemence of Childe's imagery on this topic is reminiscent of Carlyle's description of the Puritan government of England under Cromwell, when 'great quantities of dross and crypto-poisonous matter' were burnt out to secure her future progress (*History of Frederick II of Prussia*, I, 1872, 188f). There is a Protestant rectitude about both attitudes, which expresses itself in hostility to ritual: arguably the single most important aspect of most anthropological descriptions.
13. It is notable that Childe, despite his antipodean origins, made very little reference to the ethnography of New Guinea, which in the last 20 years has been the richest source of models for Neolithic life in Europe. This betrays a rather narrow, and perhaps even insecure, Eurocentrism.
14. Note that this definition would make the USSR economically a periphery, not a core, despite its political might and superpower status. The latter was achieved by massively extending its own sub-periphery, and spending a large proportion of its income on armaments. The fact that the attempt failed in the long run suggests that such economic 'laws' are ultimately determinant; but the fact that it succeeded for so long before collapsing is a warning not to be deterministic about applying them. As a realistic generalisation, one might assert that theocratic (whether Marxist or Islamic) command economies in the twentieth century are more likely to occupy peripheral rather than core positions.
15. 'Invent', because it cannot be studied directly, only reconstructed from two imperfect analogies: the European 'peasant' cultures of much later times, and the pre-urban societies of non-European parts of the world.

BIBLIOGRAPHY

Adams, R. M. 1965 *Land Behind Baghdad*, Chicago and London: Chicago University Press.

Adams, R. M. 1972 'Patterns of Urbanization in Early Southern Mesopotamia', pp. 735–50 in P. Ucko, G. W. Dimbleby and R. Tringham (eds) *Man, Settlement and Urbanism*, London: Duckworth.

Adams, R. M. 1974a 'Anthropological perspectives on ancient trade', *Current Anthropology* 15, 239–58.

Adams, R. M. 1974b 'Historic patterns of Mesopotamian irrigation agriculture', pp. 1–6 in T. E. Downing (ed.) *Irrigation's Impact on Society*, Tucson: University of Arizona Press.

Adams, R. M. 1981 *Heartland of Cities: studies of ancient settlement and land use on the central floodplain of the Euphrates*, Chicago: Chicago University Press.

Adams, R. M. and Nissen, J. 1972 *The Uruk Countryside: The Natural Setting of Urban Societies*, Chicago: Chicago University Press.

Allan, W. 1965 *The African Husbandman*, London: Oliver and Boyd.

Allan, W. 1972 'Ecology, techniques and settlement patterns', pp. 211–26 in P. Ucko, G. W. Dimbleby and R. Tringham (eds) *Man, Settlement and Urbanism*, London: Duckworth.

Algaze, G. 1989 'The Uruk expansion: cross-cultural exchange in early Mesopotamian civilisation', *Current Anthropology* 30(5), 571–608.

Algaze, G. 1993 *The Uruk World System: the dynamics of expansion of early Mesopotamian Civilization*, Chicago: Chicago University Press.

Alon, D. 1976 'Two cult vessels from Gilat', *Atiqot* 11, 116–18.

Amiet, P. 1986 *L'âge des échanges inter-iraniens, 3500–1700 avant J.-C.*, Paris: Editions de la Réunion des musées nationaux.

Amoroso, E. C. and Jewell, P. A. 1963 'The exploitation of the milk-ejection reflex by primitive peoples', pp. 126–38 in A. E. Mourant and F. E. Zeuner *Man and Cattle* (Royal Anthropological Institute Occasional Paper No. 18).

Andel, K. 1961 'Tibava – Eneolityczny zespól osadniczy u stóp Wychorlatu', *Acta Archaeologica Carpathica* 3, 39–59.

Andersen, S. H. 1983 'Monstrede åreblade fra Tybrind Vig', *Kuml* 1982/3, 11–30.

Andreeva, M. V. 1977 'K voprosu o yuzhnykh svyazyakh Maikopskoi kul'tury', *Sovetskaya Arkheologiya* 1977(1), 39–56.

Andreeva, M. V. 1979 'Ob izobrazheniyakh na serebryanykh Maikopskikh sosudakh', *Sovetskaya Arkheologiya* 1979(1), 22–34.

Angel, L. 1968 'Human remains at Karataş', *American Journal of Archaeology* 72(3), 260–3.

Anthony, D. W. 1986 'The "Kurgan culture", Indo-European origins and the domestication of the horse: a reconsideration', *Current Anthropology* 27, 291–313.

Anthony, D. W. and Brown, D. 1991 'The origins of horseback riding', *Antiquity* 65, 22–38.

Appadurai, A. 1986 *The Social Life of Things: commodities in cultural perspective*, Cambridge: Cambridge University Press.

Applebaum, S. 1954 'The agriculture of the early Iron Age as exemplified at Figheldean Down, Wiltshire', *Proceedings of the Prehistoric Society* 20, 103–14.

Artzy, M. 1994 'Incense, camels and collared rim jars: desert trade routes and maritime outlets in the second millennium', *Oxford Journal of Archaeology* 13(2), 121–47.

Athenaeus of Naucratis [Loeb Classics Edition, 7 vols] 1955–61 *The Deipnosophists* with an English translation by C. B. Gulick, London: Loeb.

Aurenche, O., Evin, J. and Hours, F. (eds) 1987 *Chronologies du Proche Orient / Chronologies in the Near East, Relative chronologies and absolute chronology 16,000–4000 B.P.* (BAR Int. Ser. 379 ii), Oxford.

Bakker, J. A. 1979 *The TRB West Group* (Cingula 5), Amsterdam: University of Amsterdam Subfaculty of Pre- and Protohistory.

Bakker, J. A., Vogel, J. C. and Wiślański, T. 1969 'TRB and other C-14 dates from Poland (Part A)', *Helinium* 9, 3–27.

Balassa, I. (ed.) 1972 *Getreidebau in Ost- und Mitteleuropa*, Budapest: Akadémiai Kiadó.

Banner, J. 1942 *Das Tisza-, Maros-, Körös Gebiet bis zur Entwicklung der Bronzezeit*, Leipzig: Archaeological Institute.

Banner, J. 1956 *Die Péceler Kultur*, Budapest: Akadémiai Kiadó.

Bar-Adon, P. 1980 *The Cave of the Treasure: the Finds from the Caves in Nahal Mishmar*, Jerusalem: Israel Excavation Society.

Barber, E. 1991 *Prehistoric Textiles: the development of cloth in the Neolithic and Bronze Ages*, New Jersey: Princeton University Press.

Barclay, G. J. and Russell-White, C. J. 1993 'Excavations in the ceremonial complex of the fourth to the second millennium BC at Balfarg/Balbirnie, Glenrothes, Fife', *Proceedings of the Society of Antiquaries of Scotland* 123, 43–210 + microfiche.

Barker, E. 1927 *National Character and the Factors in its Formation*, London: Methuen.

Barker, G. 1985 *Prehistoric Farming in Europe*, Cambridge: Cambridge University Press.

Barth, F. 1964 *Nomads of South Persia*, London: Allen and Unwin.

Barth, F. (ed.) 1969 *Ethnic Groups and Boundaries*, London: Allen and Unwin.

Bates, D. G. and Lees, S. 1977 'The role of exchange in productive specialisation', *American Anthropologist* 79(4), 824–41.

Bath-Bílková, B. 1973 'K problému påvodu hřiver – Zur Herkunftsfrage der Halsringbarren', *Památky Archeologické* 64, 24–41.

Battaglia, R. 1943 'La palafitta del Lago di Ledro nel Trentino', *Memorie del Museo Civico di Storia Naturale della Venezia Tridentina* 7.

Bauch, W. 1988 'Eine Nachbestattung der Einzelgrabkultur mit Pferdeschädel in einem Megalithgrab von Borgstedt, Kreis Rendsburg-Eckernförde', *Offa* 45, 43–73.

Bayless, T. M. and Rosenzweig, N. S. 1966 'A radical difference in incidence of lactase deficiency', *Journal of the American Medical Association* 197, 968–72.

Beale, T. W. 1973 'Early trade in highland Iran: a view from the source area', *World Archaeology* 5(2), 133–48.

Becker, C. J. 1954 'Stenalderbebyggelsen ved Store Valby i Vestsjaelland: Problemer omkring Tragtbaegerkulturens aeldste og yngste Fase', *Aarbøger for Nordisk Oldkyndighed og Historie* 1954, 127–97.

Becker, C. J. 1959 'Flint mining in Neolithic Denmark', *Antiquity* 33, 87–92.

Behre, K.-E. 1984 'Zur Geschichte der Bierwürzen nach Fruchtfunden und schriftlichen Quellen', pp. 115–22 in W. van Zeist and W. A. Casparie (eds) *Plants and Ancient Man*, Rotterdam: Balkema.

Behrens, H. 1964 *Die neolithisch-frühmetallzeitlichen Tierskelettfunde der Alten Welt* (Veröffentlichungen des Landesmuseums für Vorgeschichte in Halle, 19), Berlin: VEB Deutscher Verlag der Wissenschaften.

Behrens, H. 1973 *Die Jungsteinzeit im Mittelelbe-Saale-Gebiet*, Berlin: VEB Deutscher Verlag der Wissenschaften.

Behrens, H. 1981 'Der Walternienburger und der Bernburger Keramikstil und die Walternienburg-Bernburg Kultur', *Jahresschrift für Mitteldeutsche Vorgeschichte* 63, 16.

Behrens, H. and Schlette, F. 1969 *Die Neolitischen Becherkulturen im Gebiet der DDR und ihre Europäischen Beziehungen* (Veröffentlichungen des Landesmuseums für Vorgeschichte in Halle, 24), Berlin: VEB Deutscher Verlag der Wissenschaften.

Bekmose, J. 1978 'Megalitgrave og megalitbygder', *Antikvariske Studier* 1, 47–64.

Bender, B. 1978 'Gatherer-hunter to farmer: a social perspective', *World Archaeology* 10, 204–22.

Bender-Jørgensen, L. 1986 *Forhistoriske tekstiler i Skandinavien / Prehistoric Scandinavian Textiles* (Nordiske Fortidsminder B9), Copenhagen: Kongelige Nordiske-Oldskriftselskab.

Bender-Jørgensen, L. 1992 *North European Textiles until AD 1000*, Aarhus: Aarhus University Press.

Benecke, N. 1994a *Der Mensch und seine Haustiere*, Stuttgart: Theiss.

Benecke, N. 1994b *Archäozoologische Studien zur Entwicklung der Haustierhaltung in Mitteleuropa und Südskandinavien von den Anfängen bis zum ausgehenden Mittelalter* (Schriften zu Ur- und Frühgeschichte, 46), Berlin: Akademie Verlag.

Benecke, N. 1994c 'Zur Domestikation des Pferdes in Mittel- und Osteuropa. Einige neue archäozoologische Befunde', pp. 123–44 in B. Hänsel and S. Zimmer (eds) *Die Indogermanen und das Pferd*, Budapest: Archaeolingua.

Berciu, D. 1961 *Contribuţii la Problemele Neoliticului în Romînia în Lumina Noilor Cercetări*, Bucharest: Romanian Academy of Sciences.

Berlin, I. 1976 *Vico and Herder: two studies in the history of ideas*, London: Chatto and Windus.

Bernal, M. 1987 *Black Athena: the Afroasiatic roots of classical civilisation, volume 1: The fabrication of ancient Greece 1785–1985*, London: Free Association Books.

Bibikova, V. I. 1969 'Do istorii domestikatsii konya na pivdennomu skhodi Evropi', *Arkheologiya* (Kiev) 22, 55–67.

Bibikova, V. I. 1975 'Formen der Viehzucht bei den äneolitischen Stämmen Südosteuropas', pp. 237–45 in K. H. Otto and H.-J. Brachmann (eds) *Moderne Probleme der Archaeologie*, Berlin: Akademie Verlag.

Bill, J. and Kinnes, I. 1975 'A gold beaker from Switzerland', *Antiquity* 49, 132–3.

Binford, L. R. 1968 'Archeological perspectives', pp. 5–32 in S. R. Binford and L. R. Binford (eds) *New Perspectives in Archeology*, Chicago: Aldine.

Birdsell, J. B. 1968 'Some predictions for the Pleistocene', pp. 229–40 in R. B. Lee and I. Devore (eds) *Man the Hunter*, Chicago: Aldine.

Bíró, K. T. 1988 'Distribution of lithic raw materials on prehistoric sites', in *Acta Archaeologica Academiae Scientiarum Hungaricae* 40, Budapest: Akadémiai Kiadó.

Bisson de la Roque, F., Contenau, G. and Chapouthier, F. 1953 *Le Trésor de Tôd*, Documents de Fouilles de l'Institut Français d'Archéologie Orientale du Caire, XI, Cairo.

Bittel, K. 1959 'Beiträge zur Kenntnis anatolischer Metalgefässe der zweiten Hälfte des dritten Jahrtausends', *Jahrbuch des Deutschen Archäologischen Instituts* 74, pp. 1ff.

Bökönyi, S. 1962 'Zur Naturgeschichte des Ures in Ungarn und das Problem der Domestikation des Hausrindes', *Acta Antiqua Academiae Scientiarum Hungaricae* 14, 175–214.

Bökönyi, S. 1968 'Die geschichtliche Entwicklung der Tierhaltung in Mittel- und Osteuropa', *Agrártörténeti Szemle* 10, 1–4. (In Hungarian, with German summary.)

Bökönyi, S. 1974 *History of Domestic Mammals in Eastern and Central Europe*, Budapest: Akadémiai Kiadó.

Bökönyi, S. 1978 'The earliest waves of domestic horses in east Europe', *Journal of Indo-European Studies* 6, 17–76.

Bökönyi, S. 1979 'Copper Age vertebrate fauna from Kétegyháza', pp. 101–18 in I. Ecsedy *The People of the Pit-grave Kurgans in eastern Hungary*, Budapest: Akadémiai Kiadó.

Bökönyi, S. 1987 'Horses and sheep in east Europe in the Copper and Bronze Ages', pp. 136–44 in S. N. Skomal and E. Polomé (eds) *Proto-Indo-European: the archaeology of a linguistic problem* (Studies in honour of Marija Gimbutas), Washington: Institute for the Study of Man.

Bökönyi, S. 1991 'Late Chalcolithic horses in Anatolia', in R. H. Meadow and H.-P. Uerpmann (eds) *Equids in the Ancient World*, vol. 2, Wiesbaden: Reichert.

Bökönyi, S. (ed.) 1992 *Cultural landscape changes in south-east Hungary I: Reports on the Gyomaendröd Project*, Budapest: Archaeolingua.

Bökönyi, S. 1993 *Pferdedomestikation, Haustierhaltung und Ernährung* (Archaeolingua, Series Minor 3), Budapest: Archaeological Institute of the Hungarian Academy.

Bökönyi, S. 1994 'Über die Entwicklung der Sekundärnutzung', in *Beiträge zur Archäozoologie und prähistorischen Anthropologie: im Andenken an Joachim Boessneck* (8: Arbeitstreffen der Osteologen, Konstanz 1993): Stuttgart 1994, 21–8.

Boelicke, U. 1976/7 'Das Neolitische Erdwerk Urmitz', *Acta Praehistorica et Archaeologica* 7/8, 73–121.

Boessneck, J. 1956 'Tierknochen aus spätneolithischen Siedlungen Bayerns', *Studien an vor- und frühgeschichtlichen Tierresten Bayerns* 1.

Bognár-Kutzián, I. 1958 'Polgár-Csöshalom (Archaeologische Forschungen im Jahre 1957)', *Archaeologiai Ertesítö* 85, 201.

Bognár-Kutzián, I. 1963 *The Copper Age cemetery of Tizapolgár-Basatanya* (Archaeologia Hungarica N.S. 42), Budapest: Akadémiai Kiadó.

Bognár-Kutzián, I. 1966 'Das Neolithikum in Ungarn', *Archaeologia Austriaca* 40, 249–80.

Bognár-Kutzián, I. 1972 *The Early Copper Age Tiszapolgár Culture in the Carpathian Basin* (Archaeologia Hungarica N.S. 48), Budapest: Akadémiai Kiadó.

Bognár-Kutzián, I. See also Kutzián, I.

Bogucki, P. 1984 'Ceramic sieves of the Linear Pottery culture and their economic implications', *Oxford Journal of Archaeology* 3(1), 15–30.

Bogucki, P. 1986 'The antiquity of dairying in temperate Europe', *Expedition* 28(2), 51–8.

Bogucki, P. 1988 *Forest Farmers and Stockherders: early agriculture and its consequences in North-Central Europe*, Cambridge: Cambridge University Press.

Bogucki, P. 1993 'Animal traction and households in Neolithic Europe', *Antiquity* 67, 492–503.

Bóna, I. 1960 'Clay models of Bronze Age wagons and wheels in the Middle Danube Basin', *Acta Archaeologica Academiae Scientiarum Hungaricae* 12, 83–111.

Bóna, I. 1975 *Die Mittlere Bronzezeit Ungarns und ihre südöstlichen Beziehungen* (*Archaeologia Hungarica* 49), Budapest: Akadémiai Kiadó.

Bonev, A. 1977 'Sustoyaniya na prouchvaniyata na zlatnoto sukrovishte ot Vulchitrun', *Arkheologiya* (Sofia) 19(4), 11–19.

Bonev, A. 1984 'Datierung des Goldschatzes von Vălchitran', *Studia Prehistorica* 7, 164–77.

Boserup, E. 1965 *The Conditions of Agricultural Growth*, London: Allen and Unwin.

Bouzek, J. 1985 *The Aegean, Anatolia and Europe: cultural inter-relations in the second millennium* BC (Studies in Mediterranean Archaeology 29), Göteborg: Åström.

Bradley, R. 1971 'Trade competition and artefact distribution', *World Archaeology* 2(3), 347–51.

Bradley, R. 1980 'Subsistence, exchange and technology – a social framework for the Bronze Age in southern England c.1400–700 BC', pp. 57–75 in J. Barrett and R. Bradley (eds) *Settlement and Society in the British Later Bronze Age* (BAR Brit. Ser. 83), Oxford: British Archaeological Reports.

Bradley, R. 1989 'Deaths and entrances: a contextual analysis of megalithic art', *Current Anthropology* 30, 68–75.

Bradley, R. and Edmonds, M. 1993 *Interpreting the Axe Trade: production and exchange in Neolithic Britain*, Cambridge: Cambridge University Press.

Braidwood, R. J., Sauer, J. D., Helbaek, H., Mangelsdorf, P. C., Cutler, H. C., Coon, C. S., Linton, R., Steward, J. and Oppenheim, A. L. 1953 'Symposium: Did man once live by beer alone?', *American Anthropologist* 55, 515–26.

Brandt, K. H. 1969 'Ein neuer Holzpflug vom Walle-Typus [Mehlbergen, Kr Nienburg]', *Bremer Archäologische Blätter* 5, 17–20.

Briard, J. 1978 'Das Silbergefäss von Saint-Adrien, Côtes-du-Nord', *Archäologisches Korrespondenzblatt* 8, 13–20.

Briard, J. and L'Helgouach, J. 1957 *Chalcolithique, Néolithique secondaire et survivances néolithiques à l'Age du Bronze ancien*, Rennes: Travaux du Laboratoire d'Anthropologie préhistorique de la Faculté des Sciences de Rennes.

Brookfield, H. C. and Hart, D. 1971 *Melanesia: a geographical interpretation of an island world*, London: Methuen.

Brothwell, D. and Higgs, E. S. (eds) 1969 *Science in Archaeology* (2nd edn), London: Thames and Hudson.

Brunn, W. A. von 1959 *Die Hortfunde der frühen Bronzezeit aus Sachsen-Anhalt, Sachsen und Thüringen*, Berlin: Akademie Verlag.

Bryan, K. 1929 'Floodwater farming', *Geographical Review* 19, 444–56.

Buchholz, H. G. 1983 'Doppeläxte und die Frage der Balkanbeziehungen des ägäischen Kulturkreises', pp. 43–134 in A. Poulter (ed.) *Ancient Bulgaria*, Nottingham: Nottingham University Department of Classical and Archaeological Studies.

Buchholz, H. G. and Karageorghis, V. 1973 *Prehistoric Greece and Cyprus: an archaeological handbook*, London: Phaidon.

Bulliet, R. W. 1975 *The Camel and the Wheel*, Cambridge, Mass.: Harvard University Press.

Burger, I. 1980. 'Die chronologische Stellung der Fußschalen in den endneolitischen Kulturgruppen Mittel- und Südosteuropas', pp. 11–45 in Spindler, K. (ed.) *Vorzeit zwischen Main und Donau, Erlanger Forschungen, Reihe A* 26, Erlangen: Universitätsbund Erlangen-Nürnberg.

Burgess, C. and Shennan, S. 1976 'The Beaker phenomenon: some suggestions', pp. 309–31 in C. Burgess and R. Miket (eds) *Settlement and Economy in the third and second millennia BC* (BAR Brit. Ser. 33), Oxford: British Archaeological Reports.

Burgess, C., Topping, P., Mordant, C. and Maddison, M. (eds) 1988 *Enclosures and Defences in the Neolithic of Western Europe* (BAR Int. Ser. 403), Oxford: British Archaeological Reports.

Buringh, P. 1957 'Living conditions in the lower Mesopotamian Plain in ancient times', *Sumer* 13, 30–46.

Burrow, J. W. 1966 *Evolution and Society: a study in Victorian social theory*, Cambridge: Cambridge University Press.

Burrow, J. W. 1981 *A Liberal Descent: Victorian historians and the English past*, Cambridge: Cambridge University Press.

Burton, J. 1989 'Repeng and the salt-makers: "ecological trade" and stone axe production in the Papua New Guinea Highlands', *Man* (NS) 24, 255–72.

Butzer, K. W. 1970 'Physical conditions in eastern Europe, western Asia and Egypt before the period of agriculture', pp. 35–69 in *Cambridge Ancient History* vol. 1(1) (3rd edn), Cambridge: Cambridge University Press.

Butzer, K. W. 1972 *Environment and Archaeology*, London and Chicago: Aldine.

Butzer, K. W. 1976 *Early Hydraulic Civilization in Egypt*, Chicago: Chicago University Press.

Bylund, E. 1960 'Theoretical considerations regarding the distribution of settlement in inner north Sweden', *Geografisker Annaler* 42, 225–31.

Cantacuzino, G. and Morinz, S. 1963 'Die Jungsteinzeitlichen Funde in Cernica (Bukarest)', *Dacia* (NS) 7, 27–89.

Carneiro, R. L. 1960 'Slash and burn agriculture: a closer look at its implications for settlement patterns', in A. F. C. Wallace (ed.) *Men and Cultures*, Philadelphia: University of Pennsylvania Press.

Cassau, A. 1935 'Ein Feuersteindolch mit Holzgriff und Lederscheide aus Wiepenkathen, Kreis Stade', *Mannus* 199.

Catling, H. 1964 *Cypriot Bronzework in the Mycenaean World*, Oxford: Oxford University Press.

Caulfield, S. 1978 'Neolithic fields: the Irish evidence', pp. 137–43 in H. C. Bowen and P. Fowler (eds) *Early Land Allotment* (BAR Brit. Ser. 48), Oxford: British Archaeological Reports.

Cauvin, J. 1994 *Naissance des divinités, Naissance de l'agriculture*, Paris: CNRS.

Chang, C. and Koster, H. A. 1986 'Beyond bones: towards an archaeology of pastoralism', *Advances in Archaeological Method and Theory* 9, 97–148.

Chapman, J. C. 1983 'The "Secondary Products Revolution" and the limitations of the Neolithic', *Bulletin of the Institute of Archaeology* [University of London] 19 (1982), 107–22.

Chapman, R. 1981 'The emergence of formal disposal areas and the "problem" of megalithic tombs in prehistoric Europe', pp. 71–82 in R. Chapman, I. Kinnes and K. Randsborg (eds) *The Archaeology of Death*, Cambridge: Cambridge University Press.

Chappell, J. 1966 'Stone Axe Factories in the highlands of East New Guinea', *Proceedings of the Prehistoric Society* 32, 96–121.

Charles, J. A. 1967 'Early arsenical bronzes – a metallurgical view', *American Journal of Archaeology* 71, 21–6.

Charles, J. A. 1969 'Metallurgical examination of south-east European copper axes' (Appendix I in Renfrew 1969), *Proceedings of the Prehistoric Society* 35, 40–2.

Cherednichenko, N. N. 1976 'Kolesnitsy Evrazii epokhi pozdnei bronzy', pp. 135–50 in *Eneolit i bronzovyi vek Ukraini*, Kiev: Institute of Archaeology.

Chernykh, E. 1966 *Istoriya drevneishei metallurgiia Vostochnoi Evropy*, Moscow: Nauka.

Chernykh, E. 1971 'Spektralen analiz na metalnite nakhodki ot praistoricheskoto selishche do s. Ezero', *Arkheologiya* 13, 55–61.

Chernykh, E. N. 1978 *Gornoe delo i metallurgiya v drevneishei Bolgarii*, Sofia: Bulgarian Academy of Sciences.

Chernykh, E. N. 1983 'Frühmetallurgische Kontakte in Eurasien', *Beiträge zur allgemeinen und vergleichenden Archäologie* 5, 19–34.

Chernykh, E. N. 1992 *Ancient Metallurgy in the USSR: the Early Metal Age*, Cambridge: Cambridge University Press.

Chernykh, E. and Radunčeva, A. 1972 'Starite medni rudnitsi okolo gr. Stara Zagora', *Arkheologiya* 14, 6, 1–7.

Cheynier, A. 1936 *Jouannet – Grand-père de la Préhistoire*, Paris.

Childe, V. G. 1915 'On the date and origin of Minyan ware', *Journal of Hellenic Studies* 35, 254–75.

Childe, V. G. 1916 'The Influence of Indo-Europeans in Prehistoric Greece' (University of Oxford B.Litt. thesis, not preserved).

Childe, V. G. 1923 *How Labour Governs: A Study of Workers' Representation in Australia*, London: The Labour Publishing Company Ltd.

Childe, V. G. 1924 'A gold vase of Early Helladic type', *Journal of Hellenic Studies* 44, 163–4.

Childe, V. G. 1925 *The Dawn of European Civilisation* ('History of Civilisation' series), London: Routledge and Kegan Paul. (Successive editions thereafter: 2nd, 1927; 3rd, 1939; 4th, 1947; 5th, 1950; 6th, 1957.)

Childe, V. G. 1926 *The Aryans: A Study of Indo-European Origins* ('History of Civilisation' series), London: Kegan Paul.

Childe, V. G. 1928 *The Most Ancient East: The Oriental Prelude to European Prehistory*, London: Kegan Paul.

Childe, V. G. 1929 *The Danube in Prehistory*, Oxford: Clarendon Press.

Childe, V. G. 1930 *The Bronze Age*, Cambridge: Cambridge University Press.

Childe, V. G. 1931 *Skara Brae: A Pictish Village in Orkney*, London: Kegan Paul.

Childe, V. G. 1933 'Is prehistory practical?', *Antiquity* 7, 410.

Childe, V. G. 1934 *New Light on the Most Ancient East*, London: Routledge and Kegan Paul. (Successive editions thereafter: 2nd, 1935; 3rd, 1952; 4th, 1954; 5th, 1958.)

Childe, V. G. 1935 *The Prehistory of Scotland*, London: Kegan Paul.

Childe, V. G. 1936 *Man Makes Himself*, London: Watts and Co.

Childe, V. G. 1938 'The Orient and Europe' (Presidential address to Section II, Anthropology, of the British Association), *The Advancement of Science* 1938, 181–96.

Childe, V. G. 1942 *What Happened in History*, Harmondsworth: Penguin Books.

Childe, V. G. 1944 *Progress and Archaeology*, London: Watts and Co.

Childe, V. G. 1947 'Archaeology as a social science', *University of London, Institute of Archaeology, Third Annual Report*, 49–60.

Childe, V. G. 1949a 'The first bronze vases to be made in central Europe', *Acta Archaeologica* 20, 257–65.

Childe, V. G. 1949b 'The origins of Neolithic culture in northern Europe', *Antiquity* 32, 129–35.

Childe, V. G. 1950 *Magic, Craftsmanship and Science* (Frazer Lecture 1949), Liverpool: Liverpool University Press.

Childe, V. G. 1951a 'The first wagons and carts – from the Tigris to the Severn', *Proceedings of the Prehistoric Society* 17, 177–94.

Childe, V. G. 1951b *Social Evolution*, London: Watts and Co.

Childe, V. G. 1952 'Trade and industry in barbarian Europe till Roman times', pp. 1–32 in M. Postan and E. Rich (eds) *The Cambridge Economic History of Europe* 1, Cambridge: Cambridge University Press.

Childe, V. G. 1954a 'Early forms of society', pp. 38–57 in C. Singer, E. J. Holmyard and A. R. Hall (eds) *A History of Technology* 1, Oxford: Clarendon Press.

Childe, V. G. 1954b 'Prehistory', pp. 3–155 in E. Barker, G. N. Clark and P. Vaucher (eds) *The European Inheritance* 1, Oxford: Oxford University Press.

[Childe, V. G.] 1955 'Contributions to Prehistoric Archaeology offered to Professor V. G. Childe in honour of his sixty-fifth birthday by twenty-seven authors', *Proceedings of the Prehistoric Society* NS 21.

Childe, V. G. 1956a *Society and Knowledge: the growth of human traditions*, New York: Allen and Unwin.

Childe, V. G. 1956b *Piecing Together the Past: the interpretation of archaeological data*, London: Routledge and Kegan Paul.

Childe, V. G. 1956c 'Notes on the chronology of the Hungarian Bronze Age', *Acta Archaeologica Academiae Scientiarum Hungaricae* 7, 291–9.

Childe, V. G. 1957a 'The Bronze Age', *Past and Present* 12, 2–15.

Childe, V. G. 1957b *The Dawn of European Civilisation* (7th edn), London: Routledge.

Childe, V. G. 1958a [1957] 'Retrospect', *Antiquity* 32, 69–74.

Childe, V. G. 1958b [1957] 'Valediction', *Bulletin of the Institute of Archaeology, University of London* 1, 1–8.

Childe, V. G. 1958c *The Prehistory of European Society*, Harmondsworth: Penguin Books.

Childe, V. G. 1963 (revised edn) *Social Evolution*, London: Fontana.

Childe, V. G. 1980 [1957] letter and memoir reproduced in editorial, *Antiquity* 54, 1–3.

Chippindale, C. 1988 'The invention of words for the idea of prehistory', *Proceedings of the Prehistoric Society* 54, 303–14.

Chisholm, M. 1968 *Rural Settlement and Land Use* (2nd edn), London: Hutchison.

Chorley, R. J. and Haggett, P. (eds) 1967 *Models in Geography*, London: Methuen.

Christiansen-Weniger, F. 1967 'Die anatolischen Säpflüge und ihre Vorgänger im Zweistromland', *Archäologischer Anzeiger* 2, 151–62.

Chrpovsky, B. (ed.) 1973 *Symposium über die Entstehung und Chronologie der Badener Kultur*, Bratislava: Slovak Academy of Sciences.

Cipolla, C. 1978 *The Economic History of World Population* (7th edn), Harmondsworth: Penguin Books.

Clark, C. and Haswell, M. 1964 *The Economics of Subsistence Agriculture*, London: Macmillan.

Clark, J. G. D. 1942 'Bees in antiquity', *Antiquity* 16, 208–15.

Clark, J. G. D. 1946 *From Savagery to Civilisation*, London: Corbett Press.

Clark, J. G. D. 1952 *Prehistoric Europe: The Economic Basis*, London: Methuen.

Clark, J. G. D. 1965 'Traffic in stone axe and adze blades', *Economic History Review* 2nd ser. 18, 1–28.

Clark, [J.] G. [D.] 1976 'Prehistory since Childe', *Bulletin of the Institute of Archaeology, University of London* 13, 1–21.

Clark, J. D. 1976 'The domestication process in sub-Saharan Africa with special reference to Ethiopia', paper presented to the IXth UISPP Congress, Nice.

Clark, R. M. 1975 'A calibration curve for radiocarbon dates', *Antiquity* 49, 251–66.

Clarke, D. L. 1968 *Analytical Archaeology*, London: Methuen.

Clarke, D. L. 1970 *Beaker Pottery of Great Britain and Ireland*, Cambridge: Cambridge University Press.

Clarke, D. L. 1973 'Archaeology: the loss of innocence', *Antiquity* 47, 6–18 (reprinted in D. L. Clarke 1979 *Analytical Archaeologist*, Academic Press, 83–103).

Clarke, D. L. 1976a 'The Beaker network – social and economic models', pp. 459–76 in *Glockenbechersymposion Oberried 1974*, Bussem/Haarlem: Fibula-van Dishoeck (reprinted in D. L. Clarke 1979 *Analytical Archaeologist*, Academic Press, 333–62).

Clarke, D. L. 1976b 'Mesolithic Europe: the economic basis', pp. 449–81 in G. Sieveking, I. Longworth and K. Wilson (eds) *Problems in Economic and Social Archaeology*, London: Duckworth (reprinted in D. L. Clarke 1979 *Analytical Archaeologist*, Academic Press, 207–62).

Clarke, D. L. 1979 'The economic context of trade and industry in Barbarian Europe till Roman Times', in D. L. Clarke 1979 *Analytical Archaeologist*, Academic Press, 263–332.

Coghlan, H. H. 1961 'Some problems concerning the manufacture of copper shaft-hole axes', *Archaeologia Austriaca* 29, 57–75.

Cohen, A. P. 1985 'The Symbolic Construction of Community', London and New York: Tavistock.

Cohen, J. 1970 'The palaeoecology of south central Anatolia', *Anatolian Studies* 20, 119–37.

Cohen, J. and Erol, O. 1969 'Aspects of the palaeogeography of central Anatolia', *Geographical Journal* 135, 389–98.

Cohen, M. N. 1977 *The Food Crisis in Prehistory*, New Haven: Yale University Press.

Compagnoni, B. and Tosi, M. 1978 'The camel: its distribution and state of domestication in the Middle East during the third millennium in light of finds from Shahr-i Sokhta', pp. 91–103 in R. H. Meadow and M. A. Zeder (eds) *Approaches to Faunal Analysis in the Middle East*, Cambridge, Mass.: Peabody Museum, Bulletin 2.

Comşa, E. 1967 'Üeber die Verbreitung und Herkunft einiger von den jungsteinzeitlichen Menschen auf dem Gebiete Rumäniens verwendeten Werkstoffe', *A Móra Ferenc Múzeum Évkönyve*, Szeged 1967, 26–8.

Comşa, E. 1974 'Die Entwicklung, Periodisierung und relative Chronologie der jungsteinzeitlichen Kulturen Rumäniens', *Zeitschrift für Archäologie* 8, 1–44.

Comşa, E. 1976 'Les matières premières en usage chez les hommes néolithiques de l'actuel territoire Roumain', *Acta Archaeologica Carpathica* 16, 239–49.

Constantin, C. 1985 'Fin du Rubané, Céramique du Limbourg et post-Rubané: le néolithique le plus ancien en bassin Parisien et en Hainault', *Oxford: British Archaeological Reports*, International Series 273.

Cooke, R. U. and Reeves, R. W. 1976 *Arroyos and Environmental Change*, Oxford: Clarendon Press.

Crane, E. 1983 *The Archaeology of Beekeeping*, London: Duckworth.

Cranstone, B. 1969 'Animal husbandry: the evidence from ethnography', pp. 247–64 in P. J. Ucko and G. W. Dimbleby (eds) *The Domestication and Exploitation of Plants and Animals*, London: Duckworth.

Cribb, R. 1991 *Nomads in Archaeology*, Cambridge: Cambridge University Press.

Crosby, A. W. 1986 *Ecological Imperialism: the biological expansion of Europe, 900–1900*, Cambridge: Cambridge University Press.

D'Arcy Thompson, W. 1917 *On Growth and Form*, Cambridge: Cambridge University Press.

Dąbrowski, M. J. 1971 'Analiza pylkowa warstw kulturowych z Sarnowa, pow. Wrocławek', *Prace i Materiały Muzeum Archeologicznego i Etnograficznego w Lodzi* (Ser. Arch.) 18, 147–64.

Dahl, G. and Hjort, A. 1976 *Having Herds: pastoral herd growth and household economy*, University of Stockholm (Studies in Social Anthropology, 2).

Dalton, G. (ed.) 1968 *Primitive, Archaic and Modern Economies: Essays of Karl Polanyi*, New York: Doubleday.

Dalton, G. 1977 'Aboriginal economies in stateless societies', pp. 191–209 in T. K. Earle and J. Ericson (eds) *Exchange Systems in Prehistory*, New York: Academic Press.

Daniel, G. 1962a *The Megalith Builders of Western Europe* (2nd edn), Harmondsworth: Penguin Books.

Daniel, G. 1962b *The Idea of Prehistory*, London: Watts and Co.

Davidsen, K. 1978 *The Final TRB Culture in Denmark: a settlement study* (Arkæologiske Studier 5), Copenhagen.

Davis, E. N. 1977 *The Vaphio Cups and Aegean gold and silver ware*, New York: Garland.

Davis, S. J. M. 1984 'The advent of milk and wool production in western Iran: some speculations', pp. 265–78 in J. Clutton Brock and C. Grigson (eds)

Animals and Archaeology Vol. 3: Early Herders and their Flocks (BAR Int. Ser. 202), Oxford: British Archaeological Reports.

Davis, S. J. M. 1987 *The Archaeology of Animals*, London: Batsford.

Davis, S. J. M. 1993 'The zoo-archaeology of sheep and goat in Mesopotamia', *Bulletin on Sumerian Agriculture* 7, 1–7.

Demoule, J.-P. and Guilaine, J. 1986 *Le Néolithique de la France: hommage à Gérard Bailloud*, Paris: Picard.

Dénes, J. B., Makkay, J. and Miklós, S. B. 1989 *Békés Megye Régészeti Topográfiája: A Szarvasi Járás IV/2* (Magyarország Régészeti Topográfiája, 8), Budapest: Akadémiai Kiadó.

Dergachev, V., Sherratt, A. G. and Larina, O. 'Recent results of Neolithic research in Moldavia (USSR)', *Oxford Journal of Archaeology* 10(1), 1–16.

Deschler, W. 1965 'Native cattle-keeping in west Africa', in A. Leeds and A. Vayda (eds) *Man, Culture and Animals*, Washington: American Association for the Advancement of Science.

Deutsch, K. W. 1953 'The growth of nations: some recurrent patterns of political and social integration', *World Politics* 5, 168–95.

Diakonov, I. M. 1985 'On the original home of the speakers of Indo-European', *Journal of Indo-European Studies* 13, 92–174.

Dickson, J. H. 1978 'Bronze Age mead', *Antiquity* 52, 108–13.

Dietz, U. L. 1992 'Zur Frage vorbronzezeitlicher Trensenbelege in Europa', *Germania* 70(1), 17–36.

Dobosi, V. T. 1972 'Mesolitische Fundorte in Ungarn', *Alba Regia* 12 (1971), 39–59. (Also published separately in *Die Aktuellen Fragen der Bandkeramik*, edited by J. Fitz and J. Makkay, Székesfehérvár: Co. Fehér Museum.)

Dobosi, V. T. 1976 'Prehistoric settlement at Demjen Hegyesköbérc', *Folia Archaeologica* 27, 9–39.

Döhle, H.-J. 1994 *Die Linienbandkeramischen Tierknochen von Eisleben, Bördekreis* (Veröffentlichungen des Landesamtes für archäologische Denkmäler Sachsen-Anhalt, Bd. 47), Halle (Saale): Landesmuseum für Vorgeschichte.

Dorrell, P. 1978 'The uniqueness of Jericho', pp. 11–18 in P. R. S. Moorey and P. Parr (eds) *Archaeology in the Levant*, Warminster: Aris and Philips.

Douglas, M. 1958 'Raffia cloth in the Lele economy', *Africa* 28, 109–22.

Douglas, M. 1966 *Purity and Danger: an analysis of the concepts of pollution and taboo*, London: Routledge and Kegan Paul.

Douglas, M. 1967 'Primitive rationing: a study in controlled exchange', pp. 119–47 in R. W. Firth (ed.) *Themes in Economic Anthropology*, London: Tavistock.

Douglas, M. 1975 'Deciphering a meal', pp. 249–75 in M. Douglas (ed.) *Implicit Meanings*, London: Routledge.

Douglas, M. 1982 'Food as a system of communication', pp. 82–104 in M. Douglas (ed.) *In the Active Voice*, London: Routledge.

Douglas, M. 1987 *Constructive drinking: perspectives on drink from Anthropology*, Cambridge: Cambridge University Press.

Douglas, M. and Isherwood, B. 1978 *The World of Goods: towards an anthropology of consumption*, Harmondsworth: Penguin Books.

Driehaus, J. 1960 *Die Altheimer Gruppe und das Jungneolithikum in Mitteleuropa*, Mainz: RGZM.

Driver, H. E. 1961 *Indians of North America*, Chicago: Chicago University Press.

Drower, M. 1954 'Water-supply, irrigation and agriculture', pp. 520–57 in
    C. Singer, J. Holmyard and A. R. Hall (eds) *A History of Technology* vol. I,
    Oxford: Oxford University Press.
Drower, M. 1969 'The domestication of the horse', pp. 471–8 in P. Ucko and
    G. Dimbleby (eds) *The Domestication and Exploitation of Plants and Animals*,
    London: Duckworth.
Druks, A. and Tsaferis, V. 1970 'Tel Azor', *Révue Biblique* 77, 578 and Plate XLb.
Ducos, P. 1969 'Methodology and results of the study of the earliest domesticated
    animals in the Near East (Palestine)', pp. 265–76 in P. J. Ucko and G. W.
    Dimbleby (eds) *The Domestication and Exploitation of Plants and Animals*,
    London: Duckworth.
Ducos, P. 1973 'Sur quelques problèmes posés par l'étude des premiers élevages en
    Asie du sud-ouest', pp. 77–85 in J. Matolcsi (ed.) *Domestikationsforschung und
    Geschichte der Haustiere*, Budapest: Akadémiai Kiadó.
Dumézil, G. 1968 (4th edn) *Mythe et épopée I: L'idéologie des trois fonctions dans
    les épopées des peuples indo-européens*, Paris: Gallimard.
Durham, W. 1991 *Coevolution: genes, culture and human diversity*, Stanford:
    Stanford University Press.
Durkheim, E. 1933 *The Division of Labor in Society*, New York: Collier-
    Macmillan.
Dyson-Hudson, R. and Dyson-Hudson, N. 1969 'Subsistence herding in Uganda',
    Scientific American 220, 76–89.
Dzis-Raiko, G. A. and Chernyakov, I. T. 1981 'Zolotaya chasha
    Vulchitrunovskogo tipa iz severo-zapadnogo prichernomoriya', *Sovetskaya
    Arkheologiya* 1981(1), 151–62.
Earle, T. K. 1977 'A reappraisal of redistribution: complex Hawaian chiefdoms',
    pp. 213–29 in T. K. Earle and J. Ericson (eds) *Exchange Systems in Prehistory*,
    New York: Academic Press.
East, G. 1968 *The Geography Behind History*, London: Nelson.
Ebbesen, K. and Brinch-Petersen, E. 1973 'Fuglebaeksbanken: en jaettestue på
    Stevns', *Aarbøger for Nordisk Oldkyndighed og Historie*, 73–106.
Ebert, M. 1925 *Reallexikon der Vorgeschichte*, Berlin: Verlag Walter de Gruyter.
Ecsedy, I. 1979 *The people of the Pit-grave Kurgans in eastern Hungary*, Budapest:
    Akadémiai Kiadó.
Ecsedy, I., Kovacs, L., Maraz, B. and Torma, I. 1982 *Békés Megye Régészeti
    Topográfiája: A Szeghalmi Járás IV/I* (Magyarország Régészeti Topográfiája, 6),
    Budapest: Akadémiai Kiadó.
Eggers, H. J. 1951 *Der Römische Import im freien Germanien* (Atlas der
    Urgeschichte 1), Museum für Völkerkunde und Vorgeschichte, Hamburg.
Ellis, L. 1984 *The Cucuteni-Tripole Culture: a study in technology and the origins
    of complex society* (BAR Int. Ser. 217), Oxford: British Archaeological Reports.
Eluère, C. (ed.) 1989 *Le premier Or de l'Humanité en Bulgarie: 5ᵉ millenaire*,
    Paris: Réunion des musées nationaux.
Emboden, W. 1979 *Narcotic plants: hallucinations, stimulants, inebrients and
    hypnotics; their origins and uses*, London: Studio Vista.
Engels, F. 1985 [1st edn 1884] *The Origin of the Family, Private Property and the
    State, in connection with Lewis H. Morgan's Researches*, Harmondsworth:
    Penguin Books.
Englund, R. K. 1995 'Late Uruk period cattle and dairy products: evidence from
    protocuneiform sources', *Bulletin on Sumerian Agriculture* 8, 35–50.

Epstein, C. 1985 'Laden animal figurines from the Chalcolithic period in Palestine', *Bulletin of the American Schools of Oriental Research* 258, 53–62.

Esse, D. 1991 *Subsistence, Trade and Social Change in Early Bronze Age Palestine* (Studies in Oriental Civilization 50), Chicago: Oriental Institute.

Evans, A. J. 1909 *Scripta Minoa: the written documents of Minoan Crete*, vol. 1, The Hieroglyphic and Primitive Linear Categories, Oxford: Clarendon Press.

Evans, A. 1935 *The Palace of Minos at Knossos*, London: Macmillan.

Evans, J. 1943 *Time and Chance*, London: Longmans, Green and Co.

Evans, J. 1954 *Prelude and Fugue*, London: Museum Press Ltd.

Evans, J. D. 1987 'No. 1: the first half-century – and after', *Bulletin of the Institute of Archaeology* 24, 1–25.

Evenari, M., Shanan, L. and Tadmor, N. 1971 *The Negev: the challenge of the desert*, Cambridge, Mass.: Harvard University Press.

Falkenstein, A. 1936 *Archäische Texte aus Uruk*, Ausgrabungen der Deutschen Forschungsgemeinschaft in Uruk-Warka, Berlin: Deutsche Forschungsgemeinschaft.

Fell, C. I. 1964 'The Cumbrian type of polished stone axe and its distribution in Britain', *Proceedings of the Prehistorical Society* 30, 39–55.

Filipovski, J. and Civić, G. 1969 *The Soils of Jugoslavia*, Belgrade.

Firth, J. (ed.) 1967 *Themes in Economic Anthropology* (ASA Monographs No. 6), London: Tavistock.

Fischer, U. 1956 *Die Gräber der Steinzeit im Saalegebiet*, Berlin: Vorgeschichtliche Forschungen 15.

Flannery, K. V. 1965 'The ecology of early food production in Mesopotamia', *Science* 147, 1246–56.

Flannery, K. V. 1969 'Origins and ecological effects of early domestication in Iran and the Near East', pp. 73–100 in P. Ucko and G. Dimbleby (eds) *The Domestication and Exploitation of Plants and Animals*, London: Duckworth.

Flannery, K. V. (ed.) 1976 *The Early Mesoamerican village*, New York: Academic Press.

Flannery, K. 1994 'Childe the evolutionist: a perspective from North America', in Harris (1994), 101–20.

Flatz, G. and Rotthauwe, H. W. 1977 'The human lactase polymorphism', *Progress in Medical Genetics* 2, 203–44.

Forbes, R. J. 1954 'Chemical, culinary and cosmetic arts', pp. 238–98 in C. Singer, E. J. Holmyard and A. R. Hall (eds) *The Oxford History of Technology, Vol. 1: From early times to the fall of ancient empires*, Oxford: Oxford University Press.

Forbes, R. J. 1955 'Food, alcoholic beverages, vinegar', and 'Fermented beverages 500 BC–AD 1500', pp. 50–83 and 106–30 in R. J. Forbes, *Studies in Ancient Technology* 3, Leiden: Brill.

Forbes, R. J. 1957 'Sugar and its substitutes in antiquity', pp. 78–109 in R. J. Forbes, *Studies in Ancient Technology* 5, Leiden: Brill.

Fortes, M. and Evans-Pritchard, E. E. 1940 *African Political Systems*, London: International African Institute.

Fowler, P. and Evans, J. 1967 'Plough-marks, lynchets and early fields', *Antiquity* 41, 289–94.

Frangipane, M. and Palmieri, A. 1983 (published 1988) 'Perspectives on proto-urbanisation in eastern Anatolia: Arslantepe (Malatya)', *Origini* 12/2, 287–668.

Frangipane, M., Hauptmann, H., Liverani, M., Matthiae, P. and Mellink, M. 1993 *Between the Rivers and over the Mountains: archaeologica anatolica et mesopotamica Alba Palmieri dedicata*, Rome: Università di Roma 'La Sapienza'.

Frankenstein, S. and Rowlands, M. J. 1978 'The internal structure and regional context of early Iron-Age society in south-western Germany', *Bulletin of the Institute of Archaeology* 15, 73–112.

French, D. H. 1970 'Notes on site distribution in the Çumra area', *Anatolian Studies* 20, 139–48.

Fried, M. 1967 *The Evolution of Political Society*, New York: Random House.

Fried, M. 1978 *The Concept of Tribe*, Menlo Park California: Cummings Publishing Company.

Friedman, J. and Rowlands, M. J. 1977 'Notes towards an epigenetic model of the evolution of "civilisation"', pp. 201–76 in J. Friedman and M. J. Rowlands (eds) *The Evolution of Social Systems*, London: Duckworth.

Frierman, J. 1969 'The Balkan Graphite Ware' (Appendix II in Renfrew 1969), *Proceedings of the Prehistoric Society* 35, 42–3.

Furst, P. 1976 *Hallucinogens and Culture*, San Francisco: Chandler and Sharp.

Fyfe, H. 1940 *The Illusion of National Character*, London: Watts and Co.

Gabałówna, L. 1970 'Wyniki analizy C-14 węgli drzewnych z cmentarzyska kultury Pucharów Lejkowatych na Stanowisku 1 w Sarnowie – z Grobowca 8 i niektóre problemy z nimi związane. (Informacja wstępna)', *Prace i Materiały Muzeum Archeologicznego i Etnograficznego w Lodzi* (Ser. Arch.) 17, 77–91.

Galkin, L. L. 1975 'Odno iz drevneishikh prakticheskikh prisposoblenii skotovodov', *Sovetskaya Arkheologiya* 1975 (3), 186–92.

Gamkrelidze, T. V. and Ivanov, V. V. 1985a 'The Ancient Near East and the Indo-European question: temporal and territorial characteristics of proto-Indo-European based on linguistic and historico-cultural data', *Journal of Indo-European Studies* 13, 3–48.

Gamkrelidze, T. V. and Ivanov, V. V. 1985b 'The migrations of tribes speaking Indo-European dialects from their original homeland in the Near East to their historical habitations in Eurasia', *Journal of Indo-European Studies* 13, 49–91.

Gandert, O-F. 1964 'Zur Frage der Rinderanschirrung im Neolithikum', *Jahrbuch des Römisch-Germanischen Zentralmuseums* 11, 34–56.

Garner, B. 1967 'Models of urban geography and settlement location', pp. 303–60 in R. J. Chorley and P. Haggett (eds) *Models in Geography*, London: Methuen.

Gathercole, P. 1971 '"Patterns in Prehistory": an examination of the later thinking of V. Gordon Childe', *World Archaeology* 3, 225–32.

Gathercole, P. 1982 'Gordon Childe: man or myth?', *Antiquity* 56, 198.

Gathercole, P., Irving, T. H. and Melleuish, G. (eds) 1995 *Childe and Australia*, St Lucia: University of Queensland Press.

Gayre, G. R. 1948 *Wassail! in Mazers of Mead*, London: Phillimore and Co.

Geertz, C. 1963 *Agricultural Involution*, Berkeley: University of California Press.

Gejvall, N. G. 1946 'The Fauna of the Different Settlements of Troy: Part I: Dogs, Horses and Cattle', unpublished typescript in London University Institute of Archaeology.

Gejvall, N. G. 1969 *Lerna: a Preclassical Site in the Argolid, vol. 1: The Fauna*, Princeton: American School of Classical Studies.

Gening, V. F. 1979 'The cemetery at Sintashta and the early Indo-Iranian peoples', *Journal of Indo-European Studies* 7, 1–29.

Gening, V. F., Zdanovich, G. B. and Gening, V. V. 1992 *Sintashta: arkheologicheskie pamyatniki ariiskikh plemen Uralo-Kazakhstanskikh stepei*, Chelyabinsk: Yuzhno-Ural'skoe Knizhnoe Izdatel'stvo.

Georgiev, G. I. 1961 'Kulturgruppen der Jungstein- und der Kupferzeit in der Ebene von Thrazien', pp. 45–100 in J. Böhm and S. de Laet (eds) *L'Europe à la Fin de l'Âge de la Pierre*, Prague: Czechoslovak Academy of Sciences.

Gerloff, S. 1975 *The Early Bronze Age Daggers of Great Britain, with a reconsideration of the Wessex culture* (PBF VI, 2), Munich: Beck.

Gerloff, S. 1993 'Zu Fragen mittelmeerländischer Kontakte und absoluter Chronologie der Frühbronzezeit in Mittel- und Westeuropa', *Praehistorische Zeitschrift* 68(1), 58–102.

Gheţie, B. and Mateescu, C. N. 1973 'Utilisation des bovins à la traction dans la phase plus récente de la civilisation Vădastra', *Actes du VIIIe Congrès international des Sciences préhistoriques et protohistoriques*, 454–60.

Gibson, M. 1974 'Violation of fallow and engineered disaster in Mesopotamian Civilization', pp. 7–20 in T. E. Downing and M. Gibson (eds) *Irrigation's Impact on Society*, Tucson: University of Arizona Press.

Gilman, A. 1981 'The development of social stratification in Bronze Age Europe', *Current Anthropology* 22, 1–24.

Gimbutas, M. 1956 *The Prehistory of Eastern Europe: part 1*, Cambridge, Mass.: Peabody Museum.

Gimbutas, M. 1961 'Notes on the chronology and expansion of the Pit-grave culture', pp. 193–200 in J. Böhm and S. J. De Laet (eds) *L'Europe à la Fin de l'Âge de la Pierre*, Prague: Czechoslovak Academy of Sciences.

Gimbutas, M. 1965 *Bronze Age cultures in central and eastern Europe*, The Hague: Mouton.

Gimbutas, M. 1974 *The Gods and Goddesses of Old Europe 7000–3500 BC*, London: Thames and Hudson.

Gimbutas, M. 1977 'The first wave of Eurasian steppe pastoralists into Copper Age Europe', *Journal of Indo-European Studies* 5, 277–338.

Gimbutas, M. 1980 'The Kurgan wave #2 (c.3400–3200 BC) into Europe and the following transformation of culture', *Journal of Indo-European Studies* 8, 273–315.

Gimbutas, M. 1989 *The Language of the Goddess*, London: Thames and Hudson.

Gimbutas, M. 1991 *The Civilization of the Goddess: the world of Old Europe*, San Francisco: Harper.

Giner, C. A. 1980 'Estudio de los materiales de cestria de la Cueva de los Murciélagos', *Trabajos de prehistoria* 37, 109–62.

Giot, P-R., L'Helgouach, J. and Monnier, J-L. 1979 *Préhistoire de la Bretagne*, Rennes: Ouest-France.

Glass, M. 1991 *Animal Production Systems in Neolithic Central Europe* (BAR Int. Ser. 572), Oxford: British Archaeological Reports.

Glob, P. V. 1951 *Ard og Plov i Nordens Oldtid*, Århus: Jysk Arkaeologisk Selskab.

Glob, P. V. 1970 *The Mound People: Danish Bronze-Age man preserved*, London: Faber and Faber.

Godelier, M. 1977 *Perspectives in Marxist Anthropology*, Cambridge: Cambridge University Press.

Góngora y Martinez, M. 1868 *Antigüedades prehistóricas de Andalucía*, Madrid: Moro.

Goodman, J., Lovejoy, P. and Sherratt, A. (eds) 1995 *Consuming Habits: drugs in history and anthropology*, London: Routledge.

Goody, J. 1969a *Technology, Tradition and the State in Africa*, Oxford: Oxford University Press.

Goody, J. 1969b 'Inheritance, property and marriage in Africa and Eurasia', *Sociology* 3, 55–76.

Goody, J. 1976 *Production and Reproduction*, Cambridge: Cambridge University Press.

Goody, J. 1982 *Cooking, Cuisine and Class*, Cambridge: Cambridge University Press.

Gorman, C. 1977 'A reconsideration of the beginnings of agriculture in south east Asia', pp. 321–56 in C. Reed (ed.) *Origins of Agriculture*, Paris and The Hague: Mouton.

Gould, P. R. 1963 'Man against his environment: a game-theoretic framework', *Annals of the Association of American Geographers* 53, 290–7.

Green, M. W. 1980 'Animal husbandry at Uruk in the archaic period', *Journal of Near Eastern Studies* 39, 1–35.

Green, S. 1981 *Prehistorian: a biography of V. Gordon Childe*, Bradford-on-Avon: Moonraker Press.

Greenfield, H. J. 1986 *The Palaeoeconomy of the Central Balkans (Serbia): a zooarchaeological perspective on the Late Neolithic and Bronze Age* (BAR Int. Ser. 304), Oxford: British Archaeological Reports.

Greenfield, H. J. 1988 'The origins of milk and wool production in the Old World: a zooarchaeological perspective from the central Balkans', *Current Anthropology* 29, 573–93.

Greenfield, H. 1989 'Zooarchaeology and aspects of the secondary products revolution', *Archaeozoologia* 3, 191–200.

Grigson, C. 1987 'Different herding strategies for sheep and goats in the chalcolithic of Beersheva', *Archaeozoologia* 1, 115–26.

Grüss, J. 1933 'Über Milchreste aus der Hallstattzeit und andere Funde', *Forschungen und Fortschritte* 9, 105–6.

Guyan, W. U. 1971 *Erforschte Vergangenheit* (Band 1), Schaffhausen: Verlag Peter Meili.

Hänsel, B. 1968 *Beiträge zur Chronologie der mittleren Bronzezeit im Karpathenbecken*, Bonn: Rudolf Habelt.

Hänsel, B. and Zimmer, S. (eds) 1994 *Die Indogermanen und das Pferd*, Budapest: Archaeolingua.

Häusler, A. 1976 *Die Gräber der älteren Ockergrabkultur zwischen Dnepr und Karpathen*, Berlin: Akademie-Verlag.

Häusler, A. 1984 'Neue Belege zur Geschichte von Rad und Wagen im nordpontischen Raum', *Ethnographisch-Archäologische Zeitschrift* 25, 629–82.

Haggett, P. 1965 *Locational Analysis in Human Geography*, London: Arnold.

Hahn, E. 1896 *Die Haustiere und ihre Beziehungen zur Wirtschaft des Menschen*, Berlin: Duncker and Humblot.

Hald, M. 1950 *Olddanske Tekstiler* (Nordiske Fortidsminder 5), Copenhagen: Kongelige Nordiske-Oldskriftselskab.

Halstead, P. 1981 'Counting sheep in Neolithic and Bronze Age Greece', pp. 307–39 in Hodder et al. (eds) *Pattern of the Past: studies in honour of David L. Clarke*, Cambridge: Cambridge University Press.

Halstead, P. 1995 'Plough and power: the economic and social significance of cultivation with the ox-drawn ard in the Mediterranean', *Bulletin on Sumerian Agriculture* 8, 11–22.

Hamilton, F. E. I. 1967 'Models of industrial location', pp. 361–424 in R. J.

Chorley and P. Haggett (eds) *Models in Geography*, London: Methuen.

Harding, A. 1984 *The Mycenaeans and Europe*, London: Academic Press.

Harlan, J. R. 1975 *Crops and Man*, Madison, Wisconsin: American Society of Agronomy.

Harner, M. 1970 'Population pressure and the social evolution of agriculturalists', *Southwestern Journal of Anthropology* 26, 67–86.

Harner, M. J. 1973 *Hallucinogens and Shamanism*, Oxford: Oxford University Press.

Harris, D. R. 1973 'The prehistory of tropical agriculture: an ethnoecological model', pp. 391–417 in A. C. Renfrew (ed.) *The Explanation of Culture Change*, London: Duckworth.

Harris, D. R. 1978 'The agricultural foundations of lowland Maya civilization: a critique', pp. 301–23 in P. D. Harrison and B. L. Turner (eds) *Prehispanic Maya Agriculture*, Albuquerque: University of New Mexico Press.

Harris, D. (ed.) 1994 *The Archaeology of V. Gordon Childe: contemporary perspectives*, London: University College Press.

Harris, M. 1966 'The cultural ecology of India's sacred cattle', *Current Anthropology* 7, 51–9.

Harrison, R. 1980 *The Beaker Folk*, London: Thames and Hudson.

Harrison, R. 1985 'The "Polycultivo Ganadero" or Secondary Products Revolution in Spanish agriculture, 5000–1000 BC', *Proceedings of the Prehistoric Society* 33, 84–106.

Hártanyi, B. P. and Nóvaki, G. 1975 'Samen- und Fruchtfunde in Ungarn von der Neusteinzeit bis zum 18. Jahrhundert', *Agrartörteneti Szemle* 17, 1–65, 1967.

Hartley, D. 1964 *Water in England*, London: Macdonald.

Hartmann, A. 1978 'Ergebnisse der spektralanalytischen Untersuchung äneolithischer Goldfunde aus Bulgarien', *Studia Praehistorica* (Sofia) 1/2, 27–45.

Hartmann, A. 1982 *Goldfunde aus Europa II* (SAM 5), Berlin: Gebr. Mann.

Hartmann, F. 1923 *L'Agriculture dans l'ancienne Egypte*, Paris: Libraries-Imprimeries Réunies.

Harvey, D. 1967 'Models of the evolution of spatial patterns in human geography', pp. 549–608 in R. J. Chorley and P. Haggett (eds) *Models in Geography*, London: Methuen.

Hassan, F. and Robinson, S. 1987 'High precision radiocarbon chronometry of ancient Egypt and comparisons with Nubia, Palestine and Mesopotamia', *Antiquity* 61, 119–35.

Hatt, G. 1953 'Farming of non-European peoples', pp. 115–234 in E. C. Curwen and G. Hatt *Plough and Pasture: the early history of farming*, New York: Collier Books.

Hawkes, C. F. C. and Smith, M. 1957 'On some buckets and cauldrons of the Bronze and Early Iron Ages', *Antiquaries Journal* 37, 131–98.

Hawkes, J. J. 1982 *Mortimer Wheeler: Adventurer in Archaeology*, London: Weidenfeld and Nicolson.

Hayen, H. 1983 'Handwerklich-technische Lösungen im vor- und frühgeschicht-lichen Wagenbau', pp. 415–70 in H. Jankuhn, W. Jansen, R. Schmidt-Wiegand and H. Tiefenbach (eds) *Das Handwerk in vor- und frühgeschichtlicher Zeit*, Teil 2 (Abhandlungen der Akademie der Wissenschaften in Göttingen), Göttingen.

Herodotus of Halicarnassus [Penguin Classics edition] 1954 *The Histories* (trans. A.-de Selincourt, revised by A. R. Burn), Harmondsworth: Penguin Books.

Herre, W. and Röhrs, M. 1977 'Zoological considerations on the origins of farming and domestication', pp. 263–7 in C. Reed (ed.) *Origins of Agriculture*, The Hague/Paris: Mouton.

Hesse, B. 1982 'Slaughter patterns and domestication: the beginnings of pastoralism in western Iran', *Man* 17, 403–17.

Hesse, B. 1984 'These are our goats: the origins of herding in west-central Iran', pp. 243–64 in J. Clutton-Brock and C. Grigson (eds) *Animals and Archaeology: 3. Early Herders and their Flocks* (BAR Int. Ser. 202), Oxford: British Archaeological Reports.

Hibbs, J. 1983 'The Neolithic of Brittany and Normandy', pp. 271–323 in C. Scarre (ed.) *Ancient France 6000–2000 BC*, Edinburgh: Edinburgh University Press.

Higgins, R. 1979 *The Aegina Treasure: an archaeological mystery*, London: British Museum Publications.

Higgs, E. S. (ed.) 1972 *Papers in Economic Prehistory*, Cambridge: Cambridge University Press.

Higgs, E. S. and Jarman, M. R. 1969 'The origins of agriculture: a reconsideration', *Antiquity* 43, 31–41.

Higham, C. and Message, M. A. 1969 'An assessment of a prehistoric technique of bovine husbandry', pp. 315–30 in D. Brothwell and E. S. Higgs (eds) *Science in Archaeology* (2nd edn), London: Thames and Hudson.

Hill, C., Hilton, R. H. and Hobsbawm, E. J. 1983 'Past and Present: origins and early years', *Past and Present* 100, 3.

Hillebrand, J. 1937 'Der Stand der Erforschung der älteren Steinzeit in Ungarn', *24/25 Bericht der Römisch-Germanischen Kommission 1934/5*, 16–26.

Hobhouse, H. 1985 *Five Plants that Transformed Mankind*, London: Sidgwick and Jackson.

Hobsbawm, E. 1983 'Mass-Producing Traditions: Europe, 1870–1914', pp. 263–307 in E. J. Hobsbawm and T. O. Ranger (eds) *The Invention of Tradition*, Cambridge: Cambridge University Press.

Hodder, I. 1982a (ed.) *Symbolic and Structural Archaeology*, Cambridge: Cambridge University Press.

Hodder, I. A. 1982b *Symbols in Action*, Cambridge: Cambridge University Press.

Hodder, I. A. 1982c 'Sequences of structural change in the Dutch Neolithic', pp. 162–77 in I. A. Hodder (ed.) *Symbolic and Structural Archaeology*, Cambridge: Cambridge University Press.

Hodder, I. 1984 'Burials, houses, women and men in the European Neolithic', pp. 51–68 in D. Miller and C. Tilley (eds) *Ideology, Power and Prehistory*, Cambridge: Cambridge University Press.

Hodder, I. 1988 'Material culture texts and social change: a theoretical discussion and some archaeological examples', *Proceedings of the Prehistoric Society* 54, 67–75.

Hodder, I. 1990 *The Domestication of Europe*, Oxford: Blackwell.

Hoddinott, R. F. 1981 *The Thracians*, London: Thames and Hudson.

Höckmann, O. 1972 'Andeutungen zu Religion und Kultus in der Bandkeramischen Kultur', *Alba Regia* 12, 187–209.

Höneisen, M. 1989 'Die jungsteinzeitlichen Räder der Schweiz: die ältesten Europas', pp. 13–22 in P. A. Schüle, D. Studer and C. Oechslin (eds) *Das Rad in der Schweiz vom 3. Jt. v. Chr. bis zum Jahr 1850* (Katalog Sonderausstellung Schweizerisches Landesmuseum Zürich, 1989).

Hogbin, H. I. 1951 *Transformation Scene: The changing culture of a New Guinea village*, London: Routledge.

Hole, E. and Flannery, K. 1967 'The prehistory of southwestern Iran: a preliminary report', *Proceedings of the Prehistoric Society* 33, 147–206.

Hopf, M. 1982 *Vor-und frühgeschichtliche Kulturpflanzen aus dem nördlichen Deutschland*, Mainz: Verlag des Römisch-Germanischen Zentralmuseums.

Horton, R. 1976 'Stateless societies in the history of West Africa', pp. 72–113 in J. F. A. Ajayi and M. Crowder (eds) *History of West Africa*, New York: Columbia University Press.

Horwitz, L. K. and Tchernov, E. 1989 'Animal exploitation in the Early Bronze Age of the southern Levant: an overview', in P. de Miroschedji (ed.) *L'Urbanisation de la Palestine à l'âge du bronze ancien* (BAR Int. Ser. 527ii), Oxford: British Archaeological Reports.

Houlder, C. H. 1961 'The excavation of a Neolithic stone implement factory on Mynydd Rhiw, Caernarvonshire', *Proceedings of the Prehistoric Society* 27, 108–43.

Howell, J. M. 1982 'Neolithic Settlement and Economy in Northern France', *Oxford Journal of Archaeology* 1, 115–18.

Howell, J. M. 1983 *Settlement and Economy in Neolithic Northern France* (BAR Int. Ser. 157), Oxford: British Archaeological Reports.

Hüttel, H.-G. 1981 *Bronzezeitliche Trensen in Mittel- und Osteuropa: Grundzüge ihrer Entwicklung* (Prähistorische Bronzefunde XVI, 2), Munich: Beck.

Hughes, I. A. 1973 'Stone-age trade in the New Guinea inland', pp. 97–126 in H. C. Brookfield (ed.) *The Pacific in Transition*, London: E. Arnold.

Huxley, J. 1953 *Evolution in Action*, New York: Harper and Row.

Huysecom, E. 1986 'La question des bouteilles à collerette: identification et chronologie d'un groupe méridionale répandu de l'Ukraine à la Bretagne', *Révue archéologique de l'Ouest*, Supplement No. 1, 195–215.

Ihrig, D., Károlyi, Z. S. and Vázsonyi, A. 1973 *A Magyar Vizszabályozás Története*, Budapest: Vizdok.

Illés, A. E. and Halász, A. 1926 *La Hongrie avant et après la Guerre*, Budapest: Société Hongroise de Statistique.

Ingold, T. 1980 *Hunters, Pastoralists and Ranchers*, Cambridge: Cambridge University Press.

Ingold, T. 1986 *Evolution and Social Life*, Cambridge: Cambridge University Press.

Izbitzer, I. 1993 [in Russian] *Wheeled-vehicle Burials of the Steppe Zone of Eastern Europe and the Northern Caucasus, 3rd [4th] to 2nd Millennium* BC, Summary of Doctoral thesis, St Petersburg.

Jacob-Friesen, K. H. 1959 *Einführung in Niedersachsens Urgeschichte*, Hildesheim: August Lax, Verlagsbuchhandlung.

Jacobs, J. 1969 *The Economy of Cities*, Harmondsworth: Penguin Books.

Jankowska, D. 1980 *Kultura Pucharów Lejkowatych na Pomorzu Srodkowym*, Poznán: Adam Mickiewicz University.

Jankowska, D. (ed.) 1990 (vol. 1) and 1991 (vol. 2) *Die Trichterbecherkultur: neue Forschungen und Hypothesen*, Poznań: Adam Mickiewicz University.

Jankowska, D. and Wiślański, T. 1991 'Trichterbecherkultur im Polnischen Tiefland: die wichtigsten Forschungsprobleme', pp. 53–65 in Jankowska (1991).

Jankuhn, H. 1969 *Deutsche Agrargeschichte: Vor- und Frühgeschichte*, Stuttgart: Verlag Eugen Ulmer.

Jarman, M. R. 1971 'Culture and economy in the north Italian Neolithic', *World Archaeology* 2, 255–65.

Jażdżewski, K. 1984 *Urgeschichte Mitteleuropas*, Warsaw: Ossolineum.

Jensen, J. 1982 *The Prehistory of Denmark*, London: Methuen.

Jodłowski, A. 1971 *Eksploatacja soli na terenie Małopolski w pradziejach i we wczesnym średniowieczu*, Krakow: Muzeum żup Krakowskich Wieliczka.

Jordanov, J. and Michailova, K. 1984 'Anthropologische Daten aus zwei Nekropolen der Ockergrabkultur in Nordostbulgarien', *Studia Praehistorica* (Sofia) 7, 117–30.

Joussaume, R. 1985 *Les dolmens pour les morts*, Paris: Hachette; tr. (1988) as *Dolmens for the Dead*, London: Batsford.

Joussaume, R. 1986 'La néolithisation du Centre-Ouest', pp. 161–80 in Demoule and Guilaine 1986.

Jovanović, B. 1971 *Metalurgija Eneolitskog Perioda Jugoslavje*, Belgrade: Archaeological Institute.

Jovanović, B. 1982 *Rudna Glava: najstarija rudarstvo bakra na centralnom Balkanu*, Belgrade: Jugoslav Academy of Sciences.

Joy, L. 1967 'An economic homologue of Barth's presentation of economic spheres in Darfur', pp. 175–89 in J. Firth (ed.) *Themes in Economic Anthropology* (ASA Monographs No. 6), London: Tavistock.

Junghans, S., Sangmeister, E. and Schröder, M. 1960 *Metallanalysen kupferzeitlicher und frühbronzezeitlicher Bodenfunde aus Europa*, Berlin: Mann.

Junghans, S., Sangmeister, E. and Schröder, M. 1968 *Kupfer und Bronze in der frühen Metallzeit Europas*, Berlin: Mann.

Kaczanowska, M. 1980 'Uwagi o surowcach, technice i typologii przemysłu krzemiennego kultury Bodrogkeresztúrskiej i grupy Lažňany', *Acta Archaeologia Carpathica* 20, 19–56.

Kaczanowska, M. 1985 'Rohstoffe, Technik und Typologie der Neolithischen Feuersteinindustrien im Nordteil des Flußgebietes der Mitteldonau', Warszawa: Państwowe Wydawnictwo Naukowe.

Kaczanowska, M., Kozłowski, J. and Makkay, J. 1981 'Flint hoard from Endröd Site 39, Hungary (Körös culture)', *Acta Archaeologica Carpathica* 21, 105–17.

Kahlke, D. 1954 *Die Bestattungssitten des Donauländischen Kulturkreises der jüngeren Steinzeit*, Berlin: Rütten and Loening.

Kalicz, N. 1957 'Tiszazug Öskori Települései', *Régészeti Füzetek* 8, 1–102.

Kalicz, N. 1963 *Die Péceler (Badener) Kultur und Anatolien* (Studia Archaeologica 2), Budapest: Akadémiai Kiadó.

Kalicz, N. 1965 'Siedlungsgeschichtliche Probleme der Körös- und der Theiss-Kultur', *Acta Antiqua et Archaeologica* (Szeged) 8, 27–40.

Kalicz, N. 1968 *Die Frühbronzezeit in Nordost-Ungarn* (Archaeologia Hungarica 45), Budapest: Akadémiai Kiadó.

Kalicz, N. 1970 *Clay Gods. The Neolithic Period and Copper Age in Hungary*, Budapest: Corvina Press.

Kalicz, N. 1976 'Ein neues kupferzeitliches Wagenmodell aus der Umgebung von Budapest', *Festschrift für Richard Pittioni zum siebzigsten Geburtstag*, Vienna: Deuticke.

Kalicz, N. 1980 'Neuere Forschungen über die Entstehung des Neolithikums in Ungarn', pp. 97–122 in J. K. Kozłowski and J. Machnik (eds) *Problèmes de la*

Néolithisation dans certaines Régions de l'Europe, Wrocaw-Warsaw-Krakow-Gdansk: Ossolineum.

Kalicz, N. and Makkay, J. 1972 'Probleme des frühen Neolithikums der nördlichen Tiefebene', *Alba Regia* 12, 77–92 [also reprinted as *Aktuelle Probleme der Bandkeramik*, Székesfehérvár: County Fejer Museum].

Kalicz, N. and Makkay, J. 1977a 'Frühneolithische Siedlung in Méhtelek-Nadas', *Mitteilungen des Archaeologischen Instituts der Ungarischen Akademie der Wissenschaften* 6, 13–34.

Kalicz, N. and Makkay, J. 1977b *Die Linienbandkeramik in der Grossen Ungarischen Tiefebene* (Studia Archaeologica 7), Budapest: Akadémiai Kiadó.

Kalis, A. J. 1988 'Zur Umwelt des frühneolithischen Menschen: ein Beitrag der Pollenanalyse', pp. 125–38 in H. J. Küster (ed.) *Der Prähistorische Mensch und seine Umwelt* (Festschrift U. Körber-Grohne), Forschungen und Berichte zur Ur- und Frühgeschichte in Baden-Württemberg 31.

Kaplan, J. 1969 'Ein el Jarba', *Bulletin of the American School of Oriental Research* 194, 2–39 and Plate VII.

Karageorghis, V. 1982 *Cyprus from the Stone Age to the Romans*, London: Thames and Hudson.

Keesing, R. M. 1975 *Kin Groups and Social Structure*, New York: Holt Reinhart Winston.

Khazanov, A. M. 1984 *Nomads and the Outside World*, Cambridge: Cambridge University Press.

Killen, J. T. 1964 'The wool industry of Crete in the late Bronze Age', *Annual of the British School of Archaeology at Athens* 59, 1–15.

Kinnes, I. 1982 'Les Fouaillages and megalithic origins', *Antiquity* 6, 24–30.

Kirk, G. S. 1970 *Myth: its meaning and functions in ancient and other cultures*, Cambridge: Cambridge University Press.

Kirkby, A. V. T. 1973 'The use of land and water-resources in the past and present Valley of Oaxaca, Mexico', *Memoirs of the Museum of Anthropology at the University of Michigan 5*.

Kirnbauer, F. 1958 'Das jungsteinzeitliche Hornsteinbergwerk Mauer bei Wien', *Archaeologia Austriaca* Beiheft 3, 121–42.

Kisban, E. 1969 'Die historische Bedeutung des Joghurts in den Milchverarbeit-ungssystemen Südosteuropas', pp. 517–30 in L. Földes (ed.) *Viehwirtschaft und Hirtenkultur*, Budapest: Akadémiai Kiadó.

Kislev, M. E. and Bar-Yosef, O. 1988 'The legumes: earliest domesticated plants in the Near East?', *Current Anthropology* 29(1), 175–8.

Klages, E. 1949 *Ecological Crop Geography*, London and New York: Macmillan.

Klebs, L. 1915 *Die Reliefs des alten Reiches*, Heidelberg: Abhandlungen der Heidelberger Akademie der Wissenschaften.

Klejn, L. 1994 'Childe and Soviet archaeology: a romance', pp. 75–100 in Harris 1994.

Knöll, H. 1976 'Frühneolithische Flaschengefässe des Nordens', *Berichte der Römisch-Germanischen Kommission* 57, 1–48.

Knöll, H. 1981 'Kragenflaschen: ihre Verbreitung und ihre Zeitstellung im europäischen Neolithikum', Neumünster: Wachholz.

Koebner, L. 1966 'The settlement and colonization of Europe', pp. 1–90 in M. M. Postan (ed.) *Cambridge Economic History of Europe, vol. 1, The Agrarian Life of the Middle Ages*, Cambridge: Cambridge University Press.

Körber-Grohne, U. 1985 'Die biologischen Reste aus dem hallstattzeitlichen

Fürstengrab von Hochdorf, Gemeinde Eberdingen (Kreis Ludwigsburg)', pp. 87–162 in *Hochdorf* 1 (Forschungen und Berichte zur Vor- und Frühgeschichte in Baden-Württemberg 19).

Körner, G. and Laux, F. 1980 *Ein Königreich an der Luhe*, Lüneburg: Museumsverein für das Fürstentum Lüneburg.

Kohl, P. 1987 'The ancient economy, transferable technologies and the Bronze Age world-system: a view from the northeastern frontier of the Ancient Near East', pp. 13–24 in M. Rowlands, M. T. Larsen and K. Kristiansen (eds) *Centre and Periphery in the Ancient World*, Cambridge: Cambridge University Press.

Kohl, P. 1989 'The use and abuse of world systems theory: the case of the "pristine" West Asian state', pp. 218–40 in C. C. Lamberg-Karlovsky (ed.) *Archaeological Thought in America*, Cambridge: Cambridge University Press.

Korek, J. 1951 'Ein Gräberfeld der Badener Kultur bei Alsónémedi', *Acta Archaeologica Academiae Scientiarum Hungaricae* 1, 35–91.

Korek, J. and Patay, P. 1956 'A Herpályi-hálom kökorvégi es rézkori települése', *Folia Archaeologica* 8, 23–42.

Kośko, A. 1980 'The position of funnel beaker culture in the lowland model of Neolithisation', pp. 144–77 in J. Kozłowski and J. Machnik (eds) *Problèmes de la Néolithisation dans certaines Régions de L'Europe*, Warsaw: Ossolineum.

Kossack, G. 1964 'Trinkgeschirr als Kultgerät der Hallstattzeit', pp. 96–105 in P. Grimm (ed.) *Varia Archaeologica: Wilhelm Unverzagt zum 70. Geburtstag dargebracht*, Berlin: Akademie Verlag.

Kosse, K. 1979 *Settlement Ecology of the Körös and Linear Pottery Cultures in Hungary* (BAR Int. Ser. 64), Oxford: British Archaeological Reports.

Kossinna, G. 1941 (1st edn 1912) *Die Deutsche Vorgeschichte, eine hervorragend nationale Wissenschaft*, Würzburg: Johann Umbrosius Barth, Verlag.

Kothe, H. 1953 'Völkerkundliches zur Frage der Neolithischen Anbauformen', *Archaeologisch-Ethnographische Forschungen* 1, 28–73.

Kovacs, T. 1969 'A Százhalombattai Bronzkori telep', *Archaeologiai Értesitö* 96, 161–9.

Kowalczyk, J. 1970 'The Funnel Beaker culture', pp. 144–77 in T. Wiślański (ed.) *The Neolithic in Poland*, Warsaw: Ossolineum.

Kraus, F. R. 1966 *Staatliche Viehhaltung im altbabylonischen Lande Larsa* (Mededelingen der Koninklijke Nederlandse Akademie van Wetenschappen), Amsterdam: N. V. Noord-Hollandsche.

Kretchmer, N. 1972 'Lactose and lactase', *Scientific American* 227, 70–9.

Kristiansen, K. 1981 'Economic models for Bronze Age Scandinavia: towards an integrated approach', pp. 239–303 in A. Sheridan and G. Bailey (eds) *Economic Archaeology: towards an integration of ecological and social approaches* (BAR Int. Ser. 96), Oxford: British Archaeological Reports.

Kristiansen, K. 1982 'The formation of tribal systems in later European prehistory: Northern Europe 4000–500 BC', pp. 241–80 in C. Renfrew, M. J. Rowlands and B. A. Seagrave (eds) *Theory and Explanation in Archaeology*, New York: Academic Press.

Kristiansen, K. 1984 'Ideology and material culture: an archaeological perspective', pp. 72–100 in M. Spriggs (ed.) *Marxist Perspectives in Archaeology*, Cambridge: Cambridge University Press.

Kristiansen, K. 1987 'From Stone to Bronze: the evolution of social complexity in northern Europe, 2300–1200 BC', in E. M. Brumfiel and T. K. Earle (eds) *Specialisation, Exchange and Complex Societies*, Cambridge: Cambridge University Press.

Kristiansen, K. 1989 'Ard marks under barrows: a response to Peter Rowly-Conwy', *Antiquity* 63, 322–7.

Kruk, J. 1973 *Studia Oszadnicze nad Neolitem Wyżyn Lessowych*, Warsaw: Ossolineum.

Kruk, J. 1980a *Gospodarka w Polsce Poludniowo-wschodniej w V–III Tysiacleciu P. N. E.*, Warsaw: Ossolineum. (Translated as Kruk 1980b.)

Kruk, J. 1980b *The Neolithic Settlement of southern Poland* (edited by J. M. Howell and N. J. Starling) (BAR Int. Ser. 93), Oxford: British Archaeological Reports.

Kruk, J. and Milisauskas, S. 1981 'Chronology of Funnel Beaker, Baden-like and Lublin-Volynian settlements at Bronocice, Poland', *Germania* 59, 1–19.

Kühn, H. 1976 *Geschichte der Vorgeschichtsforschung*, Berlin: Verlag Walter de Gruyter.

Kutzián, I. See also Bognár-Kutzián, I.

Kutzián, I. 1944 *A Körös-Kultúra/The Körös Culture* (Dissertationes Pannonicae II, 23), Budapest: Pétér Pázmány-Universität.

Kuz'mina, E. E. 1974 'Kolesnii transport i problema etnicheskoi i sotsialnoi istorii drevnego naseleniya Yuzhnorusskikh Stepei', *Vestnik Drevnei Istorii* 4, 68–87.

Kyle, R. 1972 'Will the antelope recapture Africa?', *New Scientist* 23.

La Barre, W. 1972 'Hallucinogens and the shamanic origins of religion', pp. 261–79 in P. Furst (ed.) *Flesh of the Gods*, New York: Praeger.

La Niece, S. 1983 'Niello: an historical and technical survey', *Antiquaries Journal* 63, 279–97.

Lamberg-Karlovsky, C. and Lamberg-Karlovsky, M. 1971 'An early city in Iran', *Scientific American* (June 1971).

Lamberg-Karlovsky, C. C. and Beale, T. W. 1986 *Excavations at Tepe Yahya, Iran, 1967–1975: the early periods* (American School of Prehistoric Research Bulletin 38), Cambridge Mass.: Peabody Museum.

Lambrick, H. T. 1964 *Sind: a General Introduction*, Hyderabad: Sindhi Adabi Board.

Lanting, J. N., Mook, W. G. and van der Waals, J. D. 1973 'C14 Chronology and the Beaker problem', *Helinium* 13, 38–58.

Lathrap, D. 1968 'The "hunting" economies of the tropical zone of South America', pp. 23–9 in R. B. Lee and I. DeVore 1968.

Leach, E. R. 1959 'Hydraulic society in Ceylon', *Past and Present* 15, 2–25.

Leach, E. 1961 *Rethinking Anthropology*, London: Athlone Press.

Leach, E. 1976 *Culture and Communication: the logic by which symbols are connected*, Cambridge: Cambridge University Press.

Leach, E. and Aycock, D. A. 1983 *Structuralist Interpretations of Biblical Myth*, Cambridge: Cambridge University Press.

Lech, J. 1987 'Danubian raw material distribution patterns in eastern central Europe', pp. 241–8 in G. Sieveking and M. Newcomer (eds) *The Human Uses of Flint and Chert*, Cambridge: Cambridge University Press.

Lech, J. and Leligdowicz, A. 1980 'Die Methoden der Versorgung mit Feuerstein und die lokalen Beziehungen zwischen den Siedlungen und Berwerken im Weichselgebiet während des 5. bis 2. Jt. v.u.Z.', pp. 151–84 in F. Schlette (ed.) *Urgeschichtliche Besiedlung in ihrer Beziehung zur natürlichen Umwelt*, Halle:

Wissenschaftliche Beiträge der Martin-Luther Universität Halle-Wittenberg.

Lee, R. B. and DeVore, I. (eds) 1968 *Man the Hunter*, Chicago: Aldine.

Leeds, A. 1969 'Ecological determinants of chieftainship among the Yaruro Indians of Venezuela', pp. 377–94 in A. P. Vayda (ed.) *Environment and Cultural Behaviour*, New York: Natural History Press.

Leeds, A. and Vayda, A. (eds) 1965 *Man, Culture and Animals*, Washington: American Association for the Advancement of Science.

Lees, S. H. and Bates, D. G. 1974 'The origins of specialised nomadic pastoralism; a systemic model', *American Antiquity* 39, 187–93.

Legge, A. J. 1981 'Aspects of cattle husbandry' in R. Mercer (ed.) *Farming Practice in British Prehistory*, Edinburgh: Edinburgh University Press.

Le Roux, C-T. 1985 'New excavations at Gavrinis', *Antiquity* 49, 183–7.

Leser, P. 1931 *Entstehung und Verbreitung des Pfluges*, Münster: Aschendorff.

Leshnik, L. S. 1973 'Land-use and ecological factors in prehistoric north-west India', pp. 62–84 in N. Hammond (ed.) *South Asian Archaeology*, London: Duckworth.

Levine, M. 1990 'Dereivka and the problem of horse domestication', *Antiquity* 64, 727–40.

Levy, T. 1983 'The emergence of specialised pastoralism in the southern Levant', *World Archaeology* 15(1), 15–36.

Levy, T. 1992 'Transhumance, subsistence, and social evolution in the northern Negev desert', pp. 65–82 in O. Bar-Yosef and A. Khazanov (eds) *Pastoralism in the Levant: archaeological materials in anthropological perspective*, Madison, Wisconsin: Prehistory Press.

Lewicka, A. 1972 'Brandwirtschaft und Brandrodung in den Polnischen Karpathen', pp. 119–42 in I. Balassa (ed.) *Getreidebau in Ost- und Mitteleuropa*, Budapest: Akadémiai Kiadó.

Lewthwaite, J. 1981a 'Ambiguous first impressions: a survey of recent work on the early Neolithic of the West Mediterranean', *Journal of Mediterranean Archaeology* 1, 292–307.

Lewthwaite, J. 1981b 'Plains tails from the hills: transhumance in Mediterranean archaeology', pp. 57–66 in A. Sheridan and G. Bailey (eds) *Economic Archaeology: towards an integration of ecological and social approaches* (BAR Int. Ser. 96), Oxford: British Archaeological Reports.

Lewthwaite, J. 1984 'The art of Corse herding: archaeological insights from recent pastoral practices on west Mediterranean islands', pp. 25–37 in J. Clutton-Brock and C. Grigson (eds) *Animals and Archaeology: 3. Early Herders and their Flocks* (BAR Int. Ser. 202), Oxford: British Archaeological Reports.

L'Helgouach, J. and Le Roux, C-T. 1986 'Morphologie et chronologie des grandes architectures de l'Ouest de la France', pp. 181–91 in Demoule and Guilaine 1986.

Lichardus, J. 1974 *Studien zur Bükker Kultur*, Bonn: Habelt.

Lichardus, J. 1980 'Zur Funktion der Geweihspitzen des Typus Ostorf: Ueberlegungen zu einer vorbronzezeitlichen Pferdeschirrung', *Germania* 58, 1–24.

Lisitsina, G. N. 1969 'The earliest irrigation in Turkmenia', *Antiquity* 43, 279–87.

Littauer, M. A. and Crouwel, J. 1973 'Early metal models of wagons from the Levant', *Levant* 5, 102–26.

Littauer, M. A. and Crouwel, J. 1979 *Wheeled Vehicles and Ridden Animals in the Ancient Near East*, Leiden: Brill.

Littauer, M. A. and Crouwel, J. 1986 'The earliest known three-dimensional evidence for spoked wheels', *American Journal of Archaeology* 90, 395–8.

Lomborg, E. 1973 *Die Flintdolche Dänemarks*, Copenhagen: Lynge.

Lotka, A. J. 1956 *Elements of Mathematical Biology*, New York: Dover.

Lubbock, J. 1870 *The Origin of Civilisation*, London [6th edn 1902, New York: D. Appleton and Co.].

Lüning, J. 1980 'Bandkeramische Pflüge?', *Fundberichte aus Hessen* 19/20 (1979/80), 55–68.

Lüning, J. 1989 'Westliche Nachbarn der bandkeramischen Kultur: La Hoguette und Limburg', *Germania* 67(2), 355–93.

Lüning, J. and Meurers-Balke, J. 1980 'Experimenteller Getreideanbau im Hambacher Forst', *Bonner Jahrbücher* 180, 305–44.

Lüning, J. and Kalis, A. J. 1988 'Die Umwelt prähistorischer Siedlungen – Rekonstruktionen aus siedlungsarchäologischen und botanischen Untersuchungen im Neolithikum', *Siedlungsforschung: Archäologie-Geschichte-Geographie* 6, 39–55.

Lutz, H. F. 1922 *Viticulture and Brewing in the Ancient Orient*, Leipzig: J. C. Hinrichs'sche Buchhandlung.

McCormick, F. 1922 'Early faunal evidence for dairying', *Oxford Journal of Archaeology* 11(2), 201–10.

McCracken, R. D. 1971 'Lactase deficiency: an example of dietary evolution', *Current Anthropology* 12, 479–517.

McDonald, W. A. and Hope-Simpson, R. 1969 'Further explorations in the southwestern Peloponnese', *American Journal of Archaeology* 73, 132.

MacDougall, H. A. 1982 *Racial Myth in English History*, Montreal: Harvest House.

Machnik, J. 1970 'The Corded Ware culture', pp. 383–420 in T. Wiślański (ed.) *The Neolithic in Poland*, Warsaw: Ossolineum.

McNairn, B. 1980 *The Method and Theory of V. Gordon Childe*, Edinburgh: Edinburgh University Press.

Maczek, M., Preuschen, E. and Pittioni, R. 1953 'Beiträge zum Problem des Ursprunges der Kupfererzverwertung in der Alten Welt (II)', *Archaeologia Austriaca* 12, 67–82.

Madsen, T. 1979 'Earthen long barrows and timber structures: aspects of the early Neolithic practice in Denmark', *Proceedings of the Prehistoric Society* 45, 301–20.

Makkay, J. 1957 'A bihari Berettyóvölgy öskori leletei', *A Debreceni Déri Múzeum Evkönyve* (1948–56), 21–40.

Makkay, J. 1982 *A Magyarországi Neolitikum Kutatásának Uj Eredményei*, Budapest: Akadémiai Kiadó.

Malcolm, A. I. 1971 *The Pursuit of Intoxication*, New York: Washington Square Press.

Malinowski, B. 1922 *Argonauts of the Western Pacific*, London: Routledge.

Mallory, J. P. 1976 'The chronology of early Kurgan tradition (part 1)', *Journal of Indo-European Studies* 4, 256–94.

Mallory, J. P. 1977 'The chronology of early Kurgan tradition (part 2)', *Journal of Indo-European Studies* 5, 339–68.

Mallory, J. P. 1989 *In Search of the Indo-Europeans: language, archaeology and myth*, London: Thames and Hudson.

Mallowan, M. 1977 *Mallowan's Memoirs*, London: Collins.

Malmer, M. P. 1962 'Jungneolithische Studien', *Acta Archaeologica Lundensia* 2, Lund, Sweden: CWK Gleerups Förlag.

Manzanilla, L. (ed.) 1987 *Studies in the Neolithic and Urban Revolutions: the V. Gordon Childe Colloquium, Mexico 1986* (BAR Int. Ser. 349), Oxford: British Archaeological Reports.

Marfoe, L. 1981 'Cedar Forest to Silver Mountain: on Metaphors of Growth in Early Syrian Society', paper delivered to the Århus International Conference.

Marfoe, L. 1987 'Cedar Forest to Silver Mountain: social change and the development of long-distance trade in early Near Eastern societies', in Rowlands, Larsen and Kristiansen 1987.

Marx, K. 1859 *Contribution to a Critique of the Political Economy*, London.

Masson, V. M. 1976 'The art of Altyn Depe: the artistic traditions of the urbanised cultures between Sumer and India', pp. 254–62 in J. V. S. Megaw (ed.) *To Illustrate the Monuments*, London: Thames and Hudson.

Masson, V. M. and Sarianidi, V. I. 1972 *Central Asia*, London: Thames and Hudson.

Mateescu, C. N. 1975 'Remarks on cattle breeding and agriculture in the Middle and Late Neolithic on the Lower Danube', *Dacia* 19, 13–18.

Mathiassen, T. 1948 'Studier over Vestjyllands Oldtidsbebyggelse', *Nationalmuseets Skrifter, Ark.-Hist. Ser.* 2.

Mathiassen, T. 1957 'Nordvestsjaellands Oldtidsbebyggelse', *Nationalmuseets Skrifter, Ark.-Hist. Ser.* 7.

Matthäus, H. 1977/78 'Neues zur Bronzetasse aus Dohnsen, Kr. Celle', *Die Kunde* NF 28/29, 51–69.

Matthäus, H. 1980 *Die Bronzegefässe der Kretisch-Mykenischen Kultur* (Prähistorische Bronzefunde II, 1), Munich: Beck.

Matthäus, H. 1985 *Die Metallgefässe und Gefäßuntersetze der Bronzezeit … auf Zypern* (Prähistorische Bronzefunde II, 8), Munich: Beck.

Maurizio, A. 1932 *Histoire de l'Alimentation végétale depuis la Préhistoire jusqu'à nos jours*, Paris: Payot [also German translation *Die Geschichte unserer Pflanzenernährung von der Urzeit bis zur Gegenwart*].

Maurizio, A. 1933 *Geschichte der gegorenen Getränke*, Berlin: Parey.

Mauss, M. 1954 *The Gift*, London: Cohen.

Maxwell-Hyslop, R. 1971 *Western Asiatic Jewellery c.3000–612 BC*, London: Methuen.

Maxwell-Hyslop, R. 1977 'Sources of Sumerian gold', *Iraq* 39, 83–6.

Maxwell-Hyslop, R. 1982 'The Khosh Tapa-Fullol hoard', *Afghan Studies* 3/4, 25–37.

Maxwell-Hyslop, M. 1994 'Discussion' following Mulvaney in Harris 1994, 73.

Meadow, R. H. and Zeder, M. A. (eds) 1978 *Approaches to Faunal Analysis in the Middle East*, Cambridge, Mass.: Peabody Museum, Bulletin 2.

Meadow, R. H. and Uerpmann, H.-P. (eds) *Equids in the Ancient World*, vol. 2, Wiesbaden: Reichert.

Mellaart, J. 1967 *Çatal Hüyük, a Neolithic Town in Anatolia*, London: Thames and Hudson.

Mellaart, J. 1975 *The Neolithic of the Near East*, London: Thames and Hudson.

Menghin, W. and Schauer, P. 1977 *Magisches Gold: Kultgerät der späten Bronzezeit* (Ausstellung des Germanischen Nationalmuseums Nürnberg, 1977, Katalog).

Merhart, G. von 1969 *Hallstatt und Italien: gesammelte Aufsätze zur frühen Eisenzeit in Italien und Mitteleuropa*, Mainz: RGZM.

Merlin, M. D. 1972 *Man and Marijuana*, Rutherford, New Jersey: Fairleigh Dickinson University Press.

Merlin, M. D. 1984 *On the Trail of the Ancient Opium Poppy*, Rutherford, New Jersey: Fairleigh Dickinson University Press.

Merpert, N. I. 1974 *Drevneishie Skotovody Volzhsko-Ural'skogo Mezhdurech'ya*, Moscow: Akademia Nauk.

Merrillees, R. S. 1962 'Opium trade in the Bronze Age Levant', *Antiquity* 36, 287–92.

Mezzena, F. 1981 'La Valle d'Aosta nella preistoria e nella protostoria', pp. 15–50 in *Archaeologia in Valle d'Aosta dal Neolitico alla Caduta dell'Impero Romano 3500 a.v.–V sec.d.c.*, Regione Valle d'Aosta: Assessorato del Turismo Urbanistica e Beni Culturali.

Midgley, M. 1985 *The Origin and Function of the Earthen Long Barrows of Northern Europe* (BAR Int. Ser. 259), Oxford: British Archaeological Reports.

Midgley, M. 1992 *TRB Culture: the first farmers of the North European Plain*, Edinburgh: Edinburgh University Press.

Mikov, V. 1958 *Zlatnoto Sukrovishte ot Vulchitrun*, Sofia: Bulgarian Academy of Sciences.

Milisauskas, S. and Kruk, J. 1978 'Bronocice: a Neolithic settlement in southeastern Poland', *Archaeology* 31, 44–52.

Milisauskas, S. and Kruk, J. 1982 'Die Wagendarstellung auf einem Trichterbecher aus Bronocice in Polen', *Archäologisches Korrespondenzblatt* 12(2), 141–4.

Milisauskas, S. and Kruk, J. 1991 'Utilisation of cattle for traction during the later Neolithic in southeastern Poland', *Antiquity* 65, 562–6.

Milojčić, V. 1943 'Das vorgeschichtliche Bergwerk "Šuplja Stena" am Avalaberg bei Belgrad (Serbien)', *Wiener Prähistorische Zeitschrift* 30, 41–54.

Milojčić, V. 1949 *Chronologie der jüngeren Steinzeit Mittel- und Südosteuropas*, Berlin: DAI.

Milojčić, V. 1953 'Ein Goldfund der Kupferzeit aus Ungarn', *Germania* 31, 7–11.

Modderman, P. J. R. 1970 'Linearbandkeramik aus Elsloo und Stein', *Analecta Praehistorica Leidensia* 3.

Montelius, O. 1899 *Der Orient und Europa*, Stockholm: Herausgegeben von der Königl. Akademie der Schönen Wissenschaften, Geschichte und Alterthumskunde.

Montelius, O. 1903 *Die Typologische Methode* (Die älteren Kulturperioden im Orient und in Europa, 1), Stockholm: Kungl. Boktryckeriet, P. A. Norstedt and Söner.

Montelius, O. 1910 'Handel in der Vorzeit', *Praehistorische Zeitschrift* vol. II, 249–91.

Montesquieu, C. de S. 1941 [1748] *De l'esprit des lois*, Paris: Garnier.

Moorey, P. R. S. 1968 'The earliest Near Eastern spoked wheels and their chronology', *Proceedings of the Prehistoric Society* 34, 430–2.

Moorey, P. R. S. 1970 'Pictorial evidence for the history of horse-riding in Iraq before the Kassite period', *Iraq* 32, 36–50.

Moorey, P. R. S. 1986 'The emergence of the light, horse-drawn chariot in the Near East, c.2000–1500 BC', *World Archaeology* 18(2), 196–215.

Morgan, L. H. 1985 [1877] *Ancient Society, or Researches in the Lines of Human Progress from Savagery, through Barbarism to Civilisation*, Tucson, Arizona:

532

University of Arizona Press.

Morton-Williams, P. 1969 'The influence of habitat and trade on the policies of Oyo and Ashanti', pp. 79–95 in M. Douglas and P. M. Kaberry (eds) *Man in Africa*, London: Methuen.

Moseley, M. 1974 'Organisational preadaptation to irrigation and the evolution of early water management systems in coastal Peru', pp. 77–82 in T. E. Downing and M. Gibson (eds) *Irrigation's Impact on Society*, Tucson: University of Arizona Press.

Mozsolics, A. 1967 *Bronzefunde des Karpathenbeckens*, Budapest: Akadémiai Kiadó.

Mozsolics, A. 1968 'Goldfunde des Depotfundhorizontes von Hadjúsámson', BRGK 46/7 (1965/6), 1–76.

Mozsolics, A. 1973 *Bronze- und Goldfunde des Karpathenbeckens*, Budapest: Akadémiai Kiadó.

Müller, H.-H. 1978 'Tierreste aus einer Siedlung der Bernburger Gruppe bei Halle (Saale)', *Jahresschrift für mitteldeutsche Vorgeschichte* 62, 203–20.

Müller, H.-H. 1985 'Tierreste aus Siedlungsgruben der Bernburger Kultur von der Schalkenburg bei Quenstedt, Kr Hettstedt', *Jahresschrift für mitteldeutsche Vorgeschichte* 68, 179–220.

Müller, H.-H. 1994 'Das domestizierte Pferd in Mitteleuropa', pp. 179–84 in B. Hänsel and S. Zimmer (eds) *Die Indogermanen und das Pferd*, Budapest: Archaeolingua.

Müller-Beck, H. 1965 *Burgäschisee-Süd Teil 5, Holzgeräte und Holzbearbeitung*, Berne: Acta Bernesia.

Müller-Karpe, H. 1968 *Handbuch der Vorgeschichte, II (Jungsteinzeit)*, Frankfurt: Beck.

Müller-Wille, M. 1965 *Eisenzeitliche Fluren in den festländischen Nordseege-bieten*, Münster (Westfalen): Landeskundliche Karten und Hefte der Geographischen Kommission für Westfalen.

Mulvaney, J. 1994 ' "Another university man gone wrong": V. Gordon Childe 1892–1922' in Harris 1994, 55–74.

Murdock, G. P. 1967 *Ethnographic Atlas*, Pittsburgh: Pittsburgh University Press.

Murray, J. 1970 *The First European Agriculture*, Edinburgh: Edinburgh University Press.

Murray, O. 1982 'Symposion and Männerbund', *Concilium Eirene* 16, 47–52.

Murray, O. 1983 'The Symposion as social organisation', pp. 195–200 in Robin Hägg (ed.) *The Greek Renaissance of the Eighth century* BC: *Tradition and innovation* (Proceedings of the Second International Symposium at the Swedish Institute in Athens) Skrifta udgivna av Svenska Institutet i Athen, Quarto series 30.

Myres, J. L. 1906 (ed.) *The Evolution of Culture and other Essays by the late Lt. Gen. A. Lane-Fox Pitt-Rivers*, Oxford: Oxford University Press.

Myres, J. L. 1911 *The Dawn of History*, London: Thornton Butterworth.

Myres, J. L. 1935a 'The ethnology, habitat, linguistic and common culture of Indo-Europeans up to the time of the migrations', pp. 179–244 in E. Eyre (ed.) *European Civilisation: its Origin and Development*, Oxford: Oxford University Press.

Myres, J. L. 1935b 'The ethnology and primitive culture of the Nearer East and the Mediterranean world', pp. 83–177 in E. Eyre (ed.) *European Civilisation: its Origin and Development*, Oxford: Oxford University Press.

Myres, J. N. L. 1980 *Commander J. L. Myres, R.N.V.R.: the Blackbeard of the Mediterranean*, 10th Myres Memorial Lecture, London: Leopard's Head Press.

Nagel, E. 1985 *Die Erscheinung der Kugelamforenkultur im Norden der DDR*, Berlin: VEB Deutscher Verlag der Wissenschaften.

Nandris, J. 1973 'Some light on prehistoric Europe', pp. 151–61 in D. Strong (ed.) *Archaeological Theory and Practice*, London: Academic Press.

Narr, K. J. 1962 'Frühe Pflüge', *Mitteilungen der Anthropologischen Gesellschaft in Wien* 92, 221.

Nash, D. M. 1978 'Territory and state formation in central Gaul', pp. 455–76 in D. Green, C. Haselgrove and M. Spriggs (eds) *Social Organisation and Settlement* (BAR Int. Ser. 47), Oxford: British Archaeological Reports.

Needham, J. 1970 *Clerks and Craftsmen in China and the West*, Cambridge: Cambridge University Press.

Nekhaev, A. A. 1986 'Pogrebenie Maikopskoi kul'tury iz kurgana u sela Krasnogvardeiskoe', *Sovetskaya Arkhaeologiya* 1986(1), 244–8.

Nelson, C. M. 1973 'Prehistoric culture change in the intermontane plateau of western North America', pp. 371–90 in A. C. Renfrew (ed.) *The explanation of culture change: models in prehistory*, London: Duckworth.

Nemejcová-Pavúková, V. 1973 'Zu Ursprung und Chronologie der Boleraz-Gruppe', pp. 297–316 in B. Chrpovsky (ed.) *Symposium über die Entstehung der Badener Kultur*, Bratislava: Slovak Academy of Sciences Press.

Nepper, I. 1970 'Megjegyzések a Körös csoport eszközkészletének vizsgálatához', *A Debreceni Déri Múzeum Évkönyve* 1968, 79–109.

Neuninger, H. and Pittioni, R. 1963 'Frühmetallzeitlicher Kupferhandel im Voralpenland', *Archaeologia Austriaca* Beiheft 6, 1–39.

Neustupny, E. and Neustupny, J. 1961 *Czechoslovakia before the Slavs*, London: Thames and Hudson.

Newell, R. 1972 'The Mesolithic affinities and typological relations of the Dutch Bandkeramik flint industry', *Alba Regia* 12, 9–38.

Nissen, H.-J. 1987 'The chronology of the Proto- and Early Historic periods in Mesopotamia and Susiana', pp. 607–13 in Aurenche et al. 1987.

Nissen, H.-J., Damerow, P. and Englund, R. K. 1990 *Frühe Schrift und Techniken der Wirtschaftsverwaltung im alten Vorderen Orient: Informationsspeicherung und -verarbeitung vor 5000 Jahren*, Berlin: Verlag Franzbecker.

Nobis, G. 1971 *Vom Wildpferd zum Hauspferd* (Fundamenta, Reine B, 6), Cologne: Böhlau.

O'Shea, J. M. 1978 *Mortuary Variability: an Archaeological Investigation with Case Studies from the Nineteenth Century Central Plains of North America and the Early Bronze Age of Southern Hungary* (unpublished Ph.D. thesis, University of Cambridge).

O'Shea, J. M. 1984 *Mortuary Variability: an archaeological investigation*, New York: Academic Press.

Oates, D. and Oates, J. 1976 'Early irrigation agriculture in Mesopotamia', pp. 109–36 in G. Sieveking, I. Longworth and K. Wilson (eds) *Problems in Economic and Social Archaeology*, London: Duckworth.

Oates, J. 1980 'Land use and population in prehistoric Mesopotamia', pp. 303–14 in M.-T. Barrelet (ed.) *L'Archéologie de l'Iraq du Début de l'Epoque Néolithique à 333 avant notre ère*, Paris: CNRS.

Oates, J. 1987 'Ubaid chronology', pp. 473–81 in Aurenche et al. 1987.

Ørsnes, M. 1956 'Om en Jaettestues konstruktion og bruk', *Aarbøger for Nordisk*

Oldkyndighed og Historie 1952, 221–34.

Otto, H. and Witter, W. 1952 *Handbuch der ältesten vorgeschichtlichen Metallurgie in Mitteleuropa*, Leipzig: Barth Verlag.

Ovadia, E. 1992 'The domestication of the ass and pack animals: a case of technological change', pp. 19–28 in O. Bar-Yosef and A. Khazanov (eds) *Pastoralism in the Levant: archaeological materials in anthropological perspective*, Madison, Wisconsin: Prehistory Press.

Pätzold, J. 1960 'Rituelles Pflügen bei dem vorgeschichtlichen Totenkult', *Prähistorische Zeitschrift* 37, 189–239.

Panayotov, I. 1980 'Bronze rapiers, swords, and double axes from Bulgaria', *Thracia* 5, 173–98.

Panayotov, I. and Dergachov, V. 1984 'Die Ockergrabkultur in Bulgarien (Darstellung des Problems)', *Studia Praehistorica* (Sofia), 7, 99–116.

Papp, A. 1969 'Körösvidek: a felszin kialakulása és mai képe', pp. 270–4 in M. Pécsi *A tiszai Alföld*, Budapest: Akadémiai Kiadó.

Park, C. F. and Macdiarmid, R. A. 1970 *Ore Deposits*, San Francisco: Freeman.

Patay, P. 1974 'Die hochkupferzeitliche Bodrogkeresztúr-Kultur', *Bericht der Römisch-Germanischen Kommission* 55, 1–72.

Patay, P., Zimmer, K., Szabó, Z. and Sinay, G. 1963 'Spektrographische und metallographische Untersuchung kupfer- und frühbronzezeitlicher Funde', *Acta Archaeologica Academiae Scientiarum Hungaricae* 15, 37–64.

Păunescu, A. 1970 *Evoluţia Uneltelor şi Armelor de Piatră Cioplită descoperite pe teritoriul României*, Bucharest: Romanian Academy of Sciences.

Pavúk, J. 1972 'Neolithisches Gräberfeld in Nitra', *Slovenská Archaeológia* 20, 5–105.

Payne, S. 1973 'Kill-off patterns in sheep and goats: the mandibles from Aşvan Kale', *Anatolian Studies* 23, 281–303.

Pécsi, M. 1970 *Geomorphological Regions of Hungary*, Budapest: Akadémiai Kiadó.

Pécsi, M. and Sarfalvi, B. 1964 *The Geography of Hungary*, Budapest: Corvina Press.

Perkins, D. 1969 'Fauna of Çatal Hüyük: evidence for early cattle domestication in Anatolia', *Science* 164, 177–9.

Perry, W. J. 1937 (1st edn 1924) *The Growth of Civilisation*, Harmondsworth: Penguin Books.

Pétrequin, P. and Pétrequin, M. 1988 *Le Néolithique des lacs: préhistoire des lacs de Chalains et de Clairvaux*, Paris: Errance.

Piazza, A., Menozzi, P. and Cavalli-Sforza 1981 'Synthetic gene frequency maps of men and the selective effects of climate', *Proceedings of the National Academy of Sciences of the USA* 78, 2648–52.

Piddocke, S. 1969 'The potlatch system of the southern Kwakiutl: a new perspective', pp. 130–58 in A. P. Vayda (ed.) *Environment and Cultural Behaviour*, New York: Natural History Press.

Pieczyński, Z. 1985 'Uwagi o skarbie miedzianym z Bytynia, woj. Posnańskie', *Fontes Archaeologici Posnanienses* 34, 1–7.

Piggott, S. 1954 *The Neolithic Cultures of the British Isles*, Cambridge: Cambridge University Press.

Piggott, S. 1958a 'Vere Gordon Childe, 1892–1957', *Proceedings of the British Academy* 44, 305–12.

Piggott, S. 1958b 'The Dawn: and an epilogue', *Antiquity* 32, 75–9.

Piggott, S. 1959 'A Late Bronze Age wine trade?', *Antiquity* 33, 22–3.

Piggott, S. (ed.) 1961 *The Dawn of Civilisation: the first world survey of human cultures in early times*, London: Thames and Hudson.

Piggott, S. 1965 *Ancient Europe*, Edinburgh: Edinburgh University Press.

Piggott, S. 1968 'The earliest wheeled vehicles and the Caucasian evidence', *Proceedings of the Prehistoric Society* 34, 266–318.

Piggott, S. 1979 ' "The first wagons and carts": twenty five years later', *Bulletin of the Institute of Archaeology* 16, 3–17.

Piggott, S. 1983 *The Earliest Wheeled Transport, from the Atlantic coast to the Caspian sea*, London: Thames and Hudson.

Piggott, S. 1992 *Waggon, Chariot and Carriage: symbol and status in the history of transport*, London: Thames and Hudson.

Pingel, V. 1982 'Zum Schatzfund von Valčitran in Nordbulgarien', pp. 171–86 in Hänsel (ed.) *Südosteuropa zwischen 1600 und 1000 v. Chr.* vol. 1, Berlin.

Piotrovskii, B. 1959 *Vanskoe Tsarstvo, Urartu*, Moscow: Izdatel'stvo vostochnoj literatury.

Pittioni, R. 1954 *Urgeschichte des Österreichischen Raumes*, Vienna: Deuticke.

Pittioni, R. 1957 'Urzeitlicher Bergbau auf Kupfererz und Spurenanalyse', *Archaeologia Austriaca* Beiheft 1, 1–76.

Pittioni, R. 1973 'Almwirtschaft', *Reallexikon der Germanischen Altertumskunde* 1, 181–3, Berlin: Walter de Gruyter.

Pleinerová, I. 1980 'Kultovní objekty z Pozdní Doby Kammené v Březně u Loun', *Památky Archeologické* 71(1), 10–56.

Pleinerová, I. 1981 'Problém stop orby v časně Eneolitickém nálezu z Března', *Archaeologické Rozhledy* 33, 133–41.

Polanyi, K., Arensberg, K. and Pearson, H. 1957 *Trade and Market in the Early Empires*, New York: The Free Press.

Postan, M. M. and Titow, J. Z. 1959 'Heriots and prices on the Winchester manors', *Economic History Review* 2nd ser. 11.

Potratz, J. A. H. 1966 *Die Pferdetrensen des alten Orient* (Analecta Orientalia, 41), Rome: Analecta Orientalia.

Pownall, T. 1773 'A description of the sepulchral monument at New Grange, near Drogheda, in the County of Meath, Ireland', *Archaeologia* 2, 241.

Prag, K. 1978 'Silver in the Levant in the fourth millennium BC', pp. 36–45 in P. R. S. Moorey and P. Parr (eds) *Archaeology in the Levant*, Warminster: Aris and Philips.

Preuss, J. 1966. *Die Baalberger Gruppe in Mitteldeutschland*, Berlin: VEB Verlag der Wissenschaften.

Price, B. J. 1971 'Prehispanic irrigation agriculture in Nuclear America', *Latin American Research Review* 6, 3–30.

Price, R. 1993 'The west Pontic Maritime Interaction Sphere: a long-term structure in Balkan prehistory?', *Oxford Journal of Archaeology* 12(2), 175–96.

Pullen, D. J. 1992 'Ox and plow in the Early Bronze Age Aegean', *American Journal of Archaeology* 96, 45–54.

Pustovalov, S. Z. 1994 'Economy and social organisation of northern Pontic steppe/forest-steppe pastoral populations: 2700–2350 BC (Catacomb culture)', *Baltic-Pontic Studies* 2, 86–134.

Qviller, B. 1981 'The dynamics of Homeric society', *Symbolae Osloenses* 56, 109.

Qviller, B. [unpublished typescript] 'The king in Dark Age Greece and in Medieval Norway; the evolutionary significance of sympotic kingship'.

Raczky, P. 1987 *The Late Neolithic of the Tisza Region*, Szolnok: County
  Museum.
Rădulescu, D. and Dimitrescu, R. 1966 *Mineralogia Topographica a României*,
  Bucharest: Editura Ştiinţifică.
Raetzel-Fabian, D. 1986 *Phasenkartierung des mitteleuropäischen Neolithikums:
  Chronologie und Chorologie* (BAR Int. Ser. 316), Oxford: British Archaeological
  Reports.
Raikes, R. 1965 'The ancient gabarbands of Baluchistan', *East and West* 15,
  26–35.
Randsborg, K. 1970 'Eine kupferne Schmuckscheibe aus einem Dolmen in
  Jütland', *Acta Archaeologica* 41, 181–90.
Randsborg, K. 1979a 'Social Dimensions in Neolithic Denmark', *Proceedings of
  the Prehistoric Society* 41, 105–18.
Randsborg, K. 1979b 'Resource distribution and the function of copper in early
  Neolithic Denmark', pp. 303–18 in M. Ryan (ed.) *The Origins of Metallurgy in
  Atlantic Europe* (Proceedings of the 5th Atlantic Colloquium, Dublin 1978),
  Dublin: Government Stationery Office.
Randsborg, K. and Nybo, C. 1986 'The coffin and the sun: demography and
  ideology in Scandinavian prehistory', *Acta Archaeologica* 55, 161–85.
Rappaport, R. A. 1968 *Pigs for the Ancestors*, New Haven: Yale University Press.
Ratnagar, S. 1981 *Encounters: the Westerly Trade of the Harappa Civilisation*,
  Delhi: Oxford University Press.
Rausing, G. 1988 'More on the ard marks', *Antiquity* 61, 263–6.
Reichel-Dolmatoff, G. 1975 *Shaman and Jaguar: a study of narcotic drugs among
  the Indians of Colombia*, Philadelphia.
Reinach, S. 1893 'Le mirage oriental', *l'Anthropologie* 4, 539–78, 699–732.
Renfrew, A. C. 1967a 'Colonialism and megalithismus', *Antiquity* 41, 276.
Renfrew, A. C. 1967b 'Cycladic metallurgy and the Aegean Early Bronze Age',
  American Journal of Archaeology 71, 1–20.
Renfrew, A. C. 1968 'Wessex without Mycenae', *Annual of the British School of
  Archaeology at Athens* 63, 277.
Renfrew, A. C. 1969 'The autonomy of the south-east European Copper Age',
  Proceedings of the Prehistoric Society 35, 12–47.
Renfrew, A. C. 1972 *The Emergence of Civilisation: the Cyclades and the Aegean
  in the third millennium* BC, London: Methuen.
Renfrew, A. C. 1973a 'Monuments, mobilisation and social organisation in
  Neolithic Wessex', pp. 539–58 in A. C. Renfrew (ed.) *The Explanation of
  Culture Change*, London: Duckworth.
Renfrew, A. C. 1973b *Before Civilisation: the radiocarbon revolution and
  European Prehistory*, London: Jonathan Cape.
Renfrew, A. C. 1976 'Megaliths, territories and populations' in S. J. de Laet (ed.)
  Acculturation and Continuity in Atlantic Europe, Brugge: de Tempel.
Renfrew, A. C. 1987 *Archaeology and Language: the puzzle of Indo-European
  origins*, London: Cape.
Renfrew, A. C. 1994 'The identity of Europe in prehistoric archaeology', *Journal of
  European Archaeology* 2(2), 153–73.
Renfrew, A. C., Gimbutas, M. and Elster, E. (eds) 1986 *Excavations at Sitagroi,
  a prehistoric village in northeast Greece* vol. 1 (Monumenta Archaeologia 13),
  Los Angeles: UCLA.
Reynolds, P. 1981 'Deadstock and livestock', pp. 85–96 in R. Mercer (ed.)

Farming Practice in British Prehistory, Edinburgh: Edinburgh University Press.

Ripinki-Naxon, M. 1993 *The Nature of Shamanism: substance and function of a religious metaphor*, Albany: State University of New York Press.

Ripinski, M. 1975 'The camel in ancient Arabia', *Antiquity* 49, 295–8.

Roberts, N. 1977 'Water conservation in ancient Arabia', *Seminar for Arabian Studies* 7, 134–46.

Roberts, N. 1989 *The Holocene: an environmental history*, Oxford: Blackwell.

Roberts, N. 1991 'Late Quaternary geomorphological change and the origins of agriculture in south central Turkey', *Geoarchaeology* 6(1), 1–26.

Robins, R. H. 1964 *General Linguistics: an introductory survey*, London: Longmans.

Roe, F. G. 1955 *The Indian and the Horse*, Norman: University of Oklahoma Press.

Roglić, J. 1961 'The geographical setting of medieval Dubrovnik', in N. J. G. Pounds (ed.) *Geographical Essays on Southeast Europe*, Bloomington: University of Indiana Press.

Roman, P. 1971 'Strukturänderungen des Endäneolithikums im Donau-Karpathen-Raum', *Dacia* 15, 31–170.

Roman, P. 1974 'Das Problem der "schnurverzierten" Keramik in Südosteuropa', *Jahresschrift für mitteldeutsche Vorgeschichte* 58, 157–74.

Roman, P. and Németi, I. 1978 *Cultura Baden în România*, Bucharest: Institute of Archaeology.

Romer, F. 1878 *Compte-Rendu de la huitième Session: Congrès International d'Anthropologie et d'Archéologie Préhistoriques, 1876*, Budapest: National Museum of Hungary.

Rosetti, D. V. 1959 'Movilele funerare de la Gurbăneşti', *Materiale şi Cercetari Arheologice* 6, 791–816.

Rostholm, H. 1977 'Neolitiske Skivehjul fra Kideris og Bjerregård i Midtjylland', *Kuml* 1977, 185–222.

Rostovtzeff, M. I. 1920 'L'Age du cuivre dans le Caucase et civilisations de Soumer et de l'Egypte protodynastique', *Révue archéologique*, 5th ser., 12, 1–37.

Rothenberg, B.1970 'An archaeological survey in southern Sinai', *Palestine Excavation Quarterly* 1970–1, 4–29.

Rottländer, R. C. A. 1995 'Bemerkungen zu einer Abhandlung über Feuerstülpen', *Archäologisches Korrespondenzblatt* 25, 169.

Rowlands, M. J. 1971 'The archaeological interpretation of prehistoric metalworking', *World Archaeology* 3, 210–24.

Rowlands, M. J. 1980 'Kinship, alliance and exchange in the European Bronze Age', pp. 15–55 in J. Barrett and R. Bradley (eds) *Settlement and Society in the British later Bronze Age* (BAR Brit. Ser. 83), Oxford: British Archaeological Reports.

Rowlands, M. 1984 'Conceptualising the European Bronze and Early Iron Ages', pp. 147–56 in J. Bintliff (ed.) *European Social Evolution: archaeological perspectives*, Bradford: Bradford University Press.

Rowlands, M. 1994 'Childe and the archaeology of freedom', pp. 35–54 in Harris 1994.

Rowlands, M. J., Kristiansen, K. and Larsen, M. T. 1987 *Centre and Periphery in the Ancient World*, Cambridge: Cambridge University Press.

Rowley-Conwy, P. 1981 'Slash and burn in the temperate European Neolithic', pp.

85–96 in R. Mercer (ed.) *Farming Practice in British Prehistory*, Edinburgh: Edinburgh University Press.

Rowley-Conwy, P. 1984 'The laziness of the short-distance hunter: the origins of agriculture in western Denmark', *Journal of Anthropological Archaeology* 3, 300–24.

Rowley-Conwy, P. 1987 'The interpretation of ard marks', *Antiquity* 61, 263–6.

Rowton, M. B. 1974 'Enclosed nomadism', *Journal of the Economic and Social History of the Orient*, 17, 1–30.

Rowton, M. B. 1980 'Pastoralism and the periphery', pp. 291–301 in T. Barrelet (ed.) *L'Archéologie de l'Iraq du Début de l'Epoque Néolithique à 333 avant notre ère*, Paris: CNRS.

Rudenko, S. I. 1970 *Frozen Tombs of Siberia: the Pazyryk burials of Iron Age horsemen*, London: Dent.

Runnels, C. and van Andel, Tj. H. 1988 'Trade and the origins of agriculture in the eastern Mediterranean', *Journal of Mediterranean Archaeology* 1(1), 83–109.

Ruoff, E. 1981 'Stein- und Bronzezeitliche Textilfunde aus dem Kanton Zürich', *Helvetia Archaeologica* 45/48, 252–64.

Ruoff, U. 1978 'Die Schnurkeramischen Räder von Zürich "Pressehaus"', *Archäologisches Korrespondenzblatt* 8, 275–83.

Russell, K. W. 1988 *After Eden: the behavioural ecology of early food production in the Near East and North Africa* (BAR Int. Ser. 391), Oxford: British Archaeological Reports.

Ryder, M. L. 1969 'Changes in the fleece of sheep following domestication', pp. 495–523 in P. J. Ucko and G. W. Dimbleby (eds) *The Domestication and Exploitation of Plants and Animals*, London: Duckworth.

Ryder, M. L. 1983 *Sheep and Man*, London: Duckworth.

Šiška, S. 1964 'Gräberfeld der Tiszapolgár Kultur in Tibava', *Slovenská Archaeologia* 12, 352.

Šramko, B. A. 1971 'Der Hakenpflug der Bronzezeit in der Ukraine', *Tools and Tillage* 14, 223–4.

Sahlins, M. 1961 'The segmentary lineage: an organisation of predatory expansion', *American Anthropologist* 63, 322–45.

Sahlins, M. D. 1963 'Poor man, rich man, big man, chief: political types in Melanesia and Polynesia', *Comparative Studies in Society and History* 5, 285–303.

Sahlins, M. D. 1965 'On the sociology of primitive exchange', in M. Bantock (ed.) *The Relevance of Models for Social Anthropology*, London: Tavistock.

Sahlins, M. D. 1972 *Stone Age Economics*, Chicago and New York: Aldine.

Said, E. 1978 *Orientalism*, London: Routledge and Kegan Paul.

Sakellaridis, M. 1979 *The Mesolithic and Neolithic of the Swiss Area* (BAR Int. Ser. 67), Oxford: British Archaeological Reports.

Salisbury, R. F. 1962 *From Stone to Steel: Economic Consequences of a Technological Change in New Guinea*, Cambridge: Cambridge University Press.

Salonen, A. 1968 'Agricultura Mesopotamica', *Annales Academiae Scientiarum Fennicae*, Series B, vol. 149.

Samuelson, J. 1878 *A History of Drink*, London: Truebner and Co.

Sandars, N. 1983 'North and south at the end of the Mycenaean age: aspects of an old problem', *Oxford Journal of Archaeology* 2, 43–68.

Sanders, W. T. and Price, B. J. 1968 *Mesoamerica: the Evolution of a Civilization*, New York: Random House.

Sauvy, A. 1969 *The General Theory of Population*, London: Weidenfeld and Nicolson.

Scarre, C. (ed.) 1983 *Ancient France*, Edinburgh: Edinburgh University Press.

Scarre, C. 1992 'The Early Neolithic of western France and megalithic origins in Atlantic Europe', *Oxford Journal of Archaeology* 11(2), 121–54.

Schaaf, U. and Taylor, A. K. 1975 'Südimporte im Raum nördlich der Alpen (6–4. Jahrhundert v. Chr.)', *Ausgrabungen in Deutschland 1950–75*, vol. 3, 312–16, Mainz: RGZM.

Schaeffer, C. F. A. 1948 *Stratigraphie Comparée et Chronologie de l'Asie Occidentale IIIᵉ et IIᵉ millénaires*, Oxford: Oxford University Press.

Scheil, J. V. 1923 'Textes de comptabilité proto-Élamites', *Mémoires de la mission archéologique de Perse* 17.

Schietzel, K. 1965 *Müddersheim*, Cologne and Graz: Herausgegeben von Hermann Schwabedissen.

Schild, R. 1987 'The exploitation of flint in central Poland', pp. 137–50 in G. Sieveking and M. Newcomer (eds) *The Human Uses of Flint and Chert*, Cambridge: Cambridge University Press.

Schindler, K. 1993 *The Man in the Ice*, London: Weidenfeld and Nicolson.

Schlabow, K. 1959 'Beiträge zur Erforschung der jungsteinzeitlichen und bronzezeitlichen Gewebetechnik Mitteldeutschlands', *Jahresschrift für Mitteldeutsche Vorgeschichte* 43, 101–20 and Plates.

Schmid, E. 1952 'Vom Jaspisbergbau an der Kachelfluh bei Kleinkems (Baden)', *Germania* 30, 153–8.

Schmidt, H. 1902 *Heinrich Schliemanns Sammlung trojanischer Altertümer*, Berlin: Königliche Museen zu Berlin.

Schnapp, A. 1993 *La Conquête du Passé: aux origines de l'archéologie*, Paris: Carré.

Schneider, J. 1977 'Was there a pre-capitalist world-system?', *Peasant Studies* 6(1), 20–9.

Schnurkeramik-Symposium, Halle 1979, *Jahresschrift für mitteldeutsche Vorgeschichte* 64.

Schon, D. 1971 *Beyond the Stable State*, London: Temple Smith.

Schovsbo, P. O. 1983 'A Neolithic vehicle from Klosterlund, central Jutland', *Journal of Danish Archaeology* 2, 60–70.

Schubert, F. 1965 'Zu den südosteuropäischen Kupferäxten', *Germania* 43, 274–95.

Schubert, F. 1966 'Zur Frühbronzezeit an der mittleren Donau', *Germania* 44, 264–86.

Schubert, F. and Schubert, E. 1967 'Spektralanalytische Untersuchungen von Hort- und Einzelfunden der Periode B III', pp. 185–203 (appendix) in A. Mozsolics (ed.) *Bronzefunde des Karpathenbeckens*, Budapest: Akadémiai Kiadó.

Schuchhardt, C. 1944 (1st edn 1919) *Alteuropa in seiner Kultur- und Stilentwicklung*, Berlin: Walter de Gruyter.

Schüle, W. 1967 'Feldbewässerung in Alt-Europa', *Madrider Mitteilungen* 8, 79–99.

Schüle, W. 1969 'Glockenbecher und Hauspferde', pp. 88–93 in J. Boessneck (ed.) *Archäologisch-Biologische Zusammenarbeit in der Vor- und Frühgeschichtsforschung* (Münchener Kolloquium 1967), Deutsche Forschungsgemeinschaft (Forschungsberichte 15), Wiesbaden: Steiner Verlag.

Schultz-Klinken, H.-R. 1976 'Ackerbausysteme des Saatfurchen- und Saatbettbaues in urgeschichtlicher und geschichtlicher Zeit sowie ihr Einfluss auf die Bodenentwicklung', *Die Kunde* (1975/6) 26/7, 5–68.

Schwabedissen, H. 1966 (1967) 'Ein horizontierter "Breitkeil" aus Satrup', *Palaeohistoria* 12, 409–68.

Seeberg, P. and Kristensen, M. 1964 'Mange striber på kryds og tvaers', *Kuml*, 7–14.

Semple, E. C. 1932 *The Geography of the Mediterranean Region: its relation to ancient history*, London: Constable.

Sereni, E. 1981 'Per la storia delle piu antiche tecniche e della nomenclatura della vite e del vino in Italia', pp. 101–48 in E. Sereni *Terra Nuova e Buoi Rossi e altri saggi per una storia dell'agricoltura europea*, Torino: Einaudi.

Service, E. R. 1962 *Primitive Social Organization: An Evolutionary Perspective*, New York: Random House.

Service, E. R. 1968 'War and our contemporary ancestors', pp. 160–7 in M. Fried, M. Harris and R. Murphy (eds) *War: the Anthropology of Armed Conflict and Aggression*, New York: Doubleday.

Shanks, M. and Tilley, C. 1987 *Social Theory and Archaeology*, Cambridge: Polity Press.

Sharples, N. 1985 'Individual and community: the changing role of megaliths in the Orcadian Neolithic', *Proceedings of the Prehistoric Society* 51, 59–74.

Shennan, S. J. 1977 'The appearance of the Bell Beaker assemblage in central Europe', pp. 51–70 in R. J. Mercer (ed.) *Beakers in Britain and Europe* (BAR Int. Ser. 26), Oxford: British Archaeological Reports.

Shennan, S. J. 1982 'Ideology, change and the European Early Bronze Age', pp. 155–61 in I. A. Hodder (ed.) *Symbolic and Structural Archaeology*, Cambridge: Cambridge University Press.

Shennan, S. J. 1986 'Central Europe in the third millennium BC: an evolutionary trajectory for the beginning of the European Bronze Age', *Journal of Anthropological Archaeology* 5, 115–46.

Shennan, S. J. 1993a 'Settlement and social change in central Europe', *Journal of World Prehistory* 7(2), 121–61.

Shennan, S. J. 1993b 'Commodities, transactions and growth in the central European early Bronze Age', *Journal of European Archaeology* 1(2), 59–72.

Sherratt, A. G. 1972 'Socioeconomic and demographic models for the Neolithic and Bronze Ages of Europe', pp. 477–542 in D. L. Clarke (ed.) *Models in Archaeology*, London: Methuen. (*Partly reprinted here as Chapter 2.*)

Sherratt, A. G. 1973 'The interpretation of change in European prehistory', pp. 419–28 in A. C. Renfrew (ed.) *The Explanation of Culture Change*, London: Duckworth.

Sherratt, A. G. 1976a *The Beginning of the Bronze Age in the area between the middle Danube and the north Aegean* (unpublished Ph.D. dissertation, University of Cambridge).

Sherratt, A. G. 1976b 'Resources, technology and trade: an essay in early European copper metallurgy', pp. 557–81 in G. Sieveking, I. Longworth and K. Wilson (eds) *Problems in Economic and Social Archaeology*, London: Duckworth. (*Reprinted here as Chapter 4.*)

Sherratt, A. G. 1979 'Problems in European Prehistory', pp. 193–206 in D. L. Clarke, *Analytical Archaeologist*, London: Academic Press.

Sherratt, A. G. (ed.) 1980a *The Cambridge Encyclopaedia of Archaeology*, Cambridge: Cambridge University Press.

Sherratt, A. G. 1980b 'Water, soil and seasonality in early cereal cultivation',

World Archaeology 11, 313–30. (*Reprinted here as Chapter 3.*)

Sherratt, A. G. 1981 'Plough and pastoralism: aspects of the Secondary Products Revolution', pp. 261–305 in I. Hodder, G. Isaac and N. Hammond (eds) *Pattern of the Past: Studies in Honour of David Clark*, Cambridge: Cambridge University Press. (*Reprinted here as Chapter 6.*)

Sherratt, A. G. 1982a 'The first European sailing ships', *The Ashmolean* 1, 12–14.

Sherratt, A. G. 1982b 'Mobile resources: settlement and exchange in early agricultural Europe', pp. 13–26 in A. C. Renfrew and S. J. Shennan (eds) *Ranking Resources and Exchange*, Cambridge: Cambridge University Press. (*Partly reprinted here as Chapter 10.*)

Sherratt, A. G. 1983a 'The Secondary Exploitation of Animals in the Old World', *World Archaeology* 15, 90–104. (*Partly reprinted here as Chapter 7.*)

Sherratt, A. G. 1983b 'The development of Neolithic and Copper Age settlement in the Great Hungarian Plain, Part I: The regional setting', *Oxford Journal of Archaeology* 1(1), 287–316. (*Partly reprinted here as Chapter 11.*)

Sherratt, A. G. 1984a 'The development of Neolithic and Copper Age settlement in the Great Hungarian Plain, Part II: Site survey and settlement dynamics', *Oxford Journal of Archaeology* 2(1), 13–41. (*Partly reprinted here as Chapter 11.*)

Sherratt, A. G. 1984b 'Social evolution: Europe in the later Neolithic and Copper Ages', pp. 123–34 in J. Bintliff (ed.) *European Social Evolution: archaeological perspectives*, Bradford: University of Bradford. (*Partly reprinted here as Chapter 5.*)

Sherratt, A. G. 1984c 'Early agrarian settlement in the Körös region of the Great Hungarian Plain', *Acta Archaeologica Academiae Scientiarum Hungaricae* 35, 155–69.

Sherratt, A. G. 1985 'Cups that cheer: alcohol in European culture', *The Ashmolean* 8, 6–9 (reprinted in *Brewing Review*, January 1986).

Sherratt, A. G. (unpublished typescript, 1985) *Driving and Drinking: Aspects of Bronze Age Elites in Europe*, two Munro lectures delivered in the University of Edinburgh, November 1985.

Sherratt, A. G. 1986a 'The pottery of the Early Bronze Age at Sitagroi', pp. 429–76 in A. C. Renfrew, M. Gimbutas and E. Elster (eds) *Excavations at Sitagroi*, Los Angeles: UCLA.

Sherratt, A. G. 1986b 'Two new finds of wooden wheels from later Neolithic and Early Bronze Age Europe', *Oxford Journal of Archaeology* 5, 243–8. (*Reproduced here as Chapter 9.*)

Sherratt, A. G. 1986c 'The Radley "ear-rings" revised', *Oxford Journal of Archaeology* 5, 61–6.

Sherratt, A. G. 1987a 'Neolithic exchange systems in central Europe, 5000–3000 b.c.', pp. 193–204 in G. Sieveking and M. Newcomer (eds) *The Human Uses of Flint and Chert*, Cambridge: Cambridge University Press. (*Partly reprinted here as Chapter 12.*)

Sherratt, A. G. 1987b 'Wool, wheels and ploughmarks: local developments or outside introductions in Neolithic Europe?', *Bulletin of the London University Institute of Archaeology* 23, 1–15. (*Reprinted here as Chapter 8.*)

Sherratt, A. G. 1987c 'Cups that cheered', pp. 81–114 in W. Waldren and R. C. Kennard (eds) *Bell Beakers of the Western Mediterranean* (BAR Int. Ser. 287), Oxford: British Archaeological Reports. (*Reprinted here as Chapter 15.*)

Sherratt, A. G. 1987d 'The Early Bronze Age Pottery' in C. Renfrew, M. Gimbutas and E. Elster (eds) *Excavations at Sitagroi, a prehistoric village in northeast Greece* vol. 1, pp. 429–76 (Monumenta Archaeologia 13), Los Angeles: UCLA.

Sherratt, A. G. 1987e 'Warriors and traders: Bronze Age chiefdoms in central Europe', pp. 54–66 in B. W. Cunliffe (ed.) *Origins: the roots of European Civilisation*, BBC Publications.

Sherratt, A. G. 1987f [Review article] 'Two new books on early European agriculture', *Scottish Archaeological Review* 4, 134–7.

Sherratt, A. G. 1989 'V. Gordon Childe: archaeology and intellectual history', *Past and Present* 125, 151–85. (*Reprinted here as Chapter 1.*)

Sherratt, A. G. 1990a 'The genesis of megaliths: monumentality, ethnicity and social complexity in Neolithic north-west Europe', *World Archaeology* 22(2), 147–67. (*Reprinted here as Chapter 13.*)

Sherratt, A. G. 1990b 'Gordon Childe: patterns and paradigms in prehistory', *Australian Archaeology* 30, 3–13.

Sherratt, A. G. 1991a 'Sacred and profane substances: the ritual use of narcotics in later Neolithic Europe', pp. 50–64 in P. Garwood, D. Jennings, R. Skeates and J. Toms (eds) *Sacred and Profane: proceedings of a conference on archaeology, ritual and religion*, Oxford: Oxford University Committee for Archaeology. (*Reprinted here as Chapter 16.*)

Sherratt, A. G. 1991b 'Palaeoethnobotany: from crops to cuisine', pp. 221–36 in F. Queiroga and A. Dinis (eds) *Paleoecologia e Arqueologia II*, Vila Nova de Famalicão: Centro de Estudos Famalicenses.

Sherratt, A. G. 1991c 'Troy, Maikop, Altyn Depe: Early Bronze Age urbanism and its periphery'; Conference paper, Novorossiysk: to appear (in Russian) in V. M. Masson (ed.) *Majkopskaya Kultura-fenomen Drevnej Istorii Kavkaza i Vostochnoj Evropy*, Petersburg. (*Reproduced here as Chapter 18.*)

Sherratt, A. G. 1992a 'What can archaeologists learn from Annalistes?', pp. 135–42 in A. B. Knapp (ed.) *Archaeology, Annales and Ethnohistory*, Cambridge: Cambridge University Press.

Sherratt, A. G. 1992b 'The relativity of theory', pp. 119–30 in N. Yoffee and A. G. Sherratt 1992 *Archaeological Theory – Who Sets The Agenda?*, Cambridge: Cambridge University Press.

Sherratt, A. G. 1993a, 'Who are you calling peripheral? Dependence and independence in European prehistory', in C. Scarre and F. Healy (eds) *Trade and Exchange in Prehistoric Europe*, Oxford: Oxbow Books.

Sherratt, A. G. 1993b, 'What would a Bronze Age world system look like? Relations between temperate Europe and the Mediterranean in later prehistory', *Journal of European Archaeology* 1(2), 1–57.

Sherratt, A. G. 1994a 'Core, periphery and margin: perspectives on the Bronze Age', pp. 335–45 in C. Mathers and S. Stoddart (eds) *Development and Decline in the Mediterranean Bronze Age*, Sheffield: J. R. Collis Publications.

Sherratt, A. G. 1994b 'The transformation of early agrarian Europe: the later Neolithic and Copper Ages 4500–2500 BC', pp. 167–201; and 'The emergence of elites: earlier Bronze Age Europe 2500–1300 BC', pp. 244–76 in B. Cunliffe (ed.) *The Oxford Illustrated Prehistory of Europe*.

Sherratt, A. G. 1995a 'Introduction: Peculiar Substances', pp. 1–10; and 'Alcohol and its alternatives: symbol and substance in early Old World cultures', pp. 11–46 in J. Goodman, P. Lovejoy and A. Sherratt (eds) *Consuming Habits: drugs in history and anthropology*, London: Routledge.

Sherratt, A. G. 1995b 'Reviving the grand narrative: archaeology and long-term change', *Journal of European Archaeology* 3(1), 1–32.

Sherratt, A. G. 1995c 'Instruments of conversion: the role of megaliths in the Mesolithic–Neolithic transition in north-west Europe', *Oxford Journal of Archaeology* 14(3), 245–60. (*Partly reproduced here as Chapter 14.*)

Sherratt, A. G. 1996a 'Plate tectonics and imaginary prehistories; structure and contingency in agricultural origins', pp. 130–40 in D. Harris (ed.) *Origins and Spread of Agriculture*, London: UCL Press.

Sherratt, A. G. 1996b 'Why Wessex? The Avon route and river transport in later prehistoric Britain', *Oxford Journal of Archaeology* 15(2), 211–34.

Sherratt, A. G. 1996c 'Sedentary agricultural and nomadic pastoral populations (3000–700 BC)', pp. 37–43 in A. H. Dani and J.-P. Mohen (eds) *History of Humanity: Scientific and Cultural Development* (vol. II, From the Third Millennium to the Seventh Century BC), Paris and London: UNESCO and Routledge.

Sherratt, A. G. 1996 (in press, a) (in Polish) 'Gordon Childe: right or wrong?' in J. Lech (ed.) Conference volume on Gordon Childe, Warsaw. (*Reproduced here as Chapter 20.*)

Sherratt, A. G. 1996 (in press, b) 'The human geography of Europe: a prehistoric perspective', in R. Butler and R. Dodgshon (eds) *An Historical Geography of Europe*, Oxford: Clarendon Press.

Sherratt, A. G. (typescript, 1996) '"With baleful weeds and precious-juicèd flowers": Grooved Ware, grape-cups and prehistoric pharmacognosy'.

Sherratt, A. G. and Sherratt, E. S. 1988 'The archaeology of Indo-European: an alternative view', *Antiquity* 62 (no. 236), 584–95. (*Reproduced here as Chapter 19.*)

Sherratt, A. G. and Sherratt E. S. 1991a 'From luxuries to commodities: the nature of Mediterranean Bronze Age trading systems', pp. 351–86 in N. Gale (ed.) *Bronze Age Trade in the Mediterranean* (Studies in Mediterranean Archaeology 90), Jonsered: P. Åströms Forlag.

Sherratt, A. G. and Sherratt, E. S. 1991b 'Urnfield Reflections' [Review article on James et al. *Centuries of Darkness*], *Cambridge Archaeological Journal* 1(2), 247–53.

Sherratt, A. G. and Taylor, T. 1989 'Metal vessels in Bronze Age Europe and the context of Vulchetrun', pp. 106–34 in J. Best and N. de Vries (eds) *Thracians and Mycenaeans*, Leiden: Brill. (*Partly reprinted here as Chapter 17.*)

Sherratt, E. S. and Sherratt, A. G. (unpublished typescript) *The Aegean Bronze Age and the East Mediterranean: political structures and external trade* (partly incorporated in Sherratt and Sherratt 1990).

Sherratt, E. S. and Sherratt, A. G. 1993 'The growth of the Mediterranean economy in the early first millennium BC', *World Archaeology* 24(3), 361–78.

Shklar, J. N. 1987 *Montesquieu*, Oxford: Oxford University Press.

Sielmann, B. 1971 'Die frühneolitische Besiedlung Mitteleuropas', pp. 1–65 in H. Schwabedissen (ed.) *Die Anfänge des Neolithikums Va*, Cologne: Bohlau Verlag.

Sigaut, F. 1975 *L'Agriculture et le Feu*, Paris and The Hague: Mouton.

Silberman, N. A. 1982 *Digging for God and Country: Exploration, Archaeology and the Secret Struggle for the Holy Land, 1799–1917*, New York: Knopf.

Simoons, F. J. 1969 'Primary adult lactose intolerance and the milking habit: a problem in biological and cultural interrelations (1)', *American Journal of Digestive Diseases* 14, 819–36.

Simoons, F. J. 1970 'Primary adult lactose intolerance and the milking habit: a problem in biological and cultural relations (2)', *American Journal of Digestive Diseases* 15, 695–710.

Simoons, F. J. 1971 'The antiquity of dairying in Asia and Africa', *Geographical Review* 61, 431–9.

Simpson, W. K. 1959 'The vessels with engraved designs and the repoussé bowl from the Tell Basta treasure', *American Journal of Archaeology* 63, 29–45.

Skårup, J. 1975 *Stengade: ein langeländischer Wohnplatz mit Hausresten aus der frühneolithischen Zeit*, Copenhagen: Meddelelser fra Langelands Museum.

Sklenář, K. 1983 *Archaeology in Central Europe: the First 500 Years*, Leicester: Leicester University Press.

Slicher van Bath, B. H. 1963 *The Agrarian History of Western Europe* AD 500–1850, London: Arnold.

Smith, A. 1893 (1st edn 1776) *An Inquiry into the Nature and Causes of The Wealth of Nations*, London: Routledge.

Smith, C. T. 1967 *An Historical Geography of Western Europe before 1800*, London: Longmans.

Smith, P. E. L. and Young, T. C. 1972 'The evolution of early agriculture and culture in Greater Mesopotamia: a trial model', in B. Spooner (ed.) *Population Growth: Anthropological Implications*, Cambridge, Mass.: M.I.T. Press.

Smith, P. and Horwitz, L. K. 1984 'Radiographic evidence for changing patterns of animal exploitation in the southern Levant', *Journal of Archaeological Science* 11, 467–75.

Somogyi, S. 1964 'Geographical factors in the formation of alkali soils (Szik-soils) in Hungary', pp. 36–57 in M. Pécsi (ed.) *Applied Geography in Hungary*, Budapest: Akadémiai Kiadó.

Spencer, H. 1937 [1st edn 1862] *First Principles* (Thinker's Library 62), London: Watts and Co.

Spooner, B. (ed.) 1972 *Population Growth: Anthropological Implications*, Cambridge, Mass.: M.I.T. Press.

Sprockhoff, E. 1930 *Zur Handelsgeschichte der germanischen Bronzezeit* (Vorgeschichtliche Forschungen 7), Berlin: Verlag Walter de Gruyter.

Sprockhoff, E. 1938 *Die Nordische Megalithkultur*, Berlin and Leipzig: de Gruyter.

Sprockhoff, E. 1952 'Ein Grabfund der nordischen Megalithkultur von Oldendorf, Kr Lüneburg', *Germania* 30, 164–74.

Sprockhoff, E. 1961 'Eine mykenische Bronzetasse von Dohnsen, Kr. Celle', *Germania* 39, 11–22.

Starling, N. J. 1983a 'Neolithic settlement patterns in central Germany', *Oxford Journal of Archaeology* 1, 1–11.

Starling, N. J. 1983b *Studies in the Neolithic Settlement of Central Germany* (unpublished D.Phil. thesis, University of Oxford).

Starling, N. J. 1985a 'Colonisation and succession: the earlier Neolithic of central Europe', *Proceedings of the Prehistoric Society* 51, 41–57.

Starling, N. J. 1985b 'Social change in the Later Neolithic of Central Europe', *Antiquity* 59, 30–8.

Steensberg, A. 1971 'Drill-sowing and threshing in southern India', *Tools and Tillage* 11, 241–56.

Steensberg, A. 1973 'A 6000-year old ploughing implement from Satrup Moor', *Tools and Tillage* 12, 105–18.

Stevens, E. S. 1966 'Agriculture and rural life in the later Roman Empire', pp.

89–117 in M. M. Postan (ed.) *Cambridge Economic History of Europe vol. 1: the agrarian life of the Middle Ages*, Cambridge: Cambridge University Press.

Stevenson, R. F. 1968 *Population and Political Systems in Tropical Africa*, New York: Columbia University Press.

Steward, J. H. 1929 'Irrigation without agriculture', *Papers of the Michigan Academy of Science, Arts and Letters* 12, 149–56.

Stjernquist, B. 1967 *Ciste a Cordoni (Rippenkisten): Produktion-Funktion-Diffusion*, Acta Arch. Lundensia, Ser. 1(40) 6, Bonn and Lund: Rudolf Habelt Verlag and CWK Gleerups Förlag.

Stol, M. 1993 'Milk, butter and cheese', *Bulletin on Sumerian Agriculture* 7, 99–113.

Strahm, C. 1972 'Das Beil von Thun-Renzenbühl', *Helvetia Archaeologica* 3, 99–112.

Strommenger, E. 1976 'Habuba Kabir-Süd: Erforschung einer Stadt am Syrischen Euphrat', *Archaeologisches Korrespondenzblatt* 6, 97–102.

Strommenger, E. 1980 *Habuba Kabira: eine Stadt vor 5000 Jahren*, Mainz: von Zabern.

Stronach, D. 1980 'Achaemenian and Seleucid Iran', pp. 206–11 in A. G. Sherratt (ed.) *Cambridge Encyclopedia of Archaeology*, Cambridge: Cambridge University Press.

Stuiver, M. and Reimer, P. J. 1993 'Extended ^{14}C data base and revised CALIB 3.0 ^{14}C age calibration', *Radiocarbon* 35, 215–30.

Sulimirski, T. 1960 'Remarks concerning the distribution of some varieties of flint in Poland', *Swiatowit* 22, 281–307.

Swadesh, M. 1968 'Glottochronology', pp. 384–403 in M. Fried (ed.) *Readings in Anthropology*, New York: Crowell.

Szabolcs, I. (ed.) 1971 *European Solonetz Soils and their Reclamation*, Budapest: Akadémiai Kiadó.

Szabolcs, I. (ed.) 1974 *Salt-affected Soils in Europe*, The Hague: Nijhoff.

Tabaczyński, S. 1972 'Gesellschaftsordnung und Güteraustausch im Neolithikum Mitteleuropas', *Neolithische Studien* vol. 1, 31–78, Berlin: Akademie-Verlag.

Taylor, C. 1972 *The Study of Settlement Patterns in pre-Saxon Britain*, pp. 109–13 in P. Ucko, G. W. Dimbleby and R. Tringham (eds) *Man, Settlement and Urbanism*, London: Duckworth.

Taylor, F. B. 1865 *Researches into the Early History of Mankind and the Development of Civilisation*, London.

Taylor, J. J. 1980 *Bronze Age goldwork in the British Isles*, Cambridge: Cambridge University Press.

Taylor, T. F. 1985 'Bronze Age Thrace reviewed', *Antiquity* 59, 129–32.

Taylor, T. F. 1986 'Thracian Bronze Age and International relations', pp. 187–201 in *Proceedings of the 4th International Thracian Conference*, Milan: Dragan European Foundation.

Tegtmeier, U. 1993 *Neolithische und bronzezeitliche Pflugspuren in Norddeutschland und den Niederlanden* (Archäologische Berichte 3), Bonn: Holos.

Telegin, D. Ya. 1971 'Über einen der ältesten Pferdezuchtherde in Europa', *Rapports et Communications de l'URSS, VIIIe Congrès International des Sciences Pré- et Protohistoriques*, Moscow.

Telegin, D. Ya. 1973 *Seredno-Stogivska kul'tura epokhi midi*, Kiev: Naukova Dumka.

Telegin, D. Ya. 1986 *Dereivka: a settlement and cemetery of Copper Age horse-*

keepers on the Middle Dniepr (BAR Int. Ser. 287), Oxford: British Archaeological Reports.

Teuber, M. 1995 'How can modern food technology help to identify dairy products mentioned in Sumerian texts?', *Bulletin on Sumerian Agriculture* 8, 23–31.

Thapar, R. 1975 *The Past and Prejudice*, New Delhi: Publications division, Ministry of Information and Broadcasting, Government of India.

Thomas, J. 1988 'Neolithic explanations revisited: the Mesolithic–Neolithic transition in Britain and south Scandinavia', *Proceedings of the Prehistoric Society* 54, 59–66.

Thrane, H. 1962 'The earliest bronze vessels in Denmark's Bronze Age', *Acta Archaeologica* (Copenhagen) 33, 109–63.

Thrane, H. 1982 'Dyrkningsspor fra yngre stenalder i Danmark', pp. 20–8 in H. Thrane (ed.) *Om yngre stenalders bebyggelseshistorie* (Skrifte fra Historisk Institut 30), Odense: Odense Universitet.

Thrane, H. 1989 'Danish plough-marks from the Neolithic and Bronze Age', *Journal of Danish Archaeology* 8, 111–25.

Tihelka, K. 1954 'Nejstarší hliněné napodobeniny čtyřramenných kol na území ČSR', *Památky Archeologické* 45, 219–24.

Tilley, C. 1984 'Ideology and legitimation of power in the middle Neolithic of southern Sweden', pp. 111–46 in D. Miller and C. Tilley (eds) *Ideology, Power and Prehistory*, Cambridge: Cambridge University Press.

Točík, A. 1981 *Nitriansky Hrádok-Zámeček: bronzezeitliche befestigte Ansiedlung der Maďarovce Kultur*, Nitra: Archaeological Institute of the Slovak Academy of Sciences.

Točík, A. and Vladár, J. 1971 'Prehľad bádania v problematike vývoja Slovenska v dobe bronzovej', *Slovenská Archaeológia* 19, 365–416.

Todd, I. A. 1978 *Çatal Hüyük in Perspective*, Menlo Park: Cummings.

Todorova, H. 1978a 'Die Nekropole bei Varna', *Zeitschrift für Archäologie* 12, 87–97.

Todorova, H. 1978b *The Eneolithic Period in Bulgaria* (BAR Int. Ser. 49), Oxford: British Archaeological Reports.

Todorova, H. 1982 *Kupferzeitliche Siedlungen in Bulgarien*, Munich: Beck.

Tompa, F. 1929 *Die Bandkeramik in Ungarn*, Budapest: Franklin.

Tompa, F. 1937 '25 Jahre Urgeschichtsforschung in Ungarn 1912–1936', 24/25 *Bericht der Römisch-Germanischen Kommission 1934/5*, 27–127.

Tosi, M. 1974a 'Some data for the study of prehistoric cultural areas on the Persian Gulf', *Seminar for Arabian Studies* 4, 145–74.

Tosi, M. 1974b 'The problem of turquoise in protohistoric trade on the Iranian Plateau', *Studi di Paletnologia, Palaentroplogia e Geologia del Quaternario* NS 2, 147–62.

Treue, W. (ed.) 1986 *Achse, Rad und Wagen: fünftausend Jahre Kultur- und Technikgeschichte*, Göttingen: Vandenhoek and Ruprecht.

Trevor-Roper, H. 1983 'The invention of tradition: the Highland tradition of Scotland', pp. 15–41 in E. J. Hobsbawm and T. O. Ranger (eds) *The Invention of Tradition*, Cambridge: Cambridge University Press.

Trigger, B. G. 1980 *Gordon Childe: revolutions in archaeology*, London: Thames and Hudson.

Trigger, B. G. 1982 'If Childe were alive today', *Bulletin of the Institute of Archaeology* [University of London] 19, 1–20.

Trigger, B. G. 1989 *A History of Archaeological Thought*, Cambridge: Cambridge University Press.

Tringham, R. 1971 *Hunters, Fishers and Farmers of Eastern Europe 6000–3000 BC*, London: Hutchinson.

Troels-Smith, J. 1953 'Ertebøllekultur bondekultur: Resultater af de sidste 10 års undersøgelser i Åmosen, Vestsjaelland', *Aarbøger for nordisk Oldkyndighed og Historie (1953)*, 5–62.

Trump, D. 1960 'Pottery anchors', *Antiquity* 34, 295.

Uenze, O. 1958 'Neue Zeichensteine aus dem Kammergrab von Züschen', pp. 99–106 in W. Krämer (ed.) *Neue Ausgrabungen in Deutschland* (Römisch-Germanische Kommission des Deutschen Archaeologischen Instituts), Berlin: Verlag Gebr. Mann.

Uerpmann, H.-P. 1990 'Die Domestikation des Pferdes im Chalkolithikum West- und Mitteleuropas', *Madrider Mitteilungen* 31, 109–53.

Unger, H. J. and Schütz, E. 1982 'Pangaion – ein Gebirge und sein Bergbau', pp. 145–72 in B. Hänsel (ed.) *Südosteuropa zwischen 1600 und 1000 v. Chr.* vol. 1, Berlin/Bad Braunstedt: Moreland.

Uslar, R. von 1955 'Der Goldbecher von Fritzdorf bei Bonn', *Germania* 33, 319–23.

Ussishikin, D. 1980 'The Ghassulian shrine at En-gedi', *Tel Aviv* 7, 1–44.

Vajda, S. 1960 *Introduction to Linear Programming and the Theory of Games*, London: Methuen.

van Andel, Tj. H. and Runnels, C. 1995 'The earliest farmers in Europe', *Antiquity* 69, 481–500.

van Andel, Tj. H., Gallis, K. and Toufexis, G. 1994 'Early Neolithic farming in a Thessalian river landscape', pp. 131–43 in J. Lewin (ed.) *Mediterranean Quaternary River Environments*, Rotterdam: Balkema.

van Wijngaarden-Bakker, L. 1974 'The animal remains from the Beaker settlement at Newgrange, Co. Meath: first report', *Proceedings of the Royal Irish Academy* (Section C), 74, 313–83.

van Wijngaarden-Bakker, L. H. 1975 'Horses in the Dutch Neolithic', pp 341–4 in A. T. Clason (ed.) *Archaeozoological Studies*, North-Holland: Elsevier.

van der Waals, J. D. 1964 *Prehistoric Disc-Wheels in the Netherlands*, Groningen: Wolters.

Vayda, A. P. 1966 'Pomo trade feasts', *Humanités: Cahiers de l'Institut de Science Economique Appliquée*.

Vayda, A. P. (ed.) 1969 *Environment and Cultural Behaviour*, New York: Natural History Press.

Veit, U. 1984 'Gustaf Kossina und V. Gordon Childe: Ansätze zu einer theoretischen Grundlegung der Vorgeschichte', *Saeculum* 35(4), 326–64.

Venedikov, I. 1975 'Vulchitrunskoto Sukrovishte', *Izkustvo* 2–3, 2–9.

Vértes, L. 1964 'Eine prähistorische Silexgrube am Mogyorósdomb bei Sümeg', *Acta Archaeologica Academiae Scientiarum Hungaricae* 16, 187–215.

Vértesalji, P. P. 1987 'The chronology of the Chalcolithic in Mesopotamia', pp. 483–507 in Aurenche et al. (eds) 1987.

Vértesalji, P. P. 1988 'Das Ende der Uruk-Zeit im Lichte der Grabungsergebnisse der sogenannten "archaischen" Siedlung bei Uruk-Warka', *Acta Praehistorica et Archaeologica* 20, 9–26.

Vickers, M. 1985–6 'Imaginary Etruscans: changing perceptions of Etruria since the fifteenth century', *Hephaistos* 7–8, 153–68.

Vickers, M. and Gill, D. 1994 *Artful Crafts: ancient Greek silverware and pottery*, Oxford: Clarendon Press.

Vintners, Worshipful Company of, 1933 *Wine Trade Exhibition of Drinking Vessels* (Catalogue of exhibition held at Vintners' Hall), London, privately printed.

Viragh, D. 1979 'Cartographical data on the Kurgans of the Tisza Region', pp. 119–41 in I. Ecsedy 1979 *The people of the Pit-grave Kurgans in eastern Hungary*, Budapest: Akadémiai Kiadó.

Vita-Finzi, C. 1969a 'Fluvial geology', pp. 135–50 in D. Brothwell and E. S. Higgs (eds) *Science in Archaeology* (2nd edn), London: Thames and Hudson.

Vita-Finzi, C. 1969b 'Geological opportunism', pp. 31–4 in P. Ucko and G. Dimbleby (eds) *The Domestication and Exploitation of Plants and Animals*, London: Duckworth.

Vita-Finzi, C. and Higgs, E. S. 1970 'Prehistoric economy in the Mount Carmel area of Palestine: site catchment analysis', *Proceedings of the Prehistoric Society* 36, 1–37.

Vizdal, I. 1972 'Erste bildliche Darstellung eines zweirädigen Wagens vom Ende der mittleren Bronzezeit in der Slowakei', *Slovenská Archaeólogia* 20, 223–31.

Vladár, J. 1973 'Osteuropäische und mediterrane Einflüsse im Gebiet der Slovakei während der Bronzezeit', *Slovenská Archaeólogia* 21, 253–357.

Vogt, E. 1937 *Geflechte und Gewebe der Steinzeit* (Monographien zur Ur- und Frühgeschichte der Schweiz), Basel: Verlag E. Birkhauser.

Vulpe, A. 1973 'Începuturile metalurgiei aramei în spaţiul Carpato-Dunărean', *Studii şi Cercetări di Istorie Veche* 24, 217–37.

Vulpe, A. and Mihailescu-Bîrliba, V. 1985 'Der Goldschatz von Rădeni, jud. Neamţ in der Westmoldau, Rumänien', *Prähistorische Zeitschrift* 60, 47–69.

Walker, M. J. 1985 '5000 años de viticultura en España', *Revista de Arqueologia* 6, 44–7.

Wallerstein, I. 1974 *The Modern World-System: capitalist agriculture and the origins of the world-economy in the 16th century*, New York: Academic Press.

Warriner, D. 1939 *Economics of Peasant Farming*, Oxford: Oxford University Press.

Waterbolk, H. T. and Butler, J. J. 1965 'Comments on the use of metallurgical analysis in prehistoric studies', *Helinium* 5, 227–51.

Weiss, H. 1986 *The Origins of Cities in Dry-farming Syria and Mesopotamia in the Third Millennium* BC, Guildford, Connecticut: Four Quarters Publishing.

Werner, J. 1954 'Die Bronzekanne von Kelheim', *Bayerische Vorgeschichtsblätter* 20, 43–73.

Werth, E. 1954 *Grabstock, Hacke und Pflug*, Ludwigsburg: Verlag Eugen Ulmer.

White, L. A. 1959 *The Evolution of Culture: the development of civilization to the fall of Rome*, New York: McGraw-Hill.

White, L. 1962 *Medieval Technology and Social Change*, Oxford: Oxford University Press.

Whittle, A. 1985 *Neolithic Europe: a survey*, Cambridge: Cambridge University Press.

Whittlesey, D. 1944 *The Earth and the State*, New York: Holt.

Wiklak, H. 1980 'Wyniki badán wykopaliskowych w obrębie Grobowca 8 w Sarnowie w woj. Włocławskim', *Prace i Materiały Muzeum Archeologicznego i Etnograficznego w Lodzi* (Ser. Arch.) 27, 33–73.

Wilke, G. 1929 'V'lči-Tr'n', pp. 227–8 in M. Ebert (ed.) *Reallexikon der Vorgeschichte* vol. 14, Berlin: Verlag Walter de Gruyter and Co.

Willerding, U. 1970 'Vor- und frühgeschichtliche Kulturpflanzenfunde in Mitteleuropa', *Neue Ausgrabungen in Niedersachsen* 5, 287–375.

Williams-Thorpe, O. 1978 *The Distribution and Provenance of Archaeological Obsidian in Central and Eastern Europe* (unpublished Ph.D. thesis, University of Bradford).

Williams-Thorpe, O., Warren, S. E. and Nandris, J. G. 1984 'The distribution and provenance of archaeological obsidian in central and eastern Europe', *Journal of Archaeological Science* 11, 183–212.

Willms, C. 1982 *Zwei Fundplätze der Michelsberger Kultur aus dem westlichen Münsterland, gleichzeitig ein Beitrag zum Neolithischen Silexhandel in Mitteleuropa*, Hildesheim: August Lax.

Wilson, C. A. 1976 *Food and Drink in Britain*, Harmondsworth: Penguin Books.

Winckler, H. 1939 *Rock Drawings of Southern Upper Egypt*, 2 vols, London: Egypt Exploration Society.

Winiger, J. 1987 'Das Spätneolithikum der Westschweiz auf Rädern', *Helvetia Archaeologica* 18, 78–109.

Winiger, J. 1995 'Die Bekleidung des Eismannes und die Anfänge der Weberei nördlich der Alpen' in K. Spindler, E. Rastbichler-Zissernig, H. Wilfing, D. zur Nedden and H. Nothdurfter (eds) *Der Mann im Eis: neue Funde und Ergebnisse* (The Man in the Ice, 2), Vienna: Springer-Verlag.

Wiślański, T. (ed.) 1970a *The Neolithic in Poland*, Warsaw: Ossolineum.

Wiślański, T. 1970b 'The Globular Amphora culture', pp. 178–231 in T. Wiślański (ed.) *The Neolithic in Poland*, Warsaw: Ossolineum.

Wittfogel, K. A. 1957 *Oriental Despotism: a Comparative Study of Total Power*, New Haven: Yale University Press.

Wolf, E. R. 1966 *Peasants*, Englewood Cliffs: Prentice Hall.

Wolf, E. R. 1982 *Europe and the People without History*, Berkeley: University of California Press.

Woytowitsch, E. 1985 'Die ersten Wagen der Schweiz: die ältesten Europas', *Helvetia Archaeologica* 61, 2–45.

Wright, H. T., Miller, N. and Redding, R. 1980 'Time and process in an Uruk local centre', pp. 265–84 in M.-T. Barrelet (ed.) *L'Archéologie de l'Iraq du Début de l'Époque Néolithique à 333 avant notre ère*, Paris: CNRS.

Wrigley, E. A. 1962 'The supply of raw materials in the Industrial Revolution', *Economic History Review* 2nd ser. 15, 1–16.

Wrigley, E. A. 1969 *Population and History*, London: Weidenfeld and Nicolson.

Wynne-Edwards, V. C. 1962 *Animal Dispersion in Relation to Social Behaviour*, Edinburgh: Oliver and Boyd.

Yoffee, N. 1979 'The decline and rise of Mesopotamian civilisation; an ethno-archaeological perspective on the evolution of social complexity', *American Antiquity* 44, 5–35.

Yoffee, N. 1981 'Explaining trade in ancient western Asia', *Monographs on the Ancient Near East* 2.

Yoffee, N. and Sherratt, A. 1993 *Archaeological theory: who sets the agenda?*, Cambridge: Cambridge University Press.

Young, T. Cuyler 1986 'Godin Pepe Period VI/V and Central Western Iran at the end of the Fourth Millennium', pp. 212ff in U. Finkbeiner and W. Röllig (eds)

Ǧamdat Nasr: Period or Regional Style, Reichert Verlag, Wiesbaden (= Beihefte zum Tübinger Atlas des Vorderen Orients, Ser. B, Nr. 62).

Zafiropulo, J. 1966 *Mead and Wine: a history of the Bronze Age in Greece*, London: Sidgwick and Jackson.

Zaharia, E. 1959 'Die Lockenringe von Sărata-Monteoru und ihre typologischen und chronologischen Beziehungen', *Dacia* NS 3, 103–34.

Zaibert, V. F. 1993 *Eneolit uralo-irtyshskogo mezhdurech'ya*, Petropavlovsk: Nauka.

Zarins, J. 1976 *The Domestication of Equidae in Third Millennium Mesopotamia* (unpublished Ph.D. thesis, University of Chicago).

Zarins, J. 1978 'The camel in ancient Arabia: a further note', *Antiquity* 52, 44–6.

Zarins, J. 1989 'Pastoralism in southwest Asia: the second millennium BC', pp. 127–55 in J. Clutton-Brock (ed.) *The Walking Larder: patterns of domestication, pastoralism and predation*, London: Unwin-Hyman.

Zdanivich, G. B. 1988 *Bronzovyi vek uralo-kazakhstanskikh stepei*, Sverdlovsk: Izdatel'stvo Uralskogo Universiteta.

Zeuner, F. 1955 'The identity of the camel on the Khurab Pick', *Iraq* 17, 162–3.

Zeuner, F. E. 1963 *History of Domesticated Animals*, London: Hutchinson.

Zich, B. 1992 'Frühneolithische Karrenspuren in Flintbek: Aktuelles aus der Landesarchäologie', *Archäologie in Deutschland* 1, 58.

Zindel, C. and Defuns, A. 1980 'Spuren von Pflugackerbau aus der Jungsteinzeit in Graubünden', *Helvetia Archaeologica* 11(42), 42–5.

Zohary, D. 1969 'The progenitors of wheat and barley', pp. 47–66 in P. Ucko and G. Dimbleby (eds) *The Domestication and Exploitation of Plants and Animals*, London: Duckworth.

Zohary, D. and Hopf, M. 1993 (2nd edn) *Domestication of Plants in the Old World: the origin and spread of cultivated plants in West Asia, Europe and the Nile Valley*, Oxford: Clarendon Press.

Zohary, D. and Spiegel-Roy, P. 1975 'Beginnings of fruit-growing in the Old World', *Science* 187, 319–27.

Zvelebil, M. 1986 (ed.) *Hunters in Transition: Mesolithic societies of temperate Eurasia and their transition to farming*, Cambridge: Cambridge University Press.

INDEX

Aalborg (Denmark), flint source (mine), 116
Acemhüyük (Turkey), Bronze Age
   settlement, 223
Aegeo-Anatolian culture (3500–3000 BC),
   380–2, 386
Africa, west, cultivation systems in, 101
aggregation/dispersal of population, 311
agriculture
   beginnings of, 6–7
   surplus, 81–2
Aibunar (Bulgaria), prehistoric copper mine,
   126
Akkadian Empire, 459
Alaca Hüyük (Turkey), 220, 226
Albuñol, Granada (Spain), 408
alcoholic drinks, 29, 231–3, 376–402, 417;
   see also beer; wine
Aldenhovener Platte (Germany), pollen
   diagram, 235
Alföld Linear Pottery culture see AVK culture
alignments (megalithic), 357, 367–8
Alps, settlement of, 124(fig.)
Alsónémedi (Hungary), Baden culture
   cemetery, 161, 180, 233, 381(fig.), 386,
   418–19
Altyn Depe (Turkmenistan), Bronze Age
   settlement, 211(fig.), 225, 458
Andel, Tjeerd van, 21
Andronovo culture, 173, 222, 475
animal traction, economics of, 182
Annales (school of historiography), 68
anti-Semitism, 49
Archaeological Topography of Hungary
   programme, 271, 285, 293, 299
ard (light plough), 95(fig.), 200–1; see also
   plough
Argaric culture, 148
Arkaim (Kazakhstan), Bronze Age
   settlement, 222
arsenic, as alloying element in copper, 129–30
Arslantepe (Turkey), Bronze Age settlement,
   216
Ashgrove Farm, Methilhill, Fife (Scotland),
   Bell-Beaker grave, 396
Asiatic mode of production, 48
Aspergillus oryzae (fungus inducing
   fermentation), 393
ass see donkey

Aššur (Iraq), Bronze Age settlement, 192
astronomical knowledge, prehistoric, 149
astronomical orientation, of Neolithic
   settlements, 355, 358
Aunjetitz see Únětice culture
autonomism, cultural, 11–13
Avebury (England), henge monument, 148–9
AVK (Alföldi Vonaldíszes Kerámia, Alföld
   linear pottery) culture, 258, 279, 286,
   305–6
axle, rotating and fixed, 244(fig.), 246–8
Azor tomb (Israel), 207(fig.), 209

Baalberge culture, 346, 380(fig.)
Baden culture, 218, 246, 259, 281, 291,
   309, 380, 386, 437(fig.), 499
Baden-Cernavoda-Ezero complex, 17; see
   also Baden culture
Bahrein, 211
Baia Mare (Romania), copper source, 121
Balfarg Riding School, Glenrothes, Fife
   (Scotland), Neolithic ceremonial centre,
   426
Balkans, stone resources of, 109
banded flint, 112
Bandkeramik culture, 339–40, 344, 346,
   361, 362, 366, 474
   cemetery analysis, 117(fig.)
   stone resources, 109
barley as crop, 92, 394
Bat-Yam (Israel), 207(fig.)
bee-keeping see honey
beer, 9, 388, 390(fig.), 392–4
   barley, 394
   Celtic, 394
   Egyptian, 394
   emmer, 394
   see also alcoholic drinks
beer-flavouring plants, 402n
Begleitkeramik see Bell-Beaker culture
Bell-Beaker culture, 26, 147, 149, 267, 370,
   376, 384–5, 386, 422, 499
Bernburg (Germany), 203–4; see also
   Latdorf
Bernburg culture, 218, 382; see also
   Walternienburg culture
Beycesultan (Turkey), Bronze Age settlement,
   382

'big man' social system, 108, 196
bit (for horse) *see* bridle-bit
Black Sea
    history of, 21
    linguistic *koine*, in Early Bronze Age, 478
Bodrogkeresztúr culture, 259, 281, 290, 295, 308, 331, 379, 380–2
    cemetery analysis, 117(fig.), 131
    copper daggers, 131
    flint daggers, 118
Boleráz culture, 309
Boserup, Ester, 74–5, 86, 100, 188
Botai (Kazakhstan), Copper Age settlement, 214–15
Bougon, Deux Sèvres (France), megalithic tombs, 343
Březno (Czech Republic), Eneolithic monument, 231
bride-wealth, 105, 266
bridle-bit, 172, 213, 217–18, 221
Britain, Neolithic, 352
Bronocice (Poland), Neolithic settlement, 163, 202
bronze *see* copper alloy metallurgy
Brześć Kujawski (Poland), Neolithic settlement and burials, 141
Budakalász (Hungary), Baden culture cemetery, pottery wagon model, 161, 162
Bükk culture/group, 280, 286–8, 326
Bükk mountains, 260–2
Bygholm Nørremark, Jutland (Denmark), megalithic tomb, 349
Bytýn (Poland), copper hoard, 201, 226n

Calanca valley (Switzerland), plough marks, 201
calcium absorption, 208, 232
Cambridge, University of, 68
camels, 211–12
    domestication of, 11, 173
cannabis, 389, 398–9, 407–8, 411, 416, 425
capitalism, 503
Cardial (Impressed ware) culture, 22, 339–40, 474
Carnac, Brittany (France), megalithic monuments, 350–1, 367
Carpathian Basin, 255–332, 271–3
    as regional system, 260–3
    stone resources of, 109
    see also Hungary
carrying capacity, 71
cart, 161–5
cash crops, 6
Castaneda, Graubünden (Switzerland), plough marks, 201
Catacomb-Grave culture, 193, 219
Çatal Hüyük (old spelling) (Turkey) *see* Çatalhöyük
Çatalhöyük (Turkey), 7, 19, 21, 79, 87, 180, 189, 254, 358

cattle, domestication of, 254
Caucasian metallurgy, 130
causewayed (interrupted-ditch) enclosures, Neolithic, 145
Celtic language groups, 474, 483
Celts, 50, 394
    enthusiasm for ancient, 50, 54
cemeteries
    Baden culture *see* Budakalász; Alsónémedi; Szigetszentmáton
    Copper Age, 141, 265, 289–90, 308, 359–61
    see also Tibava; Tiszapolgár-Basatanya; Varna
cemetery analysis, 117(fig.), 131, 233(fig.)
Central/Northern Europe
    5000–3000 BC, 142–6
    3000–2500 BC, 146–7
centre/periphery diffusion, 83; *see also* core/periphery system
cereal cultivation, demographic effects of, 72–3
cereals
    domestication of, 90
    wild, 89
ceremonial exchange, 105
Cernavoda I culture, 24
Cernavoda III culture, 382; *see also* Baden-Cernavoda-Ezero complex
Cerny, 341–3
Cham culture, 218
Chapman, J. C., 229
chariot and chariotry, 28, 218, 219–23
Chasséen culture, 351
cheek-piece (for horse) *see* bridle-bit
cheese, 208; *see also* milk products
chiefdom, 135
Childe, Vere Gordon, 37–66, 70, 334, 337, 361–2, 370, 377, 490–505
    syntheses of European prehistory, 57–62
China, domestic animals in, 29, 198
chocolate flint, 112
Choga Mami (Iraq), early irrigation traces, 7, 96
Chorley, Richard, 68
chronology, prehistoric Europe, 20(fig.), 27(fig.), 61
Chur-Welschdörfli (Switzerland), plough marks, 201
cinnabarite (red mercuric sulphide), as paint, 115
civilisations *see individual civilisations*
Clairvaux-les-lacs Station III, Jura (France), Neolithic settlement, 205
Clark, Sir Grahame, 39–40, 102, 490, 496
Clarke, David L., 68, 158n, 198, 496
clothing, languages of, 405
coastal trading, 106–8
cocoa (beverage), 388
coffee (beverage), 388
collared flask (*Kragenflasche*), TRB vessel, 350, 415

colonialisation, internal *see* settlement area, expansion of
colonialism, nineteenth century *see* imperialism
community
    as basis of social organisation, 152
    symbolic construction of, 337
compass-drawn ornament, 221–2, 452
consumer durables, circulation of, 152
consumption
    cultural, 15–17
    elite, 17
conversion (Mesolithic to Neolithic), 361–3
Copais, Lake (Greece), 90
Copper Age, 330
    north-west European, 146
    social systems, 151, 152
    south-east European, 23, 141
copper alloy metallurgy, 129–33, 240
copper axes, distribution in south-east Europe, 127–9
copper discs, ornamental, 348
copper metallurgy, 119–29, 259
copper mining, earliest European, 126–8
copper ores
    in south-east and central Europe, 121–5
    mineralogy of, 119–20
copper shafthole axes (south-east Europe), chronology of, 125–6
cord decoration (impressed on pottery), 383, 411; *see also* Corded Ware culture
cord ornament *see* cord decoration
Corded Ware culture, 24, 146, 245, 267, 349, 370, 383–4, 386, 397, 416, 421, 422–4, 499; *see also* TRB/Corded Ware transition
core/periphery system, 10–11, 17–18, 84n, 466–7, 501–2
Cretan hieroglyphic script, 165
Criş culture *see* Körös culture
crook-ard (type of scratch-plough), 95(fig.), 166(fig.)
crop rotation, 94
Csepel Haros (Hungary), Bell-Beaker settlement, 171, 219
Csöszhalom culture/group, 288–9
Cucuteni-Tripole culture, 23–4, 369
Cueva de los Murciélagos, Albuñol (Spain), late Neolithic burial-cave, 408
cuisine, language of, 405, 412
cultivation systems, 85
    Neolithic, 237–8
    see also soil types; hoe cultivation; plough cultivation; permanent cultivation; slash-and-burn; tropical cultivation
cylinder-seal, 165(fig.), 176(fig.)

dairying *see* milking
Danube (river), history of, 274
Darwin, Charles, 36, 45, 53
date palm, 391

de Mortillet, Gabriel, 55
Dead Sea rift, 78
depas amphikypellon (two-handed cup), 391
Dereivka (Ukraine), Copper Age settlement, 170, 213–15, 227n
descent groups, 194–5
Despotism, Oriental, 48
Dévaványa (Hungary)
    excavations in, 300–2
    see also Sártó; Réhelyi Dülö
differential preservation, 203
diffusionism, 56
Dilmun *see* Bahrein
disease, 21
dispersal, of population, 311
distribution zones, for prehistoric traded commodities, 104
dolmens *see* dysser; megaliths
domestic animals, 29
    trade in, 253–4, 262
donkey (*Equus asinus*), 17–18(fig.), 209–11, 216–17
    domestication of, 11, 172–3
drinking *see* alcohol
drinking-straws, 390(fig.), 393
driving *see* chariot and chariotry
drugs *see* psychotropic substances
drum, Neolithic, 421
dry-farming, 91
dysser (Danish dolmens), 349, 364

Early Bronze Age (Hungary), 310–11
Edinburgh, University of, 38, 42
Egtved (Denmark), Bronze Age burial, 396
Egypt
    irrigation, 98
    predynastic, 209–10, 459
El 'Ubeid (Iraq), 177(fig.)
'elites', 404
En-Gedi (Israel), Chalcolithic site, 207(fig.), 209
enclosures (earthwork), Neolithic, 145, 148, 265–6, 358
Enlightenment, 3, 47–8
epi-Bandkeramik cultures/groups, 340
equids, domestication of, 170
Ertebølle culture, 345, 349, 356
Eschen-Lutzengüetle (Switzerland), Neolithic settlement, 205
Esztár culture/group, 280, 286–8
Eucharist, Christian, 404
Euphrates river
    and irrigation, 97–8
    as transport link, 10
Evans, Sir Arthur, 41, 56
evolution, as idea, 36
exchange
    ceremonial, 105
    distances, Neolithic, 110–16
    systems, Neolithic, 104, 320–2

transfer in, 105
see also settlement patterns
Ezero (Bulgaria), Bronze Age settlement, 382
see also Baden-Cernavoda-Ezero complex

Fahlerz, grey (enriched) ore of copper, 119, 130
farming, spread of, 137–8
farming systems, 76
Mediterranean, 80
feasting, 392, 406
fermentation, discovery of, 9–10
Fertile Crescent, 13, 197
fish-trap basketry, 366(fig.)
Fisher, H. A. L., 496
flint (Polish), Neolithic exploitation of, 111(fig.), 111–13
flint sources and mines, Neolithic, 190, 235–6
France, 113–15
Neolithic Europe, 112–16
Poland, 111–13
flood regimes, 93(fig.)
floodwater-farming, 95–6, 189
forest clearance, 190
Frazer, Sir James, 500
Freeman, E. A., 53
funnel-beaker culture *see* TRB culture
funnel-necked beaker, 380; *see also* TRB culture
Furchenstock (hand-ard), 168

gallery grave, megalithic monument, 356
Gavrinis, Morbihan, Brittany (France), megalithic tomb, 351, 365
gender roles, 196
Geoffrey of Monmouth, 46
geology, nineteenth-century, 52
Germans, enthusiasm for ancient, 50, 54, 55
Gerzean *see* Egypt, predynastic
Ghassulian culture (Palestine), 184, 207, 209
Gilat (Israel), 207(fig.), 209
Giv'atoyim (Israel), Bronze Age site, 209
Globular Amphora culture, 24, 162, 235–6, 382, 397
gold, 433
Grand Pressigny (France), flint source, 113–15
grape
cultivated, 391
wild, 389
see also tree crops
Graubünden (Switzerland), 201
Great Hungarian Plain, 255–332; *see also* Hungary
Greeks, enthusiasm for ancient *see* Philhellenism
grey-white-speckled flint, 112–14
Grooved Ware culture, 366, 413

Habuba el-Kabireh (Syria), Bronze Age settlement, 192

Haggett, Peter, 68
Hahn, Eduard, 53, 155, 197
Halaf culture, 230
hallucinogens *see* psychotropic substances
Hamito-Semitic language groups *see* Semito-Hamitic language groups
Harappan (Indus Valley), civilisation in, 98, 164
use of plough in, 166
Hassuna culture, 224, 230
Hatvan culture, 282–3, 291
hay, 94
hemp *see* cannabis
henbane, *Hyoscyamus niger*, 427
henge monuments, 148–9
Neolithic, 357
see also stone circles
Herder, Johann Gottfried, 48
Hermann the Liberator, statue of, 50–1, 51(fig.)
Herpály-Csöszhalom culture/group, 280, 288–9
hierarchy, social, 135
Hippocrene spring (Boeotia), 400n
history, as idea, 36
Hittite language, 476
Hlinsko (Slovakia), Copper Age settlement, 16
hoards, of bronze objects, 132
Hochdorf, near Stuttgart (Germany), Iron Age burial, 395
Hodder, Ian, 63, 158n, 337, 357, 367
hoe cultivation, 160
honey, 395–6; *see also* mead
hop (*Humulus lupulus*), 402n
Horgen culture, 246
horse bit *see* bridle-bit
horse, 17–18(fig.), 212–23, 386
as draught animal, 172
domestication of, 11, 170–1, 216–17
in North America, 193
on Pontic steppes, 213–15, 222–3
riding, 217–18
wild, 212–15
horticulture, 67, 85, 91, 100
fixed-plot, 238(fig.)
Horton, Robin, 150–1
hospitality *see* feasting
houses, Neolithic *see* longhouse; roundhouse
Hov (Denmark), flint mines in, 115
human traction, 188
Hungary, 252–332
Hungary, eastern
cultural succession, 277–83
history of research, 283
intensity of research, 283–5
landscape and geomorphology of, 274–5, 295–9
prehistoric settlement distribution, 283–93
soils and vegetation, 276–7

hybrid equids *see* mule
hydroquartzite, 114, 323–7, 324, 327, 330

Iceman (Alpine), 204, 234
   location of, 124(fig.)
identity, cultural, 45
imperialism, nineteenth-century, 52, 54
Impressed Ware culture *see* Cardial culture
incense, 406
India, domestic animals in, 188
indigenism *see* autonomism
Indo-European language groups, 49, 54, 66,
   193–4, 474–84
Indo-European languages, and culture, 58–9
Indo-European mythology, 483
Indo-Iranian language group, 475, 481–3
Indus civilisation *see* Harappan civilisation
Indus (river), and irrigation, 97–8
ingot torques *see* Ösenhalsringe
insufflator (milking aid), 177
intensification, agricultural, 74–5, 86
inter-regional pottery types, 379; *see also*
   Corded Ware culture; Bell-Beaker
   culture
intoxication, anthropology of, 405–7
irrigation, 7, 67, 70, 94–9, 224
   and flood regimes, 93(fig.)
   canal, 99
   channel, 96
   gabarband, 97
   qanat, 97
   river-basin, 97–9
   see also individual rivers
Italic language groups, 483

Jawa (Jordan), early irrigation system, 97
Jebel Aruda (Syria), Bronze Age settlement,
   17
Jericho (Palestine), Neolithic and later
   settlement, 7, 87, 95, 189, 358
Jones, Sir William, 49
Juellinge Iron Age burial (Denmark), 396

Kalabari (west Africa), 151
kammerlose Hünenbetten, 347
Karanovo (Bulgaria), Neolithic and Bronze
   Age settlement, 122–3
Karimojong (Uganda), 182
Kartvelian language group, 476
kava (intoxicating drink), 393
Kel'teminar culture, 467
Kermanshah region (Iran), 224
kill-off patterns, for secondary products, 183
kinship, as basis of social organisation, 152
Kish (Iraq), Bronze Age settlement, 178(fig.)
Knossos (Crete), Bronze Age settlement,
   178(fig.)
Körös culture, 256, 278, 285–6, 302–19,
   321
Körös-Berettyó region, geomorphology of,
   295–9

Kossinna, Gustav, 54–5, 55, 65
Kothingeichendorf (Germany), Neolithic
   enclosure, 139
koumish, 398
Kreisgrabenanlagen, 358
Krężnica Jara (Poland), Neolithic settlement,
   162
Kruk, Janusz, 88
Kryzhovlin (Ukraine), Bronze Age gold
   vessel from, 448
Krzemionki (Poland), flint mines in,
   113(fig.), 116, 235–6
Kuffarn (Austria), situla from, 390(fig.)
Kujavian graves (Neolithic long-mounds), 347
kula-ring, exchange system (Melanesia),
   106–7
Kültepe Bronze Age settlement (Turkey), 223
Kura-Arax culture, 468–70
kurilnitsa see polypod bowl
Kyjovice Těšetice Neolithic settlement
   (Czech Republic), 139

La Hoguette ware, 366
lactase *see* lactose tolerance
Lactobacillus (yoghurt bacterium), 9
lactose tolerance, 174–5, 207–8, 232
Lagunda (Italy), 163
lake-villages, circum-Alpine, 335
lakes, and early farming, 78–9, 87
language groups *see individual groups*
lapis lazuli, 459, 461
   trade in, 11, 468
Laslett, Peter, 68
Latdorf, near Bernburg (Germany),
   Neolithic tomb, 203–4
Late Chalcolithic (Anatolia) cultures, 400n
LBK (*Linienbandkeramik*) *see Bandkeramik*
   culture
Lébous (France), Neolithic settlement, 148
Lengyel culture, 112, 123, 268n, 345, 346,
   380
Lepenski Vir (Serbia), Mesolithic settlement,
   21
levees, and early settlement, 98
Limbrey, Susan, 94
Limburg Ware, 366
limnoquartzite *see* hydroquartzite
lineage-aggregates, 151
lineages, 194
linear programming models, 84n
linen preservation, 203
linguistic change, 192–3
linguistic reconstruction, 472
Linkup phase (3800–3600 BC), 378
lithicisation (of earth-and-timber
   monuments), 364
Littauer, Mrs M. A., 248n
Little Poland, Neolithic settlement in, 88
livestock *see* domestic animals
location of settlements *see* settlement
   location

Locmariaquer, Morbihan, Brittany (France), megalithic monuments, 351
Lodagaa (west Africa), 151
loess soils, and Neolithic settlements, 78
Lohne see Züschen
long barrows, 145
longhouse, Neolithic, as model for monumental long-mound, 337–8
long-mounds, 360, 363
  in France, 338–44
  in northern Europe, 347–9
Los Millares (Spain), Copper Age settlement and tombs, 147
Luther, Martin, 47
luxuries, 106, 501–2
  in pre-history, 494

McNeill, William H., 44
Maes Howe (Scotland), megalithic tomb, 148
Magan see Oman
Maikop (northern Caucasus), Bronze Age burial, and Maikop culture, 173, 215, 225, 458, 461–6, 469
Makó culture, 282, 310
malaria, 21, 79
Malta, Neolithic temples in, 148
Malthusian trap, 6
Männerbund (body of male companions), 392
margin, 17, 501–2
marginal infilling see settlement area, expansion of
maritime activities
  Mediterranean, 11
  Persian Gulf, 9
Maritime phase (2500–2000 BC), 384–5
Marx, Karl, 53
Marxism, 43, 492, 494, 495, 503
  in archaeology, 39, 57, 59, 62, 140
'mature' Neolithic communities, 140, 144
Mauern (Austria), flint-mine, 115
Maya, ancient civilisation of, 101
mead, 394–6; see also honey
meadowsweet (Filipendula ulmaria), 396
Mecsek mountains, flint from, 323–7, 331
Mediterranean (Central/West), 5000–3000 BC, 147–8
megalithic architecture, as propaganda, 362
megalithic art, representation of axes in, 116
megaliths (megalithic tombs and ceremonial monuments), 22, 143–5, 333–71
  alignments, 357, 367–8
Melanesia, 106–8, 265
mercuric sulphide, 115
Mesoamerica, cultivation systems in, 101
Mesolithic groups in north-west Europe, 23, 88, 337–9, 344–5, 361–2
Mesolithic populations, 348
Mesolithic settlements, 364
Mesolithic survival, in Neolithic Europe, 145, 365–7

Mesolithic way of life, in contrast to Neolithic, 136
metal vessels, Bronze Age, 431–56
metallogenesis, 119–20
metallurgy
  origins of, 102–3
  prehistoric, 60, 102–33
Mexico, ancient civilisation of, 101
Michelsberg culture, 346
migration, 151
milk, 174–80
  ejection reflex, 177
  exploitation of animals for, 205–8
  products, 9, 175, 178–9, 208, 232, 398
milk-churn, 207
milking, 198, 205–9, 231–3
  economics of, 182
  techniques, 175–7
millet, 92
mines, 190
  copper, see copper mining, earliest European
  flint see flint mines, Neolithic
Minho (Portugal), cart for sale, 247(fig.)
mobility, of hunters and pastoralists, 29
Modernism, 3
money, 267
Montelius, Oscar, 56
Monteoru culture, 221, 440, 451
Montesquieu, C. L. de Secondat, Baron de, 47–8
monumentality
  domestic, 356
  see also tell settlements
  funerary see megaliths
Morgan, Lewis Henry, 53, 67, 140
mould, bivalve (two-piece), 130, 240
mule, 210, 216; see also donkey; horse
Müller, Max, 53
Munţii Metalici (Romania), copper source, 121
Myres, Professor Sir John, 41, 56, 58

Nagyrév culture, 282–3, 291, 385
Nahal Mishmar (Israel), arsenical copper hoard, 9, 210, 241n
narcotics see psychotropic substances
Narmer ('King Scorpion', Egyptian Pharaoh), 209
nationalism, 3, 50
Near East, 197
  geography of, 157, 197
  prehistory of, 59, 63
  see also Fertile Crescent
neo-megalithic period, 334–5
Neolithic, primary and secondary, 365
Neolithic Revolution (beginning of farming), 59, 72, 78, 158, 503
Neolithic way of life, in contrast to Mesolithic, 136
New Archaeology, 2, 12, 62–3, 68

New Guinea, stone axes in, 105, 116
New World, cultures of, 19
Newgrange (Ireland), megalithic tomb, 148, 219, 365
Nietleben (central Germany), megalithic tomb, 420–1
Nile valley *see* Egypt
Nitra (Slovakia), *Bandkeramik* culture cemetery, 117, 264
Nitriansky Hrádok-Zámeček (Slovakia), Baden-culture burial pit and Early Bronze Age fortified settlement, 418–19
Novosvobodnaya group (late Maikop culture), 470
nuclear/margin process, 11; *see also* core/periphery system; centre/periphery diffusion
Nyírség culture, 282, 310

obsidian (black volcanic glass), 109–10, 139, 147, 257, 258, 280, 288, 321, 326, 327–30, 331
  trade in, 254
ochre-grave *see* Pit-Grave culture
Oil Crisis (1970s), 2
Oldenburg (Germany), megalithic tomb, 201
Oman, 211
onager (*Equus hemionus*), 216
  and hybrids, 210–11
  possible domestication of, 171
opium poppy, 389–90, 407–8, 411, 415–16
ores, copper *see* copper ores
oriental despotism, 48
orientation, of Neolithic monuments, 355
Ösenhalsring metal (copper type), 131
Ösenhalsringe (neck-rings, used as ingots), 131–2
Otomani (Ottomány) culture, 221, 282–3, 310, 439–41, 451, 452, 454
Oxford, University of, 41
Oxie (or A) group, 349
oxytocin, and milk ejection, 177

pack-transport, 197, 207(fig.), 209–10
package transmission, 237
passage-graves 343, 364
Past and Present (historical journal), 43
pastoralism, 29, 71, 160, 184, 187, 192–3
Payne, Sebastian, 183
Pazyryk tumuli, Altai Mountains (Siberia), Iron Age burials, 398(fig.)
periphery *see* core/periphery system
Perjámos culture, 282–3
permanent cultivation, 75
Peru, ancient civilisation of, 101
Petropavlovsk (Kazakhstan), 214–15
Peyote Cult, 401n
Philhellenism, 49–50
Phrygian language groups, 483
pidginisation, 472
PIE *see* proto-Indo-European

Piggott, Stuart, 156, 248n, 337, 498
Pit-Grave culture, 24, 171, 193, 214–15, 218, 242–5, 246, 370, 383, 408, 464, 470, 475, 481
Pitt Rivers, Sir Augustus Henry (Lane Fox), 53
Plachidol, near Tolbukhin (Bulgaria), Bronze Age burials, 242–5
plough, 197, 230
  and seeder-funnel, 165(fig.)
  cultivation, 74–5, 160, 238(fig.)
  development of, 7, 92, 93(fig.), 95(fig.), 100, 196
  distribution of, 239(fig.), 240
  early evidence for, 15–18, 165–70, 200–1, 224
  effects of, 143, 185
  Near Eastern, 165
  pictographic signs for, 164(fig.)
plough marks, 13, 167–9
pollen diagrams, 235
pollution, 403
Polyanitsa (Bulgaria), 358
polypod bowl (brazier), 411, 412(fig.), 425
Pomo Indians (California), 118
Pontic steppes, as contact corridor, 130
poppy, opium *see* opium poppy
population, dispersal and aggregation of, 311
porotic hyperostosis (bone pathology), 79
positivism, nineteenth-century, 3, 52
Postmodernism, 3
post-processualism, 3
pottery, 411
  assemblages of, 412–17
pottery assemblages and diet, 178–9
pottery types, inter-regional, 379–85
PPIE *see* pre-proto-Indo-European
PPN *see* pre-pottery Neolithic
prehistory
  as science, 52
  European, 11–14, 19–27
  near Eastern, 6–11
pre-pottery Neolithic (PPN), 6–7
pre-proto-Indo-European (PPIE), postulated language family, 477
preservation, of textile fibres, 203
primary horticultural community, breakup of, 359–61
'primitive money', 267
profanity, 403–5
property transmission, 195–6
proto-Indo-European (PIE), reconstructed language, 477
psychoactive substances *see* psychotropic substances
psychotropic substances, 6, 30, 351, 356, 364, 406; *see also* intoxication, anthropology of
purification ritual, 409

qanat, 97; *see also* irrigation
quarries, 190

Rădeni (Romania), Bronze Age gold vessels, 448–50
Radošina (Slovakia), pottery wagon model, 162
ranking, social, 134
reconstruction, linguistic *see* linguistic reconstruction
recruitment, social, 363
Réhelyi Gát, Dévaványa parish (Hungary), Neolithic settlement, 306
Réhelyi Dülö, Dévaványa parish (Hungary), Neolithic settlement, 321
Reinach, Salomon, 54–5
reindeer, milking of, 198
religion, in prehistory, 494
Renfrew, Colin (Lord Renfrew of Kaimsthorn), 62, 156
residence systems, 194–5
rice, 99, 100–1
rickets *see* vitamin D deficiency
ritual formalisation, 137
river, and irrigation, 97–9
Roberts, J. M., 44
Roberts, Neil, 19
Roessen (Rössen) culture, 341–3, 345, 346
Romantic Movement, 3–4, 48–52
rotation of crops *see* crop rotation
roundhouse tradition, 367
Rudna Glava (Serbia), prehistoric copper mine, 126
Rügen (Germany), flint source, 112–14
rye, as crop, 94

Saccharomyces (yeast), 9, 389
sacrament, 404
sacred, the, 403–4
sacred places, 404, 422
sacred time, 404
Sahlins, Marshall D., 102, 152
sail, 9
Saint-Martin-de-Corléans, Valle d'Aosta (Italy), plough marks, 200–1
salination (salinisation) of soil, 98
salt, as item of Neolithic exchange, 112
Salzburg (Austria), copper sources, 124
Samarra culture, 224, 230
Sarnowo (Poland), Neolithic tomb and cultivation traces, 14, 230
Sártó, Dévaványa parish (Hungary), Neolithic settlement, 301, 302(fig.), 306, 307, 322, 326
Satrupholmer Moor, Angeln (Germany), Neolithic finds, 231
sauceboat (drinking vessel), 391
Schalkenburg (Germany), neolithic enclosure, 139, 202
Scheibenhenkeln (disc-terminal handles), 379

Schivelbusch, Wolfgang, 15
Schliemann, Heinrich, 53
Schneider, Jane, 17, 501
Schuchhardt, Carl, 55
Scirpus (sedge), as evidence of wet environments in Neolithic, 78, 90
scratch-plough (ard), 200–1
seafaring *see* maritime activities
secondary exploitation *see* secondary products complex
secondary products complex, 150, 155–98, 199–241
    and kill-off patterns, 183
    chronology of, 169(fig.)
    definition of, 31n
    economics of, 181–3
    interactions, 12(fig.), 185(fig.), 185–6, 186(fig.)
secondary products revolution, 6, 9, 31n, 158–98, 497
secular, the, 403–4
segmentary lineages, 151
Seima-Turbino-Samussk culture complex, 222
self-sufficiency, hypothesis of, 106
Semitic language group, 476
Semito-Hamitic (Afroasiatic) language groups, 193
sesame, as crop, 99
settlement areas
    expansion of, 80–1, 151
    location, 76
    Neolithic, 191(fig.)
settlement patterns
    and exchange, 104
    prehistoric, 87–9
shaduf (pole and bucket lever), 98
shamanism, 19, 30, 406
Shari-i Sokhta (Iran), Bronze Age settlement, 211
Sheng-wen (corded-ware) pottery, China, 397, 402n
shifting cultivation *see* slash-and-burn
shrines, 404
Siassi (Melanesian tribe), 107
sieves, ceramic (strainers), 13, 206
Sintashta (Kazakhstan), Bronze Age settlement and burials, 222
Sitagroi (Greece), Neolithic and Bronze Age settlement, 382–3
situla (decorated bronze bucket), 390(fig.)
skeuomorphism, 431–56
    basketry, 366(fig.), 443
    sheet-metalwork, 381–2
slash-and-burn, 74, 75, 86, 100, 150, 188, 238(fig.)
Slavs, enthusiasm for ancient, 50, 54
Smith, Adam, 48
smoking/smoke inhalation, 409–11, 414
Snave, near Dreslette (Denmark), megalithic tomb, 200, 230

social recruitment, 363
soil types
    and cultivation system, 75
    and prehistoric settlements, 84n, 91,
        190–1
south-east Europe
    5500–4500 BC, 139–40
    4500–3500 BC, 140–1
    3500–3000 BC, 141–2
Špania Dolina (Bulgaria), prehistoric copper
    mine, 126
spelt wheat, 92
Spencer, Herbert, 35, 36, 53
Spitzes Hoch tumulus (Germany), 203–4
Spondylus-shell ornaments
    Melanesia, 107(fig.)
    Neolithic European, 117–18
spring crops, 92, 93(fig.)
spring wheat, 90, 92, 94
    definition of, 101n
    see also wheat
Sredni Stog culture, 213–14
stadial model, 12–13, 52, 70, 135, 157
stake-frame basketry, 366(fig.)
Stara Zagora (Bulgaria), copper sources,
    122–3
Steppe phase (3000–2500 BC), 282, 387
stone axes, as symbols, 116
stone circles (circular megalithic monuments;
    see also henges), 357
stone distribution, Neolithic Europe, 110–16
stone resources, Neolithic, 108–18
Stonehenge (megalithic enclosure), 367–8
Stufentheorie see stadial model
sub-Neolithic cultures, 335, 362
'subsistence', as misleading term, 5
successional social change, 139
Sümeg (Hungary), flint source (mine), 115
supersite (large, wealthy, aggregated
    Neolithic settlement), 258
surplus, agricultural, 81–2
Susa (Iran), Bronze Age and later settlement,
    164
swidden cultivation see slash-and-burn
Świeciechów (Poland), flint from, 112
Świętokrzyskie (Holy Cross), mountains
    (Poland), flint from, 112
symbolic values, of artefacts, 105
symposium, Greek, 388–92, 399, 407, 431,
    432
Szakálhát culture/group, 258, 280, 306, 322
Szatmár culture/group, 279, 285–6, 321
Szeghalom survey, 294–5
    AVK culture, 305–6
    Baden culture, 309
    Bodrogkeresztúr, 308
    Boleráz culture, 309
    Early Bronze Age, 310
    Körös culture, 302
    Szakálhát culture, 306
    Tisza culture, 307, 308

Szigetszentmárton (Hungary), 161
    cart model, 180
Szilmeg culture/group, 280, 286–8

taro, as crop, 100
tea (beverage), 388
teapot (Bronze Age pouring vessel), 391
Tekeriš (Serbia), copper sources, 123–4
tell settlements, 22
Tepe Yahya (Iran), Bronze Age site, 192
textiles
    economic significance of, 10, 81, 181, 187
    production of, 467
Three Age system (Stone, Bronze, Iron
    Ages), 52, 56, 102, 133
Thun-Renzenbühl (Switzerland), Bronze Age
    burial, 131–2
Tibava (Slovakia), Copper Age cemetery, 141
Tigris (river), and irrigation, 97–8
Timber-Grave culture, 173, 193, 222
Tisza (river), history of, 274–5
Tisza culture/group, 258, 280, 288–9, 307,
    322
Tiszadob culture/group, 280, 286–8
Tiszapolgár culture/group, 259, 281, 289,
    294, 308, 330, 360
Tiszapolgár-Basatanya (Hungary), Copper
    Age cemetery, 117(fig.), 290
tobacco, 388
traction complex, 18(fig.), 161–70, 197, 386
    animal, 201–2
    distribution of, 240
    human, 188
trade systems, prehistoric see exchange
transfer, as aspect of exchange, 105
transhumance, 29, 77, 187, 234
transport animals, 8, 11, 170–4, 208–23; see
    also camel; chariot; donkey; horse;
    wheel
TRB (Trichterbecher, funnel-beaker) culture,
    24, 143–4, 346, 414–16, 417, 436
TRB/Corded Ware transition, 422–4
tree-crops, 9, 17–18(fig.), 185, 234, 391
Trevor-Roper, Hugh (Lord Dacre of
    Glanton), 44
Tripole culture see Cucuteni-Tripole culture
tropical cultivation systems, 75, 100
Troy (Turkey), Bronze Age and later
    settlement, 26, 55, 225, 382, 458, 498
Tsoungiza, near Nemea (Greece), Neolithic
    settlement, 202
tumuli (Pit-Grave culture burial mounds),
    242–5, 281, 303(fig.), 309
turquoise, trade in, 467
Tybrind Vig (Denmark), mesolithic
    settlement, 231

Ubaid period (Mesopotamia), 184
Únětice culture, 130
Urban Revolution (beginning of towns), 59,
    70, 498, 503

urbanisation, 81–3
Uruk period (Mesopotamia), 11, 17–18,
    155(fig.), 160(fig.), 161, 164, 176(fig.),
    177, 180, 192, 207, 215, 216, 230,
    459, 461, 464, 496

Vădastra (Romania), 231
valuables, 267
    primitive, 139
Varna (Bulgaria), Copper Age cemetery, 22,
    141, 360
vase supports (braziers), 351, 410(fig.)
Vickers, Michael, 47
vine *see* grapes
vitamin D deficiency, 208, 232
Volling group, 348
Vulchetrun (Bulgaria), Bronze Age gold
    vessels, 373, 431–56, 440, 444–8,
    451–5

waggons *see* wheeled vehicles
Wallerstein, Immanuel, 501
Walternienburg culture, 382; *see also*
    Bernburg culture
warfare, in pre-history, 494
water buffalo, 100
water-spreading *see* floodwater farming;
    irrigation
Wellenbandmuster see compass-drawn
    ornament
wheat
    bread-wheat, 92
    emmer, 394
    spelt, 92

winter wheat, 90, 92
    see also spring wheat
wheel
    cross-bar, 172, 220
    models, 221, 229–30
    spoked, 172, 220–1
wheeled vehicles, 15–18, 160–5, 229, 242–8
    distribution of, 239(fig.), 240
Wheeler, Sir Mortimer, 42
Wiepenkathen (Germany), 204
wine, 388–9, 434; *see also* alcohol
winter crops, 92, 93(fig.); *see also* wheat,
    winter
Wittfogel, Karl, 99
Wolhynia (Ukraine), flint source, 112–14,
    331
Woodland period (North America), 136
wool, 17, 17–18(fig.), 180–1, 203, 233–4,
    241n, 387
    preservation of, 203
wool-sheep, 203–5, 224
world system, 136
Wrigley, Sir Anthony, 68

yeast *see Saccharomyces*
yoghurt, 208; *see also* milk products
yokes, prehistoric, 164

Zambujal (Portugal), Copper Age
    settlement, 148
Zürich (Switzerland)
    'Akad.', Neolithic settlement, 245–7
    Mozartstraße, Bronze Age settlement, 205
Züschen (Germany), 162, 163